H. M. Prison.
Reading.
. I. . 97.

...separate from the
...amire safe. as
...include with you, have read it, I
...for me. there are many reasons why I
...ice. I want you to be my literary
...have complete control over my plays, books
...a legal right to make a will I
...sustain my art, nor could be expected
...is only a child. So I turn
...for everything, and would like you to
...tell their sale will produce may be
...ion. well, if you are my literary
...of the only document that tells
...diary behaviour ~~conduct~~ with regard to
...when you have read the letter you will
...a course of conduct that from the
...olute idiocy with vulgar bravado. You
...not necessary in my life-time or
...one to sit in the Grotesque pillory
...the simple reason that I inherited for-
...tion in literature and art. and I
...to be the shield and catspaw of
...conduct. I explain it.

AFTER OSCAR

The Wit of Oscar Wilde (1997)
The Wilde Album (1997)
The Complete Letters of Oscar Wilde (2000)
Oscar Wilde: A Life in Letters (2003)
Irish Peacock & Scarlet Marquess (2003)
Coffee with Oscar Wilde (2007)
A Portrait of Oscar Wilde (2008)

Merlin Holland

AFTER OSCAR
THE LEGACY OF A SCANDAL

Europa
editions

Europa Editions
8 Blackstock Mews
London N4 2BT
www.europaeditions.co.uk

A catalogue record for this title is available from the British Library
ISBN 978-1-78770-592-0

Holland, Merlin
After Oscar: The Legacy of a Scandal

Jacket design by Ginevra Rapisardi

Prepress by Grafica Punto Print – Rome

The authorized representative in the EEA
is Edizioni e/o, via Gabriele Camozzi 1, 00192 Rome, Italy.

Printed in Italy

CONTENTS

For Emma and Lucian
with love

The truth is rarely pure and never simple.
Modern life would be very tedious if it were either,
and modern literature a complete impossibility.

Algernon Moncrieff to Jack Worthing
Act I: *The Importance of Being Earnest*

AFTER OSCAR

INTRODUCTION

This is a book about revelations. A hundred and thirty years ago my grandfather was sent to prison for being homosexual but he also championed difference in an age of conformity which the Victorians found nearly as disturbing. He pushed his subversive ideas and his subversive behaviour to the limits of what they could tolerate—and then just a little further, which they could not. He painted that drab age of industrial power with forbidden colours and put people in touch with their feelings, revealing what the Victorians wished to conceal, until they said—*All right, if it's revelations we're talking about try this for size*—and over eight weeks in the spring of 1895 they revealed every last detail of his private life and placed him where he could do no further harm, then pretended that nothing had happened. It became one of the longest continuous acts of hypocrisy in British history, and in this book are many revelations which will make people (or their descendants) uncomfortable, and it is right that they should feel a flush of embarrassment for their own or for their ancestors' hypocrisy.

This is also a book which attacks hypocrisy in many forms over more than a hundred years. I was going to stop it conveniently in the year 2000—exactly a century after my grandfather's death—but the hypocrisy continues. I have no doubt that Oscar will go on inspiring hypocrisy in various forms for decades to come. So why reveal all? What right do I have to poke around in other people's dirty linen baskets? None really; but the fact that my family's dirty linen has been washed in public for more than a hundred years goes some way towards justifying it. When my father's autobiography *Son of Oscar Wilde* came out in 1954, one of the qualities over which the critics seemed to be unanimous was that it had been written 'without bitterness,' as indeed is my book. Bitterness is not something which runs in the family.[1] But mine *is* written with a modicum of anger, channelled into storytelling. Talking about my family in private, or for that matter even in public, and telling these stories aloud would have given them an ephemeral quality open to manipulation and reinterpretation in the retelling by others. To put them into print armours them against the whims of posterity, but it requires an absolute respect for the truth which cuts both ways. The search for this truth has led to some uncomfortable discoveries about my immediate family, and I realised that if I was going to be true to my own principles, I needed to be even-handed and keep my mother's whitewash brush firmly locked in the cabinet of historical curiosities where it belongs. It has also meant revealing that some of the facts and events which my father wrote about in his autobiography owe more to his imagination than to reality, and that has been one of the hardest things with which I have had to come to terms. At some point during the writing, I referred to my work in correspondence as having to 'read between the lines of mistaken memories,' only I mistyped the word 'lines' without its 'n.' *Reading between the lies* would have made an appropriate subtitle, since that is what the story of posthumous Oscar is mostly about: debunking unverified gossip which for years has masqueraded as the truth.

After Oscar was never going to be an easy book to write, especially as the unmasking of some of the players was inevitably going to include people to whom I was even distantly related. My nights often seemed peopled by those who would do all they could to prevent me from telling their story, and sleep went from being the body's soft recompense for a hard day to the mind's nocturnal revenge for daring to tell the truth. But vivid and unsettling encounters with the spirits of those whose behaviour I was holding up to scrutiny also helped me put the truth into perspective and try to understand their motives and emotions; sometimes the reality has a depth, a poignancy even, that was lacking in the version which they had carefully polished for posterity at the time. Who am I to say, for example, that Constance, my father's mother, didn't appear to him in a dream and encourage him to tell the story of his early life? I only have my own mother's word that it was her convenient invention to make Vyvyan's story more touching. It was unlike Thelma, my mother, to have invented it; she told it to me at the time his autobiography was republished in 1988 to impress on me just how much she had been involved in persuading him to write it. Seventy years on I suppose there is a certain irony in the fact that I should now find people invading my sleep to *stop* me telling the truth.

After my father's death in 1967, my mother took solace in consulting mediums. Oddly enough (oddly, because I never really associated him with an interest in the paranormal) it was Rupert Hart-Davis, a great friend of the family and the editor of Oscar Wilde's letters in 1962, who first put her in touch with the spiritualist medium Ena Twigg. Rupert had resorted to spiritualism after the sudden death of his second wife, which helped him in the process of grieving. I was sceptical and considered it a waste of time and money but Thelma insisted on paying for me to go to a medium before letting me dismiss it out of hand. I did and the one message which 'came through from the spirit world'—long before I had even thought of trying to make a living out of writing—was that I would have to write a book about my family which would be extremely difficult. This is it.

Part of the reason why writing *After Oscar* has been so difficult is that the earlier years, for reasons which will become clear, have involved many separate stories and weaving them together into a single narrative was not necessarily the best approach. Occasionally, where they overlap, I have chosen to tell each in a single sweep rather than combining them into a fragmented chronological sequence which would have destroyed the dramatic effect. (The telling of an earlier story may have more impact when told later on, so a little mental gymnastics by the reader is sometimes necessary.) This is a radically different multi-layered biography, with the shadow of my grandfather as the main focus in each layer. I have tried to make sure that the reader can follow without difficulty how the layers are all interlinked in this three-dimensional treatment. It's the final part which has given me sleepless nights. When I started writing it twenty-five years ago, it was going to be pure fact and I resisted any attempt to persuade me that I should include *myself*. I was irrelevant to the story, and that had always been made clear to me from a very early age. But over those twenty-five years the publishing landscape has changed, and the public seems to have an insatiable desire to know what goes on in the private lives of the rich and famous. I am neither rich nor famous, and only marginally interesting as an adjunct to the continuing fascination for Oscar Wilde, but I unpacked my own life to look at Oscar's incursions into it and was surprised by what I found.

'Good artists exist simply in what they make, and consequently are perfectly uninteresting in what they are,' remarks Lord Henry in *The Picture of Dorian Gray*, a view rather contradicted by Oscar's own reputation which has swung like a weathercock in the breeze of popular opinion, or more frequently in the storm of scandal, ever since his death in 1900. Few other writers of the last 150 years have had so much attention paid to them over and above their literary output. How many other modern authors have had their witticisms printed not only on greetings cards but on every-day objects like fridge magnets? He has been used to promote everything from de-alcoholised sparkling wine to hotels where he is supposed to have stayed but almost certainly didn't, and his name graces a European river cruiser, a Norwegian aeroplane, a British freight engine, and an Irish ferry. So, I felt that to have achieved such iconic status today, after being branded a convict, a bankrupt, and an unrepentant homosexual in his short lifetime, was a phenomenon meriting a chapter of its own, as well as haz-arding an explanation for his continuing popularity.

Now, footnotes are a necessary modern evil in works of non-fiction. They persuade the reader that what is printed has a valid pedigree and is not merely a vague and unsubstantiated conjecture by the author or even, God forbid, *an invention*. I say this because some years ago in an essay entitled 'Biography and the art of lying' I did just that in order to prove the point about phantom footnotes. I referenced a perfectly plausible but entirely invented story to a non-existent manuscript in my possession and then admitted the deception towards the end of the piece. However, it didn't prevent an eager blurb-writer from quoting part of the anecdote as authentic without bothering to read to the end of the essay. That said, you have my word that no such deception has been practised in this book.[2]

I hope that you will find, as I have done in researching Oscar's very real posthumous existence, plenty to amuse, to infuriate, to fascinate, and above all to shock.

PART ONE
(1897-1900)

CHAPTER ONE
OSCAR'S RELEASE

At ten minutes past six in the morning on Wednesday 19 May 1897, by special arrangement with the prison authorities, a brougham drove into Pentonville prison. A few moments later, the blinds drawn, it clattered over the cobbles, out through the massive prison gates and into the late spring air of North London. Oscar Wilde was finally a free man. For one who had spent most of his adult life courting publicity, inventing himself afresh at every turn, it was an unobtrusive departure. It gave him a little more dignity, though, than having to pass out on foot through the wicket gate as the rest of the day's 'discharge' would do at 6:30, and the shock of his return to the outside world was somewhat tempered by the men who had come to collect him: More Adey and the Reverend Stewart Headlam. Adey, an old friend from Oscar's pre-prison days, was hardly the ideal companion for his first hours of freedom. Acrimonious letters had passed between them the previous month over Oscar's future finances, Adey's handling of which had been nothing short of disastrous as it had estranged Oscar from his wife, Constance, and nearly resulted in an unnecessary and unwanted divorce. 'He is cultivated. He is sympathetic. He is kind. He is patient. He is gentle. He is affectionate,' Oscar wrote of him at the time. 'But in matters of business he is the most solemn donkey that ever stepped . . . The harm he has done me is irreparable. He is incapable, as I have written to him, of managing the domestic affairs of a tom-tit in a hedge for a single afternoon.'[3]

Headlam he hardly knew, but it was he who, urged by his friend Adey and believing Wilde's case to be prejudged by public opinion, had stood bail for him in 1895 when friends either could not or would not do so, and it was to Headlam's house in Bloomsbury that they now drove in the brougham.

A return to Central London was far from what Oscar had had in mind when plans for his release were first discussed. Frank Harris had been to visit him at the beginning of April and with his customary expansiveness had offered him a cheque for £500 and a motoring tour through France to the Pyrenees. In a state of nervous gratitude Oscar had been quick to accept, but later turned it down when the £500 turned out to be £50 and he realized that several weeks in Harris's company would have proved something of an ordeal. 'It would be like a perpetual football match to be with him,' he later remarked to Headlam.[4] On 22 April, aware that reporters and possibly even Queensberry, the very instrument of his ruin, were planning to gather like vultures at what he called 'the ceremony of his release,' he had petitioned the Home Secretary to remit five days of his sentence on the grounds that he had already spent three weeks on remand before his first trial, but the request had been refused. The problem of Press interest became more and more acute. Cheque-book journalism, it seems, was alive and well in 1897; one American newspaper offered him any sum he wanted to give an interview over breakfast on the morning of his release, an idea which appalled him. In the end the Governor of Reading Gaol, Major Nelson, had been obliged to write to the Prison Commissioners informing them that: 'The prisoner each day becomes more hysterical and fearful of any annoyance that may be caused by the importunities of the Press.' Their response was to arrange for Wilde to be transferred discreetly on the evening of 18 May from Reading to Pentonville where the Governor had been instructed to keep the identity of his overnight prisoner a strict secret even from his staff. On hearing this, Oscar had written begging another friend, Reggie Turner, to meet him at the prison gates and take him to a hotel for a change of clothes and a pot of coffee before travelling to Southampton and across the Channel to Le Havre. Turner refused, afraid that if his family discovered they might stop his allowance, but agreed to meet Oscar a day later at the new destination which he and Robert Ross had chosen for him—Dieppe. For Oscar, however, Dieppe in early summer was a prospect which caused him about as much unease as London itself. It had become a popular resort for the British, an extension of the English south coast with Continental overtones and although it was home to a thriving artistic community, it was also patronised by an element of Society in whose eyes he was merely a perverted ex-convict and by whose narrow moral code he was sure to be treated accordingly.

The transfer between Reading and Pentonville had taken place as planned and under more humane conditions than his last transfer eighteen months previously between Wandsworth and Reading. On that occasion, handcuffed and in prison dress, he had stood for half an hour on a South London station platform in the November rain, jeered and spat at by those who recognised who he was.[5] This time he had been allowed to wear his own clothes, his sartorial dignity assured by the unexpected kindness of a sympathetic Reading Gaol wardress, Elizabeth Norris, who had pressed his suit and washed the shirt which had lain yellowing and crumpled in the prison storeroom for two years.[6] Eight hours previously, he had arrived at Pentonville with nothing to his name but the clothes he stood in. His rented house in Tite Street had been repossessed, its entire contents sold by the sheriff's auctioneers to settle unpaid debts while he was on remand; he was an undischarged bankrupt with no prospect in the foreseeable future of earning a living in England again; his wife had obtained, reluctantly, a deed of separation; and his children had been taken from him by court order.

Now he rode through the awakening streets to one of the only houses daring to give him asylum for a few hours in the city which had briefly fêted his theatrical triumphs before discovering his private homosexual life and branding him a monster of depravity. In his pocket were the statutory ten shillings gratuity from Her Majesty's Prison Service and in his hands an eighty-page letter which, by special dispensation, he had been permitted to write to

Lord Alfred 'Bosie' Douglas, the young man who had helped bring him to the pitiful state in which he now found himself. However, rules could only be bent so far and the Prison Commissioners had refused to allow such a lengthy document to be sent as routine correspondence. It was a document of such intensity—'Epistola in carcere et vinculis' he had called it—that when its full extent became known, it would affect the lives of many individuals over the next sixty years.

By 6:30 the brougham had covered the two miles to Headlam's house in Upper Bedford Place where Ada and Ernest Leverson were waiting to greet him. It was the Leversons who had opened their house to Oscar after he had been granted bail and besides lending him £500 toward the costs of his libel action against the Marquess of Queensberry, Ernest had acted as Oscar's informal, even illegal, banker during his prison sentence. Adela Schuster, one of the Wildes' family friends, had given Oscar £1,000 shortly before his conviction to ease the financial strain and Oscar with foresight had turned it over to Leverson for safekeeping. Although much of it had disappeared in legal bills, the balance should have been declared to the bankruptcy receiver as part of his assets but was not, enabling him to give his aging mother some financial assistance and ultimately pay for the costs of her funeral while he was still in prison.[7]

Whatever prison had taken from Wilde it had not dulled his charm nor the finesse of his flattery. Ada Leverson, 'The Sphinx' as Oscar used to call her, vividly remembered that early morning meeting:

> We all felt intensely nervous and embarrassed. We had the English fear of showing our feelings, and at the same time the human fear of not showing our feelings. He came in, and at once put us at our ease. He came in with the dignity of a king returning from exile. He came in talking and laughing, smoking a cigarette, with waved hair and a flower in his button-hole, and he looked markedly better, slighter, and even younger than he had done two years

previously. His first words were, 'Sphinx, how marvellous of you to know exactly the right hat to wear at seven o'clock in the morning to meet a friend who has been away! You can't have got up, you must have sat up.'[8]

Despite the appalling conditions which he had had to endure in prison, he spoke light-heartedly about the Governor and his wife, and joked about the warders refusing to allow him to read a newspaper on the train the night before. 'I suggested I might be allowed to read it upside down. This they consented to allow and I read all the way *The Daily Chronicle* upside down and never enjoyed it so much. It's really the only way to read newspapers.' In a more serious vein he seems, according to Leverson, to have sent a note to a 'Roman Catholic Retreat asking if he might retire there for six months,' a story frequently repeated but extremely unlikely; he would not have wanted to upset the elaborately laid plans of his close friends; he was hoping to be able to see his wife and children shortly; and given the sentiments expressed in his last letters from prison he wanted nothing less than to stay in England and exchange one form of confinement for another, however uplifting by contrast.

At this point, and using Leverson's book as a prime example, it needs to be said that even those who professed to know Oscar personally cannot always be relied upon to be truthful when writing about him, a fact which has become increasingly clear during the forty-odd years that I have been researching my grandfather's life and works. In some instances, understandably, it was due to their imagination recolouring grey memories of the past. In others, it has been to enhance the importance of the author, but all too often it has led biographers astray, happy to accept these first-hand accounts at face value. And why not? After all, Ada Leverson was unquestionably there on the morning of Oscar's release.[9]

Stewart Headlam's version of events, however, is far more likely to have been correct. Yes, a note was sent to a Catholic community—Farm Street in Mayfair according to Headlam—asking for a

priest to come over, possibly with a view to Oscar's desire to convert, but certainly not because he was hoping to be accepted on a
six month retreat; apart from anything else Farm Street has never
had a house of retreat. In any event the reply was a refusal, but the
incident is illustrative of one of the themes which runs throughout
this book, that of debunking unnecessarily sensationalist myths
about Oscar created and perpetuated by posterity.[10]

Other visitors came and went throughout the morning. For
Oscar who had spent two years in solitary confinement, forbidden
by prison regulations to talk to fellow prisoners, the opportunity
to converse once more was delightful. Predictably he and More
Adey missed the 10am 'Day Express' to Newhaven and the day
boat to Dieppe. With time to spare, Oscar indulged himself with a
visit to Hatchard's bookshop in Piccadilly: books, once an integral
part of his everyday life, had been a luxury behind bars and there
was another act of kindness which he needed to acknowledge. The
manager of the shop, Arthur Humphreys, had not only sent him
a lavish parcel of books for his second Christmas in prison, but
had published a limited edition of Oscar's essay 'The Soul of Man
under Socialism' within a week of his final conviction. It was a
small but significant expression of friendship and solidarity at a
moment when scandal had forced the author's plays off the West
End stage and London was trying to forget that Oscar Wilde had
ever existed.

While they were in Hatchard's Wilde was recognised, and he
and Adey had to leave in a hurry. The incident, only to be expected in the middle of a weekday in Central London, merely confirmed Wilde's fears expressed in a letter to Reggie Turner two
days before:

> I suppose I had better go to Southampton on Wednesday, by
> some station, if possible not a big London one: I mean Vauxhall
> better than Waterloo etc. So get a carriage for the drive through
> London. There are of course only two ways by which I can travel:
> either third-class, which I need hardly say, dear Reggie, I don't

mind a scrap: or first-class in a reserved carriage: it is unnecessary to explain why: you will see that while I can sit at ease with the poor, I could not with the rich: for me to enter a first-class carriage containing other people would be dreadful: they would not like it, and I would know they would not. That would distress me.[11]

However, the last minute change of plan meant that he was expected by his friends in Dieppe and not in Le Havre, so the crossing was to be via Newhaven leaving from Victoria. Rather than risk being recognized there, or even at the busy Clapham Junction, they took a cab to the next station out—East Croydon.[12] But he could not escape a bizarre coincidence. Wilde had been acquainted with Philip Cardew, a director of the London Brighton and South Coast Railway and after whose daughter he had named Cecily in *The Importance of Being Earnest*; Jack Worthing, her guardian, was found in a handbag at the Victoria Station cloakroom, 'the Brighton Line' as he insists to Lady Bracknell. Now, as he travelled down the Brighton Line for the last time, possibly even pulled by the 'Cardew,' one of the regular steam engines to make the trip, it was as though elements of his finest comedy had come to mock his departure.[13] As Oscar himself remarked on many occasions, between life's comedy and its tragedy lies but a hair's breadth.

A day in More Adey's company, whatever Oscar's misgivings beforehand, had healed much of the rawness of his feelings over what he saw as Adey's and Robbie Ross's mishandling of his affairs. He would have reminded himself how Adey had helped to secure bail for him before his final trial and had later drafted a petition for clemency during his first months in Reading. He would have remembered, too, how Ross had stood in the dreary corridor of the bankruptcy court that first autumn, waiting simply to raise his hat in silence as Oscar, handcuffed and in prison dress, passed by. Now, he was carrying what few possessions he had left in a gift from Reggie Turner—suitcases and a dressing case stamped 'S.M.' for 'Sebastian Melmoth,' the alias he had decided to adopt in his forthcoming exile.[14] A new name and a new life in another country lay across the English Channel, but so too did old friends on whose loyalty he would need to rely more than ever. So, at Newhaven where they arrived late in the afternoon, he sent a remorseful telegram to Ross:

> Arriving by night boat. Am so delighted at prospect of seeing you and Reggie. You must not mind the foolish unkind letters. More has been such a good friend to me and I am so grateful to you all I cannot find words to express my feelings. You must not dream of waiting up for us. In the morning we will meet. Please engage rooms for us at your hotel. When I see you I shall be quite happy, indeed I am happy now to think that I have such wonderful friendship shown to me.
> Sebastian Melmoth

Oscar and More dined in Newhaven before boarding the night boat and they arrived in Dieppe shortly before dawn at 4:30 the next morning. Ross and Turner were waiting on the jetty.[15] Oscar's tall figure was immediately recognisable, dominating the other passengers on deck, and as the steamer drew alongside he saw them, waved his hand and his face relaxed into a smile. His features, it seemed to Ross, had lost all the coarseness with which they had been dulled by his pre-prison life of overindulgence and he looked as he must have looked twenty years before. There was 'an irritating delay' while the gangplank was put in place and then, with what Ross described as 'that strange elephantine gait which I have never seen in anyone else,' Oscar stalked off the boat.

In his hand was a large, sealed envelope containing the letter to Alfred Douglas. 'This, my dear Robbie,' he said, 'is the great manuscript about which you know,' and as he handed it to Ross he broke into a sort of Rabelaisian laugh. Although neither man could have realized it at the time, there was a terrible symbolism in this simple act of transfer: it was as though Oscar, having come to terms with his life and committed it to paper in Reading Gaol, was demanding that Ross should share the consequences. He had been presented, so to speak, with a time-bomb which would explode with devastating effect fifteen years on. Ross already knew what was expected of him, since around the time that Oscar had finished *De Profundis*, as the Douglas letter was afterwards to become known, he had already written to Ross about it from prison asking him to have several typescript copies made before sending the original on to Douglas. But first there were other matters to attend to—breakfast and mending the broken fences of friendship.

Oscar gave Turner the keys to his luggage and asked him to complete the customs formalities while he and Ross repaired to a nearby café. When Turner reappeared, he found Oscar 'sitting at the head of the buffet table drinking his coffee and dominating the whole seasick company,' for the first, and probably the last time in his life, being 'brilliant at breakfast'; Mrs. Cheveley would not have approved. Once his luggage was cleared, Ross and Turner took Oscar to the Hôtel Sandwich where they had decked out his room with flowers and loaded the mantlepiece with books, in the centre of which was a copy of Max Beerbohm's *The Happy Hypocrite* sent to greet him on his release by the author. A few hundred pounds had been raised from various sources by Ross and Adey which must have been a huge relief to Oscar who had assumed he would be more or less destitute. Among the contributions were the £50 from Harris; £50 from Adey himself, half of which had already been spent on hats, ties, collars, shirts and toiletries; a first quarter's allowance from his wife; £50 from the composer Dal Young, who had had the courage to speak out in Wilde's favour at the time of his conviction with the pamphlet *Apologia pro Oscar Wilde*; and £111 being the balance of Adela Schuster's gift. One thing, however, was perfectly clear to Ross and Adey: under no circumstances were they going to hand over the entire sum to him without any control. In the weeks before his arrest his two plays *The Importance of Being Earnest* and *An Ideal Husband* had been bringing him in about £150 a week, all of which and more he had spent on his reckless lifestyle with Alfred

Douglas. His only fixed annual income now came from Constance and was equivalent to what he used to spend in a week. Even without Bosie to help him spend it, Oscar's past record of extravagance and lavish generosity to all around him gave cause for concern. The thought, too, that the friends would have to pick up the pieces when the release money was spent, forced Ross into the unenviable position of appointing himself banker for the next few weeks, unaware that it was a role he would be having to play for the rest of Oscar's short life. It didn't, however, stop Oscar from immediately sending small sums of money to be given to ten of his fellow inmates in Reading on their impending release.[16]

By nine o'clock all but Oscar were exhausted and excused themselves to go and sleep until lunchtime. Oscar, still living on nervous exhilaration, sat down to write a letter of thanks to Ada Leverson for her support the day before: 'I often thought of you in the long black days and nights of my prison life, and to find you just as wonderful and dear as ever was no surprise. The beautiful are always beautiful.' After lunch he and Robbie hired a carriage and drove to Arques-La-Bataille in the countryside just to the south of Dieppe. There they sat in the sunshine on the ramparts of the ruined mediaeval castle, with Oscar luxuriating in the sounds and scents of spring. For months he had anticipated this very moment:

> I tremble with pleasure when I think that on the very day of my leaving prison both the laburnum and the lilac will be blooming in the gardens, and that I shall see the wind stir into restless beauty the swaying gold of the one, and make the other toss the pale purple of its plumes, so that all the air shall be Arabia for me.[17]

Then he talked of Reading Gaol as though it were a sort of enchanted castle of which the governor, Major Nelson, was the presiding fairy. The hideous machicolated turrets became minarets, the warders benevolent Mamelukes and his friends, Ross, Turner, and Adey turned into Paladins waiting to welcome Coeur de Lion after his years of captivity. It was a truly Oscarian performance, the poet reborn, putting into practice the resolutions he had set himself in *De Profundis*: 'The important thing, the thing that lies before me, the thing that I have to do, or be for the brief remainder of my days one maimed, marred and incomplete, is to absorb into my nature all that has been done to me, to make it part of me, to accept it without complaint, fear or reluctance.'[18] It was in this positive frame of mind that he returned to Dieppe late in the afternoon, deeply touched by the loyalty and generosity of his friends and determined, without bitterness, to put his prison experience to good account as he rebuilt his life. That night he enjoyed the unaccustomed luxury of an ordinary bed with clean sheets, the final sensual pleasure of his first two days of rediscovering the outside world with its joy and colours and stimulation. It was too good to last—and it didn't.

For the first week he remained in Dieppe, but his fears about the English community's attitude towards him were soon realized. Out of consideration for his English clientele, the proprietor of a restaurant, where he had gone to dine with friends, made it obliquely clear that he was not welcome; he feared that the taint of Oscar as a regular could affect his business. People who knew him by sight but with whom he was not personally acquainted apparently crossed the street in a pointed manner as they approached him.[19] So it was partly to avoid further unpleasantness and partly to save money that he decided, persuaded by the sensible Robbie, to install himself eight kilometres up the coast in the Hôtel de La Plage at Berneval. Despite the snubs, the artistic and literary community showed more sympathy. The novelist Henrietta Stannard, who wrote popular novels under the pseudonym John Strange Winter and who was living in Dieppe at the time, asked him to call on her and her husband, which elicited an effusive letter of thanks and a bouquet of flowers from a grateful Wilde. 'France has been charming to me and about me during all my imprisonment and has now—mother of all artists as she is—given me *asile*,' he wrote.[20] One of those who had showed his 'charm' in a way that Wilde would have appreciated most of all was Aurélien Lugné-Poë who had staged *Salomé* in Paris while Wilde was in prison and who had visited him within days of his arrival in Dieppe. Nevertheless, after the initial euphoria brought on by friends and freedom, Oscar could no longer avoid addressing two relationships from his former life—Alfred Douglas and Constance, his wife.

Reggie Turner and More Adey had already returned to England by the time Oscar arrived in Berneval, so he spent the first two days there alone with Robbie Ross without whose advice the manuscript of *De Profundis* might never have survived. In the letter which Oscar wrote from prison telling Robbie what he wanted done with it, he had also asked him to become his literary executor:

> I want you to be my literary executor in case of my death, and . . . if you are my literary executor, you must be in possession of the only document that really gives any explanation of my extraordinary behaviour with regard to Queensberry and Alfred Douglas. When you have read the letter you will see the psychological explanation of a course of conduct that from the outside seems a combination of absolute idiocy with vulgar bravado. Some day the truth will have to be known: not necessarily in my lifetime or in Douglas's: but I am not prepared to sit in the grotesque pillory they put me into, for all time: . . . I don't defend my conduct. I explain it.[21]

And Robbie, even if he had only had time to read the first few pages of this long, brutally frank letter to Bosie Douglas, would have realized that it was madness to send him the original. In the first place, given Douglas's impulsive nature, he would almost certainly have destroyed it, which would have defeated the purpose of asking Robbie to 'be in possession of the only document that really gives any explanation of my extraordinary behaviour.' Once the original was no longer in existence, it would have been impossible to guarantee the authenticity of the text. Even to have sent Douglas a copy would, in Robbie's view, have been counterproductive as he was already considering the idea that Douglas might help contribute towards Oscar's upkeep. This would have been out of the question once Bosie had read what Oscar had to say about him in the letter.[22] All this must have been discussed in those two days, with Robbie impressing on his friend the importance of keeping the original for posterity. Oscar would not have been hard to convince as his instructions for copying the document specified that 'a wide rubricated margin should be left for corrections,' implying if not publication at least preservation. As it was, Robbie did hold onto the complete manuscript, publishing excerpts in 1905 and 1908, and finally deposited it in the British Museum Library in 1909, where it lay sealed for fifty years. Whether or not Bosie Douglas was sent a copy is uncertain and Robbie, depending on whether it was more expedient to admit or to deny it, changed his story several times in later years. In all probability it wasn't sent. According to Bosie he never did receive a copy, which in retrospect was a pity as it might have prevented his disastrous reunion with Oscar which took place three months later. But I anticipate.

CHAPTER TWO
AFTER THE FALL

Apart from writing to thank his friends for their gifts and their moral support (even one expressing his gratitude to Major Nelson, the Governor of Reading Gaol for treating him so humanely), one of the very first things which Oscar had done when he arrived in Dieppe had been to write to his wife.

Constance had remained astoundingly loyal to him when all around were encouraging her to distance herself and her children from the man whose public image had changed overnight from brilliant dramatist to 'loathsome importer of exotic vice.' In the middle of May 1895, between Wilde's two criminal trials, she had consigned my uncle Cyril (aged ten), and my father, Vyvyan (aged eight), to the care of a rather hysterical governess, sending them to Glion above Lake Geneva while she remained behind to pick up the pieces of her broken life. She didn't rejoin her sons until around 22 June, a month after Oscar's final conviction, and had spent some of the intervening time seeking the help of influential friends to try and make his prison life marginally less unbearable.[23] It was a brave, almost defiant gesture given the overwhelming sense of public disgust which was being expressed in the press about her husband's conduct.

Shortly after leaving England, however, Constance wrote to her friend Emily Thursfield to say that she had taken legal advice and, entirely for practical reasons, had been advised to sue for divorce. On her marriage to Oscar in 1884, she had received a marriage settlement from her grandfather which was kept in trust and provided the two of them with an income of about £800 a year. Under its terms, Oscar had a life interest in the income if Constance were to die before him and on his death it would then revert to their children, but his past behaviour showed that he could not be relied upon to act responsibly with money and the children might suffer in consequence; a divorce would annul his entitlement to it.[24] But as the summer progressed her resolve weakened, helped partly by her brother, Otho, who had written to Oscar in prison, and partly by Robert Sherard, one of Oscar's most devoted friends who had been among the first to visit him. Both were anxious to effect a reconciliation and encouraged Oscar to use one of his first meagre allowances of personal letters from prison to write asking Constance to forgive him and not to proceed with the divorce.[25] He knew that the strength of her love for him, he who had ruined *her* life as well as his own, was remarkable, and Oscar would have remembered the letter he received from her brother Otho on his marriage ' . . . if Constance makes as good a wife as she has been a good sister to me your happiness is certain; she is staunch and true.'[26] She had stood by Otho when he fell in love with their Aunt Carrie's housemaid, Nellie Hutchinson, and married her in spite of the snobbish disapproval from her extended family, so she was no stranger to family scandals.[27] Now, divorce from Oscar seemed a step which she could not bring herself to take. Oscar did indeed write and wrote again in early September, a letter conveyed as 'official correspondence' through Constance's solicitor, Sidney Hargrove, who brought it to her personally in Switzerland. It was, he said, 'one of the most touching and pathetic letters that had ever come under his eye,' and Hargrove agreed that she should stop the divorce proceedings and she and Oscar should sort matters out amicably between themselves.[28] 'His letters are touching to a degree and I cannot think that the children will suffer more by seeing him than they must in any case by the very fact of being his children,' she wrote to her sister-in-law in mid-September and a few days later she travelled from Switzerland to London to make her first visit to him in Wandsworth Prison where he had been transferred in July.[29] It was around this time that she adopted an old family name, Holland, as her new identity; a practical necessity dictated by public prejudice and concern for her children's future rather than any sense of shame on her part.[30]

Her visit to Oscar took place under terrible circumstances. 'It was indeed awful,' she wrote, 'more so than I had any conception it could be. I could not see him and I could not touch him and I scarcely spoke,' but it enabled them to start arranging their future finances without lawyers and without acrimony.[31] She offered to make him an allowance on his release in return for him renouncing his interest in her marriage settlement which he was happy to accept.[32] Back once more in Switzerland she confided again to Emily Thursfield:

> I do not wish to sever myself entirely from Mr. Wilde who is in the very lowest depths of misery. And he is very repentant and minds most of all what he has brought on myself and the boys. It seems to me that by sticking to him now I may save him from even worse and I believe that he cares now for no one but myself and the children . . . At the same time I am quite aware that I am running a certain, possibly a very great, risk. But I have my own money over which I now have perfect control and the life-interest has been renounced by Mr. Wilde in favour of the boys. So if I find it impossible to live with him I can always leave him. But, dearest Emily, I think we women are meant for comforters and I believe that no one can really take my place now, or help him as I can.[33]

Her next visit was on 19 February the following year to tell him of his beloved mother's death. Jane Wilde had died on the 3rd of the month and it was agreed that Constance was the only one who could break the news to him gently. Despite suffering from the severe symptoms of multiple sclerosis, which would contribute indirectly to her own death two years later, she made the trip to Reading Gaol where Oscar had been moved in November. It was less of a shock for him than Constance had anticipated as Oscar's mother had 'appeared' to him on the night of her death in outdoor clothes, and when asked to stay she shook her head and vanished without a word. 'I knew it already,' he said when Constance told him.[34] A year later, still touched by the memory of her visit Oscar would write: 'My soul and the soul of my wife met in the valley of the shadow of death: she kissed me; she comforted me: she behaved as no woman in history, except my own mother perhaps, could have behaved.'[35] It also gave them the opportunity to settle the details of the allowance which, the previous autumn, Constance had offered to pay him on his release. What had looked to be a simple agreement between them, though, had suddenly become complicated; Oscar had been made bankrupt in the meantime and neither of them had reckoned with the Official Receiver and the well-intentioned but misguided intervention of his friends.

By law the Official Receiver was obliged to realize even the smallest of the bankrupt's potential assets and Oscar's contingent life interest in his wife's capital could not simply be handed back to her—it had to be put up for sale. So, it was agreed that Constance should purchase Oscar's life interest from the Receiver unopposed and for a nominal sum, and in return she would make him a lifetime allowance of £200 a year and—in the event of her predeceasing him—a third of the income from her capital. After this second visit from his wife, Oscar wrote to Robbie Ross that he was happy with the arrangement:

I do not wish any opposition be made to her purchasing my life-interest. I feel that I have brought such unhappiness on her and such ruin on my children that I have no right to go against her wishes in anything. She was gentle and good to me here when she came to see me. I have full trust in her.[36]

Ross and Adey, however, supposedly looking after Oscar's interests while he was in prison and anxious that he had given away too many of his 'rights' in a fit of remorse, then decided to bid against Constance for the life interest without telling him. At £75 they were successful. Constance was furious, assuming that Oscar had gone back on his word and saw nothing for it but to sue for divorce in order to annul the marriage settlement altogether. For Oscar the prospect of further humiliation in the divorce court, in all likelihood a replay of the homosexual infidelities which had landed him in prison in the first place, was more than he could face. In a flurry of letters between himself, Adey, and Ross (which he later said should be published as *Letters from Two Idiots to a Lunatic*) he ordered them to return to Constance the life interest they had purchased. He criticized them for spending and thus wasting the funds which were intended for him on his release; and, more seriously, remonstrated with them for estranging him from his wife and children. As a result of this meddling, Constance's solicitor advised her to reduce her generous offer, to make it conditional on Oscar not 'consorting notoriously with evil or disreputable companions' and, worst of all, to give her sole custody of the children:

> I'm afraid you don't realise what my wife's character and conduct have been towards me. You don't seem to understand her. From the very first she forgave me, and was sweet beyond words to me. After my seeing her here when we arranged everything between us . . . I begged that my friends would do nothing of any kind that would imperil the reconciliation and affection between myself and my wife . . . You did not tell me the truth, you and my friends did not carry out my directions and, what is the result? Instead of £200 a year I have £150 . . . But that is not all. That is merely the common money side. My children are taken from me by an order of the court. I am no longer legally their father. I have no right to speak to them. If I try to communicate with them I can be put into prison for contempt of court. My wife also is of course wounded with me for what she considers a breach of faith on my part. On Monday I sign here a deed of separation of the most painfully stringent kind and of the most humiliating conditions.[37]

The deed of separation was brought to him by his solicitor, Arthur Hansell, and signed two days before his release.[38] Much later, in 1905, an anonymous newspaper article (obviously taking advantage of the recently published but much abbreviated first edition of *De Profundis*), maintained that Constance had come to the prison with the solicitor but without any intention of seeing Oscar. It was written by one of the warders who claimed that she asked him, nevertheless, if she could have a glimpse of her husband—presumably through the peep-hole in the door. Shortly after, she left in tears accompanied by Hansell. A lovely, heart-rending account, though it must be a complete fabrication and one swallowed, I may add, by most biographers to give poignancy to the story. The dates and content of her correspondence from Nervi on the Italian Riviera where she was then living show that she couldn't have gone to London at that time; her deteriorating physical condition would have made it difficult and she would almost certainly have mentioned it in her letters to others which she didn't. It was an imaginative invention by the warder—more unverifiable sensationalism—and now that most of Constance's letters from the period have come to light, it looks absurd.

Once in Dieppe and with no more restrictions on his correspondence, Oscar was immediately anxious to make amends with his wife for seeming so untrustworthy. His letter reached Constance on 24 May at Nervi where she was staying with her friend, Margaret Brooke, the Ranee of Sarawak. She described it to Otho at the time simply as 'full of penitence' and said she had replied, but Otho and one of the Wildes' close family friends, Carlos Blacker (both of whom she later allowed to see it), agreed that 'it was most beautiful . . . and touched with an earnestness not found in any of his published work.'[39] Unfortunately it has not survived, almost certainly destroyed, Otho later suspected, by her family or by the executor of Constance's estate and guardian to her children, Adrian Hope. Constance's own reaction to it betrayed more feeling than she was prepared to admit even to her brother: in spite of her increasing lameness, she wanted to go immediately to join Oscar in Dieppe and was only discouraged from doing so by the Ranee who advised her not to be impetuous and to wait.[40] In the end she told the would-be penitent that she would see him twice a year but made no promise at all that he could see his children. This was completely at variance with the sentiments she had expressed to Otho's second wife, Mary, eighteen months before. Instead, she sent him photographs of Cyril and Vyvyan and wrote to him weekly for a while, but Oscar was impatient and wanted—needed—more. 'It is a terrible punishment, dear Robbie,' he wrote to Ross, 'and oh! how well I deserve it. But it makes me feel disgraced and evil, and I don't want to feel that.'[41]

Why the change of mind? Constance's misgivings had started from the moment she felt that Oscar had betrayed her trust over the Official Receiver and the marriage settlement. The warm, protective tone of her letters in the autumn of 1895 showed that she was at least prepared to try and remake some sort of a life with him, but by the summer of 1896 she had become defensive, even aggressive, at what she saw as interference in her affairs by Oscar's friends, apparently with his tacit approval. The wrong-headed meddling of Ross and Adey had shaken Constance's belief in Oscar's affections and weakened her confidence that she should be the principal agent in his rehabilitation.

There were other considerations, too, which had forced her to take a hard, detached look into the future. Her family's nomadic existence in the year after Oscar's conviction, moving into increasingly modest hotels in Switzerland, Germany, and finally in Italy; the irregularity of her sons' education during that time; and the realisation that her original plan to ride out the storm for eighteen months on the Continent and then move discreetly back to England was unworkable, had all come at a cost to herself. Set against that, it seemed the principal concern of her husband and his friends was to secure Oscar's financial well-being in the case of her death. In the circumstances, this change from gentle compassion to the irritation of a woman who felt herself betrayed was only to be expected. In a letter to her brother shortly before Oscar's release she described her mood of resignation:

> I have again had pressure put upon me to go back to Oscar, but I am sure you will agree that it is impossible. I am told that I would save a human soul, but I have no influence over Oscar I have had none and tho' I think he is affectionate, I see no reason for believing that I should be able now to perform miracles, and I must look after my boys and not risk their future. What do you think I should do? The Ranee thinks he has fallen and cannot rise. That is rather like Humpty Dumpty, but then I think his fate is rather like Humpty Dumpty's—quite as tragic and quite as impossible to put right.[42]

Who was applying the pressure is not clear. It was not her brother to whom the letter is addressed; nor would it have been her confidante at the time, the Ranee, who was mindful of the problems in her own marriage; and in view of their complete antipathy towards Oscar before his trials and their feelings of revulsion thereafter it was certainly not her family. Oscar's mother, for whom she had had great affection and respect, would surely have tried to effect a reunion, but she had died the year before. Given the reference to saving a human soul, the most likely person, though one whom she would have known by reputation only, was the Rev. Stewart Headlam. He may even have suggested that she be present at Oscar's release, but if so the appeal fell on deaf ears. 'What do you think I should do?' The question, neatly sandwiched between conflicting opinions, revealed Constance still in an agony of indecision over whether she should be listening to her head or her heart. Despite these fluctuations in her feelings for Oscar, and as her name so aptly suggests, I am sure there was always an unchanging belief, as she had expressed it to Emily Thursfield, that 'no one can really take my place now, or help him as I can.' This time it was her friends, not his, who were to be the cause of misunderstandings between them. Even Bosie Douglas confirmed as much many years later: 'Mrs. Wilde was continually changing her mind about Oscar and was on the brink of making friends with him several times but that she was much influenced by women friends who mostly advised her against it.'[43]

None of those whose judgement she respected seemed prepared to do anything other than advise her to wait and see. But why? Most biographers have simply interpreted this lack of resolve as: 'She hesitated, listening to her advisers,' but the underlying reason for this misplaced advice is blindingly obvious. There was a thorny social problem. If Constance and Oscar were to be reunited, what social status were they to assume among their English compatriots on the Continent? It was unthinkable that Oscar should be accepted back into polite society as if nothing had happened: he was a bankrupt, a criminal, and a known homosexual. But it was equally unthinkable that Mrs. Holland (as she had now become) and her two sons should be ostracised on his account. The immediate answer was to make sure that on his release they were kept apart on the pretext that Oscar should be subject to a period of probation. It was pure hypocrisy. As Oscar would write to More Adey later in the year 'I was a problem for which there was no solution.'[44]

One person who might have been able to bring about the meeting between Oscar and his wife was Henrietta Stannard, the author who had asked him to call on her almost immediately after he had arrived in Dieppe. She had known them both in the days of Oscar's London successes and now entertained him on several occasions without a thought for the adverse social consequences it might have for her and her husband. In letters to friends Oscar writes of his meetings with the Stannards as news, a breakthrough in his post-prison relations with the world. There would have been nothing more natural than for Oscar to mention the reluctance of his wife to see him and, given Henrietta's complete indifference to what society thought of her befriending Oscar, she must have offered to intercede on his behalf. In a letter to the artist Louise Jopling, also a friend of the Wildes, she wrote a year later:

You know perhaps that Oscar Wilde came straight here when he was released. I did my best for him, but I am afraid it was no good. If only she would have come to him or let him go to her, I'm sure he might have been pulled up, but she was ill, something very serious internal needing serious operations and she funked it, altho' she was dying to see him. I did my level best to persuade her, but it was no good. It seemed to break Oscar up altogether for he was dying to see his boys but after he left I hear he went a regular smasher. Of course much as he had suffered in prison, his hardest times came afterwards . . . . It seems a mean thing to hit a man who is down, but the self-righteousness of some people made me very sick, I can tell you.[45]

Earlier in the year when writing *De Profundis*, Oscar had foreseen many of the difficulties he would face on his release. 'The common prisoner of a common gaol' as he described himself, 'I have come, not from obscurity into the momentary notoriety of crime, but from a sort of eternity of fame to a sort of eternity of infamy.' Unlike the petty criminals with whom he had lived for two years and who would return to their own milieu and their families to start life anew, he, by contrast, was condemned to a life of social ostracism. This he could accept as he felt it would force him to remake his life as a writer.[46] A modest, even penurious existence he had persuaded himself would be tolerable on the condition that he freed himself of all bitterness both towards Douglas for encouraging him to lead a life 'unworthy of an artist,' and towards Society for what it had inflicted upon him as a result. These were feelings which could be rationalised, understood, accepted. 'One gets no receipt for the past when one walks out into the beautiful air' he remarked a little ruefully to Frank Harris a month after arriving in France.[47] However, the part of his life which he had once taken for granted, and had assumed gratefully would be available to him when he most needed it—the fragile framework of his marriage and the affection of his wife and his children—was now denied to him. It was a bitter disappointment. Although the conventional in Wilde seldom comes to the fore, it was a useful attribute on occasion either as a platform from which to launch himself with paradoxes on his unsuspecting public, or, as in this case, a point of temporary retreat to recharge himself creatively and emotionally. Now, I'm not for a minute suggesting that Oscar and Constance would have remade a life together again for any length of time. His homosexual tendencies and his ambivalence to marriage as expressed to Robbie Ross from prison: 'For years I disregarded the tie . . . I was bored to death with the married life,' makes it clear that any reconciliation between husband and wife would have been short-lived at best, but it would have helped him to start rebuilding his shattered existence.[48] Tragically, it was not to be.

To complicate matters even further there was Bosie Douglas. Soon after Oscar's arrival in Dieppe Douglas wrote to him. The letter hasn't survived but it must have been trying to persuade Oscar to see him and to dispel any bad feeling between them. It was unlikely to have been in a similar vein as Oscar's first letter to Constance, for penitence and asking forgiveness were not Bosie's style. The only indication of its content can be surmised from the letter which Oscar wrote to Robbie Ross after he was alone in Berneval:

I had hardly any sleep last night. Bosie's revolting letter was in the room, and foolishly I had read it again and left it by my bedside. My dream was that my mother was speaking to me with some sternness, and that she was in trouble. I quite see that whenever I am in danger she will in some way warn me. I have a real terror now of that unfortunate ungrateful young man with his unimaginative selfishness and his entire lack of all sensitiveness to what in others is good or kind or trying to be so. I feel him as an evil influence, poor fellow. To be with him would be to return to the hell from which I do think I have been released. I hope never to see him again.[49]

It must have arrived at almost exactly the same time as Constance's disappointing reply to Oscar's letter 'full of penitence,' and has to be another of the great 'What if?' moments in the whole Wilde saga. Within a few days Oscar was writing back to him in a fairly neutral tone but soon he was having to fight all his better instincts not to write to Bosie every day. A week later it was 'My dearest Boy . . . yours with all love, Oscar.' A meeting planned for the middle of June had to be cancelled after word of it reached England, and a solicitor's letter warned him of the dire consequences under the deed of separation if it took place.

Constance, meanwhile, had been in touch with Carlos Blacker and his wife and was planning to spend August in Germany's Black Forest near to where the Blackers were living in Freiburg. Carlos and Oscar had been very close friends during the 1880s, so much so that he was not only appointed a trustee of Constance's marriage settlement but in 1888 Oscar dedicated to him *The Happy Prince and Other Tales*. Due to a complicated social and financial scandal in which Carlos was involved in the early 1890s, he was obliged to leave England and spent most of the rest of his life on the Continent.[50] The two men had not seen each other since Carlos had married Carrie Frost just before Oscar's trials in 1895. Carrie, homophobic and a social snob, was the daughter of an American Confederate General and thoroughly disapproved of her husband's friendship with Oscar.[51] While she was supportive of Constance during the first months after Oscar's release, her sympathy had its limits and when Oscar proposed asking Constance and his sons to join him in Berneval for a few days and then to return with them to Freiburg, Carrie must have told her husband to prevent it. He wrote to Oscar at the end of July to say that Constance couldn't make the journey because of her physical disability, though oddly enough it didn't prevent her from travelling from the Italian Riviera to the Black Forest. Oscar's reply was to suggest that he should come to Freiburg anyway to see Constance and the boys, the prospect of which must have horrified Carlos given his wife's views on the ex-convict. A further letter from

Carlos seems to have put even more emphasis Constance's illness and he told Oscar to wait until the boys were back at school and Constance was settled into her newly rented villa in Bogliasco just down the Ligurian coast from Genoa. For Carlos, at least, and given his concerns about Carrie's attitude, it was the best solution. At that point Oscar more or less gave up trying:

> My dear Friend, I am simply heart-broken at what you tell me. I don't mind *my life* being wrecked—that is as it should be—but when I think of poor Constance I simply want to kill myself. But I suppose I must live through it all. I don't care. Nemesis has caught me in her net: to struggle is foolish. Why is it that one runs to one's ruin? Why has destruction such a fascination? Why, when one stands on a pinnacle, *must* one throw oneself down? No one knows, but things are so.
>
> Of course I think it would be much better for Constance to see me, but you think not. Well, you are wiser. My life is spilt on the sand—red wine on the sand—and the sand drinks it because it is thirsty, for no other reason.
>
> I wish I could see you. Where I shall be in September I don't know. I don't care. I fear we shall never see each other again. But all is right: the gods hold the world on their knees. I was made for destruction. My cradle was rocked by the Fates. Only in the mire can I know peace.[52]

During August Oscar kept himself occupied with writing *The Ballad of Reading Gaol* and with visits from English friends, but the nights started drawing in, the friends had left and the future promised little but loneliness. From where he was living on the coast in Berneval the only decent view was towards the North, over the grey English Channel to the country which had put him behind bars. He seemed to be living out the very fear he had expressed at Oxford twenty years before: in answer to the question 'What is your idea of misery?' he had answered 'Living a poor and respectable life in an obscure village.'[53] However, he was still in touch with Bosie Douglas and they agreed to meet in Rouen at the end of the month, the first time they had seen each other since Oscar's trials. It was an emotional reunion. Bosie suggested that they take a villa together in Naples and spend the winter there. Oscar was overjoyed at the prospect and accepted, though must have known, as he wrote so poignantly only a month before to Carlos Blacker, that he was running to his ruin. Bosie offered love and danger, for which Oscar had always shown a terrible weakness, not security and respectability. Meeting Bosie in Rouen was the start of 'Part Two of the Tragic History of Oscar Wilde as devised by Lord Alfred Douglas,' Part One having opened with Douglas goading Wilde into suing his father for libel. The outcome was predictable and all the more agonizing for the onlookers as it played out in slow motion.

After that fateful meeting, Oscar had written to Carlos to say that he was going South for the winter but not with whom and gave an address in Paris where he would be spending some days on the way. Carlos suspected the worst and realised that in helping to deny Oscar access to his family he was partly responsible for this decision. In an attempt to avert the impending disaster he wrote to Oscar at once and told Constance to do the same and invite him to visit her in Nervi.[54] It was too late; their letters didn't reach him before his departure for Italy and had to be forwarded.

Once it became known that he had gone back to Bosie, all hell broke loose. To Carlos Blacker, who remonstrated with him, he wrote 'Had Constance allowed me to see my boys, my life would, I think, have been quite different. But this she would not do. I don't in any way venture to blame her for her action, but every action has its consequence.' Constance, after finally agreeing to see him, had been expecting Oscar come to her in Nervi and was furious when she found out. She wrote him what Oscar described as 'a terrible letter,' and after a brief exchange they ceased to correspond for several months. To Blacker she described Oscar's last letter to her as 'the letter of a madman who has not even enough imagination to see how trifles affect children or unselfishness enough to care for the welfare of his wife. It rouses all my bitterest feelings and I am stubbornly bitter when my feelings are roused . . . I have latterly (God forgive me) an absolute repulsion to him.' For Robbie Ross, who had been helping Oscar remake his life, the decision to return to Bosie was both personally hurtful and nothing short of madness. Robbie had been replaced in Oscar's affections by Bosie back in 1891, but after Oscar's release he had been given a new role—that of banker, adviser and literary confidant. Once more his love, and more especially now his friendship, seemed to have been cast aside. Oscar tried to justify to Robbie what he had done: 'When people speak against me for going back to Bosie, tell them that he offered me love, and that in my loneliness and disgrace I, after three months' struggle against a hideous Philistine world, turned naturally to him. Of course I shall often be unhappy, but still I love him: the mere fact that he wrecked my life makes me love him.'

Years later when my father, Vyvyan, was helping Rupert Hart-Davis to edit Oscar's letters and was going through the proofs of his father's post-prison letters, he would write in his diary:

> It has become more and more clear that Papa could have recovered and resuscitated himself had it not been for Alfred Douglas. If ever a man had an evil genius Alfred Douglas was Oscar Wilde's. And I blame my mother's family and advisers . . . They adopted the entirely wrong attitude that Papa had to go through a period of probation before even attempting to rehabilitate himself. Whereas, after his appalling prison experience, he should have come back to Mama and Cyril and me, which I think he was perfectly prepared to do at the time. In his loneliness Alfred Douglas asked to return to him; no one else did. So he clung to that man of straw and suffered a second thrust into the abyss, from which he never recovered.[55]

The consequences were inevitable. In an attempt to starve them apart, Sybil Queensberry threatened to stop her son's allowance unless they parted and, under the terms of their separation agreement, Constance did indeed stop hers to Oscar. Bosie returned to Paris in early December having persuaded his mother to pay the rent for three months on the Naples villa and provide Oscar with £200 so that he was not left destitute. Oscar read the final proofs of *The Ballad,* stayed in Italy until the first week of February and returned to Paris, chastened by what turned out to be a terrible misjudgement. As he wrote to Robbie: 'It is, of course, the most bitter experience of a bitter life; it is a blow quite awful and paralysing, but it had to come, and I know it is better that I should never see him again. I don't want to. He fills me with horror.'[56]

Although the relationship between Oscar and Constance during this period was fairly acrimonious, she nevertheless reinstated the allowance she had been giving him and even sent an extra £40 through Robbie Ross when she heard how badly off he was. She received a copy of *The Ballad* which she assumed he had asked the publisher to send her (he had) and asked Carlos Blacker, who had moved to Paris, to send news of him. Before her copy arrived she had read extracts of it in the press and wrote to her brother: 'I am frightfully upset by this wonderful poem of Oscar's, of which so far I have only seen the extracts in the *D[aily] C[hronicle]*. I hear that it was sold out the day it was published and that orders are pouring in, and that is a good thing as it means money! It is frightfully tragic and makes one cry.'[57] The day before, she had written to Arthur Humphreys, manager of Hatchard's bookshop and an old friend:

> I suppose you will not be able to get it for me? I have set my heart on getting it and I think I had better give a permanent order for every book of his that is published . . . . It is the first time that I have not had a copy of a book as soon as it is published and I am afraid that I feel it bitterly, more bitterly than I can say. For the sake of the boys I am bound to keep apart but it goes terribly against the grain, as unfortunately when I care for a person once, I care for them always, and angry as I am with him for his treatment of me, I think that if I saw him I should forgive everything![58]

It was the last book of his she would ever see. Alongside the anger and the sadness she could not help expressing her admiration and behind it all, still, the extraordinary constancy of her love for the father of her children. At the end of March she even wrote Oscar what he described to Carlos Blacker as 'a very nice letter from Constance.'[59] Less than two weeks later she was dead. She was only forty.

When I started writing this chapter, I had intended it to be merely a summary of the three and a half years from when Oscar was released from prison up to his death. It seemed wrong somehow, as the title of this book suggests, just to put Oscar into his grave without giving a brief account of those final humiliating years as a context for what was to follow. As I began condensing the facts, it became increasingly obvious that I was dealing with a story which had all the qualities of a small-scale classical tragedy— characters drawn into conflict by outside forces over which they had little control and once the plot was set in motion, impossible to halt. But in the end it was Society not Destiny which kept Oscar apart from Constance; a poignant mixture of the ancient with the modern.

After all the years that I had been studying my grandfather, I believed that I had become immune to the emotions in this final episode of his life. That was until I found the entry in my father's diary and felt his pain as I read it. Even from the restrained way he expressed himself I'm sure it was the first time that Vyvyan had confronted the reality of it all through his mother's and father's letters. More 'What ifs?' Could my father's childhood have been made happier if all those around his parents had taken the attitude of Henrietta Stannard? Probably. I can feel something of what happened in that year after Oscar's release. It's only a distant echo, a very diluted version of all their emotions, but I still feel an overwhelming sadness for them both.

M y grandmother died on 7 April 1898. She went into a clinic in Genoa for an operation seven days before and never came out. Since the early 1890s Constance had been suffering from pains in her legs, her back, and her arms as well as occasional headaches, all of which she put down variously to 'rheumatism' or 'neuralgia.' Although the symptoms were inter- mittent over the two years that Oscar was in prison, by the start of 1898 she was in continual pain. Her condition had left her virtu- ally incapable of writing by hand and she was reduced, even then with some difficulty, to using a typewriter for her correspondence. Indoors she moved slowly to avoid aggravating the condition, and outside she could only manage very short distances. At one point in July 1897 on a walk to the local station, she collapsed in the street and had to be dragged to safety by her brother.[60] It was a wretched physical state in which she found herself shortly after her fortieth birthday.

For more than a century after her death, biographers specu- lated vaguely (and even sensationally) about the nature of the ill- ness which led to her choosing ill-advised surgery to cure it. My father seems to have been the first to give any explanation for the cause of it, describing how she had tripped on a loose stair carpet in her London house and had fallen down a whole flight of stairs 'some months before leaving England.'[61] There seems no reason to doubt that it happened, but it almost certainly wasn't the cause of the slow paralysis which was taking over her body. More re- cently a 'psychoanalytic biography' of Wilde, spicing up Vyvyan's account with sensationalist conjecture, suggested that Constance may have caught syphilis from her husband early in their marriage, the tertiary symptoms of which may have caused her to lose her balance on the stairs. Logically one might then conclude that the 'creeping spinal paralysis' from which she was suffering was locomotor ataxia and syphilitic in origin.[62] It's difficult to know whether to be more amused than annoyed by such myths which implant themselves arbitrarily in the fertile soil of our family history like windborne wildflower seeds.

However, in 2014 Ashley Robins, a clinical pharmacologist from Cape Town with a long-standing interest in Oscar Wilde, suggested that we should collaborate on a medico-historical paper to conjecture more reasonably what Constance might have been suffering from and thus what ultimately killed her. Conjecture, because at this remove an accurate diagnosis was impossible but he, like I, had grown tired of seeing the same vague and medically improbable reasons given for her death. I provided the history and as many symptoms from her correspondence as I could find, and Ashley the medical expertise. His conclusion was that she had almost certainly been a victim of multiple sclerosis, a condition then only recently identified.[63] As a result it was neurogenic and not structural in origin and a surgical intervention would have been pointless, but Constance, relying on dubious medical advice, could not have known that.

By that early spring of 1898, the turmoil of her emotional life had begun to grow calmer. In September the year before, just after Oscar had gone back to Alfred Douglas, she had taken a two-year lease on the ground floor of the Villa Elvira, an imposing house in Bogliasco. For the first time since leaving London she could unpack her suitcases properly and make a home for herself and her two boys, no longer having to live out of small hotel rooms or to be dependent on the generosity of her friends and her brother for a roof over her head. Cyril and Vyvyan had settled into their second years at boarding schools, respectively in Germany and Monaco, and she at last found time to look seriously to her health.

On Constance's first visit to Genoa back in December 1895, she had put herself in the hands of Dr. Luigi Maria Bossi, a

gynaecologist who ran a small clinic in the city. Bossi was an advocate of the radical and unsound theory of the time that disorders
of the reproductive system were the cause of neurological problems in women which could be cured by gynaecologica. intervention. Exactly how he treated her that winter is not certain, but
she underwent some form of genitourinary surgery followed by
a month of complete rest in the clinic. It seemed to have relieved
some of the symptoms of which she had complained, but that was
probably a combination of rest and a period of slight remission in
the multiple sclerosis. However, she was sufficiently convinced by
the treatment to turn to Bossi again with confidence at the beginning of 1898 to consult him about something which was causing
her urinary problems and a great deal of discomfort in her lower
abdomen. Bossi prescribed a course of treatment which was ineffective and by the end of March he had diagnosed a fibroid—a
benign tumour of the uterus—and declared that surgery was the
only option left.

Given all the factors in Constance's general ill-health, it is now
perfectly clear that she was suffering from two entirely separate
disorders: there was her underlying MS making her more and
more immobile and her gynaecological problem. For Bossi this
was another opportunity to put his theories to the test—remove
the fibroid and restore his patient's mobility. She had already
written to my father in February saying that she had seen Bossi
and that 'He thinks he is going to make me walk again, but that
I shall believe when it happens,' and having suffered from what
seemed like an ever-increasing paralysis for the last two years, she
was a more-than-willing guinea-pig and her consent to the operation must have been immediate.[64] Bossi proposed operating on
Saturday 2 April.

Constance went into the clinic on the Thursday accompanied
by Maria Segré, who, although employed as her maid, had also become her companion at the Villa Elvira. As they climbed into the
carriage Constance turned to her and said, 'You know my doctor
in London told me three years ago I was not to go through with an

operation,' advice which she had been given by a doctor two years before in Heidelberg as well. Maria, already anxious, said that it was not too late to change her mind to which Constance replied with a laugh: 'It will be nothing, Maria. I think you're more afraid than I am.' She had written the night before to her close friend the Ranee in the same vein, referring merely to a 'slight operation.' Bossi operated on the Saturday as planned. Everything pointed to a quick recovery until the following Wednesday when Constance started vomiting uncontrollably, was unconscious by the evening, and died at half past seven the following morning in Maria's arms. Her brother Otho, to whom she had telegraphed the day before, arrived on Thursday evening and asked if it was too late that night to see his sister. The nurse on duty replied with a smile that it was too late, but that he could see her because she was dead. He was stunned by her apparent indifference. Had Dr. Bossi he been informed? Yes, that morning, but he said that since Constance was dead there was no point in his coming in. Where was he now? She didn't know but thought he had gone to Savona to do more operations and might be back in three or four days. Nobody was able to give Otho a satisfactory explanation for what had gone so suddenly and disastrously wrong. The death certificate simply gave the cause as 'paralysis,' which was probably correct and to-day would be termed 'paralytic ileus,' a seizing up of the digestive tract and a known complication following abdominal surgery. In Otho's mind, however, it became confused with the gradual paralysis of her arms and legs which she had been experiencing for some years, and it now seemed inexplicable that it should have killed her so suddenly.

A funeral was arranged for Easter Saturday 9 April with the help of the British Consul and his lawyer, who expressed surprise that Constance had chosen to be treated in such a 'clinic,' especially one run by Bossi who was in bad odour among his medical colleagues. The clinic's modest fees attracted less well-off patients who understood that the operations to which they subjected themselves might be partly experimental. However, this was hardly reflected in Bossi's bill for the equivalent, even then, of £140, made out with unseemly haste on the day after her death. For Otho, the overall impression was one of bungling incompetence and the opportunistic fleecing of 'wealthy' foreigners wintering on the Italian Riviera. On Constance's previous stay for nearly a month in 1895 Bossi had been happy to accept £20 but the knowledge of her friendship with the Ranee may have emboldened him to chance his luck with her estate.

Meanwhile there was no word at all from Constance's family or solicitors in London due to the Easter Holiday. In her will Constance had appointed Adrian Hope, a relative and neighbour from her London days, as her executor as well as guardian to her sons, and without his consent there was little else Otho could do except give his sister a decent burial. He chose a quiet corner in the Protestant section of the Staglieno Cemetery for her grave which he had lined in brick in the form of an underground tomb. On the coffin was painted her name 'Constance Mary Wilde.' He had made no attempt to hide her identity. After the service the Anglican clergyman who had conducted it asked whether Otho would like him to write to Mr. Wilde, an offer which was politely refused. 'I had an instinct,' he later wrote to his wife, 'that as a parson he would use his position to administer a sermon, and I thought I would spare Oscar that last humiliation.'[65]

Cyril and Vyvyan did not attend the funeral. Aside from the logistical problems of bringing the two boys from their separate schools to Genoa, Otho felt that it would have been 'useless and cruel' to have had them present, an understandable but typically Victorian attitude towards children's exposure to the reality of death. I do not know to this day whether my father in later life ever went to see his mother's grave; he never talked about it nor about her in my presence. The news was broken to him gradually by his Spiritual Father, Alfonso Stradelli, at the Jesuit College in Monaco, who said at first that Constance was very ill and then that she had died. Vyvyan wanted to know where his father was, whom by this time he had not seen for three years, but Stradelli could not tell him. And then, with the instinct of a child who knows he has been protected from an unsavoury truth, he asked the priest whether his father had been in prison. 'Yes,' replied Stradelli, 'but he is free now.' It was something that Vyvyan had suspected for a long time and a question which could never have been put so directly within the family circle.[66] He now found the truth easier to live with than the uncertainty of not knowing, and was overcome by a sense of great relief that his father was once more free. A week before she went into the clinic Constance wrote her last letter to Vyvyan:

> Father Maturin is going to bring me a rosary which he is having specially blessed by the Pope for me, so that I shall value enormously, and when I die shall leave to you! I think that I shall arrange to send Cyril into a family in the summer holidays, so I am afraid you will not see much of him. It will be expensive so we shall have to economize and live cheaply you and I, but that will not matter, will it, if we have each other? . . . Much love, my darling, from your very loving Mother.[67]

As I look through the letters that Constance wrote to my father in the final six months of her life, affectionate though they all were, none have such a loving sign-off. It's easy to interpret these things with hindsight, but I still cannot help feeling that she had a premonition of what would happen in that Genoese clinic.

Cyril, though nearly thirteen and the older of the two by a year and a half, took the news very badly and found great difficulty in expressing his emotions when writing to Otho, apart from begging to be allowed to leave Heidelberg and join his uncle's family at once. Vyvyan was more articulate and gave cogent reasons for wanting to stay on in Monaco. In the year that he had spent there he had made close friends among the pupils and even with two of the teachers at the College; he was doing well at his work; and could now converse in English, French, and Italian. They saw the decision by their guardian, Adrian Hope, to leave them both where they were for three months before bringing them back to boarding schools in England, as the pragmatic solution of a grown-up which took neither of their immediate feelings into account. Hope, incidentally, never even bothered to write to them at the time of Constance's death. Two months later Cyril still didn't have his guardian's address and wrote to Vyvyan asking for it. He wanted to know what plans were being made for his future, whether he was 'to go to a crammer or a Navy school . . . I doubt whether he will answer; he is most likely too busy.'[68]

Otho had to stay on in Genoa for ten days after the funeral before he was able meet Bossi, during which time he took legal advice about suing the clinic for negligence or at least disputing the 'butcher's bill' as he described it. The lawyer advised against legal action as the evidence was circumstantial. Short of taking a sworn statement from Bossi, exhuming Constance and conducting a post-mortem—all of which was too horrific for her brother to contemplate—there would be no case for the doctor to answer. The meeting with Bossi was inconclusive. He said that a complete hysterectomy had been discussed but that he had told Constance he was reluctant to perform so radical an operation on a woman of her age. Constance said she was 'une femme seule' with no intention of marrying again and that she would like it done; 'enlève-moi tout' were the words which she repeated several times in the course of her pre-operative consultation. However, Bossi told Otho that he had simply cut away the fibroid and that Constance had probably died from the after-effects of the chloroform, which some patients tolerated badly, and the paralytic ileus.

There was nothing more for Otho to do. It had been a major operation and not without its risks, and since Constance was persuaded that it would cure her lameness she had played it down to friends and family to avoid possible dissuasion from anyone around her. Otho removed a few of her personal possessions from the Villa Elvira but, sadly, not the blue leather case with all the letters Oscar had written to her over fifteen years and which were returned to her executor, Adrian Hope, who almost certainly destroyed them.[69] Dejected and angry, he returned to his wife in Switzerland. '*Don't* let the family push you aside; you were nearer and dearer to her than any of them and we don't want to be cut off from the boys,' Mary had written to him just after the funeral.[70] But the boys had been bequeathed by their gentle and trusting mother back to Victorian England which was far from ready to forgive the disgraceful excesses of her husband. Within a month a gravestone had been erected by the executor, which read simply 'Constance Mary daughter of Horace Lloyd Q.C.' It was in stark contrast to Otho's openness about her married past at the funeral, but it was not the first time nor the last that the English would find it necessary to whitewash Wilde's family to avoid their own discomfort. More appropriate, alongside her married name which she surely would have wanted, would have been the epitaph she chose some years before. In a letter to her close friend Georgina Mount-Temple around the time Oscar was working on *A Woman of No Importance*, she wrote: 'Here is another bit from Oscar's play which he wrote out for me last night: "Pleasures may turn a heart to stone, riches may make it callous, but sorrows cannot break it. Hearts live by being wounded." This last bit is to be graven on my tomb when I die!'[71]

Although Otho seems to have taken an instant dislike to Bossi, writing to Mary after their meeting: "I believe him in my heart to be a skunk; he gave me a bad impression. He is slimy and indefinably somewhat underbred," his view was undoubtedly coloured by his grief at Constance's death and Bossi's apparent indifference in the whole matter. As a doctor he certainly attracted criticism from colleagues both for his theories on female neurological problems and his commercial approach to surgery in his private clinic. Against that, he was later appointed professor of gynaecology at Genoa University, served as a socialist member of the Italian parliament from 1900–1904, was recognized internationally in his profession and was even made a Fellow of the British Gynaecological Society. However, none of his later achievements can excuse his misdiagnosis of Constance's condition and the unnecessary operation which led to her early death. Twenty years later nemesis struck in a bizarre fashion.

In 1918 Bossi was hauled before a disciplinary hearing of the Higher Education Council, charged with professional misconduct and unethical behaviour. He was reportedly accused of sexually molesting and seducing young female nurses and of embezzling public funds to pay employees in his private practice. The outcome was the suspension of his professorship at Genoa University for two years.[72] Bossi then left Genoa for Milan, where he continued to practise gynaecology but on 1 February 1919, he was shot dead in his consulting rooms while at his desk, his pen still grasped in his hand. The assailant was an Italian from Tunis who had accompanied his wife to the consultation, and who suspected Bossi of having an affair with her. In a fit of psychotic jealousy, after murdering Bossi, he shot his wife and then turned the revolver on himself. His suspicions were not entirely unfounded: the investigators later discovered about fifty letters which the wife, clearly obsessed with Bossi, had addressed to him. They were mostly unopened.[73]

The aftermath of Constance's death, like so much of this story, is beset with 'What ifs?' and misunderstandings. On hearing of his wife's death from Otho, Oscar at once sent him a telegram: 'Am overwhelmed with grief. It is the most terrible tragedy. Am writing,' and sent similar telegrams to Robbie Ross and Carlos Blacker asking them to come and see him. They both hurried to commiserate with him but Robbie, for some reason, later wrote to Leonard Smithers the publisher of the *Ballad*: 'You will have heard of Mrs. Wilde's death. Oscar of course did not feel it at all. It is rather appalling for him as his allowance ceases and I do not expect his wife's trustees will continue it.'[74] The allowance did continue as Constance had added a codicil to her will to that effect before her operation and Oscar was probably aware of it. It may even have been the subject of the 'very nice letter from Constance' which he mentioned to Carlos two weeks before. Robbie's remark about Oscar's lack of feeling is strange.

Most biographers seem to have taken it at face value in spite of the genuine grief which he expressed to his friends at the time and even more so later. Certainly, there had been much bitterness between Oscar and Constance over his return to Bosie the previous autumn and Oscar's insistent demands after it was over that Constance reinstate his allowance, but hostilities between them had now ceased. This was still his wife, the woman whom he acknowledged had supported him emotionally when at his lowest ebb in prison, and the mother of his children. She was dead and now any thought of ever seeing his boys again was out of the question. Had Robbie misinterpreted an apparent lack of emotion in Oscar when he arrived to console him? Oscar probably wanted to show that he was more in control of his feelings than he really was. I can't help thinking, too, that there was something almost possessive in Robbie's remark about Oscar's indifference to his wife's death. He didn't *want* Oscar to be upset over the death of the woman whom he had replaced for a while in Oscar's affections as his first homosexual lover twelve years before, still hoping to be the only one for whom Oscar had a genuinely deep affection . . . More than forty years later Alfred Douglas recounted how Oscar had told him that on the night Constance died he was tormented by sad dreams about her and that he awoke crying. 'I dreamed she came here to see me and I kept on saying "Go away, go away and leave me in peace."'[75] This story is frequently quoted to emphasise Oscar's dislike of his wife by that stage but, once again, it's too easy to take it at face value. It is far more likely that her appearance in the dreams stirred his bad conscience about the way he had behaved towards her. Her presence made him terribly aware of her goodness and his badness, which is what tormented him. As he wrote to Carlos Blacker the next day, 'It is really awful. I don't know what to do. If only we had met once and kissed each other. It is too late. How awful life is. How good you were to come at once. I have gone out as I don't dare to be by myself.'[76] A year later Oscar went out of his way to visit her grave in Genoa:

I went to Genoa to see Constance's grave. It is very pretty—a marble cross with dark ivy-leaves inlaid in a good pattern. The cemetery is a garden at the foot of the lovely hills that climb into the mountains that girdle Genoa. It was very tragic seeing her name carved on a tomb—her surname, my name, not mentioned of course—just 'Constance Mary, daughter of Horace Lloyd, QC' and a verse from Revelations. I brought some flowers. I was deeply affected—with a sense, also, of the uselessness of all regrets. Nothing could have been otherwise, and Life is a very terrible thing.[77]

Years later Robbie must have repeated his remark to my father who in turn insinuated it in a letter to Frank Harris in the 1920s: 'My mother died shortly afterwards at Genoa, of a broken heart (literally, not in the poetical sense), and my father shed telegraphic tears of Hibernian sorrow to Robbie Ross at this fresh misery an unkind fate had brought upon him.'[78] I can understand Vyvyan taking Robbie's view; he only had half the story and having grown close to him after they met properly for the first time seven years after Oscar's death, he was inclined to believe everything which Robbie told him. Constance's death had left a gaping hole in Vyvyan's life and until a more rounded picture emerged many years after, he naturally resented what he perceived to be the misery inflicted on her by his father's uncaring behaviour.[79]

The last and perhaps saddest 'What if?' is that Vyvyan might have been able to see his father again had a combination of human failings and social snobbery not prevented it. When Oscar arrived back in Paris after his disastrous interlude in Naples with Alfred Douglas, Constance wrote to Carlos Blacker to give him Oscar's address saying: 'Would it be at all possible for you to go and see him there, or is it asking too much of you? He has, as you know, behaved exceedingly badly both to myself and my children . . . but I am interested in him, as is my way with anyone that I have once known.' Carlos did indeed make contact—by letter—but hesitated about seeing him in person, largely because of his wife's disapproval. They did eventually meet but, shortly afterwards, Oscar soured the renewed friendship by touching Carlos twice for a loan. Carlos's diary at the time has several entries along the lines of 'Carrie would not allow me to see Oscar,' and although she seems to have relented at the time of Constance's death, it was one of the last times that Oscar and Carlos would ever see each other.[80] On the fringes of this deteriorating friendship was my father, son to one and a sort of adopted nephew to the other. Constance's friendship with Carlos and Carrie Blacker and the fact that the two families had spent the previous summer holiday together meant that Vyvyan came to regard Carlos much as he saw Otho, Constance's brother. One of the very first letters that he wrote after his mother's death was to Carlos, touchingly worried about the effect on his brother Cyril.[81] A second letter from Vyvyan followed less than a month later specifically asking Carlos to give his love to his father.[82] He knew that his father was alive and no longer in prison from Father Stradelli, though exactly how he knew that Oscar and Carlos were in touch is not certain. It could have been through Otho; it might even have been from Carlos himself replying to Vyvyan's first letter. In any case, Vyvyan must have been aware that his father was in Paris to ask for such a message to be passed on. Had Oscar not pestered Carlos for money alienating him as a friend, and had Carrie Blacker not poisoned the friendship still further, Carlos might have been able to bring father and son together that summer, however briefly, when Vyvyan returned to England via Paris. The Jesuit Fathers at Vyvyan's school would surely have welcomed the idea that the boy, now motherless, should at least have some contact with his father; the Rector of the College, Father Romualdo Fumagalli, had even written to Carlos as a trusted friend of the family about Vyvyan's future.[83] Perhaps I'm guilty of that anachronistic error of which I'm often too quick to accuse others—that of judging behaviour of the 1890s by the standards and practices of today. What seems to us no more than a humane gesture would have been viewed as exposing an eleven year-old boy to the corrupting influence of his depraved father.

But it could so easily have been arranged had circumstances and Puritan attitudes not interfered. According to Robbie Ross, Cyril and Vyvyan were constantly in Oscar's thoughts during his last years and he was always asking Robbie to try and find out something about them, how they were, and how they were getting on at school.[84] Towards the end, through his friend More Adey, he even approached their guardian, Adrian Hope, asking to be allowed to write them letters which could be passed on when they came of age. The reply came back that if he attempted to do so the letters would be immediately destroyed.[85] One can only imagine what extraordinary documents they would have been—*De Profundis* in a minor key with the arrogance stripped away, an attempt to seek forgiveness from beyond the grave as it would have been, like nothing else that he ever wrote. In 1954 Vyvyan wrote that for many years he had had a recurrent dream in which Oscar appeared and did just that, asking Vyvyan to forgive him for bringing so much unhappiness on his family.[86] A loving apology in writing would have been better, but a dream must have been at least some consolation.

* * *

The last two and a half years of Oscar's life were a sad reflection of what that life had been at the height of his theatrical successes just three years before.[87] 'I have lost the mainspring of life and art, *la joie de vivre*; it is dreadful,' he wrote to Frank Harris. 'I have pleasures, and passions, but the joy of life is gone. I am going under: the morgue yawns for me. I go and look at my zinc-bed there. After all, I had a wonderful life, which is. I fear, over.'[88] The pleasures and passions had now become alcohol and the low-life of Paris, and the occasional meeting with French men of letters gave a semblance of respectability to his impoverished existence. When both credit and credibility ran out with friends who 'loaned' him money, he resorted to subterfuge. On one occasion he asked Robbie Ross, who was administering it, to pay his quarterly allowance in advance citing 'a wretched inn-keeper at Nogent' who was threatening to sell his luggage for an unpaid bill. Robbie's reply hasn't survived but Oscar's next letter to him starts: 'I am so sorry about my excuse. I had forgotten I had used Nogent before. It shows the utter collapse of my imagination, and rather distresses me.' Even in adversity he hadn't lost his sense of humour.[89] Rather more reprehensible was his selling of the scenario for a new play to at least four different people, each of whom assumed it was an exclusive deal.[90]

Carlos Blacker had been working discreetly behind the scenes of the Dreyfus affair to help prove the disgraced soldier's innocence and at some point discussed the matter in confidence with Oscar. When critical reports started to appear in the press about his involvement in the affair and touched on the scandal which had forced him to leave England, he accused Oscar of spreading the rumours and broke off their friendship definitively. Leonard Smithers, who published *The Ballad of Reading Gaol* for him when no one else would touch his work, provided some badly needed royalties but the sums weren't large. He also agreed to publish Oscar's last two plays: *An Ideal Husband* and *The Importance of Being Earnest,* but the title page of each simply declared that they were 'By the author of *Lady Windermere's Fan*' pandering to British sensibilities. As Oscar wrote to him when *The Ballad* was published under his prison cell number C.3.3., 'I see it is my *name* that terrifies.'[91]

Oscar's letters from those last years, preserved mostly by his intimate friends, make melancholy reading. They comprise nearly a third of his extant correspondence and reveal him, for once, without his mask. But they also show that he was blessed with that greatest of gifts, the ability to shrug one's shoulders and smile at misfortune. One, which he wrote to his old friend Frankie Forbes-Robertson who had just married and invited him to come and stay in Wales, has the humour, beauty and sadness which so characterised him at the time:

I have nothing to offer you but one of my books, that absurd comedy *The Importance of Being Earnest*, but I send it to you, in the hopes it may live on one of your bookshelves and be allowed to look at you from time to time. Its dress is pretty: it wears Japanese vellum, and belongs to a limited family of nine: it is not on speaking terms with the popular edition: it refuses to recognise the poor relations whose value is only seven and six-pence. Such is the pride of birth. It is a lesson.

Ah! how delightful it would be to be with you and your husband in your own home! But my dear child, how could I get to you? Miles of sea, miles of land, the purple of mountains and the silver of rivers divide us: you don't know how poor I am: I have no money at all: I live, or am supposed to live on a few francs a day: a bare remnant saved from shipwreck. Like dear St. Francis of Assisi I am wedded to Poverty: but in my case the marriage is not a success: I hate the Bride that has been given to me: I see no beauty in her hunger and her rags: I have not the soul of St. Francis: my thirst is for the beauty of life: my desire for its joy. But it was dear of you to ask me, and do tell the 'king of men' how touched and grateful I am by the invitation you and he have sent me.

And, also, sometimes send me a line to tell me of the beauty you have found in life. I live now on echoes as I have little music of my own. Your old friend, Oscar.[92]

From Constance's death onwards it was little more than a slow slide into the grave. The monotony of his life in Paris was relieved with trips to Switzerland and Italy, and Frank Harris offered him three months on the French Riviera in the hope that it might rekindle some of the old brilliance, but the spark had gone. He managed with difficulty to live on the allowance Constance had bequeathed him and the charity of the few friends he had left. Bosie Douglas helped with the occasional handout, but when his father died and left him £15,000, Oscar made the mistake of suggesting that a more permanent arrangement might be considered. Bosie 'went into paroxysms of rage, followed by satirical laughter, and said that it was the most monstrous suggestion he had ever heard, that he would do nothing of the kind, that he was astounded at my suggesting such a thing, that he did not recognise I had any claim of any kind on him.'[93]

In the autumn of 1900 a recurrent ear infection became serious and needed surgery. Complications ensued and cerebral meningitis set in.[94] He was soon confined to bed and delirious, but shortly before the end Robbie Ross fulfilled a long-held promise to his friend and fetched a Catholic priest, Father Cuthbert Dunne, who baptized Oscar into the Church of Rome.[95] Aged only 46, he died the next day on 30 November 1900, and it was just the start of a very remarkable afterlife.

PART TWO
(1900-1918)

As soon as the 1898 school summer holidays began, my father and Cyril were sent back to England where they stayed with Constance's aunt, Mary Napier, while their future was being decided. Making Adrian Hope her executor and the guardian to her two boys had been the safest and most conventional option open to Constance, but in retrospect it probably wasn't the best for them. Hope was a man of great integrity and much respected as the Secretary of the Hospital for Sick Children in Great Ormond Street. He was also Aunt Mary's nephew by marriage, so there was a family connection, even if slightly distant. However, at the time of Oscar's trials Adrian and his wife Laura, neighbours of the Wildes in Tite Street, had expressed their revulsion at the whole scandal, with Laura writing in her diary that he was a 'monstrous husband' and a 'fiend.'[96] Constance had apparently begged Adrian to take on these potential responsibilities at the time she had obtained her deed of separation from Oscar and he had accepted, little thinking that within a year he would find himself having to fulfil them. The fact that Constance had already altered her own and her boys' surnames helped matters considerably. You could burn the letters that Oscar had written to you (people did) and tear the pages out of the books which he had inscribed to you (they did that too) but family was family and Wilde's children were now Hope's responsibility. It certainly wouldn't have done his standing any good if the fact had been known publicly. Had they still been called Wilde on their return to England he would doubtless have had their names changed as a priority, as much for his own sake as for theirs. His decision to wipe Oscar out of Constance's life in the inscription on her grave had already made that quite clear. Such was the need to dissociate the family from anything that could connect it with Oscar Wilde that in 1903 Hope even had their change of name confirmed by Royal Warrant and given additional importance with a new grant of arms.[97] With the best of intentions, he wanted to establish a sort of artificial pedigree which would protect Cyril and Vyvyan, then about to leave school and embark on their adult lives. Emotionally they would have been better served by Constance's brother Otho who, despite his disapproval of the way Oscar had treated his sister after prison, remained on relatively good terms with him. Oscar had sent him a copy of *The Ballad*, had received a letter of appreciation in reply and told Otho that he was 'greatly touched by what you say about it.'[98] However, Otho, twice married and living in Switzerland, had his own financial problems. He had been forced to leave England in 1891 to escape his creditors and Constance needed someone more stable and reliable to handle her estate and her children. She also wanted her boys to be educated in England, especially Cyril who had set his heart on joining the Navy.

Cyril was just thirteen when he arrived back in London to the news that 'the Navy would not have him.' The briefest of paragraphs in my father's autobiography, saying just that and giving no explanation for it, always mystified me.[99] Cyril was well-built for his age and healthy; he had been attending an English school, Neuenheim College, in Heidelberg which had a reputation for cramming the pupils who needed it for entry to the Royal Navy, the Army, and the Civil Service. In those days the Navy liked to get its hands on future officer material at an early age so applying to a special naval school at thirteen would have been perfectly normal, but such was the competition to join the 'Senior Service' that a boy's background was carefully scrutinised before he was admitted. However, though it can only be a conjecture, my discovery of a letter from Otho to his wife Mary offered a possible explanation. It seems to be one of the first effects of direct collateral damage which Oscar's scandal would have on his children. 'Cyril has lost his appointment to the Navy,' wrote Otho even before the boy's return. 'I am so sorry. All Mrs. Napier's fault for intermeddling: this was her working quietly for the children. Of course the Admiralty refused her. Digby Morant had promised to work for it and was the man to have got it if anyone could manage the thing. Poor Cyril. I am so disappointed for him.'[100] Digby Morant was then a Vice-Admiral but the two words 'Of course' say it all. Cyril was clearly rejected on the paperwork alone, and his father's name on his birth certificate almost certainly disqualified him. In case any reader should think I exaggerate, let me offer the following as evidence. A century later, as I was researching my uncle Cyril's military record in the National Archives I came across his application in 1903 to the Royal Military Academy at Woolwich. Here again he was asked to supply a birth certificate as well as enter his father's name, profession, and 'descent' on the form. He duly put 'Oscar Wilde' and 'Irish Gentleman.' Later the name was heavily blacked out (but still just discernible) and 'Father dead' substituted in another hand. Attached to the form was a Civil Service Commission envelope containing a copy of Cyril's birth certificate. It was closed with the Commission's imposing wax seal and on it was written: 'According to the evidence contained herein Mr. Cyril Holland was born in London on 5th June 1885 (eighty-five). The Civil Service Commissioners have been specially desired to regard this evidence as confidential.'[101] It also made sense of the last sentence in that brief paragraph written by my father: 'So he was entered for Radley, with a view to his going into the Army, which was not so squeamish.' Cyril must have had his suspicions about the Navy's reasons for turning him down in 1898, but when it came to completing his Army application in 1903, it would have come clear. He was, however, accepted and from 1904 until his death at the Front in 1915 during the Battle of Aubers, he served with distinction in the Royal Field Artillery.

Vyvyan's first encounter with the reality of his father's scandal, like Cyril's, came on his return to England. He had been aware that something was 'wrong' in the family throughout his exile on

the Continent and that wrongness had begun to take shape when
Father Stradelli confirmed that Oscar had been in prison. Now,
back in his Aunt Mary's house, he was delighted to find a copy of
The Happy Prince on her bookshelves: 'But I had a great shock
when I saw that the name Oscar Wilde had been scratched off the
cover and that a piece of stamp-paper had been pasted over it on
the title-page. Once more I was puzzled and wondered what it was
all about.'[102]

Constance's family, to whom the two boys were consigned,
immediately set about re-anglicising them and obliterating all
references to their father, destroying any evidence which might
possibly connect them to him. 'The first steps in that direction,'
wrote Vyvyan, 'was to give us to understand that our father was
dead. We were not told this in so many words . . . but the impression was conveyed and we accepted it as fact.'[103] However, at the
time Oscar was still alive, living in Paris, and only died two and a
half years later. They were strongly discouraged from referring to
their Irish ancestry, especially as one of Oscar's essays in dialogue,
'The Decay of Lying,' featured the two of them by their first names
and anyone familiar with it might have made the connection without too much difficulty. It was also decided that the two brothers
should be sent to separate schools so that there could be no danger
of them being overheard while discussing their past life together.
This further splintering of an already fragmented family was made
easier by the fact that Vyvyan wanted to continue his Catholic education and thus provided the staunchly Protestant Napiers with
a convenient excuse for keeping the two of them apart. At the end
of that summer, Vyvyan was sent off to Stonyhurst and Cyril to
Radley early the next year with a veil drawn over any memories of
happier days with mother and father at the family house in Tite
Street. Being told that you were an orphan, to forget a childhood
which you had scarcely left behind, and to be separated forcibly
from your only link with better times cannot have been easy for
my father.

Having been boarders for the past two years respectively in

Heidelberg and Monaco, both Cyril and Vyvyan adapted themselves well to English school life, each carrying to a different degree the family secret. Cyril was strong and athletic and threw
himself into Radley's sporting activities; Vyvyan was more cerebral
and, thanks to the education he had received from the Jesuits in
Monaco, was intellectually advanced for his age and excelled at
school-work. A far greater difference, however, lay beneath the
surface; Cyril was aware of what lay behind the unmentioned family scandal, while my father was still ignorant of it.

Cyril already had some idea having seen a newspaper placard
in London's Baker Street at the time of Oscar's arrest. As he wrote
to my father many years later, 'I asked what it meant. I never rested
till I found out.'[104] With the desire of an elder brother to protect
his younger sibling, Cyril kept the truth to himself, but in doing
so he took on a burden which he was unable to share with anyone
outside the family. The one person who might have lightened the
load was his own brother and although Vyvyan was to learn the
facts when he was eighteen, from my father's own account of their
relationship the matter was never mentioned between them. My
father seems to have kept all his brother's letters and Oscar is mentioned in them only twice merely in connection with Oxford when
Cyril visited Magdalen, 'the college father was at when he was an
undergraduate.' This decision early on, to keep what he saw as an
ugly family secret to himself, affected much of the remainder of
his short life until his death at the age of thirty. 'My own youth,'
wrote my father in 1954, 'was filled with perplexity; his with the
weight of knowledge which he was too young to bear.'[105]

In a strange way, it was just that knowledge which seemed to
work in Cyril's favour, at least as far as his relations and his guardian were concerned. He was determined at all costs 'to wipe that
stain away,' as he put it, to be a conventional young man indulging
in all those 'healthy' activities and pursuits which, like his change
of name, would distance him from anything to do with his father.[106]
This endeared him to the Hopes and the Napiers far more than
Vyvyan who, even if 'perplexed' and lacking anything equivalent

to parental affection, managed to pass his teenage years untrammelled by feelings of family shame and disgrace. As a result, he felt no need to overcompensate with exemplary good behaviour and by comparison with his brother, 'I was always the bad son of a disreputable father, who must be looked after for charity's sake and kept well in the background.'[107]

For Christmas 1898, Vyvyan was looking forward to spending time, if not with disapproving and critical relatives, at least with people he knew. Instead, he was boarded out for two fairly miserable weeks with total strangers in Southport. Cyril, by contrast, spent the holidays at Babbacombe Cliff in Devon with the Mount-Temples, old friends of Oscar and Constance and wrote to Vyvyan in the New Year that he had had 'an awfully good time.' No doubt whoever made the decision about the boys' holiday arrangements saw untold dangers in putting them together in an environment familiar from the past. The following year, after spending a more congenial summer holiday with a distant relative, Cornelia Cochrane, an aunt by marriage, Vyvyan had to pass through London on his way back to school. Adrian Hope was called on to give him a bed for the night—one of the only times that Vyvyan ever saw him. The exchange of letters between Adrian and Laura at the time makes it perfectly clear how the Hopes regarded him: 'Vivian Holland comes to me on Monday for the night. Rather a bore but can't be helped,' wrote Adrian to Laura, and a day later: 'Vivian arrives at Victoria about 5 where I shall meet him and take him home. I have asked Kellock [*their doctor*] to dine that night so he will be able to overhaul the boy before he goes back to school. I take him to Euston on Tuesday morning and pack him off to school.' Laura replied sympathetically: 'How good of you to have the little chap Vivian. I suppose he is in the spare room. I hope he will, in the fullness of time, become a priest for he would be quite off your hands.' And after putting up his ward for the night, Adrian wrote again: 'Today I packed Vivian off to Stonyhurst by the 12 o'clock from St. Pancras feeling exhausted with his ceaseless idle jabber. He never stops talking or asking questions and is full of himself and his own importance, health etc. I took a violent dislike to him, poor little chap.'[108] Earlier in the summer, Vyvyan had written to Hope telling him of the three end-of-year prizes he had won for school work. His letter was never even acknowledged.[109]

Vyvyan might have expected a little more warmth and understanding from the Secretary to the Great Ormond Street Hospital for Sick Children, the guardian into whose care his mother Constance had chosen to place him in the event of her death. Oscar, when in prison, had expressed concern at the idea of one of Constance's family taking on this responsibility for his children: 'they should not be bred up to look on me with either hatred or contempt: a guardian amongst my wife's relations would be for this reason impossible.' However, he had no say in the matter and let himself be convinced that Constance had made the right choice, writing six months later in *De Profundis*: 'She has chosen Adrian Hope, a man of high birth and culture and fine character, her own cousin, . . . with whom Cyril and Vyvyan have a good chance of a beautiful future.'[110] Hope took on the responsibility for Constance's sake but he seems to have let his disgust for Oscar affect his attitude towards his children. He saw his guardianship as a legal matter, a slightly tiresome obligation and not, as I believe Constance had hoped it would be, to give her boys, if not parental affection, at least kindness and guidance.

Even though Cyril and Vyvyan hardly saw one another during their school years, they kept in touch by letter. Cyril's letters, predictably, are full of his sporting achievements and the occasional dose of 'older brother advice' from one who is trying to conform to one who cannot see any necessity for it. He encourages Vyvyan to take up boxing saying that 'It would do you a lot of good.' Later, around the time of Vyvyan's 15th birthday, he writes: 'It is a great thing to have many friends at a public school, especially in after life. And popularity will do many things for one,' and in his letter of birthday wishes: 'I hope you will thoroughly enjoy yourself, but in so doing I hope you will show the discretion which now ought to be shown by one of your age. It is the first coming-of-age for when one is 15 one is no longer a junior.' From the tone of these letters Cyril, the golden boy, must have been alerted by family members to certain unconventional aspects of his brother's outlook on life. Vyvyan, in Cyril's eyes, was in danger of letting the side down, of undoing all the careful repair work which the Napiers had performed on the 'disgraced' family. Being a normal, intellectually and emotionally adventurous adolescent simply wasn't part of the plan. It was a theme to which Cyril would occasionally return in his letters to Vyvyan until shortly before his death in 1915. Vyvyan's letters to Cyril haven't survived, apart from the single typescript draft he kept of his long letter from 1914. Cyril's later life as a career soldier was not conducive to keeping family papers; he may also have considered his younger brother's letters a link with the past from which, with much effort, he was attempting to detach himself.

On 30 November 1900, when they had been at their respective schools for two years, their father died in Paris and short obituaries appeared in the British, Irish, and American press the day after. Just how and when the boys were told is not entirely clear but it was certainly not by the Napiers or Adrian Hope. Vyvyan wrote that he was summoned by the Rector of Stonyhurst, Father Joseph Browne, and told a day or two later. He wanted to ask about what had happened to his father but, as he said, 'my courage failed me.' Cyril was not so fortunate. *The Times* obituary appeared the very next day and was discussed by the older boys over breakfast, leaving Cyril no choice but to keep quiet and listen to their comments. To learn that your father had just died would have been bad enough; to realise that you had been deceived into thinking it two years before by your family and that grieving in another form had to start again would have been worse. Worst of all, especially for Vyvyan, would have been the thought that their father had been alive since their return to England and that they could have seen him, or at least corresponded with him, had it not been for Adrian Hope and the Napiers.

The Warden of Radley, the Revd Thomas Field, had admitted

Cyril to the school knowing whose son he was, but on the understanding that the matter was to be kept a secret. He had been a fellow of Magdalen College at the time that Oscar was there as an undergraduate and had been distinctly unimpressed by Oscar's aesthetic posturing.[111] It was probably the need for absolute secrecy which prevented him from breaking the news to Cyril personally, rather than any animosity towards his father. The secret was well-kept: Cyril's entry in the *Radley Register*, unlike those of other boys, only included his father's name for the first time in 1947. Unknown to Cyril, a boy at the school four years older than him, Louis Wilkinson, had written to Oscar in 1898 sympathising with his 'cruel and unjust fate,' which led in 1899 to a delightful exchange of letters between 'the Radley schoolboy' and the disgraced father of one of his fellow students.[112] So near and yet so far—another of those plausible 'What ifs' of the Wilde story. Had Oscar known that his eldest son was living in the same community as his youthful correspondent . . . but speculation is useless. The disguise was too effective and given Cyril's loyalty to his mother's memory and her censorious family, the discovery that his father was still alive would merely have added to his confused feelings. Many years after, on the other hand, Vyvyan would write: 'For my own part, I know quite well that if I had received a letter from him I would have answered it, family or no family, and that I would not have mentioned the fact to a soul.'[113]

One letter of sympathy which must have given the boys some comfort seems to have bypassed the carefully constructed family defences, and in his 1954 autobiography my father reproduced Cyril's reply to the writer, though, significantly, without the passages below in italics:

Dear Mr. Ross,

Thank you so much for the kind letter you sent me. It was very kind of you to give the flowers for us. I am glad you say that he loved us. I hope that at his death he was truly penitent; I think he must have been if he joined the Catholic Church and my reverence for the Roman Church is heightened more than ever. It is hard for a young mind like mine to realise why all the sorrow should have come on us, especially so young. And I am here among many happy faces among boys who have never really known an hour of sorrow and I have to keep my sorrow to myself and have no one here to sympathise with me although I am sure my many friends would soon do so if they knew. But when I am solemn and do not join so much in their jokes they stir me up and chide me for my gloominess.

It is of course a long time since I saw father but all I do remember was when we lived happily together in London and how he would come and build brick houses for us in the nursery.

I only hope that it will be a lesson for me and prevent me from falling into the snares and pitfalls of this world. On Saturday I went up to London to see Mrs. Napier and came back on Sunday afternoon. [*Vivian told me you had also written to him.*]

I first read of his death in a paper at breakfast and luckily one cannot realise so great a loss in cold print or I don't know what I should have done. [*It is only too true that 'the sins of the father visit the sons unto the third and fourth generation.'*] And yet the ordinary person reads it without emotion and quite dispassionately.

I cannot put my thoughts into words, so I will end. Yours very affectionately,

Cyril Holland[114]

Neither the original letters to the boys nor Cyril's original reply appear to have survived and the only remaining evidence is a copy of Cyril's letter transcribed manually by Robert Ross, headed 'Copy of Cyril's letter,' and omitting both the addressee and the signatory. This is odd and makes Vyvyan's explanation that it was addressed to Robbie at best improbable. On several occasions during the writing of this book I have found that what should have been truthful, first-hand accounts of events are at best unreliable and at worst mere inventions. Sometimes it is mistaken memories which are to blame; at others it is simplifications of the truth or ill-founded conjectures which artificially tie up the loose ends and conveniently round off a story. The trouble with these manipulations is that after several unquestioning repetitions by follow-my-leader biographers, myth morphs into fact and the process is difficult to reverse. Correcting them is a necessary but uncomfortable task, especially where family is concerned. This is one of them.

There can be no doubt that a letter of condolence and Cyril's reply existed; Ross was not in the habit of 'transcribing' non-existent letters, but had Cyril's letter been addressed to him there would have been no point in suppressing the names of the sender or the recipient. My father also wrote in his autobiography that Robbie Ross had sent the letter care of the family solicitor, and that it had been forwarded to Cyril for reply. That would almost certainly have been impossible as the solicitor could not have done so without instructions from Adrian Hope or the Napiers, who would have vetoed any contact being made by one of Oscar's 'disreputable' friends. Even on Oscar's death, Ross had tried to communicate with Adrian Hope through his solicitor but had received no reply until much later and then only indirectly.[115] Ross was also a compulsive keeper of correspondence and would have preserved Cyril's letter rather than just a transcript, which, I believe, is all that Vyvyan ever saw. When, over half a century later, he ascribed the original letter of condolence to his father's greatest friend it was the neatest solution, but it meant that in quoting Cyril's reply he had to suppress the sentence: 'Vivian told me that you had also written to him,' in order to make sense of writing that when he was first introduced seven years later to Robbie Ross he had no idea who Ross was. But why would Cyril have written 'Vivian told me . . . ' if he hadn't? It all leads to the conclusion that Cyril was replying to someone who wasn't Robert Ross, and that someone was almost certainly Carlos Blacker.

Nowhere in the letters which Robbie wrote to friends after Oscar's funeral does he say that he gave flowers in the name of the children, and the floral tributes and wreaths with the donors' names are listed in considerable detail. However, he does mention 'an anonymous friend who had brought some [flowers] on behalf of the children.'[116] The friend was Carlos Blacker, who wrote both in his diary and in a letter to Otho that he went to see Oscar's body and 'took him some violets from the children.'[117] In a later diary entry on 14 December Carlos records that he received a letter from Cyril and 'wrote to Ross sending Cyril's letter,' which Robbie obviously copied and showed to Vyvyan many years later.

Carlos Blacker was a good friend and occasional confidant of Constance in her last years and he had remained in correspondence with Otho since her death. He had become a sort of adoptive uncle to the two boys and Vyvyan even wrote to him after Constance died. Through Otho he would have known where the two boys were at school and there would have been nothing more natural than for him to have written to them direct to tell them about the flowers and the fact that their father had loved them. It would also have represented a posthumous gesture of reconciliation with their father after his quarrel with Oscar of two years before.

Despite their falling out over what Blacker perceived as Oscar's treachery in revealing his involvement in the Dreyfus affair to the press, Carlos was deeply affected by his old friend's death. According to his diary, over the next six years he bicycled out to Bagneux Cemetery, where Oscar was initially buried, no less than ten times to visit his grave. When he died in 1928, according to his wishes he was cremated at Père Lachaise Cemetery and his ashes placed in the columbarium, a short distance from where Oscar himself by then was buried. Not for long. Four months later, in what can only be seen as a final domineering act, his wife Carrie had them moved to the American Cemetery at St. Germain-en-Laye thus ensuring that Oscar and her husband were definitively separated.[118]

Oscar's death was widely (if briefly) reported in the British national and provincial press. A Paris correspondent for the *Daily Chronicle* telegraphed his copy to London giving details of Oscar's last days, mentioning that Robert Ross had 'nursed him' and he had been received into the Catholic Church by Father Cuthbert Dunne, an Irish Catholic priest in Paris.[119] Father Dunne would certainly not have talked to the press about such a private matter, so it must have been Robbie who provided the information in the hope that Oscar's deathbed conversion would go some way to softening the references which were bound to be made to Oscar's sulphurous past in the obituaries. It was the start of a long process of mending his friend's literary and personal reputation to which he devoted much time and effort until his own death eighteen years later.

Whether it was from the press or on the Catholic 'grapevine' that the Rector of Stonyhurst learned about Oscar's conversion, he took the initiative to write to Father Dunne:

> I am writing to ask you if it is true that you were happy enough to reconcile poor Oscar Wilde to the Church, if you could kindly send me a few lines at your leisure about his death. We have here a son of his—whom he should not have had—and the boy, who is of a sensitive and affectionate nature, is most anxious to be reassured as to his father's reputed happy end and also to have what particulars you could kindly send him. I know how busy you must be and how unfair it is to add to your burdens; but I hope you will excuse my request under the exceptional circumstances.

Father Dunne duly obliged and received a warm letter of thanks from the Rector:

> Rev. and dear Father, Your long and most circumstantial letter about the last moments of poor Oscar Wilde was a great act of charity. I wish you could have had the reward of it here by seeing the hungry delight with which his boy devoured it as I read it to him. He was quite overjoyed and is most grateful to you; he promises to write to you himself. I need hardly say that it is quite a secret here who his father is, and one dreads lest some of those wretched Society papers should get hold of the fact and drag it

and the poor boy into the world of gossip. I hope you may one day see him: he will have a great deal to thank you for.

Vyvyan did indeed write and part of his letter further supports the fact that it was Carlos Blacker who wrote to the boys about giving the flowers in their name:

Dear Father Dunne, It has given me such consolation that nothing else could possibly have done to know that my father, if not already in Heaven, is on his way there in Purgatory. Father Rector told me how kind you were to him and I bear you the greatest possible esteem for your kind aid to him. I am sure that, though in your letter to the Rector you represent yourself as the simple instrument of his being received into the Church, you spoke words of courage and consolation that had a great deal to do with father's conversion . . . . I beg you to thank Mr. Robert Ross for all he did. I have never heard of him, but from all accounts he must have been a very good man. I believe also that Mr. Carlos Blacker, who is a great friend of mine, was with my father before his death and though he refuses to tell me whether he had any part in father's conversion or not, I feel sure he must have done a great deal . . . . But thank God I have still got many friends in the world and need not think I am going to be left entirely alone. I am sure you will pray for my father and my brother too, and I in turn will pray unceasingly for you.[120]

Unfortunately both the consolation and the feeling of having 'many friends' were short-lived. A couple of weeks later at Christmas, farmed out again to distant relatives, Vyvyan found himself spending time with their neighbours' children and due to a misunderstanding one day, was sent home in disgrace. Worried about how he was going to explain his early return, as well as reflecting on the misery of being an unwanted orphan and thinking, as he put it, 'that there must be something monstrous about my family,' he decided to put an end to it all. Instead of returning to the inevitable reproaches, he wandered off into a nearby wood and lay down in a snow-drift hoping for painless oblivion. Luckily his absence was noticed in time and he was found, but complications from the exposure turned into a severe mastoid infection leaving him partially deaf and he didn't return to Stonyhurst for a year.[121]

From then on Cyril and Vyvyan saw very little of each other and seemed to drift further apart, with Cyril ever more into his self-appointed role as the cleanser of the tarnished family honour and by the beginning of 1904 he had gained his place at the Royal Military Academy at Woolwich to start a career in the army. Vyvyan, who left Stonyhurst that summer and had passed through stages of wanting to become a Jesuit monk, an engineer, and a doctor, now found himself reluctantly being pushed towards the Far Eastern Consular Service by the family. Cyril added his voice to those of the Napiers, sensing that the constraints of the Civil Service would ensure that his younger brother didn't stray onto the paths of embarrassing nonconformity: 'I think it is a pity you do not take to the Consular Service as the work is highly interesting; the posts are good and in interesting localities; there is a very distinct social standing, a thing by no means to be despised nowadays; and moreover the pay is good and the pension is the best going . . . and I think that we could mutually help one another in the two services—Consular and Army.'[122]

With Cyril in the Royal Field Artillery and most likely to be sent to the outer reaches of the Empire and Vyvyan safely isolated in somewhere like Shanghai, England would be rid finally of all living traces of the monstrous Oscar Wilde. And indeed she would have been but for a series of coincidences and the devotion of Robert Ross to the memory of his dear, dead friend.

Weaving together the different strands of a life demands a certain skill but is generally made easier when the strands naturally overlap. In the case of posthumous Oscar, this task is made all the more difficult when some of the players in the piece were determined that nothing should be allowed to overlap at all. Not only were Cyril and Vyvyan largely kept apart from each other by their own family, any of their father's friends who enquired after their wellbeing were coldly informed that they were perfectly happy and not to be disturbed. Later, my father would write: 'The lives of my brother and myself could have been made much happier after our mother's death if we had been allowed to mingle with those friends of our father who had remained loyal to him; this would have enabled us to retain much of the self-confidence of youth which was slowly drained out of us.'[123] In consequence, during all the time that Cyril and Vyvyan were at school in England they were entirely unaware of what Robert Ross was doing for the estate and the posthumous reputation of their father.

When Oscar wrote from prison asking Robbie to be his literary executor, he also said that as soon as he found he had a legal right to make a will he would do so. Unfortunately he never did and as a result he died not only a bankrupt but also intestate.[124] Even in death Oscar managed to complicate the lives of those around him.

'If I can produce one more beautiful work of art,' as he wrote to Alfred Douglas from prison, 'I shall be able to rob malice of its venom, and cowardice of its sneer, and to pluck out the tongue of scorn by the roots,' and one of the first things he had done on his release from prison was to start writing *The Ballad of Reading*

Gaol.[125] It was published nine months later by Leonard Smithers whose principal claim to fame was as the publisher of Aubrey Beardsley and the later work of Sir Richard Burton, and whom Oscar described as 'the most learned erotomaniac in Europe.'[126] There was nothing preventing a bankrupt Oscar from contracting with Smithers to publish the *Ballad* and receiving royalties from the sales, though he probably should have declared them to the Official Receiver. What he had *no* right to do, since they had been listed as part of his assets, was to sell Smithers the rights to his last two unpublished plays, *An Ideal Husband* and *The Importance of Being Earnest*, but it was not until May 1902 that the Official Receiver caught up with it. It was just one of the occasions in those last years when his need for money overcame moral considerations and one of several 'deals' which came to light after his death when the Official Receiver started to take an active interest in his copyrights. In one instance it turned out that Oscar may have given Anton Lindner, Viennese poet and friend of Richard Strauss, permission in 1900 to translate *Salomé* for Germany and Austria, though whether money actually changed hands is unclear; in another, Nino de Sanitis claimed that Oscar had authorised a translation of the play into Italian in 1901—presumably by then through a spiritualist medium. Even as late as the 1920s, when he alone was heir to the literary estate, Vyvyan used to pay an annual insurance premium to cover himself against the possibility that rights he granted might conflict with something his father had agreed while he was still alive and in desperate need of money.[127]

George Alexander, the actor-manager who had first produced the plays, paid the Official Receiver £300 in August 1901 for both the literary and dramatic rights to *Lady Windermere's Fan* and *The Importance of Being Earnest*, and with great generosity bequeathed them back to my father on his death in 1918. At the time, the Official Receiver was of the opinion 'that *Lady Windermere's Fan* had not a very long life before it and that *The Importance of Being Earnest* was practically dead.' Later, although he was under no obligation to do so, Alexander also made regular royalty payments to the estate from box-office takings. Ward, Lock & Co, the original publishers of *Dorian Gray,* bought the copyright of the novel for £10 and subsequently sold it on for £25 to Charles Carrington, a Parisian publisher of somewhat louche reputation, who exploited it to the full. By 1920, Wilde's first bibliographer, Christopher Millard, noted that 142 editions of the work had been published in 16 different languages. Richard Strauss negotiated the exclusive musical rights for *Salomé* with the Official Receiver in October 1905, though he had been working on the score as early as 1903 and maintained that under Article 5 of the 1886 Berne Copyright Convention the work was no longer protected from translation after ten years from first publication. Frederick Delius had already been asking about musical rights to *Salomé* in 1903, but enquiries with agents in Paris elicited the reply that they 'had no knowledge of Mr. Delius and on the whole would not advise entering into a contract with him.' Probably as well considering how precisely Strauss's powerful score matched the disquieting mood of the play. And then there were the piracies both at home and abroad, the pirates assuming that because Oscar had been homosexual and his works were out of favour in England, there would be neither family nor mainstream publishers to pursue them.

In short, the rights in Oscar's works were a complicated mess and were being administered by an Official Receiver who thought (doubtless because of the author's personal reputation) that they were of little financial value and who had been licensing or disposing of them accordingly. Until selling the rights to George Alexander, he was clearly unaware that Oscar's plays had continued to be produced successfully in provincial theatres, albeit mostly without the author's name or simply 'By the author of *Lady Windermere's* Fan.'[128] When Alexander revived *The Importance* at the Coronet Theatre in December 1901—Oscar's name still absent from playbills and programmes—a small weekly journal reviewing the production noted:

'On the first night it was received with such enthusiasm that stalls and pit and gallery shouted for the author: the expression, I suppose, of some strange regret, for surely, everyone knows who wrote it; even Notting Hill has heard of the greatest English playwright of our time.'[129]

Robbie, as Oscar's unofficial literary executor, knew that it was in the interests of the estate to cooperate with the Receiver, help satisfy the creditors, get the bankruptcy annulled, and take back full control of what rights were left as soon as he could. 'The function which I set myself in 1900,' he later wrote, 'was to try and get the books and plays a fair hearing and to obtain some benefit from their sale for Wilde's children,' though when he suggested as much to Adrian Hope, he was told that 'the children must not have any official benefit from their father's works, as their names are changed and it would only handicap them in life.'[130] Robbie's other concern immediately after Oscar's death was to pay the outstanding bill at the Hôtel d'Alsace. The proprietor, Jean Dupoirier, whose charity and kindness to Oscar in his last weeks were extraordinary, was owed over £100 and since it was a debt incurred after the bankruptcy he was not on the list of creditors to be paid by the Official Receiver. Frank Harris and Bosie Douglas had both promised to contribute to the bill and failed to do so. Robbie, who could not afford to pay anything from his own modest income, was hoping that the sooner the Wilde estate could be cleared of bankruptcy, the sooner Dupoirier could be paid from the rights and royalties which Robbie would then be in a position to administer. The bill was eventually paid off by Adela Schuster and George Alexander early in 1902. In the meantime he could do nothing but wait as money from rights and royalties slowly came in to pay off Oscar's British creditors, almost all of it from abroad, largely from the plays on the Continent and from Germany in particular. As Robbie would write a few years later '*Salomé* has made the author's name a household word wherever the English language is *not* spoken.'[131]

It was precisely this German enthusiasm for Wilde's works and relative disregard for the aura of scandal surrounding the man which prompted a young, anglophile journalist and translator, Max Meyerfeld, to approach Ross about the possible publication of a manuscript which—rumour had it—had been written by Wilde in prison. This was, of course, the long letter to Alfred Douglas that we now know as *De Profundis*. Oscar had given it to Robbie with instructions for making copies of certain passages to distribute to close friends, but it seems that this was never done. As a result, although a 'prison manuscript' was known to exist, its content still remained hidden from the public. Meyerfeld later recalled that he had first come across it on one of his visits to London in the Reading Room of the British Museum Library, casually mentioned under Wilde's entry in the 1901 edition of the Dictionary of National Biography: 'While in prison he wrote a kind of apology for his life, a manuscript amounting to about forty-five thousand words, now in the hands of his literary executor.'[132] He managed to get in touch with Ross through the DNB and suggested that since Oscar was so popular in Germany it would be the perfect time to treat German readers to a previously unpublished work. Robbie was not at all comfortable with the idea, despite what Oscar had written to him about making it public sometime in the future. He felt that England where 'Wilde's name unfortunately did not bring very agreeable memories to English ears,' was far from ready for this very personal document. However, Meyerfeld was not easily discouraged and persisted until Robbie, who confessed that he had begun to hate the sight of the man's correspondence, finally gave in and settled down to the painful task of producing a suitably edited version for Meyerfeld to translate and publish in *Die neue Rundschau*.[133]

The main problem with making the selection was the varied nature of the document itself. Essentially a letter addressed to Alfred Douglas, *De Profundis* is in places fiercely, and often unjustly, critical of him; but it is also a sort of confession (though as he said of it 'I don't defend my conduct. I explain it') and the closest thing we have to Wildean autobiography. It is reflective, it is philosophical, and to read it is to find him for once without his usual mask—no less endearing, perhaps even more so for all the faults it betrays. In one great sweep Oscar looks at his past glories and excesses, at his present misery and at his aspirations for the future, passing from anger to remorse, from arrogance to humility, and ends on a brief note of hope. Hope for a new life after prison which was, sadly, to be short-lived. Robbie's task was to extract a coherently abridged version which would give no indication that it was intended as a letter to Douglas, as well as to tone down the passages which he considered too arrogant or too excessively indulgent. That this first step on the way to Oscar's rehabilitation struck exactly the right note was essential. There would be no second chance. Equally important was the need to conceal its intended recipient, for if Douglas discovered that the letter had been addressed to him, he would have been perfectly capable of insisting that Ross hand over the manuscript, and even of instigating legal action if he refused. Once the editing was done and the text sent to Meyerfeld along with four carefully redacted letters which Oscar had sent him from prison, Robbie's misgivings about publishing in England began to dissolve. He sent his abbreviated version to the publishers Methuen & Co expecting that they would refuse it, but one of their readers, the prolific and versatile E. V. Lucas, recommended them to go ahead, although with a few changes to render it more acceptable to a British public. Lucas himself did the further editing, regarding the work almost as his tribute to Oscar and writing to Robbie at the time: 'I hope if I had known him personally, I should have been able to muster some of your fidelity; and I have always felt a little guilty in making no effort . . . to let him know that he had a few friends after he had left prison even among those whose names he had never known.'[134]

Robbie's decision to publish *De Profundis* almost simultaneously in England may also have been determined by the fact that the British were less insular about Continental literature than they are today and news of a previously unpublished Wilde manuscript appearing in Germany would inevitably have been commented upon. Meyerfeld's translation appeared in *Die neue Rundschau* for January and February 1905 in two instalments followed immediately by its publication in book form and he always took a certain pleasure in the fact that its publication in German preceded the English version by a full two weeks. Had it not been for Meyerfeld's persistence, the change in the British public's view of Oscar Wilde might have been far longer in coming. The first English edition of 10,000 copies was sold out within weeks and five more editions printed before the end of the year. It was widely reviewed and, despite a few carping criticisms about the artificiality of some of Oscar's sentiments, to Robbie's relief it was well received. Letters of appreciation from those to whom he had sent copies poured in. 'We all owe you thanks for having permitted us to see the man as he really was. I think *De Profundis* will live long after all that the rest of us have written will be forgotten,' wrote William Stead, editor of the *Review of Reviews*. From Laurence Housman: 'It is, for the most part, beautifully thought and written; and is the *right* sort of book to come now in order to touch the hearts of men made cruel by ignorance of human nature and history. Its reception seems to me remarkable—unprophesiable five or six years ago.' And from the man whose humanity to Oscar in prison had made it all possible originally, the Governor of Reading Gaol, Major James Nelson: 'I think it is one of the grandest and saddest efforts of a truly penitent man. One has to read but little to recognise what literature has lost in the death of a man like poor Oscar Wilde . . . . Thank you for sending me what I shall always regard as one of my most treasured possessions in my small library.'[135]

In his willing acceptance of Lucas's edit for this first English version of *De Profundis,* Robbie undoubtedly made the right decision. Oscar's assessment of himself at the height of his success starts with 'The gods had given me almost everything,' but you will not find the words which followed it in the manuscript, though they did appear in the text Robbie supplied to Meyerfeld: 'I had genius, a distinguished name, high social position, brilliancy, intellectual daring . . . I altered the minds of men and the colours of things; there was nothing I said or did that did not make people wonder . . . I awoke the imagination of my century so that it created myth and legend around me.' Of his evenings spent with the low-life of London Oscar had written: 'People thought it dreadful of me to have entertained at dinner the evil things of life and to have found pleasure in their company . . . The danger was half the excitement,' but it was felt that Oscar's openly expressed enjoyment at these encounters would do nothing for his posthumous reputation at this stage, so the next sentences were suppressed: 'They were to me the brightest of gilded snakes. Their poison was part of their perfection . . . I don't feel at all ashamed at having known them. They were intensely interesting,' and they, too, appeared only in the German translation.[136] The German text also printed Robbie's name in full where it appeared in the original, whereas the English edition merely had blanks; nor did the English include the edited four letters which Oscar had written to Robbie from prison. Including that correspondence would have been clear that this 'prison manuscript' was in fact a letter and addressed to someone other than Ross himself—something that he was most anxious not to reveal. In order to appreciate Ross's extreme caution over *De Profundis* one needs to understand the complex dynamics in the relationship between Robbie, Bosie and Oscar. Together with that letter from prison, it runs—I was going to write like a 'golden' thread but it would be better described as a scarlet, bloody one—through much of the first part of this story up to Ross's early death in 1918 and then, less violently, beyond.

* * *

Robbie Ross met Oscar sometime in 1886 when he was seventeen. The following year he went to stay with the Wildes as a paying guest in Tite Street where he most probably became Oscar's first homosexual lover. When taxed with the fact later in life he was said to have denied it but remarked cryptically that he wouldn't have minded if he had been. Between that first encounter with Robbie and meeting and falling for Bosie Douglas, Oscar appears to have had one or two homosexual relationships but they were mostly short-lived, and from 1891 Bosie became the passion which dominated his life. Introduced by Oscar, Bosie and Robbie became friends and were on good terms, though Robbie later maintained that he was constantly warning the other two of the danger they were running in the very public display of their affair. The first major disagreement between Bosie and Robbie was over Queensberry's insulting card accusing Oscar of being a sodomite. Oscar initially turned to Robbie for advice who told him to ignore it; Bosie, who detested his father, then urged Oscar to sue for libel with tragic consequences. Robbie, the voice of reason; Bosie, impetuous, self-obsessed and, to Oscar, irresistible. These characteristics would determine the interactions between all three of them until Oscar's death five years later and then between his two erstwhile lovers until 1918. Bosie's love for Oscar was essentially (but not entirely) self-centred; Robbie's was much more selfless (but not entirely either). 'Friendship is far more tragic than love. It lasts longer,' as Oscar once wrote, perhaps presciently and with both of them in mind.[137] The jealousies about who 'owned' Oscar and when, would lead to disputes, angry letters, and finally court cases. There was occasionally even violent behaviour but almost exclusively on Bosie's side, with Robbie remaining much calmer, though in the end reduced to scheming and using Douglas's unequivocally homosexual letters both to him and to Oscar to blacken his character.

Once Oscar was convicted and sent down for two years with hard labour, Robbie went several times to visit him in prison, helping to sort out his shattered life. He also made that extraordinary—even dangerous—gesture given Oscar's 'crime,' of greeting him silently in the corridor of the bankruptcy court on the day of his examination. By then Bosie, living safely on the Continent and in a misguided attempt to justify his relationship with Oscar, contented himself with writing letters to the press as well as articles for two French journals and in 1896 had to be stopped by Ross from dedicating his first published volume of poems to Oscar who found the idea 'revolting and grotesque.'[138] Robbie was only too happy to be the instrument of prevention, also dissuading Bosie from writing to Oscar and using up the allowance of letters he could receive. And so it continued. Robbie had a hand in preparing the deed of separation between Oscar and his wife, by which Constance gave her husband an annual allowance on his release, stipulating that he did not 'consort with evil or disreputable companions,' clearly with Bosie in mind. Douglas would afterwards write an angry letter to Ross accusing him of deliberately trying to separate him from Oscar.[139] Little good it did, and Oscar's and Bosie's reunion in Naples led to Robbie falling out with them both. At the time of Oscar's final illness Robbie wrote to Bosie that he was ill but it was 'nothing serious.' Two days later he sent a telegram to say that Oscar was dead and Bosie only arrived in Paris in time for the funeral.[140] Of Oscar's two main lovers, Robbie managed to be the last to see him alive. Deliberate manoeuvring or just unfortunate timing? Perhaps at such a moment it would be uncharitable to attribute ulterior motives to him, but whatever the case it allowed Robbie to sort through Oscar's correspondence and preserve certain letters from Bosie which the latter would doubtless have preferred to see destroyed. Oscar's death also left Ross unofficially in charge of his literary estate, a fact which Douglas could not dispute since Oscar had expressed it in writing. From then on Robbie found a role which Bosie could never have filled: that of rehabilitating Oscar and maximizing the value of the literary estate for Cyril and Vyvyan. In 1900, after Bosie had inherited £15,000 from his father, Robbie offered him a share in the estate if he paid off Oscar's debts. He refused and afterwards regretted having turned it down since it left Robbie entirely in charge of the posthumous Oscar.[141] There was also a radical change in Douglas's lifestyle. In 1901, having run through his inheritance, like many impoverished aristocrats of the time he decided that the solution to his financial problems was to marry an American heiress. This meant renouncing any more homosexual liaisons, a move both facilitated and complicated by falling in love with Olive Custance before leaving for the States. In Washington awkward questions were asked in the Metropolitan Club, of which he had been made an honorary member, about his friendship with Oscar Wilde. It was not the last time that his past would be dragged up to discredit him. On his return to England (without the heiress), he took up again with Olive, married her secretly and in November 1902 she gave birth to their son, Raymond. Two years later he was living the life of a respectable country gentleman at an old farmhouse he had purchased in Wiltshire, distancing himself even more from Oscar's legacy which must have pleased Robbie. Such was the background against which a heavily edited *De Profundis* was published, edited by Ross as much out of consideration for Douglas's sake as for the safety of the manuscript. Open warfare between the two men on the subject of Oscar Wilde would not be declared for a few more years.

* * *

Once *De Profundis* appeared on 23 February 1905, Douglas reviewed it, rather incongruously, in *The Motorist & Traveller* probably at the request of Frank Harris who was the editor. He saw little of real value in what he referred to as 'this interesting but rather pathetically ineffective book,' which he admits may have been written with passionate sincerity at the time but 'represents a mere mood and an unimportant one of the man who wrote it.' What good he had to say of it merely damned it with faint praise and he was clearly unaware that it was originally in the form of a letter addressed to himself. With this sudden revival of interest in his friend and lover, Bosie seized the opportunity of writing a two-part memoir for the *St. James's Gazette* on Oscar's last years in Paris, casting himself rather by implication in the role of a financial Good Samaritan, saying that stories of his supposed privations at that time were grotesquely false. 'Scarcely one of his self-constituted biographers had more than the very slightest acquaintance with him, and their records and impressions of him are chiefly made up of stale gossip and second-hand anecdotes.' The memoir was simply signed 'A,' but it was perfectly obvious to any of Oscar's good friends who had written it. One of them, Robert Sherard, a friend since 1883 and who had recorded his impressionistic memories of Oscar three years before in *Oscar Wilde: The Story of an Unhappy Friendship*, took objection to these comments and wrote to the *Gazette*:

> I have just read the articles on Oscar Wilde which appeared in your paper last week . . . and I can quite understand, that as a balm to their conscience, the friends who precipitated Wilde into the abyss should wish to persuade themselves and the public that things were not so bad with him after they had consummated his ruin and I cannot help feeling that this was the sentiment which dictated the two articles to which I refer.[142]

The squabbles over Oscar were just beginning, with Sherard cautiously referring to Douglas in the plural to imply that he was only one of several responsible for his downfall.

Because of the secrecy surrounding the original manuscript of *De Profundis*, questions began to be asked about its authenticity, forcing Ross to have a facsimile of one of the manuscript pages published in the *Daily Mirror* on 13 March. Around that time he also implied—more by omission than assertion—that it was an edited version of a letter to himself. There was a notable incident three months after publication which took place one evening at Robbie's rooms in Hornton Street, Kensington. It was recorded in his diary by the young writer Compton Mackenzie who later became a close friend of my father and incidentally the unveiler of the LCC 'Blue Plaque' on Oscar's former house in Tite Street nearly fifty years later. Robbie was reading aloud to More Adey and Reggie Turner some of the letters he had received about *De*

Profundis when Bosie came in. Robbie then started on a letter from George Bernard Shaw who, with typical Shavian contrariness, declared that the book needed to be approached from a humorous angle:

> I am half tempted to cut into the *Saturday Review* correspondence with a letter giving the *comedic* view of De Profundis. It is really an extraordinary book. Quite exhilarating and amusing as to Wilde himself and quite disgraceful and shameful to his stupid tormentors. There is pain in it, inconvenience, annoyance, but no real tragedy, all comedy. [143]

At which point, Mackenzie recalled:

> Douglas said that Shaw was probably right and Robbie got angry. Douglas criticised Wilde's life in Paris and Robbie said the one most to blame for that was Douglas himself. Douglas lost his temper, kicked the fender and marched out of the room. He came back for a moment and told Robbie he did not know what he was talking about. Then he slammed the door and presently downstairs we heard the front door slam.[144]

Ross's editing and publishing of *De Profundis* and the public recognition which he received for doing it were a source of intense irritation to Douglas, who no longer felt that he had any claim on Oscar. Later, when falsely accused in print of having abandoned Oscar after his release, Bosie was always furious and quick to point out (and prove through his bank) that he had paid several hundred pounds to Oscar in his last years in Paris. But all that was now in the past and the present help for posthumous Oscar was his growing rehabilitation, and that was entirely down to Robbie. The ill-tempered spat that evening in Hornton Street was just the start of a growing animosity between the two men.

Despite the predominantly positive reviews of *De Profundis*, one dissenting voice about its literary value came from the Church of England. On 2 April Henry Beeching, a Canon of Westminster Abbey and author of such healthy and uplifting verse as 'Going downhill on a bicycle,' attacked it in a sermon delivered on 'The Sinlessness of Christ.' He said that Wilde seemed to cast a spell on the reviewers of his book lauding it, as most had done, instead of warning against its doctrine of sin. The passage he most objected to was where Oscar writes of Christ's fascination with the sinner: 'To turn an interesting thief into a tedious honest man was not His aim . . . But in a manner not yet understood of the world He regarded sin and suffering as being in themselves beautiful and holy things and modes of perfection.'[145] Shortly afterwards Beeching heard that due to the success of De Profundis, Methuen & Co might be issuing a 'Wilde Collected Works' and, as one of their authors, he wrote urging them to 'think better of it.' In his reply, the chairman Algernon Methuen said 'It is quite clear that the spirit of the Spanish Inquisition is not yet defunct,' to which the Canon responded 'I'm not sure that the Spanish Inquisition would not have been well occupied in burning O.W. He would have made a good blaze.'[146] The Collected Works did indeed appear three years later.

Robbie's concern that news of a German translation would quickly find its way to England was well founded, and in response to a query he had to explain the slightly shorter English version in a letter to the Daily Chronicle later in the summer. It gave him an opportunity to compare English and Continental attitudes to Wilde and tell the readers that longer foreign editions had already appeared in France, Italy, Sweden, and Hungary because: 'To the English public, all Ruskinians at heart and unable to separate the man and the writer, Wilde was the author of some clever plays and epigrams, whose conduct precluded the inclusion of his name, not only in English literature, but in polite conversation.'[147]

The huge commercial success of De Profundis certainly began to change public attitudes towards Oscar, but it also brought some unexpected difficulties in the person of the Official Receiver. Having got wind of the publication, he ordered Methuen & Co not to release any of the royalties to Ross on behalf of the estate and he relieved Robbie of the first £1,000 which the book had earned. The work being part of the literary estate's assets, the estate still being bankrupt and the author not being around to claim part of the royalties as necessary living expenses, there was little that Robbie could do to contest the claim. He managed, however, to negotiate a suitable compromise: in return for handing over the royalties he was to be granted letters of administration as Wilde's official literary executor and the Official Receiver was not to dispose of any further rights in Wilde's works without his consent. This was in order not to complicate any further the acquiring of rights for Methuen's *Collected Works* which by now they had agreed to publish. On 30 July 1906 complete control of Wilde's copyrights was handed over to Ross and the application to annul his bankruptcy was granted, his creditors having been paid 20/-in the pound and with 4% interest, an outcome, incidentally, almost unthinkable today. The ultimate irony was that as one of the Queensberry heirs, Douglas would have received a part of the libel trial costs (£677 3s. 8d.) that had been owing to his father who was the petitioner for Oscar's bankruptcy in the first place.

By the time *De Profundis* was published in February 1905, it is certain that neither Cyril nor Vyvyan was aware of all that Robert Ross had been doing to re-establish their father's lost reputation in English letters. Cyril, as well as being a school prefect, had left Radley in a blaze of athletic glory, both on river and running track in the spring of 1903. After spending time at a military crammer's, Onslow Hall in Richmond, he was admitted as a 'Gentleman Cadet' to the Royal Military Academy at Woolwich in February the following year. Everything about him must have delighted the Napiers and Adrian Hope—everything which, fortunately in their eyes, belied his parentage. Vyvyan was different: more intellectual than physical, and that might lead anywhere if not properly channelled. His leather-bound, ornately gold-tooled prize books, each with its Stonyhurst crest still sit on my shelves as a reminder of how much they meant to him and how little to his guardian. As early as 1895 Constance was writing to her brother, Otho: 'Vyvyan is twice as clever as Cyril, much prettier and not nearly so nice!'[148] So, as part of the family plan to put Vyvyan out of harm's way into the Far Eastern Consular Service, no sooner had he left Stonyhurst in July 1904 than he was despatched to Lausanne for six months to brush up his French. At first sight Lausanne would not have been the obvious place to send him, but it was where Otho's first wife, Nellie, was living remarried to a Swiss doctor. Rather than boarding in a predominantly English speaking household with his aunt and two cousins and learning 'Swiss French' he would have been better off in Tours or Angers, but putting him under the care of an adult relative was considered a safer option. The unfortunate side-effect (at least unfortunate as far as the Napiers were concerned) was that his Aunt Nellie, 'a simple woman, not gifted with overmuch tact,' told Vyvyan the truth about his father. For Vyvyan who had imagined Oscar to be an embezzler, a burglar, or a bigamist, it was something of a relief to find that 'whatever my father had done had not brought distress to anyone but his own immediate family.'[149] His Swiss stay, however, came to an abrupt end after he had too much to drink one evening with student friends and had to be helped home. This was reported by Nellie to the Napiers along with other exaggerated accounts of his misdoings and he was duly ordered back to London. Needless to say it bore out all the family's fears that Oscar's younger son was 'a bad lot' and in need of institutional supervision, so it was decided that he should go to university as soon as possible. Vyvyan expressed a preference for going to Oxford because his father had been there. That was firmly vetoed because the connection might be made and his cover blown, so he was sent to Trinity Hall, Cambridge instead. The family still insisted on concealing any reference to Oscar Wilde and in the college Admissions Register for Michaelmas 1905 his is the only entry without a father's name, stating baldly 'Father deceased.' There, in an atmosphere of greater intellectual freedom, he began to discover his father's writings. The gateway to this previously 'censored' world was reading *The Ballad of Reading Gaol* for the first time, through which he moved on to other works. He apparently wrote to his brother about what he had found, and said that Cyril sent him a copy of *De Profundis* on his nineteenth birthday—possible but a little improbable given Cyril's attitude towards their dead father. And all the while there was the absurd deception which family diktat forced him to practice about his father, whose identity as an obscure anthropologist Vyvyan had invented back in his schooldays to avoid awkward questions.

After two years at Trinity Hall, my father decided that if he was to be a civil servant abroad he was wasting his time reading for a law degree, so in June 1907 he set himself up in a couple of rooms in Kensington and the following month started to attend Scoones, a crammers near Covent Garden, which specialised in preparing candidates for the Foreign Office exams. This was obviously sanctioned (and doubtless with enthusiasm) by his new guardian and the family as it brought him a step closer to being posted abroad.[150] What they had not reckoned with, however, was that in the liberal-minded environment of the university, Vyvyan would begin to discover that his father was not the appalling criminal the family had made him out to be and that far more people seemed to know who he was than he had previously imagined. Somewhat paradoxically, his most intimate friends were quite unaware of his identity. 'Before I went down I told one or two of them,' he would write later. 'When I told my great friend Joshua Goodland he said: "I always thought there was something mysterious about you. And now I know why. But what does it really matter? Your father was a great writer," and that cheered me as nothing else could have done.'[151]

It was at Scoones that occurred an event which was to change my father's life: he met a young man, Sir Coleridge Fitzroy Kennard known to his friends as 'Roy.' His father had died in 1886 when he was not even a year old and his grandfather, a banker and politician, in 1890, shortly before being officially created a baronet. As a result, the baronetcy was bestowed on his 6 year-old grandson. This chance meeting rapidly developed into a friendship and Roy told Vyvyan that he knew all about 'the guilty secret' and that his mother, Helen Carew, was anxious to meet him. After the death of Roy's father in 1886, Helen Kennard had spent ten years as a widow before remarrying, this time an Irish Nationalist politician James Carew, who was an ardent supporter of Charles Stewart Parnell, an activist in the Home Rule Campaign and who had been prosecuted and briefly imprisoned in 1889 for an inflammatory speech about the Earl of Drogheda's treatment of an Irish tenant farmer. Unfortunately his tumultuous political life took its toll and Carew died suddenly in 1903 at the relatively young age of fifty, leaving Helen widowed for a second time. It was to her house in

Hans Place, London, that Roy took my father to dine towards the end of July.

That evening Mrs. Carew spoke to Vyvyan about his father as an artist and distinguished man of letters, which he found both moving and slightly embarrassing as it was one of the only occasions on which he had heard anyone speak of Oscar with respect and he suddenly found himself being 'regarded as an object of envy instead of one of pity.' When she brought up the subject of Robert Ross and asked if Vyvyan would object to meeting him, she was astonished to find that my father had no idea who he was and, far from objecting, was eager to see him.[152]

Since 1901 Robbie had been a partner in a West End art gallery, the Carfax, which dealt in contemporary artists, among them Will Rothenstein, Max Beerbohm, Charles Conder, William Orpen and Roger Fry. It was through the Carfax that Robbie had become friends with the wealthy and art-loving Helen Carew, and she had watched with interest and admiration all that he had been doing for Oscar Wilde's estate in the past six years. That her son, by extraordinary coincidence, had become friends with my father gave her the opportunity to bring Vyvyan and Robbie together, something that the Napiers and his guardian had been at pains to prevent for so long. The meeting took place a week later at a dinner given by Mrs. Carew where Vyvyan met Robbie, Max Beerbohm and Reginald Turner who had been among Oscar's closest friends. He described it as an emotional evening and I well know a little of what he must have felt. My own father was taken from me at the age of twenty-one with too many questions unasked and unanswered, but the kindness of his old friends such as Alec Waugh and Rebecca West did much to fill that void. And I still resent the obstructive but well-meaning family blanket flung over the past by my mother, anxious that I should not learn about Vyvyan's bachelor life in the 1920s and 1930s for fear that it would somehow tarnish the image which she continued so carefully to polish. A diluted repeat of the Napier prissiness seventy years before. I often wonder what his old friend Liam O'Flaherty could have told me about Vyvyan then. He lived on seventeen years after my father's death. So many missed opportunities; so much wasted whitewash. But on one hand I'm glad since it has helped me to understand just a few of the emotions my father must have felt on meeting Robbie—an opening into the past and simultaneously a sense of closure with it.

At this point in the story there is another myth which needs exploding. In his autobiography my father described his first meeting with Helen Carew and wrote that she had been a friend of Oscar, for whose memory she retained a deep affection. He went on to say, as if to emphasise the point, that she showed him copies of Oscar's books which he had inscribed to her. Unfortunately, there is absolutely nothing to suggest that Mrs. Carew ever knew Oscar Wilde, and still less that she was one of his friends; indeed, there is a certain amount of circumstantial evidence to disprove it. There are no extant letters from him to her nor is there any mention of Helen Carew in his correspondence or in that of his immediate circle. The inscribed books which my father supposedly saw—not just one but several—have never been seen again. They are not in institutional collections nor have they ever surfaced at auction or in booksellers' catalogues. That in itself is bizarre, especially as they would have survived the later tearing out of inscription leaves by some owners of inscribed copies in order to destroy all association with the author. If Helen Carew still cherished the memory of her 'friend' in 1907, and with the growing rehabilitation of Wilde, there was nothing to prevent her from continuing to keep personalised copies of his works. The 'disappearance' of these books is not in itself proof of anything; books do have accidents but the total disappearance, especially of inscribed copies, would have been an act of wilful destruction. Given both her connection with Robbie as well as her admiration for the author, such a thing is unthinkable. After 1908, when Helen Carew gave Robbie £2,000 to fund Epstein's monumental sculpture on Oscar's Paris tomb, the association value of such copies would have been even greater. She was in no need of money so she would not have sold them, and there is nothing to suppose that she wouldn't have kept them until her death in 1928.[153] At that point, had they existed, under the conditions of her will all her books and papers passed to Freddie Smith, a protégé of Robert Ross. Freddie, through his association with Robbie and other members of the posthumous Wilde circle, would have been very much aware of the significance of such inscribed copies and made sure that they survived. If they existed, they have vanished without trace, but I don't think that they ever did.

Why did Vyvyan make out that Helen Carew had been a friend of his father? Because it was a simple explanation as to why she gave such a large sum of money for the tomb sculpture. Tying up loose ends again. And the inscribed copies? Unverifiable back in 1954, and anyway no one would have questioned his first-hand account of meeting Helen Carew and seeing his father's books inscribed to her. What I find extraordinary, given the improbability of it all, is that no one has ever queried the veracity of it. This slight distortion of the truth would be harmless enough, were it not for the fact that others have taken the liberty of embellishing it even further. Sometime in the 1950s, the rare book dealer George Sims offered for sale a copy of Oscar's poems inscribed by him: 'For Helen, the gracious lady, in homage from the poet. Jan'y. '94.' It came without any provenance—normally a disadvantage, but in this case allowing Sims to speculate opportunistically that it had belonged to Helen Carew based, obviously, on Vyvyan's statement that he had seen copies of his father's books inscribed to her.[154] He may even have consulted my father who at that time was selling off nearly his entire Wilde collection through Sims and, anxious to stay on good terms, may have agreed with his conjecture. A further instance of relying on my father's account of his first meeting with Helen Carew and her inscribed copies was almost farcical. In 1989 when a letter appeared in *The Times* about the dilapidated state of Oscar's tomb, Sir George 'Loopy' Kennard, Helen's grandson, offered to help raise a fund to restore it. We met and among other things discussed my uncertainty about his grandmother's relationship with Oscar. Loopy was adamant: they must have been good friends because she gave the money for the Epstein sculpture. I realised that against such circular reasoning it was pointless to argue my case. Loopy had had an interesting life and was a great raconteur, and when his autobiography appeared a year later he managed to blur the lines between fact and fiction. Of his grandmother and Oscar he wrote: 'She had retained the life-long affection of Oscar Wilde who inscribed her copy of *The Happy Prince* with the words "To the Happy Princess from the Unhappy Prince, with the devotion of the Author, Oscar Wilde."' Apart from the unlikelihood of his remembering the exact words over sixty years later—he was thirteen when Helen died—a worse pastiche of Wildean style would be difficult to imagine.[155] But thus do innocent inventions in the story of Oscar breed and multiply.

Further evidence that Helen Carew and Oscar Wilde are most unlikely to have been friends is supplied by Robert Ross. When Robbie edited Oscar's first *Collected Works* with Methuen & Co in 1908, he preserved most of the author's original dedications in each volume, but in addition he honoured two women: Adela Schuster and Helen Carew. Schuster had given Wilde £1,000 at the time of his arrest and was very supportive of him while in prison. Robbie's long dedicatory note in *The Duchess of Padua* is accordingly effusive and connects her closely with Oscar. Not so the dedication to Helen Carew in the volume of *Reviews*, addressed simply as 'Mrs. Carew' and from which it is clear that she has become Robbie Ross's friend in recent years; had she been Oscar's, Robbie would not have usurped the privilege.

It brings us back to the question of why, if Helen Carew was not a good friend of Oscar, did she give such a substantial sum to Robbie (nearly £200,000 in today's terms) for the monumental tomb sculpture in Père Lachaise Cemetery? That she enjoyed Wilde's work, was non-judgemental about his life and admired all that Robbie was doing for his posthumous reputation and his children was already answer enough. She was also extremely rich. But I believe that there was another less obvious reason for her

gift. Her second husband, James Carew, and Oscar Wilde shared
a common interest in Irish Nationalism and both believed in the
cause of Home Rule. They had both attended meetings of the
Liberal Party's Eighty Club in the late 1880s, were listed among
the guests in the newspaper reports and must have known each
other. In particular they were present at the widely reported meeting at which Parnell spoke on 8 May 1888.[156] In the context of
Irish Nationalism, it seems perfectly plausible that the subject of
Oscar Wilde would have come up in conversation between Helen
and her new husband after their marriage in 1896. Later, having
got to know Robbie Ross and one of Oscar's sons, her sympathy
for Wilde had increased together with the realisation that both he
and her late husband had been badly treated by the British and,
partly as a result, had both died young. While she may have felt
that funding such a monument to her late husband was not entirely appropriate, to do so for Oscar Wilde would, in her mind,
commemorate both of them with their views on Ireland and be
a subtle gesture of defiance towards the establishment on their
behalf.

Whatever the motives which lay behind Helen Carew's extremely generous gesture—and I think one can assume that a close
friendship with Wilde wasn't one of them—her chance meeting
with one of Oscar's sons and introducing him to Robert Ross was
certainly a contributing factor. For my father the meeting with
Robbie was a pivotal moment in his life. He felt he had found a
friend, someone he could confide in, rely on and above all in whose
company he would never have to worry about 'the family secret.'
'Suddenly, with the entry into my life of Mrs. Carew, I found myself,
within the space of a few days, no longer the friendless haunted
creature I had been for years, but in the midst of well-wishers
in the literary and artistic world of London.'[157] Under Robbie's
influence it wasn't long before Vyvyan abandoned his studies at
Scoones, Robbie no doubt horrified by the idea of Oscar's son being banished to the Far East to live out his life as a petty Consular
official. Having lived for so long under the suffocating restraints

of his family and guardians, I don't imagine Vyvyan needed much persuading. Cyril however, by then a Second Lieutenant in the Royal Field Artillery, was another matter. Robbie naturally wanted to meet Oscar's other son, though Vyvyan was apprehensive about making the introduction given that both parties held radically different opinions on how the rehabilitation of Oscar should be brought about: Robbie by emphasising his stature as a great man of letters and Cyril by his own clean-living lifestyle as an army officer 'serving King and country.'[158] My father needn't have worried. The meeting was a success and the two of them became good friends based on a mutual respect for each other's point of view. Cyril would later write to Robbie from India where he had been posted with his battery, saying: 'Poetry is for the gods and I am a soldier . . . I seldom read that tragic document [*De Profundis*]. I hate it, Robbie. More, I hate it and cannot believe it,' but he then goes on to say 'You and those others were loyal indeed. The more I experience of life in all its sordid vulgarity and mediocrity, in all its cowardice and egotism, the more I realize the nobility of your conducts.'[159]

The other liberating influence in Vyvyan's life at that moment was undoubtedly Roy Kennard. He was almost exactly the same age as Cyril and it seems as though Vyvyan suddenly found himself with the affectionate and sympathetic elder brother which circumstances and his family had conspired to deny him for so long. Roy, too, was destined for a career in the Foreign Office, though he felt quite unsuited to it as his inclination was to literature rather than to politics. It was a feeling with which Vyvyan was finding himself more and more in tune and created a close bond between them at once. He had kept an extensive diary during his time in Lausanne and had edited his college magazine while at Cambridge, but until then he knew that any admission to his family that he could be considering a life in letters would have been greeted with severe disapproval. It might have linked him to his disgraced father which they were anxious to avoid at all costs. Not long after their first meeting and those two dinners which were destined to alter the course of Vyvyan's life so radically, Roy was sent off to Hannover to improve his German as part of the preparation for his Foreign Office exam. From there he wrote regularly to Vyvyan, slightly pretentious letters in a vaguely poetic vein and from their content I imagine that my father replied in a similar fashion. In one of them Roy quotes Vyvyan as writing that he had 'broken off all the shoots which cling to conventionality' and that he is enjoying 'thought, contemplation, writing, everything that makes life worth living.'[160] It must have been one of those sudden, intense friendships which infect twenty year-olds who discover that they share a common love of words and an equally strong dislike of conformity. Their friendship continued until Roy's death from the cumulative effects of heroin in 1948, and although my father saved all his letters over those four decades, infuriatingly Vyvyan's side of the correspondence was never kept. There exists, however, a locked, leather-bound diary in which my father recorded much of what he felt at that time about his friendship with Roy, and about his new-found pleasure in creative writing, although that should read 'exists in part' for the diary has been mutilated.

When I returned to London in September 1974 after living in Beirut, I stayed for a while in the family flat which I had left four years before. My mother, Thelma, was on holiday and glad of a house-sitter while she was away, and since I had already decided that I was no longer going to be stonewalled about the family's past, I took advantage of her absence to go through some of my father's papers. Until then, any suggestion that I might do so on the pretext that I wanted to find out more about his pre-war life—he had already been dead for seven years—was always met with 'Well you can ask me,' and with that the matter was closed. It was then that I found the locked diary and its key.

Vyvyan had started it in September 1907 and I remember being taken aback by the nature of what I was reading. He had recorded what seemed like an almost romantic happiness that he had experienced in Roy's companionship and a sadness that Roy had gone abroad. I felt indiscreet as I turned the pages until I realised that these were feelings I, too, had had towards a very close friend at exactly the same age. Later, when we were separated by continents, we wrote to each other; we shared more than just a past; I understood. Unfortunately Thelma didn't, decided that posterity would put the wrong interpretation on what Vyvyan had written and tore out the pages. God forbid that anyone should ever think that Oscar Wilde's son might have had homosexual tendencies. As I write this fifty years later and worry about false memory, I'm reassured by a single page, which escaped her depredation, written four years later when my father was depressed and living in Spain. He must have written to Roy at the time who replied from the Embassy in Teheran:

> But who should I write to if not to you? . . . Above all and through all remember me as your friend. At one of my lowest moments when I nearly shot myself at Baku, I remember writing 'To have a friend who knew the worst of one and who, if one asked him to come, would do so without thinking of what he knew and without telling anyone—'. Do not forget that I am here if ever you want me.[161]

Alongside that friendship was Robbie Ross's growing affection for Vyvyan. In his first, rather avuncular letter to my father, Robbie wrote: 'I hope you realise how very fond I am of you simply because you are your father's son, and I am sure I shall become very fond of you on your own account . . . . I was very glad to hear from Mrs. Carew that you had told your guardian of our meeting,' and he went on to say that he was delighted to hear that Vyvyan had literary aspirations and would like to see anything he had written.[162] It is not difficult to imagine the rebellious pleasure my father must have felt in informing his guardian that despite all attempts to prevent it, he had finally made contact with one of Oscar's closest friends and literary executor.

This opening up of a new life for Vyvyan was not an unmitigated success. Certainly it gave him a degree of self-confidence which had eluded him until then; it also put a stop to the Civil Service career for which he would have been utterly unsuited. At the same time it nurtured a growing sense that he might have inherited a little of his father's love of words, even if not his genius, encouraging him to believe that he could start writing for a living alongside the modest amount of income generated by his father's literary estate. As a result, he began to take a fairly carefree attitude towards life. In one of the early entries in his 'locked' diary he describes trying to write a lyrical fairy-tale, being unsatisfied with the result and starting to read Oscar's essays, *Intentions*, 'the great works of him who knew the value and the beauty of his tongue,' as he calls them, which merely brought on a fit of depression. No mention, significantly, of his father by name, the years of family conditioning still having an apparent stranglehold on his freedom of expression. A month later, on 19 September, instead of being at Scoones he was sitting at home reading and writing, Balzac-like in a dressing-gown, when unexpectedly Cyril appeared. Vyvyan, with no time to hide his literary efforts, anticipated an older-brother lecture about wasting his time, but instead Cyril approved of his writing and they spent the rest of the day and evening together. 'Cyril was a new Cyril,' he wrote. 'I think I was new to him. At last we have found things in common. I hope to see him often in the future. I haven't been to Scoones for two days. I am not going on the third. When Mr. Meinertzhagen [his guardian] comes back he shall know all. I am going to write at last!'[163] Sadly the new relationship with Cyril did not develop as Vyvyan had hoped; his brother's sense of duty and conventional behaviour was too ingrained to countenance what he saw as Vyvyan's irresponsibility.

That autumn Vyvyan finally came of age and theoretically neither family nor guardian could dictate to him any longer. In abandoning his studies at Scoones he had already anticipated this and the family rather pointedly ignored the occasion of his birthday and made no offer to celebrate the event. Robbie Ross, however, made up for it by giving a splendid dinner at his house in Kensington attended by a number of Oscar's old friends. Shortly after, almost as if to emphasise his new independence, Vyvyan left on a five month-long holiday in the US and Canada and, by his own admission, spent a good deal of money that he could ill-afford. On his return to London Cyril informed him that according to a rumour circulating in the family, Vyvyan had been sent down from Cambridge for some unspecified wickedness; they clearly weren't going to let my father's claim or his new-found independence go unchallenged. Robbie, more gently critical of what he saw as Vyvyan wasting time and money when he should have been thinking about his future career, persuaded him to continue studying for the Bar. My father duly asked his former tutor at Trinity Hall if they would allow him to return and complete his degree and it was there that he spent most of 1909. In contrast to Vyvyan's somewhat haphazard existence, Robbie had been working extremely hard at Oscar's rehabilitation since taking over officially as Wilde's literary executor, a daunting task now made the more rewarding having met and befriended his two sons.

CHAPTER FOUR
RETURN FROM PURGATORY

When Robbie Ross made Oscar a deathbed promise to look after his literary estate and make sure that his Paris creditors were paid as a matter of honour, he could have had little idea of the complications it would involve. Until 22 February 1906 Robbie had no official status as the literary executor and until the end of June that year no proper control of the copyrights, but with the debts paid off and the estate solvent, he could then take a more active role. The extraordinary success of *De Profundis* had encouraged its publisher, Algernon Methuen, to sign up for a multi-volume *Collected Works* under Robbie's editorship and he signed a contract in February 1906 stipulating that it had to appear within two years.

The texts themselves, with the exception of the last two volumes *Reviews* and *Miscellanies* which contained a mixed bag of Oscar's occasional writings for periodicals, essays and lectures all of which had to be tracked down, presented relatively few problems. Securing the permission to include the book-length works from their original publishers was another matter altogether. On the one hand John Lane of the Bodley Head and original publisher of *Salomé, Lady Windermere's Fan, A Woman of No Importance,* and *The Sphinx*, was extremely reasonable over granting permission for those works in which he still held rights. On the other, Charles Carrington, the Parisian publisher who had bought the rights to *Dorian Gray*, rather than taking a permission fee or a royalty wanted to sell the entire copyright back for £425. This neither Ross as the estate nor Methuen as the publisher could afford, and despite the latter's strong disapproval of the work he always regretted turning down the investment given its later world-wide popularity. In the end it appeared as part of the fourteen volume set under Carrington's own imprint and he simply took a royalty on the sales.[164] Leonard Smithers' widow tried to sue Robbie for including *The Ballad of Reading Gaol* in the volume of *Poems* which was somewhat ironic given that her husband had carried on printing totally unauthorised editions long after Wilde's death. She was unsuccessful.[165]

It was their varied but complementary interests in Wilde which brought together three men around that time and made the preparation of the *Collected Works* far easier than it would otherwise have been: Robert Ross, the literary executor; Walter Ledger an eccentric and impassioned collector of everything Wilde had ever written in all forms and all languages; and Christopher Millard a more modest collector, scholar and bibliographer. In 1902 Ledger, who had started to compile a bibliography of all Wilde's writings, had written to Bosie Douglas asking him for information 'as an authority on Wilde's works.' Bosie, duly flattered by the epithet but knowing that this was not his field referred him to Ross.[166] Millard, quite brazenly for the time, seemed to make little secret of his own homosexuality and had even written to *Reynolds' Newspaper* in Wilde's defence shortly after his conviction (admittedly signed only with his initials) saying: 'Why does not the Crown prosecute every boy at a public or private school or half the men in the Universities? In the latter places 'paederism' is as common as fornication and everybody knows it.'[167] In the summer of 1904 Christopher Millard together with Robert Sherard made a pilgrimage to Wilde's grave at Bagneux. It was probably Sherard's account of his close (heterosexual) friendship with Oscar published two years before which brought them together and that, in turn, led to Millard being introduced to Robbie as well. All that remained was for Robbie to introduce the two bibliographer-collectors and the triangle was complete. He did, and by the end of the year Christopher Millard and Walter Ledger were exchanging long letters on the finer points of Wilde bibliography.[168] Ledger, recognising that Millard was the more methodical, seems to have abandoned his own project and concentrated instead on building up his collection. This turned out to be mutually beneficial as each had different contacts among the booksellers; the rarer items that Ledger bought, Millard could add to his bibliography; those that Millard could not afford he passed on to Ledger. Both shared information about piracies—and there were plenty—with Ross who took legal action to stop them. Ledger specialised in collecting the magazines in which Wilde's essays and reviews had first appeared. This not only helped complete the bibliography but also enabled Millard to put together the volume of *Reviews* for the Methuen edition, a task which had been delegated to him by Robbie Ross. This three-way friendship made an important contribution to Robbie's editing of the *Collected Works*, the publication of which in 1908 would play a significant role in re-establishing Oscar's reputation in the literary world. Robbie dedicated the last volume in the collection, *Miscellanies*, to Ledger in recognition of his help, though Millard who did much of the donkey-work in tracking down the occasional writings only appears fleetingly in Robbie's introduction to the *Reviews* under his pseudonym 'Stuart Mason.' This was sad but necessary.

At the end of April 1906 Millard was arrested in Oxford on a charge of 'gross indecency,' the same offence that had put Oscar behind bars in 1895.[169] He was unsure how his family would take it and wired to Robbie for help, whom until that moment he had never met in person. Robbie went up to Oxford to give what support he could, and again a week later when the case came up before the local magistrate. He only stayed in court for an hour, writing afterwards to Ledger that listening to the evidence was too painful as it must have brought back memories of Oscar's arrest eleven years before.[170] Although there was no intimacy between him and Millard as there had been with Oscar, it was not in Robbie's nature to ignore an appeal from a fellow homosexual in trouble despite the danger of doing so. Millard's own family organised and paid for his defence counsel, though in the end he was convicted and sentenced to three months with hard labour.

When he was released Robbie found him work at the *Burlington Magazine,* continued to use him for research on the Methuen edition, and even used him occasionally as his secretary; such was his sympathetic and generous nature. Unfortunately, when open warfare later broke out between Robbie and Bosie Douglas, it would be used against him as circumstantial evidence of his own homosexuality—guilt by association with Millard's less than discreet sex-life. As Robbie wrote somewhat ruefully at that time: 'I have assisted and found employment for people in my own social position who have served terms of imprisonment for moral or other offences. I have to admit that I have constantly been told that in the circumstances it was unwise for me to do so.'[171]

In the meantime Robbie had other worries now that he was officially Oscar's literary executor. Piracies were rife, and chasing down the pirates, seizing their stock, and occasionally taking legal action was tedious. Leonard Smithers, who had published Wilde after his release from prison when no mainstream publisher would touch him, was one of the main offenders.[172] Certainly he had provided Oscar with some badly needed cash in those last years, and with dubious moral logic he probably felt that making money from his illegal editions was by way of repayment. But piracies, even if they reached a public which Methuen's *Collected Works* never could, were not part of the rehabilitation exercise and were money lost to the estate. Far worse were the foreign publishers who were quite open about their appropriations, either assuming that the estate wouldn't notice and, even if it did, wouldn't go through the complicated procedure of prosecuting internationally. The most blatant of these infringements took place in the United States in 1907 when A.R. Keller published a fifteen volume set entitled *The Writings of Oscar Wilde*, introduced by Richard Le Gallienne.

Poet, novelist and critic, Le Gallienne, despite not being part of Wilde's homosexual coterie, was very friendly with him from 1887 and at one time a reader for Wilde's publisher John Lane at the Bodley Head. They professed a mutual admiration for each other's work but after 1893, when Le Gallienne wrote a generous review of *Salomé,* they seem to have drifted apart. Regardless, at the time of Wilde's trials he dissuaded John Lane from withdrawing Wilde's books from his list saying that he was much too good a writer to drop, whatever the Philistines might say about it. Robbie was first alerted to the American edition by a widely circulated prospectus in which it was stated that Le Gallienne had been 'a life-long friend of Oscar Wilde and his college chum at Oxford,' an absurd claim since he would have been twelve when Oscar left Magdalen in 1878. That Robbie might have overlooked, but what he could not forgive was the inclusion of two works wrongly attributed to Wilde merely for sensationalist reasons: there was a translation of Barbey d'Aurevilly's novel *Ce qui ne meurt pas* and a homoerotic short story 'The Priest and the Acolyte' about which Edward Carson had unsuccessfully cross-examined Oscar at the Queensberry libel trial back in 1895.[173] It was suggested in the prospectus that although the authorship of the short story was in question, it was included because Le Gallienne (described as 'the editor') was 'confident that it could have been written by no other man.' There was also the matter of money, since Keller had made no attempt to seek permission from the estate and, worse, his edition would eat into the sales of the Methuen *Collected Works,* half of which was being earmarked for the United States. One completely laughable aspect of Keller's edition was the proud boast in the prospectus that 'To obtain the complete text of all of Wilde's dramatic works [*which included such rarities like* Vera *and* The Duchess of Padua], constant recourse has had to be made to translations of them into French and German.' The same principle was obviously applied to their version of *De Profundis,* translated back into English from Max Meyerfeld's German of 1905 by a Dr. Henry Zick, and which rendered one of the best-known and beautifully cadenced passages: 'I awoke the imagination of my century so that it created myth and legend around me: I summed up all systems in a phrase, and all existence in an epigram,' into the tin-eared: 'I stimulated and fructified the imaginative power of my century, and myths and legends crystallised about my person.

I expressed and condensed the philosophical systems into one phrase, all being into one epigram.' Not surprisingly Robbie wrote an angry letter of protest to the *Times Literary Supplement* about the claims in the prospectus, motivated partly by his annoyance at seeing his own carefully prepared edition scooped by an American publisher. It was, coincidentally, just a week or two before he would meet and befriend my father for the first time.

Le Gallienne was no fly-by-night hack and, from his response to Ross's letter several months later in the *TLS*, he was clearly embarrassed by the verifiable misstatements and misattributions. His only involvement, he wrote, was to provide an introduction and he denied being the editor or having any knowledge of the contents of the edition or even of the prospectus. Given Keller's reputation as a publisher, none of that was surprising. In fact, the introduction was both balanced and fulsome in its praise of Oscar's genius as a man and as a writer. An extract from the introduction in the prospectus, which for some reason was omitted from the edition, might even have been written by Ross himself. It highlighted the remarkable influence of Wilde's writings 'in the two most intellectual countries of Europe—France and Germany,' saying that it was a status until then achieved only by Shakespeare, Byron, and Dickens. Robbie, it must be said, did adopt a more apologetic tone in the final letter of their exchange. These were battles which had to be fought but they were time-consuming and, as Robbie emphasised, he was fighting as much for Wilde's family as for his reputation.[174]

Aside from chasing the pirates, the preparation of the *Collected Works* proceeded apace, the first six volumes being published on 13 February 1908 and the next five on 13 March. A month later Vyvyan returned from his long North American trip to 'some disapproval of my gallivanting and wasting my time in America' from Robbie Ross.[175] Like so many passages in my father's autobiography—and there will be more in the later years—behind a simple sentence or two, or at most a paragraph, something is intimated but nothing is revealed. It seems perfectly clear that in the relatively short time that Robbie had known Vyvyan, he had begun to treat him like a son. It was Robbie, after all, who was providing Vyvyan with an income—small though it was—from the estate, and taking nothing for doing it: the father giving his son an allowance and voicing gentle disapproval that his progeny was squandering the money and not making more of an effort to find some gainful employment.

With no clear idea of what he was going to do with his life, Vyvyan must have felt a certain amount of discomfort, guilt even, at seeing Cyril now a fully-fledged, working officer in the Royal Artillery, Robbie handling all the problems of Oscar's literary estate, and his new-found friend Roy Kennard about to enter the Foreign Office. He had already decided to finish his law studies, but returning to Cambridge didn't happen immediately. Contrary to what my father remembered in his autobiography it wasn't until January 1909 that he went back. For the remainder of 1908 he lived in London where, presumably through Robbie, he 'met most of the literary and artistic figures of the time.'[176] That seems to be a slight exaggeration but what is certain is that he had a far greater sense of belonging in that world than in the suffocatingly conventional one in which his family would have preferred him to remain. Robbie Ross recognised this and was partly to blame for encouraging Vyvyan's literary efforts, perhaps wanting to see if he could rekindle some of the father's literary flair in the son. I write 'to blame' with some reluctance due to all that Robbie was doing for Oscar's memory, but that encouragement combined with my father's rebellious streak and a genetic inclination towards the written word, meant that that Vyvyan would spend the next few years discovering that he was not destined to become a creative writer. A pity his father wasn't alive to give him the advice he gave to an aspiring author twenty years before:

> As regards your prospects in literature, believe me that it is impossible to live by literature. By journalism a man may make an income, but rarely by pure literary work. I would strongly advise

you to try and make some profession, such as that of a tutor, the basis and mainstay of your life, and to keep literature for your finest, rarest moments.[177]

Both Cyril and Vyvyan were 'cursed' with a desire to express themselves in writing, doubtless passed on through the genes of their father. Cyril fought against it because he felt he ought to, but when he gave in to it his style was laboured and contrived as letters to his brother and others from India would later show.[178] Vyvyan initially resisted because he was made to feel that he should, and after several false starts he became an exceptional translator between the wars and in later life a perceptive and witty diarist. It was sad that Robbie, who died too young in 1918, didn't live to see the eventual success of what he had encouraged so many years before.

During the late spring and summer of 1908 Vyvyan reapplied himself, if a little half-heartedly, to his law studies in preparation for returning to Cambridge and then, on the pretext that he had been 'working very hard and needed a holiday,' he spent most of the month of September in Venice with Roy Kennard who had just passed his Foreign Office exams. There he decided to experiment with calling himself Vyvyan Wilde, supposedly at Kennard's suggestion but Robbie Ross almost certainly had a hand in it too. Through dealing with foreign publishers Robbie knew that on the Continent there was no stigma attached to the name as there was in Britain, and if Vyvyan was to try claiming his true family name, Venice was an ideal place to test people's reactions. It was a city with a constant stream of international visitors to whom Wilde's works would be familiar but most probably not that he had been married with children, an unexpected fact which might well have worked to my father's advantage had not a young homosexual Frenchman committed suicide in the middle of Roy's and Vyvyan's holiday.

Roy and Vyvyan spent a fortnight enjoying themselves on the Lido before moving into the city and it was there, at 2 am on 24

September, that the twenty-one year-old Raymond Laurent shot himself in despair at his unrequited passion for a young American man, Langhorne Wister (not Langhorn Whistler as frequently and erroneously reported) who left Venice the day after.[179] In itself this tragic event should not have affected their stay: there was nothing to suppose that they had met Laurent. But, once again, my father's autobiography leaves much unsaid behind the two short paragraphs describing his Venetian holiday. All that he says about being openly his father's son is that 'I was constantly being sought out by reporters from Italian newspapers who wanted me to give them interviews. So I abandoned the experiment.' There is no reason to doubt his word, but rather than just for being Oscar Wilde's son, it seems likely that reporters, vaguely hoping for a homosexual scandal, may have wanted to see if there was any connection to be made between Vyvyan 'Wilde' and Laurent's suicide. This is not as far-fetched as it may sound for three months later an obituary of Raymond Laurent appeared in a newly founded French literary magazine *Akademos* in which it was alleged: 'Apart from the customs official who was on duty near the golden statue of Fortune [*at the punta della Dogana*] only one other person, who happened to be passing by, heard that gunshot in Venice and gathered up the still warm body of poor little Laurent; it was Vivian [*sic*] Wilde, son of the great poet.'[180] The obituary had been written by the founder of *Akademos*, Count Jacques d'Adelswärd-Fersen, himself also homosexual, who had met Laurent early in 1908 and had offered him a job as the editorial director, a post which he sadly never filled. Nowhere in the detailed local newspaper reports at the time is there any mention of my father as having been the first to find the dead man, and the customs officials—there were three of them, not one—who arrived on the scene immediately afterwards would certainly have recorded the fact and taken his details.[181] Besides, it was highly improbable that Vyvyan would have been so far from his hotel and wandering about on the other side of the Grand Canal at two in the morning. Bringing Oscar Wilde even vicariously into the story gave it an added piquancy and the imaginative detail was almost certainly supplied by the nineteen year-old Jean Cocteau who happened to be in Venice at the time and had met my father experimenting with his confiscated family name.[132] Cocteau figures semi-anonymously as 'M. Jean C.' in the obituary and he must have supplied Adelswärd-Fersen with the details, both real and imaginary, on his return to Paris. Cocteau was fascinated by Oscar Wilde and had already begun writing a dramatic adaptation of *The Picture of Dorian Gray* that year; Laurent, an Anglophile who had visited England twice, had written an essay on Wilde and aestheticism which was later published in 1910.[183] Given the two men's interest in Wilde and the fact that the number of foreign visitors to Venice was minute in proportion to today's mass tourism, it is more than likely their paths would have crossed once Vyvyan's presence in the city became known. Writing nearly half a century later, my father may have forgotten why journalists were anxious to interview him. Perhaps homosexual scandals in the family had caused him enough grief, and memory decided that, even though he had not been directly involved, erasure was the best policy; perhaps it was simply advisable to gloss over the affair in his 1954 memoir in which the word homosexuality does not appear once. Taking back his family name had done Vyvyan no favours.

There was a bizarre sequel to the story. The Paris correspondent of a German periodical picked up on the *Akademos* obituary and, wrongly reading that Raymond Laurent was the pseudonym of Vyvyan Wilde (Holland), declared him to be dead. Fortunately, they corrected the mistake in the following number saying that there was clearly something fateful about the name Wilde since occasional rumours surfaced about the father being still alive and here they were already sending the son to the underworld.[184]

The reference to Oscar's survival was to articles which had started to appear in newspapers a few years before—needless to say not in the British press which on the whole was quite happy to be certain that he was still six feet underground in Paris's Bagneux Cemetery. In 1903 a German actor and author of Gothic horror novels, Hanns Heinz Ewers, published a surreal account of a meeting with Oscar in a grotto on Capri. Oscar recounts events from his trial and imprisonment and describes how he has become the dream-object of a grotesque legless and armless monster which seems to accompany him everywhere. The article was headed with the author's name and (Capri) in brackets implying that the copy was filed from there, so it is unclear whether we are supposed to believe that the encounter actually took place then, or in 1897 when Oscar was with Bosie in Naples, or indeed at all.[185]

Ewers' account appeared in book form the next year and it wasn't long before other fictitious memoirs and even 'sightings' were being published. In 1905 there appeared a ludicrous volume entitled *Osrac, the Self Sufficient* written by one J. M. Stuart-Young, in which a lamentably bad verse-tribute to Oscar is framed by his clearly invented memoir of the man, some indifferent poetry of his own and a brief assessment of *De Profundis*. By 1899, when he was eighteen, Young, a working-class Mancunian (the hyphenated Stuart was later added to imply middle-class respectability), was already a fake spiritualist medium and convicted embezzler and forger. After six months in Strangeways Prison he embarked for West Africa where he would spend most of the rest of his life, and from where *Osrac* was written. In it he maintained that, aged fourteen, he had met and dined with Oscar at the Savoy, and that he had corresponded with him, reproducing as proof a badly forged and clumsily phrased letter. Aged eighteen he visited him in his Paris exile and by twenty he 'had read most of the pages in manuscript' of *De Profundis* although at the time it was closely guarded under lock and key by Robert Ross. Such inconsistencies abound on almost every page of the memoir. To be charitable, it was a well-meaning if slightly ill-conceived attempt by one homosexual to pay tribute to another, though with its blatant fabrications the author can hardly have expected it to be taken seriously by those who had known Oscar even slightly. Unfortunately that didn't prevent one of Wilde's more eminent biographers, Hesketh Pearson, from taking the 'memoir' at face value in 1946. [186]

On the other side of the Atlantic a twenty year-old college student, George Sylvester Viereck, who had been obsessed with Oscar Wilde since his school days, wrote an article for the *New York World* based on rumours that Oscar might never have died. The *World*, then a major player in the field of 'yellow journalism,' turned it down as being too sensational even for its attention-grabbing columns, so Viereck perversely offered it to one of the foremost literary journals of the time, *The Critic,* where it appeared in their July 1905 number as 'Is Oscar Wilde Living or Dead?'[187] As a precocious schoolboy Viereck had contacted Alfred Douglas when the latter had come to New York in 1901, and they had remained sporadically in correspondence. In the article, doubtless prompted by the US edition of *De Profundis* published earlier in the year, Viereck quotes an unnamed woman whom he met during the interval at a theatre and who told him in confidence of the rumour that Oscar was alive and living in a Spanish Monastery. Three months later in a New York bookshop he says that he shared this astonishing news with one of the sales assistants who, far from being surprised, confirmed that he has seen Oscar in the City only two weeks before and had spoken to him. Viereck then offers his own theory for Oscar's possible survival: that his huge popularity in France and Germany was specially engineered to allow the author 'to return to England wreathed with continental laurels.' In support of this (and with dubious logic) he then quotes a paragraph from one of Oscar's prison letters to Robbie in which he compares his return to the outside world as a man risen from the grave. The letter, says Viereck, only appearing as a supplement to the German edition of *De Profundis,* had to be suppressed in the English version, so as not to reveal Oscar's intentions. The *New York Times* picked up the story and treated it with appropriate scepticism and no more was heard of Oscar's presence in the City; with his cover blown he obviously took the boat back to Cadiz or Barcelona.[188]

It was left up to the *Los Angeles Examiner* three years later to attempt an explanation of how Oscar might have avoided the grave. In a full-page, unsigned article it was suggested that some days before his death a dying man was substituted for Wilde who went briefly into hiding in London and finished up in Italy. The ruse was carried out with the full knowledge of Robbie Ross and with the help of the American coloratura soprano Sibyl Sanderson who was then performing at the Paris Opéra. Although Sanderson had died in 1903, the circumstantial evidence was apparently provided by the *garçon d'étage*, Jules Patuel, one of the Hôtel d'Alsace employees. He maintained that four days before Oscar had died he had seen Sanderson half-carrying a man up the hotel stairs. Patuel had not seen the man's face clearly but Sanderson said to him 'It is Monsieur Wilde who is very ill; I will take him to his room,' and that was the man whom they buried on 3 December 1900. Everything about the article was preposterous. The rumour of Oscar being alive 'whispered about the ateliers and salons of Paris and London . . . a thing believed by nine-tenths of those who knew Wilde' was absurd, and 'men and women who reported that they had met Oscar Wilde in their wanderings. Not one or two, but dozens—Americans, French and English' was pure invention. He had been seen in Venice, Naples, and at a little villa outside Milan and an unnamed artist friend, who had known him in his heyday, met him in Palermo where Wilde admitted the subterfuge, said he was revelling in his posthumous fame and that he had nearly finished a new novel.[189]

It was the suggestion of a Wildean 'renaissance' in Italy which may have prompted an Italian newspaper to run an article in March 1909 along much the same lines—'Oscar Wilde sarebbe vivo?' (Could Oscar Wilde be alive?). The journalist, Gabriele Gabrielli, wrote that there had been rumours of a mysterious and elusive person being seen in the cafés and theatres of Turin whom many thought to be Oscar Wilde. He was described as elegant and reclusive, but Gabrielli had no idea who had first started this rumour. One of the people willing to testify was a certain Alfredo Martinelli, a Neapolitan who had met Wilde in Naples in 1897 when he frequented the Café Gambrinus and was convinced he had now seen his unmistakable face again in Turin. However, when 'Wilde' realised that he was being watched intently he hurried off down a side street and Martinelli never saw him again. Adding his own touch of mystery to the story, Gabrielli described how he himself, while reading the *Gazzetta del Popolo*, found an advertisement in which a certain Roberto Chiltern was looking for an elegant and secluded villa on the outskirts of Turin on the very same days when the sightings occurred. He went on to explain that Robert Chiltern was the main character in Wilde's play *An Ideal Husband*, whose efforts to redeem himself for a mistake made as a young politician led him to think that this could indeed be Wilde using the name of one of his own characters just as he used the name Sebastian Melmoth when he came out of prison. All slightly more credible than Sibyl Sanderson half-dragging a dying substitute up the stairs of the Hôtel d'Alsace, but still firmly in the realms of pure fantasy.

The nearest real-life event which could be compared to a 'resurrected' Oscar around that time was the subscription dinner given in Robbie's honour at the Ritz on 1 December 1908 to celebrate the publication of the *Collected Works*. It was a gathering of the good and the great under the chairmanship for the evening of Sir Martin Conway, with whom Robbie had become friends through the art world. In his opening speech Conway, an extraordinary polymath—art critic, mountaineer, cartographer and politician—thanked the assembled company who had shown their support of Robbie by purchasing their dinner tickets and caused much laughter with his analysis of the guests:

> The Chairman, after submitting the loyal toasts, announced that the gathering was composed of 36 journalists and critics, 5 actors, 11 art connoisseurs, 5 Government officials, 20 authors, 4 editors, 12 poets, 4 dramatists, 7 artists, 4 publishers, 4 men of science and medicine, 2 clergy, 4 lawyers, and many other people whom he could 'not put into a definite category'[190]

A very eclectic mix which would have appealed to the ghost of the man they were honouring besides Robbie himself. H. G. Wells proposed the toast to 'Our Guest' and said that Robbie had stood up for Oscar at a time when the whole hurricane of public opinion was against him, and had roused against himself the cruellest thing in modern life—righteous indignation. Robbie's response was moving and humorous by turns but characteristically modest throughout. He said that had he not been Oscar's literary executor, nobody but his close friends would have heard of him and it made him very mindful of the eighteenth century poet John Gay's lines: 'I hate the man who builds his fame / On ruins of another's fame.'[191] He went on to praise Max Meyerfeld as the inspiration behind publishing excerpts from *De Profundis* which helped to secure Wilde's reputation in Germany and he announced, to cheers, the anonymous gift of £2,000 (from Helen Carew) to erect a suitable monument to Oscar once his remains had been moved to Père Lachaise Cemetery. Finally, of that gift and of the dinner in his honour he said that he would like to take them: 'as symbols that in after years it will be my privilege to boast that I was the occasion, though never the cause, of giving back to Wilde's children the laurels of their distinguished father untarnished save by tears.'[192] It was the only oblique mention of Cyril and Vyvyan who were, of course, present, nor did their names appear anywhere in the press reports of the dinner afterwards. There was, however, one very noticeable absentee that evening. Alfred Douglas.

For several months prior to the Ritz dinner the uneasy relationship between Alfred Douglas and Robbie Ross had been further deteriorating. Back in March 1907, Pamela Wyndham, one of Bosie's cousins and married to Edward Tennant (later Lord Glenconner), persuaded her husband to buy a mainstream, rather conventional literary magazine, *The Academy,* and install Douglas as the editor. The following year Douglas made the fatal mistake of hiring T. W. H. Crosland as his assistant editor, an experienced and clever journalist but a hypocritical moralist who, though himself an adulterer and self-confessed alcoholic, found repugnant everything that Oscar Wilde had stood for. During the next six years Crosland's influence over Douglas was disastrous, encouraging his already quarrelsome temperament to tip into belligerence and litigation. Crosland's aversion to everything Wildean extended, unsurprisingly, to Robbie Ross who had been a regular contributor to *The Academy* since 1905. When in May 1908 Robbie was commissioned to review a play by a friend of his, Maurice Baring, Crosland altered it to such an extent that it was turned into disagreeable comments on the play coupled with a snide remark about George Bernard Shaw's Irish loquacity. Robbie was furious, as there was just enough of his style left in the unsigned piece for it to be clear that he had had a hand in writing it.[193] He returned the cheque for his fee and declared that it was the last time he would write anything for the magazine. Later that summer, he and Bosie met at a weekend house party and when Bosie brought up the subject of the mutilated review, Robbie told him that he felt a little more courtesy was owed to an old contributor and a violent argument ensued. Their host later said that he would never have the two of them in his house again; a pattern repeated on more than one occasion over the next few years.[194]

Around the same time, *The Academy* published an article clearly penned by Douglas, and no doubt to the fury of Crosland, headed 'The genius of Oscar Wilde' which applauded Methuen's initiative in issuing the *Collected Works* and was lavish in its praise of their author. A week later in a remarkable *volte-face,* an article entitled 'A literary scandal' appeared in which Douglas wrote that it was ridiculous Methuen should be excluding *The Picture of Dorian Gray* from their edition of Wilde's works.[195] It would seem that Robbie had told Bosie in confidence about the problems he and Algernon Methuen had had to get the rights from Carrington in Paris. Unfortunately Douglas had his facts tangled as *Dorian Gray* was indeed included in a uniform volume with the rest of Wilde's works and all he managed to do was to embarrass Ross and antagonise him still further by making public a private conversation.[196]

It was against this background of literary sniping and not long after the final two volumes of Methuen's *Collected Works* appeared on 15 October 1908 that some of Robbie's friends felt that a public dinner should be held in his honour to celebrate all that he had achieved in the past eight years since Oscar's death. Reginald Turner, who was one of the organisers of the Ritz dinner, informed Bosie who apparently replied with an abusive letter both about Ross and the event and refused to participate. Even if Bosie didn't want to attend the dinner—and it was understandable that he might have felt uncomfortable in that company of Ross's well-wishers—he couldn't bring himself to offer even a grudging word of acknowledgement for Robbie's work in trying to restore Oscar's literary reputation.[197]

Early in 1909 Bosie's wife, Olive, who had always been fond of Robbie but was aware of the tensions between him and her husband, wrote and asked him to lunch. Robbie replied formally that he was otherwise engaged prompting a rather plaintive letter from Olive who was clearly hoping to reconcile the two of them. This led Robbie to detail the reasons for their estrangement which, apart from the quarrels outlined above, also included his irritation that Bosie had recommended the public buy the pirated American edition of Oscar's works because as he said (errone-ously) the Methuen edition had excluded *Dorian Gray*:[198]

> It is because I do not wish to quarrel with him in the future that I have avoided him and shall avoid meeting him . . . . I have no hostile feelings whatever because I know Bosie too well and have known him too long. But I decided some time ago to deny myself the privileges coincidental to friendship with him.

Olive showed the letter to her husband and in stark contrast to the measured tone of Robbie's letter, Bosie immediately replied to what he called 'the extraordinary farrago of impudent rubbish' and said that the feelings were entirely reciprocated:

> I gave up going to your house because I disapproved of your views, your morals and most of your friends. My own views have changed and I do not care now to meet those who are engaged in active propaganda of every kind of wickedness from anarchy and socialism to sodomy.[199]

Robbie's solicitor, Sir George Lewis, advised him not to reply and to ignore the unpleasant insinuations. Had the matter finished up in court, apart from Robbie's own reputation, it could well have revived the whole scandal of 1895 which Robbie wanted to avoid for the sake of Cyril and Vyvyan. In political terms diplomatic re-lations had been severed and it was merely a matter of time (in fact just under a year) before an incident would lead to the outbreak of hostilities. Their feud might have erupted even sooner had Douglas made a more careful examination of the expanded version of *De Profundis* in Methuen's *Collected Works*, for Robbie had all but named him as the recipient. In his preface, written in the form of a letter to Max Meyerfeld, the translator of the German edition,

Robbie stated that the work was 'cast in the form of a letter to a friend not myself . . . Contrary to a general impression it contains nothing scandalous . . . a large portion of it is taken up with business and private matters of no interest whatever'—a serious misrepresentation in view of what was to come. Furthermore, in the new German edition which appeared a year later, Meyerfeld—presumably with Robbie's approval—stated quite openly that the letter was written to Alfred Douglas and, more significantly, included in the text the words omitted in all editions until then: 'neither you nor your father, multiplied a thousand times over, could possibly have ruined a man like me . . . Terrible as what you did to me was, what I did to myself was far more terrible still.'[200] Although Douglas spoke French and had friends in Paris who would have alerted him to something similar appearing in France, German was a closed book to him and Ross knew it; there was little danger and much long-term advantage to be derived from this form of guerrilla warfare.

By the middle of 1909 the first stage of Robbie's rehabilitation of Oscar was complete. The thousand copy print-run of the *Collected Works* on hand-made paper had sold so well that Methuen had to put out a second edition to satisfy popular demand: smaller in format, cheaper in price but uniformly bound and still stylish in design. With the £2,000 from Helen Carew and royalties coming in from the publishers, Robbie's next objective was to give Oscar a permanent resting place with an appropriate memorial and to remove his remains from the temporary grave at Bagneux. Accordingly, he purchased a *concession à perpetuité* in Père Lachaise Cemetery where he and my father went to be present at Oscar's reburial on 20 July. A simple enough event one would have thought, but the details of which inevitably became clothed in the gaudy apparel of myth and exaggeration. There was no contemporary description of what happened by the only two people—Vyvyan and Robbie—who were there apart from the gravediggers and the officials. However, the most dramatic account came from Frank Harris in his 1916 biography of Oscar who claimed to have had it directly from Robbie Ross. Robbie apparently told him that despite being advised to put quicklime in Oscar's coffin so that only his bones would survive and make a later transfer easier, when the coffin was opened it was exactly the reverse and the body had been preserved: 'Oscar's face was recognisable, only his hair and beard had grown long. At once Ross sent [Vyvyan] away, and when the sextons were about to use their shovels, he ordered them to desist, and descending into the grave, moved the body with his own hands into the new coffin in loving reverence.'[201] One, there is no way that quicklime could have 'preserved' the body rather than hastening its decomposition; two, it is medically nonsensical to suggest that hair continues to grow after death; and three, the idea that Robbie, with his slim build, would climb down into a narrow grave and himself move the remains of a man over six feet tall is simply absurd. The story smacks of myth-making, even hagiography—the exhumation of St. Oscar the Sinner nine years after his burial, his corpse still intact. Whether Ross really did provide Harris with these fantastical details, or whether Harris took something more realistic and embellished it—which we know he was quite capable of doing—Ross read the first edition of his book and sent Harris a list of comments but correcting this account of Oscar's reburial was not among them.

There were two others who might have been at Père Lachaise on that day: Alfred Douglas and Vyvyan's brother, Cyril. Given the escalating tensions between Robbie and Bosie, it was hardly surprising that Bosie was not informed of the reburial. Vyvyan, by then quite aware of the part Douglas had played in his father's disgrace, would have felt extremely uncomfortable had he been there, and for Robbie this was a family affair. But why no Cyril? Now a fully-fledged lieutenant in the Royal Artillery, he was stationed at Woolwich and could easily have made the trip to Paris, but it would have meant taking leave and questions might have been asked about the purpose of it. No one at the barracks knew who his father was, and both Robbie and my father were acutely

aware that if ever it became known it could affect his army career.[202] Nevertheless, it was unthinkable that Cyril should have
been kept in the dark, and given his own feelings towards his
father it was probably agreed between them that Vyvyan alone
should be the family presence. After the reburial, all that remained
was for the sculpture to be completed and placed over the grave.

At the Ritz dinner when Robbie announced Helen Carew's
anonymous gift of £2,000 for a monument to Oscar in Père
Lachaise, he said that it came with a condition, namely that the
work should be carried out by 'the brilliant young [American]
sculptor, Mr. Jacob Epstein.' Having studied for three years in
Paris, Epstein came to London in 1905 with a letter of introduction
from Auguste Rodin to George Bernard Shaw, who in turn passed
him on to Robert Ross.[203] Robbie then enlisted the help of one of
the former partners in the Carfax Gallery, William Rothenstein, to
promote Epstein's work in England and before long he had landed
his first major commission—to carve eighteen over-life-size figures
for the façade of the new British Medical Association building in
the Strand. The BMA wanted portrayals of famous medical men
but Epstein was having none of it. He wanted to create symbolic
figures rather than dully representational ones: 'I was determined
to do a series of nude figures and surgeons with side whiskers, no
matter how eminent, could hardly have served my purposes as
models.' It was a sentiment with which the man whose memory
he was soon to honour in Père Lachaise had been entirely in sympathy. Hadn't Oscar said in his lecture on 'The Decorative Arts':
'to see the statues of our departed statesmen [substitute 'medical
men'] in marble frock coats and bronze, double-breasted waistcoats adds a new horror to death'?[204] At the time of their unveiling in the summer of 1908, the BMA statues caused public uproar
and much comment in the press, the matter even briefly reaching
the House of Commons, but eventually the statues were left in
place and the storm subsided.[205] It was against this background
that Epstein was awarded the commission for Oscar's tomb.

The question has often been raised as to why Ross would have risked courting controversy in this way, but reading between the lines of his speech at the dinner and assuming that my conjecture about one of the reasons Helen Carew wanted to provide the money for a monument is correct, the answer becomes obvious. This was a subtle gesture of defiance entirely appropriate to celebrate the memory of a man who had spent half his life defying Victorian 'respectability.' Even if Ross had influenced Mrs. Carew in her choice of artist, for him to declare that her funding was conditional on Epstein carrying out the work would have been absurd if not true, since she herself was present as the dinner. It was also to be installed across the Channel in the relative safety of artistically adventurous France 'la France, mère de tous les artistes' as Oscar once described her.[206] 'Relative safety' is probably the appropriate phrase since in the event, quite literally 'from beyond the grave' he managed to create a minor scandal with his new monument in 1912 when it was finally erected. But in the meantime, Robbie had other concerns.

In November 1909, and almost certainly anticipating possible claims by Bosie about the ownership of the *De Profundis* manuscript, Robbie deposited it in the British Museum Library for safekeeping with the stipulation that it was to be closed for fifty years. He reckoned that enough had now been published to satisfy public curiosity, and that by 1960 Douglas would no longer be alive to object to Oscar's brutally candid comments about him. Such was Oscar's sulphurous reputation, however, that before accepting the document, the Director and Principal Librarian Frederic Kenyon, had it read by the Archbishop of Canterbury who was one of the trustees.[207]

Earlier in the year Douglas had quarrelled with one of his friends, and although Ross could not have anticipated it at the time, as part of the collateral damage he would later find himself involved in an ugly dispute on Oscar's behalf. In the summer of 1909, *The Academy*, which Bosie was editing, ran into financial difficulties. Freddie Manners-Sutton, who was a good friend of Bosie and godfather to his son, had mentioned some time before that if ever the magazine was in need of money he would try to help out. Bosie unwisely despatched his tactless deputy editor Thomas Crosland to ask Freddie for £500 to tide them over a liquidity problem, which was phrased more as a demand than a request, and which Freddie turned down saying he considered that Bosie was drawing too large a salary as the editor. When Crosland reported back to him, Bosie was furious and wrote Freddie an ill-tempered and vitriolic letter finishing up 'I beg to inform you that neither I nor Olive will ever speak to you again and that I forbid you to come to this house. Furthermore, I will tell you quite plainly that I consider you to be a dirty, low, huckstering, Jew-minded pimp.' That on its own Freddie might have ignored, but Crosland compounded the injury by writing in two successive weekly issues of *The Academy* that Manners-Sutton (by implication and without actually naming him) was connected with two publishing houses 'which carry on two very different classes of business.' One of them produced 'dubious stories of a highly spiced character' just keeping on the right side of the Law while the other specialised in high-toned 'religious works and translations of various Christian liturgies.' Freddie asked for an apology to be printed in the next issue to say that he was not the person referred to, which Crosland refused to do. More inflammatory correspondence followed and finally Freddie had no choice but to sue Crosland for criminal libel. Crosland's plea of justification, prompted by pure malice and later described by Manners-Sutton's counsel as 'a more disgraceful document never came from the hand of any member of the legal profession,' concerned Freddie's alleged debauching of a possibly under-age girl five years before. This was intended to show that he was a man of low life, a hypocrite, and not a Christian. The full trial at the Old Bailey only came on in February the following year and was an extraordinary display of mud-slinging by both parties. Bosie was called as a witness for Crosland's defence, and since it was he who had provided the details for Crosland's plea of justification, he was foolish not to imagine that his own life might come under scrutiny—which indeed it did on the third day. Prosecuting counsel, Marshall Hall, said that Bosie had taken up with Oscar again after his release from prison, suggesting thereby that Bosie did not exactly have a spotless moral character himself. Bosie responded that Oscar told him he was the only friend he had left in the world and so he stuck to him until he died, paid his funeral expenses, buried him and, moreover, the man who could 'rake up the filth of 18 years ago [*actually 13*] was a blackguard.'[208] In the end, the jury acquitted Crosland of the libel charge. However, the case came to Robbie's attention and Bosie's lies and exaggerations about his role in Oscar's last years, widely reported in the press and implying that he was the only friend Oscar then had left, were more than he could stomach. He wrote to Marshall Hall offering to come forward and disprove Douglas's testimony, but the case had already closed. Even though Douglas continued, at that point, to believe that Oscar was a great writer, he couldn't stand the idea that it was Ross and not himself who now seemed to be centre stage and if that meant rewriting history, he had little conscience about doing so.

Four months later Douglas was in court again, this time as the plaintiff, suing the Anglican clergyman, Dr. Robert Horton for claiming in print that *The Academy* had taken on a Roman Catholic bias. Horton's solicitors having heard of Ross's offer to Marshall Hall asked if he would be prepared to give evidence as to Douglas's character in this new case. Although it's unclear how this could possibly have strengthened Horton's defence, Robbie, still smarting from the extraordinary mendacity Bosie has shown in the Manners-Sutton trial, was prepared to give vent to his anger if the opportunity arose. Wisely, Robbie's own solicitor, Sir George Lewis, dissuaded him from doing so, but somehow rumours of it reached Douglas who tried to enlist the help of More Adey, still a good friend both to him and to Ross. Adey wrote back saying that he would rather not be drawn into their quarrel eliciting a characteristic Douglas reply which ended 'As far as I am concerned both you and Ross can go to hell.'[209] As it was, he lost the case and was forced to sell *The Academy* to pay his costs.

Terminating friendships acrimoniously was one of his specialities and all too frequently, as in this case, Oscar can be found lurking in the shadows.

A month after the Manners-Sutton libel trial Robert Ross wrote to André Gide to compliment him on his recently published booklet *Oscar Wilde: in memoriam*, and since it expresses perfectly Robbie's state of mind at the time it is worth quoting extensively:

> Some day, perhaps, I shall publish letters of Oscar Wilde to myself, . . . This may one day become necessary in order to refute the lies of Alfred Douglas. You no doubt heard reported in a recent libel action that he swore in the witness-box that he was unaware of Oscar Wilde's guilt, and that he was the 'only decent friend who remained with Oscar Wilde.' You know perfectly well that Alfred Douglas was the cause of Oscar Wilde's ruin both before and after his imprisonment. I would like to have pretended this was not the case, out of old friendship and regard for Douglas: and the fact that I had quarrelled with him personally would not have affected my determination to let the world think he was really the noble friend he always posed as being. But since he has taken on himself, in his new character of social and moral reformer, to talk about Oscar Wilde's 'sins' (in most of which he participated) and has betrayed all his old friends, there is no longer any reason for me to be silent.[210]

It signified the end of the friendship between Ross and Douglas—definitively—and the start of a very ugly war of attrition.

CHAPTER SIX
VYVYAN TRIES TO FIND A PURPOSE IN LIFE

I have often wondered whether my father was fully aware of all that Robbie was going through protecting and rehabilitating Oscar in the years after he and Vyvyan first met. I suspect that he wasn't, and that to some extent he was sheltered by Robbie from Alfred Douglas's worst excesses. By the time these two finally fell out with one another, although Vyvyan was twenty-three and a responsible adult, I'm sure Robbie felt that he had suffered enough as a child without wanting to burden him further with the sordid squabbles between his father's friends. As it was, this Wildean Punch-and-Judy show would continue among the friends and the enemies for more than another three decades, until Douglas's death in 1945.

I struggle to write about my father in those early years of the twentieth century for many reasons, not least because he seemed to be living a somewhat unfocussed and irresponsible life off his share of the Wilde estate which Robbie, unpaid, had been administering with great care and much trouble. In the context of the Ritz dinner, there is a brief paragraph in Vyvyan's autobiography praising Robbie's efforts as literary executor and his achievement in getting the *Collected Works* published, but it is written fifty years after the events it describes, and with surprisingly little indication of how grateful he was feeling to Robbie at that time.[211] In his early twenties and freed from the stifling conventionality of his mother's family, it was understandable that Vyvyan would rebel, go travelling and, with Robbie's encouragement, even try to write for a living. Given the ambivalence he felt towards his father's memory, for a while he probably considered the income from the estate a form of just recompense for the misery which

Oscar had brought on his family, and if there was one thing which Vyvyan inherited from his father it was the ability to spend money which he didn't have.[212] That said, at the height of the Douglas vendetta against Ross in 1914, Vyvyan, far more conscious by then of all that Robbie had so selflessly achieved, went into court as a character witness for him and described him as a second father. All this could go beyond mere conjecture if only Vyvyan's letters to Robbie had survived, and why they didn't is something of a mystery.

Robbie Ross was a meticulous keeper of letters and papers which were preserved in his family after his death until they were sold in the late 1960s to a Wilde collector in America, Mary Hyde (later Mary Eccles), who in turn left them to the British Library in 2003. An inventory of the papers made before they were sold lists no less than 224 correspondents, among them substantial quantities of letters from Aubrey Beardsley, Max Beerbohm, Edmund Gosse, Somerset Maugham, John Singer Sargent, H. G. Wells, and William Rothenstein. This 'Ross Archive' enabled Robbie's niece by marriage, Margery, to compile a selection of the letters as her tribute to him in 1952, *Robert Ross: Friend of Friends*, a book unfortunately symptomatic of its time in that it simply ignored anything in Robbie's life of a controversial or scandalous nature and even those letters only touching on some of the legal wrangles he had to endure were redacted accordingly. My father gave Margery Ross some valuable help while she was working on the book and in return she gave back to him the surviving letters which he and Cyril had written to Robbie. Of Vyvyan's there were very few: half a dozen from the Front in 1915-1916. There had certainly been many more. It is inconceivable that, alongside all the other correspondence, Robbie would not have kept Vyvyan's first letter to him which he described as being 'almost as charming as meeting you . . . Your handwriting is so absurdly and pleasantly reminiscent [of Oscar's].'[213] The most likely explanation is that the others were destroyed after Robbie's death in 1918—in all probability by Vyvyan himself—as many of them, especially those between 1909 and 1913, didn't show my father in the best light. He was in close touch with Robbie's brother and executor, Alec, about the hand-over of all Wilde-related material and it was often customary to offer letters back to their authors if they were still living; either that or Vyvyan simply asked to have them returned and made his selection for posterity. The letters from the Front, written in the obligatory pencil, were kept as interesting and harmless historical documents—Oscar Wilde's second son, like his older sibling, doing his duty for King and Country.[214]

As one of Oscar Wilde's children, my father's life was inevitably going to attract a certain amount of unhealthy interest. Vyvyan's family had wanted to spare him this unwelcome attention by changing his name and attempting to eradicate every last connection with his parent, but Oscar's genes were all-too powerful. Vyvyan was not genetically suited to being the civil servant his family wished him to be, nor a businessman or financier. He was encouraged to read Law at Cambridge but always seemed to be a reluctant student and was happiest when writing.[215] Unfortunately this wasn't the success he had hoped for, and from Robbie's side of the correspondence it is clear that his financial problems and his future were discussed in painful detail. Unsurprisingly, Vyvyan preferred to treat this period of his life in London rather sketchily in his second memoir, *Time Remembered,* and his letters were probably 'disappeared' for the same reason.

After spending a final year at Cambridge in 1909, and with a view to becoming a barrister, Vyvyan spent a few months at a country solicitor's office in Hereford learning, as he put it, something about 'the other side of the law.' In April 1910, just about the time that Ross and Douglas were breaking off their friendship for good, Vyvyan returned to London and set himself up in a flat in Chelsea. There he continued his legal studies in a desultory way, spending more time with artists and writers than with his law books. 'It was not a very productive year,' he wrote of the time with laconic understatement and, as if to prove it, he covers the next eighteen months of his life in *Time Remembered* with a few anecdotes about H. G. Wells, Henry James, and Herbert Beerbohm Tree, and a short, makeweight chapter on life in Edwardian London.[216] As a result, in the spring of 1911 he failed his Bar Finals, found himself heavily in debt to tradesmen and moneylenders and had to leave the country to escape his creditors and possible insolvency proceedings. Contrary to what he wrote, it was not merely as a result of failing an exam and wanting a foreign environment without social distractions that Vyvyan went to spend six months in Spain between October 1911 and April 1912.

What right do I have to reveal what my father was at pains to conceal? Is it so significant a part of the posthumous Oscar story that it needs to be told? Insofar as it emphasises yet again the difference between the two sons, one wanting to claim what little of his father's artistic temperament he might have inherited and the other desperately anxious to distance himself from it at all costs—yes. Besides, safely preserved in institutional archives, the circumstantial evidence exists. As Robbie Ross wrote to Walter Ledger in the autumn of 1911, he was obliged to sell various important Wilde manuscripts at Sotheby's the previous July in order to help Vyvyan pay off some of his debts despite the fact that Vyvyan had already mortgaged his half of the Wilde literary estate to his brother: 'Poor Vyvyan Holland has come a fearful smash. He has been reprehended by his brother and I have had to send him off to Spain which has made a sudden and unpleasant strain on my resources. The sale at Sotheby's which I made really on his behalf was not enough and he has bartered his share of the literary estate long ago.'[217] Shortly before Vyvyan left the country Robbie wrote to him, deeply concerned about the financial mess in which Vyvyan found himself:

Conceal from your creditors that you have a contingent interest in anything. It will be fatal if I am 'garnisheed' by the official receiver in bankruptcy. That is what Cyril dreads so much. He does not want it to come out that either of you derive monies from your father's works. It really might damage Cyril's career in the army.

Personally I would not mind except that I don't want your creditors to get hold of the Estate in any way.[218]

A week later, on 27 September, Cyril embarked for India. It wasn't his brigade, the 26th at Aldershot, which was posted; it was just Cyril. They simply replaced him with another lieutenant and he in turn replaced another junior officer in the 17th at Secunderabad. An individual posting at his request? Not impossible but a strange coincidence in the circumstances. In fact Robbie was so concerned for Cyril that he checked the *Army List* for the period and discovered to his relief that there were no less than thirty-seven Hollands listed so the likelihood of Cyril's real identity being discovered was slim, especially if he were serving in India.

In 1959 my father sold all the letters he had received from Robert Ross, the other side of the correspondence which 'disappeared.' Why, if Vyvyan had wanted to conceal an awkward and embarrassing period in his life, did he bother to keep half the evidence and, even more incomprehensibly, why did he sell them? By the time of Robbie's death in 1918 Vyvyan had grown deeply fond of him; he had become like a parent and represented the only surviving link with an obliterated past. Keeping Robbie's letters was a way of preserving his memory irrespective of the criticisms of Vyvyan that Robbie may have voiced in them. But forty years later, desperately short of money and still suffering from the effects of his bankruptcy in 1955, Vyvyan decided to sell them. Interest in Oscar Wilde and his circle had grown in the previous ten years and items even peripherally associated with him were becoming collectible. However, before disposing of them my father made and kept transcripts for himself—selectively. He ignored all those which Robbie wrote to him in Spain and seems to have copied only a single paragraph—the one printed above—from the letter he received before he left England and even destroyed the original rather than selling it with the rest. Quite illogical, at first sight, to let the unexpurgated correspondence out of your control and only keep the doctored version if you were anxious to conceal things. But, when money is short, papers with a hint of scandal inevitably fetch more than those which have been sanitised. No doubt Vyvyan reckoned that by the time anyone was interested in the detail of how his father's downfall affected his sons, he would be long gone and it wouldn't matter. He was right on the first count and wrong on the second. It *does* matter but for a different reason: sixteen years after Oscar's conviction Cyril and Vyvyan were, to differing degrees, still having to live with 'the secret.'

Robbie wrote to Vyvyan in Spain on 14 February 1912 mildly exasperated by the son's profligacy as he had been by the father's thirteen years before: 'Have you had any writs or threats forwarded from your flat? I don't exactly know how things stand now. I am distressed that you should be leading a somewhat futile life from your own account and you must be terribly bored,' but still signed it 'Always yours affectionately.' Ten days later he wrote again to say that Cyril 'has very generously given me enough money to pay the money-lenders with interest; but of course you understand that he was not obliged to do this, so . . . you must write and make acknowledgments to him.' Cyril in turn wrote to Vyvyan from Secunderabad on 20 March in a slightly sarcastic vein: 'What a quaint life you seem to be leading. Rather fascinating for a short time I should think but dull unless done with some purpose. I suppose you will write some delightfully untrue romances about your sojourn among the Southern races.'[219]

As it turned out my father did write, but rather too truthfully. He kept a diary for the six months he spent in Spain and his diary style by then had started to become reflective and interesting rather than just a dull record of daily events. I remembered reading it at the same time I had found the 'locked' diary of 1907. There was a fair amount about his amorous adventures with the young women of Madrid but he would certainly have commented on his 'exile' from England which, unaware of his financial difficulties as I was back in 1974, I would have overlooked. But alas, when I opened the Spanish diary for the first time in twenty-five years, I found that Thelma had ripped out ninety pages at the beginning. My mother had been at work with her bucket of family whitewash yet again. Not content with ensuring the 'locked' diary contained nothing that could possibly be interpreted as Vyvyan having homosexual tendencies at twenty-one, she was determined to suppress his rampant heterosexuality at twenty-four. Following *that* rather distasteful sexual scandal back in 1895, a hundred years later it was important to her that the Holland/Wilde family should be seen to be squeaky clean and sexless.

If the remains of his diary are anything to go by, the reality of Vyvyan's time in Spain was rather different to the romanticised adventure he portrays in *Time Remembered*. He was constantly short of money and having to pawn valuables to tide himself over until funds were transferred from England. His study of the law texts which would have enabled him to retake his Bar Finals seems to have been abandoned completely for a rich diet of European literature, still intent as he was on making a life in the world of letters. And on top of everything else he came down with a severe bout of Malta Fever and was laid low for a month. Before it was properly diagnosed he wrote 'I have a horrible suspicion that the whole thing is merely a question of "breaking up" after my debauched life of the last few years,' an uncomfortable echo of what Oscar had written from prison: 'I let myself be lured into long spells of senseless and sensual ease. I became the spendthrift of my own genius, and to waste an eternal youth gave me a curious joy.' Like his father before him, he went into a self-imposed exile, but unlike his father his transgression had not taken him to prison and after six months' absence he returned to England. 'My return was not heralded by drums or any loud fanfare of trumpets,' he wrote a touch evasively. 'I came in by the back door,' and that was as close as he would come to the truth about his Spanish exile.[220]

On his return to London at the end of March 1912, Vyvyan decided that he might as well finish off his legal studies and try to find work as a barrister. Having made over his share of the Wilde royalties to Cyril in return for the payment of the major part of his debts, he was living off the small quarterly income from a trust fund, most probably what was left over from his mother's estate. He spent the remainder of 1912 preparing for his Bar Finals and just scraped through with a Third Class at the beginning of November. He was called to the Bar on 18 November as the 'son of Wills Wild [Holland] deceased' the same designation under which he had been admitted to Lincoln's Inn in 1905. The shame and secrecy continued.

At the beginning of 1913 Vyvyan started his pupillage but it didn't last long. He was bored with the law and the only lasting effect of having passed the qualifying exam was to enable him to put 'Barrister' against the question 'Profession' on any form he had to fill in over the next fifty years. He tried writing again, but apart from a short story in the *Morning Post* which Cyril rather flippantly and unhelpfully put down to the result of nepotism (Robbie Ross had been a contributor to the paper for some years), literary success eluded him.[221] "If I set myself to write a fairy tale . . . I would find myself drifting into a kind of imitation of my father's works and comparing them so unfavourably with stories like "The Happy Prince" that I would destroy them . . . I did my best, but it was no good.' In the spring of that year, tired, as he said, of sitting around and doing nothing, he seems to have set off for Portugal on some madcap scheme to help restore the Portuguese monarchy. I write 'seems' because there is absolutely no evidence for it happening apart from a single paragraph in *Time Remembered* and a passing reference to it in a letter from his brother hoping he 'had a jolly time in Portugal.' The 'buccaneering friend' who accompanied him is never mentioned by name.[222] Unlike the Spanish 'exile,' he kept no diary which was unusual for him at that time, though perhaps understandable due to the politically sensitive nature of the undertaking. He didn't even leave a brief account of the escapade once he returned to England and it is mentioned nowhere by Robbie Ross in his voluminous correspondence. Perhaps it happened; maybe it nearly did. Apart from that one paragraph in his memoir, I never heard it referred to again when my father was alive.

It was a period in my father's life when he felt lost, torn between what he felt was expected of him and what his genes were urging him to do:

> Robbie Ross used to try to obtain jobs for me, but I suppose I was too wayward and he aimed too high. I was perfectly prepared to start at the bottom and to work my way up, but Robbie, with the best possible intentions, did not want me to do anything that would lower my father's dignity, for what it was worth, in the eyes of the world, and he refused all offers of menial employment, and I still had nothing to do.

For the next two years, by his own admission, Vyvyan drifted along aimlessly, still trying to write but becoming disheartened by the regularity with which his articles and stories came back with 'The Editor regrets' slips.[223] There was, however, one high point in this otherwise depressing existence: in the summer of 1913 he met a young woman, Violet Craigie, whom would become his first wife. When they became engaged at the beginning of October, Vyvyan told Robbie who said he was delighted but also concerned, not for Vyvyan but for his future bride on account of his unpaid debts and lack of future prospects.[224] Robbie, presumably as part of the 'normalising' of the Wilde family, decided to publicise the engagement in the announcements columns of *The Times*, which unfortunately then led to considerable press interest and much to Vyvyan's embarrassment his appearance on a *Daily Sketch* newspaper placard. The family were furious, accused Vyvyan of undoing their years of hard work trying to dissociate him and themselves from everything to do with Oscar Wilde and pointedly boycotted the wedding which took place on 7 January 1914. Cyril, with whom by now Vyvyan had fallen out, only heard of the engagement through their solicitor and wrote to Robbie expressing a marked lack of enthusiasm at the news.[225] He also wrote a somewhat terse letter from India to his brother on the day of the wedding, finishing up: 'I trust that you will prove yourself more loyal to your wife than, in the past, you have done to those many friends whose good offices on your behalf you now persistently ignore.' Robbie in the middle of a very nasty legal battle with Alfred Douglas nearly didn't attend, but since Vyvyan had asked him to be his best man, he took the risk fearing that Douglas might appear and cause a scene. Thankfully that didn't happen. Apart from being married, Vyvyan's life went on as unfruitfully as before until 4 August when Britain declared war on Germany and he at last found himself with a purpose—fighting for his country. Meanwhile another war was being waged in the Law Courts of London, a war which had been started two and a half years before and at the centre of which, yet again, was Oscar Wilde.

Chapter Seven
The Brothers Exchange Letters

In his 1954 autobiography my father reproduced part of a letter which his brother had written to him from India. It was in response to one from Vyvyan about their childhood and he quoted from Cyril's letter largely to explain, in Cyril's own words, the latter's stoical attitude towards life and his determination, as he put it, to wipe away the stain on the family honour brought about by their father. Vyvyan simply refers to his own letter in passing and in 1954, many years before the start of the vogue for 'miserable childhood' memoirs, I can understand his reluctance to do any more than refer to it obliquely as part of the story. It has survived as a typescript draft, amended by Robbie Ross to whom Vyvyan must have showed it for his advice before sending it on to Cyril. Nevertheless, I feel that both letters in their entirety poignantly reflect what it must have been like to have grown up as orphans in the Edwardian era with the poisonous influence of Oscar Wilde still lurking in the collective memory of that self-righteous society.

The letters need to be read together with two of the chapters in Vyvyan's *Son of Oscar Wilde,* 'Return from Exile' and 'Adolescence' which fill in the details and explain some of the references. Both the facts and the emotions in Vyvyan's letter were still as real to him forty years later when he was writing about them in his autobiography, but in 1954 restraint was the order of the day for a British public which still regarded the 'stiff upper lip' as an admirable quality. Vyvyan had just married his first wife, Violet, and as described in the previous chapter, the unwanted publicity in the Press caused an uproar in the family. The reaction in Cyril's letter was rather less extreme but still disapproving.

23 February 1914

Dear Cyril,

I have been meaning to write to you for some time but I shrank from the task for many reasons. In the first place I doubted, and still doubt, what I have to say will interest you. Secondly, I felt the difficulty which one always experiences after a long cessation of correspondence, the difficulty of picking up threads and explaining the silence. Above all I was afraid that you would apply to my letter those epithets and adjectives which you always apply to any action of mine—such as 'hasty,' 'ill-judged,' 'hysterical,' 'shallow' etc.

But I certainly owe you an apology for not writing to you when I was first engaged to be married. As a matter of fact only Ross and a few intimate friends of mine were aware of it. I understand that the news first reached you through Ross who indicated to me that you did not seem particularly pleased, though he did not show me your letter. Consequently, I did not think that you would welcome a letter from me.

Certain notices of the marriage, moreover, appeared in the Press identifying me with my father. As Ross and Hargrove will confirm, I had nothing to do with these notices. Of course I was at once accused, without any enquiry, by the Napiers and Meinertzhagen of having deliberately inserted them. In the meantime Meinertzhagen, Lizzie and various friends of my mother, who had accepted invitations to the wedding, seized the opportunity of my marriage for venting their traditional hatred of me by writing me insulting letters and announcing their intention of abstaining from being present at the ceremony, a deprivation from which I readily recovered. I was fortunately able to convince Hansell, by letters received by Barber of the *Morning Post,* that my identity—though not necessarily yours—was well-known in Fleet Street. And that directly the marriage was announced photographers, without asking my permission, immediately supplied the illustrated papers with portraits of myself and Violet.

You must not imagine that I am making any grievance that

family friends did not attend the wedding: they were invited merely from politeness, not from affection; and, as I suspected, did not even go through the form of sending me a wedding present.

I have been very happy with my wife until the last week when she unfortunately contracted blood-poisoning and has been very ill, necessitating the expense of nurses and doctors; but I will not bore you with domestic details which probably will have no interest for you.

On the other hand I am going to inflict on you certain suggestions which may possibly explain to you why there has been a gulf between us in the past; and I will ask you to believe that, curious as it may seem, I do so simply on account of the great affection which I have always had for you. I want to explain at least my attitude from one side of the gulf which has never dissipated the affection with which I still and shall always regard you.

You may remember that in 1896 mother began to have leanings towards Catholicism and suggested that both of us should go to a Catholic school. You were strong, healthy and athletic: I was weak and always in bad health, besides being horribly miserable at Neuenheim, so I embraced the idea with enthusiasm. I was just ten years old. You wisely refused and remained at Neuenheim. I went to Monaco where whatever of the English schoolboy I may have had in me was painlessly knocked out.

I returned to England in 1898, at the same time as you did, and was at once regarded with pious horror by the Hopes and the Napiers, those pillars of the Anglican church. Of course my manners must have been foreign, and my physical weaknesses and delicacy were un-English and galling to the stiff-necked Napiers who were so delighted at possessing a relative who was a peer.

You went to Radley: I to Stonyhurst.

Do you realise that for the next six years—perhaps the most important in a boy's life—I was denied the social advantages of my caste and almost entirely the society of my social equals?

Do you realise that through the entire time that I was at Stonyhurst my holidays were always spent either as a paying guest in some wretched family, who wanted me only because of the money which was paid to them for my keep, or I was herded among a lot of ill-bred foreigners from Stonyhurst and other schools whose homes were too far off to permit of their returning for the holidays and whose moral standards were those of the card-sharper and the bar-loafer?

I was deprived of all human affection and sympathy. I was treated like a leper and a pariah by those whose duty it was to have accorded me the reality as well as the simulation of affection; and my character became crippled by the neglect and unkindness of those who were *paid* to do a duty which should have been exercised by the Napiers and the Hopes.

For six years I never had a single friend of my own age. I could give you countless instances of the humiliations I went through, of the longings I had that some one should take some interest in me. The Napiers, who cordially disliked me, openly showed their feelings. The only people who ever treated me decently were Mrs. Cochrane and Lady Low and they were the only elder friends of my childhood, the only real friends I was allowed to know, who turned up on my wedding day to wish me luck.

I want to speak particularly of the attitude of the Hopes. Until two years after my mother's death I never saw either Adrian or Mrs. Hope. At the end of my first year at Stonyhurst I wrote and told Adrian Hope that I had been the top of my form during the entire time; he never even answered the letter. I saw him only three times from my mother's death until his own [1904]. The first time was at Cottesmore Gardens; the second time was at More House on the only occasion I ever went there; and the third time at the hospital in Great Ormond Street. I have never had a letter from him in my life. He was the man into whose hands my darling mother had confided me. I believe there was a daughter called Esmé, with whom you were the greatest friends. Do you know that I never saw her? You used to call Mrs. Hope 'Laura.' When I started to follow your example, Lizzie told me to call her 'Mrs. Hope.' I asked why you called her 'Laura.' It was explained to me that 'it was quite different.' Do you think that I do not remember these things? However much you may scout the idea, slights and insults are a great reality to a sensitive child. Adrian Hope, I have since found out, said in answer to an enquiry as to what had happened to your younger brother, that he was 'going in the same way as his father.' There was never any foundation for this assumption and had he looked a little nearer home, he would have been reminded that his own father was hardly a paragon of all the virtues and was found to have even pawned the Victoria Cross which should have lain on his coffin at his funeral.

A little time ago I saw Mrs. Cochrane who repeated to me that Lizzie had told her that Bill [*Napier*] refused to allow his son to know me because I had introduced him to bad men. I have only twice seen Arthur since he left Wellington, and on each occasion it was with Trelawney Reed and Ivan Campbell and a lot of other disreputable ~~sodomites~~ people to whom I had been introduced by your friend Laura Hope—men with whom I, the black sheep, would have nothing to do.

Luckily, I can laugh at that sort of thing now, but ten years ago I could not. I have no desire to know either Bill or his son.

All through my life you have been held up before me as the good elder brother, the pattern of which I fell so short. I am supposed to have wandered away from the good influences which surrounded you; the real truth is that I was never allowed to wander into them.

Because the Meinertzhagens and the Napiers know none of my present friends they conclude that all of them must be bad. They should remember that they refused to have anything to do with me as a child. For them I was always the bad son of a disreputable father, who must be looked after for charity's sake and kept well in the background. Can you wonder that I made friends of my own who did not regard me as a pariah or as a person to be pitied?

I was ill at ease with the Napiers and the Meinertzhagens, not (as they thought) because I was unused to decent society, but because I was conscious that they disliked me and that they would rather that I was not there. Can you wonder that my visits gradually ceased?

I cannot forget that during all the time I was being boarded out with baby-farmers and in shady homes there were dozens of people—Ross's mother and sister, Mrs. Carew and others—who would have been only too glad to have welcomed me to their houses and given me that affection and welcome for which I hungered.

I cannot forget that Adrian Hope and the Napiers in answer to the questions of these friends merely intimated via Hargrove that I could not be seen and that I was quite happy where I was.

I do not wonder that Ross spoke so bitterly to me of Adrian Hope as a professional philanthropist when we first met at Mrs. Carew's with Roy Kennard.

I have tried to forget the unhappy days of my childhood and early youth. My method of forgetting may not always have been wise. Am not ashamed to have had mistresses; but I own to having been feckless and extravagant and foolish and hard; but I think I can claim some excuse. I was continually on the defensive and I am too well aware that my nervousness in the presence of people who disapprove of me makes me leave a bad impression.

And then, my dear Cyril, you are not entirely without blame. All the time that you were at Radley and at 'The Shop,' I looked up to you and admired you more than anyone else in the world. You were the link with happier days before mother died. But any attempt I made at friendliness with you was met with ridicule and contempt, the somewhat natural contempt of a strong boy for a weak one: but you forgot that I was your brother and you did not know that you were the only person in the world for whom I cared one straw. I was gradually retiring further and further into myself and became a fatalist and a pessimist.

I only beg that you will not put down the above letter to hysteria and weak-mindedness. If you think for a moment, you will see that everything in it is quite true. The fundamental thing that I want you to realise is that I have always compared my lot with yours in my mind and that I have always realised the instinctive dislike with which all my mother's friends have regarded me, a dislike which is made the more galling to me because the people concerned preen themselves on their righteousness and the noble way in which they have always endeavoured to keep me on the right path as they understand it.

But their kindness has always been the kindness shown by a workhouse master to an inmate or by a prison chaplain to a prisoner.

You must also bear in mind, in judging me, that until I was 18 I never knew the history of my father, the history you knew so well; and that therefore the iron of that tragedy never really entered into my soul, as it did into yours.

My one desire now is that you should try to understand me a little, to be more tolerant towards me, to show more interest in me besides the kindness you have shown me and which I appreciate, in assisting me over financial difficulties.

Always your most affectionate brother,

Vyvyan Holland

And Cyril's reply when Vyvyan's letter finally reached him months later:

Royal Artillery Mess, Trimulgherry, Deccan   3 June 1914

My dear Vyvyan,

I have received your letter of Feb. 23rd—I enclose the envelope, by which you may see its little Odyssey.

Your letter is frank and manly. I will answer you in the same spirit. As a matter of fact I wrote you a prodigiously long letter putting my point of view and expressing a hope that we might arrive at a better understanding. I was brought to this by your silence about your marriage of which I heard from Hargrove and not from Ross who never writes to me. But it was an unsatisfactory epistle—too egotistical in fact—so I destroyed it. I was then just off to China.

Now let me first of all dispel some illusions in your mind. You have informed me of some facts of which I was not aware, so we'll be quits yet. After the usual diatribes against members of what we are pleased to call 'family,' you state that you were 'denied the social advantages of my caste and almost entirely the society of your social equals.' In the first place it is really news to me that Stonyhurst is filled with ill-bred foreigners. Secondly, I was not aware that Mrs. Carew, Ross's mother and sister and others offered to take you. I never knew to this moment that Ross had either a mother or sister living.

Though I thought the Bills [*William Napier's family*] horrible people, I imagined you were happy there. At any rate you kept up your acquaintance afterwards with members of the family. You say that for six years you never had a single friend. The Cochranes wouldn't thank you for that. But let that pass. What you say is true. But while I admit at once that I never realised you were so miserable, I must correct your entirely erroneous belief that I, *au contraire,* was surrounded with friends and affection.

How often did I ever stay with the Hopes? Never, not once. How often did I see Adrian? Seldom enough. But what of that? Why did Laura, a woman in middle age go on slaving at pictures after his death? For bread and butter. Adrian was a hard and conscientious worker. He had a father too. I suppose you've never heard of Colonel Hope, VC. Never heard of how they all fought, father, son, brother, sister? Adrian had his tragedy too, believe me. He was almost kind to me and honestly laboured on *our* behalf. Before I became a cadet I never stayed with the Napiers—a couple of days perhaps *en route* for school. I was jolly enough when I was with cousin Bill, but he went to the South African war. You think I had a splendid time with giggling Maud and pale-faced Arthur? I spent my days wandering alone in Portsmouth, longing to get back to school. Do you think I had friends at school? My last year perhaps, because I was a power in the land—respect and fear but affection none.

I was nine years old when I saw the first placard [*about their father's arrest*]. You were there too, in Baker Street *en route* for Seymour Street (Napiers). I asked what it meant. I never rested till I found out.

Do you suppose that a proud, self-willed, sensitive boy, who had travelled across Europe alone at 11½ years, had been abroad for 3, had been his mother's confidant, who bore this burden of a secret, do you suppose he found mates and friends in the Lower School at Radley? Was I an aimiable person? No, distinctly not. But here's the difference, Vyvyan. I wanted love too. but I lived alone in my own pride. I defied the world. I never sat down and wept. Nay—more. I sometimes resented an affection shown me as I imagined—falsely—it was intended as a substitute for that of our beloved mother. You say you have had your humiliating moments. My first year at school, my hand against my fellows, I sat at breakfast in the big hall at the table of the senior prefect. Before me was the high-table. A 'don' read out the news of OW's death. The prefect looked it up now in his paper. It was discussed. Though the iron entered into my soul, I never gave a sign. Believe me, Vyvyan, I too have suffered and none the less because unexpressed. I can wear a mask better than many. Moreover I have never been afraid.

A lot of satisfaction it was to me to be held up as an example to you, a fact of which I was ignorant until you told me some years ago. I knew my Dickens well enough even then to detest the very thought. I wander on, you see, through your letter, *seriatim.*

You complain still of want of friends. But you were years younger than I was when you first made the acquaintance of such charming people as Ross, Mrs. Carew and others. I was 20 when I first made the acquaintance of a soul outside the family circle. I was 19 when I was introduced to a girl of my own age for the first time—then to be laughed at, for another cadet inveigled me to his rooms when his 'people' were there, as a joke, they having been prepared to meet a surly bear.

You went to the 'Varsity'; I to 'The Shop.' You spent your life in London; I in the Officers' Mess. By this time at any rate we should be quits on that score. No, no, Vyvyan, it has not been all so simple, all so one-sided as you make out. You say I too had my share of blame. I admit it. I am sorry for it. I ask you to forgive me. But I hadn't learnt to be affectionate in the school of sorrow. We seldom met and then under unfavourable circumstances. But our natures are poles asunder. We quarrelled in the nursery where mother took my part, nurse yours. I have had the fortune to be gifted with a strong physique. You have suffered terribly in health, I know. And you complain that not sufficient allowance was made you for this I believe you there too. But is it logic to expect others to make allowances for you while you yourself, now, at years of discretion make none for others? You plead your own case like a lawyer, but you condemn your 'enemies' unheard and dismiss them in passion. Are you really so blind as to think that all the fault lies with the Hopes, the Napiers, the Meinertzhagens? In your heart of hearts you must know how trying you were, how difficult it was to deal with you.

You seem to forget, too, what they had suffered in 1895. Do you know how much our mother was loved? Do you realise what it all meant to them? You admit that you are sensitive; sensitive people are not easy to understand. Because they failed to understand, they lost sympathy for you. But did you help them, aye, my fidgety Phil? Well something too much of this. I will now tell you what I wrote last January and never sent.

When I returned to England in 1898, I naturally realised our position more fully. Gradually, I became consumed with the idea that I must retrieve what had been lost. By 1900, it had become my settled object in life. I told Ross many years ago in one of our rare meetings of this. I told him that by his magnificent labours and self-sacrifice he had almost accomplished my end. But he cannot do all. All these years my great incentive in life has been to wipe that stain away; to retrieve, if may be, by some action of mine, a name no longer honoured in the land. The more I thought on this, the more convinced I became that, first and foremost, I must be a *man*. There was to be no cry of 'decadent artist,' of 'effeminate aesthete,' of weak-kneed degenerate. That is the first step. For that I have laboured, for that I have toiled. As I roughed it month after month last year in the terrible plateau of Tibet, as I trekked hour after hour, day after day, but lately, over difficult country in dangerous times, when I was weary and ill with dysentery and alone in a strange and barbarous land, it was this Purpose which whispered in my ear: "It is the cause, my soul, it is the cause." Many years ago, I laid to heart the awful truth we hear in *Hamlet* 'Purpose is but the slave to memory, of violent birth, but poor validity.' This has been my purpose for sixteen years. It is so still. I have often fallen away. I have despaired, I have cursed my fate and mocked at the false gods. It is my purpose still. I am no wild, passionate, irresponsible hero. I live by thought, not by emotion. I ask nothing better than to end in honourable battle for my King and Country.

Ross has never forgiven me my puritanical, proud, contemptuousness of years ago. But I saw what I thought to be my destiny and way of life and acted accordingly. It has not been easy. I work alone, unencouraged, unknown. But I want none of these things.

But here's the rub, Vyvyan. As I have watched you year by year, I have continually said to myself: 'Does he realise the task before him? And if so, is this the way to set about it?' It is that, that and nothing else which has made me drift further and further away from any possible sympathy with you. Aye! Vyvyan, I say that I can never feel sympathy towards you until I see you working for the cause. 'Tis a bitter cry. But my life is wrapt up in this. This is all my personal ambition. I should be the last to ask or to expect of you that you should go about this business as I do myself. Every man his own method. But you have never given me a sign. Moreover to control destiny one must conquer self.

I have had bitter thoughts about you sometimes. I have often said hard, cruel words of you. I have taunted you to your face. I meant it then; I mean it now. But then it was in wrath and now more in sorrow than in anger.

What shall become of this in years to be? Surely, surely you would not have me *pity* you? I ask you to rise and put your armour on and fight the fight, for the true success is to labour.

Your affectionate brother

Cyril Holland

It was the last letter Cyril wrote to Vyvyan before he was posted back to Europe at the start of the First World War. Vyvyan showed it to Robbie who commented: 'I admire his pride and strenuous determination. Unhappily, family problems are not solved by one member of the family trekking across Tibet, though it may produce excellent effects on the character of the person trekking, as Cyril claims,' but he seemed relieved that the brothers had been able to air their differences and make peace with each other.[226] It was a timely exchange, for less than a year later Cyril was dead, killed on the battlefield for his King and his Country, though leaving the 'stain,' as he saw it, on the family honour for Vyvyan to deal with.

CHAPTER EIGHT
A TALE OF TWO TESTICLES

It has always struck me as a terrible irony that on the first day of Oscar's libel action against the Marquess of Queensberry, the *Pall Mall Gazette* published a review of *Books Fatal to Their Authors* by Peter Ditchfield and within a few hours Oscar was being cross-examined by Edward Carson on *The Picture of Dorian Gray*. The Marquess's defence had included it as part of their plea of justification and tried to establish the fact of Oscar's homosexuality by association with the homoerotic elements in his work. Oscar defended himself forcefully against the suggestion, but the matter was raised again in the Crown trials which later prosecuted him and sent him to prison. Seventeen years on, and although not directly the author, Robbie Ross provided the source material for a book which would do *him* almost as much harm as *Dorian Gray* had done to his friend.

In 1910, a young author and journalist, Arthur Ransome, was commissioned by the publisher Martin Secker to write a critical study of Oscar Wilde. Ransome's cousin, Laurence Binyon, Assistant Keeper of Prints and Drawings at the British Museum, advised him that the first thing to be done was to get the goodwill of Robbie Ross. Binyon was a good friend of Ross, whom he knew through their connections in the art world, and effected the introduction. Robbie was impressed with the young man's credentials and promised to give him all the help he needed, in particular allowing him access to much unpublished material. By this time several books had been published on Wilde but all of them by authors who had either known him personally or who had been in the orbit of the friends and acquaintances, and Robbie felt that Ransome's book would be all the better for being written by one entirely without preconceptions on the subject. Despite it being a critical study of Wilde as a writer, Ransome quickly realised that he could not ignore the life, especially as he would have to deal with *De Profundis,* but it was agreed between him and Ross that no mention should be made of Douglas by name. Ross certainly showed Ransome copies of letters written to him by Wilde about Douglas and also confirmed statements about the two of them made by previous biographers, but from then on their recollections about Ross's collaboration diverge significantly. Ross later stated that he refused to read the proofs of the book because he did not wish to be held responsible, by default, for anything which was written; Ransome stated categorically that when the proofs arrived in January 1912 Ross did read them. Ross was adamant that he had not shown Ransome the typescript copy of *De Profundis* (the original by then being locked up in the British Museum), while Ransome said that he was not only shown the copy but allowed to take it away and read it at leisure. The book was dedicated to Robert Ross who said that Ransome never asked if he might do so, which seems possible but highly improbable.[227]

When *Oscar Wilde: a Critical Study* appeared on 16 February, Bosie Douglas immediately read it and at the beginning of the chapter on *De Profundis* he found it described as being 'a letter . . . not addressed to Mr. Ross but to a man to whom Wilde felt that he owed some, at least, of the circumstances of his public disgrace. It was begun as a rebuke of this friend, whose actions, even subsequent to the trials, had been such as to cause Wilde considerable pain.' That, combined with the discovery that Robbie Ross was acknowledged effusively for his help and even worse that Ross was the object of the dedication drove Douglas into a fury. He immediately wrote to Robbie to ask if *De Profundis* had indeed been addressed to him and not, as he had always been led to believe, to Robbie with abusive references to himself which Robbie had chosen to suppress in the printed edition. Robbie's solicitors replied on his behalf saying that the fact had never been concealed, and that following Oscar's instructions their client had kept the original and sent Douglas a copy in 1897. That was almost certainly untrue but difficult to prove one way or the other fifteen years later. Bosie admitted he had received a long letter from Robbie at that time (on another matter altogether) but which he had destroyed after reading the first half dozen lines. In fact, Bosie might have had his suspicions had he read Robbie's introduction to the slightly expanded version included in the *Collected Works* of 1908: '*De Profundis* . . . is cast in the form of a letter to a friend not myself.' The ill-will escalated rapidly and on 13 March Bosie issued a writ for libel against Arthur Ransome, the publisher Martin Secker, and the Times Book Club who were the distributors.[228] Although legally Bosie could not attack Robbie directly just for giving Ransome help in writing the book, this indirect approach through everyone else involved was the next best thing. Robbie stated later that he had felt no compunction about telling Ransome what he saw as the truth about Oscar's and Bosie's relationship post-prison, especially after Bosie had tried to make out in the Manners-Sutton case that he that had been the only friend left to Oscar after 1897.[229] The libel trial didn't take place until over a year later and in the meantime Oscar was causing quite enough trouble elsewhere.

Although Jacob Epstein had been commissioned to create the monument for Oscar's tomb back in 1908, he wasn't satisfied with his preliminary sketches and didn't start work on what he would refer to as the 'demon-angel' until September 1911.[230] By the following June it was in a sufficiently finished state for Epstein to invite the public and the press to view it at his Chelsea studio. The overall reaction was largely positive, which Epstein found especially pleasing as he was still smarting from the adverse criticisms levelled at his commission for the new British Medical Association building in the Strand. The national papers modified outright praise with epithets such as 'unconventional' and 'curious,' but the critic on a provincial newspaper grasped exactly the spirit of what Epstein had set out to achieve: 'In its suggestion of remorseless strength it is ancient, even primeval, but in its needless and imperious force, and intangible and intellectual quality, it is modern. It is this indefinable, nameless, dual attribute, which makes Mr. Epstein's imaginative work one of such singular power,' and predicted that the French, more open 'to the mysterious and the startling' would more readily accept 'this admirable tribute to the wayworn man of genius who sleeps in alien soil.' Unfortunately he was mistaken.[231]

At the beginning of July the largely finished monument was crated up and transported to Paris where the problems began. The French demanded that customs duty of £120 be paid on the value of the stone which Epstein, who was responsible for the installation, had not anticipated. A petition was drawn up in England, signed among others by George Bernard Shaw, H. G. Wells, Robert Ross, and Leon Bakst who had just created the costumes and sets for *Salomé* at the Théâtre du Chatelet, in an attempt to get the French authorities to waive the charges. It was unsuccessful. Epstein, who had followed his sculpture to Paris to oversee its erecting over Oscar's grave, not only had to pay the duty but found that unexpected technical problems arose with setting it up and delayed him further still with putting the finishing touches to it. As a result, he was in danger of losing another commission to which he had committed himself: sculpting two granite lions for the government buildings in Pretoria and for which the architect had already reluctantly granted him an extension. Still in Paris in mid-September, he lost the South African commission, and suspected it was not just the delay but also that 'no doubt frightened by the row in Paris, the South Africans threw me out.' It was not the last of the troubles Oscar's 'demon angel' would cause him.[232]

On the morning of 16 September, he arrived to work on the monument and discovered to his horror that the angel's male genitals had been covered with a lump of plaster. On going to the office of the cemetery director, Paul Henriot, he was informed that it had been done because the sculpture was considered 'indecent' for a cemetery. Henriot had referred the matter to the *préfet de la Seine*, Marcel Delanney, and the *directeur de l'École des Beaux*

Arts, the painter Léon Bonnat, who had decided that the genitals should be covered until an official decision had been made (it being France) by the Comité Technique et d'Esthetique of the Préfecture. Neither of these authorities would have bothered with the internal affairs of Père Lachaise in the normal course of events, so it was clear that Henriot, concerned about a possible scandal which a funerary sculpture with prominent testicles might cause, had approached two higher ranking officials to give weight to his argument. His concern that Catholic sensitivities could be offended by what might be regarded as gratuitous nudity in a cemetery, a place for religious contemplation, was a legitimate one as Oscar had shocked enough in his life without having his sulphurous reputation perpetuated beyond the grave. But one of the cemetery surveyors, M. Hedequer assured a reporter from the *Pall Mall Gazette* that it had nothing to do with Wilde himself: 'We admire the genius of the deceased, but we wish to avoid all opportunity for scandal.'[233]

Epstein, furious that his sculpture should have been censored in this way, chipped off the plaster and continued putting the final touches to the headdress and face of the angel. However, since the artist had shown he was determined not to allow French bureaucracy to interfere with his sculpture more drastic measures were clearly necessary, and shortly afterwards the entire tomb was shrouded in a tarpaulin.

Undeterred, Epstein took off the tarpaulin to finish his work until the cemetery director posted a *gardien* to prevent him from removing it. Thereafter he was obliged to work in fits and starts according to the latter's presence or absence, and in the meantime the *'couilles de taureau,'* as they were exaggeratedly described by Henri Gaudier-Brzeska, started to become something of a cause célèbre.[234] In a complete reversal of British prudery and the French acceptance of the avant-garde, newspapers in Britain—even provincial ones—rallied to Epstein's defence pointing out that no objections had been raised when the sculpture had been on public view in London.[235] Robbie Ross, who until then had taken no part in the dispute (preoccupied as he was with Bosie Douglas's impending libel case), sent an amusing letter to the *Pall Mall* Gazette saying that he regarded 'the arrest of the monument' as a logical outcome of the Entente Cordiale, the French now subscribing to what they perceived to be the English view of Art—'Propriety before everything'—and finished: 'I hesitate to say that the rest lies in the lap of the gods, because that is precisely the part of the statue to which exception is taken.' In Paris, a young Anglophile author, Cecil Georges-Bazile, who had translated *An Ideal Husband* into French earlier in the year, wrote an article in *Comœdia*, the major cultural newspaper of the time, echoing the British point of view:

> [Oscar Wilde] had the right to believe that he was forever rid of all the tiresome affronts he had suffered at the hands of the enemies of genius, those blinkered materialists who had tried—and by what foul means!—to fell that great mind . . . . but the prisoner of Reading Gaol is today the prisoner of M. le Conservateur du Père Lachaise . . . What is the point in trying to prevent his great flight into immortality?[236]

It was an encouragement for those in French literary and artistic circles to protest at this bureaucratic censorship, but few, initially, could be bothered. Epstein wrote in his autobiography that Auguste Rodin had refused to lend his voice in support, although the *Cambridge Daily News* reported that Rodin had indeed remarked: 'The monument is novel and the authorities have a horror of anything new,' which seems more likely since it was Rodin who had, after all, sent him to London with a letter of commendation to George Bernard Shaw seven years before.[237] Meanwhile French officialdom took its inexorable course and on 25 October the impressively styled 'Comité Technique et d'Esthétique des Services d'Architecture et des Promenades et Plantations de la Préfecture du Departement de la Seine' foregathered at Oscar's tomb to examine the sculpture. It was unanimously agreed by those present that the monument was 'une œuvre bizarre que le Comité juge peu esthétique et de gout douteux' but not such that it could be described as 'shocking' or 'indecent.' However, since some members had not been present it was decided to adjourn the meeting until a full committee could decide, which then took place on 13 December. Photographs were produced; it was noted that 'certain families' had protested at such nudity in the cemetery; and the committee decided unanimously that it could not be allowed to remain in its present state.[238] In the preamble to the discussion it was stated that the plot in the cemetery had been acquired by 'Mme Oscar Wilde' which would have amused Robbie. Bosie's reaction, had he been told, doesn't bear thinking about.

For the next two months there was very little heard about the matter on either side of the Channel. Robbie Ross, concerned that his tribute to Oscar's memory might be about to unravel, approached Epstein about modifying the genitals which the sculptor resolutely refused to do saying that there was absolutely nothing indecent about it. The Préfecture Committee met again on 26 February 1913 and this time decided that as they did not consider the sculpture to be a work of art, its nudity was offensive and unless it was covered or changed (presumably castrated) within a fortnight, it would be removed from the cemetery.[239] As a result Georges-Bazile wrote another piece for *Comœdia* on 21 March appealing strongly for all writers, artists and sculptors to sign a petition drawn up by the newly founded periodical *L'Action de l'art* in protest at what he described as an attack on the freedom of artistic expression.[240] Ross, feeling increasingly stressed and with the Douglas/Ransome libel case about to open at the High Court, capitulated and commissioned the sculptor Cecil Howard to produce a bronze plaque in the form of a butterfly which, to satisfy the Parisian authorities, would be fixed between the legs of the 'demon angel.' But the plaque was not considered to be firmly enough attached and the tarpaulin was kept in place, until the occult philosopher and ceremonial magician, Aleister Crowley, was determined to take a hand in the matter.

In November 1913 Crowley was living in Paris and, aware of

the controversy surrounding the 'arrest' of the Epstein sculpture, decided to perform an unofficial unveiling in defence of what he called 'an insult and outrage to the freedom of art.' He printed a manifesto 'Au nom de la liberté de l'art' which he had distributed around Paris, inviting sympathisers to attend his unveiling on 5 November at midday. Warned that a guard might be mounted to prevent him getting close enough to carry it out, he went the evening before and attached a length of fine wire to the tarpaulin so that it could be pulled off from a distance by a fellow conspirator just as Crowley reached the climax of his panegyric. On the day there was no guard, no confrontation and about twenty people turned out in the drizzle to watch. It was something of an anticlimax which Crowley described as 'a disheartening success.' He also managed to upset Epstein who wrote to *The Times* saying that he would have preferred the monument to remain veiled until its butterfly 'fig-leaf,' attached against his express wishes by Ross, had been removed. A short while after, Crowley went back to the cemetery to see if the tarpaulin had been replaced (it had) and took the opportunity to remove the butterfly which, as he pointed out, was doubly insulting as it had been the emblem of the painter James Whistler with whom Wilde had notoriously quarrelled in 1890. Once back in London, Crowley, in evening dress and wearing the butterfly as a codpiece suspended from his neck by a long cord, marched into the Café Royal where Epstein happened to be dining and was able to tell him that his sculpture was now, indeed, as he had originally conceived it.[241]

Epstein, his 'demon angel,' and the Café Royal didn't stay out of the news for long. Bosie Douglas's first and worst book on Oscar Wilde, *Oscar Wilde and Myself* was being prepared for publication around that time and Bosie wanted to include an illustration of Epstein's sculpture. The book was largely a riposte to Arthur Ransome's and given the combination of Douglas's well-known irascibility in matters Wildean and Epstein's slight paranoia over all the difficulties associated with the monument, Epstein's response, though somewhat extreme, was understandable. He delivered a letter to Douglas at the Café Royal in which he had written: 'If you attack my monument to O. W. in any way derogatory to me in England I shall have you in the Courts. Should you disregard this warning I shall spoil the remains of your beauty double quick.' Douglas summoned him to the Marlborough Street Police Court on 2 January 1914 for threatening behaviour and had him bound over to keep the peace.[242] As for the monument, the tarpaulin remained in place until the outbreak of war seven months later when it was quietly removed; the world had more important things to think about than an angel's testicles in a Paris cemetery.[243]

When Bosie Douglas issued his writ for libel over Ransome's book on Wilde in April 1912, it was at the prompting of his former colleague and deputy on *The Academy*, T. W. H. Crosland who detested everything to do with Oscar and by extension Robert Ross who had played a considerable part in helping Ransome with his research. Martin Secker, the publisher, immediately apologised and withdrew leaving Ransome and the Times Book Club to defend the action by pleading justification on the basis of what Oscar himself had written in the still unpublished parts of *De Profundis*. As evidence for the defence, these sections criticising Douglas which Ross had suppressed were central to the case, but the original manuscript had been under lock and key in the British Museum Library since 1910, meaning Ross's typewritten transcript was the only version immediately accessible. Under the duty of disclosure this evidence had to be made available to the prosecution and Robbie deposited a copy with his solicitor Sir George Lewis from whom Douglas obtained it at the beginning of November.

Litigious though Douglas had already proved himself to be, when he issued the libel proceedings that spring I don't believe he intended to obtain anything more than an apology, the withdrawal of Ransome's book, and perhaps some financial settlement. Back in 1902 Robert Sherard, one of Oscar's oldest friends and his first biographer, had made a statement similar to the one Douglas was objecting to, also without referring to him by name. He wrote of Oscar's return to Bosie after prison: 'His funds had all run out, he had nowhere to go, and all the while his friend was pleading, fretting, menacing . . . And so, in the end, the meeting came about.

It took place in a hotel in Rouen. The consequence was a natural one and a few days later it became known that Oscar Wilde had resumed the friendship which had brought disaster and ruin upon him.' Bosie consulted his solicitor about Sherard at the time, but took no action. Another writer, L. C. Ingleby, assessing Wilde's life and work in 1907, said of his immediate post-prison months: ' . . . all would doubtless have gone well with him had it not been for certain malign influences which had already been prominent factors in wrecking his life, and which now appeared again . . . that is to say, certain companions it was most unwise of him to see or recognise, once more entered his life . . . ' [244] Given his mild paranoia about anything written concerning himself and Oscar, I find it most improbable that Bosie had not read the book or at least that some friend wouldn't have alerted him to the passage in question. Again, he took no action. During that summer of 1912—the case would not be heard until the spring of the following year—the publisher John Lane said in correspondence with Bosie that he had Ross's assurance (quite clearly a lie) that he was not responsible for Ransome's libel. This, Bosie accepted and replied: 'Whatever may have occurred between us I have too great a recollection of former friendship to wish to do him harm if it can possibly be avoided. It was quite another thing when I believed that he was actively assisting this scoundrel Ransome. Now that I am assured this is not the case, I am anxious to avoid doing anything to hurt him.'[245] It was a conciliatory attitude which changed dramatically after the disclosure of the documents in November.

Apart from the unpublished portions of *De Profundis*, Robbie had also offered as evidence the letter Oscar had written to him in early 1898 once he returned to Paris after his disastrous reunion with Bosie in Naples:

Bosie, for four months, by endless letters, offered me a '*home*,' He offered me love, affection, and care, and promised that I should never want for anything. After four months I accepted his offer, but when we met at *Aix* on our way to Naples I found that he had no money, no plans, and had forgotten all his promises . . . . the bald fact is that I accepted the offer of a '*home*,' and found that I was expected to provide the money, and that when I could no longer do so, I was left to my own devices.

It was an oversimplification of what happened, but it was Oscar's view of events; along with *De Profundis* it would certainly support Ransome's statement that Bosie had caused Oscar 'considerable pain' both before and after his downfall.

It is not hard to imagine Bosie's fury on reading both documents and realising that it was indeed Robbie who was backing Arthur Ransome against him. In the space of a week Bosie wrote Robbie three vitriolic letters, the first of them addressed to 'Robert Ross, bugger and blackmailer' and referring to *De Profundis* as 'the letter with all its plain lies and obvious absurdities concocted by the filthy swine Wilde in prison for the express purpose of giving him a hold over me and my family' and to Robbie as 'the foulest, dirtiest and meanest skunk that ever drew the breath of life.' In the second, he disputed the facts of Oscar's post-Naples letter saying 'Your name shall go stinking down the ages and I will make you so that no decent man or woman in England will sit in the same room with you.' And in the third, he accused Robbie of purposely engineering the libel through Ransome saying that 'My libel action against Ransome henceforth becomes an action against you.' He went on: 'You have corrupted and debauched hundreds of boys and young men in your life and have gone on doing it right up to the present time,' and challenged Robbie to sue him, threatening to repeat in public what he had written in the letter.[246] He didn't have to wait long.

Later that month, Robbie received an invitation from Lady Glenconner to a soirée on 29 November at her house in Westminster at which the guests of honour were to be the Prime Minister, Herbert Asquith, and his wife Margot who was Pamela Glenconner's sister-in-law. Robbie was able to move in such exalted political circles because of his position in London's art world, and especially because he was extremely discreet about his homosexuality. Knowing that Pamela and Bosie were cousins and anxious to avoid the possibility of a public scene, Robbie consulted a number of friends about whether he should go and all urged him to accept as, in the circumstances, it was impossible to imagine that Bosie would have been invited as well. However, ten minutes after arriving, Robbie was conversing with the author Marie Belloc Lowndes when Bosie appeared and started shouting abuse at Robbie, among other insults: 'You have got to clear out of this. You are nothing but a bugger and a blackmailer!' An ugly situation was saved by Margot Asquith, the host's sister, who left the party with Robbie and took him back to the safety of No 10 Downing Street. Bosie left shortly afterwards but not before he had used the opportunity to 'explain' his behaviour to the other guests and further abuse Robbie in his absence.[247]

Bosie had long since renounced his homosexual past and in 1911 had become a Catholic, so as a recent convert he regarded Robbie's Catholicism as incompatible with his sexual orientation and consequently a sham. He also resented more and more Robbie's ever-growing hold over the posthumous Oscar, and the disclosed documents had now provoked him beyond endurance. He showed the unexpurgated *De Profundis* to Crosland who was so incensed by what he read that he immediately set about writing a vicious attack on it which he published in December as a pamphlet entitled *The First Stone*. Composed in free verse it was an extraordinarily spiteful condemnation of Wilde, mocking *De Profundis* and accusing him of every vice imaginable: 'We are told that the complete work is not "for this generation." Until the race of men get rid of the last vestige of moral sense it ought not to be for any generation. I have read every word of it and shuddered as I read. A blacker, fiercer, falser, craftier, more grovelling or more abominable piece of writing never fell from mortal pen.'[248] It was a perfect opportunity for Crosland to further his crusade against every foulness that he felt Wilde represented and at the end he suggested an alternative inscription for Wilde's tomb: 'OSCAR

FINGAL O'FLAHERTY WILLS WILDE, WHOSE SOUL WAS ALL A SIN, WHOSE HEART WAS ALL A LUST, WHOSE BRAIN WAS ALL A LIE.' Bosie claimed to have no knowledge of what Crosland had written until he saw it in proof, which is probably correct; not that he would have tried to prevent Crosland from publishing, but there was always the possibility that as an attack on one of the disclosed documents in the pending libel action, it might have been considered as trying to influence the jury and consequently contempt of court.[249]

Reactions to *The First Stone* were varied and extreme. The Irish author, Lord Dunsany wrote to Crosland: 'The MS of *De Profundis* must make messy reading. It's a pity that the author of *The Fisherman and his Soul* should have had so nasty a mind,' and in another letter an unspecified Dignitary of the Church said 'It puts into words exactly my own thoughts on a horrible subject.'[250] By contrast, in February the following year, the London salon hostess Gwendolen Otter hit back with a pamphlet of her own, *The Writing on the Ground,* in which she assumed that it was Bosie who had put Crosland up to writing *The First Stone* and, without naming him, took Bosie to task over it: 'We have all recently been shocked by a striking and terrible example of the lowest depths ever reached by any human being in meanness and disloyalty to a friend [*Wilde*] . . . this despicable creature [*Douglas*] does not stop at mere lies and slander—he hires a jackal, a low lackey [*Crosland*] to help him in his ghoulish task of desecrating the dead.' Gwen Otter included in her pamphlet the poem 'A Slim Gilt Soul,' an indictment of Douglas's hypocrisy, which her friend Aleister Crowley had published three years before in his collection *The Winged Beetle* and to which Crowley added his own stinging condemnation by citing the more overtly homosexual passages in Douglas's earlier poetry. These libels were far more serious than those contained in Ransome's book, but since Bosie had been declared bankrupt in the middle of January on the petition of a moneylender, he lacked the resources to do much about it. The battle lines between the friends and the enemies of Oscar Wilde, not merely the squalid feuding between Bosie and Robbie, were being drawn up for a long war.

The Ransome case came on at the High Court on 17 April 1913 before Mr. Justice Darling and lasted four days. From the outset the judge 'suggested that ladies should leave the court because of the character of the evidence they might otherwise have to hear.'[251] In his opening for the prosecution the young barrister for Douglas, Cecil Hayes, inevitably had to remind the jury about Wilde's rise to fame and fall from grace and his client's involvement in the whole sorry affair. It was, he said, a painful thing to have to do as the case of Oscar Wilde was one of the most unpleasant episodes of the last generation. In such cases there was always a 'before' and an 'after' when even a man's friends stampeded to dissociate themselves from him. But there were a very few who, perhaps heroic, perhaps foolish, and without the slightest sympathy for the cause of the man's downfall continued their friendship, and Alfred Douglas was one of those. He went on to say that Douglas, just starting on a literary career, had been pleased to meet such a well-known man of letters and that Wilde, 'though distinguished in the literary world, was only a Bohemian and literary adventurer who wanted to get into society.' Their friendship was therefore understandable, but it was absurd to suggest that a boy of 21 would have had a bad influence on a man of the world aged 38.

Bosie cannot have felt comfortable about such a public rehearsal of the facts, although he must have been aware that what he regarded as a libel would have to be put into context. He could easily have withdrawn his action once he'd had sight of the disclosed documents and from the start his wife, Olive, was strongly against him going to court over it anyway. A blind desire to get even with Robbie Ross, though, had clearly clouded his reason.[252] If that was uncomfortable, worse was to follow when the parts of *De Profundis* which Robbie had previously suppressed to spare Bosie's feelings were read out in open court. Before that, though, Bosie went into the witness box to give evidence.

He produced his bank book to show that he had given Oscar some £380 and a good deal more in cash after Oscar's release from prison in order to prove that he had not, as Ransome alleged, deserted his friend and left him penniless. But it was under cross-examination that things began to unravel. When asked by Ransome's counsel for the defence, James Campbell, whether there was anything immoral in the relationship, Douglas flatly denied it, whereupon Campbell read out the compromising letters Oscar had written to Bosie and which had been used back in 1895 in the Wilde v. Queensberry libel trial. At this point Mr. Justice Darling intervened and made a strong appeal to the Press to make their report as disguised as possible. These questions had to be asked, but it would do incalculable harm to public morals if they were published. The cross-examination continued with Campbell asking Douglas if he had corresponded with Henry Labouchère, the editor of *Truth,* in defence of homosexuality and Wilde in particular shortly after his conviction. Douglas said he couldn't remember, but was then forced to admit it when faced with his original letter of which he said he was now ashamed. He was also questioned about an article written in a similar vein for *La Revue blanche* in Paris in June 1896 which, again, he denied writing until faced with the proof of it. It was then that Douglas must have asked himself whether taking the matter to court had been altogether wise and protested that it was 'shameful that all these things should be raked up now when I am trying to lead a decent life with my wife and child.' Shortly after, the defence produced the original manuscript of *De Profundis* released, exceptionally, from the British Museum as evidence that Wilde had indeed felt that 'he owed some, at least, of the circumstances of his public disgrace' to Douglas. He was asked to verify the handwriting which he did and with that, Wilde's unflattering account of their relationship was read aloud to the court. It was the first time that Bosie had seen the letter which Oscar had written during his last months in prison. He had obviously read much of it when a copy of it had been disclosed in November the year before as part of the defence, but to hear Oscar's condemnation (whether justified or not) of his selfish behaviour exposed to the world must have been particularly galling. Moreover, he would have remembered how, in a fit of anger only a few months before the trial began, he had destroyed more than a hundred and fifty of Oscar's letters to him—letters written when their relationship was at its most intense.[253] After fifteen minutes Douglas, evidently distressed, asked the judge if he might sit down, which Mr. Justice Darling agreed to, and then if he might leave the box. This, Darling refused to allow saying that unless Douglas was unwell, he was there to listen to the evidence. When the trial was resumed the next day with more readings from *De Profundis* the judge, noticing that Douglas was not in court, stopped the proceedings and had him sent for. Douglas's excuse was that he had not wanted to hear it read and was told by Darling that if he absented himself from court again when he was supposed to be a witness, the jury would be instructed to enter judgement against him. Under cross-examination by Mr. Campbell, Bosie declared that the letter had been written to curry favour with the governor of the prison and went on to describe it as 'the most horrible, meanest and most disgusting document I have ever read in my life. Here I am ruined and hunted down by all sorts of brutes. This is the height and depth of treachery and meanness and vileness after I had made all those sacrifices for him.'

As the trial progressed it became less a question of whether Bosie had abandoned Oscar and more a question of whether he had been addicted to the same homosexual practices and, by extension, contributed to Oscar's downfall as Ransome had stated. Compromising letters from Bosie to Oscar, one comparing the relative merits of Neapolitan, Roman, and British rent boys, were produced under protest from Bosie that they had not previously been disclosed by the defence. Robbie Ross had found and preserved them at the time of Oscar's death. After Oscar's conviction had Bosie described it in writing as 'the greatest romantic tragedy of the age' despite knowing that he was guilty as charged? Well, yes. In his closing speech for Ransome's co-defendant, the Times Book Club, the brilliant advocate and later Lord Chancellor, F. E. Smith told the jury not to be misled by the plaintiff's hysterical protests that the evidence which the defence had produced was ancient history. It *was* ancient history, but however long ago it might be, it related to the very period of which he had come to court to complain and the plaintiff had chosen to rake up the whole odious story himself. 'With regard to Oscar Wilde, that unhappy child of genius, years had passed since his fall and men were beginning to be glad to think of the artist rather than of the man's life,' said Smith. 'And now this legacy of infamy had been resurrected—unnecessarily resurrected again.'

Cecil Hayes, Douglas's counsel, asked in closing why neither Ransome nor especially Ross had been called to give evidence. Ransome, obviously could not substantiate his claims personally as he had not known Wilde. The disclosed documents were his justification and if he had been put in the witness box he would have been forced to admit under oath that Ross had provided much of this information. This could have led to Ross being forced to give evidence, which is exactly what Douglas was hoping for so that as much mud could be thrown at Ross as the defence was slinging at him. As the judge pointed out, Ross was not a party to the action and if the defence chose not to call him that was their decision, but it meant that Hayes could not cross-examine him.

Mr. Justice Darling's summing up on the last day was largely a model of bias against the plaintiff. He was even-handed about *De Profundis* saying that it would be a great mistake to take all that Wilde had written as the truth, but it did not follow that it was all false either. However, he made the same point as F. E. Smith, that Douglas could scarcely complain about documents being produced which were twenty years old when they dated from a period to which Ransome alluded in his supposed libel. He also re-read to the jury one of Douglas's letters to Wilde the content of which he said 'a decent pagan at the time of Pericles would not have referred to.' Douglas's bad behaviour throughout the trial undoubtedly contributed the judge's lack of impartiality but it may well have been aggravated by some of the disparaging remarks about Darling's poetry which Douglas had published in *The Academy* at the time he was editing it a few years before—for example: 'We are irritated by the prosy, didactic kind of sonnet affected by Mr. Justice Darling and hailed as the product of blinding genius by the *Westminster Gazette*.'[254] The jury took just under two hours to find in favour of the defendants with costs.

If anything good can be said to have come out of this sordid replay of the Wilde affair it was that some of the unpublished parts of *De Profundis* became known long before they otherwise would have been, giving Douglas the opportunity, however hysterically, to dispute some of the more exaggerated facts. It also allowed him to demonstrate how much money he had given Wilde after his release. As Cecil Hayes said on Douglas's behalf in his opening speech, this was not a matter about which, as a gentleman, he would have wanted to boast, but since the production of his bankbook was to try and clear his name of allegedly leaving Wilde penniless, he did it. That book might later have been destroyed and the full story of the post-prison relationship between Bosie and Oscar might have remained incomplete. [255]

Fortunately for Arthur Ransome his legal expenses, which should have been paid by the bankrupt Douglas, were borne by Robbie Ross, but finding himself caught in the Wildean cross-fire like others later was a distressing experience, especially as the case had been pending for an entire year.[256] Only ten days after Douglas's writ for libel was issued, Ross had written to Ransome asking if he had taken the precaution of having a bill of sale made out for his furniture and effects: 'I don't for a moment think it will be necessary, but it is just as well to be prepared.' It was a slightly underhand means of avoiding seizure of his assets by the bailiffs if he had lost the case and couldn't pay the costs.[257]

The result of losing his case against Ransome was to make Bosie Douglas more determined than ever to destroy Robbie Ross, despite what he had written to John Lane the year before about not wanting to harm a former friend. After the disclosure of the documents in evidence, Robbie already suspected that financial gain had become one of the main motives for Bosie's action. [258] In the end, however, it was not only Oscar's reputation which had been dragged through the courts yet again, but Bosie's own which had suffered in consequence. His past had caught up with the new image he now liked to cultivate of a clean-living, morally upright Catholic. There was little he could do about the existence of the overtly homosexual letters which had been read out in court, but if he could lay hands on the manuscript of *De Profundis*, he might be able to ensure that no further use was made of it. [259]

As I explained before, until this time I do not believe that my father, Vyvyan, was fully aware of how much Robbie was suffering in his role as Oscar's literary executor. In Robbie's extant letters to him there is no mention at all of the problems that Ransome's book were causing apart from a vague reference just after the libel writ to being 'fearfully worried about my private affairs.' Indeed, they are mostly concerned with trying to help Vyvyan sort out his life after his return from Spain in April 1912; just another worry for Robbie to cope with.[260] Accounts of the trial were not just confined to the London broadsheets but widely reported in the provincial press from Dundee to Belfast to Cardiff and even internationally in the Parisian daily *Le Temps,* so it could hardly have escaped Vyvyan's attention. But fifty years later in his second volume of memoirs, he dismissed the Ransome case rather flippantly as: 'It was all very stupid really and . . . only another example of Douglas's love of litigation.'[261] Significantly though, it was the first major court case since the 1895 débâcle to have paraded the less attractive aspects of his father's life before a general public and, judging from the subsequent support he gave to Robbie in the latter's war with Bosie, it must have aroused in him for the first time a surprising degree of family loyalty as well as unbounded admiration for Robbie.

The effect of it all on Douglas was rather less uplifting. 'It was

losing the Ransome case that made me take the fearful risk of publicly and persistently libelling Ross till I forced him into the open
to prosecute me.'[262] It was this determination to 'smash Ross' as he
put it, which would occupy him off and on over the next five years
and was believed by many to have contributed to Robbie's death
from heart failure in October 1918.

CHAPTER TEN
KICKING OSCAR'S CORPSE

There was a time not long ago when, rather perversely, I used to enjoy defending Bosie Douglas against those who took the simplistic view that he was spoilt, selfish, and largely responsible for Oscar's downfall. *Perversely* because it was the last thing that anyone expected from a descendant of the man he was supposed to have ruined. Oscar fell in love with a beautiful young poet and had to take the consequences—socially, legally, and emotionally. Bosie was certainly mercurial and after one quarrel Oscar even wrote of his behaviour: 'By the terrible alchemy of egotism you converted your remorse into rage,' but back then Bosie was never hurtful in a calculated way and I felt I had no right to be judgemental. However, the more I reflected on Bosie's increasingly aggressive attitude towards Robbie Ross once the truth about *De Profundis* became known, the less objective I became. 'The terrible alchemy of egotism' had now converted jealousy into rage and rage into the desire at all costs to destroy Robbie, the man who was salvaging Oscar's reputation.

Furious at having lost his libel action against Arthur Ransome, Douglas wanted to appeal against what he regarded as an unjust verdict, but since he had been made bankrupt and could not provide security for the costs, the matter had to be dropped. With scant regard to the realities of copyright law, in November 1912 he had tried to bring a case against Methuen & Co claiming the royalties on their publication of *De Profundis*.[263] Now, at his public examination in June, he declared that the manuscript of *De Profundis* was his property by right, that it was worth £5,000, and should not be in the British Museum at all. It was the first of several unsuccessful claims he would make to gain possession of it. He then resorted to print and commissioned his old colleague Thomas Crosland to ghostwrite a book for him entitled *Oscar Wilde and Myself*, which was intended as a lengthy retort to *De Profundis.*

Robbie heard about this privately at the end of August and immediately applied for an injunction to prevent Bosie from publishing in his book any of Oscar's letters or the suppressed parts of *De Profundis*, which in Britain were all firmly in copyright and subject to permission from the literary estate. He also learnt that Douglas was intending to bring out an edition of the suppressed parts of *De Profundis* in America with his own commentary, which was worrying since the copyright laws in the United States were far more lax and would have allowed Douglas to publish and then claim the copyright in his own name. With this in mind, Robbie immediately arranged for a typescript of the unpublished sections to be sent over to New York and for it to be published by the literary agent Paul Reynolds. Only fifteen copies were printed (of which two were deposited at the Library of Congress to secure copyright), with twelve sent to Ross and one offered for sale by Reynolds to satisfy the US laws of publication and prove 'public availability.' The single copy for sale was priced at what was considered the prohibitive amount of $500 and, apparently, was bought within days by an unknown purchaser.[264] The remaining copies were distributed to Robbie's friends and people with a particular interest in *De Profundis,* among them Algernon Methuen, Christopher Millard, and Viscount Haldane, the man who had arranged for Wilde to have writing materials while in prison.[265]

Bosie, with his literary counter-offensive to Oscar's prison letter temporarily thwarted, resorted to less ethical tactics. Even before the Ransome trial had come on in April, Bosie's junior counsel in the case, Harold Benjamin, presumably on his client's instructions, had tried to bribe a young man, Norman Farr to give evidence that he'd had sexual relations with Ross. Farr, a twenty-five year old medical student and ex-public schoolboy from St. Paul's School, had consulted Robbie a few years before about some pictures, but

otherwise the two men had hardly met. Naturally enough, Farr
refused and reported the matter to Robbie who took no action.
Now, in the middle of August, Farr came again to Robbie with
far more disturbing news. The Director of Public Prosecutions,
Sir Charles Mathews had been to see Farr's old tutor at St. Paul's
with a letter from Douglas accusing Robbie of having corrupted
boys from the school over the past twenty years. There seemed no
lengths to which Douglas would not go to blacken Ross's character and even have him arrested and prosecuted under the same
law which had put Oscar in prison in 1895. The accusation was
briefly examined by detectives from Scotland Yard but they didn't
pursue it, though it forced Robbie, who was preparing to go to
Moscow for the Russian premiere of *Salomé*, to put off his departure for a couple of weeks 'in order not to give the impression of
running away' to avoid arrest.[266] It didn't, however, stop Douglas
from spreading the rumour that this was exactly why Robbie had
left the country.

Even worse news greeted Robbie on his return at the beginning
of October. Christopher Millard, who had been acting as Robbie's
secretary on and off for some time, had found himself implicated
in the arrest of a rent-boy during Robbie's absence. Early in the
morning of 18 September the seventeen year-old Charles Garratt
had been picked up by the police in Oxford Street for being drunk
and importuning passing men. At the magistrates' court hearing he
had called Millard, with whom he had been dining the evening before, as a character witness, but it didn't prevent him from getting
a three month sentence with hard labour and Millard from getting
a severe dressing-down by the Magistrate for being a bad influence
on the boy. To the delight of Douglas and Crosland it was reported
in *Reynold's News* on 21 and 28 September and Douglas sent a
press cutting to Ross's solicitor, Sir George Lewis, with the first of
a series of abusive and libellous letters.[267] Although they had failed
with Farr, they assumed that if Millard knew Garratt, it stood to
reason that Ross did as well and they may have had sex. Even if
they hadn't, with sufficient financial incentive Garratt might be

'persuaded' to say that they had. Their attempt to denounce Ross directly to the DPP and have him arrested for 'gross indecency' under the 1885 law had not been a success, but Douglas and Crosland hatched a new plan. By declaring publicly and in correspondence to third parties that Ross was 'a filthy bugger,' they would finally provoke him into taking legal action, just as Queensberry had done to Wilde twenty years before. While Queensberry had made the famous accusation on his visiting card and then hired detectives to scour London's homosexual underworld for evidence to justify it, Douglas and Crosland were already trying to line up a suborned witness—Charles Garratt—in the expectation of Ross suing for libel. They lost no time in getting permission for a solicitor to visit him in prison to suggest that if he were prepared to swear a statement that he both knew Ross and had had a sexual relationship with him, he would be 'looked after' when he came out. Garratt, sensing something to his advantage, prevaricated and said he would consider it on his release which took place on 10 December when he went immediately to Millard and reported what had happened. Meanwhile, Ross had been obliged, reluctantly, to dismiss the sexually indiscreet Millard as his part-time secretary and Douglas, presuming that he would be bearing Ross a grudge, had even approached Millard offering to purchase any letters which might compromise his former employer. Millard refused. Garratt was pressured once more by Douglas and Crosland into swearing a statement compromising Ross, which he agreed to and then refused to sign. Scotland Yard was briefly involved but due to Garratt's criminal record they decided he was unreliable and chose to drop the matter. Crosland then persuaded Garratt's mother to issue a writ charging Ross with indecent assault on her son which was duly served on Robbie on Christmas Eve but later withdrawn for lack of evidence. Robbie, still resisting the dangerous temptation to sue Bosie for his libellous outbursts, instead approached Oscar's old publisher John Lane with a proposal to issue the unpublished parts of *De Profundis*:

The book would contain a very controversial preface by myself; it would contain also a very contentious appendix dealing with the quarrel between Douglas and myself . . . I can undertake that there will be nothing obscene in the book, but there would be much that is libellous; and in our agreement I would, of course, guarantee you against any consequences of a financial kind . . . The book must not be announced beforehand but be put on the market quite suddenly, so that a large number of copies could be sold before Douglas or his family were able to obtain an injunction.[268]

Sensibly, Lane refused to play standard-bearer for Ross in what had become an ugly war with Douglas. To add to the stress Robbie was feeling, he arrived back from Christmas in Scotland to find that Douglas had taken rooms in the same block of flats as himself and on the same floor. On being questioned, the hall-porter admitted that Douglas, who had been asking about Ross's movements and his visitors, had insisted that Ross should not be told either about his enquiries or his presence in the building. Robbie, on friendly terms with the owner and explaining the tense situation, managed to have Douglas turned out the following day, but not before discovering he had bribed one of the waiters to steal some of his papers and a chambermaid to remove some of his handkerchiefs, presumably to be planted on Garratt as 'evidence' of Ross's relationship with him. And at the root of all this melodramatic cloak-and-dagger behaviour was Douglas's anger over Ross's handling of De Profundis.

On a happier note, Robbie attended my father's wedding on 7 January as his best man, though he took the precaution of having a number of detectives 'disguised as guests and members of the theatrical profession' both at the church and the reception, worried that Douglas might show up uninvited and make a scene. He didn't.[269] Two days later, Crosland wrote to Ross challenging him to resign as Wilde's literary executor. He accused Ross, in the promoting of Wilde's works to rehabilitate him as a serious literary figure, of being no more than 'one dirty sodomite bestowing lavish whitewash upon another.' More provocation which Robbie continued to ignore. When he didn't respond to that, Crosland sent another letter informing him that Douglas had written exposing Ross's homosexual life to, among others, members of the judiciary, the DPP, the Prime Minister, and the editor of the *Morning Post,* H. A. Gwynne.[270] Robbie's connections in high places ensured a certain immunity from these accusations, made as they were to people who were beginning to regard Douglas as slightly unhinged and he was all too conscious that suing for libel could easily take him down the same disastrous route as it had done for Oscar in 1895.

But Douglas and Crosland were not going to give up easily. Although suborning Garratt and persuading his mother to bring an action on behalf of her son had not proved a success, they did make one more attempt to get the Garratts to play their game. Charlie Garratt had been living at home with his mother since Christmas, and Douglas had been paying Mrs. Garratt ten shillings a week for her son's keep to make sure that he stayed up in Leicestershire where Ross could not get at him. On 6 February mother and son were brought down to London to swear fresh statements, with a sum of £1,000 in possible 'damages' being mentioned for Ross's supposed corruption of the boy. At the last minute Garratt, realising that if the truth came out he could be in very serious trouble for perjury, ran off, was arrested a week later for importuning again and sentenced this time to six months. While he was in prison, Ross's solicitor paid him a visit and Garratt told him the whole story of how Douglas and Crosland had tried to suborn him. This put an entirely new complexion on the affair as it would enable Robbie to sue the two of them for criminal conspiracy and avoid the risk of having his private life held up to scrutiny in a libel action. He duly got Sir George Lewis to issue proceedings on 24 March, though unwisely, and almost incomprehensibly, he also sued Douglas for criminal libel at the same time for publicly calling him 'a bugger and a blackmailer.' The writ could not be served on Douglas for on 4 March he had fled to France where he stayed for the next six months to avoid appearing at the Old Bailey on charges of breaking a court order to stop his continual libelling of his father-in-law. Had he attended, he almost certainly would have been sent to prison. All of this litigation would involve Robbie in a tangle of legal problems for the whole of the next year, lose him his job and start to destroy his health.[271] However, with Douglas safely in France, Robbie could indulge in a little literary sniping and on 19 March he published with Methuen & Co the *Selected Prose of Oscar Wilde* in which he took extracts from almost all Wilde's works, gave them appropriate titles, justified his 'temerity' in doing so in his preface, and said 'Though unlike one of Wilde's other friends I cannot claim to have collaborated with him or to have assisted him in any of his plays,' meaning, of course, Douglas.

The committal proceedings for the conspiracy case started on 27 April at the Marylebone Police Court. Only Crosland attended, Douglas being worried that if he returned from France he would be arrested over the matter with his father-in-law. Garratt, who by now had come firmly onto Ross's side, was brought up from Pentonville prison to give evidence and absolutely denied ever having seen Ross before the moment they faced each other in court. Robbie's relationship with Oscar was inevitably bought up and much was made of his selfless administering of the Wilde literary estate, his support for Arthur Ransome when Douglas had sued for libel the previous year and his use of the suppressed parts of *De Profundis* all of which had increased Douglas's growing resentment of him. This, maintained the prosecution, had led to Douglas and Crosland's plans to destroy Ross's reputation by attempting to suborn Garratt. The hearings dragged on throughout May with Crosland becoming increasingly indignant and badly behaved, shouting at the prosecuting counsel and occasionally being rebuked by the magistrate. The case was sent for trial at the Old Bailey and opened on 27 June. Once again, Oscar was dragged in and Robbie cross-examined on why he had continued to befriend a man of Wilde's reputation. Christopher Millard gave evidence about how Douglas had offered him money to steal compromising letters from Ross and had said that all he wanted to see was a newspaper placard with 'Arrest of Robert Ross' which would ruin him. Both Millard and Ross were cross-examined on whether they thought *The Picture of Dorian Gray* was an immoral book, a line of questioning presumably intended to associate them with Dorian's unnamed depravities and merely repeating what Edward Carson had asked Oscar at his failed libel action against Queensberry back in 1895. It prompted the judge to ask Robbie if *he* thought there was such a thing as an immoral book to which Robbie replied 'Lord Alfred Douglas's poems, for instance,' which infuriated Crosland who 'shouted an excited but incoherent protest' from the dock. Crosland's defence over his association with Garratt was that he just had the boy's best interests at heart; he was helping him to return home, give up his filthy way of life and possibly get him some compensation for being 'debauched' by Ross and Millard. On his hounding of Ross, he said he regarded Wilde's works as 'dangerous' and felt that 'The whole movement to whitewash Oscar Wilde and propagate his works by his disciples was repulsive' and that his determination to expose Ross was in the public interest as it would 'interfere with the Wilde movement.' In the end it came down to whom the jury believed was telling the truth: Crosland pretending to be leading a moral crusade when in fact he was just doing Douglas's bidding to ruin Ross, or the prosecution's main witness, Charlie Garratt, who in one of his first statements for Douglas had claimed he was a student at an agricultural college and his mother a landowner, when in fact he was a part-time rent-boy and his mother a charwoman. The judge, Horace Avory, although having to be as impartial as possible in his summing-up, could not resist the suggestion that by associating himself with Oscar Wilde, Robbie Ross could scarcely complain if assumptions were made by Crosland about his character and his relationship to Garratt. The fact that Avory had been a junior on the prosecuting team at Wilde's criminal trials may have coloured his view of the whole matter. It took the jury a mere thirty minutes to find Crosland and the absent Douglas not guilty and Oscar had, once again, found himself in court.

For Robbie the outcome verged on the disastrous—financially, socially and professionally. Since 1912 he had held the position of Adviser to the Board of Inland Revenue on picture valuation for estate duty but, given the scandalous nature of the trial, on the day that the verdict was announced he felt obliged to write to Sir Matthew Nathan, Chairman of the Board, and offer his resignation as a formality. Unfortunately, what Robbie considered a formality and hoped might be refused was clearly seen with some relief by Nathan who replied on 8 July: 'In view of all the disagreeable features of the case which you thought it necessary to bring to trial, it will, I think, be advisable in the best interests of the Government department which I represent, that you should do as you suggest.'[272] Apart from being the object of Bosie's rage and jealousy, Robbie was beginning to experience the secondary effects of his loyalty to Oscar. However, he also received a large number of letters about the injustice of the verdict including a telegram from the Prime Minister: 'Losing a case is an awful bore. I have got one coming on which I shall lose. You come to our garden party. We shall love to have you. Asquith.'[273] Quite surprisingly, given the vaguely sulphurous odour which still clung to the name of Wilde, discreet homosexuality of the type which Robbie embodied was generally tolerated among the liberal-minded upper classes and it was precisely this which had infuriated Bosie. For Robbie, perhaps the most heart-warming gestures of all came from Oscar's two sons, my father Vyvyan and my uncle Cyril. On Sunday 5 July, the day before the verdict was announced, Robbie sent Vyvyan a telegram asking him to come up to London and to be with him the next day. I'm sure that by now my father had begun to realise the extent of Bosie Douglas's persecution and equally the extent of Robbie's devotion to Oscar's memory, and he went straight up to town to give him what support he could. He also stayed on for about a week afterwards to act as a sort of amanuensis, dealing with the aftermath of the case and all the correspondence it had engendered. Robbie's letters of thanks both to Vyvyan and his wife Violet show how much he appreciated my father's help and presence:

> My dear Vyvyan, If I said all I felt towards yourself, this letter might compromise us both. I won't say I'm grateful, because gratitude is the father of boredom. But for you, I would be still sprawling over my papers and boxes in Bury Street, or in bed with a nervous break-down. You really carried me through a physical and mental crisis . . .

And to Violet:

> It was so good of you to spare Vyvyan at telegraphic notice. You have no idea what a real consolation his presence was to me during the last days of the trial, and how indispensable were all his activities on my behalf. My instinct told me he would be the only friend who would not get on my nerves just at that moment. His sympathy, tact and gentleness, his unenforced cheerfulness and humour always touched with genuine sympathy, will never be forgotten by me. If anything could have made a hideous disaster a beautiful memory, it was dear Vyvyan's friendship and support.[274]

Cyril, still posted in India with the Royal Field Artillery, must have read about the committal hearings in month-old newspapers, as he wrote to the family solicitors on 1 July saying he insisted that all Robbie's legal expenses should be paid out of the Wilde Estate's royalties and if that did not cover them, then the shortfall should come out of his personal income. 'You will inform Mr. Ross that this is no Quixotic offer. It is profoundly serious. I regard the quarrel as mine as much as his. My honour is more to me than money.' Robbie, though deeply touched by Cyril's gesture, turned it down.[275]

As if the intrigues of Douglas and Crosland weren't enough to keep Oscar's name disagreeably in the news every now and then, there was the Chelsea Town Hall fiasco. In 1910, a couple of years after the Borough of Chelsea had opened its new Town Hall building, the then Mayor, Christopher Head, proposed that since there were four large empty panels in the main hall, the Council should consider filling them with paintings representing celebrated figures associated with the borough. The Chelsea Arts Club was consulted and agreed to run a competition to find suitable artists to do the work, the brief being that each panel should be devoted to a particular theme: 'Politics, Religion & Science,' 'Art,' 'History,' and 'Literature.' The artists, once selected, set to work and by early 1914 the very large canvases, each 256 x 357 cm, were finished and installed. It's not certain how the figures depicted in each painting were chosen—by the artist or by the Club's competition committee—but, in any case, it was clearly *not* by the Borough Council, at whose meeting on 29 April Councillor Henry Wright, described in the press as 'one of the temperance stalwarts of the borough,' expressed the following forceful opinion about the presence of a seated Oscar Wilde in the panel representing 'Literature': 'I do not think that that panel, at all events, should remain any length of time, and one of the characters should be blotted out. As a native of Chelsea, I think that our Town Hall was not erected for the exhibition of criminals.'[276] He put forward a motion that either the artist should substitute another figure or the picture should be taken down, and at the next meeting on 13 May there was much heated discussion on the subject with some ill-tempered remarks made both about Oscar Wilde's morals and the quality of the painting. An amendment was put forward simply to have the panel removed and, when put to a vote, was carried overwhelmingly by 22 to 3. The Chelsea Arts Club was said to be 'up in arms' at the decision and Councillor Harwood, in contrast to Councillor Wright, accused his fellow members of behaving like self-righteous Pharisees, stating that if they were going to be consistent in their moral judgments, they should be removing George Eliot and Henry VIII as well. Fortunately, following letters of protest from the public, a policy of 'wise and masterly inactivity' by the Council ensured that the painting remained in place. Councillor Wright, with his 'hysterically Victorian attitude,' raised the matter once more in July and again in May 1915, but died a month later. The panel can still be seen where it was originally installed.[277]

On 17 July 1914 Alfred Douglas's book *Oscar Wilde and Myself* in which, astonishingly, he 'claimed' to have been unaware of Oscar's homosexuality until the time of the 1895 trials, finally appeared. Even Bosie's more recent and comparatively sympathetic biographers have been unanimous in their condemnation of it, and to give him his due, Bosie did finally repudiate it himself.[278] Crosland's own loathing of Wilde in his text was undisguised: 'This statement of Wilde [an aphorism from the 'Preface' to *Dorian Gray*] shows us clearly the nature of the man's mind, which was a shallow and comparatively feeble mind incapable of grappling unaided with even moderately profound things, and disposed to fribble and antic with old thoughts for lack of power to evolve new ones.' He went on to say: 'He believed that he had supreme gifts and that he had squandered them . . . His remorse over the squandering of these alleged gifts was at times ludicrous to behold.'[279] *Oscar Wilde and Myself* was essentially Bosie's scream of rage at not being able to reply to Oscar's accusations of his self-centred behaviour in the then unpublished parts of *De Profundis*, and in it he issues a challenge to Robert Ross to publish the letter in its entirety together with his own running commentary. Needless to say, Ross ignored the provocation.

Whilst the outbreak of the First World War in Europe put an end to the controversy over Epstein's sculpture for Oscar's tomb, as well as any real notice of Douglas's odious book in the press, and the silliness of the Chelsea Council over having Oscar 'sitting' permanently in the Main Hall, it did not halt the vicious dispute between Ross and Douglas. Robbie's action against Bosie for criminal libel was still pending, and when Bosie returned to England a month after war had been declared he was immediately arrested and remanded in custody for five days before the case was sent for trial at the Old Bailey where it opened on 19 November. Why

Ross, after losing his criminal conspiracy case against Crosland and Douglas, persisted with this one is half a mystery. If he withdrew from the prosecution, he opened himself to yet further hounding by Douglas who was likely to broadcast the fact as a tacit admission of Ross's guilt. If he continued and won, it would put an end to Douglas's attacks, but if he lost there was the danger that he himself might face prosecution for 'gross indecency.' It was a calculated risk and threatening to become a replay of Oscar's action against Douglas's father back in 1895. Bosie might plead justification by pointing to Robbie's discreet relationships with Freddie Smith, who had lived with him as his 'secretary,' or Christopher Millard who, although convicted of homosexual offences in the past, had never been sexually intimate with Ross. Neither man, however, would give evidence against him, and since Ross was not in the habit of picking up rent-boys in Piccadilly, Douglas would be forced to rely on circumstantial evidence from the past and probably rake up the whole Wilde affair once again, to imply that Ross was guilty by association. As I write, I feel an overwhelming sense of *déjà vu* at the way Oscar's name was about to be dragged through the courts yet again merely to gratify Douglas's desire to take revenge on Ross for the way he handled *De Profundis*.

The libel case ran for just over a week and during that time Robbie was examined, cross-examined, and re-examined for nearly three days. His counsel had to replay the whole Wilde scandal in his opening for the prosecution in order to show Ross in the best possible light as Oscar's staunch friend and literary executor. His publication of the expurgated *De Profundis* had been a great success, enabling him to clear Wilde's estate of bankruptcy and provide some income for his children but he had never received any remuneration for his work as the executor. The deterioration in Ross's and Douglas's relationship was attributed principally to the Ransome case the year before, and to Ross's use of the unpublished passages of *De Profundis,* critical of Douglas who, as a result, was 'filled with ungovernable rage' and started writing Ross highly abusive and libellous letters.

When asked in cross-examination why he had not taken action before, Ross replied that he did not feel it worthwhile to take proceedings against a man who made libelling others a profession. He also denied publishing the expurgated *De Profundis* to show Wilde as a repentant sinner but rather to give the general public a more favourable view of him as a serious man of letters. He was followed into the witness box by Douglas who admitted that Wilde had had a very bad influence on him, and that he was constantly in the company of depraved men: 'I was so corrupted by the teaching of Wilde and Ross, that I condoned it and got to think nothing of it at all.' Under cross-examination he said it had been a pernicious attitude to take up and that he now repudiated it:

'You put yourself in the class of Wilde's friends who did not practice his vices?'
'Yes.'
'And you put Mr. Ross in the class of those who did?'
'Yes.'
'Why do you want to prove it?'
'In the public interest.'
'Is that your only reason?'
'It is not the whole reason. I should not have denounced Mr. Ross if he had not given me the most intolerable provocation.'
'Is it a mixture of morals and revenge?'
'No. I have no ill-feeling towards Mr. Ross.'[28]

An extraordinary exchange given what is known of Bosie's life before 1900 as well as the vicious letters he had sent to Robbie in the previous two years. Among the fourteen mostly tainted or unreliable witnesses for the defence, Douglas's team called an Inspector West from Scotland Yard who testified that in the years he had been patrolling the West End, Ross was known to him as 'an habitual associate of sodomites and male prostitutes.' The author Ralph Straus later wrote to Robbie to say that he knew West, was sorry about his perjury and, had he known, he could have asked several men from the Yard to appear and contradict it.[281] H. G. Wells and Edmund Gosse appeared as character witnesses for Robbie and described him as a thoroughly honest, moral and unselfish man, and my father testified that Robbie had been like a second father both to him and his brother who was then fighting at the Front in France. All three witnesses said that they were good friends with Freddie Smith and saw nothing abnormal in his relationship with Robbie which, it must be said, suggested that their definition of sexual normality was somewhat different from the one current at the time.

In his summing up, which was unsympathetic to both parties, Mr. Justice Coleridge reminded the jury that they were trying Lord Alfred Douglas and not Robert Ross and that their quarrel had come about 'because both parties seem to have been clamorous to obtain all the notoriety that could attach to Wilde and his writings and to put them before the public in as large a measure as possible.' He referred to them disparagingly as persons who 'have fluttered round Oscar Wilde, as moths flutter round a candle,' which must have infuriated Robbie who, as he had made clear in his speech at the Ritz six years earlier, had done his utmost to remain as unassuming as possible in his running of the literary estate.[282] The judge also said of Robbie's evidence 'I waited and waited, but I waited in vain for any moral expression of indignation or horror at the practice of sodomitical vices,' and that, despite keeping an open mind on the matter, he could not recall anything to indicate that Ross disapproved or that he viewed that kind of vice with disgust.[283] The jury retired for an hour and a half when the foreman announced that they were unable to agree on a verdict. The judge instructed them to make a further attempt which was again unsuccessful and the case was held over for retrial until the next sessions. However, before the case was due to come up again, Ross sensibly indicated that he wished to enter a plea of *nolle prosequi* and withdraw the prosecution if the other side would agree. After negotiations it was settled that Ross would pay Douglas's costs and would cease using old documents to discredit him and in return Douglas would stop his libellous attacks on Ross.[284] He hadn't managed to get Ross arrested for homosexuality, but he regarded the outcome as a sort of victory since the implication was that he had justified his libels and permanently blackened Ross's reputation.

Yet his triumph wasn't to last long. In the first few months of 1915, Edmund Gosse and a few others of Robbie's friends decided to present him with a testimonial and raise a subscription to help him financially. Although Robbie's family had covered many of the legal costs incurred in the previous two years, he was still badly out of pocket from his battles with Douglas and Crosland and the loss of his job at the Inland Revenue as an indirect result. The organisers were quite overwhelmed by the response to their appeal and the text of an 'Address and Presentation to Mr. Robert Ross' was published in several national newspapers on 29 March. It carried the signatures of over three hundred names in the world of literature and the arts as well as peers and politicians, including the Prime Minister, Herbert Asquith, and £760 had been raised. Robbie, in his typically modest way, insisted that the money be used to fund a scholarship in his name at the Slade School of Fine Art at University College London, though the committee held back £50 to present him with a gold repeater pocket watch as a personal reminder.

Douglas, predictably, could not let the occasion pass without comment and wrote a letter to *The Globe* reminding its readers that Ross had withdrawn his libel action four months before, was by implication guilty of the offences which were the basis of the libel, and asked whether the Prime Minister, as one of the signatories, was aware of the fact. Of course he was, since Douglas had written him an abusive letter about Ross back in January, outlining the case, referring to him again as 'a bugger and blackmailer,' and more or less threatening to expose the Asquiths' friendship with Ross unless they stopped receiving him socially. On 15 April Douglas sent a telegram to Andrew Bonar Law, opposition leader at the time:

Please ask the Prime Minister to explain to the House of Commons on what grounds and with what motive he organised and signed a public testimonial with gift of money to Robert Ross for whose record see today's Times and Telegraph and see also my plea of justification entered last November and still on the file of the Old Bailey. Copy of this telegram sent to the King. Lord Alfred Douglas.[285]

Having had no success on that front, on 21 May he sent Winston Churchill a copy of his January letter to Asquith suggesting that if Churchill used the information to oust Asquith, he could then be in a position to lead the Liberal Party.[286] There seemed to be nothing at which Douglas would stop in order to make Ross a social pariah.

Meanwhile, Robbie had one last battle to fight. Thomas Crosland had brought an action against him for malicious prosecution over Robbie's case of the year before against himself and Douglas for criminal conspiracy. The trial started on 13 April, lasted for four days and was mostly a re-run of the previous one. Crosland's counsel tried to make out that the conspiracy case was merely an attempt by Ross to destroy his client who had described Ross's rehabilitation of Wilde as 'propagating his doctrines' and whitewashing his offences. Crosland insisted, as before, that his interest in Charlie Garratt was entirely altruistic and his only concern was to help the young man put his rent-boy existence behind him and start life afresh. Given the background details to which we now have access, this was a shameless lie. Under cross-examination Crosland said he objected strongly to Ross putting out a 'shilling edition' of Wilde's works leading to 'the spreading of Wilde's doctrines . . . among the "cheap" public, the street public—office boys and others. I thought that the publication of Wilde's works in this cheap form was a danger to public morals.' He then went on to say that Ross had an ulterior motive in promoting Wilde's works and not just a literary one and that *Dorian Gray* 'was a very foul work.' In his summing up, the judge, Mr. Justice

Bray, concluded that Ross had every reason to believe Garratt's story about being used as part of the conspiracy to discredit him and there was therefore no element of malice in his prosecution of Crosland and Douglas. He then withdrew the case from the jury and gave judgment in Robbie's favour.

Even though it brought Robbie's legal battles to an end, it did not stop Bosie from continuing to snipe at him in print. Two pamphlets appeared within a year of the Crosland trial: *The Antidote* No. 4, Vol. 1 on 12 June 1915 and *The Rossiad* on 8 February 1916. Both were attacks on Robbie Ross and the Prime Minister, Herbert Asquith for continuing to befriend him, and a chronology of the various court cases and the events leading up to them. Little public notice was taken of either as Douglas remarked in his 'Note' to the third edition to *The Rossiad*. Still spewing bile, he wrote a sort of repetitive supplement to *Oscar Wilde and Myself* entitled 'The Wilde Myth' which contained yet more invective against Ross. It was set up in type late in 1916, but the publisher refused at the last minute to have it printed.[287] By this point Robbie must have grown immune to Bosie's rantings about him, if indeed they were even brought to his notice. I, too, grew tired of reading about them in the end, and I could sense just a little of the constant stress Robbie must have felt during six years of continuous warfare with the man whose friendship he had once enjoyed. Loyalty to Oscar and the desire to see him and his works rehabilitated in the eyes of the British public had come at a heavy price.

Vyvyan, like so many of his countrymen, assumed that the war would be over by Christmas and in the general surge of patriotic fervour to serve 'King and Country' he applied for a commission in the Interpreter Corps. Being quite fluent in French and Italian and competent in German due to his early education abroad, his application was successful. However, a month later he was informed that the British Expeditionary Force in France now had enough interpreters, but that he was entitled to keep his commission and could apply for a position in any other branch of the Service where it would be favourably considered. The choice was obvious. Cyril's artillery brigade had been ordered back to Europe in September and he was already in Northern France, so by the beginning of December my father found himself a Temporary Second Lieutenant in the Royal Field Artillery. Shortly after, he wrote to tell his brother the good news and Cyril, unable to resist playing the role of elder sibling and by now promoted to Captain, replied with some brotherly advice:

> You will forgive an 'Old Gunner' if I remind one of your vivacious and imaginative temperament that a meticulous attention to detail and a conscientious performance of every duty is a surer road to success than an occasional display of brilliant powers . . . It has been an ever-recurring mistake of young officers to endeavour to master the command of armies before they know how to deal with a squad.[288]

And he finished up: 'Buy cheap clothes out of government stores. This is not Piccadilly.'

That was Cyril, convinced as ever that Vyvyan, unless admonished, might somehow bring the family into disrepute. It was one of the last letters he wrote to my father. Four months later, on 9 May 1915, he was shot through the head by a German sniper while in the infantry trenches, though what he, an artillery officer, was doing there has always seemed a mystery. Apparently, British heavy guns had been bombarding the German front line and as the Germans bolted, Cyril picked up a wounded infantryman's rifle and started shooting at them. I don't know whether putting his head over the parapet in that way was bravery or just recklessness, but he paid with his life.[289] Reflecting on it and on Cyril's letter to Vyvyan the year before in which he said that his 'incentive was to wipe that stain away; to retrieve, if may be, by some action of mine, a name no longer honoured in the land,' there is a certain tragic sense to it. As my father later wrote 'If it was any consolation to me, I think that was the way he wanted to go.'[290] There is, however, something which needs correcting in Vyvyan's view of his brother and it may as well be corrected here. In *Son of Oscar Wilde* he wrote that Cyril was unpopular with his brother officers and that he was considered pompous and intolerant. After Vyvyan's book appeared, Malden Studd who had been one of Cyril's contemporaries at Woolwich and by then a retired Brigadier, wrote to the publisher, Rupert Hart-Davis to say that this was certainly not the case. On the contrary, he said, Cyril was pleasant, well-liked and respected. He went on to say:

Sometimes when the port had gone round after dinner, Cyril would entertain us with stories of travel etc. and all of us sat throughout listening and wondering at the way he had of keeping us interested in all he said. We did not know it at the time, but he certainly inherited some of his father's genius and charm.[291]

Cyril's adult life is something of an enigma. He carried around with him what he perceived as the immense and secret burden of his father's shame—secret because were it ever to be known who his father had been, he was convinced that it would ruin his career in the Army for good. Part of his attempt to atone for his father's 'sins' was to lead a life whose watchword was self-denial. There was a short time around 1906/7 when it seems Cyril fell in love, and had it lasted it might have changed this ascetic outlook. In a letter to Vyvyan of November 1906 he writes of 'my lady-love— *un cas sérieux*—no money, or I would marry her *sur le champ.*'[292] The object of his affection was Margaret Maitland who had also been orphaned at a young age, in her case at sixteen, so there was a common bond between them. Her letters to him have not survived, but his to Margaret have, and they show an emotional side to Cyril which is totally absent from all his other extant correspondence. By the summer of 1907 he is addressing her as 'My very dearest Margaret' and signing off 'I live in hope that I may see you soon . . . With my very deepest love and affection.' Although the feeling was mutual according to her granddaughter, sadly Margaret was also looking to marry into financial security and by 1909 their relationship came to an end. On 26 October that year Cyril wrote to her: 'My dear Margaret, May I come down to see you this Friday? I will try to be neither sentimental nor gloomy and do my utmost to be thoroughly commonplace. Yr very affect: friend Cyril.' They must both have realised that marriage under the circumstances was not possible and, sometime after, Margaret met Cecil Whitaker, got engaged and married him in July 1912. Two months before her marriage, Cyril was writing to Vyvyan from India: 'My attitude towards women is this. Being human, they are imperfect as works of art; intellectually they are fatiguing; economically a burden. Eh bien, je m'en fiche!' And implicit in his cynicism seems to be an acceptance of the fact that because of his heritage he wasn't made for happiness.

I suggested earlier that Cyril may have requested a posting with the RFA to India to avoid any possible connection with his brother's financial difficulties; I wonder now whether there might not have been an element of the 'Foreign Legion Syndrome' about his transfer as well—leaving England behind and all the memories of what might have been with Margaret. His last letter to her (like so many of his letters a bizarre mixture of Kierkegaard and Baedeker) was from India in 1913, a year after her marriage: 'I feel sure that your present life must be full of such joy, such hope, such promise for the future. You know how sincerely I desire that the one woman who has really cared for me and helped me should be herself happy.'[293] In the event of his death, Cyril had asked for his Sam Browne belt to be sent to Margaret and, after the war was over, she went to visit his grave in the St. Vaast Military Cemetery in Northern France. She kept the belt hanging over the back of her writing-desk chair until the end of her life in 1975. Her granddaughter, Margaret Stewart, still hangs it over the back of hers to this day.

* * *

Vyvyan, in the strange parlance of the time, 'had a good war.' He saw action in 'the Gunners,' survived, was mentioned in despatches four times, and was awarded a military OBE. Even fighting in France, though, Vyvyan could not escape the legacy of his father. Not long after his brother's death, he had heard—probably from Robert Ross—that Robert Sherard was planning to bring out his third volume on Oscar, *The Real Oscar Wilde*, and was wanting to include pictures of him and Cyril. It was doubtless something which had been discussed between Ross and Sherard and was intended to show Oscar in a more 'normal' light as a family man, but Vyvyan was having none of it and wrote to the publisher, Werner Laurie asking him not to include them. If it was a book on Oscar's work, he argued, logically they had no place and if it was what he called a 'sensational biography' he did not wish either '[my] brother's memory or my own present life to be dragged to light in it.' Laurie complied and Vyvyan wrote back somewhat apologetically to thank him and to say that he looked forward to their meeting so that he could explain the reasons for his request and reassure Laurie that there was no intended disloyalty to Oscar.

It was typical of his continuing and complicated ambivalence towards his father at the time.[294]

As Vyvyan later wrote in *Time Remembered*, with Cyril's death he felt the last link with his true family had snapped and Robbie became closer than ever, both as a father-figure and a friend. Vyvyan being at the Front, it was Robbie who dealt with the business of tidying up Cyril's estate and kept a sort of paternal eye on Vyvyan's wife, Violet. Since the business of war was just as brutal but in a strange way more 'gentlemanly' back then, Vyvyan also asked if Robbie could send him half-a-dozen bottles of whisky via Fortnum & Mason 'who have an excellent service to the Front.' He also explained that it had a practical as well as a pleasurable purpose: 'One not only becomes popular, but one has more chance of life if one provides whisky, as no Major would ever be fool enough to send a subaltern who provides whisky on a dangerous errand.' The ever-benevolent Robbie obliged. Vyvyan's feelings for Robbie at this time are perfectly exemplified by the closing words of his last surviving letter from the Front: 'With my fondest love and all my most loving thanks, Robbie dear, for all your forbearingness [*sic*] with me and my family. Always affectionately yours, Vyvyan.'[295] He had been a trial to Robbie between 1910 and 1913, as sons so often are to their fathers, though in his case teenage self-centredness manifested itself ten years later than normal. Now, at last, having witnessed all that Oscar's most devoted friend had done and suffered on his behalf, Vyvyan could express his heartfelt gratitude. Unfortunately, there was one last broadside which the British Establishment would fire at poor Oscar's memory before the war was over.

Early in 1918 Robbie licensed the avant-garde theatrical producer, Jack Grein, to stage three private performances of *Salomé*, private because it was still subject to the Lord Chamberlain's ban of 1892 when Oscar had hoped that Sarah Bernhardt would take the title role for the London première, but which never took place. The idea, according to Robbie, was that if it were a success, they could then apply for a licence for public performances.[296] His thinking was that apart from making extra money for the estate, it would also contribute to Wilde's reputation as a serious playwright. In the event, it was to achieve almost exactly the opposite. The actress whom Grein had chosen to play Salomé was the Canadian, Maud Allan, a dancer whose performance in her *Vision of Salomé* had taken London by storm ten years before and who, as a result, had found herself being received in the highest echelons of British Society. She had even been befriended by the Prime Minister and, given her reputedly bisexual tastes, there were rumours of an affair with his wife, Margot Asquith. In the meantime, Maud's career had fizzled out, so an offer for the forty-five year-old to take the leading role in Wilde's play was irresistible.

On 26 January, the independent and strongly nationalist MP, Noel Pemberton Billing had published an article headed 'The Forty-Seven Thousand' in his right-wing newspaper, *The Imperialist*. He claimed that there existed a 'Black Book of sin' in the *Cabinet Noir* of a certain German Prince containing the names of 47,000 prominent English men and women who practised vices which 'all decent men thought had perished in Sodom and Lesbia.' The implication behind the article was that the British war effort was being undermined by the Germans and 'that there had been many persons who had been prevented from putting their full strength into the war by corruption and blackmail and the fear of exposure.' The public reaction to the article was more one of amusement and incredulity than the outrage which Billing had anticipated, but a fortnight later, when the *Sunday Times* announced the performances of *Salomé,* he saw an opportunity to make his accusations of 'depravity' even more specific. In the 16 February edition of his paper, by now rebaptised *The Vigilante*, there appeared on the front page a short paragraph headed 'The Cult of the Clitoris':

To be a member of Maud Allan's private performances in Oscar Wilde's *Salomé* one has to apply to a Miss Valetta of 9 Duke Street Adelphi W.C. If Scotland Yard were to seize the list of these

members I have no doubt they would secure the names of several
of the first 47,000.

Like Queensberry's insulting card left at Oscar's club in 1895 it
was a provocation and like that card, it had the desired effect.
Jack Grein saw the offending paragraph on 5 March and, having showed it to Maud Allan, they consulted their solicitors and
immediately started proceedings against Billing for criminal libel.
Robbie Ross tried to dissuade them from taking legal action, mindful of the libel trial five years before when Alfred Douglas had
failed in his prosecution of Arthur Ransome.[297] The circulation of
The Vigilante was small and for subscribers only, and if Grein and
Allan had merely ignored the implied accusation of Maud's lesbi-
anism, it would have been forgotten in a week. Robbie was also
concerned—rightly as it turned out—that bringing the matter to
court would simply be another excuse to attack Oscar Wilde for
his morals and his work for its 'decadence.'

The trial opened on 29 May and lasted for six days, the charge
against Billing being that he had published a false and defama-
tory libel concerning Maud Allan: 'Meaning thereby that the said
Maud Allan was a lewd, unchaste and immoral woman and was
about to give private performances of an obscene and indecent
character so designed as to foster and encourage obscene and unnatural practices among women.'[298]

Billing in turn entered his plea of justification: 'The tragedy
Salomé is a stage play by one Oscar Wilde, a moral pervert, is
an open representation of degenerated sexual lust, sexual crime,
and unnatural passions and an evil and mischievous travesty of a
biblical story.' It went on to say that 'The textual presentation of
such play by any person or persons whatsoever would be highly
deleterious and prejudicial to public morality and to the interests of purity in the public life of this country generally.'[299] After
four years of war, Billing was clearly intending to tap into patriotic feeling. He conducted his own defence, objected from the
start to Mr. Justice Darling judging the case, and was frequently

reprimanded by Darling on points of legal procedure and the irrelevance of some of his more sensational evidence. With a Mata Hari-like *femme fatale*, a captain discharged from the army as insane, high-ranking politicians dragged in for good measure and the whole case suffused with the heady perfume of sadism and a lesbian scandal, in places the verbatim account of the trial reads like a modern-day film-script with an 18+ certificate.[300]

After counsel had opened for the prosecution and examined Maud Allan, Billing started his cross-examination by asking about her brother who had raped, disfigured and murdered two young women in San Francisco and had been hanged for the crimes in 1898. Allan and her counsel both protested at this line of questioning, but Billing maintained that he would call witnesses to prove that sadism and degenerate sexual lust were hereditary and had a direct bearing on the case. He also implied that Allan only understood the meaning of the word 'clitoris' because of her sexual inclinations, since its use in 1918 was otherwise mainly medical and anatomical. It soon became clear that he was trying to imply that Allan might be a sexual pervert and a sadist for wanting to play the part of Salomé, which then set the tone for the next six days, during which Oscar Wilde and his 'repulsive and blasphemous' play was as much on trial as Billing was for his alleged libel.

Eileen Villiers-Stuart was called as a witness by Billing and claimed under oath to have seen the famous 'Black Book' and that the names of both Mr. and Mrs. Asquith were in it as well as that of Mr. Justice Darling himself. It later turned out that she had perjured herself, that she had been employed initially by the Government to entrap and compromise Billing to end his political career, but had since switched her allegiance to Billing and his moral crusade as well as becoming his mistress. Another witness for the defence, Captain Harold Spencer, who had brought the 'Black Book' to Billing's attention and collaborated with him on *The Vigilante*, concocted a story about seeing it when he became ADC to Prince William of Wied while on secondment to the International Commission in Albania, an employment later flatly denied by the

Foreign Office. Billing also called Alfred Douglas as a witness in order to discredit Wilde and his play. When asked what Wilde's intention had been in writing the play, Douglas said 'I can say that he intended the play to be an exhibition of perverted sexual passion excited in a young girl.' And to the question of whether Wilde was a sexual and moral pervert he replied 'Yes. He admitted it; he never attempted to disguise it after his conviction,' and after further questioning Douglas said 'I think he had a diabolical influence on everyone he met. I think he is the greatest force for evil that has appeared in Europe during the last 350 years.' Since none of this was strictly relevant to the libel, the prosecution, aware that Douglas would probably try to vilify his former lover as he had done in other court cases since 1913, was prepared and retaliated with the overtly homosexual love-letters which Oscar had written him in the 1890s. Not to be outdone, Billing in his closing speech counter-attacked and said that counsel for the prosecution had 'stood up and licked his lips with satisfaction as he read out all the sordid filth written to that child [*Alfred Douglas*]—the love letters of Oscar Wilde who ruined him.' He went on to say that his witnesses had demonstrated 'that this social leper, Oscar Wilde, had founded a cult of sodomy in this country, and travelled from end to end of it perverting youth wherever he could,' and asked the jury if it would be right to find him guilty when he was merely trying to stop the further spread of Wilde's 'evil influence' by denouncing his play *Salomé*.

In his summing up, Mr. Justice Darling said in error that Douglas had written (as opposed to merely translating from Wilde's French original) the sadistic scene when Salomé kisses the severed head of John the Baptist, causing Douglas to jump up and shout 'You are a liar, a damned liar. If you say it outside the Court, I will prosecute you.' This was followed by loud cheers from the public and Darling ordered Douglas's removal from the Court. Shortly afterwards, the jury retired for an hour and on their return brought in a verdict of 'Not Guilty' at which the public gallery erupted in a great outburst of cheering and stamping of feet.

Darling, who by this time had more or less lost control, ordered everyone out of the gallery and the Court to be cleared and told Billing he was discharged. Douglas, too, was cheered as he left the Court. For him it was another well-merited blow to Wilde's reputation and therefore indirectly to Robert Ross.

With my father still in France, poor Robbie, though just an observer this time of the damning of Oscar Wilde in public, had no one to turn to for support. Towards the end of the trial, he wrote to Vyvyan: 'London has lost all interest in the War for the moment. In tubes, trains and Clubs you hear of nothing but the Billing case . . . I only hope, dear Vyvyan that *you* don't mind. Oscar's works have now stood the shock of ages and his permanent position in English literature and drama must compensate for all the rest.' After Billing's victory Robbie wrote again, this time in reference to the recent death of Sir George Alexander:

> Alexander has fulfilled his promise and has bequeathed to you *Earnest* and *Lady Windermere's Fan*. I fear it will prove but a barren legacy. The Billing case has ruined the Wilde Estate. Douglas, having ruined your father twice, has now effectively ruined the property on which he always cast greedy eyes . . . Everyone has cancelled their contracts for the dramatic or cinema rights in the plays or books.[301]

Four days later he wrote to Charles Ricketts: 'The English, intoxicated into failure, enjoyed tearing poor Maud Allan to pieces, simply because she had given them pleasure, and kicking Oscar's corpse to make up for the failure of the Fifth Army.[302] Thankfully Vyvyan wasn't in London at the time to read the daily reports in the press about the trial and its witnesses' expressions of disgust about his father and his works. So unaware was he of the whole sordid farce that he even wrote to Robbie in the middle of the month asking what the original libel had been about.

Once the trial was over, Robbie, in a very uncharacteristic manner, sent a grossly libellous letter to Sir Charles Mathews, the

Director of Public Prosecutions starting: 'I write to congratulate you on the complete rehabilitation of your protégé, Lord Alfred Douglas,' hoping that Mathews might sue and Robbie would be in a position to expose what he regarded as the collusion between Douglas and Mathews. He particularly resented Mathews' repeated investigations into his private life on Douglas's vindictive 'information' about his homosexuality. Mathews seems, sensibly, to have ignored the letter.[303] The Billing trial had threatened to unravel much of the careful work which Robbie had been doing to rehabilitate Oscar in the previous twelve years and his disappointment and depression show in his correspondence at the time. Friends who visited him that autumn said that he was looking tired and worn. In his professional capacity as an art critic and dealer he had been preparing for a trip to Australia to advise the National Gallery on its collections, but viewed the prospect of the long sea voyage and the six-month absence from London with a mixture of pleasure and apprehension. On 5 October Robbie went for a rest in the late afternoon and when his housekeeper came to wake him for dinner, she found him dead from heart failure. Sadly, his touching devotion to Oscar's memory and the stresses of the previous six years had taken their toll and, as he jokingly but poignantly suggested to Siegfried Sassoon a while earlier, his epitaph should probably read 'Here lies one whose name was written in hot water.'[304]

Vyvyan was in Paris at the time and read of Robbie's sudden death in a newspaper. Not being a close relative there was no question of him getting compassionate leave to attend the funeral which he found deeply upsetting:

> He was my greatest friend and whenever I got into trouble, which I did with great frequency, he always came to the rescue. I was devoted to him and I wonder how he could have put up with me; his death was a great blow to me and I felt that another of the strings that bound me to life had snapped.

Ten days later he received a telegram to say that Violet, his wife, had been 'dangerously injured by fire' and this time he was granted leave to return to London. However, on the train from Folkestone, he read that she had been taken to hospital where she had died of her burns the night before. It was a classic case, like the death Sir William Wilde's two illegitimate daughters nearly half a century before, of an evening gown catching alight at an open fire:

> I sat in the train and thought of the people who had died in such a short space of time: my brother, Robbie Ross and now Violet, and I felt that I was once more alone in the world, as I had been years before on my return to England from Monaco. I do not think I mourned particularly, I was too numb, and it all seemed to be fatalistic and pre-ordained.[305]

When he was alive Robbie had regarded Cyril and Vyvyan more or less as his own grown-up children: Vyvyan was the wayward one, the prodigal son, whom he loved as he had loved Oscar, with all his faults; Cyril he loved for his integrity and his sense of purpose in life—'his pride and strenuous determination' as he described it to Vyvyan—but never with the same understanding that he had for his less reliable brother. 'Dear Cyril's letters always make me feel like a Balkan State receiving assurances and advice from the Russian Government,' he wrote to Vyvyan at the beginning of the War.[306]

Shortly after my father first met Robbie Ross in 1907, he came of age. Now with Robbie's death, he was forced to take that step again but this time into a rather different adulthood, assuming the responsibility for his father's literary estate which had so challenged Robbie for the past eighteen years.

PART THREE
(1918-1945)

CHAPTER ONE
VYVYAN TAKES CONTROL

After an extended bout of Spanish flu following the deaths of Violet and Robbie, Vyvyan returned to France where he remained until he was demobbed on 28 July 1919. He felt a mixture of relief that it was all over and he had managed to survive, but he was also profoundly aware that it had been a terrible waste of four years. 'I felt lost, a dog without a master, with no one to tell me what to do and when to do it, and no one to care whether I appeared on parade or not,' he wrote, lamenting how army life had crushed his independence.[307] Added to this was the dreadful sense of *déjà vu* from his childhood, the realisation that he had no family to whom he could turn to help ease him back into civilian life. It must have been unbearably depressing, but this time he knew that to honour the memory of those who had been dear to him, his wife, Cyril, and Robbie, he needed to start afresh.

The problem, as he explained in his second memoir, was that he really didn't know where to begin. Despite being called to the Bar and attempting, rather unsuccessfully, to write for a living, before the War he had achieved very little, so at the age of thirty-three he found himself unemployable.[308] It was then that Richmond Temple came into his life. Temple, seven years younger than my father, had been a young (but strictly heterosexual) protégé of Robert Ross. Having left school at fifteen, he managed to find himself jobs first in Canada and then India before returning to Europe and serving in the Royal Flying Corps, until he was invalided out in early 1918. Aged only twenty-seven and cultivating an entirely fictitious reputation for being a brilliant businessman, he relieved my father of some £4,000 which was rapidly lost in an ill-considered venture importing unsaleable goods from post-War

Germany. Vyvyan's only consolation was that Robbie and others had convinced him of Temple's business prowess, fooled into believing it themselves. Thus, divested of any capital he had, my father realised he would be reliant more than ever on the income from Oscar's copyrights: 'I was, I suppose, fortunate that my father's estate was beginning to pay, and I could not help thinking it sad that he should have died in comparatively straitened circumstances while I, his younger son, should reap a belated harvest from his works.'[309]

There was also a certain irony in the fact that of the three people who had benefited from Oscar's royalties, Vyvyan had been the most improvident. At the time of his financial troubles in 1911/12, he had exchanged his share in the estate for Cyril to bail him out. When Cyril died in 1915, in his will he left Vyvyan's share back to him and his own half to Robbie Ross. When Robbie died in 1918 he bequeathed Cyril's share to Vyvyan who then became the sole beneficiary of the Wilde estate. Mindful of where his financial irresponsibility had landed him before, Vyvyan took himself in hand and even kept income and expenditure 'ledgers' for the years 1921-24 into which he seems to have entered every last detail, even down to the cost of presents for the women in his life. The income from Oscar's works in those four years totalled £5,751, enough to live on comfortably without being in regular employment, and it enabled Vyvyan to take over the estate and the copyrights from where Robbie had left them in such good order at the time of his death two years before.

With peace restored in Europe after four bloody years of war, the reconstructed world of the 1920s was determined to enjoy itself, and that included accepting, even celebrating, that diversity in the arts and literature which it had so often disparaged before. The seeds so carefully sown by Robert Ross to re-establish Oscar's reputation, had germinated, flowered and were being appreciated by a less fettered society. But with that flowering, came a renewed interest in the man's work and an inevitable spate of piracies, so Vyvyan issued through his solicitors, Parker Garrett & Co, a

circular updating the one issued in 1908 by Robbie which now
listed all authorised editions alongside works ascribed to Oscar but
never written nor translated by him. Booksellers were warned that
offering for sale any unauthorised or spurious publications would
lead to their being prosecuted. Even if it halted the sale of piracies
in English, it did nothing for those beyond the reach of the Law in
Europe, except in France and Germany with whose publishers the
estate under Robbie Ross had always had good relations. Unable
to replace the first editions of Oscar's works which my father had
been forced to sell off in the 1950s, forty years ago I decided to
collect cheap foreign piracies instead—the number I have amassed
for the period 1920 to 1950 is astonishing. Publishers in Turkey,
Latvia, Greece, Russia, Portugal, Italy, and Yugoslavia as well as
America must have assumed that because Oscar was gay, he would
have had no heirs to claim their rights. Parker Garrett enlisted
the help of the Society of Authors and the League of Dramatists
over the next thirty years during which the copyrights still had to
run and were able to exercise some control over performances of
the plays. The BBC, for example, was very correct in requesting
permissions, leading to some unlikely broadcasts over the Foreign
Services such as a 25 minute version of *Salomé* in Hindustani and
a 35 minute version of *The Importance of Being Earnest* in Arabic.
Publishing, however, was far more difficult to control and as the
Society of Authors explained 'So many of these foreigners take advantage of the fact that they are not easily get-at-able and . . . simply withhold all royalties until they are worried for them.' Nor was
any of it was made easier by the haphazard distribution of rights
by Oscar's receiver in bankruptcy back in the early years of the
century.[310] My father must have begun to feel some of the burden
that Robbie had shouldered between Oscar's death and his own
eighteen years later, but the task wasn't all negative—there was
the positive side, too, continuing Robbie's work of rehabilitating
Oscar through his writings.

Back in 1911, six years after the publication of the much
abridged *De Profundis*, Robbie had planned to bring out a

collection of Oscar's letters to him all written after his release from prison. The aim was to put his friend's last years into proper perspective, to balance what he called the sombre accounts of certain biographers with the fact (shown in these letters) 'that the world, even in its less noble manifestations, was still full of pleasant places and pleasant moments for him.' Unfortunately it was Robbie's falling out with Alfred Douglas which initially halted the project and then the War intervened before he could arrange for their publication, so it was left to Vyvyan, More Adey, and Christopher Millard to complete it for him. Whether or not they relied on a text prepared by Robbie is uncertain and probably immaterial anyway; the principal consideration was to avoid stirring Alfred Douglas into legal action yet again. Between May 1897 and his death three and a half years later, Oscar wrote 130 letters, postcards, and notes to Robbie who, more than ever, became his close confidant, adviser, and reluctant banker. Inevitably he expressed strong feelings about Bosie's behaviour towards him at the time, feelings often unfairly intensified by money worries and even an element of anger at having allowed himself to be drawn back to his young lover and nemesis. Even though Robbie's original explanation for publishing them had to be changed slightly with Millard's preface now stating: 'The letters stand not only as examples of Wilde's delightful epistolary style, but as a tribute to the devoted friendship of Robert Ross,' all of the derogatory comments about Bosie still had to be suppressed.[311] For example in Oscar's first letter to Robbie after his release he wrote of Bosie: 'I have a real terror now of that unfortunate ungrateful young man with his unimaginative selfishness . . . To be with him would be to return to the hell from which I do think I have been released. I hope never to see him again.' Quoted in its proper context, it would only have emphasised Robbie's 'devoted friendship,' but fear of litigation prevented the editors from including such passages. Their concern was well justified, with Bosie was back in court in November 1921 suing the *Evening News* for libel. Earlier in the year on 4 February and acting on a telephone tip-off, the paper had announced the

'Sudden Death of Lord Alfred Douglas.' The news item was accompanied by an unflattering obituary in which it was stated that 'He might have done anything and, his poetry excepted, he did nothing and worse than nothing,' and referred to him as 'this poor bewildered man who . . . will perhaps only be remembered by the scandals and the quarrels in which he involved himself.'

Despite briefing Douglas Hogg, one of the most able barristers of his time and a future Lord Chancellor, the *Evening News* lost the case and was ordered to pay Bosie's costs and damages of £1,000. Inevitably Oscar was dragged in yet again, not only on account of his own trials and downfall, but also for the part that he played posthumously in all of the 'scandals and quarrels' mentioned by the newspaper. To Bosie's discomfort, the overtly homosexual letters written both by him to Oscar and by Oscar to him (and which were used in the Ransome and in the Pemberton Billing trials) were produced and once again read out in court to justify the defence's description of him as degenerate, though as part of his settlement the jury recommended that they should be destroyed to prevent any further use of them.[312] Oscar would feature in several more legal actions before the Second World War but, thankfully, in respect of his works and no more on account of his morals.

I imagine my father must have felt quite ambivalent about resuscitating Robbie's project to publish Oscar's post-prison letters. On the one hand it was now a tribute to Robbie, to whom Vyvyan owed so much: the successful rehabilitation of his father as an author; his own rescue from the dull life of a civil servant mapped out for him by his family; and, not least, the affection and emotional stability torn from him so early in life which Robbie had later provided. On the other, there was the pain of reliving through those letters the period when he might have seen his father and, worse, when his father was writing to Robbie: 'I have heard from my wife: she sends me photographs of the boys—such lovely little fellows in Eton collars—but makes no promise to allow me to see them; she says *she* will see me twice a year, but I want my boys.'[313]

Vyvyan wrote to his friend Edward Heron-Allen a couple of years later: 'Personally I should never have published them at all. I did so in the first place because it was Ross's earnest wish that they should be published and in the second place because I did not feel justified in destroying them and if they are not destroyed, they are bound to be published sooner or later.' In fact, until they were sold to the American collector, William Andrews Clark in 1929, so candid were some of the suppressed passages about Douglas, that Vyvyan made provision in his will that they should join the manuscript of *De Profundis* locked up in the British Museum.[314]

They appeared in two slim volumes, *After Reading* and *After Berneval*, each in 475 copies and together covering just one year after Oscar's release up to 14 May 1898, as well as a very limited and less censored edition of only 23 to secure copyright in America. They sold out more or less immediately on publication and a third volume was planned but the idea was abandoned. Best to leave Oscar full of good intentions about new literary work following the success of *The Ballad*, rather than depicting the last, sad and unproductive years leading to his death as the remaining letters would have done. Despite the slightly fuller American versions, it was a very biased view which would not be fully rectified until *The Letters of Oscar Wilde* was published in 1962 and, in some ways, worse than useless; when you expurgate documents and advertise the fact with ellipses and dashes for the sake of exactitude, people automatically want to know what it was that you were trying to hide. In the meantime, there was another of Robbie's projects which needed completing: foreign editions of the complete *De Profundis*. It was, in a sense, the continuation of Robbie's feud with Douglas which Vyvyan was taking on, but having seen what it did to Robbie, he was naturally worried about the consequences.

Back in 1904, Max Meyerfeld had persuaded Robbie Ross to allow him to publish a much-censored German edition of Oscar's prison letter to Bosie Douglas including the four very revealing letters from Oscar to himself which didn't appear in the first English edition of *De Profundis*. In his slightly expanded version of 1909 Meyerfeld even named Bosie as its intended recipient long before it was generally known, and then tried to persuade Robbie to let him have more and more material with which he intended to show Bosie as the arch-villain in the Wilde saga. From the time of the Ransome trial onwards, this suited Robbie perfectly, as he had failed to enlist John Lane's help in December 1913 to publish the complete text of *De Profundis* with a commentary. Permitting a foreign publisher to do the job for him had the advantage of being beyond the jurisdiction of the English courts as well as helping to blacken Douglas's character to an even wider public on the Continent where Wilde and his works were held in high regard. It was around this time that Robbie agreed Meyerfeld should have access to the texts of any unpublished material three months before it was due to appear in England so that a German translation could be put out simultaneously. The war had effectively put a stop to any such publications, but now Meyerfeld wrote to my father, whom he had met with Robbie years before, asking if they could resuscitate the planned projects, namely Oscar's post-prison letters to Robbie and the complete *De Profundis*. It seems that Vyvyan ignored the request, concerned presumably at the possible consequences these 'unexpurgated' projects might have. Meyerfeld then asked Christopher Millard to intercede on his behalf, aware that Vyvyan respected Millard's judgement and his knowledge of Robbie's past intentions.[315] It was a successful move, though it was not until May 1924 two years later that Meyerfeld finally went to London and Vyvyan gave him access to a complete typescript of *De Profundis*.[316] The translation was made and published early in 1925 as *Epistola* which, said Meyerfeld, was more in keeping with Oscar's half-humorous suggestion to Robbie that it should be known as the 'Epistola: In Carcere et Vinculis' (Letter from prison and in chains).[317] It was the first 'complete' version of *De Profundis* in any language to be made widely available to the public though, based as it was on Robbie's inaccurate transcript, it was seen to have numerous errors and omissions when the original manuscript was released in 1960.[318]

After a tense start to their relationship—Meyerfeld having told Vyvyan initially to name his royalty terms then accusing him of being grasping when he refused a flat payment of £100—they reached an agreement and by June 1925 Meyerfeld was back in London translating the American version of the post-prison letters.[319] Given Vyvyan's initial ambivalence about publishing the letters at all, it might seem a little surprising that he also gave Mayerfeld access to another twenty-seven letters from Oscar's last years. Once again, I feel sure that Millard used his influence on my father pointing out that the ones chosen combined humour, beauty and sadness, especially the one in which Oscar describes his visit to Constance's grave. As expected, Mayerfeld's preface was unsparing in its anti-Douglas sentiments:

> As in the theatre of the Middle Ages, where characters are depicted as being torn between the forces of good and evil which fight for the possession of their souls, so Oscar Wilde found himself torn between the good and the evil friend. Bosie was the evil one. And just as in the Morality and Mystery plays, where the weak character feels drawn to the force of evil, the real Mystery here is that Bosie wins the fight.[320]

If the publication of these letters had passed more or less unnoticed in England and America, it was not the case with the complete German translation of *De Profundis*. Attention had been drawn to it in a long article by Meyerfeld in the *New York Times* describing the genesis of his edition where it must have caught the eye of the notorious copyright pirate Samuel Roth, who duly printed a substantial amount of the unpublished work in the July 1926 issue of his quarterly periodical, *Two Worlds*.[321] Less than half of *De Profundis*, it purported to have been 'Translated from the German by Lord Ramsgate,' whose fictional identity could have belonged in the pages of Hilaire Belloc's *Cautionary*

Tales, and whose tin-eared translation was a complete travesty. Vyvyan had seen Roth's forthcoming translation advertised in the February issue of *Vanity Fair* and told his solicitors to get tough on the periodical, especially as a correct typescript would need to be made for the typesetters if it was to be official. Roth made a derisory offer (as he usually did) of $150 and when that was turned down, he simply had it translated from Meyerfeld's German. The Society of Authors (who knew all about Roth's activities) declared that it wasn't worth pursuing a pirate unless he was full of money, which elicited the response from Vyvyan: 'I see great days ahead for book piracy if this is the firm attitude taken up by the Society of Authors.'[322]

In France, however, matters were much more complicated. In October 1925, Henry Davray—a French man of letters and highly regarded translator of British authors—wrote to Vyvyan asking for permission to publish the unexpurgated *De Profundis* in French. Davray had sent Oscar some books together with a sympathetic note on his release from prison in 1897 and, much praised by Oscar, had made a translation of *The Ballad* shortly after it first appeared the next year. They met on a number of occasions after Oscar settled in Paris and in 1905 it was Davray who translated the heavily censored version of *De Profundis* put out by Robbie Ross. Davray who was a regular correspondent for the French literary magazine the *Mercure de France*, followed and reported on any 'Wildean' news from then on and wrote at length on the Ransome trial of 1913. In his article, he quoted much of Oscar's letter to Robbie condemning Bosie Douglas's behaviour after their disastrous reunion in Naples.[323] There was no longer any question about whose side he was taking in the increasingly bitter Ross/Douglas feud and a year later when Ross was in Paris, he provided him with evidence to show that Douglas had perjured himself in one of their recent court cases. In a letter written at the time to Stuart Merrill, another of Wilde's friends from his Paris days, Davray wrote of Douglas: 'Really, that filthy toad, that horrid little viper is a total disaster for anyone who crosses his path.'[324] It was against this background that Davray felt the time was right for the French to have the full text of *De Profundis*. However, negotiations stalled over the details of royalties and in the interim another translator of Wilde's works, Cécil Georges-Bazile, put out an unauthorised translation entitled *Clamavi ad te* to mark the 25th anniversary of Oscar's death at the end of November. Georges-Bazile's work was no more than the 1905 edition together with the unpublished extracts which had been read out in court at the time of the Ransome trial and reported in the press. When Davray became aware of this early the following year, he put pressure on my father to take legal action against Georges-Bazile so that he, Davray, could put out an authorised and therefore complete version of the work. Vyvyan duly took the matter up through his solicitors, but rather than having Georges-Bazile's edition suppressed, which is clearly what Davray had wanted as it would leave the market clear for his own version, Vyvyan started to negotiate some form of compensation and royalty. Davray then went quiet and by the end of July had simply published his own French version of the expanded *De Profundis*, stating clearly in his preface that Robbie Ross had given him permission to do so before the war and had even provided the sources he had used. As a result, Vyvyan was faced with two simultaneous piracies in France and started legal proceedings against both them. However, on 25 July Cécil Georges-Bazile suddenly died aged only 36 and my father, to his credit, tried to withdraw the legal action writing to his solicitor: 'Can nothing be done to stop this writ? I really don't want to persecute a lot of wretched women who are probably struggling hard to make both ends meet now that the breadstealer is dead. The only object of the writ was to give Georges a moral sandbagging. My virulence does not extend to mishandling his women.'[325] Not so with Davray of whom he was determined to make an example to discourage further piracies. The legal proceedings rumbled on for another three years with Vyvyan forced to concede that Davray may well have had Robbie's approval for the complete edition, especially as he quoted unpublished and inflammatory passages about Douglas from Oscar's post-prison letters to Robbie which he could only have had from the recipient

himself, but he should nonetheless produce the evidence.[326] Even
Frank Harris, with whom Vyvyan was corresponding at the time,
interceded on Davray's behalf: 'I hear from Davray you are suing
him about the copyright in De Profundis. I am sure that the difficulty has come through Robert Ross because I can assure you that
Davray is scrupulously honourable, and he was a good friend of
your father's. I have known Davray now for 30 years and hope that
there can be no real trouble between you; make it up—please.'[327]
In the end they did make it up; I still have the copy of *Oscar Wilde:
la tragédie finale*, Davray's account of Oscar's last years, containing
a pitiless indictment of Alfred Douglas and which he inscribed to
my father.

There were numerous other attempts to publish unauthorised
translations of *De Profundis* in the 1920s, some of which Vyvyan
and his solicitors were able successfully to have suppressed. In
some cases, though, the circumstances were more complicated. At
the beginning of 1925 Max Meyerfeld sent Vyvyan a play by Carl
Sternheim, *Oskar Wilde: Sein Drama*, which was essentially a dra-
matized re-run of Oscar's disastrous relationship with Bosie complete with rent-boys, court case, and even the brief appearance of
a journalist named Holland, which can't have pleased my father.
The play was due to be produced in Berlin in March. Vyvyan's
solicitor, Martin Holman, wrote to the Society of Authors asking if
anything could be done to prevent it being staged but feared that
any attempt to do so would simply give it extra publicity:

> Lord Alfred Douglas could stop it as he is still alive, but that
> would give it a *succès de scandale* and he might also try to prevent
> further distribution of the full de Profundis . . . . I did hope that
> with poor Ross's death all this poisonous business would come
> to an end. There are apparently "Literary Gents" in Berlin, even
> of high standing, who are prepared to make money out of any-
> thing. The play went ahead notwithstanding but only ran for ten
> performances.[328]

Despite being on his guard over piracies as well as generally mis-
trustful about foreign publishers and authors, there were occasions when Vyvyan seemed if not to enjoy then at least to respect
the interest shown in his father. One such was the visit at the end
of 1928 of a Japanese literary critic and academic, Honma Hisao.

Born in 1886, the same year as my father, at the age of twenty
Honma had started to take a keen interest in Oscar Wilde after
attending a lecture at Waseda University by Hogetsu Shimamura
on 'Aestheticism in England.' As a graduate he wrote articles on
the aesthetes and the *fin de siècle* in England for *Waseda bungaku,* the prestigious review of the University's Department of
Literature, in which he published the first Japanese translation of
the abridged *De Profundis* in 1911 and brought it out as a book
the following year. Alongside teaching at the university, he succeeded Shimamura as editor-in-chief of the review in 1918, but
his real interest still lay in Oscar Wilde and his circle. So, in 1928,
in preparation for completing his doctoral thesis, he travelled to
England where he spent nearly a year tracking down survivors of
the 1890s and anyone who'd had close contact with them. Among
others he met and interviewed Arthur Symons, Holbrook Jackson
and Max Beerbohm who, in his incomparable style, inscribed a
copy of the recently published *The Dreadful Dragon of Hay Hill*
to Honma with 'From a member of one vulgarized civilization to
a sympathetic member of another.' All this might have remained
just a mothballed memory had it not been for a strange photo I
discovered among my father's papers seventy years after it had
been taken. Strange, because the two people in the photograph
seem almost to be ignoring each other. Vyvyan is sitting on a sofa
looking away from the camera. He seems uncomfortable. On
one of the sofa's arms is perched a Japanese gentleman in formal
morning dress looking straight into the lens. On the photograph
are some characters in Japanese which would, presumably, have
explained the occasion, but finding out was low on my list of priorities. Judging by my father's age and his clothes, it was sometime
in the 1920s and since he was obviously not interacting with the

other sitter, I assumed that he had probably agreed, if somewhat unwillingly, to humour a Japanese fan of Oscar's works who happened to be in London.

I contacted the Oscar Wilde Society of Japan and asked if anyone could recognise the other sitter. But of course—it was Honma Hisao a professor of comparative literature who had founded the Society in 1975. This was no mere fan of my grandfather then, but a serious academic who had travelled to Europe in the 1920s (I still couldn't put an accurate date to it) to research Wilde and his world at a time when he was still not really considered by the British as a major literary figure. Another twenty years would go by before I learned more about him. I was looking into the convoluted publishing history of *De Profundis* and came across a reference to an article in the *Japan Review* referring to Honma as the first translator of the work into Japanese.[329] I wrote to the author, Yoko Hirata, in the hope of finding out more about the man himself and after a brief exchange of correspondence, she revealed (in the most charmingly modest fashion) that Hisao Honma had been her grandfather. Through her I learned how he had visited Europe in 1928/29 and had made contact with Vyvyan through Dulau & Co, the booksellers in Bond Street, who were selling an enormous collection of Wilde books, manuscripts, and related material which had belonged to Robbie Ross, Christopher Millard, and my father. I learned, too, that Vyvyan must have been sufficiently impressed with Honma's serious interest to have given him one of the locks of his father's hair cut off by Robert Ross after Oscar's death, a gesture he only ever made to one other person, the actor Micheál Mac Liammóir. My father also gave him access to the parts of *De Profundis* which until then had been suppressed in English and were only available in French and German—another sign of the high esteem in which he held his visitor. They met not once but at least four or five times at the end of 1928 according to my father's pocket diaries of the time, and Honma wrote about it in 'Talking with Oscar Wilde's son,' a chapter of his book *Impressions of Europe*.[330] When he interviewed Arthur

Symons, having expressed a particular interest in Oscar Wilde, he was asked by Mrs. Symons how the law in Japan would deal with such a case of homosexuality: 'I answered that since it belonged to the sphere of private life, the law would not take it up as a case for trial at all. She nodded in agreement and said that that was how it should be.' From Honma's point of view, Oscar had done nothing illegal and therefore should not have been tried and imprisoned. He would doubtless have expressed the same view to Vyvyan, and my father must have felt that he could talk openly about the subject with Honma in a way which would have been impossible with his heterosexual fellow countrymen and which would have strengthened the rapport between them. In addition to allowing Honma access to the suppressed part of *De Profundis*, Vyvyan also agreed to provide him with an introduction to a proposed Japanese version, an idea which, in other circumstances, he would have shied away from. Honma never did produce a full translation, but he quoted extensively from it in his 1934 doctoral dissertation.[331]

Short though their acquaintance was, those meetings with 'the son of Oscar Wilde' would have a profound and long-lasting effect on Honma. During the Second World War, when the bombing of Tokyo became imminent, he sent the lock of Oscar's hair together with books which Vyvyan had given him and his own copy of that famous photograph, signed by Vyvyan, to his home town of Yonezawa for safe keeping. Sadly, other treasured mementos from his European trip were left behind and destroyed. After the war, in spite of having switched his academic interests from British aestheticism to the literature of the Meiji era in Japan, he continued to buy any books of Vyvyan's which were published and on his death in 1981 he bequeathed his Wilde collection to Jissen University where he had been teaching in his retirement. Of the eighteen books by my father in the university library, fifteen came from Honma's collection and the library now preserves very carefully and reverently both the photograph and that lock of hair. On his 1882 lecture tour of America, Oscar Wilde announced his intention of going on to Japan but never actually made it; he would doubtless be amused to think that a small part of him made the trip nonetheless. Had I not been intrigued by that strange photograph and the series of serendipitous discoveries which followed, I might never have known about Honma Hisao, and I would have missed an important piece in the complex historical puzzle of *De Profundis*.

V yvyan's life in the 1920s was strangely similar to the double life he had been forced to lead as a teenager in the early years of the century, though it was now made more complicated by the death of Robbie Ross. Whilst alive, Robbie had managed the Wilde literary estate and passed the entire income from it over to Cyril and Vyvyan without taking a penny. He had played an extraordinarily selfless role, one which had allowed Oscar's two children to benefit financially from their father's works without having to suffer directly from any of the adverse effects of his still scandalous reputation. Other than close friends and family, few people had been aware of the link between the two Hollands and Oscar Wilde. In Cyril's case as an army officer, this concealment had been particularly important. Now, however, as the literary executor and sole beneficiary of the estate, my father had little choice but to reveal his heritage, but he still did so unwillingly. For example, when he was editing the two collections of Oscar's post-prison letters to Robbie Ross for publication in America, he wrote to Christopher Millard:

> In thinking things over I do not think that it is any use my signing the copies. If I could sign as V[yvyan] W[ilde] it would be right and proper, but I have an innate loathing of *noms de plume* and a still greater loathing of *noms de camouflage*. To sign as VW would be silly unless I meant to adopt the name . . . . I want to remain, as far as the American edition is concerned, in the background.[332]

Corresponding with Frank Harris a few years later about the latter's biography of Oscar and correcting some of the mistakes for a new edition, he insisted: 'I do not want you to acknowledge my interference anywhere in the book. I have a perfect craze for anonymity and self-effacement. Even in my translations from the French, by which I largely make my living, I never put my name on the title page.'[333] Paradoxically, though, given Vyvyan's reluctance to associate himself publicly with his father, it is more through the surviving correspondence about Oscar's estate than through personal letters that I have been able to piece together a picture— albeit very fragmented—of my father's life back then.

By the time I came on the scene and was old enough to take an interest in his past life, for him it was a distant memory and blurred by the intervening years. There were occasions when I caught a glimpse of it, as in the summer of 1962 when we walked round 'his' Chelsea in the early mornings together, but it was a superficial version, sanitized for a teenager. He wrote occasional diaries in the 20s and 30s, but only when abroad, so they told me where he had been, whom he had met and something about his travelling companions, but very little about himself. He was a meticulous preserver of letters written to him by close friends, something he doubtless learned from Robbie Ross, but of his own letters to those friends, relatively few have survived. He kept up a long correspondence with Roy Kennard, the son of Helen Carew who paid for Oscar's tomb in Paris and who had first introduced Vyvyan to Robbie Ross, but my father's letters to Roy have disappeared, probably down to indifference on the part of his executors. His letters to the Irish author Liam O'Flaherty, were destroyed by Liam before he died in 1984, and those to Charles Scott Moncrief were destroyed by Charles himself three years before his death in 1930.[334] In both cases the other half of the correspondence has survived, and begins to make sense of the conjectures I have always made about Vyvyan's state of mind at the time. Cyril's aim in life, and one which he expressed in that letter to his brother of 1914, was to wipe away the stain which their father's disgrace had brought on the family honour by 'being a man' and a soldier. Vyvyan's approach was entirely different and one of which Cyril, doubtless, would have thoroughly disapproved: he was going to make it quite clear in every possible way that he was a thoroughgoing heterosexual. Liam's and Charles's letters are witty, bawdy, gossipy, and laced with sexual innuendo on their own and their recipient's amorous adventures. Insofar as lengthy exchanges of correspondence tend to mirror each other, Vyvyan's must have been too—a fact confirmed by the survival of nine of his letters to Charles which he wrote between the 'bonfire' of 1927 and Charles's death.[335] He had much in common with Charles; they were both translators and linguists, they both loved French literature, and they had both known and loved Robbie Ross. I'm sure that the close relationship they enjoyed helped Vyvyan to a better understanding and acceptance of his own father's sexuality.

Another regular correspondent between the wars was Edward Heron-Allen, a friend of Oscar and Constance in the 1880s who subsequently became a friend of my father in the 1920s and a sort of mentor to him as Ross had been until his death. He was twenty-five years older than Vyvyan and an extraordinary polymath with interests including marine zoology, violin-making, Persian literature and palmistry but also literary erotica of which he had a fine collection. When he died in 1943, Vyvyan was one of his executors and made a point of 'cleaning up' the voluminous Heron-Allen papers, clearly including his own letters.[336] My father seems to have kept only two, a slender testimony to their twenty years of friendship. The others? Probably of too *risqué* a nature to be allowed to survive. He also, exceptionally, seems to have destroyed Heron-Allen's to him. There was no knowing where they might end up if not suppressed. Judging from Vyvyan's other correspondence, they likely contained nothing more scandalous than a few playful references to their respective lady-friends (promiscuous in my father's case and adulterous in Heron-Allen's) and their common interest in erotic books, but Vyvyan probably felt that the later 'rediscovery' of their correspondence might lead to further disagreeable comments on the family.[337]

Having lost his wife at the end of the war, Vyvyan seems to have been in no hurry to remarry. Among his lovers at that time—sequential rather than simultaneous—were Iris Barry, the film critic and historian, Kathleen Hale, the artist and author of the *Orlando* books, and Rebecca West; he seemed determined to lead the life of a strictly unattached, heterosexual bachelor.[338] Many years later, Marie-Jacqueline Lancaster, grand-daughter of Adrian Hope (Vyvyan's guardian), told me that in order to avoid any pressure to form permanent relationships, he used to intimate that he had an unwell wife living somewhere in the country—a convenient variation of the Jack/Ernest Worthing deception from his own father's comedy.

It was around this time, too, that my father started to build up an extraordinary library of erotic literature, mostly French from the 18th and 19th centuries which, far from being for clandestine enjoyment, he took great pleasure in sharing with others, further reinforcing his image of 'healthy' heterosexuality. The French author Julien Green, whose books Vyvyan translated, confirmed as much when he visited Vyvyan in 1936:

> Lunched today with Vyvyan Holland at his charming little house on the corner of Carlyle Square in Chelsea. Our conversation turned almost at once to Felicien Rops and even as we were starting on the sherry, Vyvyan Holland showed me, or rather started to show me, one of the most extraordinary collections of erotic books that I have ever seen. It's apparently the thing which interests him most in life. He loves, or says he loves, women . . . I stayed until five o'clock and all around us on the sofa, the chairs, everywhere, lay these beautifully bound erotic books.[339]

Vyvyan was never a 'clubbable' sort of man in the St. James's sense of the word, preferring the company of intelligent, creative women to that of hearty upper-class men. However, in the 1920s my father joined a couple of 'dining' clubs, such as the Sette of Odd Volumes and the Omar Khayyam Club, neither of which had fixed premises but which met several times a year in fashionable restaurants when a paper was read by a member to his fellow diners. On election to the Odd Volumes, a new member had to choose a pseudonym reflecting his profession or one of his interests and adopt a little pictorial cartouche representing it. In his self-deprecating way, Vyvyan called himself 'Idler' and his cartouche was a sloth hanging from a branch. Belonging to clubs fulfilled, in part, his desire to be accepted; to come in from the cold and no longer to feel the sense of social ostracism brought about by the family scandal. They were his way of being sociable without having to be Oscar Wilde's son; there was a common interest which united everyone and who you were was largely irrelevant. It must have compensated, too, for his lack of family. He had little or no contact with his uncle Otho's children, although for some years from 1921 he made an allowance of £100 a year out of the Wilde royalties to one of Otho's sons, Eugene.[340] He hardly knew his maternal grandmother, who had physically and mentally abused Constance as a teenager, though when she died in 1921 he attended her funeral out of a sense of family obligation. His only other close blood-relation was Dorothy (Dolly) Wilde, the daughter of Oscar's brother Willie, and of whose existence he was completely unaware until he returned from the war when she was already in her mid-twenties. They got on in a cousinly sort of way, but by the end of the decade the relationship had soured because Dolly, unlike Vyvyan, had been able to keep the family name and consistently put it to good use as 'Oscar Wilde's niece' in Natalie Barney's queer literary circle in Paris. Barney even reported her as saying: 'I am more like Oscar than he was like himself,' and my father told Rupert Hart-Davis that she was often introduced in Paris as 'la fille d'Oscar Wilde' a title, according to Vyvyan, which she was seldom at pains to deny and which must have been particularly galling for him.[341] On one occasion when Dolly asked him why he didn't love her more, he replied 'My dear Dolly, I would never dare be a *beau* to a *gousse*'—the dated French slang meaning 'a walker to a lesbian.' Matters weren't improved when Vyvyan discovered that she passed off some of his witticisms as her own: 'Of her half-hearted cock-teasing proclivities I once told her that one of her great faults was that she was always taking her horse to the water and then refusing to let him drink: a week later I found her laying claim to have said this herself.' She died of a drug overdose in 1941, and Vyvyan wrote at the time that he begrudged every bloom of the flowers that he sent to the funeral which he didn't attend. 'This is not so much because she disliked me personally, as that I hate all the hoodoo about "family." I have no family feeling whatever.'[342] The emotional wounds of an orphaned childhood were a very long time in healing.

Then there was the full-length portrait of Oscar by the American artist Harper Pennington which had hung in the back drawing-room of the Wilde's house in Tite Street. It had been saved by the Ernest and Ada Leverson from the sheriff's sale of Oscar's possessions when he was on remand in 1895 and passed subsequently to Robbie Ross, who in turn left it to Vyvyan. I am sure that Vyvyan had it for a while when he returned from the war, felt uncomfortable with it, and decided to dispose of it. As a very large painting, he was reluctant to hang it in his sitting-room and thus draw attention to the fact that Oscar was his father. He knew Millard had contacts in the library and collecting world and asked him to help dispose of it. In 1922 B. F. Stevens & Brown offered it to Henry Huntington in California, but he refused to buy it. It was eventually purchased by Harrison Post who donated it to his partner William Andrews Clark for his Los Angeles library.

This wasn't the first time my father had disposed of a piece of family memorabilia. When Oscar was reburied in Père Lachaise Cemetery in 1909, Robbie Ross removed the name-plate from the original Bagneux coffin and gave it to Vyvyan who less than a year later had passed it on to the collector, Walter Ledger.[343] Why? Perhaps it was too macabre a souvenir or maybe just part of his need to show that 'bits of his father' were unimportant to him though, deep down, they weren't even at that time.

In 1928 Vyvyan sold through the London booksellers Dulau & Co most of the Wilde books and manuscripts left to him by Robbie Ross, ostensibly because he did not want to be bothered by the increasing number of researchers wanting access to original Wilde materials. The catalogue makes no mention of his name and simply refers to him as 'The Younger Son of Oscar Wilde,' showing that he was still reluctant to be identified directly with his father.

Almost nothing about Vyvyan's relationship to his heritage nor his handling of his father's literary estate was to appear in his second volume of autobiography. When it was published forty years later, despite being advertised as by the 'author of *Son of Oscar Wilde*,' readers might reasonably have expected more revelations about Oscar's 'afterlife.'[344] But in retrospect it is hardly surprising, for by the time it appeared in 1966 my father had finally managed to put being 'the son of . . . ' behind him for good, so resurrecting it for a curious posterity has been left to me, a hundred years on.

On the cover of *Hutchinson's Magazine* for October 1921 there appeared a startling announcement: 'Remarkable literary discovery. New unpublished work by Oscar Wilde.' Inside, spread over just five pages was a short play set in Burma: 'For Love of the King' which had apparently been discovered in Paris by Henry Noble Hall, special correspondent of *The Times*. He had been approached by one, Mabel Cosgrove, who claimed not only to have grown up with Oscar Wilde and his elder brother Willie (despite being born in 1873, some twenty years after them), but to have been briefly engaged to Willie and subsequently 'remained on terms of intimacy with Lady Wilde.' This astonishing catalogue of lies was offered up in order to authenticate the typescript of the play which she said had been sent to her by Oscar for her 'amusement' at the end of November 1894, together with a letter explaining its origins. Twice widowed, Mabel Cosgrove also adopted her two married surnames (Mrs. Chan Toon and Mrs. Wodehouse Pearse), depending on whether she was trying to sell her forgeries or escape her creditors. Her first husband, Chan Toon was the son of a successful Burmese businessman and had been called to the Bar at the Middle Temple in 1888. He and Mabel married in 1893 and he was certainly not a 'Nephew of the King of Burma' as she would later maintain, adding to her ever-growing list of fantastical claims. Her second husband whom she married in 1911, Armine Wodehouse Pearse, had been killed in France shortly before the Armistice in 1918. It was to 'Mrs. Chan Toon' that the accompanying letter had been addressed, suspiciously over-emphasising the Burmese connection:

My dear Mrs. Chan Toon,

I am greatly repentant being so long in acknowledging receipt of Told on the Pagoda. I enjoyed reading the stories, and much admired their quaint and delicate charm. Burmah calls to me.

Under another cover I am sending you a fairy play entitled "For Love of the King," just for your own amusement. It is the outcome of long and luminous talks with your distinguished husband in the Temple and on the river, in the days when I was meditating writing a novel as beautiful and as intricate as a Persian praying-rug. I hope that I have caught the atmosphere.

I should like to see it acted in your Garden House on some night when the sky is a sheet of violet and the stars like women's eyes. Alas, it is not likely. I am in the throes of a new comedy . . . .

I was at Oakley Street on Thursday; my mother tells me she sends you a letter nearly every week. Constance desires to be warmly remembered, while I, who am bathing my brow in the perfume of water-lilies, lay myself at the feet of you and yours.

Oscar Wilde

To anyone even slightly familiar with Oscar's letters now that much of his correspondence has been published, this florid pastiche of his style is absurd, but since both the play and the letter were only typewritten, there was no chance of verifying them by a study of the manuscript. Aside from these blatant fabrications, there is a simple anomaly which no one seems to have noticed: Oscar is thanking Mrs. Chan Toon for a book of stories (rather tardily, so probably received in early November 1894) which, from its title page, was only published in 1895.

None of this seems to have bothered The Century Magazine in New York, to which she sold the American rights and which published it with lavish oriental illustrations in December 1921. The editor did, however, preface the play with the following note: 'In the instance of the discovery of so interesting an unpublished manuscript, there is always the possibility that some may question its authenticity . . . . It will, in any event, be diverting to watch the critics discuss the question of its genuineness.' Like collectors of dubiously attributed Wildeiana, who try to ensure their pieces are publicly exhibited as often as possible to dispel any doubts about their provenance, Mabel Cosgrove, in having *For Love of the King* accepted by literary magazines on both sides of the Atlantic, was doing just that. And it worked. By early November 1921 she had persuaded Methuen & Co, the publishers of Oscar's *Collected Works*, to print the play as a supplementary volume. To add weight to the story she even maintained that Robert Ross had written to her wanting to include it with the other works back in 1908, but Mrs. Chan Toon, as she still was then, felt that such a 'personal gift' should remain unpublished. Surprisingly, Methuen accepted all her inventions but still remained cautious; she asked for a one-off payment of £200, but when the contract was signed on 7 November, she had settled for £50 promising to produce the manuscript the next day—which she never did. It wasn't until 26 May the following year that the publishers finally received, not the promised manuscript, but a typed carbon copy from Cosgrove's solicitors with handwritten corrections. Understandably they asked whether these corrections had been made by Wilde himself and, through the solicitors, received the reply that, no, they had been made by Cosgrove but with Wilde's approval. Nor did they ask to see the letter from Robert Ross which would have helped to support her claims and so, on 19 October, it appeared in a binding uniform with the rest of Oscar's works and the edition of 1000 copies was over-subscribed before publication.[345]

The reception of *For Love of the King* by the press was at best lukewarm. The *Evening Standard* described it as 'hastily written, lazily exuberant stuff'; the *TLS* asked: 'We cannot help wondering whether Wilde would have cared to see this . . . put out among his collected works'; and the *Weekly Dispatch* said sniffily: 'Wilde's passion for sensuous effects—riots of colour, gorgeous jewels, indescribable perfumes, and so forth—finds full play in this Eastern setting . . . but it cannot be said to add to his literary reputation . . . . but probably he himself did not take the task very seriously.' Surprisingly, Christopher Millard, who had by now become the acknowledged expert on Wilde's writings, did not query its authenticity, especially given his later claim that he 'had promised Robert Ross to keep an eye on the Oscar Wilde estate' and admitted that he 'thought Wilde might have scribbled it off.'[346] Three weeks after publication, and presumably on the strength of the sell-out edition, Mabel Cosgrove, tried her luck with Methuen once more and offered them the film and stage rights for £1000 on condition they paid within seven days. The offer was turned down, but the resourceful Cosgrove still managed to exploit them a few months later by assigning them to her unsuspecting landlady in lieu of unpaid rent.

News of the 'unpublished' work by Oscar Wilde reached the ears of the American bibliophile William Andrews Clark, with whom my father was already in contact, and he wrote to Vyvyan asking for details. Vyvyan replied saying that its publication had come as a complete surprise to him and continued: 'There appears to be no doubt whatever of the authenticity of the manuscript. My father was a great friend of the lady in question and had a good deal of correspondence with her.'[347] When I first read this letter in the Clark Library archives, I was astonished. What motive could my father have had to be so misleading? He was not trying to sell the manuscript/typescript because it wasn't his to sell, and since he was in regular touch with Millard at the time they must have discussed its provenance. One possible explanation was that if Methuen had seen fit to publish without his permission as Wilde's literary executor, far from questioning the authenticity he would give it his backing and then claim royalties on the sales.[348] What Robbie would have said of this somewhat unethical attitude hardly bears thinking about.

The amount of attention paid publicly to the whole affair was relatively small and *For Love of the King* might simply have remained classified as Wilde apocrypha, had Mabel Cosgrove not tried to pass off more Wilde forgeries a couple of years later. She offered a London bookseller six letters purportedly written by

Wilde to her which were blatant forgeries: one was dated three years after Wilde's death and another mentioned that he had just won the Newdigate Prize for poetry at Oxford when Cosgrove would have been five. The bookseller suggested she should offer them to Christopher Millard as an antiquarian dealer, which she did, emphasising that she was the original owner of *For Love of the King* and little suspecting that he was the pseudonymous 'Stuart Mason' and the most knowledgeable Wildean specialist of the time. Millard already had his doubts about the play and these letters simply confirmed them.[349]

On 28 June 1925, the day after her visit, Millard wrote to Methuen, saying that Cosgrove had tried to sell him forged Wilde letters and had told him that the typescript of the play had corrections in Wilde's handwriting—quite a different story from the one she had told the publishers two years before. An examination of the typescript, said Millard, would establish once and for all whether it was authentic or not. He took the trouble to emphasise that even if the work proved to be a forgery, he was sure that Methuen had acted in good faith. They complied and having seen the typescript, Millard wrote to *The Times* detailing why there should be serious doubts about whether Wilde had ever written the play and in a separate covering note explained that the case was far stronger than he had presented it, but that it would now be up to the publishers and Mabel Cosgrove to produce their counter-evidence to prove its authenticity. *The Times* returned his letter with the excuse that it had no room to print it. Millard sent it on to the *Times Literary Supplement* whose editor expressed misgivings about printing it because of the possible legal implications. Millard was sure that the real reason for their refusal was a reluctance to upset the publishers and lose advertising revenue. He made one last attempt to publicise his findings by writing in more forceful terms to *Hutchinson's Magazine,* the original publishers, directly accusing Cosgrove of fraud and suggesting that they take legal action. He also expressed the hope that she might sue for libel, thus exposing the whole affair. They took no action. No one seemed anxious to become involved in Millard's crusade, for that is what it had become. So, mindful of his promise to Robbie Ross, on 28 July he printed a four-page folio circular entitled 'Who wrote *For Love of the King*?' reproducing his entire correspondence with Mabel Cosgrove, Methuen & Co, and the press. There were, incidentally, two editions of the circular: the first referred to 'Mr. Vyvyan Holland, who is Oscar Wilde's only surviving son and his father's literary executor' but Vyvyan objected to having his relationship to Oscar stated openly and Millard was forced to reprint before many had been distributed, calling him merely the 'literary executor.'[350] The circular for sale to the public was priced at one penny and Millard offered to send copies of it free of charge to all the main London bookshops together with a poster to be displayed: SENSATIONAL CHARGE OF LITERARY FORGERY. WHO WROTE 'FOR LOVE OF THE KING' OSCAR WILDE OR MRS. CHAN TOON? Exposing the forgery had taken on a degree of urgency since Cosgrove had persuaded William Rider & Sons to announce publication of her memoir entitled *Oscar Wilde as I Knew Him*, which would have been a work of total fiction but in the end, thankfully, never materialised. Unfortunately, Millard's impatience to expose the forgery led him to be incautious in the wording of his covering letter of 17 August to the booksellers: 'With the assistance of Mrs. Chan Toon this eminently respectable firm of publishers has succeeded in foisting on an unsuspecting public 1000 copies of a book at 8/6d for which, but for Oscar Wilde's name and the imprint of Methuen & Co Ltd, no one would have paid 8½d.' The publishers responded by placing an announcement in the Personal Columns of *The Times* on 29 August saying that they would continue to sell the book until forgery could be proved and warned Millard through their solicitors of the potentially libellous nature of his statement. Undeterred, Millard issued one of his catalogues early in 1926 offering a copy of the book for sale and repeating in the description his accusations of 'a forgery foisted on an unsuspecting public by an unscrupulous woman now serving a sentence of imprisonment for theft.' Mabel Cosgrove had indeed been arrested and tried for stealing £240 in £10 notes from her landlady and sentenced on 12 January to six months in prison. Methuen, who had run out of patience, finally issued libel proceedings.

The case was tried from 9-11 November and centred almost entirely on whether Millard had libelled Methuen in declaring that they had 'foisted' a work of forgery on a paying public and thereby called into question the honesty of the publishing house. Methuen's main witness was its chairman, E. V. Lucas who still maintained (he could hardly do otherwise) that the play was by Wilde. He admitted to having written the publishers' preface but refused to sign it saying that he regarded the work as 'awful tosh.' Millard's defence counsel pointed to the anomalies in Mabel Cosgrove's account of how she had come by the play and the chronological absurdity of maintaining she had been on terms of intimate friendship with the Wilde family, all of which Methuen should have verified as genuine before publishing. Unfortunately, none of this carried any weight with the jury who found in favour of Methuen and Millard was ordered to pay £100 in damages, all the trial costs, and bound by an injunction to refrain from further comment on the matter. Although he had lost the case, Millard did admit to Walter Ledger that he never really anticipated winning since it was his libel which was being judged and not Mabel Cosgrove's forgery. Nonetheless, he had the satisfaction of exposing Cosgrove as a fraudster and probably prevented her from taking in others with her imagined links to the Wilde family and her Wilde 'manuscripts.' It did not stop her, however, from trying to sell an alleged interview sometime later which she had had with George Bernard Shaw.[351] She also wrote to the War Office in 1936 from an address in Inverness enquiring about Vyvyan's military service and was told that the details were confidential, but if there was another elaborate scam in the making, it never materialised.

Millard was not a wealthy man and the costs of the libel action would probably have bankrupted him had my father and others not come to his rescue. Vyvyan started a fund to which forty-five friends and admirers from the world of letters put their names and bailed him out, including names such as H. G. Wells, Shane Leslie, and Holbrook Jackson. In recognition of their generosity, Millard printed an elegant note of thanks listing the donors which he sent it to all of them.[352] Speculating on what the dead might think about the actions of the living is a fairly hackneyed exercise, but in the case of Oscar Wilde it is not inappropriate. Petty criminals and forgers fascinated him and in 1886 he prepared and delivered a lecture on Thomas Chatterton who had 'created' the poetry of the fictional mediaeval monk Thomas Rowley before being exposed by Horace Walpole and committing suicide by arsenic at the age of seventeen. I don't know whether Oscar would have approved of the literary efforts of Mabel Cosgrove, but as the improbable author of the much quoted 'Imitation is the sincerest form of flattery which mediocrity can pay to genius,' he would certainly have been flattered.

The fact that Oscar's tarnished reputation had recovered sufficiently by the early 1920s to make him an interesting (if not entirely acceptable) literary figure partly accounts for why Mabel Cosgrove managed to fool so many people with her inventions and lies. It was a time when anything in the way of books and manuscripts connected with him were being sold for increasingly large sums at auction: the 423 items of the John B. Stetson Oscar Wilde Collection, for example, made over $46,000 at the Anderson Galleries sale in New York in April 1920. The climate was ideal for forgers who knew that with antiquarian desirability and high prices, potential customers would tend to let excitement overcome caution, which is exactly what happened when William Figgis, the owner of Dublin's prestigious Hodges Figgis bookshop, received a letter dated 5 April 1921 purporting to come from André Gide in Paris. The writer was offering Figgis a number of Wilde manuscripts including that of *The Importance of Being Earnest*, as well as letters written to him by Wilde. Figgis was extremely interested but asked first to see them on approval and took no further action until the autumn. The London booksellers Maggs Brothers received a very similar letter only a few days later from the same Paris address, but this time purporting to come from Pierre Louÿs who offered them the manuscript of *Salomé* as originally written in French by Wilde, whose grammatical quirks Louÿs had helped polish up at the time it was written back in 1891. Maggs purchased it but soon established that the paper on which it had been written was made in America and not in circulation until fourteen years after Wilde's death. They then obtained the address of the real Pierre Louÿs in Paris and wrote asking for an explanation, which elicited an immediate telegram from Louÿs to say that someone must be impersonating him. However, he seemed reluctant to take any action, aware of the time and inconvenience that would be involved. As far as Maggs were concerned that was the end of the matter. Not so Figgis and the false André Gide. Figgis had initially been more cautious than Maggs, but by October had convinced himself that the manuscripts he had been offered were genuine and duly paid for *The Importance of Being Earnest* and various letters from Wilde to Gide. By now, 'Gide,' perhaps worried that his cover might have been blown by his dealing with Maggs as 'Louÿs,' had changed his mailing address from 11 rue Scribe (the address of American Express) to 4 rue Ventadour (Munroe & Co Bankers) and asked for the cheques to be made out in the name of D. Hope 'my secretary.' Although the London bookseller, Davis & Orioli, to whom Figgis had tried to sell on some of the manuscripts, returned them as spurious, Figgis was still convinced of their authenticity. Even when *The Importance* was found to be incomplete, 'Gide,' professing himself to be equally surprised, came up with the plausible and complicated explanation that Robert Ross (conveniently dead) had sold Act 2 to Octave Mirbeau (also dead) whose family probably still owned it. He added that Mme Mirbeau was away in Florence and that he would enquire on her return, leaving himself time to fabricate it. Duly, by the end of the year 'Gide' had written the missing part as well as the complete manuscripts of other works including *The Ballad of Reading Gaol* and shamelessly offered them all to Figgis as a complete package. Meanwhile, at the beginning of December, Figgis had been in London and showed his purchases to Maggs who saw that the 'Gide' and 'Louÿs' manuscripts were in the same hand and immediately alerted Figgis to that fact that they were probably dealing with the same forger. Figgis then decided that a face-to-face meeting was called for and in the first week of January, made his way to Paris. There, through Frederic Harrison (a former employee now managing Brentano's bookshop), he met Dorian Hope who claimed to be André Gide's secretary, and who explained that Gide himself was unavoidably absent in Italy. Although Figgis and Harrison seemed satisfied with Hope's bona fides, there must have been some residual doubt as they ascertained the real André Gide's address and paid him a visit unannounced. It rapidly became clear that Hope was the author of an elaborate fraud and Gide vowed to take immediate action which he did, lodging a complaint with the police on 7 January.

Harrison continued to string Hope along in order to help the police track him down and the case came to court on 1 June 1922. On 8 June judgment was given in Hope's absence for fraud, attempted fraud, and for bouncing a cheque on the Hôtel du Volga in the rue de Seine where he had been living. He was described as Dorian Hope, a twenty-five-year-old American student, from Richmond, Virginia and sentenced to three years in prison and a fine of 500 francs.[353] Astonishingly, Figgis still held out hope that not all the manuscripts he had purchased were forged: 'In looking back now on the whole incident it seems very strange to me that the question of genuineness in the MSS was not allowed to drop forthwith. Their provenance was proved bad which should have been sufficient. As it was, the question lingered on for several months.'[354] In June Figgis took the manuscripts to London to show the bookseller Christopher Millard who declared them to be genuine and purchased a couple on his own account for resale, but a few weeks later, having seen the 'Louÿs' forgeries which Maggs Bros had kept, was forced to recant and write grovelling letters of apology to his customers, and especially to Figgis:

This letter is more painful for me to write than it will be for you to read . . . I see in a flash all the forger's blunders which I tried to explain away . . . Yet so convinced was I of the genuineness of all these letters and manuscripts that I found explanations that satisfied me . . . Of my own feelings I cannot speak and of course I shall never again put myself forward as an expert on Wilde manuscripts.[355]

By now 'Dorian Hope' had disappeared and Millard started to put it about that he strongly suspected Hope of being Fabian Lloyd, the son of Constance Wilde's brother Otho and consequently Oscar's nephew by marriage. It was a neat explanation and seemed to tie up of all the loose ends, despite the obvious age discrepancy, Fabian by then being thirty-five.

In 1884, to the snobbish disapproval of his relatives and two weeks after his sister had married Oscar, Otho Lloyd had married his aunt's housemaid, Clara 'Nellie' Hutchinson. The marriage took place in Lausanne, far from the gossip-mongers of London, but they agreed to divorce four years later when their second child Fabian was just a year old. Nellie, anxious to maintain her bourgeois status, rapidly got remarried to a respectable Swiss doctor and Fabian, understandably something of a problem child with all the family upheavals, was sent off to board at a college in St. Gallen in the hope that institutional discipline would tame him. In the long term it had precisely the opposite effect giving him a life-long disregard for authority and disdain for his mother's bourgeois aspirations. Between 1909 and 1915 he lived largely in Paris where he started to associate with the artists of the Surrealist and Dadaist circles, and he became the amateur light-heavyweight boxing champion of France by a walk-over in 1910 but never won another fight thereafter. In 1912 under the pseudonym of Arthur Cravan he started writing and publishing a proto-Dadaist literary magazine called *Maintenant* in the third number of which appeared a piece entitled 'Oscar Wilde est vivant!' It was an imaginary account of an evening spent getting drunk on cherry brandy with his uncle by marriage who told him that he had just finished four plays for Sarah Bernhardt. In 1915, to avoid the French conscription, Fabian left for America by way of Barcelona where, to make some badly needed money, he went six rounds with the world heavyweight champion, Jack Johnson. Arriving in New York in early 1917 he met and fell for the artist Mina Loy whom he married a year later in Mexico. Then, with Mina pregnant and the two of them nearly penniless, Fabian despatched her on a boat to Buenos Aires where he promised to join her a month later. He was never seen again, variously reported as being lost at sea in a small boat, murdered by Mexican pirates, or killed in a bar brawl. A picaresque life and a mysterious disappearance which lent itself perfectly to his possible resurrection in Paris as the forger of Wilde manuscripts, and it was this explanation which remained more or less undisputed for the next sixty years.[356] My own theory is that the prospect of becoming father to a child and stepfather to two others by Mina's previous marriage, was more than his vagabond nature could handle, so he changed his name once again and started anew somewhere he was entirely unknown. In reality Fabian Lloyd/Arthur Cravan was entirely innocent of Millard's charges and the perpetrator of the forgeries was a young American named Brett Holland.

Brett Holland (no relation) was born in Fork Union near Richmond, Virginia in 1898 and spent his childhood between there and Gaston, North Carolina. By 1916 he appeared to be making a part-time career for himself as an in-store female impersonator, a skill which he would later put to good use at a naval 'entertainment evening' after enlisting in the US Naval Reserve Force at the end of 1917. In early 1920 he moved to New York and found employment in the poetry department of the publisher G. P. Putnam's Sons, doubtless helped by having some of his verse published in the *Richmond Times* the year before, a line of which, lifted verbatim from one of Oscar Wilde's own poems, already shows how well he knew the latter's works. In New York he made friends with another young poet, Augustin Lardy, who died in the spring of 1920, whereupon 'Dorian Hope,' as Brett Holland had now started to style himself, asked Lardy's mother to let him have any of his friend's manuscript poems and he would arrange to have them published by his employer. This was duly done in the summer, but they appeared under Hope's own name and with the title *Pearls and Pomegranates* (another phrasal borrowing from Oscar, this time from his fairy tale 'The Nightingale and the Rose') and having obtained a passport under his new alias, he set sail for Europe at the end of August. True to form he gave his London address on the ship's manifest as The Ritz but stayed at a boarding house in Earl's Court. On board, he made the acquaintance of Michael Fallon, the Roman Catholic Bishop of London, Ontario, by the use of whose name he contrived to meet Alfred Douglas. It was not the only time he would latch onto a public figure with a view to some form of personal advantage. Douglas eventually saw through him and in March 1921 printed a warning to the readers of *Plain English*, the magazine he was editing at the time, that Sebastian (another alias) or Dorian Hope had been telling people that he was the Assistant Editor of the magazine which was entirely untrue. By this time Hope had reached Paris where bad news from America did not take long to reach him. *Pearls and Pomegranates* had been reviewed in the *New York Times*, quoting a poem which caught the attention of one, Miriam Vedder. She recognised the verses as her own and complained to the publisher who immediately withdrew the book from sale. As it was, Miriam Vedder and Augustin Lardy had been friends and had exchanged poems on a regular basis. Since some were unsigned carbon copies, Mrs. Lardy could not have known that the manuscripts she passed on to Hope were by two authors, one of whom was still alive and who, by sheer chance, saw her poem in the *New York Times*. Much was made of the plagiarism in the press including the unpaid tradesmen's bills Hope had left behind, with it all being reported at exactly the time Hope was starting to masquerade as Pierre Louÿs to Maggs and André Gide and to Figgis.[357]

Since his dishonesty had now been made public and he was

embarking on a more criminal career with his forgeries, on 20 April 1921 Hope took the precaution of having his passport amended at the American Consulate in Paris. Originally designating the British Isles, France, and Italy as destinations, he asked for Spain, Portugal, Scandinavia, and Switzerland to be added. Should he need to make another 'disappearance,' the more countries in which to do it, the better. As the Wilde manuscripts scam ran its course, and Hope became aware that the French police were actively looking for him, on 8 March 1922 he had even more countries added to the list including Hungary, Albania, Greece, Egypt, and India. Once his conviction in the Paris courts for fraud was official, he was liable to be arrested and staying in France became impossible. So he moved back to London, 'buried' the aliases of Dorian and Sebastian Hope, destroyed his passport and applied for an emergency one in the name of Brett Holland giving his address as Magdalen College, Oxford (Oscar's alma mater) where he claimed to be 'studying.' The college, needless to say, has no record of him at all under any of his aliases. The newly resurrected Brett Holland then decided to return to the States but since the name Holland had been linked with Hope in the matter of the New York unpaid debts, he travelled via Canada conveniently giving Bishop Michael Fallon's address as his interim destination.

The rest of Brett Holland's short life was spent less in outright criminal activity and more as a sort of literary conman. Back in America he persuaded Emanuel Haldeman-Julius, publisher of the popular 'Little Blue Books' imprint, to allow him to edit several volumes which owed more to Holland's imagination than to historical fact, most of them centring around his entirely fictitious friendship with Sarah Bernhardt. Having reinvented himself yet again with the suitably French-sounding name of Sylvestre Dorian, he concocted *Oscar Wilde's Letters to Sarah Bernhardt* and wrote of his own relationship with the actress in *Sarah Bernhardt as I Knew Her*, both of which are larded with unattributed epigrams and phrases from Wilde's works. He claimed to have known her for the last five years of her life—she died on 26 March 1923—and to have seen her on a weekly basis for the last two, all of which is in direct conflict with what we know for certain about his own life. In an act of astonishing effrontery given his own past activities, he also contributed an article to the January 1925 issue of the *Haldeman-Julius Monthly,* the publishing house's newsletter, entitled 'The plagiarism of Oscar Wilde' which started: 'To declare that Oscar Wilde was a plagiarist would be like running through the streets and enthusiastically proclaiming to a jaded world that the sky is blue or that two and two make four.' He spent much of his time from 1926 onwards as the European correspondent for various press associations like the North American Newspaper Alliance filing copy, for example, about the latest women's fashions in Paris on which, given his earlier penchant for cross-dressing, he would have been well-qualified to comment. Partly resident in Brussels, he appears to have latched onto Professor Auguste Piccard, the physicist and explorer who was teaching at the Free University and was due to undertake a lecture tour of America in January 1933. Dorian accompanied him to the States describing himself variously as the professor's business manager, biographer, travelling companion, and translator. They parted company when Dorian sold the details of a private dinner party conversation between the professor and the aviator Charles Lindbergh to a newspaper for $40. Unable to resist the lure of literary invention, one of his final contributions to the genre was to forge correspondence between himself and Rudyard Kipling but which only came to light when sold at auction in 1936.[358] Holland/Hope/Dorian was killed on 23 April 1934 when his car left the road and overturned near Fayetteville, North Carolina. In the car with him was Private James Richards, 27, an enlisted soldier from the local military barracks at Fort Bragg, who also died. Their common interest is unlikely to have been the finer points of lyric poetry.

The obituary which appeared in his home town newspaper might well have been written by Brett Holland himself, so full was it of exaggerations and untruths, doubtless gleaned from publicity material for the lectures he was then delivering: the biographies of Lillie Langtry, Isadora Duncan, and Auguste Piccard which he had never written; the non-graduate of Oxford University; the fictitious 'residences maintained in Paris, Nice and Brussels.'[359] So ended the Walter Mitty-like life of one of Oscar Wilde's most prolific forgers. The final irony was that as an ex-serviceman and as 'one of those few who have served our nation with dignity and honour,' he enjoyed a free burial in Arlington National Cemetery. His mother, a government clerk in Washington at the time, would have known how to apply and thus ensured that her son was remembered as a 'good American boy.' Most of his 'creations' are now safely in captivity with institutions or responsible owners, but occasionally a couple of them surface for sale and are duly recognised as forgeries and withdrawn, to the huge disappointment of the vendors whose ancestors, more often than not, purchased them in America in the 1930s. One such collection was doing the rounds in New York in June 2007, identical in style to the Gide/ Louÿs forgeries of 1921, even with the 'wrong' purple ink which Oscar never used. A forged letter from Oscar to Pierre Louÿs (probably from the same collection) was 'floated' at Bonham's in San Francisco a few months before to test the market but was withdrawn as a forgery before the sale and is now safely in the Clark Library at UCLA. As a result, the New York manuscripts were exposed as fakes and I suggested to the dealer handling them that the owners should do the ethical thing and give them to an institution like the Clark.[360] The suggestion was dismissed and for all I know the 'original manuscript' of Oscar's 'The Happy Prince' is still at large. The afterlife of Brett Holland has thus proved to be almost as long-lasting as that of the man whose manuscripts he was so adept at forging.[361]

CHAPTER FOUR
FRANK HARRIS'S *LIFE OF WILDE*

In 1916 there appeared, privately printed in New York, a two-volume biography of Oscar Wilde entitled *Oscar Wilde: His Life and Confessions.* The author was Frank Harris and it was more of a literary docu-drama than a carefully researched life, with Harris reproducing complete pages of improbably verbatim conversations with Wilde who had died sixteen years before. Harris had been working at the idea of such a biography since shortly after Wilde's death, though in the first instance he felt Robbie Ross should produce most of it and that he and Douglas should contribute a few pages each:

> Douglas and I had a long talk to Humphries of Hatchard's in regard to the book to be written about Oscar. The foundation of it—three-fourths of it—should of course be your diary, and no one could do this work better than you yourself. I would like to confine my work to an appreciation of his genius and lovable nature . . . . A sonnet or two from Douglas and a few pages from myself might add something to it; but, of course, the main thing will be yours.[362]

In light of later events the idea of these three collaborating on a life of Wilde is hilarious, but it came to nothing which was probably just as well.

Frank Harris and Oscar first became friends in 1891 when Harris was editing the *Fortnightly Review* and published Oscar's essay 'The Soul of Man Under Socialism.' At the time of Oscar's libel action against the Marquess of Queensberry, Harris agreed to give evidence on Oscar's behalf to refute the Marquess's claim that *The Picture of Dorian Gray* was an obscene and sodomitical novel, though in fact he was never called as a witness. He did, however, strongly advise Oscar not to proceed with the action. In between Oscar's two criminal trials he also offered him a chance to jump bail and even cover the bondsmen's losses, but his offer was turned down. Harris visited him in prison, gave him some new clothes and a generous cheque on his release and, later, when Oscar was living an impecunious existence in Paris, invited him to spend three months on the French Riviera in the hope that it might rekindle some of his friend's old brilliance. Sadly, it didn't. In 1899 Oscar even dedicated the published version of *An Ideal Husband* to Harris: 'a slight tribute to his power and distinction as an artist, his chivalry and nobility as a friend.' In short, Harris was nothing if not generous, and even if he didn't know Oscar as well as Ross did, he was certainly well-qualified to write his biography.

He started work on it in the winter of 1909/10 when he was staying as a guest of his friend Lord Grimthorpe at the Villa Cimbrone in Rapallo. Completed in three months, the proofs of a first draft ran to 320 pages and as he wrote to the artist Augustus John at the time: 'I had to write it; it was in me and now I have done it I feel better . . . . Oscar had been in me ten or fifteen years and I had to get rid of him.'[363] Harris was well aware that he needed Robbie Ross's permission to publish the letters which Oscar had written to him and, more importantly, Robbie's advice and good-will, so he wrote to him accordingly in July 1911. Robbie's reply was cautious. Yes, Harris had his permission to publish the letters, but no, he didn't want to read the proofs as he didn't want to take any responsibility for opinions and conclusions with which he might possibly disagree. Additionally, he suggested that Harris should only say he had 'the permission of Wilde's literary executor and administrator' and not mention him by name. He knew that Harris would not be treating Alfred Douglas lightly in the Wilde story and there was no point in further exacerbating his already strained relationship with Douglas by being seen to ally himself too closely with the author. He finished his letter by saying 'I am sure that your proposed work will be far more interesting than anyone else's.'[364]

By 1913 Harris's book had grown to 450 pages in proof and he was already planning publication; in the meantime Douglas's failed libel action against Arthur Ransome and his biography had taken place and now Ross saw Harris's *Life of Wilde* as a useful weapon in the open warfare between himself and Douglas:

> I am very anxious that all the facts in your forthcoming book should be pedantically accurate . . . . However, there are a heap of things I must talk to you about and I would rather that it was delayed a little . . . I want to be able to say when it is published that I have read it, that everything in it is *true* and that I might only differ on small points of opinion or estimate of Oscar.[365]

In December, assuming that Ross might have changed his mind over publicly associating himself with the book, Harris wrote to him again saying that he would like to use his name both in a prospectus and the preface as having given permission for Oscar's letters and also as having endorsed the book itself. Robbie was distinctly unhappy with the idea. Despite the help he had given Harris, the Ransome trial had shown him the lengths to which Douglas was prepared to go in order to injure him for officially giving support to a Wilde biographer. A prospectus, he added, would allow Douglas to apply for an injunction to prevent publication of anything which might reflect badly on him. As a precaution, he even suggested that Harris backdate asking permission for the letters to 1906 when Robbie became the official literary executor so as to predate his quarrels with Douglas.[366]

Robbie seems to have changed his mind frequently over whether or not to read Harris's book in proof, depending on the progress of his court cases with Douglas and Crosland. He remembered the unpleasantness which arose out of the Ransome trial and the arguments over the extent to which he had or hadn't helped the author and feared being the object of Douglas's fury yet again over

Harris. In April the following year he asked Harris to send the latest proofs to Christopher Millard, adding 'No doubt if I am passing and he is out, I shall call and have a squint at them.' At least if ever questioned under oath he would be able to say that Harris had never sent him proofs, nor had he read them. Nevertheless, he continued to answer queries until Harris left for New York in October 1914.

At that time, Harris was more or less forced to leave Europe because of his publicly expressed pro-German and anti-British sentiments, but it made publication of his *Life of Wilde* something of a logistical problem. The proofs were corrected and now ran to 600 pages, but the British printer was made aware of certain libellous statements in the book (presumably those concerning Douglas) and consequently refused to print it. It finally appeared in two volumes, 'Printed and Published by the Author' in New York in the summer of 1916, but even there Harris ran into difficulties. Before publication Harris had submitted the proofs to John Sumner, the Secretary of the New York Society for the Suppression of Vice who pronounced it disreputable:

> I am returning herewith the proofs of your proposed publication . . . . I read the matter carefully up to the point where the litigation between Mr. Wilde and the Marquess of Queensberry terminated so abruptly and regret to have to express the opinion that the publication and sale of this work would be a violation of our state laws . . . . I believe that the book in its present form would make an appeal entirely on its salacious qualities.[367]

Once the book was ready Harris was anxious to get it distributed in England but the problem, as ever, was Alfred Douglas. At the slightest hint of a disparaging remark, he was liable to serve the author and bookseller with a writ for libel and Harris's *Life of Wilde* contained plenty. As such, the book had to be promoted by word of mouth and copies made discreetly available, so Harris appealed to his young friend and admirer, the author Hesketh Pearson, for help. Pearson sent out copies to various authors and critics who might be persuaded to write favourably about it, notably H. G. Wells, Arnold Bennett, Joseph Conrad, Rudyard Kipling, and John Galsworthy, all of whom distanced themselves from it. The one exception was Bernard Shaw who wrote Harris a long letter of appreciation about his meetings with Oscar and a candid assessment of his life and works, saying of the book that it was 'the best literary portrait of Wilde in existence.' Although as an endorsement it was not originally intended for publication, Shaw realised that the use of his name in a popular edition of Harris's biography would increase its sales dramatically in America and gave him permission to use it. Harris wrote delightedly about this to Robbie Ross and at the same time asked him to provide any corrections he felt necessary and some personal views of his own.[368] He also said that Douglas was trying to peddle a new book in America entitled 'The Wilde Myth' which had been turned down by the publisher Martin Secker in London as simply being a replay of his 1914 mendacious and self-justifying *Oscar Wilde and Myself*. By this time Robbie, badly bruised after his legal wranglings with Douglas and knowing that Harris's book was only published in America, was now happy to comply with a list of corrections including a few well-aimed criticisms of Douglas.[369] The second 'popular edition' of Harris's book duly came out in early 1918, again privately published by the author, and with 'Criticisms by Robert Ross' and 'Memories of Oscar Wilde by Bernard Shaw' as an appendix. Harris had Shaw's contribution advertised in gold blocking on the front cover and, if one believes his estimates of selling over 40,000 copies, it certainly helped promote the book in America. When Harris's book first appeared in 1916, Douglas wrote to one of his many correspondents that he hadn't seen a copy and didn't want to; by early 1918 he said that he was going to obtain a copy of the book, take it to a magistrate with his solicitor and get a warrant for Harris's arrest on a charge of criminal libel. Then as a counterblast (and since he had been unable to get his *Wilde Myth* into print), Alfred Douglas reissued *Oscar Wilde and Myself* early in 1919 with a new preface in which he wrote: 'I was born into this world chiefly to be the instrument, whether I would or no, of exposing and smashing the Wilde cult and the Wilde myth.' In 1921, still frustrated that he could not drag Harris through the courts and expose what he regarded as the lies written about him, he wrote: 'I am powerless to prevent the circulation of Harris's book (since it is published in America), though of course if he ever returns to England I shall immediately take criminal proceedings against him.'[370]

Harris returned to Europe in January 1923 having written and published the first volume of his semi-pornographic autobiography *My Life and Loves* which he hoped was going to make his fortune, but he hadn't reckoned with the obscenity laws of the countries in which he was hoping to sell it. Printed in Germany and 'published' in Paris, it was confiscated in France, Italy, Britain, and America. By early 1925, he was seriously short of money and living in Nice when he heard that Alfred Douglas was in town staying with Gladys Brooke, wife of the third White Rajah of Sarawak whose mother-in-law, the 'Ranee,' had been Constance Wilde's friend and confidante during her last years in Italy.[371] Harris was quite friendly with the Dyang Muda—to give Gladys her official title—and started besieging her flat in the hope of meeting Douglas and being able to sort out their differences which would allow him to sell his *Life of Wilde* in England. In February, Reginald Turner, an old friend of Douglas, Ross and Wilde, had been in Nice and pointed out to Harris several errors in his book, which he otherwise regarded as an excellent and vivid literary portrait. In particular, he said, the facts surrounding Oscar's death and reburial in 1909 which had been provided to Harris by Ross were hugely over-exaggerated. Turner also told him that Ross's animosity towards Douglas would certainly have coloured much of what he had told Harris about the relationship between Oscar and Bosie after prison and this set Harris thinking about other misinterpretations and mistakes he might have made by relying on Ross's help.[372] He knew there was a big market for the book in

England, but he was also aware that Douglas would immediately start libel proceedings against anyone who tried to sell it because of the way he had been depicted. Yet Harris's motives for wanting to pacify Douglas weren't entirely materialistic. He'd had unsolicited praise for his book and, even allowing for some extra Harris-style 'colouring' of the facts, he wanted it, broadly speaking, to be as accurate a tribute to Oscar's life as possible.[373] It was entirely consistent with what he had written in his introduction:

> Oscar Wilde was a friend of mine for many years: I could not help prizing him to the very end: he was always to me a charming, soul-animating influence . . . . The whole story is charged with tragic pathos and unforgettable lessons . . . . No book could have been written more reverently than this book of mine.

At first Douglas refused to have anything to do with Harris, but gradually came round to the idea that it would be in their common interest to set things right and they met around 14 March.[374] A week later Douglas wrote Harris an extraordinary letter which started 'Dear Frank, Fate, or Providence, has brought us together after all these years. You asked me to see you, and after much hesitation I did so.' And continued:

> I have now convinced you that nearly all that is said about my relations with Wilde in the American edition of your book Oscar Wilde: His Life and Confessions in the financial way is entirely untrue . . . . Now to come to the moral (or immoral) part of the story. I think it is a hard thing, and an unfair thing, that I should be forced, as I am now being forced by your widely disseminated accusations, to tell the real truth which, I freely admit, I have not told so far. I have always denied that I ever had any immoral relations with Oscar Wilde. I owed it to myself, to my mother, to my wife, to my son and to all my family and friends to deny it to the last . . . . I did with him and allowed him to do just what was done among boys at Winchester and Oxford. It is hateful to me now to

speak or write of such things, but I must be explicit. Sodomy never took place between us, nor was it thought or dreamt of. Wilde treated me as an older boy treats a young one at school, and he added what was new to me and was not (as far as I know) known or practised among my contemporaries; he 'sucked' me . . . . For at least six months before he went to prison no such thing happened between us, nor was it so much as hinted at after he came out two years later when I met him again.[375]

And he finished the letter: 'You are at liberty to make any use you like of this letter, and I have no objection to its being published.' For one who had shown himself to be deeply suspicious of other people's motives, this confession in writing to Harris, himself not the most discreet of correspondents, seems unusually out of character. Douglas had spent the previous twelve years fighting strenuously against all attempts to brand him as immoral, especially in the various court cases in which he was involved. And yet here he was admitting to Harris that he and Oscar had indulged in oral sex together. It was probably this confession that prompted Harris to give Bosie a copy of the first volume of his autobiographical *My Life and Loves* in which he describes his own heterosexual exploits in fairly graphic detail. Douglas's next letter is even more surprising:

Dear Frank, It's no use. I simply cannot read your book. I think it is too dreadful for words. Leaving out all the dirty part, I think it would be very interesting . . . . I have read about 80 pages and honestly it has made me cry . . . . I always used to like you and at one time I almost adored you (25 years ago). My mother could tell you how I wrote about you and thought you a most wonderful man. Then came all this estrangement, and now I've met you again and find that I'm still awfully fond of you. But this book, my dear Frank, breaks my heart.[376]

And he signs off 'Your real friend, Alfred Douglas.' He was

fifty-five at the time but the letter reads as though written by a disillusioned young man half his age. It reveals a pattern occurring several times in Douglas's life: his need for a father figure, the older man he admired and whose approbation he sought but with whom, inevitably, he quarrelled, from his own father onwards and then Oscar Wilde, Frank Harris, and finally, a few years later, George Bernard Shaw.

After several meetings it was agreed that the two of them should write a joint preface to Harris's book correcting what Bosie regarded as the errors about himself. The principal errors to which he objected were that he didn't leave Oscar penniless in Naples after their disastrous reunion; that Oscar wasn't largely unproductive in his writing when they were together; that he wasn't responsible for introducing Oscar to the rent-boys of London's gay underworld; and that although he had encouraged Oscar to sue his father for libel, he had paid all the expenses of the court case. In the draft preface, Douglas's side of the story was couched in the form of a long letter to Harris, 'bookended' by some rather grovelling apologies by Harris about how he regretted having been taken in by Wilde's and Ross's falsehoods: 'Now, when I review the whole case, I have to admit that in many essentials I misjudged Lord Alfred Douglas again and again, and did him grave injustice.'[377]

The preface complete, Douglas returned to London with a copy and waited for Harris to order its printing as a separate publication to accompany every volume sold of his remaining stock of which he still had 300 copies. Once Harris's *Life of Wilde* was out of print, the preface would be incorporated into a new edition and the errors corrected. That, at any rate, seemed to be the basis on which an agreement had been reached. However, Douglas had consulted a couple of publishers who advised him that the book should be rewritten or, at the very least, the offending pages should be reprinted with annotations, as few people would bother to read the separate preface, and he wrote as much to Harris. Harris, meanwhile, was beginning to have doubts about some of the corrections on which Douglas was insisting, especially after receiving a letter from Reggie Turner in which he stated:

> It is this wild and blind method of over-stating his case which has always damaged Bosie, Robbie Ross indulged in a similar error and made it impossible for any sane person to work with either of them in the long run. Vituperation and cleverness don't ride over every obstacle, though they do take people a long way. In their relations to each other, Douglas and Ross were two impossible people and the truth would never be got from either of them, for they didn't want truth. They only wanted to prove their point and even when evidence was produced against, would retreat to obstinate assertion. The horror of the whole thing was that it was a personal quarrel or rivalry between the two and they cared very little about Oscar's reputation in the struggle.[378]

Nevertheless, both Douglas and Harris were agreed that the preface should be put out as soon as possible, but a further difficulty arose when Harris's English printer refused to print it because of what he considered to be Douglas's libellous remarks about Sir Edward Clarke, Oscar's counsel in the 1895 libel trial. Although Douglas had corrected some of Harris's 'errors' in his long contribution to the preface, he used it to brand *De Profundis* as a 'dreadful piece of cold-blooded, malignant malice, hypocrisy and lying' and to rehearse what he saw as the unfairness of using it in the Ransome case in 1913. It was also gave him a chance to attack Ross generally and to criticise Clarke for promising and then failing to put him into the witness box to testify on behalf of Oscar against his father, which to me always seemed improbable. The damning of his father's character might have been vaguely relevant to the case, but as a witness he could then have been cross-examined by Edward Carson which would have been as disastrous as it was for Oscar himself: a good reason for Clarke not to have called him. It was the truth of Queensberry's libel which was being tried and not the behaviour of the man himself, but having been refused the opportunity to vent his hatred of his father in court, Douglas used a large part of the preface to do exactly that.[379]

As a result of the English printer's refusal, Harris sought legal advice and was told that attacking Clarke would be extremely rash, that Douglas's self-justification was far too long and that it would be more convincing if Harris was to write the preface in his own name, rather than Douglas trying to rehabilitate himself. At the end of July he wrote all of this to Douglas who agreed with some reluctance, but when he received the watered-down revised preface with most of his criticisms of Ross, Clarke, and De Profundis removed, he reverted to his previous insistence that Harris rewrite the book or he would prosecute anyone who tried to sell it in its present form in England. This Harris refused to do, and the correspondence became increasingly belligerent with both sides maintaining entrenched positions and trading insults. At length, Douglas simply told Harris that he was going to print and publish their preface as it stood, since it more or less constituted an apology by Harris for what he had written. Harris retaliated by threatening to publish Douglas's first letter of March confessing to the physical relationship he had had with Oscar. The New Preface to the Life and Confessions of Oscar Wilde in its original form duly appeared in the late autumn of 1925 and effectively prevented any possible reconciliation between the two men.[380] Douglas had managed to find a mouthpiece for his pent-up anger and Harris was still unable to sell his Life of Wilde in England. As Harris wrote to him at the height of their quarrel: 'You have inherited your father's terrible temper and incalculable character. You've quarrelled with everyone; you have the most imperious temper I've ever met, with a tongue of extraordinary cleverness to make your outbursts unforgettable if not unforgivable.' Douglas even tried to have the New Preface published in America, but Harris heard about it and put pressure on their common friend, George Viereck, to prevent it.[381]

In February the following year Harris put out a version of De Profundis with The Modern Library in New York and prefaced it with a vitriolic introduction about Douglas's character. While admitting that *De Profundis* does not give a fair and sympathetic portrait of Douglas, with Wilde's insisting on the 'singular self-ishness and rank malignance of his friend,' he says that it is curiously justified by Douglas's subsequent writings, especially in his self-deluded 1914 autobiography *Oscar Wilde and Myself* which he describes as 'an appalling production, livid with hate, from start to finish, and even falser to fact than Oscar's extravagant disdain.' The first edition of Douglas's *New Preface* having sold out, he reprinted it in September 1927 with a 'Note to the Second Edition' counterattacking Harris for 'his hideous lies and black-hearted perversions of what he has always known to be the truth.' It became uncannily like the Ross/Douglas feud of ten years before, squabbling over poor Oscar's corpse and a perfect example of what Reginald Turner had described in his letter to Harris. Fortunately, there was the English Channel between them but even that did not prevent Douglas (before they stopped corresponding) from threatening Harris: 'don't forget that it would only be necessary to pull one or two very little strings to have you turned out of France.'[382]

At the end of February 1926 my father, having read the *New Preface*, wrote to Harris saying: 'I am not, nor have I ever been, particularly impressed by the hysterical spite of Lord Alfred Douglas, and I have, indeed, never read his book *Oscar Wilde & Myself*.' He pointed out a few minor errors in the *New Preface* and finished up: 'This letter is written in no spirit of enmity towards you, but only to protect you against the insinuations of that extremely clever man Douglas. If only he had turned his talents to something useful he might have become a great man.' He immediately received an effusive reply from Harris giving the whole story of the *New Preface* fiasco, though somewhat skewed, as one might expect, by Harris's point of view. 'My only desire in this book [his *Life of Wilde*] was to tell the truth,' he wrote, 'and that I had and have a deep affection for Oscar Wilde and his memory. I have never met a more delightful companion and I have said so convincingly, I think . . . . I am very glad that your whole judgment of Douglas is very much the same as mine. I have never met such an all-hating nature.'[383] Vyvyan's reply to Harris, characteristic of his attitude at that time towards the whole Wilde story and its aftermath, merits quoting in its entirety:

> My dear Frank Harris, Many thanks for your letter and for your assurance that you do not believe everything that Alfred Douglas says. I particularly do not want you to quote me as having said anything to anybody about anything, ever, in your book; at any rate not in the capacity of Oscar Wilde's son. Having, vicariously and at an early age, disowned my father's name, it is, I am quite sure you will agree, ridiculous of me to try and champion him under the *ægis* of Vyvyan Holland. Your life of my father is the only one I have ever read, and the only reason that I read it is that Robbie Ross said it was so good. The whole melancholy affair is, as far as possible, better left alone by me. It is different for others. But I myself have suffered too much in the endless quarrels of the last twenty-five years. My poor father never did himself or anyone else half as much harm as Douglas has done to his memory and to others. I hope to be over in Paris next week. Will you be back? Yours very sincerely, Vyvyan Holland.[384]

In a later letter Vyvyan complained of Harris's slighting description of Constance at the time of her marriage to Oscar as 'a young lady without any particular qualities or beauty', and said that Harris gave the impression 'that she was hideous, stupid, ill-bred and impecunious. Whereas she was singularly beautiful, much better bred than my father and possessed a perfectly adequate income upon which my father lived for many years and out of which she made him an allowance after his release. The charge of stupidity is one from which I am unable to defend her, in view of the fact that she married my father!' Harris apologised, and promised to write more fairly of her in future but asked Vyvyan if he would consider contributing a chapter to a revised edition of his *Life of Wilde* on the relationship between Oscar and Constance which, he said, was one of the main things missing in the book. As always, my father refused on the pretext of wanting to preserve his anonymity but he was perhaps wary that by associating himself with Harris he could become a target for more Douglas litigation. In the event, the unflattering description of Constance has remained in all editions of Harris's book to this day.

One surprising fact became clear from their correspondence early on: my father's admiration for Harris and his writing. He told Harris that he had an almost complete set of his works and would very much like Harris to inscribe them all for him. He also praised Harris's *My Life and Loves* of which he owned volumes I & II by the time they start corresponding and later asked Harris to sell him inscribed copies of III & IV once they were published in 1927. My surprise was to come across these letters after reading what my father had written about him in his 1954 memoir, *Son of Oscar Wilde,* thirty years later: 'I knew him when I was a young man and I thought that he was the most sinister and repulsive person that I had ever met. His book about my father has already been exposed as a concatenation of lies, and it should join his other books of reminiscences in the dustbin,' and that Robert Ross had told him that Harris's *Life of Oscar Wilde* was 'a thoroughly bad book.'[385] More whitewash applied all too liberally in the 1950s to 'clean up' what was left of the Wilde family. Heaven forbid that Oscar Wilde's son should have approved of an 'unreliable' biography of his father written by Frank Harris whose reputation by then was that of a semi-pornographer and liar because of his steamy autobiography *My Life and Loves*. Vyvyan had best distance himself and do so in print.

The Harris/Douglas feud continued over the next few years but with rather less intensity. After falling out with Harris over the *New Preface*, Douglas tried to make sure that no bookseller in England would sell his *Life of Wilde* and threatened any who tried to do so with prosecution for libel. Most apologised and came to financial agreements out of court; he managed, for example, to get

Hatchards of Piccadilly to pay him £200 for selling a single copy.[386] But Douglas was determined to make a public example to deter further sales and he employed a detective agency to purchase a copy from Harrods' book department and then sued them for distributing libellous material. The store offered £25 in compensation which Douglas refused, took them to court and won his case with £100 in damages.[387] After Douglas published his *Autobiography* in 1929 expressing, yet again, his feelings about Harris's iniquity, Harris responded by persuading a New York publisher, Covici Friede to reissue his *Life of Wilde,* with a toned-down version of the *New Preface,* but also printing in full Douglas's letter of five years before, openly admitting his short-lived sexual relationship with Wilde. In full, that is, but without the phrase about oral sex which not even Harris could bring himself to include. A year later Harris was dead, unreconciled with Douglas to the last.

What are we to make of Harris's biography of Oscar Wilde? Posterity has formed a picture of Harris as a rogue, a braggart and a liar, a reputation based partly on his scandalous *My Life and Loves* rendering unreliable much of his non-fiction. Harris himself anticipated this as early as 1927 when writing to a correspondent: '*My Life*, that you thought "great stuff", has killed the sale of all my other books in America and England,' and since his *Life of Wilde* was first published, nearly every other biographer of Wilde has questioned its veracity.[388] However, we should remember that Harris showed Oscar great loyalty and kindness in his last years and probably knew him as well as anyone then, a fact Bernard Shaw recognised in his assessment of the book. His enthusiasm for Harris's *Life of Wilde* showed remarkable perception at the time and, qualified by a note of caution to read it as an impressionistic and personal view, still holds good. Weeded of self-interest and the wilder flights of Harris's imagination it provides a technicolour element which only a personal friend could have brought to a portrait of Wilde and which will always be lacking in the grey photo-realism of modern biography. In January 1899 when Oscar Wilde was staying in Nice at Frank Harris's expense, Harris describes showing him a picture in a paper of Lord Curzon on his arrival in Calcutta as Viceroy of India driving in a state carriage drawn by four horses with outriders and escorted by cavalry:

> 'Do you see that?' cried Oscar angrily; 'fancy George Curzon be-
> ing treated like that. I know him well; a more perfect example of a
> plodding mediocrity was never seen in the world. He had never a
> thought or phrase above the common . . . . Close the eyes of all of
> us now and in fifty years hence, or a hundred years hence, no one
> will know anything about Curzon: whether he lived or died will
> be a matter of indifference to everyone; but my comedies and my
> stories and The Ballad of Reading Gaol will be known and read
> by millions and even my unhappy fate will call forth world-wide
> sympathy.'[389]

Amen to that, even if they weren't Oscar's exact words.

CHAPTER FIVE
INVENTIONS & FALSE MEMOIRS

Despite what Robbie Ross wrote to Charles Ricketts after the Pemberton Billing trial in 1918 about the British public taking pleasure in 'kicking Oscar's corpse,' by the 1920s what the British saw as the less attractive aspects of Oscar's life, revisited so often in the law courts during the previous decade, had largely been forgotten or at least forgiven. It suddenly became fashionable to include in one's memoirs a paragraph or even a whole chapter on Oscar Wilde; how the author had enjoyed his friendship, had sympathised with his fate, and had perhaps even given him moral or financial support when the crash came and later during his exile. Given his unpleasant reputation in the twenty years after his death, it was understandable that, with a few notable exceptions, none of this should have been admitted during that time. Meanwhile, most of those who could have confirmed or denied at first-hand what was written—Oscar himself, Constance, Robbie Ross—were conveniently dead, so the truth of it was never questioned. At best, some of the anecdotes are embellished to enhance the teller's own role in the story, and at worst they are improbable and border on fiction; perhaps not with any real intention to deceive, but passed down in family lore and enshrined in fact with regular repetition. One obvious offender was Gladys Palmer.

Oscar and Constance were good friends with Walter and Jean Palmer whose family owned the famous Huntley & Palmer's biscuit factory in Reading. The Wildes were regular house guests at the Palmers in Sunninghill and my father wrote about his visits there in *Son of Oscar Wilde*, describing how he and Cyril were in awe of the Palmers' daughter Gladys, who was slightly older than them. There is also evidence in the form of photographs taken of Oscar and Constance with the Palmers in their garden.[390] This much is not in doubt. In 1929 Gladys Palmer had her memoirs, *Relations and Complications,* ghosted by Kay Boyle in which she claimed to remember Constance and the two boys staying with them when 'Uncle Oscar,' as she called him, arrived looking 'so old and so sad' to ask her father to lend him four hundred pounds for his trial. And she continued:

> It was not until many years later that I was to know how very deeply he was rooted in the affections of both my father and mother; how they helped him both financially and morally during his trial; or that I was to read and revel in the long and devoted correspondence with my mother. All of these letters begin by addressing her as 'Moonbeam I' and are signed 'Moonbeam II' and his tender charm and wit are as real here as they were in those days when he used to scramble over the gardens and through the house with us like a mad boy.[391]

Everything about this rings so false that it's difficult to know where to start unpicking it. If Oscar really did ask Walter Palmer for a loan, it would have been for his libel action against Queensberry, not for the subsequent criminal trials at which Sir Edward Clarke represented him *pro bono*, and in addition, at the time of the libel trial both Cyril and Vyvyan were still in school. There is absolutely no evidence that the Palmers helped Oscar 'both financially and morally' and he would certainly have acknowledged the fact somewhere in his correspondence. Besides, as a pillar of the local Establishment and with ambitions to become an MP (which he did in 1900), Palmer is more likely to have distanced himself from such a scandal in the making. As for Oscar signing his letters 'Moonbeam I,' the idea is laughable. If Gladys—who clearly implied that Uncle Oscar's letters still existed at the time of writing—treasured them so much, why were they not kept safely for posterity until her death in 1952, if indeed they existed at all?

Similarly, the zoologist Peter Chalmers Mitchell recalled being in a café at Fontainebleau in the late 1890s with two friends when Oscar came in and sat at a table nearby. Mitchell recognised him and remarked on it to the others who got up to leave, saying that he was probably there under a false name and that his hotel should be warned. Mitchell, on the other hand, went over to Oscar's table and introduced himself as a friend of Robbie Ross and spent two hours talking to him before suggesting that they should all dine together that night. 'No,' said Oscar, 'Your friends, would not stand it. But thank you and good-bye.' One of those friends happened to be Arthur Waugh (the publisher and father to Alec and Evelyn), and who related a rather different version of the story when asked by Alec as a schoolboy if he had ever met Oscar Wilde. He remembered Wilde coming into the café, looking around and walking out, whereupon Mitchell got up and followed him and returned ten minutes later to castigate the other two for apparently snubbing Oscar because of his scandal. The friends defended themselves on the basis that they hardly knew the man and protested at Mitchell's excessive self-righteousness. Arthur Waugh's version was told to Alec some twenty years before Mitchell put it into his autobiography in 1937 and as Alec later wrote:

> My father's account of the incident is far likelier to be correct. He was . . . very far from being the man to turn against anyone who was in trouble. It is clear to me that Mitchell confused what might have happened or rather what he would like to have happened with what did happen. I recall the anecdote here because it exemplifies the danger of accepting even what is known as first-hand evidence.[392]

Nor did the French hesitate to embellish or invent their relationships with Oscar during his last days in Paris. In a 1925 interview for a German magazine to mark the twenty-fifth anniversary of Oscar's death, Paul Fort, the Symbolist poet who had got to know Oscar during his long stay in Paris in the winter of 1891, claimed that he and his wife were the only friends Oscar had in his last days. [393] He described how Oscar couldn't stand being in hospital (which he never was), had been taken back to his room in the Hôtel d'Alsace and how all the flowers he had in his room had been provided by Fort and his wife. It was an extraordinary fabrication, totally ignoring the care and attention lavished on Oscar as he was dying by his two closest friends at the time, Robbie Ross and Reggie Turner. Just as inventive was the interview headed 'Oscar Wilde died in my arms' given by Jean Dupoirier, the owner of the Hôtel d'Alsace to mark the thirtieth anniversary of Oscar's death.[394] He, too, ignored the presence of Reggie and Robbie in his account maintaining that he slept in Oscar's room during his final days and was there the moment he died at nine in the morning. He could be forgiven for getting the time wrong thirty years later—it was ten to two in the afternoon and Reggie and Robbie had been with him since five-thirty that morning—but not for saying that it was he who had washed and laid out the body when this distressing business was carried out by Oscar's two friends. It was a pity that Dupoirier, of whom Robbie wrote: 'I can scarcely speak in moderation of the magnanimity, humanity and charity of the proprietor of the Hôtel d'Alsace,' should have wanted to exaggerate his role in Oscar's demise. The fact that he turned Father Cuthbert Dunne, the Irish Passionist priest who received Oscar into the Catholic Church on his deathbed, into the local parish priest from St. Germain-des-Prés one can charitably put down to French catholic chauvinism.[395]

These are merely a few instances of mistaken memories and fabricated anecdotes which started to appear once Oscar had been accepted back, posthumously at least, into literary and artistic society. Then came the hypocrites like Lillie Langtry. She was a year older than Oscar and by the time their friendship really started when Oscar came down from Oxford in 1879, she had been the talk of London for two years. Neither of them belonged by birth in the upper echelons of society, but each aspired to it and realised in different ways that the other could be instrumental in achieving that goal. Lillie's star was very slightly on the wane; Oscar's was definitely in the ascendant and for several years they served each other's purpose and cultivated a genuine friendship.[396] Yet, at the time of Oscar's downfall she made no attempt to offer either financial or moral support and was heard to remark 'I always found Oscar Wilde a terrible bore.' So long as 'his name was surrounded by a vague fog of obscenity' in Christopher Millard's words, she chose to distance herself from her former friend. That was until his partial rehabilitation in the 1920s, when she capitalised on the past friendship by keeping an empty chair at her dining-table in Monaco, explaining that it was 'In memory of dear Oscar.' And when someone criticised this honouring of a convicted homosexual, she replied sharply 'You fool, you don't understand. Oscar was a very versatile man.'[397]

By way of contrast, in 1917 John Coulson Kernahan published *In Good Company*, a collection of essays on personalities he had known including Swinburne and Wilde. Kernahan was an author and journalist who worked as a literary adviser to Ward, Lock & Co, the publishers of *The Picture of Dorian Gray* which is how he met Oscar. They were not close friends but had a mutual admiration for each other's work, and Kernahan's frank and sympathetic portrait of Oscar was unusual for the time. Shortly after Wilde's death he had wanted to dedicate a book to his memory but his publisher adamantly refused to issue a book with Wilde's name on the dedication page and strongly advised Kernahan to give up on the idea of ever writing a chapter on his memories of the man. Sixteen years later, a visiting friend who had also known Wilde saw an inscribed photograph of him on Kernahan's mantlepiece and said: 'If I were you I should put that thing out of sight and, if you happen at any time to hear his name mentioned, I should keep the fact that he had been a friend of yours to yourself.' Thus provoked, he did indeed write the chapter for *In Good Company* and included several of Oscar's letters to him, though redacted to exclude the parts he considered unimportant. The missing parts were restored for Oscar's *Complete Letters* once the originals had come to light, but one omission struck me in particular; the sentence 'As for the photograph, I will send you one with pleasure.' Kernahan was happy to describe a signed photo on his mantlepiece but clearly drew the line at admitting that it was he who had asked for it.[398] It was bold enough of him to write about his friendship with Oscar as early as 1917, without appearing to be a late-Victorian groupie.

Then there was Natalie Barney. In *Aventures de L'Esprit*, which she published in Paris in 1929, she recalls meeting Oscar Wilde back in 1882 on his American lecture tour. She was five years old at the time and in what she calls her 'First Adventure' she remembers being in a seaside hotel fleeing from a group of small children when Oscar scooped her up as she ran past and held her out of their reach before sitting her down on his knee to tell her what she recalled was a wonderful story. When her mother came to take Natalie away, Oscar complimented her on the girl's lovely complexion, her dress and how she had listened so attentively to his words. Could she have remembered that amount of detail nearly fifty years later? It's possible, allowing for a degree of artistic licence, though improbable; but very convenient by the time she had become one of the most prominent lesbians of the 1920s Paris scene and was in a relationship with Oscar's niece, Dolly Wilde. In her memoir Natalie goes on to say that as a teenager when she learned Oscar had been sent to prison 'I wrote to him in Reading Jail [sic] in the hope of comforting him as he had comforted me and reminded him how he had protected me.'[399] If that first encounter had been so important and she really had taken the trouble to write to him in prison, why had she made no attempt to get in touch with him only a couple of years later? His presence in Paris wasn't exactly a secret and, at the age of 22, she had been living there from 1898, already no stranger to scandal having started her first lesbian relationship at 17. Perhaps befriending a bankrupt ex-convict and homosexual was a step too far even for her but, at least, unlike some of the others, she never pretended to have done so when she hadn't. It's interesting, though, that her childhood encounter with him didn't find its way into any of her books before 1929.

Complete fabulists in the posthumous life of my grandfather are fortunately rare and more or less instantly detectable thanks to his real life being so well documented in reliable memoirs and his own letters, but occasionally the boundaries are cleverly blurred with the obvious intention to deceive. Such was the case of Arthur Henry Cooper-Prichard. Prichard (the hyphenated Cooper a later addition to confer status) was born in Jamaica in 1874. His father was a colonial civil engineer and he was sent back to be schooled in England from the age of eight and spent his holidays with his maternal aunts and grandmother in West Kensington. He later had a varied career as an actor, professional numismatist and occasional author. In 1930 there appeared in the *Cornhill Magazine* an article entitled 'Reminiscences of Oscar Wilde' by Professor A. H. Cooper-Prichard. In it the author recounted how, improbably aged eleven in the 1880s, he was taken to see Ellen Terry and Henry Irving in *Faust* at the Lyceum Theatre and wrote a dreadful poem about it which his aunts, with whom he was staying, insisted on him reading to Oscar Wilde who 'in his informal way dropped in to tea.' His embarrassment was doubled by the arrival of Irving and Terry themselves 'both family friends' to whom he had to read it again. His youthful literary credentials thus established, he went on to say:

> As I grew older I saw more of Wilde, and not only in my own grandmother's drawing room, where I also again often met him, his mother and my grandmother having been bosom friends from girlhood, when they had been schoolmates in the same young ladies' seminary . . . . I do recollect some few of the things he said to me personally, mostly on the occasions of my dropping in upon him unexpectedly during the daytime . . . . In this way, too, we had many cosy talks together on Literature.

The 'Reminiscences,' which the *Cornhill* presumably published as a genuine record, reappeared a year later as 'My introduction to Wilde,' a sort of justificatory preface to a volume entitled *Conversations with Oscar Wilde*. The volume itself was a collection of ten farcical exchanges between Wilde, Prichard, and such absurd characters as Lady Wyndebagge, Lady Flapdoodle, and The Earl of Dodderington, with the odd historical personage like James Whistler, Walt Whitman, and William Morris thrown in for good measure. As Prichard wrote at the end of that introduction, 'Imagination is the gift of describing as fact what has not really happened,' which is tantamount to a confession that what follows is pure fiction. At this point even the 'Reminiscences' begin to unravel. Prichard's grandmother and Speranza were born eight years apart, one in Islington, London and the other in Dublin; there is no way they were 'bosom friends from girlhood'; Oscar's 'long, beautiful hair and his aesthetic way of dressing' as described by Prichard were both discarded after his marriage in 1884; Prichard's 'Professorship' never existed, and so on. *Conversations with Oscar Wilde* is an elaborate spoof with just enough credibility in the introduction to fool the unwary, and an amusing period piece by someone who admitted wanting to cash in on the current vogue for reminiscences of Oscar Wilde.[400]

Reinventing Oscar Wilde was but a short step from allowing Oscar to reinvent himself—through the spirit world—and in June and July 1923 a medium, Hester Travers Smith, daughter of Edward Dowden the former professor of English at Trinity College Dublin, claimed to have communicated with Oscar Wilde through 'automatic writing.' This consisted of a medium—herself—guiding the hand of an 'automatist'—a Mr. 'V'—to record Oscar's words. Mr. V, it later turned out, was Samuel Soal, a parapsychologist later charged with the fraudulent manipulation of data in paranormal experiments. 'Oscar' seemed to be well-informed about contemporary literature and its authors claiming to have known Mrs. Chan Toon, the forger of the play *For Love of the King*, some years before, and was brutal in his scathing remarks about others. Of Arnold Bennett he said:

'Of his characters, one may say that they never say a cultured thing and never do an extraordinary one. They are, of course, perfectly true to life—as true as a bad picture.' When asked his opinion of *Ulysses* he replied: 'Yes, I have smeared my fingers with that work . . . . It is a singular matter that a countryman of mine should have produced this great bulk of filth . . . . It gives me the impression of having been written in a severe fit of nausea.' His criticism of the Sitwells was considered too malicious to be repeated, and of George Moore's *Hail and Farewell* he said 'The enquiring mind of Moore has induced him to lay his friends and enemies thus on the table, in order that he may have the opportunity of observing their entrails while they are still alive. An accurate method, but rather a severe tension for the unfortunate subjects, who have to undergo this ordeal in the cause of literature.' He detested the Epstein sculpture above his tomb in Père Lachaise Cemetery, 'which in its monstrous want of taste does homage to the man whose monstrous want of morals suggested the design' and, somewhat ungraciously since their country had largely helped his literary rehabilitation, was rude about the Germans: 'Though I have forgiven the world the humiliations that were heaped upon me, and though I can forgive even that last insult of posthumous popularity that has been offered me, I find it hard to forgive them for translating my beautiful prose into German.' So many were the attacks on prominent men in the literary world that Hester Travers Smith took legal advice and was informed that she certainly could not print these things without exposing herself to an action for libel. It was advice which, fortunately for us, she ignored and *Psychic Messages from Oscar Wilde* appeared in April the following year.[01] Travers Smith also recorded some less controversial messages, for example the very first in which Oscar compares the twilight world his spirit inhabits with the world he left behind. Although it read like slightly pastiche Wilde with phrases from *De Profundis* thrown in, it clearly impressed Arthur Conan Doyle who was a prominent figure in spiritualist circles at the time and who declared: 'This is not merely adequate Wilde. It is exquisite Wilde. It is so beautiful that it might be chosen for special inclusion in any anthology of his writings.'[402] But then he *had* been duped by the 'Cottingley Fairies' hoax a few years earlier.

Before she stopped communicating with Oscar's spirit, Travers Smith did manage to get Oscar to start dictating a new play to her: 'I suggested a play to him three weeks ago. A week ago he gave me the characters and the plot, but the dialogue is coming slowly because he rewrites almost every sentence.'[403] My father got to hear of it and had his solicitor contact the Society of Authors, giving rise to some unusual correspondence:

> Mr. Holland has already written to me to enquire whether, if the play is produced, he as the author's surviving son, will be entitled to royalties. I fancy that as a point of law the claim will be quite a novel one, as also the alternative question whether, in the event of royalties not being forthcoming, an injunction to restrain Mrs. Travers Smith and her friends from producing the play could be obtained and on what grounds.[404]

The play, so far as one can tell, was never staged and Vyvan's claim was never tested in law. Hester Travers Smith did, however, 'take' Oscar to the Theatre Royal, Haymarket on 29 November 1923 to see a production of *The Importance of Being Earnest* and published his review of the play. He noticed some good performances and said of the audience: 'They felt that [the author] was a shade *démodé*, but they looked on him as a curio worthy of a dark corner in the drawing-room.'

Hester Travers Smith's well-publicised conversations with Oscar spawned a few more reappearances over the following years, among the most notable was the revisiting of his old rooms at Magdalen College, Oxford. An Australian undergraduate and ice-hockey Blue, described as 'not a man given to aesthetic fancies' and who occupied the rooms, claimed to have seen Oscar's ghost late one night dressed in a long jacket and a loose, flowing tie. He walked up and down but refused to speak and then faded away. Maybe not given to aesthetic fancies but perhaps a little too much to the 'amber nectar,' one feels.[405] The most bizarre of all was the appearance in 1928 of *The Ghost Epigrams of Oscar Wilde* taken down in automatic writing by Lazar whose identity nearly a century later still seems to be a mystery. It was issued by the New York avant-garde firm of Covici Friede among whose other publications that year was Radclyffe Hall's controversial lesbian novel *The Well of Loneliness*. The epigrams included such gems as 'All faithful husbands have kidney stones' and 'Love, like the measles, attacks only the young,' as well as an editorial note stating: 'The epigrams contained in this book have never appeared in any book of epigrams or aphorisms selected from the works of Oscar Wilde. These are set down as they came from the Master.' I fear that 'the Master' would not have been too happy at the appropriation of his name to front the book's two hundred and eighty-five pathetic attempts to emulate his own sparkling witticisms.

L ate in 1928 the London antiquarian booksellers in Bond Street, Dulau & Co were selling a huge number of Wilde books, letters and manuscripts which had belonged to Robert Ross, Christopher Millard, who had died the year before, and my father who still insisted on being described in the catalogue merely as 'The Younger Son of Oscar Wilde.' Aware of Alfred Douglas's litigious nature, the company took the precaution of submitting to him all the letters which Robbie had received from Oscar while in prison and after his release, many of which were openly critical of Douglas. Dulau even included a notice in the front of the catalogue saying that he had raised no objection to their sale which looked suspiciously as though it had been drafted by a solicitor in case he forgot or changed his mind, but which Douglas claimed to have written himself to show his complete indifference to their content.[406]

Douglas had known that Oscar's long letter from prison, *De Profundis,* had been addressed to him ever since its part disclosure as evidence at the Ransom trial in 1913 and he had claimed it as one of his assets during his public examination in bankruptcy later that year.[407] In total ignorance of copyright law he even started an action against Methuen & Co, the publishers of *De Profundis,* to pay him royalties on past and future sales.[408] Both claims were rejected. However, now that the full texts of Oscar's letters to Robbie had become available he found further ammunition for his ownership claim in the letter written to Robbie from prison on 1 April 1897. In it, Oscar had told Robbie to make several copies before sending the original on to Douglas, though in the same letter he seems to contradict himself by saying 'you must be in possession of the only document that really gives any explanation of my extraordinary behaviour with regard to Queensberry and Alfred Douglas.' Seeing Oscar's instructions to Robbie in writing for the first time prompted Douglas to renew his demand that the British Museum should give him what he considered by right to be his property. On 22 May 1929 the Director of the Museum, Sir Frederic Kenyon, passed the request to the Treasury Solicitor, one of the government law officers, in whose opinion the Trustees of the Museum should refuse to part with the manuscript unless ordered to do so by a Court of Law, so the Museum stood firm once more. Remarkably, in getting the Treasury Solicitor's opinion, the Museum wrote that 'The Trustees have no great interest in the matter; the entire contents of the manuscript have been published abroad and the possession of the MS itself is not a matter of great importance, but they desire to know their legal position.' Six months later, in November 1929, Douglas threatened to start legal action unless *De Profundis* was handed over to him within seven days, but it was an empty threat since he was short of money and still an undischarged bankrupt, so for the time being he was unable to press the matter further.[409]

Sixteen years previously, when Bosie Douglas first became aware of Oscar's bitterness towards him in *De Profundis*, part of his motive for getting possession of the manuscript was to make sure that no more of it was published and possibly even to destroy it. In the meantime, *The Suppressed Portion of De Profundis* had been published as well as two complete versions in German and French so any further attempt at concealment was pointless and his incentive was as much financial as wanting to put his own side to the story for posterity. Although Ross had made the copies that Oscar had requested, there was no guarantee they were complete or accurate (as it later turned out they were neither) and Douglas had no access to them anyway. Obtaining the original document would have allowed him to make a totally accurate copy for future reference and then realise its considerable monetary value as a Wildean manuscript.

Back in 1925, the eccentric scholar and bookman, A. J. A. Symons approached Douglas for help with two books he was writing: *An Anthology of 'Nineties' Verse,* which was published in 1928 and *A Bibliography of the Writers of the Eighteen-Nineties,* which never was, and they had corresponded regularly ever since. Then in 1930, with my father's complete backing as heir to the Wilde estate, Symons proposed writing an entirely new life of Wilde, free from the petty squabbles and bias which characterised much of what had been written about Oscar until then. He and my father were close friends and members of a bibliophile dining club, the 'Sette of Odd Volumes' and Vyvyan had complete confidence that Symons would make an admirable job of the biography. The fact that Symons had become something of an epistolary confidant to Douglas over the previous few years was very much in his favour since Douglas's co-operation was essential to the whole undertaking and as soon as Douglas got to hear of it he wrote to Symons saying 'I shall be pleased to come and help over the Wilde book.'[410] It also set Douglas off in a new direction in his attempt to claim possession of the *De Profundis* manuscript. If, with my father's support, he was to renew his claim, he felt it would strengthen his case considerably and as a compromise he was would allow Symons to include the full version of *De Profundis* as an appendix to the biography. There was one further stipulation: that Douglas should be allowed to exercise some control over the editorial matter.

Towards the end of 1931, Douglas wrote about *De Profundis* to his friend Edward Marjoribanks, a Conservative MP and barrister who had acted for him in the Harrods libel case three years before. Marjoribanks consulted his stepfather Lord Hailsham, the previous Lord Chancellor and ex-officio one of the Museum's trustees, who sent back a message: 'Tell Lord Alfred that I consider he ought to have it and I shall so advise the law officers of the Crown.' Douglas also heard that the Treasury Solicitor, still advising the Museum, seemed prepared to concede an important point: 'Admitting that Ross misappropriated the MS (which we without prejudice are prepared to admit) he stole it from Wilde and not from you.'[411] Douglas wrote at once to Symons urging action and saying that a claim made in the joint names of himself and my father (probably the last thing the authorities would have expected) would be irresistible. What happened next is uncertain. It is possible that my father and Symons went cold on the idea, concerned that once Douglas gained possession of the manuscript he might destroy it, although it was more likely he would sell it as he was desperately short of money. At any rate, Symons was distracted from Wilde, while he finished his great life of Frederick Rolfe, published in 1934 as *The Quest for Corvo*. When the matter of *De Profundis* resurfaced in 1938, it became clear that Symons's biography of Wilde was on ice and that he and my father were hoping to bring out a stand-alone edition of *De Profundis*, or possibly to include it in a volume of Wilde's collected letters, but in either form with a minimum of editorial matter. To this Douglas now refused to agree.

If there was anything consistent about Lord Alfred Douglas it was his inconsistency, especially regarding *De Profundis*. His priorities fluctuated wildly between matters of principle when he felt attacked and matters of profit when he felt exploited. 'I'm afraid I can't consent to your bringing out the *De Profundis* letter like that,' he wrote to Symons in May 1938. 'I understood you were embodying it in your book and explaining the absurdity and unfairness and spite of most of it. Even so, I didn't like it, but I consented to please you. To bring it out by itself, merely for you and Vyvyan to make money out of it, seems to me rather a tall order!' And fifteen months later: 'I loathe the idea of its being published. It is not pleasant to have a mass of abuse and a whole heap of utterly untrue statements about me broadcast all over the world . . . . On the other hand I don't say that I may not agree to its publication on certain conditions which would include a considerable share in the gross receipts for me.'[412]

It was a period during which Douglas felt under siege. In 1935 a play, *Le Procès d'Oscar Wilde* by Maurice Rostand, son of Edmond, the author of *Cyrano de Bergerac*, was staged at the

Théâtre de l'Œuvre. Bosie came to hear of it through his friend
in Paris, Gladys Brooke, and wrote to the author saying he considered it an act of '*mauvaise foi*' on Rostand's part that he was
represented as the villain of the piece, and that far from abandoning Oscar after prison, he had stood by him and even given him
money.[413] Given that the three-act play merely covered the lead-
up to Queensberry's insulting card, the trials and finally a scene
in prison when Oscar is visited by Frank Harris, this accusation
seemed slightly bizarre. However, in the last act Harris, in an attempt to blacken Douglas's character, tells Oscar that young Bosie
is unlikely to stand by him on his release, which then leads straight
into Oscar starting to compose and read aloud the long recrimina-
tory *De Profundis*. For Douglas the combination of Harris's conjectures, which he thought an audience might well remember as
fact, together with the start of that letter which for Douglas was
still a running sore, must have been especially irritating. Matters
weren't helped by having Harris as one of the main characters in
the play. But Bosie had grown tired of fighting French authors'
misinformation about his relationship with Oscar and might have
contented himself with a sharply worded letter to some French
literary magazine, had the director of the Gate Theatre in London,
Norman Marshall, not decided to stage an English version of
the play. Douglas told Marshall that he objected strongly to the
production which he described as a 'travesty of the truth and a
deliberate misrepresentation of well-known and often-recorded
facts.' Marshall, aware of Douglas's litigious nature whenever he
felt himself libelled, wisely cancelled the production and commissioned one of the actors, Leslie Stokes to team up with his brother
Sewell and write a new three-act play along much the same lines
but which Douglas would find acceptable. Once written and approved the Stokes brothers also offered him a share of the profits
which, to his later regret, he declined. To make matters worse,
he discovered that the manuscript of his *Autobiography*, which he
had given to Symons as a present a few years before, had been sold
by the latter, secretly, to Hugh Walpole.[414] The idea that Vyvyan

Holland might now attempt to make money out of *De Profundis* was anathema to him, and he gave Methuen & Co notice that if they published he would obtain an injunction and sue for damages. He even believed misguidedly that his family would be able to prevent publication after his death. A ludicrous stalemate had been reached, with my father holding the copyright, the British Museum holding the sealed manuscript and Alfred Douglas holding an effective right of veto.

The full English version of *De Profundis* was never published in Douglas's lifetime. A so-called 'complete' version was published in 1949 by my father based on the inaccurate typescript left to him by Robbie Ross, but it wasn't until the manuscript was finally released to the public in 1960 that the full text could be published in *The Letters of Oscar Wilde* two years later. One final attempt to claim possession of the manuscript was made by Douglas's literary executor, Edward Colman, in 1982. Colman had cleared the estate of bankruptcy in September 1981 and together with Harford Montgomery Hyde, one of the doyens of Wilde studies at that time and who had written extensively about the history of *De Profundis*, yet another application was made to what had now become the British Library to hand over the manuscript. Once again, the Library took advice from the Treasury Solicitor and refused to part with it unless ordered to do so by a judge. The cost of litigation was more that the estate was prepared to risk, so Hyde suggested they enlist the help of a wealthy collector who would bankroll the legal costs in return for the prospect of owning this iconic manuscript at a reasonable pre-agreed price to be paid to the estate. The obvious choice was the American Mary Hyde, whose Wilde collection was the finest in private hands at that time. The only problem was that Mary had grown close to David Eccles, a fellow member of the exclusive Roxburghe Club and Chairman of the British Library, and when she married him the following year there was too great a conflict of interests for the plan to be carried out. The manuscript remains to this day safely preserved in the British Library.

De Profundis was the last prose work that Oscar Wilde ever wrote. To read it is to find him for once without his mask: no less endearing, perhaps even more so for all the faults it betrays. In one great sweep Oscar looks at his past glories and excesses, at his present misery and aspirations—mostly unrealised—for the future, passing from anger to remorse, from arrogance to humility. He wrote it under appalling conditions and in places was severely critical of his young friend and sometime lover, who spent (some would say wasted) more than thirty years defending himself from what he saw as its 'grotesque lies and misrepresentations.' The history of *De Profundis*, like the letter itself, is a catalogue of emotions and ironies, of greed and selfishness, of accusations and injustices. It blighted the lives of Robbie and Bosie and caused much distress to my father when its copyright was nearly 'stolen' from him in the 1950s. Yet its survival against many odds has left us with what is one of the most beautiful and moving of all Wilde's writings, and certainly the most poignant.

In 1929 Bosie Douglas had published his *Autobiography*. Not content with publishing the *New Preface to "The Life and Confessions of Oscar Wilde"* against Harris's express wishes four years before, Douglas decided that his settling of old scores needed a wider audience than the limited distribution of the *New Preface* had given it. Although he more or less repudiated his vicious attacks on Oscar in *Oscar Wilde and Myself,* the new targets for his rancour were Frank Harris and Robbie Ross. Harris was able to defend himself and did so admirably in his introduction to the Covici Friede reprint of his *Life of Wilde* the following year:

Lord Alfred Douglas recently published his *Autobiography* . . . . He attacks nearly everyone he has ever known or met. His father and his father-in-law are alike the objects of his venomous petty spite. Wilde and Ross, of course, are scourged as homosexualists dozens of times. He lies about me on nearly every page and is not ashamed to contradict himself a few pages later . . . . 'Frank Harris is my great traducer, the man who has done more than anyone else

to blacken me and calumniate me in the eyes of the whole world.'
He is mistaken: it is Lord Alfred Douglas who is his own chief
accuser and calumniator. Had he not been a remarkable poet, I
would not have troubled to mention his name, so little did I think
of his character.[415]

Douglas's book became the prelude to a decade of squabbles between Oscar's friends and acquaintances, his admirers and his
detractors, a sort of Punch-and-Judy show of literature with pan-
tomime overtones and Bernard Shaw, who was involved on the
fringes, regarded the whole thing as a huge joke. He was right
when he said that at least in one respect they were unanimous:
each one of them vouched for the shameless mendacity of all the
others.

Robert Sherard was one of the first to start the endless contro-
versies of the 1930s going. Sherard and Oscar first met in Paris
in 1883 where Oscar spent three months after his year-long lecture tour in America. They rapidly became friends though they
saw each other infrequently thereafter as Sherard spent most of
his time in France or Corsica. After Oscar's conviction, Sherard
visited him several times in prison, and at Oscar's request (and
to Douglas's fury) in August 1895 intervened to prevent Douglas
from publishing an article in the *Mercure de France* defending
his relationship with Oscar, which included intimate letters that
Oscar had written to him.[416] Sherard wrote three books about his
friend, of which the first in 1902 was partly autobiographical at a
time when very few people in England would have dared admit
they knew the disgraced Wilde let alone take pride in a friendship
with him. As a thoroughgoing heterosexual, his spaniel-like devotion to Oscar's memory was touching, but I don't think he ever
had any proper empathy or understanding for the sexual side to
Oscar's nature. For example, in his third book published in 1917
he writes: 'Wilde had been "experimenting" in certain kinds of
aberration for three years before he met Lord Alfred Douglas and
afterwards succumbed to the mania,' but says that he himself never

saw anything of it. In Sherard's three books, Douglas was only occasionally mentioned by name and his part in Oscar's downfall was only suggested by implication. In return, Douglas's comments about Sherard in his *Autobiography* were dismissive but entirely without the venom he reserved for Harris and Ross. It was against this background that Sherard seems to have announced to various people of his acquaintance (mostly by sending them newspaper reports anonymously), that the French had made him a Chevalier of the Légion d'Honneur. Douglas must have been among them as he wrote back to Sherard via a newspaper editor in October 1929 to congratulate him and say that he had heard Sherard was now 'on our side in the matter of poor Oscar Wilde.'[417] He was right and from that point on they joined forces in a campaign to discredit Frank Harris entirely.

In fact, Sherard had written to my father the year before after having read Harris's book and said 'I intend to take up the cudgels again and shall be able to expose Harris as a liar and fraud who simply wrote his book to make money out of your poor father's tragic history.' My father wrote back to thank him but said: 'Frank Harris is rather an extinct volcano. His 'Life and Confessions' of himself have banished him for ever, I'm afraid, from the realms of serious literature. Personally, I always think that it is better to ignore all these things. If one grows indignant it merely shows that one considers them seriously.'[418] What irritated Sherard, apart from the embellishments and inventions, was the way in which Harris tackled Oscar's homosexuality head-on, whereas he had approached it as something abnormal and not to be discussed in any detail. In *Oscar Wilde: His Life and Confessions*, Harris described a long conversation between Oscar and himself on a train to Nice in December 1898 when Oscar argued for the superior beauty of a boy's body over that of a girl, taking his latest young man, Maurice Gilbert, as an example.[419] There was an element, too, of Sherard feeling upstaged by Harris's reconstructions from memory of his conversations with Oscar, as reflected in the 'confessions' of the title, implying that his friendship was much closer than the one

Sherard had enjoyed. So, having read Douglas's *Autobiography*, Sherard set to work demolishing Harris's *Life of Wilde* page by page, which also involved a certain amount of criticism aimed at Bernard Shaw for endorsing it. Shaw, in his 'Memories of Oscar Wilde,' which he allowed Harris to include in the second edition of the *Life and Confessions*, had referred to Oscar ending up as 'an unproductive drunkard and swindler' to which Sherard had taken great exception and was determined to 'prove' that he was wrong. Three years later 'George, Frank and Oscar' was finished. Finding a publisher for it, though, was another matter. American publishers refused to consider it partly due to the Depression and the publishers he approached in London, who even bothered to read it, turned it down according to Sherard because 'the public is interested only in Wilde as perverted, a criminal and a monster and not in the least in the Wilde . . . whom I have known, admired and loved for over fifty years.'[420]

In order that his work should somehow be preserved for posterity, Sherard offered the typescript to the British Museum Library which elicited the response from the director: 'I regret to say that I do not think my Trustees would entertain it . . . . the subject is one surrounded by so much acrimonious controversy that they would, I am sure, prefer not to be in any way involved in it. They have recently suffered so much annoyance in connexion with *De Profundis* that they would hardly be disposed to consider favourably any fresh proposal concerning its author, or books relating to him.'[421]

Once Sherard had decided to fight for Oscar's reputation he lost no opportunity to attack anyone whom he felt had besmirched it. One particular offender was André Gide. As Sherard wrote to Reginald Turner in April 1933:

As for me the battle I began for our mutual friend 38 years ago is waging still and my main occupation in my old age is beating back the hyaenas from, and shooing off the vultures from poor Oscar's grave . . . . I am preparing to vindicate Oscar's memory against

Harris's atrocious lies about 'his friend' which but for G. B. Shaw would have gained credence nowhere but which now tinge and taint everything that is written about Wilde . . . . Unfortunately, unless his biography is proved word for word to be pure, malicious fabrication-as my book, with documents à l'appui proves it to be-Wilde's name will go down to posterity utterly disgraced. But worse than Harris even is this filthy liar André Gide whom I am tackling next.[422]

In 1926 Gide had published *Si le grain ne meurt,* an autobiographical account of his early years which included meeting Oscar and Bosie in Algiers in January 1895. He described how Oscar, believing him to be innocent in homosexual matters, procured for him an Arab youth and one for himself with whom they each spent half the night. This published account of Oscar's sexual activities was more than Sherard could stomach, and he believed that most of what Gide had described was exaggerated or even invented and, even if it wasn't, he was going to try and prove that it was. While doing his research in early 1933 Sherard came across a recently published book on Gide's life and works by Léon Pierre-Quint from which he learned that Gide had been made an Honorary Foreign Fellow of the Royal Society of Literature back in October 1924 to replace Anatole France who had died a few weeks before. He had been proposed by Edmund Gosse and elected unanimously. Sherard immediately wrote to Professor W. H. Wagstaff, the Hon. Secretary of the RSL to say that he found it incredible that Gide had been elected 'shortly after [he] had published his indescribably filthy autobiography under the title *Si le grain ne meurt* . . . or that he should be allowed to enjoy that honorific position any longer.'[423] In fact, Pierre-Quint was mistaken (and Sherard didn't check it) since *Si le grain* was only available commercially two years after his election. But Gide *had* published *Corydon* in 1924, a series of four Socratic dialogues on the subject of homosexuality, which caused a considerable stir in French literary circles at the time, hence the possible confusion of titles.

The RSL acknowledged Sherard's letter and said that the matter would be brought before the Council at their next meeting in late October 1933. To maintain the momentum of his accusations about Gide, on 7 October Sherard sent the RSL another letter saying that 'Gide is the centre of a circle of the vilest corruption amongst young people, and this is admitted by even his warmest admirers,' and to emphasise the point he sent the RSL a pamphlet *Un Malfaiteur: André Gide*. This pamphlet, published two years before, was written by Étienne Privaz who was described by Sherard as 'the unfortunate father of a youth who in 1929 committed suicide as the result of gorging himself on André Gide's loathsome books in which sodomy and masturbation are not only condoned but recommended to young people.' As a result, at the next council meeting on 18 October, a sub-committee was formed to look into the matter. Its report was unanimously adopted on 8 November and the following day a letter was sent to Gide: 'Dear Sir, I am instructed by my Council to inform you that the Honorary Fellowship of this Society, which was conferred upon you in 1924, has now terminated. Yours faithfully, W. H. Wagstaff. Hon. Secretary.' Gide, slightly bemused by the terseness of the letter wrote to his English translator, Dorothy Bussy, saying 'Have I been sacked? I imagined one was "immortal" for life! As at the Académie française.'[424] Many of Gide's later biographers have either been mystified by the sudden removal of his RSL Honorary Foreign Fellowship or have put it down to his Communist sympathies, but it is perfectly clear from the Council minutes that Robert Sherard's correspondence denouncing Gide's 'pestilential books' and their promotion of homosexuality was at the root of it.

Not content with stirring up trouble at the Royal Society of Literature, Sherard also wrote to the Irish Prime Minister, Eamon de Valera and the US President, Franklin Roosevelt, warning them about the evil influence Gide's literature could have on the youth of their respective countries and enclosed the two pamphlets which he himself had published that year: *André Gide's Wicked Lies About the Late Mr. Oscar Wilde in Algiers in 1895*, and

Oscar Wilde 'Drunkard and Swindler': A Reply to George Bernard Shaw.[425] The second of these he had printed to air his views on Shaw's endorsement of Harris while still trying to find a publisher for 'George, Frank and Oscar.' There is something quite touching about Robert Sherard's furious protection of his dead friend's memory but occasionally he comes across as mildly unhinged. Oscar's homosexuality was so distasteful to him that he simply lashed out at anyone who did more than mention it incidentally in print. Sherard reprinted his two pamphlets in expanded form the following year as *Oscar Wilde Twice Defended* in which he makes the astonishing claim that 'the unfortunate Wilde was doubly the victim of syphilis' inherited first from his father Sir William and reinforced by another dose of the disease contracted from a prostitute during his time at Oxford. This, says Sherard, puts the lie to Gide's story about him and Oscar picking up two Arab youths in Algiers because the 'kindly, humane, fatherly Oscar Wilde' would never have done such a thing knowing himself to be thus infected. Four years later in an unpublished typescript Sherard recants and declares: 'Were I writing his life anew, I could with an easy conscience towards my public omit all reference to a disease [syphilis] which is still looked upon by the hypocritical and the ignorant as a proof of depraved character.'[426] But the damage was done and later biographers have occasionally used Sherard as an unimpeachable source for giving poor Oscar the disease. In the end Sherard did manage to get 'George, Frank and Oscar' published. It appeared in 1937 as *Bernard Shaw, Frank Harris & Oscar Wilde*, and he even persuaded Douglas to write a preface, which can't have been difficult since the whole purpose of the book was to expose what he saw as Harris's lies and exaggerations. Although Douglas thoroughly approved of Sherard's motives for writing the book, he nonetheless sounded a note of warning:

> I still think you try to prove too much in it. It is no use trying, at this date, to "whitewash" Oscar from things which he would have admitted and gloried in himself. One of these days I should

like to talk to you about this. But I would love to see the book published . . . . I recognise absolutely that you are the one friend of Oscar who admired and loved him from the standpoint of the normal man, and in an entirely disinterested way.'[427]

Unfortunately Sherard took no notice of the advice and his method of discrediting Harris was largely one of nitpicking, inflicting as much damage on himself as on Harris with his own inaccuracies. As Douglas wrote to A. J. A. Symons after publication: 'The book has a lot of good stuff in it, but of course dear old Sherard will persist in thinking that things about O. W. which I *know* to be perfectly true, and which he would not have denied himself, are absurd and unbelievable!'[428] Douglas's own regard for the truth wasn't much better since he used his preface to take a swipe at Ross, accusing him of having 'faked up' part of *De Profundis* for publication.

Of all the relationships which developed in these years among the admirers and the detractors of Oscar Wilde, none would appear more improbable than the friendship between Alfred Douglas and Bernard Shaw. Their correspondence began in 1931 after Shaw had read Douglas's *Autobiography* and his *New Preface* to Harris's *Life of Wilde*. It seems unlikely that he had bothered to purchase them and more probable that Douglas had sent them to him to make amends for a slightly prickly exchange he had had with Shaw back in 1908 when he was editing the *Academy* and had given a bad notice to *Getting Married,* Shaw's latest play. Shaw now replied in a friendly enough tone, which encouraged Douglas to ask him in the interests of fairness, and having contributed to Harris's book, if he would be prepared to write a short preface to a new edition of his own *Autobiography*. 'What! YOU among the preface hunters!' replied Shaw. 'Have you *no* self-respect?' but told Douglas he could use his previous letter suitably edited so as not to give offence to any third party. Even though it was quite critical in places, Douglas did use it as a gesture to keep friendly with Shaw and their correspondence continued for a while on less controversial subjects such as Shakespeare and Douglas's poetry.[429] Then in October 1937, Shaw wrote to him saying he had heard that Nellie Harris, Frank's widow, was more or less destitute and that one way of giving her some income would be to reissue Frank's *Life of Oscar* for which he would add a preface and edit the text to take out the offensive references to Bosie. But would he agree to it? Douglas replied that in fact Nellie had been to see him about a year before and he had already agreed provisionally subject to certain conditions, mainly that passages critical of himself be corrected or omitted. Shaw set to work using a copy of the book annotated by Douglas and in late January 1938 he sent the revised text off to the publishers Constable & Co with a note saying: 'Here at last is the accursed job finished. I think it is lawyer-proof now. Far from libelling Douglas, it gives him his first coat of whitewash.' Shaw's preface was masterly. Harold Nicolson wrote on publication: 'Mr. Shaw's loyalty to his friends is as passionate as his vegetarianism. In his delightful preface he manages to be loyal to Alfred Douglas, loyal to Wilde, loyal to Frank Harris and loyal to Robert Ross. The dexterity of this combination of incompatibles leaves one agape.' Shaw himself admitted that he'd had fun writing it and in poking gentle fun at Robert Sherard in response to Sherard's disobliging remarks about him in *Bernard Shaw, Frank Harris & Oscar Wilde* the year before: 'His reckless impetuosity of attack and the vitality and endurance with which he keeps it up through fifty thousand words of invective, produce an exhilarating impression of a man who lives in a permanent rage, . . . and the more ungovernable his furies, the more impossible it is to dislike him. One cannot be angry with Don Quixote.'[430] When Douglas received his pre-publication copy he was incensed: most of what he regarded as the offensive passages had been left in. He considered taking legal action for libel but decided against it out of friendship for Shaw. Instead, he demanded that Constable & Co recall the whole edition and reprint without the passages to which he had objected. In the end, a compromise was reached whereby the publishers did stop selling the book and ordered a reprint with just half of one chapter removed.

In the late 1920s and throughout the 1930s, these endless disputes over Oscar's reputation and the resulting fall-out were not just confined to the friends. In spite of his plays being staged and works being more widely read, in some circles he was still considered to be 'not quite nice to have known.' Robert Sherard, wanting confirmation that Oscar had been friendly with the Duke of Newcastle and had stayed at Clumber Park, wrote to the Duke and received the reply: 'It is, unfortunately, true that Oscar Wilde was an occasional visitor to Clumber in the late 80s, but I would be much obliged if you would let the matter rest and take no notice of the statement.' It didn't stop Sherard from quoting His Grace in *Bernard Shaw, Frank Harris & Oscar Wilde*.[431] David Hunter-Blair had been a contemporary and good friend of Oscar in the 1870s at Oxford. While there, he converted to Catholicism, later joined the Benedictine Order at Fort Augustus and eventually became its Abbot. In 1932 he was intending to give a lecture to the Catholic Poetry Society entitled 'Oscar Wilde as I knew him' but an influential member and Vice-President of the Society, Alfred Noyes, wrote to Hunter-Blair and said it would be a scandal if he were to deliver it and the meeting on 19 April was cancelled.[432] Hunter-Blair was so upset by this intolerant attitude that he still felt obliged to refuse a request for help from A. J. A. Symons three years later:

I regret to say that I cannot contribute in any way towards your proposed life of Oscar Wilde. Three or four years ago I prepared a very complete account of my Oxford friendship with him: his near approximation to the Catholic Church, his visit to Rome with me and much else of interest. I had intended reading this as a paper to a well-known Catholic society and afterwards publishing it. But owing to the very strong representations made to me by one whom I could perhaps call the head of the English Catholic laity at that time, I was practically (or morally) obliged-very much against my will, to abandon all idea of either reading my paper or publishing my recollections. Unfortunately I still feel myself bound by the promise I then made and therefore I must ask for your quite definite promise that you will not, in your forthcoming volume, make any mention of my name or of my former friendship with Wilde; or publish any letter which I may have written to him.[433]

Perhaps the most regrettable 'rejection' of Oscar around this time was by his *alma mater*, Magdalen College. Walter Ledger, who with the help of Robbie Ross and Christopher Millard had built up an extraordinary collection of Wilde's works in many editions and languages, died in December 1931 and asked that ·this collection be offered after his death to a library such as that of Magdalen. Ledger had apparently offered it to them while he was still alive, but they had turned it down and Ledger had not altered his will. This proved to be slightly embarrassing for his friend and executor, Donald Cree, when he approached them and Magdalen repeated their refusal to take it. Cree then wrote to Sir Michael Sadler the Master of University College where he himself had studied:

> An old friend of mine, whose executor I am, made during his life a wonderful collection of the writings of Oscar Wilde (a perfectly beastly person except for his writings) . . . . Now he wanted it given to some body of a semi-public nature and for the collection to be bound together and called the Robert Ross Memorial Collection. During his lifetime he offered the collection to Magdalen but they, for very obvious reasons which I learned today, refused. I suppose Univ. would not care for it. OW was such a very unpleasant person that I feel rather diffident about the whole matter and only wish that he had specialised in Kipling or some other healthy-minded writer.[434]

Sadler, a progressive educationalist and modern art collector, replied at once: 'Many thanks for your letter which interested me very much. I knew Ross quite well and had a deep respect for him. There is a sort of curse attached to almost everything about Oscar

Wilde . . . . Personally I should like to do anything in my power
to commemorate Ross.' After a brief exchange of letters, Sadler
wrote to Cree that the Fellows of the College were delighted to
accept the gift which would then be placed on a permanent but
revocable loan in the Bodleian Library. Cree, however, did offer
a word of warning on the use of the manuscript material which
was included: 'While Alfred Douglas lives, it will be as well to act
with caution, as he appears to like to discuss his past at frequent
intervals either in court or elsewhere.' The gift was publicly acknowledged in the 1930-31 issue of the *University College Record*
as 'a unique and very valuable collection of books and papers il-
lustrating the literary movement in England during the nineties of
the last century' but, sparing the feelings of its readers, without
any mention of Oscar Wilde's name. The collection lay, little used
or recognised, in the stacks of the Bodleian until it was reclaimed
by University College in 2013, and its full significance is now recognised and promoted by the college librarian, Elizabeth Adams.

The 1930s had been Douglas's decade. By the time they were
over, most of the contestants in the battle for Oscar's soul had retired, limping, from the fray. Only Douglas was left standing and
he predictably wanted the last word, which he managed to have
in two books on the subject: *Without Apology* and *Oscar Wilde: A
Summing Up*. In both he resuscitated most of the same old quarrels and brought out the same old weapons with which to fight.
He couldn't resist the occasional snipe at Harris and his 'abominable book,' and found a new enemy in W. B. Yeats who failed to
include him in his *Oxford Book of Modern Verse*, but not being
overburdened with modesty he consoled himself for the perceived
insult by writing in *Without Apology*: 'I suspected that I was a
great poet when I was twenty-three and as the years went by my
suspicion became a conviction.' He also took the opportunity to
repudiate yet again the ill-conceived publication in 1914 of *Oscar
Wilde and Myself* which had so often been held against him in turn
by those whose books he had attacked for their lies.

Douglas's last years were full of ill health and empty of money but he did manage one last claim for libel, this time against the British Museum Library for circulating Harris's book. The Museum was unable to claim 'legal deposit' as a defence because it had purchased a copy of Harris's 1918 second edition with Shaw's 'Memories of Oscar Wilde.' In an internal memo the Treasury Solicitor wrote of his previous experience of Douglas: 'Lord Alfred was invariably out for damages and nothing else. In fact he had, for years, been living on damages collected in respect of these libels,' and suggested settling for £100 and costs. It was accepted.[435] Douglas suffered a serious heart attack in the autumn of 1944 and was taken by friends, Edward and Sheila Colman, to convalesce at their farm near Lancing where he died six months later on 20 March 1945. Oscar once wrote to Bosie at the height of their 'affair' in 1894 'I find that forgiving one's enemies is a curious morbid pleasure,' something he must have finally discovered for himself as he had Masses said for Harris, Ross, and even Sherard at various times, though one wonders whether it might not have been partly to shorten his own time in purgatory as much as theirs.[436] It marked the end of the quarrels over Oscar's life between his friends, but trouble of a very different sort was already brewing for my father.

PART FOUR
(1945-1967)

CHAPTER ONE
AUSTRALIA

By 1948, my father's life seemed to be taking a turn for the better. In 1943 he had remarried, this time to a glamorous Australian woman twenty-four years his junior, Thelma Besant who in 1945 had produced the son my father had so much wanted; Lord Alfred Douglas, the last player in the Oscar 'Punch and Judy show,' had died in 1945 leaving the way open for a full edition of *De Profundis*; and since 1942 there had been major West End revivals of *The Importance of Being Earnest*, *An Ideal Husband*, and *Lady Windermere's Fan* (the latter running for more than eighteen months) as well as British and American films of the plays both for general distribution and for television. Between 1944 and 1948 the estate had received £29,495 in royalties, more than the total of the preceding thirty years. For the first time Vyvyan felt himself well-off and didn't hesitate to spend the proceeds accruing from his father's work, though on such substantial sums he naturally had to pay income tax as well as surtax, effectively reducing them in most years by more than half. [437]

In the spring of 1947 my mother, Thelma, who had been working for the international cosmetic company Cyclax since before the War, organised a fashion and beauty pageant to celebrate the fiftieth anniversary of the company's foundation using Doris Langley Moore's collection of period costumes (now safely housed in the Victoria & Albert Museum). It was such a success that Thelma was invited to spend a year travelling in Australia and New Zealand to promote Cyclax with similar shows on a smaller scale. Vyvyan decided that he and I should travel with her, a long and expensive trip only made possible by the exceptional royalties he was receiving at the time, and in late July that year we set off on the six week sea-voyage. He later estimated the fares alone must have cost over £1,000 in 1947 prices. I wonder whether we would have gone, or indeed whether my mother would have abandoned us for a year, had she and my father known what the new Labour government had in store.

On our arrival in Melbourne, the press coverage over ten days was enormous, helped no doubt by some sleuth uncovering Thelma's link with Buckingham Palace. During the War, alongside organising charity events for the Red Cross and the Armed Forces as well as developing camouflage creams for the army, my mother had managed Cyclax's beauty salon in Mayfair. Among her more prestigious clients were Ladies of the Royal Household, one of whom was marrying her daughter at Windsor Castle in the autumn of 1944 and asked my mother to do the young bride's make-up on her wedding day. Thelma, who had already noticed the remarkable 'English rose' complexion of Princess Elizabeth from her war service photos of her in the Women's ATS, saw this as a possible entrée to the Palace itself, though Royal protocol obviously demanded absolute tact and a diplomatic approach.[438] How she pulled it off was never revealed, but the bride's make-up was clearly remarked on and a word in the right ear led to my mother being invited to Buckingham Palace on 14 November 1944 to advise the 18 year-old Princess on general skin care and the use of make-up. It was a role she was to fulfil off and on over the next twenty-two years, giving first the Princess and then the Queen regular face treatments, as well as advising on cosmetics and their colour coordination with the Queen's wardrobe for Royal tours and special occasions, the most important of which was to be the Coronation. This connection between Cyclax and the Palace had been treated with the utmost discretion back in England and at no point was it hinted at in the London pageant or the surrounding publicity. Once it was out in the open, Thelma had little choice but to play along and play it down, terrified that the emphasis on her being 'Princess Elizabeth's beauty adviser' would be attributed to her wanting the publicity and the Palace would terminate the arrangement as soon as she returned to Britain. In the event, as her press-cutting book shows, she managed the journalists quite skilfully and parried any awkward personal questions about the Princess by concentrating on her perfect complexion, so much so that for weeks before the Royal marriage Australian women were queuing to be made up 'like the Princess.'[439] The Palace, to Thelma's relief, showed that it saw no harm in her promotion of the Royal skin by replying to her wedding cable with one of its own:

> THE PRINCESS ELIZABETH DESIRES TO THANK YOU FOR THE VERY KIND MESSAGE OF CONGRATULATIONS WHICH GAVE HER ROYAL HIGHNESS MUCH PLEASURE . . . PRIVATE SECRETARY.[440]

Thelma loved every column inch of publicity she generated, which was far beyond anything her employers had ever expected.[441] For Vyvyan, who had spent the last forty years shunning publicity of any sort, the situation was as novel as it was uncomfortable. He seemed distinctly ambivalent about the idea on one hand of playing consort to 'Miss Thelma Besant, the famous beauty specialist' while on the other he was being billed as 'a noted gourmet,' 'one of the best translators from the French in England' and, inevitably, as 'Oscar Wilde's only surviving son,' occasionally elbowing my mother out of the limelight. Unlike the British press around that time, which was always ready to remind its public of the reasons for Wilde's downfall, the Australians managed to put Vyvyan at ease by concentrating on the positive and literary side of his father rather than on his personal failings. Though he couldn't have known it at the time, it was the start of a coming to terms with his family history which would culminate in his writing *Son of Oscar Wilde* six years later. He was able to talk proudly about 'retaining cherished first editions of almost all his father's works'[442] which would have been an unthinkable comment to have made to the newspapers in London. Just as he was in Continental Europe, so in Australia Oscar Wilde was treated as a writer and an artist. Any passing references to his downfall were made in a matter-of-fact manner rather than the salacious and judgmental one characteristic of the tabloids back home. 'Vyvyan Holland—his name was changed when that fierce, blinding light of notoriety drenched his father's fame and wit—is the absolute opposite of any mental picture of that magnificent, flamboyant writer,' was about as close as Australia came to criticism.[443]

Fans of Oscar Wilde, not inhibited by his mixed reputation as they would have been in England, addressed him on the subject quite freely. It was another point of view, unencumbered with the moribund leftovers of Victorian propriety, and to begin with he seemed slightly unsure of how to deal with it. When someone sent to his hotel a volume of Oscar's *Essays and Lectures* to sign, my father wrote in his diary: 'Such fame! I never know what to put on these occasions. In fact life becomes more and more embarrassing daily. I feel like an animal at the zoo and am constantly expecting someone to thrust a bun at me stuck on the end of an umbrella.'[444] Towards the end of the Hollands' Antipodean tour in May 1948, on one day Vyvyan declared that he was in a hot and cold sweat at the prospect of having to talk to the press before the Australian film première of Alexander Korda's *An Ideal Husband*, and yet on the next that 'This is the worst week for publicity that we have ever had,' bemoaning the lack of it rather than the quality. Ten days later in Brisbane a waitress in their hotel exclaimed, 'I saw you both on the Movietone News yesterday. Oscar Wilde's son! What a thrill!' prompting the comment in Vyvyan's diary: 'It was one of the more embarrassing moments of my life.'[445]

For fifty years in England my father had seen Oscar Wilde's reputation swinging like a weathervane in the breeze of popular opinion or more often in the storm of scandal; his work and his life were kept tactfully at arm's length from one other. Even though there were revivals of the plays and new editions of the works, in the background there was still hushed talk of perversion, scandal, prison and disgrace. Now, after ten months spent in Australia and New Zealand, Vyvyan discovered that there were people who took an entirely different view of his father. One can read it between the lines of his diary. His account of that tour in his later memoir, *Time Remembered*, says nothing of this and instead reads like a travelogue interspersed with a few amusing anecdotes, but at the end of the chapter devoted to it is the following statement: 'I had for some time thought of writing a book about my early life, but I had avoided doing so for fear of turning the knife in old wounds. But on my return to London I settled down to try and recapture my childhood.'[446] Vyvyan's experience of the Antipodes was to change his life almost as radically as Oscar's had been changed by his own year-long lecture tour of America in 1882.

Our return from Australia, however, was a return to the nation in which some eminent people continued, in Robbie Ross's words, to enjoy kicking Oscar's corpse.[447] In July 1948, a couple of weeks before our arrival back at Tilbury, a book had appeared in the Notable British Trials Series entitled *The Trials of Oscar Wilde*. Its editor was Harford Montgomery Hyde, a lawyer who had taken an interest in Wilde ever since occupying his old college rooms at Magdalen in the late 1920s. He had started collecting Wilde books and manuscripts before the War and as a result became a recognised authority on the subject. His edition of Oscar's three trials was, broadly speaking, just a rehash of Christopher Millard's *Three Times Tried* which had appeared in 1912 and with which Millard intended to dispel 'a vague fog of obscenity in which truths, already sufficiently repulsive, have been covered by inventions even more hateful.'[448] Hyde with his barrister's knowledge of legal proceedings and the formal modes of address by counsel to the bench, transformed reported into direct speech, made some conjectures about which passages from Wilde's works were read aloud to the court, and added a sentence or two from the newspapers of the time. He never acknowledged his debt to Millard other than stating that his work had been long out of print. There was very little new in the volume; practically all of it had been published before (apart from a useful, informative introduction putting it all in context), but for my father it was something of a blow.[449] It was not entirely unexpected as he had corresponded with Hyde the year before and refused him permission to quote from *De Profundis*. The recent revivals of the plays and the increasing public acclaim of Wilde as a writer had unquestionably helped Vyvyan to look less harshly on the legacy of his father, but now the whole scandal was being set out afresh. Sir Patrick Hastings, one time Attorney-General, used the occasion to write an odious and undisguisedly homophobic piece in the Scottish press which started: 'For half-a-century the name of Oscar Wilde has been a byword in our language. It typifies all that is degraded in human life and at the same time remains the centre of a controversy whether or not it is for the general good that the glare of publicity should be directed upon a social cesspit.' And finished: 'It is idle to argue that his offence is more pathological than criminal. Such a man is a social leper, and as such should be regarded.'[450] It gave me my first taste (happily unremembered) of what it was to have this man as my grandfather. 'Not long after Harford published *The Trials of OW*,' my mother later wrote to Hyde's wife, 'there was the usual deleterious press publicity from our point of view. The woman I had looking after Merlin at the time, told me that they were ostracised by parents and nannies. Merlin was of course not old enough to know anything about this, but I think you will sympathise with my discomforture.'[451] The news of who my grandfather was even found its way to the ears of my kindergarten teachers. I happened to be very good friends with Simon Ward-Jackson, the son of my godfather and took to putting an arm around his shoulders when we were out walking in our school 'crocodile.' A stop was soon put to this and we were told not pair up together. Perplexed, Simon told his mother who many years later reminded me of the incident. For Vyvyan to have been 'Oscar Wilde's son' in Australia was one thing; in England the fact was best unmentioned and being 'Oscar's grandson' aged six wasn't much better.

One afternoon in August, as we were wandering round the Open Air Sculpture exhibition in Battersea Park, we ran into

Maurice Lancaster, an old friend who was on the staff of *Time Magazine*. He had a couple of photographers with him wanting illustrations for a feature on the exhibition and, to my father's horror, suggested including us in the shots. 'That sort of thing is all very large and fine in Australia, but in England one must draw the line somewhere,' he noted. A few days later he remarked that Thelma was 'disgruntled because we are not moving in high society; I cannot make her believe that the combination of my being Oscar Wilde's son and very poor is an insuperable obstacle.'[452] To have described himself as 'poor' on the receipts of the Wilde estate in the previous few years would have been absurd, but he was in fact anticipating the financial catastrophe which was fast approaching.

On 6 April 1948, while we were still in Australia, the Chancellor of the Exchequer Sir Stafford Cripps presented his annual Financial & Economic Statement ('the Budget') to Parliament. For some time there had been talk of a capital levy or wealth tax, but it was a sensitive political issue as well as being impracticable in the short term because of the logistical difficulties of nationwide valuation. Instead, he proposed a one-off 'Special Contribution' a tax on the investment income of individuals for the year 1947-48 which was intended to help revive the economy, severely drained by six years of war. Under the heading of investment income fell Vyvyan's royalties, the capital asset being Wilde's remaining copyrights. At the top end, the tax payable was 50% and into this bracket fell nearly half of his royalties from the period. Unfortunately, it had been the most lucrative year ever for the Wilde estate with net proceeds of nearly £8,300. Alexander Korda had made a film of *An Ideal Husband; The Importance* had been made into an American television film; and in a separate production John Gielgud had played it in New York and toured it across the States. Although Vyvyan had made provision to pay his tax and surtax, he couldn't have foreseen the 'Special Contribution'—which was in effect being levied retrospectively—and the income from which to pay it had already been spent. He commented wryly that he would have been better off in some ways, and certainly in less of a financial mess, had his father's plays been less successful.[453]

The Chancellor had stated in his Budget speech that he was aware the tax could be seen as a charge on capital and that the sale of assets in many cases might be the only way to pay it. Vyvyan therefore nursed a vague hope that he and his solicitor might argue a case for exemption or at least a substantial reduction in the amount levied as the 'asset' of copyright was far more nebulous and unrealisable than a portfolio of shares. Prepared for the worst, that autumn he started to take desperate measures. He tried to persuade Korda to buy film rights in *Salomé,* simultaneously playing him off against De Mille in Hollywood though neither showed much interest, aware that the rights would fall into the public domain in two years' time. He then approached Binkie Beaumont, the theatrical producer at H. M. Tennant, with a proposal to purchase the acting rights to Wilde's four major plays for a lump sum, though was met with much the same response. Tennant had staged the immensely successful 600-performance run of *Lady Windermere's Fan* in 1945-47 and Binkie was well disposed towards Vyvyan, but felt ultimately that the post-War revivals were still too recent to warrant further investment in the plays.[454]

The attempted fire-sale of his father's plays being a disaster, Vyvyan turned his attention to one of Oscar's works which still had life in it beyond the normal term of copyright—*De Profundis.* Of this long letter to Alfred Douglas, which had been the cause of so many recriminations and so much pain over the years, more than half was still unpublished in England. My father had inherited one of the typewritten transcripts made originally by Robbie Ross and offered to produce from it the first unexpurgated version in English for Methuen & Co. Douglas was no longer alive to threaten legal action for libel as he had so often done in the past, and while there was no immediate hurry to secure copyright for the unpublished material it was, as Oscar himself had said in a letter to Robbie: 'the only document that really gives any explanation of my extraordinary behaviour with regard to Queensberry and Alfred Douglas.'[455] As well as generating some badly needed income, I suspect Vyvyan saw in it something of a public antidote to the 'damage' caused by Hyde's publication of the Wilde trials.

Francis Queensberry, grandson of the 'screaming scarlet marquess' and Bosie's nephew, had shown some interest in publishing the previously suppressed passages of *De Profundis* in a book he was writing with Percy Coulson which, he led my father to believe, was largely about his Uncle Alfred. A bibliophile and collector (somewhat bizarrely) of Wilde books and manuscripts, Francis was altogether a more civilized creature than his pugilist grandfather, and he and Vyvyan had become friends. My father had some misgivings about the use of *De Profundis* in this context, partly because Methuen & Co had the publishing rights on the abridged version and might claim a sort of first refusal over the rest, and partly because it would reduce the impact of his own first English publication of the complete text. When Queensberry sent the typescript of his book *Oscar Wilde and the Black Douglas* to my father for approval, Vyvyan was surprised to find that it was more of a 'pamphlet on Oscar Wilde' than a life of Douglas and that Francis had dedicated it to him 'in sincere friendship.' This made preventing the extensive use of the new material somewhat awkward:

> Francis Queensberry has now finished his life of Uncle Alfred and is going to dedicate it to me! This is a real bit of poetic justice; not only that, it will probably prove conclusively whether there is any survival after death, as if there is, both the old Marquess and Alfred himself will undoubtedly return and encompass Francis's death in circumstances of extreme agony.[456]

A compromise was reached and Vyvyan's edition came out in October 1949 with Queensberry's book publishing a month later, but it was not the first time nor the last that Oscar's prison letter would put a strain on friendships. In any event, it transpired that Ross's typescript was both faulty and incomplete and it wasn't until the manuscript was unsealed by the British Museum in 1960 that the first accurate version could be published. Reviewing *De Profundis* in *The Listener*, Herbert Read referred to Douglas as 'the most complete cad in history,' a description which enraged Marie Stopes, the birth control pioneer. Stopes, whose improbable friendship with Bosie had started in 1938, responded by branding the book as 'the hysterical and deranged outpourings of Oscar Wilde . . . then in a condition bordering on insanity owing to the excessive shock to his self-esteem of prison and the exposure of the abnormal and filthy practices, which he had been indulging in with stable boys.'[457] Her outburst led to further correspondence from readers condemning her 'bigoted moral fervour,' none of which did anything to help Vyvyan in coming to terms with his family history. It was the first time he had publicly associated himself with his father in print and it had led almost at once to controversy. On a happier note a copy of *De Profundis* sent to John Gielgud prompted the following:

> I am greatly touched by your kind gesture in sending me the beautifully bound volume of *De Profundis*. My association with you, slight though it has been, has been so invariably cordial and charming, and I like so much to think that, in however humble a way, I have been a small contributor to the awakening of an increasing appreciation of your father's unique genius. The more I read and hear of him, the more I salute the sweetness of his character and his splendour of achievement against such fearful odds.[458]

They were words which others might well have applied to Gielgud himself four years later when he had his own brush with the same law which had sent Oscar to prison in 1895.

In March 1949 the Inland Revenue confirmed that Vyvyan's substantial 1947-48 royalties were subject to the Special Contribution and he was going to have to find £3,600. All he could see was the prospect of a downward spiral into insolvency. Although there would certainly be a few more royalties coming in before they fell into the public domain at the end of 1950, and these could be used to stave off any legal proceedings from the Revenue for recovery of the Special Contribution debt, they would also be subject to income-and surtax in due course and then what? It seemed just a matter of time.

Regular entries in his diary at the time veer between dark humour and despair:

> I awoke just before dawn and lay awake brooding with horror over the financial situation. I do not care much for myself as I could always get a job (well-paid) as the hall-porter of a French brothel or even as a Cook's man which, though less paid than the former, is always worth a couple of thousand a year. I am worried to death about Thelma and Merlin; at the rate at which we are proceeding, I imagine we shall begin to sell our possessions towards the end of 1951 and that by the end of 1954 we shall be destitute.'[459]

It would turn out to be prophetically accurate.

CHAPTER TWO
WRITING *SON OF OSCAR WILDE*

I n May 1949, at the end of Chelsea Week, I had gone with my father to watch a hot-air balloon take off from the Duke of York's barracks in the King's Road. 'I adored the whole thing because it took one back to the nineteenth century and its culture and learning and smoothness of life,' he wrote in his diary, and after dinner that evening he decided 'whomever it might annoy or hurt, that I would write down the history of my unhappy childhood,' and then wrote the first 1500 words.[460] However, the constant worry of unpaid tax and other debts, together with the regular reminders of how the British public as a whole still seemed to view his father, effectively meant that committing his memories to paper took far longer than he anticipated. His Australian experiences the year before had undoubtedly given him the incentive to start, but what began as an exercise in laying to rest some painful childhood memories, soon took on a rather different role: that of keeping him afloat financially and of presenting his father in another light to a public which still tended to regard Oscar as a model of selfishness and depravity.

Another year passed before he resumed the writing of it, and when he did it was with certain misgivings. Behind the scenes Thelma was working on several of Vyvyan's oldest friends, among them Alec Waugh and Freddie Birkenhead whose judgement in literary matters she knew he trusted. In May 1950 Thelma lunched with Alec and reported back that he felt sure the book would be an immediate success in America. Vyvyan was not convinced: 'The main difficulty about this is that I must either give names, which would open me up to dozens of libel cases or give no names and then the book would be unutterably dull. It seems to be the sort of book that could only possibly have a *succès de scandale*.' He had also accepted a job working full-time for a public relations firm owned by Richmond Temple which specialised in the hotel industry and he was disinclined to spend his leisure hours working on a memoir which he was beginning to feel would have little interest for the general public. Temple had been Robbie Ross's protégé and, as detailed in Part Three, Chapter One, it was he who had separated Vyvyan from the little capital he possessed and lost it in an ill-conceived business venture. Why my father agreed to work for a man from whom he had parted company so acrimoniously in the 1920s I have never discovered, but Vyvyan's legal training, his knowledge of wine and food, and his literary background all suited him perfectly for the job. I suspect it was partly down to a guilty conscience on Temple's part since he knew of my father's financial difficulties, and with the Inland Revenue snapping at his heels, Vyvyan had little choice but to accept, but it meant putting the book to one side.

All this was taking place against a backdrop of public indifference to Oscar Wilde or even dislike of him as an individual. My father's publication of the first (purportedly complete) English edition of *De Profundis* at the end of 1949 was received in a largely lukewarm manner. Compared with our view of the work today and our better understanding of its author, it's clear that some of the reviewers had difficulty in concealing their animosity. We tend to forget that Wilde was still regarded by much of the literary establishment of the early 1950s as talentless, superficial and perverted, and extracts from reviews at the time confirm it:

'*De Profundis* . . . is like a distorting mirror in which the faults of Douglas are extravagantly swollen so as to offset the responsibility of the older man for the disaster which overtook them both.'[461]

'Wilde writes to the friend he held responsible for his ruin in accents that are often undignified, conceited and rancorous.'[462]

'One asks oneself . . . how such a stylist could have written on the same page terse vigorous prose of which any writer might be proud and shoddy purple patches that would have been blue-pencilled in an undergraduate essay.'[463]

'*De Profundis* reads like the pitiful nagging of a forsaken mistress at her former lover. It is an attempt to plumb emotional depths by an essentially shallow mind . . . It is understandable that Lord Alfred should have preferred to prevent publication in his lifetime. It is rather less easy to comprehend what anybody should have bothered to repair the omission thereafter.'[464]

Reading these press cuttings and others, carefully preserved by Vyvyan in a scrapbook, I could imagine how he must have felt at seeing Oscar's letter from prison described in such unflattering terms. What was the point of writing about his childhood memories and linking himself even more closely to a father who aroused such antipathy?

A year later, on 30 November 1950, the fiftieth anniversary of Oscar's death passed almost without comment in England apart from a long article in the *Times Literary Supplement* by John Sparrow which concluded: 'Apart from one perfect play, one memorable poem and the new full version of *De Profundis*, Wilde left little with which, as literature, posterity need seriously concern itself. He was a brilliant writer of letters and teller of stories and master of the epigram and the aphorism,' and he agreed that Wilde's self-assessment as having put his genius into his life but only his talent into his works was seen by most critics to be all too correct. In Paris, by contrast, Oscar was remembered with four days of literary events organised by a 'Comité d'Honneur' which included such illustrious names as André Maurois, Sacha Guitry, and Jean Cocteau. It was also an appropriate anniversary on which to place Robbie Ross's ashes into Oscar's tomb in Père Lachaise Cemetery as he had requested in his will thirty-two years before. Until then it had been impossible to do it for fear of Bosie Douglas causing a scene, although it could probably have been done discreetly without Douglas's knowledge. Vyvyan was invited to attend, but he refused to go, and my mother went in his place so that there was at least some 'Wilde family' presence. Given all that Robbie had done for Oscar's legacy and the affection in which Vyvyan had held him, this has always seemed strange to me, but there were many factors behind his refusal, some more emotional than others. He hated having to attend functions labelled as 'Oscar Wilde's son'; he decided on the advice of friends that it would be 'undignified' for him to go—though I don't quite follow why; and since no one was prepared to pay for his travel, he resented having to spend the money, especially as it was on the very day that the royalties on Oscar's works were coming to an end.[465] No amount of persuasion on my mother's part would make him change his mind, so it was she who went, together with Margery Ross, Robbie's niece by marriage who carried his ashes to Père Lachaise. During her stay in Paris, my mother was taken to the Hôtel d'Alsace which was still being run by the daughter of Jean Dupoirier, the proprietor who had been so generous to Oscar in his last days. Mlle Dupoirier had carefully preserved two mementos from 1900: one of Oscar's shirts embroidered with the initials SM (Sebastian Melmoth was his pseudonym in exile), and his false teeth and these she offered to Thelma who gratefully accepted the first but turned down the second as being too macabre. Had it been my father I know he would have taken neither, so the shirt has survived somewhat against the odds.

By the start of 1951, Vyvyan still hadn't returned to his autobiography and the family financial situation was growing worse by the day. He entered newspaper competitions, did the football pools, put money he couldn't afford on the horses and started to sell his books as well as the stamp collection which he had built up over many years. There was—though not under the same dreadful circumstances—an uncomfortable echo of the dispersal of Oscar's possessions at his house in Tite Street while he was awaiting trial. 'Long after I am dead Merlin will rail against his daddy, whom he loves now, for having left him defenceless; very much in the same way as I rail against my own progenitor today, though I loved him dearly when I was Merlin's age.'[466] I never did. All I did feel was a sense of profound sadness and sympathy at what he must have endured and it was to be in large part thanks to reading the memoir which he was hesitating to write. The end of the year brought a tidal wave of bad news. Within the space of two weeks before Christmas he received a final notice from the Inland Revenue for the unpaid Special Contribution; Richmond Temple ended his employment at the PR consultancy; and, with no prior warning, St. John Ervine's *Oscar Wilde: a Present Time Appraisal* suddenly appeared in the bookshops. Ervine's book, while promising in its blurb to be an objective assessment of Wilde the dramatist and writer, did nothing of the sort. On the contrary much of it was a vicious and unrelenting attack on both Oscar's life and his work. Ervine spat his venom at Wilde with all the resentment of one literary man for another whose work he despises because it has been more successful—and in his view unjustifiably so—than his own. I suppose one should hardly be surprised to find an acerbic Unionist Ulsterman writing about a witty Republican Dubliner's style as being 'in the manner of an author of servant girls' novelettes,' nor describing the well-known portrait of Oscar and Bosie at Oxford as 'a frightful photograph . . . [showing] Wilde looking like an overblown bookie with a pretty barmaid at Epsom . . . That man, bulging out of his tightly-buttoned striped suit, was not designed for tragedy. Intended for a farce, he was miscast in tragedy.' Even less does he spare poor, loyal Robbie Ross, to whom he attributes an unduly large proportion of blame in Oscar's downfall, and refers to him as a 'small, obsequious sodomite . . . [who] had many of the excellent virtues of a Norland nurse.' And in concluding his *Present Time Appraisal* Ervine cannot resist delivering his *coup de grâce* 'Wilde came into the world with a small talent and made little of it. He did worse than that. He cast such pearls as he had before swine, and then wallowed with the swine at the troughs in the sty.'[467] Normally restrained critics such a Jocelyn Brooke were incensed: 'Mr. Ervine's book is the most sustained and belligerent diatribe against Wilde, the man, that I have yet read, rivalling in some of its more bombastic passages the epistolary frenzies of the "Scarlet Marquess" himself. It seems extraordinary that poor

Wilde should still be capable of provoking such hysterical fury.'[468] Harold Nicolson, took issue with Ervine's assessment of Wilde in exile as being 'vulgar, wicked, lustful, untruthful, selfish and coarse' and asked 'Why does the Red Hand of Ulster deal this unhappy man these resounding smacks now that he has been dead for more than half a century?'[469] Moreover, Nicolson had been a friend of Robbie Ross and took the spiteful descriptions of him as a personal slight. For Vyvyan it was doubly painful to see his father so savaged and Robbie, who had done so much for Oscar in his lifetime and then for his posthumous reputation, so scurrilously attacked, making it that much harder for him to start writing again about his early life.

In an odd way it was the very awfulness of Ervine's book which may have pushed Vyvyan into tackling the subject from a different viewpoint, in order to counteract this entirely negative portrayal of Oscar Wilde as an author as well as a human being. By the second week of January 1952, my father had started pulling together the threads of his life in exile in 1895/96. Another very public blow to Oscar's reputation then came on 24 February: the *News of the World* ran a 2500 word piece in its series of notable British trials by Travers Humphreys who had been junior counsel on Wilde's legal team in all three trials in 1895. Entitled 'The Importance of Being Oscar Wilde: Disaster at the Height of his Fame,' it covered only the trials, reinforcing the image of Wilde as a pervert and criminal, everything which Vyvyan was keen to avoid being emphasised. The only mention of his work was a repeat of Ervine's unflattering conclusion about his lack of talent. It infuriated my mother and prompted my father to write to Radley College 'to see if there is any record of Cyril's athletic prowess to be had; I think that a record of his activities may do a great deal to counteract Pop's so-called degeneracy.'[470] In what way he imagined that Cyril's masculinity was going, retrospectively, to counterbalance his father's perceived degeneracy was unclear. He did, indeed, include a whole catalogue of his brother's athletic achievements in the finished book, though it was used in a more subtle way to show how Cyril's determination, even then, 'to restore the family honour' would affect his whole life. As he put it to my father in the letter he wrote from India in 1914, 'I became obsessed with the idea that . . . first and foremost, I must be a *man*.'[471]

Earlier in the New Year Binkie Beaumont had suggested that Vyvyan might like to work with the screenwriter, Paul Dehn, and revamp *A Woman of No Importance* in order to make it less sententious and more in line with the humour of Oscar's three other society plays. He was also offering a 'small courtesy royalty.' Vyvyan was uncomfortable with the idea due to the probable reaction of the critics, but should it succeed it would provide some instant income, so he overcame any scruples he may have had and set about it. The 'new' play was staged in February 1953 to a predictably mixed reception by the critics, but it gave Vyvyan a little badly needed money and, above all, it gave him another excuse *not* to get on with his memoir. Encouraged by this brief excursion into drama, in June he started writing a comedy of his own which he sent to Beaumont in July. It came back rejected as being too slight and lacking in characterisation despite what Binkie called 'the wit and the really skilful writing.' Meanwhile money was growing ever shorter; the bank was refusing to cash his cheques; a visit was made to the pawnbrokers 'for the first time in forty years'; and two treasured Beardsley drawings were sold to pay the rent. My mother, still convinced that the autobiography was the solution to their current problems became more forceful:

> I was driven out of bed at 7 am by Thelma urging me to write about my early life. I can imagine nothing so horribly macabre and gloomy, or anything that would do Merlin more harm. If I were alone in the world, I would write it for posthumous publication . . . But I can see nothing but sorrow arising from it now.[472]

He soon gave in and noted on 22 Sept 1952 that he had written 'nearly 3000 words covering most of my first six years and not drawing very much on my imagination either.' It was that last phrase which, when I first read it sixty years after he had written it, seemed to be putting the key to the door of a secret room in my hands, but I wasn't sure that I wanted to open it for fear of what I would find. Was it possible that a few parts of this book, my father's memoir which for years had made his early life so real for me, could be mere inventions? For a while I buried the thought and just followed Vyvyan's false starts and prevarications through the pages of his diary, Desultory bits of research and writing interspersed with articles on wine and food for *House and Garden* and a monthly 'Lettre de Londres' for the Parisian *Nouvelles Littéraires,* brought him into the New Year when Thelma started to take a more active (if not altogether helpful) role in the matter. 'We discussed the autobiography and quarrelled violently over it. Thelma wants it to be largely a life of papa, which would only mean lifting it bodily from Hesketh Pearson etc., which would get damning reviews. I still think the whole proposition is rather unwise.'[473] As I read of his reluctance to start writing, I understood and sympathised as I realised that the original motive, a cathartic revisiting of an unhappy childhood, had largely given way both to the need for money and to effect a credible make-over of Oscar through the eyes of his son. It was never going to be easy, but having to regard the writing more as an obligation just made it more difficult. By the end of January he had settled down to writing in earnest and in order to give a historical perspective to the Wilde family, he had started to tackle what he called the Prologue: 'I have got to expand that first chapter of my book, however fictional it may seem. On the other hand, I must not put the Wilde expert off by being too far-fetched.'[474] In the published book Vyvyan attributed the family name to a Dutch soldier of fortune, a Colonel de Wilde who had settled in Connaught after fighting the Irish under William III. He also maintained that Oscar was named after the King of Sweden on whom Sir William had performed a successful cataract operation just after Oscar's birth and who consequently agreed to become godfather to the new arrival. I can remember repeating these stories until I was about thirty because (as was intended) they sounded somehow impressive, yet as I conducted my own research into Oscar and the family, I realised that there was no historical evidence for them whatsoever. Vyvyan's diary entry merely confirmed my suspicion that, on the contrary, what was generally accepted to have been the Wildes' origins was an enterprising builder who had gone from Durham to Dublin in the eighteenth century to seek his fortune. My father more or less owned up to the invention six weeks later when he was briefly hospitalised with an uncontrollable nose-bleed: 'I was washed this morning by a small dark nurse who looked exactly like a young Speranza [Oscar's mother] and said she came from Durham. She is probably a near relative of mine.'[475] I began to realise that the key to what I imagined to be a secret room was redundant; the door was wide open; it was all in front of me in those diary entries and it would be up to me to put this uncomfortable discovery properly in context.

For the next six months Vyvyan worked at the book more or less full-time, though concerned that it would be too short and that he would still be having to rely more on his imagination than his memory and none of it made any easier by Thelma's adverse criticisms. She wanted the book to be more 'dramatic.' 'So be it.' he wrote. 'I told her that it was going to be the thriller of the year and that I proposed to call it "No Orchids for Mrs. Wilde". Phrases like 'I think I can spin it out if I use a bit of imagination, but I shall have to be careful how I romance about Stonyhurst and Trinity Hall,' and 'I finished the first draft of Chapter 2 with a lot of invention and padding,' continued to worry me, though by mid-June his mood had changed for the better: 'I am now thoroughly enjoying writing my book. It is lovely reliving the past and remembering all the things one has forgotten.' However, once he had written his way past the death of his mother and his return to England in 1898, he realized, in more senses than one, that he was on his own: 'From now onwards there is no more talk of mum or dad and the interest centres on the psychology of the growing lad . . . The enemy in our midst is the time factor. I must get money somehow to pay the rent.' Fortunately the material problems were temporarily solved at the end of July by Rupert Hart-Davis Ltd paying a generous advance of £500 for the book, but the disagreements over which aspects of Vyvyan's early life it should cover were only just beginning.

Having encouraged my father from the outset, my mother unaccountably had no constructive criticism to make. 'Thelma thinks the book pedestrian, unconvincing and dull. This rather upsets me as she is the public that I want to get at. However, I don't suppose it matters much so long as publishers are prepared to make advances.'[476] The publisher was in favour of Vyvyan dropping in as many literary names as possible and even suggested incorporating a version of the long essay he had written in 1930 on Ronald Firbank, one of his close friends at Cambridge. Vyvyan resisted arguing it would totally unbalance to book. Spencer Curtis Brown, his agent, was more in tune with Vyvyan's view that it should be a largely introspective book about losing his father and then finding him posthumously, but there was a fine line between being Vyvyan Holland and Vyvyan Wilde; still the old reluctance to be identified as his father's son. This in turn led to an argument over the title. Vyvyan was clinging to the semi-anonymity of nearly sixty years and wanted it called 'Grief Forgotten' after lines from Swinburne. Spencer, quite rightly, said that *Son of Oscar Wilde* was essential if it was to sell: '"Grief Forgotten", though a perfectly good title for a novel, is quite unilluminating as a title for a non-fiction work. It might be the title of a sad travel book, or the biography of a third century saint.' Spencer had his way.

There were still occasional glimpses of public discomfort—if not outright homophobia—expressed about his father which Vyvyan encountered as the book neared completion. He wrote to Portora School in Enniskillen for details of Oscar's achievements as a schoolboy and received a lengthy letter from the headmaster, Douglas Graham, including the sentence 'We are proud that your father came from this school.' Vyvyan asked if he might use it as a quotation, but in his apologetic reply Graham explained that

the 'vehemently narrow-minded and old fashioned' school gov-
ernors would rather he did not, 'especially as the whole subject
of homosexuality is at the moment coming before the public and
they must consider the prejudices of the parents and potential parents of boys here.'[477] In the same letter Graham told how Oscar's
name had been painted out on the scholars' board at the time of
his conviction and how an Old Portoran recalled seeing a previous headmaster, armed with hammer and chisel, chipping away
at a window reveal in a classroom where Oscar had carved his
initials.[478] Years later and for reasons to do with Oscar's attraction to Catholicism, I contacted Father Holt, the archivist at the
Jesuit Church in Farm Street, Mayfair. He told me he had been
a history teacher at Stonyhurst in the early 1960s and had once
seen 'V. Holland' carved on a school desk. During a history lesson he had asked the boy sitting there if he had any idea who 'V.
Holland' was. Naturally he hadn't, which was then an opportunity
to teach the class about Oscar Wilde, the family's change of name,
and to explain Vyvyan's presence at the school—a perfect example
of living history. I'm sorry that my father never knew; it would
have amused him to think that a minor schoolboy naughtiness,
similar to Oscar's, had helped contribute a little to his own father's
rehabilitation.[479]

He eventually delivered the typescript to his agent on 14
October but the relief at having finished was almost immediately
blighted by two events in quick succession. On 16 October—
ironically on Oscar's birthday—an arrest warrant was issued for
Lord Montagu who was accused of committing offences with boy-
scouts earlier in the year at Beaulieu. Then, on 21 October Sir
John Gielgud appeared in court and was fined for 'cottaging' in
Chelsea the evening before. The newspapers went to town on the
two cases, giving them front page exposure and causing Vyvyan to
write despairingly 'I wish, oh! how I wish that the Press had not
chosen this particular time to start a [anti-] "queer" campaign . . . I
am afraid that my own wretched book will only feed the flames, if
it ever gets so far as being printed.'[480] Matters were not improved

by his publisher asking for large parts of the book to be rewritten. The original version hasn't survived so it's impossible to tell how the focus was changed, but it was clear that Vyvyan began to regret having written the book at all. Milton Waldman, Hart-Davis's editor, regarded any adolescent reminiscences which couldn't be directly linked to the whole Oscar story as irrelevant. In retrospect he may have been right, but having been encouraged to write the book Vyvyan found it irksome that he was now being asked to take second place to his father in what was intended to be an autobiography. Despite its title, *Son of Oscar Wilde* was supposed to give Vyvyan a life of his own rather than putting him further into the shadow of his father. Far from being the healing voyage into his past, which for years I made it out to be, by Christmas 1953 it was clearly becoming a nightmare with the agent, the publisher, and my mother all pulling him in different directions.

Whatever I may have thought later about my mother and her endless and tiresome attempts to whitewash her father-in-law, when times were hard in the family she did manage to keep us from sinking beneath the flood of creditors in which we always seemed to be on the point of drowning. The end of 1953 was no exception. The directors of Cyclax in Australia, with whom she had started her career in cosmetics before the war, were keen to get Thelma back 'Down Under' to coincide with the Queen's first Royal Tour of their country in February-March the following year. Initially, the head-office in London refused to let her go, but eventually gave in and on 6 January Thelma set off for five months, with all expenses paid and earning three times her London salary. I'm sure she felt ambivalent about having to spend so much time away from her family, especially when men were still expected to be the main breadwinners, but my mother was never publicity-shy. She was proud in a necessarily discreet way of her connections with the Palace and Australia always fêted her as one of their own for making a successful career in London. When she married Vyvyan, she knew that it would open all sorts of social doors into the world of arts, entertainment, and literature, but I don't think

she ever reckoned on the money running out, nor the scandals being resuscitated. 'If I had known about the Wildes' filth, I would
never have married into the family,' Vyvyan recorded her as saying two days before leaving for Australia.[481] Charitably one should
put it down to the stress of everything that was going on in her life
at that moment, but my father certainly wouldn't have written it
down if she hadn't said it and one can imagine his feelings when
she did.

The next five months saw Vyvyan at an all-time low. Despite
the re-writes which he had undertaken in December the publisher
was still not happy with the book and asked for yet more chapters to be redone. He scrapped much of his schooldays, though
later fought to have them restored, and began to hate the book
which, against his better judgement, so many people had encouraged him to write. In fact, his editor insisted on so many changes
that he felt the book no longer had the stamp of his own personality. Fortunately for posterity, he rebelled and reinstated some of
the excisions, but much of what he thought and felt in those early
years, things a publisher today would insist on, must have finished
up as scrap paper. His financial situation was dire with creditors
threatening legal action every week that went by, staved off only
by Thelma remitting some of her salary from Australia along with
morale-boosting letters. One debt, however, was the greatest worry
of all and in early February the Inland Revenue finally issued a
writ for £3,068 for Vyvyan's unpaid 'Special Contribution' on his
1947/48 royalties. Twice in the space of a month he writes that
had it not been for Thelma and me he would have ended it all: 'If
I live another year, I shall be in the workhouse, in the Bankruptcy
Court or behind bars. What an unholy mess I have made of my
life! Nevertheless, let us buckle on our armour and make one last
effort.'[482] Thelma also had problems of her own. Apart from the
immensely long days she was spending promoting Cyclax in public, she had issues with the press. The company was determined to
make as much capital as possible out of the connection with the
Queen, but occasionally overstepped the mark resulting in a curt

dressing down by the Palace and the instructions not to use the title 'Queen's Beauty Adviser' again. Articles in the press linking her to the Queen also referred to her occasionally as being married to the son of Oscar Wilde as if this was somehow going to add to her celebrity, and though it may be reading too much into the Royal ticking-off to imagine that this association was unwelcome, given the way Oscar had been dragged negatively into the public eye so often at that time, it was not improbable.

To sap Vyvyan's morale even further, 1954 started with the re-arrest of Lord Montagu on further homosexual charges after the jury had disagreed at his trial in December. Also arrested were Peter Wildeblood, a foreign correspondent on the *Daily Mail,* and Michael Pitt-Rivers, Montagu's cousin. Even the magistrates' court hearings made headlines in the Sunday papers three weeks in a row and the press was delighted to help stir up the public on the 'problem' of homosexuality until the three of them came up for trial in March and continued it thereafter with the debates in Parliament over reforming the law and the appointment of the Wolfenden Committee. None of this gave Vyvyan any confidence that his book would be well received. He worried that parts of it in which he had tried to 'humanise' Oscar as a father and described his conviction and sentence as being unnecessarily severe, would be seen as some sort of apology for homosexuality. The publisher shared his concerns. The year before, Vyvyan had written to Boris Brasol in New York asking for permission to quote a passage from his 1938 biography of Oscar Wilde. In the introduction Brasol had listed some of the most famous gay men in the history of the arts and made an eloquent and moving plea for the understanding rather than the persecution of homosexuals. By May 1954, with the public debate on homosexuality at its height, Rupert Hart-Davis felt it advisable to leave it out though it appeared in the page-proofs, as did the previously unpublished photograph of Oscar in Greek costume taken in Athens in 1877. That, too, disappeared from the final book. One can only assume that the publisher felt that 'Oscar in a skirt' (the traditional Greek *fustanella*) might give rise to ill-informed comments about his effeminacy. However, the Brasol quote, together with a Publisher's Note giving the whole background to Oscar Wilde's trials was briefly summarised in the American edition, something that was deemed impossible for the English one, in which, incidentally, the word homosexuality never appears. A further significant difference was between the frontispieces. In the US edition I am shown, aged seven, sitting on my father's knee. In the English edition Vyvyan is on his own. Again, one can only conjecture, but I'm sure my parents were just being over-protective in case it somehow affected me to be shown as the grandson of a notorious homosexual and America was far enough away not to matter. Curtis Brown tried in vain to interest the British press in serialising some of the book but there were no takers. However discretely it handled the subject, the idea of 'promoting' a book which was associated with homosexuality was clearly distasteful.

After correcting the page-proofs my father started on the index but abandoned it after two days as he felt it would make the book too unemotional and analytical.[483] It was his way of countering what he felt had been the editor's attempts to turn it into a post-Oscar historical document. Vyvyan wanted people to read it as the chronicle of a young life turned upside down by the disgrace of his father.[484] From then on it should have been just a question of waiting for the day of publication and the reviews, except that being the centenary year of Oscar's birth, there was yet another unpleasant surprise with which to cope.

Lewis Broad, who had written a competent biography of Winston Churchill, was planning to bring out a life of Oscar entitled *The Friendships and Follies of Oscar Wilde* just in time for the centenary of his birth in October. In June, when it was nearly in page-proof, Broad wrote to Vyvyan asking effectively for blanket permission to quote from *De Profundis* as well as from many of Oscar's letters still in copyright. The title had already put my father on his guard, particularly after St. John Ervine's vicious attack three years before, and he asked for sight of the proofs to see in what context the quotations would be used. He seems more or less to have made up his mind to refuse permission from the outset because of the title: 'I really cannot have a book of that title appearing at the same time as my own pathetic little volume,' he commented.[485] An increasingly acrimonious correspondence ensued in which Vyvyan accepted Broad's assurance that his work was not hostile and censorious, but pointed out to him in a letter that 'no one would have wanted to write about the follies of Oscar Wilde had he not been a celebrated author and that to write about them without connecting them to his art must necessarily give a very one-sided picture of him.'[486] After the proofs arrived at the end of July, Vyvyan's worst fears were confirmed: there was nothing in the book which was new; the emphasis, he wrote to Broad, was largely on Wilde's sex life, the trials and the imprisonment, to the exclusion of any of his literary achievements.[487] It highlighted all those elements in his father's life which he had been at pains to skirt round in *Son of Oscar Wilde* and while he couldn't actually suppress Broad's book, by refusing permission to quote copyright material he could effectively dissociate himself from it. In retrospect it was classic 'obstructive literary heir' behaviour, but given all that Vyvyan had had to put up with, the current strength of homophobic feeling in the country, and the adverse effect it could have on his own book, it was understandable. Broad's text was also littered with factual errors which Vyvyan had no intention of pointing out, leaving them as ammunition for the reviewers in due course. Rupert Hart-Davis, apprised of the situation, brought forward the publication date of *Son of Oscar Wilde* so that the two books were not likely to be reviewed together—a tactic which was almost entirely successful. The reviewers of Vyvyan's autobiography were unanimous in their praise for a deeply moving story told with restraint and entirely without bitterness. Lewis Broad's *Friendships and Follies*, by contrast, was treated as competent, impartial, brutally frank in its assessment of his subject and, yes, somewhat careless with his facts. Today it would be considered a slightly sensationalist pot-boiler, though with some astute, if blunt, insights regarding Oscar's relationships to his wife and friends. Three years later, Broad's book was issued in paperback even more provocatively entitled *The Truth About Oscar Wilde*. To depict Oscar in his last years as a charming, unscrupulous cadger with rather too much affection for *la fée verte* was unfortunately accurate but, done without a trace of sympathy, it was more than my father wanted to hear.

CHAPTER THREE
UNPICKING *SON OF OSCAR WILDE*

U ntil I started reading his diaries, I had always assumed my father's autobiography was a relatively uncomplicated, if at times disturbing trip down memory lane; I was quite unprepared for the emotional see-saw between pleasure and pain which he clearly experienced during the writing of it. My realisation that the task had been more complicated than it first appeared came in stages and at each one I tried to explain away, or at least understand, the uncomfortable discoveries I made. It wasn't his self-doubts, which any writer will recognise as part of the process, nor the fact that they were compounded by some fairly derogatory assessments of the man whose son he happened to be. No, what I found far more disturbing was that where memory failed him, imagination was summoned to replace it. All autobiography is to some degree embellishment, mostly to enhance the image of the author, but in this case certain improvements on reality were added to dramatize or authenticate a story where later research has revealed them to be superfluous and even misleading. Yet did it matter? This was Vyvyan's story as he told it and I shouldn't be tampering with it. And had he not left us with a nineteen-volume, three-million-word diary I wouldn't be. 'I hope it will survive me for many years,' he wrote, 'because, mingled with a great many uninteresting facts, there are a few illuminating passages which would be a pity for some future generation to lose.'[488] In that diary, however, are clear indications that Vyvyan is having to invent certain things and a couple of generations ago short-sighted literary heirs might well have made a bonfire of the diaries to preserve the integrity of the printed memoir. My mother, who had custody of them for nearly thirty years after his death, first resorted to a razor blade and then to Tippex to suppress the which she found too frank. The entry for 21 Jan 1953 about fictionally 'expanding' his first chapter was a case in point.[489] Mutilating Vyvyan's diaries, after the hopes he had expressed about their survival, was bad enough, but to destroy them would be a form of unthinkable literary vandalism.

Getting at the truth about my family, however painful, as well as exposing those whose sensationalist conjectures about it are based on the flimsiest of evidence, is what I have spent half my life trying to do, and I found myself having to be faithful to my own principles. It was surely better that I correct some of the errors myself and explain sympathetically the reasons for the fabrications rather than leaving it for some stranger years later to declare tactlessly: 'Look! Vyvyan Holland was a liar.' But getting my head around the task has not been easy and although I know it's the right thing to do, I still can't help feeling a slight pang of conscience and disloyalty.

It started some years before my mother's death when a reprint of the book was in hand with Oxford University Press and I was arguing with Thelma about the text of an introduction which they had asked me to write. I knew she had been instrumental in getting him to write the book and wanted to give her credit for it. 'Not only did I get him to write it,' she told me, 'but it was my idea that Constance should appear to him in a dream and tell him to do so. It sounded better.' I only had her word for it but nowhere in Vyvyan's diaries between 1948 and 1953 does he mention such a dream and since he frequently recorded his dreams, he almost certainly would have done had it happened. On the contrary, in several entries for 1953 he writes that Thelma is taking over the start of the book to make it less 'dull.' I didn't find my mother's admission particularly shocking; it was a sort of poetic licence, but it *did* start me looking for other passages which seemed strange or which didn't quite fit with the facts as I knew them.

At the time Richard Ellmann was finishing his biography of Oscar in 1986, I went through all Constance's letters to her brother

Otho for material I thought might be useful to him. Immersing yourself in someone's correspondence makes you quickly familiar with their style of writing, and when I reread *Son of Oscar Wilde* before writing my introduction I was struck by a quote from the letter Constance wrote to Vyvyan about his father shortly before her death in April 1898. 'Try not to feel harshly about your father; remember that he is your father and that he loves you. All his troubles arose from the hatred of a son for his father, and whatever he has done he has suffered bitterly for.' It didn't ring true; there was something stilted and unnatural about it that wasn't Constance's style, especially to her eleven year-old son, but I put the slightly admonitory tone down to her wanting to make an important point. I knew that the American collector Mary Eccles (née Hyde) owned all Constance's letters to Vyvyan, so when I next visited her I asked to see them expecting to find that Vyvyan had misquoted his mother. The letter wasn't there. Mary, too, had read about it in Vyvyan's book and was expecting to find it when she acquired the letters, but her catalogue entry specifically noted its absence from the collection which she had purchased in 1971, four years after my father's death, from an English antiquarian bookseller, George Sims.[490] My mother certainly hadn't sold them; indeed, she was incensed when she heard they had been sold and tried in vain to find out where they had come from. It was unthinkable that my father had sold them when he was alive and even if he had, Sims, who specialised in Wilde material, would have been able to sell them to any one of half a dozen collections in the US within days. Why sit on them for more than four years? Simple. He didn't, but whoever had them waited a discreet amount of time after Vyvyan's death before putting them on the market. Whether they were stolen or lent by Vyvyan to someone who conveniently 'forgot' to return them, we'll probably never know, but his diary established the moment he realised that he no longer had them. On 20 June 1953 he wrote: 'The devil of it is that I have lost all my mother's letters to me. I know I had them once and I am pretty sure they went down to Chetnole in a suitcase, with all my photographs which I also want urgently.' Chetnole in Somerset was where his old friend (and later my godmother), Betty Richards lived and to whom he had sent certain valuable possessions for safe-keeping during the War. Six months after writing about their disappearance, he and I went to visit her but of the suitcase there was no sign nor, as far as I know, did it ever turn up. This all leads to the uncomfortable conclusion that Vyvyan simply made up the quotation since he had no access to the letters while writing the book, and unless it was subsequently lost, the letter doesn't appear to have existed anyway. There is no doubt in my mind that Constance would have said something very similar to Vyvyan when she visited him at his school in Monaco in February 1898. She may even have written it in a lost letter which Vyvyan tried to recall from memory; they were sentiments entirely in keeping with her feelings at the time and had expressed in correspondence to several friends—anger at Oscar's behaviour but continuing love for the father of her children. Vyvyan could simply have written that he vividly recalled his mother telling him not to think too harshly about his father, which would have been enough to convince, instead of the artifice of trying to authenticate it with a non-existent letter.

One of the more dramatic incidents my father recounted in his book was his expulsion together with his mother and brother from the Swiss hotel where they were staying in the summer of 1895 after Oscar's last trial and conviction. Apparently the manager of the Righi-Vaudois at Glion, on learning that they were related to the infamous Oscar Wilde and realising that if his other clients were to find out it might be bad for business, asked them to leave. As Vyvyan's first taste of the 'fall-out' from the scandal, it was a hugely repeatable family story and for years I did just that. However, in 2008 I went to lecture in Lausanne, and with Glion being a short distance away I visited to the local archives to see if I could find out more about Vyvyan's stay there. It was intended to be an emotional in-the-footsteps-of piece of research, but what I discovered turned the story upside down. In the 1890s Montreux, the nearest large town, published a weekly newspaper entitled *Le Journal et*

Liste des Étrangers which recorded the arrivals, departures, and continuing presence of foreign guests in the local hotels. Vyvyan and his brother Cyril are listed as having arrived about 18 May and Constance about 22 June. They stayed until 14 September, the entire time in the same hotel—l'Hôtel du Parc. Clearly no one asked them to leave, so why the story about the hotel manager telling them to pack their bags? And why the Righi-Vaudois? Without the advantages of instant internet research, and short of making a special trip to Switzerland to remind himself, Vyvyan must simply have selected the most likely hotel from a guide-book of the period, assuming his mother had done the same. The Hôtel du Parc—the building still exists—was originally built by Henri Nestlé, the Swiss chocolate magnate, as a summer residence of comfortable proportions for his family. After his death in 1890 it was bought by the nearby Hôtel Bellevue, converted into the hotel annexe and given a separate name. Glion at that time was a very fashionable summer resort, even frequented by European royalty, so most hotels were booked out months in advance and it is certain that Constance had no easy task finding rooms at a few weeks' notice. However, the Parc had opened for the first time on 12 May and Constance was no doubt grateful to find any accommodation at all and took what was offered. Being separated from the mainstream hotel guests and thus feeling somehow excluded can only have confirmed to the eight year-old Vyvyan that he and his family were somehow 'undesirables,' as he put it in his book, and that it was all to do with his father. The memory of the perceived 'exclusion' sixty years later was still so strong that it had transformed itself more dramatically into an eviction.

Apart from those odd diary entries in which my father confesses to supplementing memories of his early life with touches of imaginative colour, there were others which proved more worrying. In 1951 Thelma played secretary for Vyvyan answering a letter from a Dane who was writing a thesis on Wilde for his English literature degree in Copenhagen and 'wanted to know who he was and what he was like. Luckily Thelma enjoys doing this kind of thing. The letter was very largely about myself and my early recollections of Papa which amount to about s.[weet] f.[uck] a.[ll]'[491] Years later, when Micheál Mac Liammóir asked him to write a programme note for his one-man show *The Importance of Being Oscar* he was even more explicit about his lack of real childhood memory:

> Today I tried to write a piece 'Oscar Wilde by his son' for Micheál Mac Liammóir . . . a very difficult job to do, as everyone has written about Papa ad nauseam and everyone is really sick of him. So I had to invent stories about Papa playing with us. I really doubt very much if he ever went up to the nursery. He was rather bored with children, and I can really only remember one occasion when I saw him in the dining room after luncheon. And, of course, coming into the house: the gigantic figure.[492]

I first read that with dismay and began to wonder how much of the chapter in *Son of Oscar Wilde* entitled 'The Happy Years' could be relied on. Did Oscar not go up to the nursery and play with his children after all? Filling in the outline of dimly remembered life in Tite Street with stories of Oscar mending toys and crawling around the nursery floor playing animals was one thing, but more or less to deny it twelve years after writing it, and to do so in a diary he hoped would survive him, was incomprehensible. Fortunately, there is a contemporary letter which shows that Vyvyan's original account, even if a little coloured in the telling, must have been largely truthful. When Oscar died in 1900, Carlos Blacker wrote to both Cyril and Vyvyan to inform them, and in his reply Cyril evokes memories of his father: 'It is of course a long time since I saw father but all I do remember was when we lived happily together in London and how he would come and build brick houses for us in the nursery.'

There is nothing to suppose that Cyril, then only fifteen, would have had any reason to exaggerate only a few years after.[493] Another account of how much Oscar enjoyed entertaining children was given by Gladys Palmer, daughter of Walter and Jean Palmer (of the eponymous biscuits) with whom the Wildes used to stay in Reading. In her autobiography she describes the visits of 'Uncle Oscar' to their house: 'I regarded him as an overgrown boy and loved him to come to the house because he belonged not only to the conversation of the grown-ups, in which, I always remember he had the *parole*, but he was equally my playmate.' She remembered, too, when Cyril and Vyvyan were staying how 'he would crawl under the tiger-skin rug and pursue us through the halls while we screamed and fled from him in half-terror.'[494] And what of the famous tea-party given for the 15 *gamins* at Berneval in 1997 when he was just out of prison to celebrate Queen Victoria's diamond jubilee?[495] Hardly the behaviour of one who was bored with children; more likely that of a man desperately missing his own as shown in his letters of the time.

Having given such a sympathetic portrait of his father in *Son of Oscar Wilde*, why in 1965 did Vyvyan want to destroy the image he had created? Even allowing for a few imaginative embellishments, I think my father's memory served him better than he realised, especially given what Gladys Palmer and his own brother had each remembered of Oscar. Any attempt to explain it at this distance in time can only be conjecture, but I offer it for what it's worth. When Vyvyan started writing his memoir, it was both a revisiting of his childhood to heal some of the wounds, as well as a desire to show his father in a more favourable light. It was the fusion of these two aims which expressed itself in the depiction of Oscar as a gentle giant, a man who loved his children (which he undoubtedly did), who played with them in the nursery and who had an endless supply of stories to tell them. In short, a man far removed from the archetypal, Victorian *paterfamilias*. Vyvyan idolised his father in order to rediscover him emotionally and did it by turning the exceptional in their relationship into the norm. I know, because I did it too. I lost my father when I was twenty-one, not as early as Vyvyan lost Oscar, but I'm sure our emotions were similar. For years after his death I over-romanticised the relationship with my father because I needed to remember him uncritically, with love and fixed by a few vivid memories. I *wanted* my father to have been affectionate and close, so, like the palaeontologist, I took those fragments of real memory, added a missing piece or two, fleshed it out and, as far as I could without deceiving myself, made it real. I suspect that Vyvyan did the same. I'm sure that Oscar's nursery visits took place, but they weren't every day and precisely because of that they were memorable. By the time 1965 came round and he was writing Mac Liammóir's programme note, Vyvyan's recall of what took place over seventy years before might well have dimmed and he felt the need to question the parts he had coloured in. He was simply being true to his own principles and being honest with himself in his diary: 'However humiliating it may be, it must be truthful and it must be a faithful account of all your activities . . . One indiscretion suppressed, one conceal-ment and the diary ceases to have any interest at all.'[496]

One of the hardest parts of writing *After Oscar* has been to 'correct' what my father said. It's not that he wanted deliberately to mislead, so setting the record straight is not saying 'You were a liar'; it is saying 'I understand why you embellished a few things at the time of writing.' In the end, the reality behind them is often more poignant than the way Vyvyan chose to depict them. The fact that Constance and her boys weren't actually told to pack their bags and leave a Swiss hotel doesn't matter; the fact that my father still felt it sixty years later and why, is what's important. Do I have the right to say this or should I just be perpetuating the myth? Even breaking the myth can be instructive especially in this case for what it tells us about the enduring 1950s homophobia and the continuing echoes around the whole Wilde story, but having to do it is troubling. I take down *Son of Oscar Wilde* from the book-shelf and see the inscription 'For Merlin with fondest love from his Daddy. September 1954' and I feel a jolt of perfidy at what I'm doing though I know it has to be right.

There are two sequels to this story: one which moved me a little and one which moved my father far more. In 1982 I needed to renew the American copyright in the book. It wasn't automatic in those days and I had to fill in forms and apply to the Library of Congress. One afternoon not long after, the phone rang:

'This is the Library of Congress Copyright renewals. Is that Mr. Holland?'

'It is. Is it about my father's book?'

'Yes, there's a small error on your form which could invalidate the renewal and since there isn't time for me to send it back to you, may I have your permission to correct it?'

'But of course, please do. How very kind of you to go to the trouble of ringing. I'm extremely grateful.'

The error was corrected and I asked if this was all part of the Congress service:

'No,' said Rita Aufricht, 'not normally, but I've always been fascinated by Oscar Wilde and had no idea that he had a family so I guess I was curious and felt this was the safest way to make sure you kept the copyright.'

I offered to send her a copy of the book by way of thanks. She gave me her address and we rang off. A couple of months later I received a long and touching letter of appreciation from her in which she wrote how part of her own childhood had been similar to Vyvyan's and drew my attention to a single sentence whose significance I had somehow always overlooked. 'The perpetual consciousness that there is no one to whom you are the most important person in the world.' When I read it again, for just a moment it was as if I could hear my father talking to me. Afterwards his book seemed to have an extra poignancy which I had never noticed before.

A year after the English edition appeared, a French translation was published. It was read by Lucien Wormser who lived at Issy-Les-Moulineaux just outside Paris and who wrote to my father a remarkable letter of which the following is an extract in translation:

It so happened that I saw your father nearly every day for several months on end. I was ten or eleven years old at the time, a rather small, shy, quiet little boy. My own father did not like his work interrupted by a mid-day meal, and he used to send my mother and me out to lunch 'Chez Bechet,' a small restaurant run by Monsieur Bechet and his wife at No. 42, rue Jacob [around the corner from the Hôtel d'Alsace where Oscar was living in Paris]. In those days, the ground floor was frequented by casual visitors, but the first floor was kept for regular clients. My mother and I went there every day, and the table reserved for us was the one next to 'Monsieur Sebastien' [Oscar's pseudonym in exile] whose personality attracted my mother very much, as she noticed that there was a certain style about him which was lacking in the other clients. He ate with his back to the far wall, silent and alone.

As we occupied neighbouring tables, we used to nod to him on arriving and on leaving, or he would nod to us if we were there before him. My mother held him up to me as a model of deportment, elegance and good breeding, and often used to talk to me about him on our way to the restaurant. What was the sorrow that weighed him down and made him so sad? He must be very unhappy; what had happened to him? My mother, who was as tender-hearted as she was pretty, worried about him. She would have liked to have talked to him, but he himself never talked.

I must describe Monsieur Sebastien as he appeared to me. The first thing that struck me was the width of his shoulders, and his height; he was like a man who had been very big but was wasted by illness. His face must have been handsome, indeed it retained traces of this; but his features were extremely tired. He made gentle movements with his hands. I think that his eyes, which he seldom raised, must have been a rather dark blueish-grey, but I do not have a very good eye for colour. It was an expression of great kindness, but of infinite weariness.

He ate what Madame Bechet put before him, and she looked
after him like a child. She would prepare special dishes for him
and kept coming to see whether he was eating them. If things
were not going to her liking she would say: 'Come on, Monsieur
Sebastien, you must not give up!'

One autumn evening, while putting on my overcoat after finishing my meal, I clumsily upset something, perhaps a salt-cellar,
on Monsieur Sebastien's table. He said nothing, but my mother
scolded me and told me to apologise, which I did, distressed by
my clumsiness. But Monsieur Sebastien, sensing my embarrassment, turned to my mother and said: 'Be patient with your little boy, One must always be patient with them. If, one day, you
should find yourself separated from him . . . ' I did not give him
time to finish his sentence, but asked him: 'Have you got a little
boy?' 'I've got two,' he said. 'Why don't you bring them here with
you?' My mother interrupted, saying: 'You mustn't ask questions,
Lucien!' 'It doesn't matter: it doesn't matter at all,' he said, with
a sad smile. 'They don't come here with me because they are too
far away.' Then he took my hand, drew me to him and kissed me
on both cheeks. I bade him farewell, and then I saw that he was
crying. And we left.

While kissing me, he had said a few words which I did not
understand. But on the following day we arrived before him and
a bank employee who used to sit at the table on the other side of
us asked us: 'Did you understand what Monsieur Sebastien said
last evening?' 'No,' we replied. 'He said, in English: 'Oh, my poor
dear boys!'

The bank employee went on to say: 'I am almost certain that he
is a great English writer who became mixed up in a scandal which
rocked England.' My mother retorted that she could not imagine
such a sympathetic man being mixed up in a scandal, and he replied: 'When a man is too successful, people are envious of him.'

A few weeks later, Monsieur Sebastien ceased to go there.
Thanks to the other client who was the only one to witness what
had happened, I realised that I had been given those two kisses

vicariously. I was just at the age at which you had last seen him. I ask myself whether my clumsiness was not, perhaps, well-timed, since it was an opportunity for him to send you an indirect message.[497]

Whatever agonies my father had gone through in the writing of *Son of Oscar Wilde*, I tell myself that they must have been worth it just to have received that letter alone. Two kisses finally delivered to the right address fifty-seven years after they were sent. I wonder if Oscar was thinking about the nursery in Tite Street that day . . .

Although the fiftieth anniversary of Wilde's death on 30 November 1950 had come and gone with very little to commemorate it in England, it was felt by a number of people that the centenary of his birth should not pass in the same indifferent manner. A small committee was formed in 1953 under the chairmanship of the MP Harford Montgomery Hyde (an avid Wilde collector, and at the time still a friend of my father), with a view to placing a commemorative 'Blue Plaque' on Wilde's former house at 34 Tite Street; it was originally No. 16 but had been renumbered in 1931. The initiative was largely that of Irene and Eric Barton, a bookselling couple from South London specialising in the life and works of Oscar Wilde. Five years previously Irene had written to *The Times* strongly objecting to the omission of Wilde's name from other local notables in the official programme of 'Chelsea Week' in May 1948. She asked if it were not now possible to 'honour one famous resident of this borough with a commemorative plaque? Oscar Wilde has contributed a great deal of enjoyment to people of all classes, and quite recently there have been revivals of his plays. Overseas visitors would be moved and interested to see a blue plaque outside No. 16 Tite Street.'[498] This suppression of Wilde by the Borough was oddly reminiscent of the fiasco in 1914 regarding the murals of famous Chelsea residents in the Town Hall when it was proposed that the image of Wilde be replaced with a figure less controversial. If the suggestion for a plaque was made in time for an unveiling to coincide with 30 November 1950, it fell on deaf ears. Two months after Irene's letter, Sir Patrick Hastings' stinging review of Hyde's *The Trials of Oscar Wilde* appeared and it seemed to reflect a general, uninformed opinion about Wilde's private life which had been made so disastrously public in 1895. Even if theatregoers had flocked to see the latest post-war revival of *Lady Windermere's Fan*, about the author's morals it was best not to enquire, let alone celebrate the man in so open a fashion.

In May 1953 the Bartons wrote to Montgomery Hyde to ask if he would support their proposal to the London County Council for one of its 'Blue Plaques.' His reply was not encouraging and he warned that while being in favour of the idea himself, he doubted the LCC would give its consent. Undeterred, the Bartons first approached the freeholders of the house in mid-June who replied on 6 July that 'provided nothing except that Oscar Wilde lived at 34 Tite Street is put on the plaque' they would agree to it being erected. The following day Irene Barton wrote to W. G. Fiske, the Chairman of the Town Planning Committee, at the LCC who replied within a week that he would put it to the Committee at its next meeting and was 'hopeful of a favourable outcome.' Permission was indeed granted and the Bartons were informed of the fact on 28 July.[499] Compared to the problems they would later face in finding someone to unveil it, obtaining the official consent had been quite painless.

In early August Eric Barton wrote to my father to give him the good news saying that he and his wife 'both very much hope that you will unveil the plaque next year.'[500] The very thought was anathema to Vyvyan. The fragile sense of pride in his father, which his Antipodean experiences had given him, had all but evaporated in the last five years. The disappearance of the Wilde royalties, impending bankruptcy and a climate of increasing homophobia in Britain had all taken their toll, but the Bartons could hardly have known that such a proposal would have met with my father's outright refusal to be the unveiler and consequently the focal point of the ceremony. Fortunately, as part of the research for his autobiography, Vyvyan had just been corresponding with Max Beerbohm about how they had first been introduced and whether Max had been present at the twenty-first birthday party thrown for him by

Robbie Ross. Max replied that he would have liked very much to have been there but wasn't invited, adding: 'I always remember with deep pleasure the meetings I have had with you—all too few though they have been.'[501] It opened the way for my father and Eric Barton to write to him proposing that as one of the last people alive to have known Oscar well, he would be the ideal person to unveil the plaque. Max's answer in mid-September was disappointing: he was deeply honoured but regretted that he was too old to travel.[502] He did, however, suggest that they ask Sir John Gielgud as one of the most eminent actors of the time and one who had both played in and directed successful post-war revivals of Wilde's plays, a suggestion prompted no doubt by Gielgud's visit to Max in Rapallo the month before. Barton wrote at once to Gielgud who replied on 1 October that he would be very glad to perform the unveiling and two weeks later Eric and Irene met my parents for the first time to discuss who should be approached to form an organizing committee. Vyvyan in the half-jocular, half-cynical manner he used as a form of self-protection in matters to do with his father recorded in his diary: 'In the evening Mr. & Mrs. Barton came to see us to discuss papa's plaque in Tite Street. They seem to think that the unveiling will be almost as important as the Coronation, except that the crowds will probably be much larger.'[503] The committee once formed consisted of the Bartons, Thelma & Vyvyan, Max Beerbohm, Francis Queensberry and his younger brother Cecil Douglas (both grandchildren of Oscar's nemesis, the 9th Marquess), André Maurois (with whom Vyvyan had corresponded in the 1920s), Guy Edmiston (the Mayor of Chelsea), and Louis Wilkinson (the Radley schoolboy who, under the pretence of running the 'Ipswich Dramatic Society,' had written to Oscar in 1899 about dramatizing *Dorian Gray*), with Montgomery Hyde as chairman.

The following day, ironically Oscar's 99th birthday, the morning papers reported that a warrant had been issued for the arrest of Lord Montagu of Beaulieu on charges of 'committing an unnatural offence' with two youths. Montagu was in America on business at the time but returned via Paris and was arrested three weeks later at London Airport. He was taken to Lymington Magistrates Court where a crowd of 250 had gathered and booed him on his arrival. A celebration of the life of Oscar Wilde who had been arrested and imprisoned for similar offences in 1895 began to look rather misplaced But just when things seemed bad, they suddenly became a great deal worse. On the night of 20 October, John Gielgud was arrested for 'cottaging' in Chelsea. He appeared the next day at West London Magistrates' Court, gave his name as Arthur Gielgud, was fined £10, and told to go and see his doctor for advice. There the matter might have ended had a reporter from the *Evening Standard* not recognised him and by lunchtime the paper carried the story on its front page. 'Poor John!' wrote my father in his diary. 'I am afraid that will take some living down. The awful thing is that he has been definitely co-opted to unveil dad's plaque in Tite Street, and I really do not see how he can do it, or how we can refuse to let him do it.'[504] Vyvyan immediately informed Max who replied:

I was much distressed at reading the cutting that you sent me about John Gielgud. What a very tragic thing to have happened! You are of course absolutely right in feeling that in the circumstances the unveiling of the plaque could not be done by him. I should think you have very likely had a letter from him of his own accord to this effect. Whom do you think of in his stead? Laurence Olivier perhaps? But he might chivalrously feel that he could not do what was to have been done by his friend and rival. What writers do you think would be appropriate? It has occurred to me that the best man of all for the occasion would be yourself.[505]

Gielgud himself realised the dilemma and solved it by writing to Eric Barton:

I am sure you will understand that in the present circumstances I am not a suitable person to perform the ceremony of unveiling the Wilde plaque, and, seeing as I am to withdraw, I shall be glad if you will approach someone else to undertake it. There are many notable men in the theatrical and literary world who I am sure would gladly preside on such an occasion—I greatly regret the inconvenience I have put you to in the matter.[506]

The week after Gielgud's appearance in court he was due to open in *A Day by the Sea* at the Royal Court Theatre in Liverpool. There was much agonising between him and the producer 'Binkie' Beaumont as to whether he should let an understudy take over but in the end it was decided he should face the first night audience regardless. Many years later Beaumont's biographer, Richard Huggett, ignored the very subdued reception that opening night in Liverpool and merely described Gielgud's entrance on the first night in London a month later: 'To everybody's astonishment and indescribable relief, the audience gave him a standing ovation. They cheered, they applauded, they shouted.'[507] By contrast the reception in Liverpool, according to a news agency telex of the time which my father had carefully preserved with other cuttings, was somewhat different: 'Almost unnoticeably, in one of the most cleverly contrived moves on to the stage, Sir John Gielgud took the floor. There was no applause; there were no boos; a faint suggestion of a sigh.'[508] Manipulating history to prove what a liberal-minded, tolerant society we were about homosexuality in 1953 is pointless when contemporary evidence suggests quite the opposite. In a vicious piece in the *Sunday Express*, John Gordon referred to homosexuals as 'human dregs' and proposed that Gielgud should be stripped of his knighthood conferred five months before in the Coronation Honours list. David Maxwell Fyfe, the Home Secretary, called a conference of magistrates and urged them to get tough on homosexual offenders.[509] Vyvyan, who had sent a message of support to Gielgud for that first night and received a heartfelt note of gratitude in reply, noted in his diary that the *Daily Express* had been trying to get hold of him about the plaque 'I suppose they see a salacious story in it . . . . I am afraid this Gielgud affair is going to kill my book, the plaque on Tite Street and the whole O.W. Centenary next year.'[510]

Anticipating Gielgud's withdrawal, my father thought of sounding out Harold Nicolson while lunching at the Beefsteak Club. He felt it best to raise the subject verbally in the first instance, but was unable to catch him alone and the opportunity passed.[511] Next to be approached was the actress Edith Evans who had played Lady Bracknell to Gielgud's Jack Worthing in the legendary 1939 revival of *The Importance of Being Earnest*. She wrote back saying that as a woman she did not feel qualified to do it and that 'it would be better if you had a man to perform this ceremony.' She also advised that it might be sensible in the prevailing climate that the unveiling be postponed.[512] Louis Wilkinson suggested that the committee move away from actors whose fame he considered rapidly transient: 'In fifty years' time few will know of Sir Laurence Olivier or Michael Redgrave,' and proposed that they ask Francis Queensberry as a gesture of reconciliation between the two families: 'It would be of lasting literary-historical interest, the Lord Queensberry of 1954 doing public honour to Wilde, redressing the insults and injuries . . . inflicted by the Queensberry of 1895.'[513] Neither Vyvyan nor the Bartons were in favour of such an idea, with my father pointing out it was a Wilde and not a Douglas centenary that was being celebrated.

For the next four months, there appears to have been no further attempt to find anyone of note to unveil the plaque. Given the press coverage of the Gielgud and Montagu affairs and the public debate surrounding them with the tabloids stirring up a climate of extreme homophobia, it was hardly surprising. 'I am beginning to think,' wrote my father, 'that the plaque had better just appear one morning, having been unveiled surreptitiously at 3:30am by the policeman on the beat.'[514]

On 16 December Lord Montagu was acquitted of some of the charges against him but the jury could not agree on a verdict and a retrial was ordered, keeping the matter in the public eye to my father's continuing unease. 'It is really so like the Wilde trials that it horrifies me,' was his comment.[515] Montagu was rearrested in January along with Peter Wildeblood and Michael Pitt-Rivers and all three committed for trial at the next Hampshire assizes where they were found guilty on 24 March of 'gross indecency' and sentenced, Montagu to a year and the others to eighteen months imprisonment. As in Wilde's trials fifty-nine years before, it was the testimony of the young men with whom they had committed the offences and who had turned Queen's evidence which sent them to prison. Significantly T. S. Eliot, to whom the Bartons had written in early March asking if he would care to unveil the plaque, replied a few days after the Montagu trial opened to decline, giving as his excuse 'that the person chosen to unveil the memorial should be a wholehearted admirer and I have never been a warm admirer of the work of Oscar Wilde.'[516] On a more positive note Max Beerbohm had sent Vyvyan a short message to be read out at the ceremony praising Oscar's genius as a conversationalist, but there was still no one prepared to do the unveiling.

The next to be approached was Laurence Housman who, like Max, declared himself at the age of eighty-nine too old and unfit to travel, but also sent a message to be read out on the day. He must have been delighted that Oscar was to be honoured in this way, for it was he who had written to Robert Ross on the publication of *De Profundis* in 1905: 'Perhaps before we die a tablet will be up in Tite Street on the house where he used to live.'[517] Laurence Olivier refused saying that he would be filming in October and was not sure where he would be on the day of the centenary. Bertrand Russell declined to take part saying that that although he was 'thoroughly appreciative of the proceedings' he had to be abroad in October. Reading between the lines of E. M. Forster's letter of refusal to take 'so prominent a part in the proposed ceremony,' it is clear that as a discreet homosexual himself he seems to have been extremely worried that by being openly associated with such a commemoration he might attract the unwelcome attention of the newspapers. While admiring Wilde, Forster considered the unveiling of a plaque to be fraught with difficulty at a time of 'ill-judged prosecutions' by the Government and 'venomous activities in certain sections of the press.' He asked whether the committee might not be better advised to invite a woman to perform the unveiling, 'preferably an eminent actress.'[518] As a result, the Bartons approached Sybil Thorndyke, but she, too, turned them down, and Irene Barton's suggestion to Vyvyan of asking Evelyn Waugh 'of all unsuitable people' was dismissed out of hand.[519] It was finally left to my father to write to an old and dear friend whom he had known since the 1920s, the author Compton Mackenzie. Even though 'Monty' had never met Oscar, he had known several of the 'Wilde Circle'—Robbie Ross, Reggie Turner, and Max Beerbohm—and he was eminently suitable. 'He would make a good speech and is a prominent figure in the world of artists and authors; he has also been on the stage,' wrote Vyvyan.[520] Monty was abroad when the letter arrived and recorded in his memoirs that at first he refused but at last gave way, though there would seem to be a little artistic licence employed there for dramatic effect, as his letter of acceptance saying he would be proud to preside at the unveiling, is dated the day after his return. Max Beerbohm, who had earlier praised Mackenzie's *Sinister Street,* thoroughly approved and wrote to Vyvyan in September: 'There couldn't be a better choice.'[521]

With the problem of finding someone to unveil the plaque finally resolved, you would have thought that my father's mood might have changed, but the public debate (if one can call vitriolic editorials about the 'vice' or even the 'disease' of homosexuality which appeared in the popular press 'debate') made him more and more uneasy about celebrating the centenary of Oscar's birth. In May there had been a heated exchange in the House of Lords about homosexual law reform during which Earl Winterton had referred to homosexuality as a 'filthy, disgusting and unnatural vice,' deploring the way theatregoers had treated a 'well-known actor of the present day' with such leniency, later even mentioning Gielgud by name and saying that he was not in the least prepared to apologise for the comment. He argued that contrary to the new tolerant view, prison was indeed a deterrent. Homosexuality, which had been rife at Oxford in the 1890s due to the influence of Oscar Wilde and his associates, had been all but eradicated by the time he was there ten years later because of Wilde's conviction and imprisonment.[522] The Lords' Debates weren't just confined to *Hansard* and *The Times* Parliamentary Reports but splashed over the pages of the *Daily Mail* and the *Daily Sketch*. It is difficult to imagine what Vyvyan's feelings must have been to read about such attitudes towards his own father. He was clearly dreading the centenary event.

Since the sudden death in April of his brother, Francis Queensberry, Cecil Douglas had been taking a more active role in the committee. Encouraged by Louis Wilkinson he proposed saying a few words of a conciliatory nature at some stage in the proceedings. My father was not in favour of the idea for the same reasons he had turned down the suggestion of Francis doing the unveiling, but eventually agreed that Douglas should speak at the lunch which was to be held at the Savoy afterwards. To add to my father's discomfort, Douglas also contributed £25 towards the general expenses of organising the plaque and the lunch, leading Vyvyan to comment that, since there was no way in his present financial difficulties that he could afford to match it with a contribution of his own, it made the family look mean.[523] The last, quite pointed refusal to participate in the centenary celebrations came from Cecil Day Lewis (later to become Poet Laureate in 1968) to whom the Bartons had written asking if he would write a poem for the occasion. 'To write a poem of that sort, with any hope of success' he replied, 'one must feel some sort of affinity with the subject, and this is, alas, lacking in my case.'[524] Miron Grindea the eccentric and gifted editor of the little magazine *Adam* came to see my father three weeks before the unveiling and said that French writers were appalled that no committee of literary people had been set up in England to organize commemorative events dismissing the Bartons somewhat petulantly as *sans instruction*. He partly rectified matters in the autumn number of his magazine with tributes from France and Belgium saying in his editorial:

> More than half a century after the writer's death, the name of Oscar Wilde is still mentioned in many quarters with a prurient disdain and a shameful ignorance of his creative achievement . . . .
> At any rate it was symptomatic that four times as many foreign writers as English contemporaries deemed it important to pay in our pages a tribute to Wilde.[525]

In contrast to the general indifference, even distaste, shown by many of the literary and artistic elite in Britain for celebrating the centenary of Oscar's birth, in France a committee had been formed under the patronage of the Minister of Education, Jean Berthoin. It consisted of five members of the Académie française, including André Maurois, and a galaxy of those in the French world of the arts, some of whom, like Paul Fort, had known Wilde personally. A week of events preceded the anniversary and culminated in the laying of flowers at the grave in Père Lachaise and an evening of speeches and readings from Wilde's works on the day itself at the Sorbonne. Messages were read out from those who were unable to attend but wished to show their support, among them Jean Cocteau who wrote; 'Oscar Wilde a payé cher d'être Oscar Wilde, mais c'est le comble de luxe d'être Oscar Wilde. Il est naturel que ça coute cher. On n'honorera jamais assez l'auteur de *La Ballade de la Geôle de Reading.*'[526] Sacha Guitry's message summed up in a sentence the difference between English and French attitudes to the man: 'Nous devons nous enorgueillir qu'Oscar Wilde ait choisi la France pour refuge.'[527] In Dublin the centenary was marked with the unveiling of a commemorative plaque on 21 Westland Row, the house where Wilde was born before his family moved to the more prestigious Merrion Square shortly afterwards. Lennox Robinson, the playwright and stage director, much involved with the Abbey Theatre, made a speech emphasising Wilde's Irishness. He concluded by saying that it was especially fitting that Dublin

1 Carlos Blacker (left), dedicatee of *The Happy Prince*
and the actor Norman Forbes-Robertson, both close friends of Oscar
in his early days in London.

2 Jean Dupoirier and his wife, proprietors of the Hôtel d'Alsace
who were unfailingly kind to Oscar in his last years.

3 One of the last photos of Constance in exile aged 38 in Heidelberg, 1896.

4 Ada Leverson who met Oscar on his release from prison.
'How marvellous of you to know exactly the right hat to wear at 7 o'clock in the
morning to meet a friend who has been away,' he remarked.

5 Cyril (left) and Vyvyan *Holland*, as they had become, in Heidelberg in 1896.
These were the photos Constance sent to Oscar on his release.
'She sends me photographs of the boys – such lovely little fellows
in Eton collars.'

6 Oscar's last table in the Hôtel d'Alsace in Paris.
Not used for creative work but for writing begging letters to friends.

7 Leonard Smithers, who published *The Ballad of Reading Gaol* under Oscar's prison number C.3.3. 'I see it is my name that terrifies,' Wilde wrote to him.

8 Constance's grave in Staglieno Cemetery, Genoa.
She died on 7 April 1898.
The words 'Wife of Oscar Wilde' were added
by her great niece only in 1963.

9 Oscar on his deathbed, taken by his young friend Maurice Gilbert.
Of his bedroom decor he declared:
'The wallpaper and I are fighting a duel to the death; one of us has to go.'

10 Oscar's first grave in the Parisian suburb of Bagneux.
His friends could only afford a 'sixth class' burial at the time.

11 Robbie Ross (left) and Reggie Turner, the two loyal friends
who were with Oscar at the time of his death.

12 Cyril aged about 13 with his great aunt Mary and her daughters in Kensington around the time of his return to England in 1898.

13 Vyvyan at Babbacombe Cliff, the home of Lady Mount-Temple, friend of the Wildes and close confidant of Constance. After his return to England and the general indifference of his guardian and his mother's family, Vyvyan often found a sympathetic refuge at Babbacombe.

14 Brought up in Switzerland, Vyvyan's cousin Fabian Lloyd became by turn a boxer, a poet, and a Dadaist magazine editor. He was later (falsely) credited with the 1920s Wilde manuscript forgeries and disappeared mysteriously in 1919.

15 Alfred Douglas and his wife Olive (née Custance) in their Hampstead house, probably around 1908.

16   Robert Ross on the eve of the Ritz dinner given in 1908 to celebrate
his publication of Wilde's *Collected Works*. He holds a copy of *De Profundis,*
heavily expurgated at that time because of its criticisms of Douglas,
and only published in its entirety in 1962.

17   Jacob Epstein's monumental sculpture for Oscar's tomb in Père Lachaise caused outrage when first installed because of the flying angel's nudity, and the authorities ordered it to be covered until the genitals were concealed or modified.

18   Arthur Ransome leaving the Old Bailey in April 1913 after winning the case brought against him by Alfred Douglas. Douglas considered he had been libelled in Ransome's biography of Wilde.

19 Lord Alfred Douglas, aged 43, after the Arthur Ransome libel trial
and about the time *Oscar Wilde and Myself* was published.
The book, largely a disparagement of his former friend,
was ghosted for him by his journalist colleague Thomas Crosland.

Christopher Millard

Oct. 1916

20 Christopher Millard, who wrote the first and finest bibliography
of Oscar Wilde under the name of Stuart Mason.
He was a close friend of Robbie Ross and subsequently of my father Vyvyan.

21 Cyril in his Royal Field Artillery officer's uniform about 1912.

22 Vyvyan and his wife Violet. They married in January 1914 but had hardly
a year together before he left to fight in France.
She died in an accident in 1918 before he was demobbed.

23   Newspaper placard announcing Vyvyan's marriage, much to the displeasure
of his remaining family for linking him to Oscar Wilde.
They refused pointedly to attend the ceremony as a result.

24   Staff Captain Vyvyan Holland 3rd Corps 1918.

25 T.W.H. Crosland, Douglas's assistant editor at *The Academy*
who detested everything Oscar Wilde stood for
and conducted a personal vendetta against Robbie Ross.

26 Maud Allan, an exotic dancer who was due to play the leading role in a private theatre performance of Wilde's *Salomé* in 1918.

27 Noel Pemberton-Billing libelled Allan in his right-wing newspaper
The Vigilante, implying she was a lesbian. This led to one
of the most sensational trials of the period.

28 Oscar's tomb in Père Lachaise, *les parties nobles*
of the 'flying demon angel' still intact.

29 Vyvyan (right) and Hisao Honma, who came to London in 1928 to find and write about the survivors of the 1890s Aesthetic Movement. Vyvyan gave him a lock of Oscar's hair cut off at the time of his death by Robbie Ross.

30 A 'new play' by Oscar Wilde discovered in 1921. Many people were fooled into believing it to be genuine, eventually leading to yet another posthumous Wildean court case.

SENSATIONAL CHARGE OF LITERARY FORGERY

WHO WROTE

'FOR LOVE OF THE KING'

OSCAR WILDE

OR

MRS. CHAN TOON?

PRICE ONE PENNY

31 A forged letter to André Gide (left) and a genuine one to Frank Harris. The forger tried too hard; in exile, Oscar would never have had the funds to buy monogrammed stationery.

32 Professor Auguste Piccard celebrates his birthday in New York in 1933.
Shifty 'Paris forger' and conman Brett/Hope/Dorian (3rd from left) looks on.

33 Dorothy 'Dolly' Wilde, Oscar's niece, who had no qualms about trading on the relationship in 1920s Paris.

34 André Gide, whose memoirs concerning Oscar caused much controversy in the 1930s. His fellowship of the Royal Society of Literature was rescinded.

35 Alfred Douglas in 1932 still trying to gain possession of the *De Profundis* manuscript and fighting the biographers of Oscar Wilde for his own reputation.

36 Alfred Douglas in the 1940s. He lived most of his last years alone in Worthing.

37 Robert Sherard, friend of Oscar from 1882, whose touching devotion to his memory resulted in four biographical works about him.

38 (Next page) Frank Harris at home in Nice in the late 1920s. He was generous to Oscar while in exile, but his 1916 biography *Oscar Wilde: His Life and Confessions* would be the cause of untold disagreements among Oscar's friends.

39 My parents, Thelma and Vyvyan, in London towards the end
of the Second World War. They married in 1943.

40 My father and myself in 1953, a photo portrait taken for the frontispiece
of his 1954 autobiography *Son of Oscar Wilde*. It was only included
in the US edition, it being considered 'unwise' to link me to the Wilde story
in the UK edition, where Vyvyan appeared alone.

41 Rebecca West in 1964. She persuaded my father to allow Oscar's letters to be published unexpurgated which, at first, Vyvyan had been reluctant to do.

42   Thelma, my mother, at the height of her career as a beautician in 1955.
It was she who encouraged Vyvyan to face the task of writing his autobiography.

43 Oscar's tomb in Paris after 1961 when the angel's prominent testicles were knocked off. Over the years the French have embellished the story so much that the truth of how it happened is now completely obscured.

44   The premiere party for the 1960 film *The Trials of Oscar Wilde*.
Vyvyan is on the right next to Lionel Jeffries while Peter Finch cuts the cake;
John Fraser (2nd from left) is next to Ken Hughes, the director and screenwriter.

45   Lord Cecil Douglas, my father, and David Queensberry dine
at the Café Royal on 4 December 1959
to discuss their role as historical advisers on Ken Hughes' film.

46 Rupert Hart-Davis, who edited *The Letters of Oscar Wilde* in 1962.
It became the benchmark for published literary correspondence
and contributed hugely to Oscar's continuing rehabilitation.

47 In Beirut 1972: Wondering how much longer
I would have to go on selling paper rather than writing on it.

48 In London 1972: Thelma holding court to a group of young people
as Oscar Wilde's daughter-in-law.

49   Alice Guszalewicz as Salomé in Strauss's opera performed in Cologne in 1906. It was reproduced in Ellmann's 1987 biography of Wilde as a pictorial scoop: 'Wilde in costume as Salomé.'

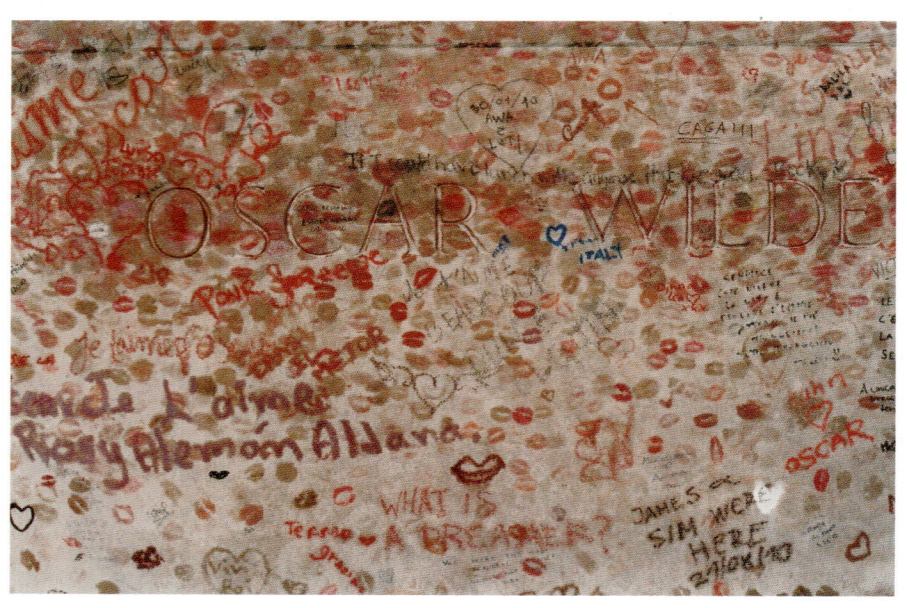

50 & 51
(Previous page and here) Oscar's fans show their appreciation,
but with scant regard for Jacob Epstein's work of art.
It was fully classified as a French Historic Monument in 1995,
and cleaned and protected from the kissers in 2011.

52 With John Gielgud who unveiled a plaque at the back
of the Haymarket Theatre on 3 January 1995 to commemorate
the centenary of the first night of *An Ideal Husband*.

53 Ireland's 'stamp of approval' for the Wilde family: Oscar by Toulouse-Lautrec (1980); Oscar and his works—to commemorate the centenary of his death (2000); the bicentenary of Lady Wilde's birth, issued on International Women's Day 2021.

When Oscar Wilde called for the Champagne waiter, he was only after One thing.

Exquisite, decadent, sensual and frivolous. Like Oscar Wilde, Perrier-Jouët is all these things. The most sought-after champagne of the naughty 1890s (in a good year we gleefully sank a million bottles), its elegant chardonnay character is equally at home in the 1990s. In fact, you never know when you might fancy it (as Oscar might have said).

GRAND BRUT
PERRIER~JOUËT
A EPERNAY-FRANCE

54 Oscar's favourite champagne house, Perrier-Jouët, distributed 30,000 of these double-size postcards around the clubs, bars, and hotels of London's West End in late 1994, just before his window in Poets' Corner was dedicated.

55 & 56   (This page) The 'performers' at the Poets' Corner ceremony.
(Left to right) Michael Denison and Judi Dench who read 'The Handbag Scene'
from *Earnest*; John Gielgud who read from *De Profundis*;
Seamus Heaney who delivered a specially written oration.

57 The window unveiled.
'Neither in nor out and facing both ways at the same time.'

58 & 59
(Here and next page) Commemorating the centenary
of Lady Wilde's death with a new panel on the family grave
in Mount Jerome Cemetery. (Left to right) Donald Ross, Lucian Holland,
Sarah Holland, Mary O'Rourke (the unveiler), and Ulick O'Connor.

IN MEMORIAM

JANE FRANCESCA, LADY WILDE
SPERANZA OF *THE NATION*

WRITER, TRANSLATOR, POET AND
NATIONALIST, AUTHOR OF WORKS ON
IRISH FOLKLORE, EARLY ADVOCATE OF
EQUALITY FOR WOMEN AND FOUNDER
OF A LEADING LITERARY SALON.

BORN DUBLIN 27 DECEMBER 1821
DIED LONDON 3 FEBRUARY 1896

WIFE OF SIR WILLIAM
AND MOTHER OF

WILLIAM CHARLES KINGSBURY WILDE
BARRISTER AND JOURNALIST
1852 - 1899

OSCAR FINGAL O'FLAHERTIE WILLS WILDE
POET WIT AND DRAMATIST
1854 - 1900

ISOLA FRANCESCA EMILY WILDE
1857 - 1867

Tread lightly, she is near
Under the snow,
Speak gently, she can hear
The lilies grow

IN THE VAULT BENEATH
REST
THE REMAINS OF
JOHN FYNN
OF BALLYMACBOON CO. MAYO
WHO DIED IN DUBLIN
MAY 30TH 1849
AGED 64 YEARS
AND ALSO
THOSE OF HIS SISTER
EMILY
WIFE OF
TOBIAS BIRCHALL
WHO DIED 29TH MARCH 1868
AGED 70 YEARS

60   Appearing to lecture Vanessa Redgrave on the subject of 'Speranza'
Lady Wilde when she unveiled a plaque to her in Oakley Street, Chelsea in 2000.
Vanessa played Lady Wilde in the 1997 biopic *Wilde*.

61 Maggi Hambling enjoying a cigarette with her memorial to Oscar in Adelaide Street opposite Charing Cross Station.

62 Lucian Holland, Stephen Fry and myself at the unveiling of Maggi Hambling's 'A Conversation with Oscar Wilde' on 30 November 1998.

63 Together with Simon Callow we frame Melanie de Brocquy's bust of Oscar at No 1 Merrion Square, the Wilde's family home in Dublin.

64 With Seamus Heaney at the unveiling of Danny Osborne's sculpture of Oscar Wilde on Merrion Square, Dublin. in 1997.

65 With H.M. Queen Camilla, then Duchess of Cornwall, at Oscar's 'Birthday Party' in 2015. Her great-grandfather, Alec Shand, was said to have been briefly engaged to my grandmother, Constance, in 1879.

66 Oscar, insouciant, reveals a side of Victorian England which it would rather he hadn't. Caricature by Mexican artist Gonzalo Rocha.

67 & 68
Always on the move, Oscar's name christens many forms of transport from ferries
to freight engines. Here, Oscar is pictured above on a Rhine cruise ship and as
one of Norwegian Air's 'Tail Fin Heroes.'

69   Rehabilitation of a sort. Fans pay tribute to 'Saint Oscar'
on the door of his tomb in 1994.

should honour him in this way and that 'we should emphatically claim him this morning as a great Irish writer.'[528]

In the weeks leading up to the London ceremony, Vyvyan stead-fastly refused to consider taking any active part in the proceedings saying that he did not even want to sit at the top table with the committee, let alone make any sort of speech. Louis Wilkinson in a letter to Vyvyan of 28 September wrote 'It is very good that you are coming on 16th' from which one can only conclude that one moment my father was seriously considering staying away from the event altogether. Even as late as 3 October he was writing to Rupert Hart-Davis, the publisher of his autobiography, 'You are lucky not to be coming to the October 16 festivities. I wish I could avoid them. I may do so yet. I feel a slight migraine coming on already.'[529]

The night before the unveiling, after the plaque had been put in place, it was discovered that no one had thought to provide any sort of 'veil' which could be removed at the critical moment. Consternation all round until Irene Barton managed to enlist the help of a local garage mechanic with a ladder, who, being Irish himself and learning that the plaque was for Oscar, flatly refused any payment for the job. Somewhat inappropriately, given British attitudes towards him and all he had stood for in the eyes of the Establishment, the only cloth to be found at that late stage was a small Union Jack.[530]

Arriving at Tite Street early on the morning of 16 October, my father heard the following exchange between a smartly dressed woman and a policeman: 'What time does this binge start?' she asked. 'Kick-off at 11:15' he replied. 'The ceremony was, at any rate, starting off on the right foot,' wrote Vyvyan.[531] And continued: 'Merlin did not, of course, know what it was all about, but he was much impressed.' I must have had at least some idea since earlier in the summer, aged 8, my father and I had been walking down Shaftesbury Avenue and passed the theatre where Noel Coward's musical adaptation of Lady Windermere's Fan was playing. I noticed Oscar's name on the billboards and asked 'Was should honour him in this way and that 'we should emphatically claim him this morning as a great Irish writer.'[528]

In the weeks leading up to the London ceremony, Vyvyan steadfastly refused to consider taking any active part in the proceedings saying that he did not even want to sit at the top table with the committee, let alone make any sort of speech. Louis Wilkinson in a letter to Vyvyan of 28 September wrote 'It is very good that you are coming on 16th' from which one can only conclude that one moment my father was seriously considering staying away from the event altogether. Even as late as 3 October he was writing to Rupert Hart-Davis, the publisher of his autobiography, 'You are lucky not to be coming to the October 16 festivities. I wish I could avoid them. I may do so yet. I feel a slight migraine coming on already.'[529]

The night before the unveiling, after the plaque had been put in place, it was discovered that no one had thought to provide any sort of 'veil' which could be removed at the critical moment. Consternation all round until Irene Barton managed to enlist the help of a local garage mechanic with a ladder, who, being Irish himself and learning that the plaque was for Oscar, flatly refused any payment for the job. Somewhat inappropriately, given British attitudes towards him and all he had stood for in the eyes of the Establishment, the only cloth to be found at that late stage was a small Union Jack.[530]

Arriving at Tite Street early on the morning of 16 October, my father heard the following exchange between a smartly dressed woman and a policeman: 'What time does this binge start?' she asked. 'Kick-off at 11:15' he replied. 'The ceremony was, at any rate, starting off on the right foot,' wrote Vyvyan.[531] And continued: 'Merlin did not, of course, know what it was all about, but he was much impressed.' I must have had at least some idea since earlier in the summer, aged 8, my father and I had been walking down Shaftesbury Avenue and passed the theatre where Noel Coward's musical adaptation of Lady Windermere's Fan was playing. I noticed Oscar's name on the billboards and asked 'Was

Oscar Wilde your father?' 'Yes,' said Vyvyan, apparently dreading
the sequel, but to his relief I was content to leave it at that.[532] By
the time the ceremony was due to start between four and five hundred people had gathered in Tite Street, which was now closed
to traffic, and the nurses from the Victoria Hospital for Children
opposite crowded to the windows for a grandstand view. The
stage was well represented by Edith Evans, Dorothy Tutin, Peggy
Ashcroft, Margaret Rawlings and Isabel Jeans, as well as Michael
Redgrave, Micheál Mac Liammóir, and Esmé Percy (later listed
on the Savoy lunch seating plan as Miss Esmé Percy, which as
Vyvyan commented, 'must have given him a kick'). Among the
writers were Alec Waugh, Rebecca West, Sacheverell Sitwell,
T. S. Eliot and E. M. Forster, these last two despite their previous
refusal to take a prominent part in the unveiling. Augustus John,
predictably ostentatious in black felt hat and flowing cape, turned
up with his 'niece' who was rumoured in fact to be another of his
illegitimate daughters.

Before unveiling the blue plaque Monty Mackenzie spoke
movingly of Oscar's career and downfall. He described how he
discovered Wilde's writings as a teenager which seemed to open
up a whole world of sophistication, a world 'which was coming
to life again after the long, long sleep of the later Victorian age.'
He then read the two tributes to Oscar specially written for the
unveiling, the first by Max Beerbohm:

> I suppose there are now few survivors among the people who
> had the delight of hearing Oscar Wilde talk. Of these I am one. I
> have had the privilege of listening also to many other masters of
> table-talk—Meredith and Swinburne, Edmund Gosse and Henry
> James, Augustine Birrell and Arthur Balfour. Gilbert Chesterton
> and Desmond MacCarthy and Hilaire Belloc—all of them splen-
> did in their own way. But assuredly Oscar in *his* own way was the
> greatest of them all—the most spontaneous and yet the most pol-
> ished, the most soothing and yet the most surprising. That his talk
> was mostly a monologue was not his own fault. His manners were

very good: he was careful to give his guests or his fellow-guests many a conversational opening; but seldom did anyone respond with more than a very few words. Nobody was willing to interrupt the music of so magnificent a virtuoso. To have heard him consoled me for not having heard Dr. Johnson or Edmund Burke, Lord Brougham or Sydney Smith.

and the second by Laurence Housman:

I am very glad that this memorial meeting is being held for so good a purpose. Oscar Wilde was incomparably the best talker I have ever met. But he was not only the best talker, he was also the most courteous and the most charming. His unhappy fate has done the world a signal service in defeating the blind obscurantists: it has made people think. Far more people of intelligence think differently to-day because of him. And when he wrote his *Ballad of Reading Gaol* he not only gave the world a beautiful poem but a much-needed lesson in goodwill, pity, pardon, and understanding for the 'down and out.'[533]

Finally, Monty recalled the sheriff's public auction which had taken place in the house behind where he now stood when Oscar was on remand and awaiting his trial. Everything was sold down to 'A very large quantity of toys' and 'A rabbit hutch.' At this point, Monty looked over to his friend, my father, and was overcome with emotion, but recovered himself and continued 'I don't believe we should let such a thing happen today. And I don't think it could. Today we are better and we have all of us had this great lesson. Some men of this world have had excessive suffering and I think Oscar Wilde was one of those.' And with that he unveiled the plaque which, as the *Irish Times* said, 'was greeted with wet eyes and loud cheers.'[534]

It was then the turn of Guy Edmiston, the Mayor of Chelsea and Basil Marsden-Smedley, Chairman of the Chelsea Society who both made brief speeches about Chelsea's proud tradition of

being home to those who practised the Arts in every form, especially painters and authors. Honouring Oscar Wilde in this way was long overdue, said Marsden-Smedley. He was an eccentric in the best sense of the word and Chelsea needed more eccentrics like him. He added that in the past Chelsea had had 'something to be sorry for' in its attitude towards Oscar Wilde, but now he felt that this memorial was putting things right. 'I hope that at last we have done credit, although rather late in the day, to this great name,' he concluded and with that the main ceremony was over.

Sometime after the war, No. 34 had been converted into flats and now, to the horror of the tenants, the VIPs who had attended the ceremony wanted, understandably, to visit the house where the subject of the plaque had lived. Dorothy Boness, who lived on the ground floor with her husband and three children, was startled when the Mayor came up the steps followed by a troop of distinguished visitors and asked 'I suppose it's all right for us to look over the house?' and before she knew it they were inside. What had been the Wilde's dining room on the ground floor at the back, was now the single bedroom for the whole Boness family. Lilian Allan, the first floor tenant, said 'If we'd have known they were coming, we'd have made the beds and polished the place from top to bottom. As it is, they're seeing everything in a terrible state. They may be only interested in it historically, but we housewives are proud and don't like our homes to be seen like that by strangers.' Mrs. Boness's husband, a pastrycook at Blackfriars, arrived home to his wife who exclaimed 'The Mayor's in the kitchen!' 'What about it?' he said. 'Has he had my dinner? That's the main thing!'[535] A spirit of Wildean comedy seemed to have returned the house for a brief moment, though my father almost certainly wasn't part of it. Revisiting his childhood home would have been too painful and there is a noticeable absence of such a visit in his otherwise detailed description of the day.

The celebration lunch at the Savoy was attended by more than 160 paying guests. For the benefit of those who hadn't been able to come to the unveiling Monty Mackenzie re-read the tributes

from Max Beerbohm and Laurence Housman as well as two others from Walter de la Mare and Allan Aynesworth who had played the part of Algernon in the 1895 production of *The Importance of Being Earnest*. In the letter which accompanied his tribute, Housman said that his *Echo de Paris,* a short book partly about his imaginary meeting with Wilde in 1899, was one of the books he was most glad to have written. Monty also placed Oscar among the greats of 'English' theatre—Sheridan, Goldsmith, Shaw, and Wilde—adding 'There is one thing about them all that we have to face up to I'm afraid: they are all Irish.' Cue for laughter and loud applause. The Irish Ambassador, Frederick Boland gave a vivid sketch of Wilde's Irish background and of his special debt to his nationalist mother, Speranza. Paul Boyer, the French cultural attaché read a tribute from André Maurois and according to the *Manchester Guardian* the German cultural secretary, Eugen Gürster 'put a British audience to shame by saying that not a week passed without one of Wilde's plays being performed somewhere in Germany. "His plays," said Herr Gürster, "belong to the very foundation of the German repertory theatre."'[536] Cecil Douglas spoke briefly saying:

> These few words of mine, in view of the name I bear, are meant as some small restitution to Vyvyan and his family for the way my family behaved all those long years ago . . . If I have helped to bury any hatchets or settle any feuds, it is not only what I wanted to do but what my brother, Queensberry [Francis who had died in April] would have wanted me to do as well.[537]

David Queensberry, Cecil's nephew who had recently inherited his father's title as 12th Marquess, had been on the acceptances list but was laid low with flu. John Gielgud was invited but was filming that day and couldn't come. His reply expressed genuine regret at not being able to attend, as did those of John Betjeman, John Cowper Powys, Noël Coward, Joyce Grenfell, Christina Foyle and many other notable figures.[538] By a curious turn of fate the unavoidable absences of John Gielgud and David Queensberry were pleasingly rectified forty years later when John unveiled a plaque on the Haymarket Theatre to mark the centenary of the first night of *An Ideal Husband*. David and I were both there when a journalist from *The Times* came up to me all excited and asked 'Is this the first time for a hundred years that the Holland and the Queensberry families have been talking?' 'No,' I said, 'my father and David's father knew each other well.' 'Pity,' said the journalist somewhat crestfallen. 'There's no story in a friendship. I was hoping you'd been feuding all this time.' Despite Vyvyan's initial misgivings, he appears to have enjoyed the day which centred on his father's qualities and achievements rather than the disaster of his personal life, and so it seems did I, though for less exalted reasons:

> Hosts of distinguished people in the world of art, literature, the theatre and society were present. The only people omitted seem to have been the Press and quite rightly too.[539] At the last moment Mr. Dulanty, the ex-Irish Ambassador, did not turn up and his place, next to me, was occupied by Mr. Merlin Holland . . . I have since ascertained that Mr. Dulanty refused to come some weeks ago and that the whole stunt was worked by Thelma. Thank God no one noticed that we were sitting together and that no nonsense appeared in the Press about it. However, it all seemed to leak out at the end because Merlin, planting himself in the chair that had been recently vacated by Harford Montgomery Hyde M.P. sat serenely signing menus with all the aplomb of a lesbian authoress at a Foyle's luncheon for a long line of elderly people queuing up for the favour.[540]

I went back to my little boarding school near Midhurst obviously very full of myself and the attention that had been unexpectedly paid to me and must have regaled my young contemporaries with exaggerated stories of how I had been signing menus at the Savoy all afternoon. I still remember being told sharply at the time to stop my noisy boasting which obviously had a profound effect as I

spent the next five years at different schools being asked by people
to speak up as they couldn't hear me. However, not everyone was in
agreement about the centenary honouring of Oscar. At ten o'clock
in the evening, two days after the unveiling, a tin of light blue paint
was hurled at the plaque. One of the residents thought it might
have been a student prank, but no one was ever charged with the
offence. The 'Peterborough' column in the *Daily Telegraph* on 18
October carried a paragraph entitled 'No inspiration for Wilde'
which described Compton Mackenzie's address as dull, uninspir-
ing and lacking in spontaneity and suggested that Vyvyan might
have been a better choice of unveiler, but apparently he hadn't
even been invited to speak. It was an ill-informed and unnecessary
sneer and one which, it later transpired, was premeditated by the
columnist even before the ceremony had taken place.[541] Worse
still were the comments of a Bromyard magistrate, Mr. W. R. Lyon
who told a meeting of the Worcestershire Magistrates Association
on 27 October that the recent 'glorification' of Oscar Wilde was
'a disgraceful public spectacle' and sent out all the wrong messages. 'Oscar Wilde was nothing more or less than a dirty common
criminal. He was convicted of one of the filthiest crimes.'[542] It was
a view echoed by a female reader in the letters columns of the
Daily Sketch a week later: 'Could it be that those responsible are
not aware of his filthy life?' though she was quickly taken to task
by three others with more tolerant views. Seventy years later it is
unthinkable that such comments could be made publicly. Nearly
nine, I was protected from them, but Vyvyan was not and at a time
when he was having to be very public himself about his relationship to Oscar, such raw hostility towards his father must have been
deeply hurtful.

There was, however, one particularly cheering moment that
day for my father and it came from a very unexpected direction.
Towards the end of the lunch a very old friend of his, the novelist
and critic Rebecca West, noticing that Vyvyan was not as happy
a she felt he should have been, asked him instinctively if he was
worried about educating me.[543] It turned out that her instinct was

entirely right as that very morning he had received a notice of intended bankruptcy from the Inland Revenue. Rebecca then offered to pay my school fees and, with the combination of seeing Oscar publicly celebrated in London for the first time and knowing that my education was assured, Vyvyan was completely overcome with emotion.[544] My mother, in an oddly predictable way, was furious at the thought of having someone take over a part of her parental responsibilities even though she might not have had the means to fulfil them herself, and it was the cause of disputes between her and my father for several days. She eventually came round to the idea, but her reaction of anger coupled with embarrassment at having to see me educated by someone else, while understandable, was uncharitable. I only found out about the arrangement quite by accident seven years later.[545]

On 30 November 1950, prompted that day by articles in the press about the 50th anniversary of Oscar's death, Rupert Hart-Davis had written to Vyvyan suggesting that he publish a volume of Oscar Wilde's letters. 'He was obviously a wonderful letter-writer and I feel that his letters ought to be collected . . . You of course would be the ideal editor . . . '[546] Vyvyan, who was feeling somewhat besieged by matters Wildean at that moment, uncharacteristically didn't reply for over six weeks. When he did reply on 15 January it was to tell Rupert of all the difficulties there had been over the years with putting together collections of his father's letters, not merely with tracking down the originals, but with questions of ownership, copyright, and the need for suppressing derogatory passages (especially in the later letters) about Alfred Douglas who, predictably, would have sued for libel had they not been. With Douglas no longer alive and no more royalties on Oscar's works coming in, the prospect of being able make some money out of this unrealised 'asset' must have been tempting. However, since he was working more or less full-time in Richmond Temple's public relations office, he would have had little time to spare for the research and editorial work that it would entail—hence the delay in responding to Rupert's offer. I think, too, that he was uneasy about the openly homosexual content of much of the post-prison correspondence. A publisher would want to include all but the most banal and undatable letters and that meant coming to terms with having Oscar's private life dragged before the public again at a time when homosexuality was being regarded as a distasteful social problem. In fact, Oscar and his letters had been a problem one way or another since 1894 when blackmailers came to his house in Tite Street to try and extort money from him for an intimate letter which he had written to Bosie Douglas. Another letter to Douglas was used by the defence lawyer, Edward Carson to prove justification in Oscar's failed libel action against the Marquess of Queensberry for calling him a sodomite. And *De Profundis* was perhaps the most damaging of all, but Oscar could hardly have suspected its being used as such a vicious weapon after his death in the feud between Robbie and Bosie, notably in the Arthur Ransome libel trial of 1913. The publication by my father in the early 1920s of Oscar's post-prison letters to Robbie, censored to the point of being almost colourless, was a mistake but undertaken in memory of Robbie, who had been planning it before his death in 1918. Vyvyan had also permitted the publication in German, French, and Japanese of the unexpurgated *De Profundis,* carrying on in a sense the war against Douglas which Robbie had started in 1913. It was a subtle means of making Oscar's somewhat one-sided views on Alfred Douglas available to a wider audience in countries outside the jurisdiction of the English courts. Methuen & Co had planned to issue Oscar's letters in 1937 in two volumes with A. J. A. Symons and my father as editors but the project came to nothing. This was partly because Symons, whose biography of 'Baron Corvo' had been so warmly received in 1934, was side-tracked by wanting to write Wilde's biography too. In the end Symons died in 1941 before either work was completed. Incidentally, the contract with Methuen for the letters contains a significant alteration: the clause in which the author guarantees that the work 'contains nothing of an objectionable or libellous nature' has had the word 'objectionable' scored through. Even then, Symons and my father were clearly aware that the overtly homosexual nature of some of the letters might present a problem.[547] It is small wonder, then, that Vyvyan seemed slightly hesitant to embark on yet another project to publish his father's letters. In the event, the matter seems to have been dropped until after Vyvyan had delivered *Son of Oscar Wilde* and a contract was finally signed in July 1954.

My father was happiest—even if he occasionally regarded the occupation as an addiction and an obsession—as a translator and a writer. He didn't have the necessary rigorous discipline to be an editor of letters. Rupert must have realised that and appointed Allan Wade, who had just finished editing the letters of W. B. Yeats for him, to do the job. I suspect in the interim that he may also have been nervous about Vyvyan's lack of distance from the subject; intimate knowledge in such a case can be an advantage, but fidelity to family sometimes gets in the way and, as previous history showed and later events proved, Vyvyan as editor would have been a disaster. Allan Wade had known Yeats personally, but they weren't related and his edition of Yeats's letters became a benchmark of excellence for published correspondence.

As soon as the contract was signed Allan and my father set to work tracking down as many letters as possible from the obvious sources: universities, public libraries, and individual collectors, some of whom were known to Vyvyan personally, the most prominent among them being Harford Montgomery Hyde. It was Hyde who had agreed to chair the committee organizing the celebrations to mark the centenary of Oscar's birth later in the year and who at the time was probably considered the doyen of Wilde studies, not only for his knowledge on the subject but also on account of his extensive collection of manuscripts, letters, and books. Rupert, Allan, and my father knew they would have to rely on Hyde's goodwill both to supply the texts of the letters he owned as well as helping with editorial queries—a somewhat one-sided arrangement on the face of it since he was not being offered any sort of advisory fee. What they were unaware of, however, was that Hyde was perfectly happy to cooperate, realising it would in fact be very much to his advantage as he had already been planning an 'in prison' sequel to his 1948 book on Oscar's trials and needed my father's help.[548]

Earlier in the year Hyde, who had been the MP for North Belfast since 1950, had written to the Home Secretary, Sir David Maxwell Fyfe, asking to see the Home Office papers relating to

Oscar Wilde's imprisonment which, in theory, were closed for 100 years. Fyfe, who was incidentally well-known for his reactionary views on homosexual law reform, replied on 4 March to say that he could not allow access to them. Hyde repeated his request at the end of May and received the same answer.[549] Thinking that he might get further by airing the matter in the House of Commons, on 24 June 1954, Hyde put down a Parliamentary Question asking why the file of official correspondence relating to Wilde's imprisonment should not be made available to the public. Fyfe, still refused to give access stating that it might give pain to living descendants.[550] Hyde then approached my father, presumably with the same explanation: 'for the purpose of conducting a genuine piece of historical research,' and Vyvyan duly wrote to the Home Secretary on 7 July to say that he could speak for all living descendants of Oscar Wilde and had no objection to Hyde having access. It was, on the face of it, a mutually beneficial operation. As a Member of Parliament Hyde knew whom to approach and how to set about it and my father's blessing on the application was essential or the file would remain closed. Vyvyan had just signed the contract with Rupert Hart-Davis to publish Wilde's collected letters and the background details of his two years in prison would be editorially invaluable. Hyde had also stated in the House that 'this correspondence is of considerable interest to students of English penal history and prison conditions in the last century,' a piece of sophistry which, as it turned out, was wasted on the Home Secretary and permission was still withheld.[551]

However, the autumn, saw the appointment of a new Home Secretary, Gwilym Lloyd George, and at the end of November he wrote to Hyde saying that in view of a recent change in policy regarding departmental records he had decided to let Hyde see the papers. His department must also have informed Vyvyan who wrote a note to Hyde a day or two later, 'When you see the OW papers, do you think that you could take me with you?'[552] Vyvyan, although he was unaware of it, had served Hyde's purpose which was to get access to the file and make as much use of it as possible.

On 10 December my father and Montgomery Hyde went to the Home Office together:

> It was really quite thrilling, as no one had looked at it for nearly sixty years, and it contained three petitions from Papa to the Home Secretary, the first two for the reduction of his sentence as he feared he was going mad and the third, towards the very end, for his release at some time different to the usual one as he feared a demonstration and masses of reporters . . . . I shall try to get $5000 for the story in America . . . . I shall have to watch Harford, however, as he is quite capable of stealing a march on me.[553]

Since the petitions amounted to over 3000 words, my father requested photostatic copies to be made, but the Home Office only agreed to make transcripts and, given the sensitive nature of the files, to send them only to Vyvyan as Wilde's son. Hyde, whose declared interest until then had merely been historical research, realised that he might not easily gain access to them again and, on the pretext of wanting to recheck certain details and without telling Vyvyan, went back the same afternoon and copied them out by hand.[554] Within a week (and unknown to my father), Hyde who had already been discussing a newly edited version of *De Profundis* with the managing director of Methuen, Alan White, made a radical new proposal to the publisher for a volume containing not only Wilde's long letter to Douglas, but all his letters to other friends like Robbie Ross, Reggie Turner, and Robert Sherard as well as the petitions themselves. White wrote about it enthusiastically to Vyvyan, outlining the scope of the book and its suggested title 'Oscar Wilde in Prison.' Vyvyan's decidedly negative response was a mixture of his old concern about dragging his father's name through the mud again, as Hyde had managed admirably to do with his book on the trials in 1948, as well as the prospect of his own edition of *De Profundis* being replaced by Hyde's and consequently having to share half his royalties on the work.[555] The first of these worries seems slightly inconsistent with his own intention to publish the petitions in America, but his files show that they would have been heavily edited and accompanied by his own commentary; the second was more understandable, as just over a month previously he had finally been served with a bankruptcy notice by the Inland Revenue for £3,077. As he later admitted to Rupert Hart-Davis, he should perhaps, have expressed himself more forcefully to White than he did but, in a state of extreme depression over his finances and on the assumption that Methuen, having been Wilde's publisher since 1908, would show him more loyalty, he did not.[556] My father, though not naïve, was basically of too trusting and gentle a disposition. The idea that someone like Hyde, whom he had been seeing regularly for several years, could really go behind his back and harm him, especially in the delicate matter of his complicated feelings about his father, was dismissed; Methuen went quiet and the project appeared to have been shelved.

The start of 1955 brought worse news financially. The Inland Revenue, tired of waiting, forced an interview at the end of January in Worthing for Vyvyan to explain how he was proposing to pay the arrears of tax which had been rolled forward from when he had been forced to pay the Special Contribution:

> We were interviewed by a young man named Lewis, clad in sports clothes. His personal appearance was reasonable, but his mental attitude was so utterly without any charm or co-operation that it would have frozen the hinges of hell. We spent nearly three mortal hours with him in a brick-lined cell and when we left I really, for the first time in my life, felt suicidal.[557]

Vyvyan's proposal, whatever it may have been, was turned down and the Revenue announced they were starting bankruptcy proceedings. His solicitor said he could not see what the Revenue hoped to gain from forcing the issue as Vyvyan's only tangible asset was his ability to write, which would be affected adversely by the stress of bankruptcy. My mother made a last impassioned plea on 6 February, offering to devote part of her own earnings to paying off the tax bill. This, too, was rejected. When I first learned about it years later, I wondered, like the solicitor, what point there was in publicly humiliating my father in the days when bankruptcy was a social catastrophe, and when the Revenue would have recouped more by letting Thelma and Vyvyan pay it off. I suppose they wanted to make an example of him, *pour encourager les autres*, as Voltaire described the shooting by the British of Admiral Byng, but given the subsequent publicity, I still ask myself whether the Establishment didn't want to get in a final word about the son sixty years after it had dealt with the misdeeds of the father.

The bankruptcy then took its course. The petition was served on 25 February and on 22 March Vyvyan went before the assistant official receiver at the Bankruptcy Court in Carey Street 'a pleasant and sympathetic man . . . who kept on referring to my illustrious sire as "your dad" . . . and he promised to keep Papa's name out of everything.'[558] The receiving order once made, Vyvyan knew that within days a court official would be arriving at the family flat to make an inventory of any assets, so immediately after the interview he went to see Montgomery Hyde who had offered to store the few remaining bits and pieces of Wilde-associated silver in his House of Commons locker for the duration. I would like to think, as my father clearly did at the time, that it was a generous and confidential gesture to a friend in trouble, but given Hyde's subsequent duplicity, it was clearly more of a move to make Vyvyan indebted to him.[559] A bailiff duly arrived the following morning, but since the flat was rented, the furniture mostly Thelma's and the bailiff was looking for objects of obvious value, the only result was to leave Vyvyan exhausted and depressed.

On 29 April 1955 he was then adjudged bankrupt. The day before, with the press having got wind of the matter, it made front page headlines in the *Daily Mail*: OSCAR WILDE'S SON FACES CAREY STREET and within three paragraphs the paper had managed to drag in my mother: 'His wife, Thelma, is the Queen's consultant on make-up and beauty preparations.' By the time of his public examination two weeks later Vyvyan had made the newspapers in France, Italy, Spain, Australia, and New Zealand; I know because I still have the file of crumbling press cuttings he kept. There must have been a small degree of *déjà vu* for Vyvyan with the public exposure and the social stigma attached to it in those days; at least he knew I would not be much affected since he wasn't in prison with his wife and children in exile on the Continent. Nonetheless, as he wrote in his diary when he put me on the train back to school: 'I also had a rather haunting suspicion that when I saw Merlin's face at the railway carriage window, I was looking on it for the last time.'[560]

The collateral damage caused to my mother's career by the piece in the *Daily Mail* was immediate and dramatic. Earlier in the year she had applied in the name of Cyclax for the award of a Royal Warrant for beauty products, three years having elapsed since the Queen's accession. Although Cyclax was not mentioned in the article, the Managing Director was furious, accused Thelma of bringing the name of the company into disrepute and doing it irreparable harm, removed her from the board of directors, and told her to take a month off while they decided what to do with her. He also wrote, without her knowledge, to the Palace to disassociate Cyclax from Thelma Holland's problems and officially withdraw the Royal Warrant application. Thelma in turn blamed Vyvyan telling him: 'Owing to you I have been publicly disgraced and branded as a liar and a cheat,' which was somewhat unfair and unnecessary as he noted, but understandable given the state of affairs.[561] It was only after some months that Thelma (through Bobo Macdonald, the Queen's dresser and whose confidence she enjoyed) managed to persuade the Palace of her complete innocence and of her regret at the incident. In the end my mother continued to advise the Queen on skin care and also kept her job at Cyclax—today she would no doubt have received thousands in compensation—by the expedient of demanding reinstatement and an increase in salary for all the good publicity she had brought them over twenty years. They granted her both, but it was no thanks to her father-in-law dragging her onto the front page of the *Daily Mail*.

On 11 May, Vyvyan was summoned to appear at the Bankruptcy Court in Carey Street for his Public Examination. Threatened with immediate imprisonment if he failed to appear, he arrived far too early and filled in the time reconnoitring escape routes to avoid 'the Press ghouls' as he called them. At the examination Mr. Registrar Cunliffe expressed the opinion that since the bulk of the debt was due to an unforeseen tax on earnings from the copyrights which in the meantime had expired, the debtor might be described as improvident, but certainly not extravagant. A year later, granting Vyvyan his discharge the same Registrar was reported as saying: 'I take the view that there is a very strong degree of misfortune in this case.'[562] However, the law was the law and allowed for no exceptions. The examination concluded, Vyvyan made his exit through the boiler-room, thus avoiding the Press who were indeed waiting to take unflattering pictures to attach to yet more sensationalist pieces linking him to his father and, by implication, to the very public debate on relaxing the laws on homosexuality.

Once Vyvyan's bankruptcy had become more or less inevitable by the start of 1955, he had redoubled his efforts to knock Oscar's petitions from prison into some sort of publishable form in which they could be sold. Yet there was a terrible conflict of interests in his own mind: on the one hand there was a desperate need to make money out of their discovery in order to stave off the Inland Revenue; on the other there was his unresolved and exceedingly complex attitude towards his father. There was resentment at having to live in Oscar's shadow, as well as some residual anger at his irresponsibility and the resulting destruction of the family. But in contrast to this, there was also an element of pride in his father's literary achievements, a natural love for a man who had been an affectionate father, and the desire to protect him against further sensationalising by biographers and the press. In some ways it threatened to be a repeat of his 1920s editing of Oscar's post-prison letters to Robbie Ross which, so anodyne did they become, would have been better unpublished, In the first petition which Wilde wrote to the Home Secretary in July 1896, for example, he was proposing to omit the key words in brackets from the following passage:

THE PETITION OF THE ABOVE-NAMED PRISONER HUMBLY SHEWETH [*preceding words printed*] that he does not desire to attempt to palliate in any way the [terrible] offences of which he was [rightly] found guilty, but to point out that such offences are forms of [sexual] madness . . .

giving as his reason that they 'show a spirit of cringing hypocrisy' and that 'It seems to me that unless some sort of editing of this sort can be done, the publication of the petitions might do more harm than good. And if they are published only in the United States, who is to know any better?'[563] I confess once more that I have found it difficult to reveal this behind-the-scenes view of my father's attempt to censor something Oscar wrote, but in mitigation of the offence, one has to put it in context and remember that he was doing so at a time when public homophobia in Great Britain was particularly widespread. Besides he did come round to the idea, over the next seven years during which he and Rupert Hart-Davis were editing the letters, that his father depicted with all his faults and weaknesses was a better policy than wasting whitewash, which one day was bound to be wiped off.

On 24 February 1955 Vyvyan had written to the Home Office requesting permission to use the petitions in a book or an article which was immediately granted, subject to sight of the material by the Home Secretary. Then, since he had heard nothing more from Methuen about 'Oscar Wilde in Prison,' he wrote to Montgomery Hyde on 4 April to outline his proposal for publishing the petitions, asking for his help with some of the background and offering him a fee, adding 'I think that the explanation ought to be in my own name, particularly as the original correspondence [*with the Home Office*] came from me.'[564]

He wrote twice more on 14 and 19 April, but Hyde did not respond to either letter and since Vyvyan was by then in the throes
of bankruptcy with his creditors' meeting and his public examination looming, the matter seems to have been dropped. He
little suspected that the reason for Hyde's silence was that having
gained access to the prison files through Vyvyan he was hard at
work on such a book himself, and by 19 May had already signed
a contract for it with Methuen.

Shortly after his visit with Vyvyan to see the petitions at the
Home Office and his proposal to Methuen of the radical new
'Oscar Wilde in Prison,' Hyde had written to the Home Secretary
asking if the permission granted in November also included in-
specting the files of the Prison Commissioners. His letter, mentioning Vyvyan by name to imply that the request was coming from
both of them, was written entirely without my father's knowledge.
Gwilym Lloyd-George replied saying that he would arrange to
have the files placed at Hyde's disposal. Hyde obviously inspected
them and copied yet more material for his proposed book and, six
months later, on 12 July he sent his first draft of 'Oscar Wilde in
Prison' for the Home Secretary's approval which was forthcoming, with a few minor amendments, on 13 September.[565] By late
September Hyde was busy finding illustrations for the book and
even asked the Home Secretary if a photograph of Wilde in prison
dress existed in the official archives. 'If such a photograph were
available, I think it would add very considerably to the interest
of the book.'[566] There wasn't one and I don't like to imagine my
father's reaction if there had been and if Montgomery Hyde had
published it. Vyvyan was quite unaware of Hyde's activities despite seeing him on a regular basis at the time.

Allan Wade had died suddenly in July and for a brief period
Rupert Hart-Davis considered replacing him with Hyde as the
editor for Oscar's letters, but Hyde's parliamentary business took
up too much of his time and, fortunately, the idea was abandoned.
However, he, Rupert, and Vyvyan continued to correspond on
matters Wildean throughout 1955 and at some stage Rupert

promised Hyde that once the page proofs of *The Letters of Oscar Wilde* had been corrected, he could have the photostatic copies of all the letters that he had assembled in lieu of a fee. On the surface it was a satisfactory working arrangement between the three of them and never the faintest whisper of Hyde's book, the proofs of which by the end of November 1955 he had already corrected.

The first that Vyvyan heard of it was over a lunch at the Beefsteak Club with Freddie Birkenhead in January the following year: Freddie mentioned that an advertisement had appeared in a book-trade paper for 'Oscar Wilde in Prison' as forthcoming from Methuen and was surprised that Vyvyan knew nothing about it. Vyvyan immediately rang Montgomery Hyde to ask him what was going on. Hyde was out and rather than ringing back, he wrote a somewhat evasive letter saying that he had been meaning to get in touch about progress on the Methuen project and assumed that since a year had passed and that Vyvyan had not published the petitions himself, he would have no objection to Hyde doing so. He also said that he was intending to dedicate it to my father. Vyvyan was incensed and wrote back accusing Hyde of being secretive about the nature of the book which Hyde had told him was to be on the prison system generally and in which he wanted to include 'certain passages from the petitions to show up the hideous torture of solitary confinement. But from that to quoting the whole petitions verbatim is quite another matter':

> As you know, I always do my best to suppress the sordid things about my father, and these petitions seem to contain more sordidness than anything else . . . I have not even dared to show them to Thelma, and I am horrified to think of what her reactions would be if they came out in print. And the thought of them getting into Merlin's hands is even more distressing. I do not want all this business of suppurating ears and failing eyesight. I gave you my reasons for this. You brushed them aside, but I still stick to them. They will revive all these syphilis stories which I am always trying

to kill. I am sure that you will see my point of view. It is all very fine for other people, but I am the constant object of vulgar curiosity on the part of people who want to know about my morals, health and way of life, and this same curiosity is also, in a minor degree, carried on to my son whom it is my duty to protect. It has always been my earnest hope that in the course of time my father will be remembered for his works and not as a drunken homosexual with suppurating ears, shedding crocodile tears and fawning upon the authorities from a prison cell obsessed with indecent thoughts and riddled with syphilis.[567]

Vyvyan also warned Hyde that Rupert Hart-Davis would not be at all happy to discover unpublished letters from Oscar to his friends trickling out before the full-scale publication of *The Letters of Oscar Wilde* on which they were still working.

It is just possible that the matter might have been resolved had it not been for a paragraph in the gossip columns of the *Daily Mail* on 15 February, which can only have been leaked by Hyde himself, though he later denied it. The piece implied that Hyde had been responsible for discovering the petitions and that Vyvyan was being obstructive about their publication. From that moment my father took a firm stand, supported totally by Rupert. Methuen was caught in the cross-fire as Hyde's book was already type-set and in page-proof and Alan White had all along assumed that Hyde had been keeping my father informed. 'I do not blame Alan White in any way whatever,' Vyvyan wrote to Rupert. 'When he was handed the manuscript of a book dedicated to me, how could he have imagined that I knew nothing about it? The more I think about it, the more convinced I am that Harford's idea was to shoot first and apologise afterwards.'[568] The correspondence grew increasingly acrimonious with accusations flying back and forth and the positions of both parties becoming ever more entrenched. Vyvyan compared the possibility of my seeing displays of 'Oscar Wilde in Prison' in a bookshop window to Cyril seeing the newspaper placard

'Oscar Wilde Arrested' in Baker Street in 1895 and suggested that it might have a similar psychological effect on me. Hyde wrote back saying that I might just as readily see a copy of *The Ballad of Reading Gaol* and that the effect would be the same.

Hyde's next move was an attempt to drive a wedge between my father and Rupert Hart-Davis. He reminded Rupert of the help he had provided in tracking down some of Wilde's letters and made vague reference to the existence of others. Rupert stood firm:

> You always said that you would help with the *Letters*, so your present offer to help only if Vyvyan and I agree to your using this mass of copyright material [*it was 18,000 words*] naturally looks rather more like a threat than a promise. Needless to say, I shall be sorry not to have your help, but there it is.[569]

In the meantime, Vyvyan's financial difficulties had taken a turn for the better. His solicitor, Richard Butler, a fellow member of the Beefsteak Club, who had been working *pro bono* for Vyvyan since the year before, had been negotiating with the appointed trustee in bankruptcy, Torquil Macleod, for Vyvyan's discharge and a sum of £400 was finally agreed on. Still counting every shilling that passed through his pocket, Vyvyan was clearly not in a position to pay such a sum himself but was able to make the offer thanks to the generosity of an old friend, Alec Waugh. Alec had recently sold the film rights to his novel *Island in the Sun* and, flush with money, loaned my father £800 to obtain his discharge and put him back on his feet; in return Vyvyan agreed to assign all his royalties to Alec until the debt had been paid.[570]

Then, at the beginning of May, Macleod announced that an offer of £500 had been made for all the Wilde copyrights which Vyvyan controlled. As the trustee it was his duty to realise as much money as possible for the creditors from the bankrupt's assets, and the unpublished letters of Oscar Wilde (including, of course, the petitions), *De Profundis,* and one or two other unpublished manuscripts were a potential source of income. Although the identity of the buyer was confidential, there was only one person who could possibly have had the knowledge to make such an offer—Harford Montgomery Hyde.

Hyde had written to Macleod on 4 May making his offer and stating: 'My interest in the matter springs from the fact that for many years I have made a particular study of Oscar Wilde's life and writings and am regarded in the literary world as being by way of an authority on them.' No mention, of course, of the real reason for acquiring the copyrights which was to have unfettered control over the letters and the petitions he wished to use in 'Oscar Wilde in Prison.' He went on to say:

> Although you are not officially concerned with what happens to the copyrights after their disposal, I think it may interest you personally to know that, should I acquire the rights, I am considering handing them over with any accrued royalties to Mr. Holland's only son, Merlin Holland, when he comes of age, as a 21st birthday present.[571]

All nicely altruistic but hardly in keeping with the very confidential letter he wrote to Alan White at Methuen two days later:

> I am determined to make every effort to secure the surviving Wilde copyrights from Vyvyan's trustee in bankruptcy. It is an opportunity which is hardly likely to occur again and besides their value as a long term investment, their acquisition would solve all our immediate difficulties. I hope therefore that you, or rather Methuen's, can come in on the deal, possibly on a fifty-fifty basis. I don't see how we can lose over this, even if we have to pay a bit more than £500 in the end, as all the rights have between 35 and 50 years to run, and I am sure that a combination of our two selves is the most profitable method of exploiting them . . . If it comes off Vyvyan and Rupert will be madder than hornets, which will be just too bad! Hence, I have impressed the need for utmost secrecy on the trustee while the negotiations are proceeding. I need hardly

tell you to put this letter, if you keep it, on the kind of file your brother used to keep in the last war![572]

The gloves were off and, somewhat unwillingly, the trustee had to take the part of referee. Hyde was clearly determined that his book should appear at all costs. Vyvyan was equally determined that it shouldn't, especially as he now had firm evidence of Hyde's deviousness.

On 13 March, increasingly concerned at the escalating disagreement, my father had written to the Home Office requesting that they withhold permission from anyone attempting to publish the petitions in full. Clearly embarrassed, they replied after nearly two months revealing that Hyde had actually submitted a draft of 'Oscar Wilde in Prison' to the Secretary of State the year before and that permission had already been given insofar as it concerned a public record.[573] Vyvyan now found himself forced to match Hyde's offer. Macleod was prepared to give Vyvyan precedence as the original holder of the rights, particularly as he had expressed his concern about them being controlled by someone outside the family. Hyde then lunched Macleod at the Garrick, upped his offer to £750 and craftily suggested giving an undertaking that no use of the rights would be made 'except with the consent and approval of Methuen and Co, the publishers of Oscar Wilde's works in this country since 1905.' With Alec's loan Vyvyan was again in a position to match Hyde's increased offer saying to Macleod that he was anxious 'to prevent the publication of a certain book, prompted by a great desire to spare his eleven year old son some of the agonies which he himself has experienced during his life.' Again Macleod exercised his discretion in favour of Vyvyan, saying that he 'must have respect for this very human appeal.' Undaunted, Hyde offered £1,000 and insisted that this should include the copyrights of Sir William and Lady Wilde, as well as those of Constance and Vyvyan, all of them further assets which Macleod was legally obliged to realise as well. At this point Rupert, by now considering the whole business something of a *cause celèbre* and as much his own fight as Vyvyan's, generously guaranteed the extra £250. More importantly, though, he took legal advice on the validity of his contract for *The Letters of Oscar Wilde* with Vyvyan as an undischarged bankrupt, found that it was entirely watertight and put Methuen on notice of the fact that he fully intended to seek an injunction if they published Hyde's book including the petitions and copyright letters. The whole purpose of Hyde's acquiring the copyrights was now thoroughly undermined. A few days later Rupert had a meeting with Alan White and, as a concession, agreed that if Hyde stopped bidding up the copyrights and changed the title of the book, he would be permitted to publish it six months after the appearance of *The Letters of Oscar Wilde*. Hyde conceded defeat and withdrew his last offer. It had, however, cost my father £350 more than expected to obtain his discharge from bankruptcy, which finally came through on 1 July.

When the battle for the Wilde family copyrights was over, Vyvyan wrote a touching letter of thanks to Richard Butler for having helped him *pro bono* over the last year. In his reply Butler said:

> My partners and I have felt that not only because of my personal friendship with you but, if I may say so, on grounds of 'poetic justice' we should not make you any charge for our fees. Please believe me when I tell you that we have been only too pleased to give you a helping hand, and I venture to think that my old master in the law and founder of our firm, the late Sir Charles Russell, whose name must be only too well known to you in another connection, would have been the first person, if he were alive to wish to help you.[574]

The 'other connection,' of course, was that Charles Russell had acted as the Marquess of Queensberry's solicitor in 1895.

I don't know whether Vyvyan ever did pay Alec Waugh back in full. If he didn't, it could only have been because Alec wrote off the debt to an old and dear friend. I suspect that may have been the case, because he was already suggesting in March 1957 that he reduce the amount by £300 if Vyvyan would help him with a book on wine which appeared two years later. The amount was disproportionate to the work involved as Vyvyan noted when Alec made the offer.[575] It seems that Harford Montgomery Hyde, or 'Judas' as he subsequently became in the long correspondence between Rupert and Vyvyan over *The Letters of Oscar Wilde*, couldn't resist one last sniping shot at the Wilde copyrights. On the same day that he finally withdrew his offer, he spoke to the Standing Committee in support of an amendment which had been tabled to the 1956 Copyright Bill. The amendment would have put unpublished letters into the public domain fifty years after their author's death, whereas until then they were protected until first published. After a short debate and considerable opposition, the amendment was withdrawn. 'One can see how Hyde's mind works,' wrote Vyvyan in his diary.[576] Hyde's 'Oscar Wilde in Prison' did finally appear in 1963 as *Oscar Wilde: the Aftermath* and, to be fair, it brought together a considerable amount of useful and original material which, once the *Letters* had been published and a whole new picture of my grandfather was emerging, seemed relatively harmless. It has to be admitted, too, that had it not been for Montgomery Hyde gaining access to the prison petitions and forcing the issue over them, they might never have been printed in the 1962 *Letters* and Vyvyan might never have come round to the idea of Oscar warts and all as Rupert Hart-Davis slowly encouraged him to do.

Hyde still tried to publish it under the title of 'Oscar Wilde in Prison' and my father still protested, citing the fact that he didn't want me, by then aged 17 and probably even more impressionable to such things, to have to cope with explaining 'Oscar Wilde' and 'Prison' to any of my contemporaries who might ask. As it was, I received a copy on publication from a totally unexpected source which helped me to take the first steps towards feeling comfortable with Oscar as a grandfather.

Chapter Six
Publishing Oscar's Letters

Once the dust had settled after the 'Great Copyright Theft That Wasn't,' an uneasy truce was declared. Vyvyan and Rupert needed 'Judas' Hyde for help with editing the letters; Hyde, as some collectors can be, was a vulture but a singularly rapacious one and knew that my father, who wasn't yet in the clear financially, still owned a few odds and ends of Wilde related material. There was no point in severing ties completely if there were other treasures to be had at knockdown prices, even if he now had to purchase them in a roundabout fashion. Three years before, he had bought a very rare copy of Oscar's first play, *Vera*, which had belonged to Robbie Ross who bequeathed it to Vyvyan. He offered my father £30 for it. Vyvyan's letter of acceptance makes me sad and angry by turns: 'Do you think the *Vera* is worth £30? Probably more like 30 shillings! I would cheerfully take that for it, as I happen to be more than usually hard up.'[577] Within three days it was on Hyde's bookshelf with a full, signed provenance by my father. The fact it would be worth 500 times that today is immaterial; it's just that it feels like a toned-down version of the 1895 sheriff's sale of all Oscar's possessions when he was on remand awaiting his first criminal trial. I suspect that my father, though he needed the money, felt the same. Then there was Oscar's letter to W.B. Yeats. Allan Wade wrote to Vyvyan just after the LCC plaque was unveiled on the family house in Tite Street to say that he had been in touch with Georgie, Yeats's widow, who had sent him the single surviving letter written by Oscar to her husband. Once he had transcribed it, she said, she would like him to give it to Oscar's son.[578] Touched by the gesture, Vyvyan wrote to thank her and sometime in 1955 that, too, went Hydewards.

Even more generous was the gift from Charles Du Cann, author, criminal barrister and small-time Wilde collector. He rang Vyvyan on 13 December 1954 and asked him to authenticate a volume of Oscar's poems inscribed to Constance: 'To a poem from a poet,' which he had found in a bookshop. Vyvyan did so and Du Cann made a present of it to him on the spot. My mother told me years later that it had been earmarked for me on my 21st birthday, but financial pressures and the silver-tongued Hyde diverted the book. It finished up being sold on with the rest of Hyde's collection to his namesake in America, Mary Hyde, in 1962.

On 28 January 1956, when Vyvyan first wrote to Hyde expressing surprise and dismay after learning about the imminent publication of 'Oscar Wilde in Prison,' the tone at the end of the letter was conciliatory: 'I feel sure that we shall be able to hit upon some *modus vivendi* . . . let us get the matter cleared up soon.' But Hyde was determined that his book should include the unpublished prison petitions in full, despite what my father felt about them. Vyvyan wrote twice more, on 4 and 12 March increasingly indignant at what he regarded as Hyde's underhand behaviour:

> Why, when I was seeing you continually in London and frequently asked you when we were going to see the Home Office files again, did you always give me evasive answers, and why did you never mention the fact that you had already obtained copies of all the documents (not only of the petitions) and were proposing to publish the petitions in full, when you knew quite well that to do so would be to act in direct opposition to my expressed wishes?[579]

Thereafter, as far as I know, my father never wrote or spoke to Hyde again. All further communication about the *Letters of Oscar Wilde* or Hyde's book was conducted at arm's length through Rupert Hart-Davis or Alan White. Hyde even wrote to White on 3 September 1962 in a tone of injured innocence trying to maintain that he had had no interest at all in securing the royalties for himself when he tried to purchase Vyvyan's copyrights, conveniently forgetting the highly confidential letter he had written to White six years before. The intermediary for Hyde's purchases of Wildeana appears to have been the book dealer George Sims to whom Hyde had introduced Vyvyan back in 1953. The correspondence between Sims and my father about all that was sold between 1956 and 1962 makes depressing reading.[530]

Cleared of his bankruptcy, Vyvyan was able to devote much more time to helping Rupert with finding and editing his father's letters. After the sudden death of Allan Wade, Rupert found himself having to take over the editorial work: 'Vyvyan Holland, a charming chap but unsuitable as editor, offered to take the job on, and the only way tactfully to stop him was to do it myself,'[581] but at that point he cannot have had any idea of the difficulties he would face nor how long it would take him. For a start there were the editorial problems: Oscar rarely bothered to date his letters and ordering them chronologically when they had been preserved by the recipient without envelopes and postmarks, sometimes required an extraordinary depth of research based on the slimmest of clues in the letter itself. For example a passing reference to a recently published book might be the only evidence to go on but it would at least indicate a year. A visit to the British Museum Library to see the 'date received' stamp in the copyright deposit copy could narrow it down to the space of a month or two, but it was all immensely time-consuming and had to be done without the aid of the digital facilities we take for granted today. Getting negative photostats from public libraries and individual collectors in America took an age even after managing to track down the originals. It often started with auction catalogues from the 1920s and relied on the goodwill of antiquarian booksellers, their memories and a sprinkling of trade gossip. A large collection of miscellaneous Wilde material had been loaned by Vyvyan in the 1930s to A. J. A. Symons for his never-completed Wilde biography and after Symons' death during the War his brother Julian and my father corresponded about its return but nothing was ever concluded.

Julian Symons sat on it until 1966 when he finally sold it to the Clark Library, but editorially it would have been particularly useful as it included many letters addressed to Oscar which would have helped to date his replies.[582]

Then there was the problem of the forgeries. Some had already been exposed, especially those created by the 'Paris Forger' of the 1920s, which were sophisticated enough to have fooled even the bookseller and specialist Wilde dealer Christopher Millard. As explained in Part Three, Chapter Three, until recently they were thought to have been done by my first cousin once removed, Fabian Lloyd, but were in fact the work of a small-time American conman, Brett Holland (no relation) who went by the various aliases Sebastian Hope, Dorian Hope, and Sylvestre Dorian. With so many genuine originals passing through his hands, Rupert managed to avoid being taken in by the forgeries still in circulation in the 1950s. Most of them are now safely in captivity, but even today one or two resurface and fool the most practised of auctioneers.[583] A further series of forgeries purporting to be letters from Oscar during his last years in Paris to his publisher Leonard Smithers, had been doing the rounds for some time as well. It was said they were done by Smithers himself after he had gone bankrupt and was desperately in need of money. They made little attempt to emulate Oscar's 'once Greek and gracious handwriting' which had deteriorated into a scrawl by 1899, and any doubts as to their authenticity were defended on exactly those grounds. That the forger had situated Oscar's address at the Hôtel d'Alsace incorrectly in the non-existent 'avenue des Beaux-Arts' instead of the 'rue' seems to have been largely overlooked by those gullible enough to buy them. A collection of letters allegedly written by Wilde to Sarah Bernhardt was published in the mid-1920s in the American 'Little Blue Books' series, but without the research advantages of the digital age Rupert would not easily have been able to link the name of the editor, Sylvestre Dorian, with the 'Paris Forger.' He and my father agonized for some time over including them as they were rather too sententious and larded with laboured aphorisms, not to mention the whole style which lacked the lightness of touch that characterised Oscar's other correspondence. In addition, there were even whole sentences lifted almost verbatim from his works written at a date later than the letter itself. My father, by strange chance had translated Lysiane Bernhardt's memoir of her grandmother back in 1949 and now wrote to her asking if the originals of these letters still existed and, indeed, whether they had ever existed at all. She told him that Sarah had always kept letters from interesting people, but despite inheriting all her grandmother's papers there were none from Oscar to be found. Rupert, seemingly blinded by the exciting prospect of including correspondence from one iconic figure of the 1890s to another was still not convinced and the forgeries even reached galley-proof stage before my father persuaded him to remove them. 'They lack the light-hearted jollity of most of OW's letters; this may be accounted for by the fact that they are translations and bad translations at that. Somehow they seem too pompous and too turgid.'[584]

The owners of original letters were generally cooperative about allowing the texts to be printed, as were auction houses when they came up for sale. The vulgar financial argument that unpublished letters would lose their resale value when published—largely put about for obvious reasons by the auction houses themselves—hadn't yet pervaded the market. Even when it did by the 1980s, the best of Oscar's letters always showed themselves proof against such devaluation. However, one person had his reasons for withholding letters from Rupert in order to negotiate a curious deal—the son of Carlos Blacker. Carlos and Oscar had known each other in London in the 1880s and had been such close friends that in 1888 Oscar dedicated to him his first collection of stories *The Happy Prince and Other Tales*. In 1890 Carlos, who by then was living beyond his means with a long-term mistress and in need of money, was persuaded to underwrite an American Land Development scheme. The scheme failed but not before Carlos had involved the young Duke of Newcastle and his brother as collateral sureties for his debts. When these were called in and the Duke forced to cover them, in a fit of pique he accused Carlos of cheating at cards. With his life in shreds Carlos fled abroad in 1893 and took up with Carrie Frost a wealthy American girl, whom he had known previously, abandoning his mistress and leaving her penniless. At this point Oscar stepped in and, apart from attempting to mend the rift between Carlos and Newcastle, helped the mistress financially to the tune of about £50. After Oscar's release from prison the roles were reversed. Carlos had married Carrie and had settled in Paris, whereas Oscar was lonely and short of money—never the best attributes to display when wanting to renew a friendship—and before long they had quarrelled irrevocably. There were undoubtedly faults on both sides and part of their falling-out was due to Carlos believing that Oscar has betrayed him over his behind-the-scenes activism in the Dreyfus affair, which the latter strenuously denied. Oscar then unburdened himself in two letters to Robbie Ross, hurt that Carlos 'had broken off our friendship in a coarse, offensive letter' and recounted in detail how he had stood by Carlos in his own trouble.[585] It was in return for suppressing these unsavoury details of Carlos's past that 'Pip' Blacker agreed to make available Oscar's letters to his father. Significantly, these letters to Robbie were the only ones which Rupert censored in the whole volume. When I came to revise and expand Oscar's letters in 2000, Carlos's grandchildren, anticipating that I would restore the deleted passages, arranged for a book to be published on the subject the year before, whose sole purpose (though they denied it) was to vilify Oscar and sanctify Carlos.[586] Among its many errors both of fact and of judgement, it quoted selectively from the offending letters ignoring Carlos's reprehensible treatment of his mistress and the help that Oscar gave him at one of the lowest points in his life.

From early on, Rupert's apparent concern for the sensitivities of the Blackers but not of the Hollands led to some light guerrilla warfare in the correspondence between him and my father. Despite their relatively harmless content, Vyvyan was concerned about the overtly homosexual nature of some of Oscar's letters from the post-prison period, mainly when he was corresponding with his two friends Robert Ross and Reginald Turner. Though he tended to regard Oscar's dalliances with young men in his last years as an undeniable fact, in the 1950s it was still something of open secret and he was anxious that it shouldn't be made obvious by publishing Oscar's own words on the subject. At first Rupert tried to reassure him that the more obvious passages would 'be lost in the great mass of the book, and anyhow we can discuss them later.' But Vyvyan was so easily convinced sure that the critics would ferret them out and highlight them in reviews: 'I suppose we shall fight over this until the end.'[587] My father kept bringing the subject up in a more or less light-hearted fashion with Rupert either ignoring the comments or repeating that it was nothing to worry about until April 1960 when the galley proofs of the last letters started coming in and decisions had to be made as they were corrected and started going to page. On 26 April Vyvyan confided to his diary: 'No one pretends that Papa was not slightly inclined towards homosexuality, but I do not want to plug the point that he and all his friends were utterly blatant about it. The suggestion I would like to put over is that he regretted it but really could not help it.'[588] I'm sure that entry must have been occasioned by a conversation he and Rupert had had that day, as Rupert's letter of the same date began countering Vyvyan's objections more and more firmly: 'You must trust my editorial judgement. I am quite certain that the book will be a major contribution to literature and should be considered as such.'[589] Until then Vyvyan had been adamant that some of them should be omitted or at least slightly expurgated, but in the meantime two major feature films on Oscar were about to be released and my father started to have doubts about the stand he was taking. Only three days later he would write 'The *Letters* are reaching the salacious period, but the two films now reaching completion have pretty well dispersed any mealymouthedness that might have been in the air, and it does not really seem to matter what goes in now.' But they were still only doubts. In early June he wrote to Rupert worried about including parts of the petitions from prison: 'They are far too cringing and there is always an element of doubt in some people's minds which these candid confessions would dispel.'[590] I talked to Rupert about it thirty years later and he told me that by then, in the six years he had been working with my father, he had come to look on him as a friend, and because he saw and understood Vyvyan's emotional turmoil about it all, he found it difficult to put too much pressure on him. When they met on 13 June to discuss what was to be done, however, Rupert was finally able to win Vyvyan over to integral publication and no suppressions. Any lingering doubts he may have had were dispelled by an exchange of letters with his old friend Rebecca West, to whom he wrote a few days later:

> Rupert Hart-Davis is publishing, early next year, all the letters of Oscar Wilde that he has been able to assemble for over five years. Among them is a large number of letters written during the last two years of his life to his main homosexual friends, Robert Ross and Reginald Turner. These letters leave no doubt in the mind that O.W. took his pleasures where he could find them. They are mostly in public libraries in America and are bound to be published at some time. Personally, I think that it is better that they should be published now, with explanatory notes by ourselves than in bare fashion by unsympathetic editors. Thelma does not agree, and thinks they ought to be censored; but she is thinking only of their repercussion on Merlin, who will probably not be much interested anyway.[591]

Rebecca, whose judgement in such things he trusted implicitly replied by return of post:

> As for the letters, I feel for Thelma over this. It is a hateful thing to have to face, and I also feel for your unfortunate father, who cannot have written those letters with any idea that one day all could read them. But I feel strongly that it is far better that your father's letters should be published by a reputable publisher,

who would vie you some control over the editing, rather than nameless wolves and jackals should get hold of them in the future . . . Thelma cannot hope that Merlin can fail to learn that his grandfather was homosexual and I wonder if he will not be wearied of the subject by the very excess of attention which is given it. (Your poor father—he also wrote, didn't he? Sometimes one would never guess it.)[592]

Vyvyan also sent her some examples of the passages he had been intending to remove which elicited the reply: 'Seriously, I think you should leave these passages in. They are very period—so period that they are really not shocking any more. And I have a dread of the letters being hawked about by people like Frank Harris as an "unexpurgated version of what the cowardly son suppressed."'[593] If my mother still needed convincing that this was the right course to take, it was certainly Rebecca's opinion which did it, and Rupert was relieved that this final obstacle had been overcome. Unfortunately, not quite; there was still the matter of *De Profundis*. When Robert Ross had deposited it in the British Museum Library in 1909, he had embargoed it for fifty years. The typed copy which he had made before doing so and which Vyvyan had used for his 'complete and accurate' version in 1949 was revealed to be far from it when the manuscript was finally opened to the public on 1 January 1960. There were several hundred errors and a thousand words omitted, most of which were fiercely critical of Alfred Douglas, and the entire letter needed careful rechecking against the manuscript. It meant a further delay during which extra letters materialised and which Rupert, after his marathon effort to put Oscar's letters into print, was reluctant to omit. Page proofs only started to come through towards the middle of the following year and the book was finally published more than eleven years after Rupert had first suggested the idea to my father.

In retrospect this long gestation was a blessing. Had Oscar's letters been published in the mid-1950s before the Wolfenden Committee had delivered its report on homosexual law reform and at a time when tolerance in Britain for same sex relationships, let alone understanding and acceptance of them, was at a low point, the book would certainly not have had the acclaim it did in 1962. I often wonder, too, when Rupert suggested the project to Vyvyan back in November 1950 whether he could have been aware of just how frankly Oscar was writing to Robert Ross and Reggie Turner about his amorous adventures after his release from prison. I suspect not. Once committed to the publication, though, it was a tribute to his patience and his campaign of persuasive diplomacy with my father that enabled Vyvyan to come to a more sympathetic understanding of his own father's sexuality. Small things of apparently superficial importance gradually won Vyvyan over, such as Rupert's inspired choice of section headings: 'Instead of the melodramatic chapter-titles (which occur in all biographies of your father—"Success", "Disgrace" etc.) we shall have nothing but plain place-names, which seem to me altogether fitting for a book of this sort.'[594]

Three months before publication, though, the Labour MP Leo Abse introduced to Parliament a private member's bill on 9 March 1962, the intention of which was to decriminalise homosexuality. It was legislation which had already been recommended by the Wolfenden Report nearly five years before, but the Government, concerned that public opinion was strongly against any such measure being taken, had simply shelved the matter. As it was, Abse's bill was 'talked out,' and Abse even accused the Cabinet of killing off his initiative as being too controversial.[595] It was against such a background, with Conservative MPs such as John Wells and Charles Doughty referring to homosexuals in House of Commons debates as 'repugnant' and 'abominable' and suggesting that prison was the only possible 'treatment' for them, that Oscar Wilde's letters appeared on 25 June 1962.

On receiving his first copy Vyvyan wrote a letter to Rupert which, knowing all that he had gone through, still moves me every time I read it:

My dear Rupert, How can I thank you for your really magnificent labour of love for my father? I had expected something *good,* but not as good and as splendid as that. And you concealed from me (you rogue!) that you had discovered all those photographs which no one had ever seen! *Where* did you find them? I am quite amazed by the book, and very touched by the inscription. I shall treasure it as long as I have to live as your most beautiful production. I want to go on writing, but I really do not know what to say. This is really the final tribute to my father and it will always be a lasting tribute to yourself.[596]

And signed himself, exceptionally, with his full name 'Yours ever, with affection, Vyvyan Holland.' From his reply it was evident that the whole affair had left Rupert with an affection for Oscar and *de facto* he became an adviser to all who studied and wrote about him for the rest of his life:

My dear generous Vyvyan, It's a long time since anything brought tears to my eyes, but I must confess that your letter did. Above everything I did so want to please and satisfy *you,* after all your help and patience and trust, and to know that you are in fact pleased makes me very happy. It was indeed a labour of love, for the more I read of and about your father, the fonder I grew of him, and the more I admired his generosity, tact, kindness, humour and total lack of malice. He may have had some of the faults that go with genius, but to me they are none of them faults that matter, and his fine qualities will survive. I shall be most disappointed if he is not now hailed as the great letter-writer I believe him to have been. I hope you and Thelma will have a little dinner of celebration with me before publication day—and then I will tell you all about the illustrations, which I was indeed keeping up my sleeve as a surprise for you! I will telephone and suggest a date. Love to you both. Rupert.[597]

Rebecca West, not known for her sympathy with homosexuals

generally, wrote to my father paying her own very special tribute to the book:

> May I say that the impression left on me by the letters is that it was not just advisable that they were published, it was necessary. [They] show him as a) a most charming creature, b) an affection-ate creature, c) a really gifted creature, and d) a victim, brother of Phèdre. I don't think anybody could read the volume without lik-ing your father more than before. I would think that from Merlin's point of view it was admirable that this clear view of his grandfa-ther should be put before us. He no longer, for one thing, appears as primarily a homosexual, which anybody could be, as there was no bravery involved, since people have been that throughout the ages (and I understand from a zoologist that the giraffes are al-ways at it, which I would give anything to see). He was a sweet and delightful person and the letters show it . . . Oh, God, it is a volume which throws a light on the precariousness of the human condition—it is a great book. I didn't expect to feel so intensely about it.[598]

In contrast to the general praise showered on the volume, the *Sunday Express* in a piece entitled 'WAS THIS MAN REALLY SO HARD DONE BY? IN HIS OWN WORDS—THE STARK TRUTH ABOUT THE DOWNFALL OF OSCAR WILDE,' simply concentrated on Oscar's last years and what Vyvyan referred to as 'the boy question' as he feared certain reviewers would. It was the only paper which sneered at what it called Oscar's 'absurdly inflated claims to ge-nius.' The reviewer, Robert Pitman, pointed out that:

> 'The accepted tragedy—[that] the sordid British Philistines trod Wilde into the mud and the grave for being slightly different, for being less vulgar, less boorish and infinitely more cultured than themselves,' was merely the standard image of Wilde's story, cre-ated by 'two films, a dozen radio and TV programmes and endless pathetic books'. The reality, as shown in this correspondence, was

'a terrifying record of callous depravity made still more terrifying because Wilde . . . seriously imagined that such behaviour set him above the ordinary philistine English.'

For the *Western Mail*, the Welsh dramatist and critic Saunders Lewis wrote:

> His wit and vast sense of fun never deserted his judgment of himself even in his hours of despair. For example it was suggested to him [*by Robert Ross*] after his wife's death that he should marry again. He answered: 'As regards my marrying again, I am quite sure that you will want me to marry this time some sensible, practical, plain, middle-aged boy, and I don't like the idea at all. Besides I am practically engaged to a fisherman of extraordinary beauty, age eighteen. So you see there are difficulties.' Anyone who can't delight in the sheer mischief of that ought to leave literature alone and go and play bingo. [599]

One reviewer obviously picked up on a sentence in Rupert's introduction in which he said that although Vyvyan did not wholly approve of the decision to publish the letters unexpurgated 'he has nobly allowed me to carry it out.' Cyril Connolly ended his review in the *Sunday Times* with the words: 'Mr. Vyvyan Holland deserves a word of special thanks for allowing the letters to be printed in their entirety.'[600] It must have seemed to my father like the final vindication of all his agonizing over whether or not to censor some of the correspondence and his decision in the end not to do so.

CHAPTER SEVEN
ETON

Four years after Rebecca West made her extraordinarily generous offer to my father at the Centenary lunch, I found myself starting the Michaelmas Half (their strange locution for a term) at Eton. In the balmy days of the post-War revivals and films of Wilde's plays and with royalties still payable on the copyrights, my father, in an uncharacteristically far-sighted moment, put my name down for Eton twelve years before I was due to go there. In those days entrance to the school was largely dependent not on academic merit but on a bizarre form of nepotism: so long as you passed the Common Entrance Exam, if your father had been to the school or you had a sibling there, you were more or less guaranteed a place. If not, it was at the discretion of the individual housemasters and most of them were as selective about future pupils as the parents were about the masters themselves, the houses with the best reputations filling up years in advance. The house to which I was assigned was run by a brilliant classicist, D. P. Simpson who himself had been at Eton as a scholar and who was once reputed to have dropped only four marks in his end of term exams. My parents had been to the school to meet him two years before and had been distinctly unimpressed by him. 'Thelma took a dislike to Mr. Simpson who is a typical schoolmaster: academic, verbose, self-opinionated and abrupt,' Vyvyan wrote of the meeting, adding that Thelma's colonial snobbishness overcame any misgivings she may have had, and that *he* would have preferred me to go to a local grammar school.[601] Brilliant though David Simpson may have been and possessed of a very amusing, dry sense of humour, he should never have been *in loco parentis* to impressionable teenage boys. I spent the next five years defying what I saw as his heavy-handed authority which I might have accepted had it been balanced with an equal measure of encouragement and inspiration. Instead, any sign of non-conformity or individuality was repressed, which made me 'trail my coat,' as Simpson described it to my parents, all the more frequently. Another boy who passed through his hands a few years after me would later write that 'Simpson thrived on belittling his boys, cutting down their egos, preventing them from exercising any creativity,' so my experience wasn't unique.[602] Matters weren't helped by my father remarking on the style of one of Simpson's letters as reminding him of the comedian, Jimmy Edwards, which can't have endeared him (and, by extension, me too) to my housemaster.[603] It would be too easy in retrospect to exaggerate these things and explain the reasons for our personality clash in facile terms. Might he have resented the fact that neither of our families could have afforded Eton's education, but that he had earned it as a scholar, whereas I was there by courtesy of one of my father's old friends? Was he perhaps mildly homophobic, disapproving of everything to do with my grandfather and, like all public school housemasters of that time, having to be acutely aware of any signs of homosexuality among the boys in his care? Either seems improbable though not impossible and he knew of my link to Oscar since Vyvyan had given him a copy of *Son of Oscar Wilde*. Oscar's reputation at this time bore no resemblance to what it is today: he was seen as a late Victorian oddity, a witty fellow with a couple of good plays to his name, and the author of some light fiction, but little else apart from his 'perverted' private life over which it was best to draw a veil.

About a year after arriving at Eton I gave up playing the piano. I was never going to earn a living as a musician but I had won a couple of small prizes at my previous school and enjoyed making music whether at the piano or singing. However, the combination of having a new teacher who was principally an organist and insisted on making me play hymn tunes 'for practice,' which bored me to distraction, and not having a piano at home, made progress dishearteningly slow, so I stopped. A friend of my mother who got to hear of it bought me a ukulele and taught me the basics since she played one herself. I was in heaven. I could make music; I could sing. It was small and it was portable and I took it back to school, though in a matter of weeks it was discovered and confiscated by Simpson who wrote to my father asking him to remove it when he next came down to see me.[604] On two occasions I wanted to audition for the school play, but since housemasters had to be consulted concerning all extra-curricular activities, the idea was firmly vetoed. Any deviation from the norm was regarded as a minor offence or even as a provocation, which was worse, and in my case probably true. Regular skirmishes took place over the length of my hair. I never wanted to wear it Beatle-length; that would have been too extreme an outrage, but that it should have been the subject of correspondence was a measure of how seriously the subject was taken: 'He is doing all right,' Simpson wrote to my father, 'apart from the inability to control his hair; he finds extraordinary difficulty in conforming about this, but I hope he will look human when you see him . . . I had to make a personal visit to the hairdressers to ensure that, in spite of his manoeuvres, his hair got properly cut.'[605]

Why do I write all this? I suppose because none of it would have happened had those royalties from the post-war revivals and films of Oscar's plays not come at just the wrong moment, attracting punitive levels of tax and tipping my father into bankruptcy. Rebecca would never have been so generous to her old friend, and I would have been educated perfectly well by the State. Eton was far from being academically one of the best private schools in the country at that time. It was a bastion of privilege, with the brightest pupils carefully groomed for Oxbridge and the rest being groomed for life outside and the old boy network. I fell, properly speaking, into neither category. As a result, there was a side of me which wished that I could have led a normal upper middle-class existence like the rest of the boys around me; a father in a liberal profession, a nice house, being part of the crowd and wearing the same uniform of easy confidence in one's background. Instead of which it was the perpetual consciousness of not fitting in at a time when conformity at school was still the least complicated option. I was thrust into a milieu in which I belonged neither socially nor economically and was constantly having to dissimulate, to pretend that I was at ease with it all and yet explain away the gaps. Mild eccentricity, a little disobedience, but kept sufficiently in check to avoid serious trouble, and a few untruths drew attention away from my more obvious deficiencies More difficult to conceal was the fact that on visiting days my parents used to arrive on a number 704 Green Line bus which stopped outside the School Office. Thirty years later that would probably have been regarded as the height of cool but to my lasting shame I neither met them nor saw them off from the bus-stop. When my father first accepted Rebecca's offer to educate me, he wrote 'There is only one sin for which I would never speak to Merlin again and that is snobbery'; fortunately it was only a mild dose and I recovered quite quickly as soon as I left.[606]

Looking back, I must have been quite conscious that Oscar was my grandfather, but I'm fairly certain that most of my contemporaries were unaware of the family connection until I was at least halfway through my time there. I had been told that if someone asked, the easiest way to avoid any awkwardness was to reply 'Yes, that's right; he was my father's father,' and steer the conversation away by saying 'I never knew him. He died a long time ago.' Surprisingly, I don't remember questioning why the subject was to be avoided because having him as a grandfather didn't feel like a guilty secret. Reading now what was written in the Press at that time and the views expressed during the House of Commons debates on the 1957 Wolfenden Report, I can understand why my parents might have felt concerned. On 26 November 1958, at the first Commons debate on the report, there was still a strong feeling that public opinion would not stand for reform and some speeches were peppered with emotional words such as 'repugnance,' 'perversion,' 'disease,' 'cure,' and 'social evil,' especially from MPs like James Dance representing Bromsgrove. Oscar, described by one MP as being a singularly objectionable individual, arrogant and ungenerous and playing no part in society, was held up as a good example of why any relaxing of the law was undesirable.[607] Another debate took place on 29 June 1960 on a motion to implement those recommendations of the report concerning homosexuality as soon as possible, with MPs like Godfrey Lagden expressing openly homophobic views and declaring that any change in the law would be a disaster for public morals. It was soundly defeated by 99 to 213 and the law was not changed until seven years later.[608]

Unlikely as I was to have read *Hansard*, the popular press was another matter. Aged thirteen and just into my second year at Eton, I wrote to my parents on 17 November 1959 to ask if they had seen the piece in the latest *Daily Mail* about a film which was due to be made on Oscar's life and, if not, would they like me to send it to them. Of course they were already aware of the article but had only just learned about the proposed film themselves. The article started 'Oscar Wilde's life story, which the cinema has always been afraid to touch, is to be filmed at last,' and went on to say that it would start at the peak of his success and cover his downfall through to the criminal trial and jail and would carry an 'X' certificate. Vyvyan's comment was 'Merlin cannot have many more illusions about his grandfather,' and added that ominous though the 'X' certificate was 'it is some comfort as none of Merlin's friends will be allowed in.'[609] Thelma was furious the producers hadn't been in touch with the family before making a public announcement, but she appeared more worried at the effect that it might be having on me. The following weekend she came to Eton to talk to David Simpson and to make sure I was not being affected by it. Apparently she asked me if I knew what the word homosexuality meant, to which I replied 'No, not really,' and it seems that no further explanation was forthcoming.[610] The idea that the whole of Oscar's scandal was to be resuscitated once again, and for a far wider public than Montgomery Hyde's *Trials of Oscar Wilde* in 1948, must have worried Vyvyan and brought back a few painful memories which not even his autobiography published five years before had been able to ease. The end of his diary entry for that day reads: 'Merlin is almost exactly the same age that I was when papa died, but then I had not seen my father for over five years. I often wonder what would have happened between Cyril, myself and him if he had lived. I imagine Cyril would have repudiated him and that I would have tried to help him.'[611] A couple of weeks later Simpson wrote to my father to say: 'I still feel pretty sure that Merlin is going to have nothing to worry about in this connection.'[612] I have never been certain whether this was to do with being Oscar Wilde's grandson and the publicity for the film due out the following year, or whether they thought I might be showing homosexual tendencies myself. Apart from that, I have no real memory of Oscar impinging on my life at school, though there was one incident a couple of years later . . . Ever since two films on Oscar's life had appeared in 1960, (and presumably by then I *had* found out what the word 'homosexuality' meant) Thelma had brainwashed me into believing that the trial was a mockery, the charges all made up and the witnesses had lied through their teeth.[613] So when one of my classmates told me that my grandfather was 'nothing but an old poofter' and continued to taunt me beyond endurance about Oscar's sexuality, I thumped him to protect the family 'honour,' was caught in the act by a prefect, answered back and was soundly caned for my trouble. I might have appealed with explanations, but I felt it would have landed me in even deeper water.

In May 1963, at the beginning of the summer term, the book which Montgomery Hyde had wanted to publish in 1956 as 'Oscar Wilde in Prison' finally appeared as *Oscar Wilde: the Aftermath*. I probably wouldn't have known about it had I not been sent a copy quite unexpectedly and by someone who, as far as I was concerned, had no idea about my relationship to Oscar. For all my father's attempts to protect me from the family scandal, he didn't reckon with my first serious girlfriend who sent it to me shortly after publication with, as an ultimate irony, the inscription 'I hope you enjoy reading this.' I distinctly remember being slightly shocked that she knew and I didn't know that she knew, a feeling which quickly gave way to relief that the 'secret' wasn't one any longer and that it wasn't my fault. Teenage passions being what they are, we split up not long after and I responded by sending her a specially bound edition of Oscar's fairy tales, inscribed with a suitably sentimental quote from one of his poems. It was the first time I recall feeling that I hadn't obeyed the parental injunction to keep my head down where Oscar was concerned, but that my disobedience was of no matter.

It was during my last year at school that an accident on the rugby pitch changed my whole view of why I was being educated and almost certainly was instrumental in getting me a borderline place at Magdalen, my grandfather's old college at Oxford. I was strong for my age and enjoyed that instant feeling of exhilaration which sporting success always brought, but one afternoon I finished up at the bottom of a scrum, my right leg in agony and the kneecap seriously damaged. The injury was badly diagnosed, incorrectly treated and for the next nine weeks instead of playing sports in my spare time, I was more or less confined to my room. At first, I became depressed and introspective but then, overnight, my priorities changed. I was going to show those who kept insisting my English prose was lamentable—Simpson being my principal critic—that I could write. I wish I could say that I had suddenly discovered my literary heritage; after all, my father was a writer, as had been my grandfather, and even aged nine and a half I had asked my parents 'When I grow up do I *have* to be a writer?' but the truth was more banal.[614] I simply wanted to try and prove my detractors wrong; it was intended as a sort of constructive defiance. I read copiously and transcribed passages which I found striking or beautifully written from Aldous Huxley, Graham Greene, and Lawrence Durrell in the vague hope that I might be able to absorb some of their genius. This all coincided with the study of a German set text for the term, Thomas Mann's

Tonio Kröger, a novella which followed the life of a self-conscious teenager with his inner conflicts and emotional crises through to being a successful writer with the dualities in his nature still unresolved but harnessed as a creative force. Identifying immediately with Tonio, it opened a door for me onto a whole new world—that of literary criticism and appreciation. I began a love affair with words and my reports suddenly sprouted phrases like 'penetrating remarks about literature,' 'ingenious and original,' 'the literary critic of the form.' The short-lived euphoria of some sporting victory had given way to a much deeper and more enduring satisfaction, that of knowing I had achieved my aim—to confound those who had dismissed my literary capabilities. Alastair Graham, a dynamic young Eton master, was given the unenviable job of building on my late-found enthusiasm for literature to cram me for university entrance and despite a poor mark in German language at 'A' level, I managed—as it turned out through the literature papers—to get an interview at Magdalen.[615] I remember the President of the College, Tom Boase, a remarkable art historian and sometime director of the Courtauld, saying to me at the time, 'Well, your German needs working on, but you obviously have a feeling for the literature and we're not just looking for scholars in this college; we're looking for people we think we can turn into scholars. We'll let you know.'

A week later I was offered a place. I'm not quite sure why Magdalen was chosen; it seemed to go against the continuing advice of my parents to play down my relationship to Oscar and applying to his old college was asking for a snide paragraph in a gossip column if the Press ever got to hear of it. Oddly enough, it may have been Vyvyan's idea. When he himself went to university in 1905 he had wanted to go to Oxford because his father had been there, but this was vetoed by his guardian for precisely that reason and he was sent to Cambridge instead. I think he may have derived a sort of vicarious pleasure from the idea that his own son could now do what had been forbidden to him.[616] It was all the more satisfying since David Simpson seems to have told him that my chances of getting a place were negligible and he may well have written an adverse report about me to the College. 'We went to see Simpson, who was obviously disgruntled about Merlin getting into Magdalen after being so sure that he would fail to do so. Indeed, he expressed unutterable surprise. I really don't like Simpson all that much.'[617]

So, I left Eton behind me. My five years there prepared me mentally for a world in which, though I didn't know it at the time, I would never have a place. Many years later when I first met Rupert Everett, he told me how, for half of his early life, he had felt an outsider because of his homosexuality. It was a feeling that I knew, though for different reasons, and almost for the first time I understood, as he must have done, that being this outsider was not 'bad blood' or some terrible character flaw of my own, but just the way things were.

The gradual public realisation in the early 1960s that Oscar Wilde was, after all, quite an important cultural figure, certainly made my teenage years infinitely more bearable that those which my father had been forced to live through after 1900. Nonetheless, in 1961, at the age of sixteen and in a country where homosexuality was still a crime, it was not always easy to live under the shadow of a grandfather who, in his own premonitory words from his Oxford days, ended his life both famous and notorious.[618] I was weighed down with what I perceived as the burden of others' expectations of me, as well as the fact that Oscar had been a convict, a homosexual, and a bankrupt, labels which still carried some of the same stigma as they had in 1895. I was inevitably torn between his literary achievements, in which I took a certain family pride, and his private life with which, in my teenage emotional immaturity, I was still coming to terms. A number of events around that time contributed to the growing public awareness of Oscar's downfall and imprisonment. Two films had appeared almost simultaneously in 1960 both of which were 'X' rated, though in places laughably inaccurate and sanitised and neither of which I saw until I was in my thirties. From the start they were in litigation with each other over questions of copyright and to the delight of the press it turned into yet another posthumous trial in which Oscar unwittingly found himself involved. Later that year Vyvyan published a pictorial biography of Oscar in which he was marginally more open about the relationship between his father and Alfred Douglas than he had been in his autobiography, though the story he told was still far from the truth. Significantly, it is the only one of his books he never inscribed to me at the time of publication. Lastly, the editing of Oscar's letters was nearly complete. The volume was duly published in 1962, finally giving the most frank portrait to date of my grandfather but one which, as a result, was also the most sympathetic. Needless to say every one of these events had its attendant controversy, and in 1961, perhaps anticipating my reaction to them, my father first handed me a copy of his autobiography which he had touchingly inscribed to me on publication day seven years before, knowing that one day he would have to give it to me.

It wasn't like Vyvyan to have engineered the right moment; it just happened. I was home for the summer holidays and it was a very hot August. My father was regularly getting up at half-past-five to write when he could avoid the main heat of the day, and one morning early—sleep having deserted me and inspiration probably failing him—he suggested we go for a walk in Hyde Park. As most teenagers, I was not an early riser by nature so the quiet city in pale sunlight was a new experience for me and as there was scarcely any traffic we could converse with little more than the dawn chorus for background. The pleasure of having my father to myself for two hours rapidly turned into an almost daily routine and sometimes we varied our route and walked through the empty streets of Chelsea. He would reminisce about his life between the wars, often prompted by passing a house where he had been a regular guest. He showed me the Wilde's house in Tite Street with its blue LCC plaque, and the Royal Hospital Gardens where he and his brother had played as children. With the difference in our ages—he was then seventy-five and I fifteen—it might have been difficult to relate to a father so much older, but it was not so. To me he represented a bygone age which fascinated me and I never tired of his anecdotes and explanations. I even found that I could trigger some of them, with variations of course, a second time around a few days later by subtle manipulation of our conversation or of our route that morning. One of my favourites was about transport in London before the First World War and his sudden realisation one day that there were more motorised vehicles in Piccadilly than horse-drawn ones; another was about the lamplighters who turned on the gas street-lamps at 'lighting-up time' with their long poles and of whom there were still a few in Chelsea and Knightsbridge even then. It was after one of those tours of Chelsea that he gave me *Son of Oscar Wilde*, my oblique introduction to who my grandfather really was.

Very recently I came across an entry in his diary which he had made about two months beforehand in June: 'Merlin telephoned today; about time . . . Actually we have now lost him. The trusting times when he and I walked the streets of Chelsea hand in hand and later arm in arm, have now gone, and it will not be long before he leaves the nest and flutters away on his own.'[619] Our early morning walks that August helped me to discover my father, and if they gave him half as much pleasure as they gave me, it's also good to think that they may have made him see that his rueful prediction about his 'fledgling' son wasn't to be realised for a while longer.

CHAPTER EIGHT
THE TWO OSCAR WILDE FILMS

In May 1960 two films on my grandfather's life and trials opened within a week of each other at London cinemas. The newspapers were ecstatic not so much about the films but about the fact that they could play off the merits of one against the other and, as a bonus, one production company had tried to take out an injunction to prevent the other company from distributing its film and was suing for breach of copyright. Oscar was back in court three times over.

With the publication of the Wolfenden Report in September 1957 and the debating of it in Parliament a year later, the whole question of homosexuality had become a public issue. The probability, therefore, in pre-digital age that two film-makers might simultaneously be tempted to tackle such a controversial subject without each other's knowledge was quite high. However, it might never have happened had Alfred Douglas not complained back in 1936 about being traduced in a French play about his relationship with Oscar Wilde.

The full story about Douglas's objection to the way in which he was depicted in Maurice Rostand's *Le Procès d'Oscar Wilde* when it was staged in Paris is given in Part Three, Chapther Six, but it was the sequel to that story which became the indirect cause of one of the 1960 films being made. By the mid-1930s Douglas had begun to tire of threatening people for libelling him so he contented himself in the case of Rostand merely with a letter correcting the facts. But when an English version of the play was announced at the Gate Theatre, he told the director Norman Marshall that he objected most strongly and Marshall, aware of Douglas's litigious reputation, wisely cancelled the production and instead commissioned a new version which would prove less offensive to him. By the time it was finished the main actors were no longer available and the leading role of Oscar Wilde was offered to the young and virtually unknown Robert Morley.

Refused a public licence by the Lord Chamberlain (the censor of plays until 1968) because of its subject matter, the play still had to be staged at the Gate, a private club theatre, and its success in the autumn of 1936 launched Morley's career. In 1938 it transferred to the Fulton Theatre in New York with Morley still playing the lead. It was there that an American scriptwriter, Joseph Eisinger, saw the play several times and felt it would make a magnificent film, although he realised that censorship laws on both sides of the Atlantic would probably prevent a film on homosexuality from being distributed. The War then intervened and it wasn't until the late 1950s that Eisinger approached an American producer, Robert Goldstein, who suggested there was a better chance of raising the money and making the film in England and introduced Eisinger to Warwick Films. Meanwhile, quite independently, and with the Wolfenden report's recommendations made public, Montgomery Hyde had been trying to interest the American actor/director Gregory Ratoff in making a film based around his 1948 book *The Trials of Oscar Wilde*, though nothing had yet been concluded between them. By the autumn of 1959, for reasons unclear, Warwick Films had decided to break off negotiations with Eisinger and Goldstein and make the film with an English director and scriptwriter, Ken Hughes. Here the waters become muddy. Eisinger and Goldstein were furious at having their project hijacked by Warwick and seem to have teamed up with Ratoff to make a rival film. It later transpired from the legal papers that Harold Huth, one of the Warwick producers, offered Goldstein a 'sweetener' of £2,500 to settle the dispute but in spite of that, Vantage Films, the company set up by Eisinger, Ratoff, and Goldstein, went ahead with casting and preparations for filming.[620] Warwick, in order to steal a march on Vantage, then went public with its plans and announced its forthcoming film to the press in mid-November. The article which, writing from school, I offered in all innocence to send to my parents, appeared in the *Daily Mail* on 17 November. In it, Ken Hughes was reported as saying that they would be talking to the Queensberry family with whom they could be facing problems, since the Marquess would be portrayed as the villain while Oscar would be shown as deserving pity, 'a genius living in a superficial fantasy world.' No concern, you notice, for the Wilde family at dragging him through the mire of a Victorian scandal yet again. I find it strange that Warwick films made no attempt to contact my father at all before publicising their film in this way, though had they done so he might well have taken offence and refused to have anything to do with it. Laurence Olivier, Alec Guinness, and John Gielgud were all floated as names to take the lead, which led to Vyvyan noting sarcastically in his diary 'And why not Terry Thomas or Gilbert Harding with his moustache shaved off?'[621] Within two days, however, Warwick films had been in touch and on 20 November Vyvyan and Cecil Douglas, nephew of Alfred Douglas and uncle of the then Marquess, went to meet the director and producers to discuss their possible involvement as 'technical and historical advisers.' Warwick's intentions were clearly to obtain a sort of *de facto* endorsement for their film by ensuring that members of the Queensberry and Wilde/Holland families were exclusively tied up and unavailable for the rival film, and since my father had in fact been working as an adviser on historical films at Pinewood Studios on and off for the last three years, he knew the ropes and felt he was in a strong position to negotiate a reasonable fee. He thought, rather unrealistically, that he might get £5,000 but in the end it was £500 for his advisory services and £500 for his name which, in the appalling financial state the was in at the time he had no choice but to accept. As he noted, the important thing was that he had some sort of say in the script.[622] Shortly after, the actor David Tomlinson whom Vyvyan had known from his time at Pinewood, rang and invited him to lunch at the Savoy. The conversation soon turned to the subject of the 1936 Gate Theatre play which, though my father didn't yet know it, was the basis of the rival film being produced by Vantage. Tomlinson tried to get Vyvyan to endorse the play or at least meet the authors, both of which he resolutely refused to do. Had Tomlinson been aware of Vyvyan's hostility to the play when it was first staged, he could probably have saved himself the expense of a meal. It was an oblique move by Vantage attempting to counter the *Daily Mail* publicity by Warwick, but it failed. The initial skirmishes were taking place between the two companies and would erupt into full scale war by the following spring but my father was quite oblivious to the fact.

On 4 December 1959 Warwick, in order to mark its territory even more assertively, arranged a 'publicity dinner' at the Café Royal with my father, Cecil Douglas, David Queensberry the twenty-eight year-old 12th Marquess, the producer Harold Huth, the director Ken Hughes and a journalist from the *Daily Mail*. There was still no sign of a contract and Vyvyan was growing nervous that he, Cecil and David were simply being used to give the film a sort of multiple family blessing and that Warwick might shortly inform them that they were no longer needed. He needn't have worried, as signing up the descendants of the Queensberry and Wilde families exclusively as 'historical advisers' was part of Warwick's game plan to make life for their rivals as difficult as possible. Apart from blocking Vantage's access to the individuals whose endorsement of a film would be invaluable, Warwick also tried to prevent them from using historical material which, as they believed, was still protected by copyright—the verbatim account of the trials.

The first comprehensive account of the three trials which Oscar went through in 1895 was published anonymously as *Oscar Wilde: Three Times Tried* in 1912 by Christopher Millard. It was the only one in existence until Montgomery Hyde published his 1948 book, *The Trials of Oscar Wilde,* almost all of which was taken from Millard, but with scant acknowledgment of the fact. Millard's edition by then was long out-of-print and quite rare. Hyde's book had been published in their Notable British

Trials Series by William Hodge & Co of Edinburgh, whom Hyde assured that he had been granted permission to use Millard's work by the original publishers, though it later turned out he was unable to produce any evidence for it. By 1959 Hyde's adaptation of Millard was regarded as the main authority on the trials and had doubtless been discussed at the Café Royal dinner, so Harold Huth duly rang James Hodge on 15 December proposing £250 for the exclusive film rights in Hyde's book. Negotiations went back and forth over three months and an agreement was finally reached on 17 March the following year. In the meantime Vyvyan had received his contract at the beginning of February together with the film script which he started to read, describing it as 'completely illiterate' and by the middle of the month he had sent off ten pages of general comments and dialogue corrections.[623] Sadly they have not survived or, knowing my father, I imagine they would have been humorous and acute and largely ignored. Irving Allen, Huth's co-producer on the film, was memorably reported as saying: 'If I get a literate script, I throw it in the wastepaper basket.'[624] In early February Warwick finally informed my father that another company was also planning to shoot a film on Oscar, a fact that they concealed from James Hodge until the moment they had signed up the film rights to Hyde's *Trials* six weeks later, and even then, in Mr. Hodge's words, 'they mentioned casually that another film company might be contemplating making a film on Oscar Wilde and that they would be looking into the matter.'[625] The very same afternoon that Warwick acquired the rights they sent a threatening letter to Vantage to say that they would be applying for an injunction and would start an action for breach of copyright unless Ratoff, Eisinger, and Goldstein immediately undertook to have nothing further to do with the rival film. Predictably no undertaking was forthcoming and an injunction was applied for the next day. The *Daily Mail* immediately reported the outbreak of hostilities and quoted Warwick as saying they had paid 'around £1000' for the film rights, four times the real figure presumably to over-sensationalise matters. At the beginning of April the *Evening Standard* started a nine-part serialisation of Warwick's film script over two weeks, an extraordinary move by today's standards when production companies tend only to feed out advance 'teasers' at carefully controlled intervals. In view of all the publicity, my mother wrote to Sir Sidney Harris, President of the British Board of Film Censors, asking him to take the family's feelings into consideration when viewing the films for certification. The letter hasn't survived but knowing my mother's feelings at the time it was undoubtedly couched in terms of 'I have an adolescent son at school who could be deeply disturbed by . . . ' and in due course he replied sympathetically to say he was keeping a careful eye on both films. Later, when both films were released, and the papers were full of them, my mother came to Eton once again to see if it was affecting me. I have no recollection of it but my father noted that 'Merlin remains calm.' I rather wish I'd kept a diary myself at the time, though I doubt there would have been any revealing introspective remarks in it of the type 'It's quite difficult having famous parents,' which I was supposed to uttered sometime around then.[626] On 6 April Vyvyan made his first visit to Elstree where the Warwick film was being shot:

> Spent the afternoon on the set representing the foyer of the St. James's Theatre—of course not remotely resembling it. Peter Finch, in response to applause, waving his hand at the audience like a heavy-weight boxer. All the ladies in stiletto heels and all the men, looking like stable-boys, smoking cigars. Pretty lamentable, but it could have been worse. Speranza was a thin, undistinguished looking frailty; Bosie frankly a cockney pansy; Queensberry a rather large benevolent comedian; Mama I could not even distinguish; and the poor Sphinx [*Ada Leverson*] a shabby nonentity.[627]

Although employed as an historical advisor he was only asked to visit to the set once more at the beginning of May. Despite his professional experience advising on historical films, this seems odd, but clearly Ken Hughes and Irving Allen considered they had bought his tacit consent rather than his advice and in the finished film it showed.

It was at this point that Warwick began to press James Hodge about the sources which Montgomery Hyde had used for his book. Hyde had to admit that his version was very largely based on Millard and maintained that the original publisher, Cecil Palmer, had given him permission verbally to use the material. There was no paperwork and Hyde's assertion would have been useless in a court of law.[628] Palmer himself had died in 1952 and the publishing house no longer existed so the matter was unverifiable. There was, however, one further possibility: even though the publication had originally been anonymous, it was generally known to have been Millard who had collected and edited the material. He had died in 1927 so his work would still have been protected for the fifty-year copyright term which was valid at the time. Warwick's solicitors traced Millard's sole surviving executor and on 25 April they also purchased what they believed to be the film rights to *Oscar Wilde: Three Times Tried*. Not wasting a moment and confident that by purchasing rights in both books an action against Vantage for breach of copyright could not fail, the next day they withdrew their previous application for an injunction and reissued it including William Hodge & Co as joint plaintiffs but without informing them—a fact which only came to light at the injunction hearing three weeks later. This was almost certainly done to give weight to their claim against Vantage and because Hodge's agreement with Warwick would have included an indemnity clause, for any claims against them over granting the exclusive film rights. It would later cost them dearly. While the dispute with its threats of legal proceedings grew increasingly vicious, the two Oscars, Peter Finch for Warwick and Robert Morley for Vantage, provided some light relief. When asked by the *Daily Mail* about the battle between the two films Morley replied facetiously, 'I should have thought two films were better than one. I'd be quite happy to appear in both.'[629] And when Jack Bentley, the showbiz columnist on the *Sunday Pictorial* made no secret of visiting both sets on the same day, Peter Finch said that even if the film companies were at each other's throats, the actors certainly weren't: 'Give Bob Morley my love. He and I are the best of pals. In fact, for a joke, we were arranging that each of us should turn up at the wrong studio one day,' and Bentley reported that Ratoff's 'explosive statement was largely unprintable.'[630]

At the hearing on 16 May for the interim injunction by Warwick to prevent Vantage from showing their film until the matter of copyright had been sorted out, the general duplicity on both sides was evident. Sir Andrew Clark for the defendants referred to Warwick's last minute acquisition of the film rights as 'a couple of rusty old swords picked up cheap in a junk shop' and pointed out that the idea was filched by the plaintiffs from the defendants in the first place. Warwick's counsel pleaded that the injunction was necessary because Vantage was a 'straw company' with £100 capital and two shares of £1 and would never be able to pay the substantial damages which would ensue if they distributed their film but were found to have breached copyright in the two books in question.[631] In the end, the application was rejected by the judge who said pointedly that there was not much to choose between the moral conduct of the parties in this matter of cut-throat competition. From then on it was a race to the screens.

Vantage were first to premiere on 22 May. 'The most talked about film in the history of the cinema,' and 'Theirs was a relationship the world could not—*would* not tolerate,' screamed the advertisements. The proceeds for the evening were being donated, somewhat incongruously, to the Moroccan Earthquake Relief Fund, a publicity stunt whose sole purpose seemed to be able to link the film with the names of the Foreign Secretary, Selwyn Lloyd, and some members of the Moroccan Royal family who attended. Shot in black and white, it was the 'cheaper' of the two films, and being the shorter it was criticised for not building up the main characters enough before concentrating on the trials.

Morley had more of the presence and the corpulence of Oscar than Finch and managed the endless epigrams with some skill but was not unreasonably described by one critic as playing the role like 'a rather wrinkled Billy Bunter in appearance and an over-confident small boy in manner.'[632]

Both had their frankly ridiculous moments. The Vantage film made a whole scene out of an incident mentioned in passing by Oscar in *De Profundis*—Bosie while at Oxford was blackmailed over a compromising letter he had written to a young man and had appealed to Oscar for help. In reality, Oscar simply put Bosie in touch with his solicitor who settled the matter. The film, how-ever, has Oscar posing as a plain-clothes police inspector, arriving at Bosie's rooms in Oxford and frightening the blackmailer into returning the letter. The result is a hilarious, even vaguely credible vignette, although total fiction. The Warwick film, taking advan-tage of its technicolour, has Constance meeting her husband at the gates of Pentonville prison with a green carnation which she places lovingly into his buttonhole, before taking him to Victoria station in a cab and waving him off on the train to France. Bosie, meanwhile, stands in the background on the platform being ig-nored by everybody. Cinematographic licence to simplify the truth is one thing, but as a portrayal of the day of Oscar's release it was totally ludicrous. Queensberry's defence barrister, Edward Carson, whose deadly tenacity caused Oscar to abandon his libel action and led to his arrest, was played passably well by James Mason with an Irish brogue (which indeed he had) but his inter-pretation was limp by comparison with that of Ralph Richardson who was well cast by Vantage in the role.[633] John Neville, at thirty-five, was too old and too well-behaved to do justice to the part of Bosie Douglas, whereas John Fraser at twenty-nine in the Warwick version was closer to Douglas's real age and played him with a near-perfect combination of arrogance and irascibility as a spoilt young aristocrat. The opinion of the critics was divided, but overall Warwick's was deemed to be the better production. The Warwick film for some reason didn't manage to get a West End premiere but opened nationally a week later, though there was a press screening a few days before which my father attended:

> It was distinctly better than the Morley film, but it was full of absurdities. Peter Finch was efficient as Papa but has not got the necessary breeding. James Mason as Carson was not a patch on Ralph Richardson . . . . The whole film was so unreal to me because I knew nearly all of the chief characters and of course the characterisation was quite fantastically wrong . . . . The only one that I really recognised was myself having 'The Happy Prince' read to me.[634]

Years later at an Oscar Wilde Society lunch meeting in 1995, John Fraser recalled how he had played Bosie Douglas in the film and how, at that screening, Vyvyan had been 'overcome with emotion.'[635] I'm afraid Fraser's memory owed more to his imagination than to reality as Vyvyan's diary entry implies. I am not suggesting that this reflects badly on Fraser; it's just that people, in all innocence, like to embellish the past. When it comes to stories involving Oscar, whether in his lifetime or posthumously, the temptation to do so seems irresistible. Fraser *wanted* Vyvyan to be moved by the film in which he had played, but my father, as I remember him, was very seldom 'overcome with emotion' and on this occasion, if indeed he was, it could only have been from seeing a travesty of the facts.

Derek Monsey, a critic who praised Warwick's film unreservedly, even referring to it as 'a tremendous film, one of which the British film industry can—and should—be proud,' lamented the fact that it was not granted a West End début and suggested his own credible conspiracy theory:

> I have no doubt that a number of highly plausible reasons can be given for this. But is it a coincidence that of the dozen or so major cinemas which make up the great prestige shop window for films in Britain, only two or three are controlled at the moment

by British companies? And that the Morley film, now in the West End, is backed by a powerful American company, while the ostracised Finch film is not?[636]

All perfectly possible since open warfare had broken out between the two production companies, and one cannot discount any form of skulduggery by Vantage to queer the pitch for their competitors.

On 18 July Warwick started a High Court action against Vantage for breach of copyright claiming they had acquired the exclusive film rights in both Hyde's and Millard's accounts of Oscar's trials. Irving Allen told Cecil Douglas that he believed he could get £250,000 in damages from Vantage and to strengthen their case he asked my father to provide some hard evidence of Millard's authorship.[637] Having known Millard personally while he was working on his trial book, Vyvyan was able to swear an affidavit to that effect and backed it up with some of Millard's correspondence buried in Oxford's Bodleian Library, but having seen Warwick's *modus operandi* he made sure of his fee before handing over the evidence. Vantage, determined to fight all the way, then demanded 'Further and Better Particulars of the Statement of Claim' which involved an immense amount of work by Warwick's legal team comparing the two books with Vantage's script and listing every occurrence they regarded as an infringement. It was clearly a delaying tactic to enable Vantage to carry on distributing their film in the meantime. And so the costs mounted up.

As for the films, neither was a box office success. The bigger-budget Warwick film won a few awards and did well in the south of England, but in Leeds, Birmingham and Manchester it was booed, and it was a complete flop in America except in the eastern states. It lost Warwick £250,000 and contributed to making their tied distribution company, Eros Films, bankrupt in June 1961 to the tune of £400,000.[638] Vantage were struck off the Companies Register in 1965. The litigation dragged on for seven years, with the case finally heard in June 1967 and judgment given in favour of the defendants because the film rights in the two books which Warwick purchased were deemed invalid. The publishers William Hodge & Co, having been joined in the action as co-plaintiffs found themselves owing legal fees of nearly £1,000 just for selling the exclusive film rights in Hyde's book on Wilde's trials, which they never owned in the first place, although they believed in good faith that they did. Hyde never was able to produce either a written agreement nor any correspondence relating to a verbal one from Cecil Palmer (if indeed he ever had one), allowing him to use most of Millard's original book in his own. It might well have changed the outcome of the copyright action. As a lawyer himself such carelessness seems improbable to the point of plain fabrication. It was just another trial in which Oscar found himself unwittingly involved long after his death and an unedifying glimpse behind the scenes of the film industry throughout.

CHAPTER NINE
VYVYAN'S LAST YEARS

The last eight years of my father's life, from 1960 on, were considerably happier than the previous decade had been. Happier maybe, but not wealthier; he was still absurdly short of money and was taking almost anything which was offered to him in the way of work. In July the previous year, Walther Neurath of Thames & Hudson asked if Vyvyan would be interested in contributing an Oscar Wilde volume to their series of Pictorial Biographies. This was partly due to the success of *Son of Oscar Wilde* and partly, as Neurath explained, due to Oscar's popularity in Europe where translations of the series were more or less guaranteed. The terms were good—only 20,000 words, an advance of £300 and delivery by 1 December—so he accepted at once but immediately started to worry about three things: where to find the illustrations, how to give the text originality, and how to deal with Douglas, the trials and the post-prison years. Despite receiving two thirds of the advance on signature, which was unusual but solved his immediate financial problems, Vyvyan didn't seem in any mood to get down to the writing. A simplistic explanation for this would be that he still had various long-term commitments to magazines and newspapers for which he had been writing regular articles on wine, as well as having to work on the accounts of Slenderella, the English branch of an American 'slimming' company, which my mother was running. I can't understand why she was ever appointed its managing director; she was extremely capable and well-respected as a leading cosmetician and beauty adviser, but as a businesswoman she was a disaster. Behind the scenes, my father was trying to keep the finances in order spending whole days each month balancing the books. I can still feel his frustration at having to do what he must have regarded as utterly uncreative work, but necessary in order to make it appear that Thelma was exercising proper control of the company as it was her salary which was paying our rent. By mid-November, a fortnight before he was due to deliver his text, another excuse conveniently presented itself: Warwick Films was fishing for his support as an historical adviser for their Oscar Wilde film. These were certainly valid reasons to put off starting the pictorial biography, but in reality it was the old story of having to face up publicly to his father's homosexuality, and especially at a time when his battle with Rupert Hart-Davis over censoring some of the overtly gay letters was coming to a head. It was also his first attempt to write what would be a potted biography of his father which, given the nature of the Thames & Hudson series, would necessarily include a great many generalisations which needed to be accurate. A diary entry when he at last got down to the writing reflected some of his concern: 'So far my difficulty has been mainly that until 1888 he seems to have done nothing but prance about, and it is very hard to build him up entirely on antics and horseplay.'[639] A slightly harsh assessment of the father by his son, but not untypical of a general public view at that time; the revaluation of Oscar wouldn't begin for another decade. Eventually, with no more 'justifiable' procrastination possible, Vyvyan delivered his text at the beginning of March 1960. As to be expected, he skirted around the real nature of his father's relationship with Bosie Douglas, writing that after their first meeting: 'Oscar Wilde immediately took a liking to the young man and a close friendship sprang up between the two.' This in turn, he explained, gave rise to 'certain rumours' which led the Marquess of Queensberry, Bosie's father, to accuse Oscar of 'unnatural practices.'[640] Nowhere in the book (as was the case in *Son of Oscar* Wilde six years before) does the word 'homosexuality' appear and one of Oscar's petitions from prison for his early release, written on an official form and used as an illustration, had the section detailing crime, sentence, conduct etc carefully scalpelled out. My father clearly considered that even the offence of 'gross indecency,' as it was quaintly called in 1895, was too uncomfortable to be mentioned. I only discovered this thirty-seven years later when I published my own small pictorial biography and used a copy of the Thames & Hudson illustration for the rough make-up. When the photo I had ordered from Oscar's prison file in the National Archives came through and didn't fit the allotted space, it was immediately obvious why. Just another sad reflection on how Vyvyan was still being affected by it all sixty-five years after the events.

On publication most critics were guardedly positive, though some criticised the illustrations, which had been largely chosen by the publisher, as wrongly captioned or simply irrelevant. It was the *Birmingham Daily Post* in a review entitled 'Tragedy Obscured' which cut through to the heart of the problem:

> What ought to be the most intriguing point about this book—that the author is Wilde's surviving son—is the one that creates the greatest reservation. Mr. Holland tells the story neatly and elegantly, but he tells it coyly with an excess of filial respect that, however admirable in itself, masks the deeper issues of the tragedy. We would, in fact, hardly know that Wilde was charged with homosexual offences, referred to here as "charges under a section of the Criminal Law Amendment Act of 1885."[641]

Ever since the universally good reception given to *Son of Oscar Wilde* in 1954, there had been murmurings about a sequel. *Son of Oscar Wilde* finished with the reburial of Oscar in his permanent plot in Père Lachaise Cemetery in 1909, but what happened to his son in the intervening fifty years? According to Vyvyan it was mainly Thelma who encouraged him, but until August 1961 he had hardly written a word. It was a long-term project which had to make way for work which was more immediately remunerative. Having delivered his book on Oscar Wilde for Thames & Hudson, he persuaded them to take a biography of Goya based on an unused film synopsis he had written a few years before; he continued writing regular articles on wine for *Good Housekeeping* and the newly launched *Sunday Telegraph*; and there was work as a publishers' reader on wine and food books. Apart from being hampered by his financial worries, there was also a sense of *déjà vu* about the whole undertaking. As he had experienced when writing *Son of Oscar Wilde,* unless he included interesting and even slightly personal revelations about others as well as exploring some of his own emotions in relation to his father's legacy, the book would just be a sterile and lifeless memoir. Against that, there was the perfectly understandable desire that it should be an account of Vyvyan Holland's life rather than Vyvyan Wilde's. He finally settled down to writing it in the autumn, though with misgivings about how good it was and also apprehensive about Thelma's declared intention to go through the manuscript and 'correct' where necessary—for which read 'censor.' Even if Thelma had let Vyvyan write the pictorial biography without interfering, she was definitely going to have her say about the second volume of his autobiography.

Shortly before Christmas 1961 my father had completed about 50,000 words and sent them with a rather diffident letter to Rupert Hart-Davis. He had already admitted to himself that the content was not up to much, but since Rupert was in the middle of editing the letters and had published *Son of Oscar Wilde*, Vyvyan felt it was only courteous to offer him the sequel. Rupert must have read it at once and in the voluminous correspondence he was carrying on with George Lyttleton expressed his dismay: 'During the holiday I have read . . . the second autobiographical venture of Vyvyan Holland, Oscar's son, which, alas, is very thin and banal. I don't know how on earth to tell him without hurting his feelings.'[642] However, in his usual diplomatic way, he did tell Vyvyan and his response came as no surprise: it was too dated for him to publish. Nevertheless, he offered some advice on improving it and in his reply Vyvyan thanked him for his frank criticism and offered to rewrite it: 'The trouble is, I suppose, that Thelma rather objected to certain passages, which did not seem to tally with the pure upright life of a British gentleman. But, then, what is one supposed to do when one isn't married or anything?'[643] He admitted there was almost nothing about his first wife: 'One of the chief difficulties about it is that there is no mention of my first wife. It was rather deliberately suppressed by Thelma who will not admit it now. She says she only hinted.'[644] He also wondered whether all references to his activities in the First World War should be suppressed as being rather remote and asked Rupert for more advice. It came. Cut out all the part about the First World War and give us some stories about interesting people you have known. Early in the new year Vyvyan added 2000 words about Violet, his first wife (of which only 1000 survived in the end), but his heart wasn't in it. He felt that it was like writing *Son of OW* all over again with Thelma objecting to accounts of his personal life between the Wars and Rupert telling him to delete the parts which he found dated—everyone pulling in different directions and Vyvyan in consequence becoming more and more depressed about the whole venture. 'It was hopeless from the start with . . . the First War being so dated and my own life so very imperfect after the early years. I ought to have remembered that my first book had so much about my father in it that it sold for curiosity's sake.'[645] Fortunately in the rewrite he ignored some of the advice and didn't delete the chapters on the First World War, as they turned out to be among the most lively and readable in the whole book. As for 'interesting people who are still alive [they] are so difficult . . . I seem to have seen them all in their more relaxed (to say the least of it!) moments and I am pretty sure they or their descendants would hate to be included.'[646] Some were included in the end, but merely as the subject of a rather bland description or a lifeless anecdote or two. Every time I read in Vyvyan's last chapter that one of his reasons for writing *Time Remembered* was 'so that when my son reads it he may know something more about me than most sons know about their fathers,' I feel a slight pang of resentment towards . . . well, towards whom? My mother for making sure the life of Oscar Wilde's son comes over as squeaky clean? A little, but she was acting for the best as she saw it, especially given how the press latched onto anything even mildly sensational to do with Oscar Wilde or his offspring. Rupert for getting him to delete some of the dated material as being unpublishable for that time? A little too, though what we are left with has become a fascinating snapshot of an era seen through Vyvyan's eyes. Prevailing attitudes towards Wilde at that time and his posthumous reputation? Certainly, because Wilde had got his comeuppance in 1895 and who really cared in 1962 how Vyvyan had coped with the echoes of the scandal in the intervening years? All this, further aggravated by Thelma telling him not to bother finishing it, made Vyvyan want to destroy the manuscript. In the end he simply abandoned it for eighteen months and concentrated on writing wine articles.[647] When he had recovered from this mauling and decided pick up the threads in April the following year, the slimming business Thelma had been running had just gone into liquidation and she was in no mood to give him encouragement: 'Thelma says that my second book is "old hat" whatever that may mean and that whatever I do to it will be no good. This is rather depressing as I thought I might be able to pull it together,' and it was abandoned yet again.[648] Fortunately other work came in—a revamp of Oscar's collected writings for Collins with an introduction, and a translation of Auguste Escoffier's 703-page *Ma Cuisine* which, though Vyvyan had promised himself no more translating, was too well-paid to turn down.[649] Two more years of false starts would go by before he made what he knew would be the last attempt to complete this second volume of memoirs, and still my mother went on pulling them apart: 'I now know quite well that I am no author with Thelma over my shoulder criticising every word I write and sneeringly approving of every third sentence. Oh! to hell!'[650]

As I write this, I try to make sense of it all. Was my father exaggerating, going against his first principle in 'Keeping a Diary' which was to be scrupulously truthful?[651] I don't want to believe it, but equally I don't want to believe that Thelma, having been the one to encourage him in the first place, could have been so callous in her attitude when Vyvyan was so clearly full of self-doubt and in need of reassurance. But she was angry. Angry at herself for the failure of her business, disappointed with my father for not being more of a literary success (to say nothing of the financial implications) and probably fearful that another bank-ruptcy was just around the corner. In spite of it all, by August 1965 the book was finished and, certain that it would be turned down, he sent it to Victor Gollancz. Within a couple of weeks it had been accepted for publication and Vyvyan was thrilled: 'Even Thelma now regards me in an entirely new light, though she is still bossy,' my father wrote with some relief at the time.[652] Gollancz wanted him to make the book a little more substantial so Vyvyan offered to add two more chapters on his war-work in the French service of the BBC and the family's year-long visit to Australia in 1947. The first of these was as interesting in its way as his experiences in the First World War. The second, however, almost certainly instigated by Thelma, gave her the cue to make Vyvyan indulge in some name-dropping so that the book would have good sales in Australia. This he resolutely refused to do and, as a result, the chapter reads in places like a Michelin guide to the Antipodes.

Far more dramatic was Thelma's attempt to interfere just as the book was being typeset. She had rejoined her old cosmetics company Cyclax after the failure of the slimming business in 1963 and in the autumn of 1965 she undertook a promotional tour of Canada for them. While in Vancouver she was contacted by a Mrs. Fitz James whose father, George Foley Shaw, had been a District Inspector in the Royal Irish Constabulary in County Roscommon. She related that on one of his periodic visits to London's Scotland Yard in 1906 her father had apparently unearthed documents in the police files which proved beyond doubt that Oscar Wilde had been blackmailed. Despite being told the case was closed, he took copies of the papers 'intending to clear Oscar's name.' A few days later he died in his hotel in mysterious circumstances. He was found tied to a chair, gagged, and with a chloroform bottle by his side. All this was recounted to Thelma by Gladys Fitz James, Shaw's daughter.

In a letter overflowing with breathless excitement, Thelma's wrote to Vyvyan from Canada about her latest discovery and suggested he include the story as a sort of epilogue to his book and that they should try to check out the Scotland Yard files and even if they didn't exist or were destroyed, it sounded a plausible story. In his reply Vyvyan put his foot down very firmly: 'I have brought my book to a grand finale, and I don't want to end up with an effort to make out that papa was not homosexual, or to "clear his name". It would be impossible to do so, in view of the petitions from Reading Gaol, in which he admits everything.' Thelma, who frankly knew very little of the detail of Wilde's trials, and what she did know she ignored, wouldn't let it go: 'Any book needs publicity and if it was true about Scotland Yard and could be found out, it would be worthwhile: "SON CLEARS FATHER'S NAME. FANTASTIC COINCIDENCE IN THE WILDE STORY" etc. Headlines.' And she went on to say that if Oscar was blackmailed it meant that the witnesses in his criminal trial were paid which, of course, made no sense at all. For once Vyvyan was not going to be talked into doing what he felt instinctively was wrong: 'My policy with regard to papa has always been to ignore, as far as possible, the whole shabby business. I never discuss his sex life with anyone, and I do not see any use in trying to resurrect his corpse and try to whitewash it . . . everyone who has studied the matter knows that Queensberry kept the witnesses and coached them in what to say. No. Leave it alone, I say.'[653] And with that the matter was dropped.

Coming across the story more than fifty years later in my parents' correspondence, I was intrigued by the idea of a fellow Irishman wanting to clear Oscar's name so soon after his disgrace. The Shaw family connections all stood up to scrutiny, as did the sudden death of George Foley Shaw in a central London hotel in 1906, but that was where fact morphed into fiction. He had retired from the RIC in 1899 so it was highly unlikely that he would have had access to London police files seven years later. From papers found in his room, it was clear that he had gone to London to work with a political association on the forthcoming general election. At the inquest, the hotel chambermaid said that she had found him lying dead on his bed fully clothed and with a near-empty bottle of chloroform beside him. He had been in the habit of taking it as a cure for insomnia and a local chemist testified that Shaw had purchased the chloroform that very afternoon supposedly to put down a large dog. A verdict of death by misadventure was recorded.[654]

Even if the story related by Gladys Fitz James to my mother had a few elements of truth to it, the dramatic conclusion was clearly a complete fabrication. The Shaw family may have been aware of the Wildes' connection with Roscommon (Sir William Wilde was born in Castlerea), so they were probably aware of Oscar's fate in 1895, hence his cameo appearance to give more depth to the story. One likely explanation is that the invention of a 'conspiracy' was to protect Gladys, then only sixteen, from learning the truth about her father's death. A suicide, or at best a suspicious accidental death, carried with it a social stigma in those days, so instead, her father had died like a hero attempting to see justice done. Either that, or the family's imagination had been hard at work improving the story over the years, especially after the 1940s when Oscar had become 'nice to know' again. It is an object lesson in how myths about Oscar grow and establish themselves, and how disentangling fact from fiction, far from being a graceless exercise in dullness, often reveals the hidden motives of those who need to embellish as well as those who want to believe in the embellishments. It was certainly one of the first occasions when Thelma felt that her crusade to sanitize the family was about to be vindicated.

What more might my father have told us about his life between the Wars had he not been discouraged from recounting events and adventures which, as he wrote to Rupert Hart-Davis, 'did not seem to tally with the pure upright life of a British gentleman'? There was obviously a need for discretion as many of those whose unconventional paths he had crossed were still alive in 1965, but above all it wasn't part of Thelma's game-plan that her husband should admit having frequented the louche and the racy in the '20s and '30s. What of his friendship with the Irish writer Liam O'Flaherty who gave Vyvyan the manuscript of one of his darker short stories inscribed 'Written to amuse Vyvyan and hoping it does. (Our motto "Two Bucks Rampant"), Paris 1932'? No, best draw a veil over that. By her own admission to me years later it was Thelma who insisted on the inclusion of the words at the end of the *Time Remembered*: 'So given good health, a nice home, plenty of books, a good meal with my family or with friends, with whom would I change?' The Oscar Wilde story needed a nice, clean, Hollywood happy ending. What, too, of the fortnight in 1938 which Vyvyan had spent travelling in the Nationalist-held area of Spain during the Civil War? He went on a special pass, ostensibly as a journalist, and kept a diary possibly with a view to publishing an account of daily life in war-torn Spain on his return. In Burgos he met up with an old friend, the actress Frances 'Bunny' Doble who was having an affair with Kim Philby, then correspondent for *The Times* but already feeding Nationalist information to the Communists. They all dined together on several occasions. The diary, cautiously factual because it was subject to censorship on his departure, records nothing of the conversations, but knowing my father he would have still been able to supplement his written account from memory. However, with Philby's defection to Moscow barely three years before Vyvyan was writing *Time Remembered* and the spy scandals of the '60s erupting almost yearly, recalling even a chance encounter with a Soviet spy was probably a more appropriate subject for a tabloid 'I once met . . . ' piece than as a short chapter in Vyvyan's memoir. I shouldn't complain; he left enough in diaries and the letters which did survive for me to fill in some of the blanks and, as he hoped, I probably do know more about him than most sons know about their fathers just from this second memoir alone. The fact that Vyvyan couldn't or wouldn't write about the quarrels between Oscar's friends and his enemies on his behalf in the first half of the twentieth century is more understandable. It has also allowed his own son to set the record straight.

Just after *Time Remembered* was published in the spring of 1966, a major exhibition of Aubrey Beardsley's work opened at the Victoria & Albert Museum. It was the first time that his work had been exhibited in such a comprehensive manner and it helped to spark a renewed public interest in the *fin de siècle* and the 1890s. It was curated by Brian Reade, Deputy Keeper of Prints and Drawings at the museum who had succeeded James Laver, one of Vyvyan's greatest friends. It was almost certainly through James that Brian Reade found out about my father's two remaining Beardsley drawings, one of Émile Zola and one of Ellen Terry which he asked to borrow for the exhibition. At one time, up until his bankruptcy, Vyvyan had owned several major Beardsley works, encouraged as a young man to collect them by Robert Ross. But like so much else they had to be sold and these two were all he had left. I think he had kept them because of their curious and rather charming provenance. Towards the end of the War Vyvyan had invited the theatrical impresario C. B. Cochran to dinner during the course of which Cochran had accidentally knocked over a bottle of wine. It must have been an exceptional bottle judging from the letter which accompanied these two drawings as a gift the next day apologising for his clumsiness.[655] Cochran had been a childhood friend of Beardsley which is probably why he owned them. Despite the huge success of the exhibition and the fact that Vyvyan's book was promoted as being 'By the author of *Son of Oscar Wilde*,' its sales were poor so Vyvyan turned his attention to another project—a book of limericks with humorous, tongue-in-cheek explanations for the story behind each one and illustrations by George Sprod. He wrote to me in Vienna, to where I had escaped for the summer, asking for my opinion as what he called 'one of the young generation' and saying that Thelma considered limericks out of fashion and that no one would dream of publishing them. I was aged 20 and it was one of the first letters that I ever had from him asking for my advice rather than giving me

his. I wrote back and told him that I didn't really consider myself
'typical of the younger generation' but I was sure it would sell
as a Christmas book the following year. The only proviso, I said,
was that he should include a few naughty ones 'to satisfy (with
apologies to John Masefield) "the dirty British mind with its smut-
caked outlook, ploughing through the pornographic shelves with
glee."' We were, after all, in the middle of the Swinging Sixties;
the *Lady Chatterley* case had come and gone six years before and
I felt that a severely bowdlerised version would be completely out
of tune with the permissive zeitgeist. A few months later, once it
was finished, he wrote again saying 'It contains veiled indecency
in every line, and I have included many limericks which would
be quite unpublishable in their original form, but by the slight
alteration of the operative part of the anatomy have become print-
able. The joke is that anyone who knows the original will be able
to read between the lines.'[656] I knew that such subtlety would be
seen merely as outdated and prudish so it was with a heavy heart
that I went back to Oxford that autumn carrying the manuscript
with me to read on the train. As I suspected, the ones I had hoped
to see included were not so much veiled as cleaned up or simply
omitted. Two months earlier Vyvyan had already bemoaned my
mother's predictable interference: 'Thelma insisted on going over
my limerick book so far as it has gone, in spite of my oft-repeated
dictum about unfinished work and the classes of people to whom
it ought not to be available. Alas! I am afraid the young lawyer
named Rex is definitely out.'[657] I consoled myself with the fact that
when the book appeared the following year, ten days before his
death, he gave it to me with 'Rex' duly written out in full on the
title page—I still treasure it as his parting gesture of subversion, a
shared confidence, an acknowledgement that he agreed with me
but circumstances had prevailed.[658]

Once Vyvyan had signed the contract for his limerick book
with Cassell's that autumn and had paid off his current debts with
the advance, he was uncertain about how he was going to make
enough money to survive. He wasn't entitled to a state pension;

there were no more historical advisory jobs on films in the offing; he was bored with writing about wine which he said was just becoming repetitive; and tired of writing about his father having said all he wanted to say. Relief came in the form of an offer to go to New York with all travel and living expenses paid plus some TV appearance fees, to accompany the V&A Beardsley exhibition which was due to transfer to Huntington Hartford's Gallery of Modern Art the following February. After some slightly woolly negotiations about the fees and expenses it was agreed that Thelma should accompany him, at her insistence I am sure, since she was a great deal more media-savvy than Vyvyan. As it turned out the fees were craftily put towards their living expenses by the Gallery, but at least my father was paid decently for rewriting the subtitles to the hugely camp 1923 Alla Nazimova film of *Salomé* which, supposedly inspired by Beardsley's art, was to be shown during the exhibition. This led to Vyvyan being interviewed for an arts programme on CBS television in which, largely to justify his presence in New York it would seem, Vyvyan claimed to have been taken by his mother to see Aubrey Beardsley shortly before he died in 1898.[659]

The first time I heard this interview many years later I was slightly shocked because it was clearly a total fabrication. For a start, even if it were true, why did Vyvyan not write about it in *Son of Oscar Wilde* fourteen years earlier? It was perfectly harmless as an anecdote and would have made a strong link between Vyvyan and one of the major cultural figures of the 1890s—as, indeed, was intended that day in New York. The idea that he had forgotten about the meeting in 1953 and suddenly remembered it again in 1967 is ludicrous. There are several other reasons to suppose that such a visit never took place. In February 1898, his mother, Constance, went to visit Vyvyan for a week in Monaco where he was in a Jesuit boarding school. She was very unwell suffering from multiple sclerosis and could only walk with difficulty, but she made the trip as a consolation for not having seen him at Christmas. On account of her illness she felt that she was unable to cope with both her sons at the same time, so it was only Cyril who had spent Christmas with her. There is no evidence to suppose that Constance ever met Beardsley in London, let alone that she was friendly enough to visit him as an invalid three years after her husband's disgrace. Her artistic friends were far more conventional like the Burne-Joneses and she would have classed Beardsley as one of Oscar's 'disreputable friends' as she called them. So, the idea that Constance, who had gone to Monaco to spend time with her son, would have said to him 'Oh, poor Aubrey Beardsley's dying of tuberculosis; let's go and pay him a visit. He's down the road in Menton,' is absurd, as is the idea that eleven year-old Vyvyan would have had any interest in doing so. Vyvyan said in the CBS interview that Beardsley had asked to see him, but how would Beardsley have known where to contact Mrs. Holland as she had become? Even supposing he had, she had far more important things on her mind than taking her son to visit one of her estranged husband's friends who was dying of a mildly contagious disease.

Apart from doing a couple of TV appearances herself on beauty and fashion, Thelma had accompanied Vyvyan to New York to shield him from the American press and shield him she did. A number of papers ran fairly harmless interviews with Vyvyan using the obvious hook that he was the son of the man who was the friend of Aubrey Beardsley, but concentrating more on Vyvyan's own life and writing, and in a couple of cases Thelma turned it into a sort of double act, answering questions on my father's behalf. Her intentions were good and probably prevented him from being traduced by reporters, since he regarded interviews as friendly conversations and could be very incautious in his replies. In one instance a journalist from the *Kansas City Star*, Joseph Kaye, wanted to concentrate on Wilde's trials and imprisonment and the change of name:

> Mr. Kaye was quite the most unpleasant reporter we have met yet. He admitted he knew nothing about either myself or about Oscar

Wilde and kept trying to talk about homosexuality, in which effort he was skilfully side-tracked by Thelma, who, sensing my embarrassment, did most of the talking. He kept on trying to make me say that it was a handicap to be the son of Oscar Wilde and I kept on saying that, on the contrary, it was rather fun. He was trying to muck-rake.[660]

Some of Thelma's interventions, apart from showing that she hadn't forgotten to pack her whitewash, were astonishingly misleading. When Vyvyan was pressed about how it was to live with such a difficult heritage, Thelma waded in: 'Almost anyone we meet does not associate us with that background. We are the Hollands and that is how we are known.' She then declared that I, who was studying at Oxford, was proud of the name Wilde and was thinking of changing my own surname to Holland-Wilde.[661] Thank God it wasn't in the *New York Times* and picked up by the British press; having been brainwashed for so long about keeping a low profile, nothing could have been further from my mind. I'm just glad I only came across that interview fifty years later and wasn't aware at the time that I had been co-opted, unknowingly, onto the clean-up team. And yet everywhere Thelma went, she handed out at any opportunity the extract from Boris Brasol's book about famous gay men in history which she had typed out by way of a Holland press release before leaving London.[662] Too many conflicting signals. Too selective an acceptance of history. What was I supposed to make of such contradictions when they impinged on my life?

Writing about the New York episode has made me see more clearly than ever that as he grew older, my father had a tendency, whether in public or in writing, to embellish or even to invent certain things about his early life to render it more interesting. We're all guilty of it at times, but in Vyvyan's case it makes biography a nightmare because people assume that his first-hand account must be the truth. Parts of it went hand-in-hand with Thelma's crusade to present her 'special' view of the family so, reconciling family versions of past events with what I was discovering later to be the truth was, to say the least, confusing. Now, many years on, confusion has given way to guilt and a sense of disloyalty about setting the record straight and showing how the echoes of 1895, faint though they are, can still be heard more than a century later.

On 27 July 1967, nearly ten years after the publication of the Wolfenden Report, the Sexual Offences Act was finally passed. It largely repealed clause 11 of the 1885 Criminal Law Amendment Act under which my grandfather was convicted and it was the end of an extraordinary political marathon run by the Welsh Labour MP Leo Abse who spent five years steering it through Parliament as a Private Member's Bill. To the very end, a number of reactionary Conservative MPs tried to wreck the bill by 'talking it out' and using language such as 'utterly disgusting and degrading,' and 'homosexuals are perverts.' The House of Commons had sat all night on 3 July thrashing out amendments, some MPs questioning why so much precious time was being spent on such a triviality when more important matters needed their attention. I can't help wondering how Vyvyan must have felt when reading such reports in the newspapers, as he must have done so often in the previous twenty years, and realising that even in 1967 some people still regarded his father as depraved and a pervert. But at least he lived to see the repeal of the law which sent Oscar to prison and nearly destroyed his family; he died just seventy-five days later, having lived nearly the whole of his life with that very law on the statute book.

The trip to New York in February had not been as lucrative as my parents expected; indeed, without the personal link to Beardsley, which Vyvyan invented, from a publicity point of view there might well have been fewer interviews and even less in the way of earnings. However, the balance left over from the fees kept the family more or less afloat until the summer and it allowed Vyvyan and Thelma to have a short holiday in France at Semur-en Auxois not far from where I was studying at the University in Dijon, and for me to spend a few days with them. My mother would sunbathe by the lake and so I had my father to myself. I was twenty-one, becoming vaguely civilized as a human being, and found I could enjoy his company as a friend rather than just having to be his son. It was a strange combination of those early morning walks around Chelsea six years before and the breakthrough letter asking what I thought about his limerick book. If ever I feel uneasy about the Beardsley fib, I tell myself that without it I might never have had those last memories of being so close to him towards the end of his life. Before I left to go back to Dijon, he slipped me a tenner which I knew he could ill-afford and said 'Don't tell your mother.' I never did. It was one last secret we shared.

My father died on 10 October 1967 after falling down the steep stairs of the Beefsteak Club. He had just been lunching with Alec Waugh to discuss some final points about Alec's book *Wines & Spirits* before the manuscript went to the publishers. With his knowledge of wine Vyvyan would have been more than happy to help Alec as an old friend, but there was the added pleasure of being able to repay Alec in kind for his immense generosity in saving my father's copyrights from being sold off eleven years before. Whether my father had a stroke and fell or whether he fell and the fall resulted in a massive haemorrhage to the brain was never established. Thelma, with her clichéd disapproval of Vyvyan's old friends from before the War, later maintained that Alec had probably encouraged him to drink too much at lunch and that had been the cause of it.[663] He was taken to Charing Cross Hospital, which was then around the corner in William IV Street, and by early evening he was unconscious. Thelma saw him in the late afternoon and told me that he just said: 'I want to go to sleep now,' and shut his eyes. I came down from Oxford summoned by telegram to find Thelma and Peta Everett sitting at the dining-room table, very tearful and well-oiled with only a couple of inches left in the whisky bottle. Peta, a new-found friend, was in charge of the public relations for Lenthéric where my mother had started working that summer. I was sober and Peta definitely wasn't, so Thelma told me to go out and find her a taxi and make sure she got home safely. As we neared her mansion block in

Hammersmith, she asked if I had been to see my father on the way in from Oxford. 'No,' I replied. 'Then go to the hospital now because I don't think he'll last the night' she said, and gave me enough money to go to Charing Cross, keep the taxi waiting, and take it back home again. I've never forgotten that night. For a long time it would come back to me in dreams. The darkened ward; the kind Sister who shouldn't have let me in because hospitals were so much stricter about visiting hours then; my father lying on his side breathing very heavily and rapidly. I remember kissing him and telling him I loved him however much of a trial I had been in the last few years. Vyvyan did die in the night and I was eternally grateful to Peta for making me go. Not so my mother. When I got home, having been away for at least an hour and a half, her first angry reaction was to ask if 'that Peta' had seduced me. When I expostulated in a fury that I had been to see my father she was even angrier and didn't speak to Peta for days. It felt as though she had wanted to be the last one to have seen him alive, not me, and someone had interfered without consulting her. I wish I could remember whether I made a point of thanking Peta. I hope I did, but if not it didn't matter as I found a very roundabout way of doing it many years later through her nephew, Rupert.[664]

When I talked to friends about my father, I used to joke that he was immortal, but if ever he did go, it would be after a good lunch with an old friend. At least I got half of it right and thanks to Peta Everett helping me go and say goodbye, I'm sure the grieving was that much easier. It was only one evening two months later, back at Oxford that I realised how much I missed him.

When my father died my mother went to pieces, and although I remember very little of the days that followed, it seems that I took charge of all the funeral arrangements. I must have felt it my duty to do so in that rather old-fashioned tradition as 'man of the house' now that my father was no longer alive, since it was my name listed on the death certificate as the 'informant' at the Chelsea Register Office. I also instructed the undertakers and must have made them put it all in my name so that my mother didn't have to deal with it. Rebecca West and her husband Henry Andrews had been in London on the day Vyvyan died and Henry said to me that if I needed 'help' with the funeral arrangements just to ask. A month later, knowing Thelma couldn't pay and that we would probably have to negotiate a loan, I wrote and asked Henry if he could 'help us out of this difficulty temporarily.'[665] To this day I still feel a flush of embarrassment reading that letter. He and Rebecca had given me an education and were still helping me through university and here I was asking for help with my father's funeral. Henry settled the undertakers' account and wouldn't hear of us paying him off. Vyvyan's legacy to Thelma was a £10 gas bill and he left me with a load of unanswered questions. That was the state of the 'Wilde inheritance' at the end of 1967.

Not long after Vyvyan's death, Rupert Hart-Davis put Thelma in touch with a well-known medium, Ena Twigg. At the start of 1967 Rupert had been devastated by the sudden death of his wife, Ruth, and had found great comfort in Mrs. Twigg's apparent ability to communicate with her in the spirit world. He recommended Thelma to try and contact Vyvyan in the same way. A séance was arranged and among other things Vyvyan 'told' Thelma that he didn't mind what she did with his ashes: she could scatter them anywhere.[666] Thelma had been thinking of scattering them on his mother's grave and when I told her the following summer that I was going to be passing through Geneva she asked me to try and find it. No reference to the site let alone the name of the cemetery, and with my own knowledge of family history being fairly basic at that stage I found nothing. It was only later that I discovered she had been confusing Geneva with Genoa so it wasn't surprising. Then Vyvyan stayed imprisoned in his urn for a few years before Thelma announced that she had scattered most of them in the private gardens opposite where we lived in the Boltons and that she thought we could disperse the rest 'on the quiet' in Cannizaro Park in Wimbledon. The reasoning for the first was that Vyvyan had been happy there in his last years; fair enough, but if one isn't a local resident, one has no access. For the second she said it was appropriate because 'Vyvyan had played there as a child' which I found fairly tenuous—once or twice maybe; I never heard him mention it. It used to be the grand garden of Cannizaro House, the home of Adela Schuster, 'the Lady of Wimbledon' as Oscar called her, who gave him £1,000 at the time of his trials. I went along with it to avoid arguments but felt strangely unemotional. It was as if I had no say, no father. Many years later I got the urn with barely a teaspoonful of ashes still inside and took it with me to France. I was going to Burgundy so I buried them above the Château du Clos de Vougeot beside the *grand crû* Musigny vineyard, which meant something to both of us. I can remember the spot to this day and I can visualise the act of doing it. I'd have liked to be able to pay my respects to my father, to be able to go somewhere and stop my life for five minutes and think about him once in a while—every two or three or even five years, just knowing that was where his mortal remains were scattered, but I can't. And that makes me sad. I feel excluded, just like I did with my grandfather. A no-go area. I understand why they wouldn't let me anywhere near Oscar. It was far too dangerous in the 1960s for a young man who was related to him. But my father?

As a sadly moving postscript, Dr. A. W. J. Houghton, a consultant physician in Shrewsbury, wrote to Vyvyan in that summer of 1967 saying how much 'in advanced middle life I find increasing pleasure and solace reading the works of your famous and distinguished father.' He added how, in his view, Oscar's shortcomings were of minor importance alongside his literary genius and that he would like to leave a sum of money in his will enough to provide for flowers to be laid on Oscar's grave annually on his birthday.[667] The letter must have been sent via a publisher where it lay around for weeks and only arrived after Vyvyan's death. I discovered it thirty years later in a pile of unanswered correspondence. I wish he had read it.

PART FIVE
(1968-2024)

CHAPTER ONE
(AFTER) OXFORD

I went up to Oxford in the Michaelmas Term cf 1964 and the shock of being treated like a young adult rather than a rebellious schoolboy was oddly stimulating. A close friend from school matriculated at the same time as I did and finished up with rooms almost next to mine in the college. Richard Collins was a talented gymnast who had been offered place to train for the Mexico Olympics had he not been given a place at Magdalen. Neither of us having a girlfriend in Oxford and both enjoying each other's company, we spent a great deal of time together as a result. When we weren't having to produce weekly essays for our tutors, we drank good wine, played cards, watched sunsets, reinforced one another's youthful prejudices, and regularly stayed up half the night to argue about the state of the world. In short, we were unashamedly but not ostentatiously sybaritic. A visit to the theatre in our first term where the Royal Ballet was performing on tour convinced Richard with his muscular physique that he should try to make a career in dancing which, indeed, he spent the rest of his too-short life doing. Small wonder that a friend of ours told us with a laugh that he had been asked: 'Do you think Richard and Merlin are queer?' Amusement quickly gave way in my case to mild panic that someone had made the Wilde/Holland connection and, on the visible evidence of what seemed quite an intimate friendship, had jumped to conclusions. I was less concerned about my sexuality being questioned than having to cope with being the 'grandson of Oscar Wilde.' Although I hadn't realised it fully until then, being 'Holland' rather than 'Wilde' was a huge psychological advantage unlike what it had been for my father sixty years before at Cambridge. He had been at pains to conceal his father's name because of the continuing shame attached to it; I preferred to be discreet about it to avoid being the object of curiosity. At Oxford, having talked my way into Oscar's old college, and partly because Vyvyan had had dealings with Magdalen over some Wilde letters held in the archives, I was less anonymous. Years later I heard from a fellow undergraduate that she had met me at a drinks party and had been quite struck by the family resemblance, but far more by the fact that I was quiet and somewhat reserved and not at all what she had expected a grandson of the flamboyant and loquacious Oscar to be.[668] Thankfully I was quite oblivious to the possibility that anyone outside my immediate circle knew of the connection and I'm sure I benefited from my presumed anonymity. Carrying the name openly with the inevitable 'Another Wilde at Oxford' label would have been too much to handle. Maybe I exaggerate with hindsight and forget that Oscar Wilde was far from being the iconic figure he has become today, but an incident still stands out in my memory.

In 1967, an American postgraduate, Jules Ryckebusch, was wanting to start a literary magazine called the *Fall River Review* and somehow managed to get contributions promised for the first number from the likes of John Updike, Isaac Asimov, and Allen Ginsberg. He wrote asking if I would contribute a piece on my grandfather and aestheticism and I replied saying that since I was studying French, I would much rather write on how France had influenced Oscar's work, a subject I felt at least competent to research. Jules accepted enthusiastically and in much excitement I wrote to my parents. It was a mistake. They wrote back with the only letter I ever received signed by both of them telling me not to do it: 'This is not only a family matter, but something that could be very deleterious to you in any future career you wish to take up,' and full of dire warnings about how the 'lascivious Press' would take advantage of me and how I was in some sort of danger of profiting from 'reflected glory.'[669] I couldn't see the logic, it being what the trade referred to as a 'Little Magazine,' but having caused enough trouble with adolescent stroppiness and not wanting any more grief, I abandoned the idea. It was another twenty-one years before I would pen anything publicly about my grandfather.

In the end, the magazine never appeared for lack of funding, but the fact Jules had asked me, meant he believed I had something to say, so I would have been a contributor to the further understanding of my grandfather rather than a mere exhibit in the Wilde freak show. To that extent it was a valuable first lesson in finding a place where I could feel comfortable with my heritage. I was becoming aware that I had to exist in my own right rather than just as an extension of Oscar Wilde for other people to gawp at and in those early days of coming to terms with it all, I was already trying to find a niche in which to be at ease. The story did have a slightly embarrassing sequel forty-four years later. In 2011 I tracked down Jules who had gone on to a university career and asked him to confirm what I had remembered and also why he had written. He said he had been prompted to write by seeing a picture of Oscar in the collage of personalities on the sleeve of the Beatles' album *Sgt Peppers Lonely Hearts Club Band* and thought it would be interesting to have an article by his grandson relating him to the popular culture scene. At the same time he told me that although he had completed a Master's thesis on Oscar's plays at the University of Massachusetts, he had been forced to abandon a Doctoral dissertation a year or two later because of Vyvyan's rumoured intransigence over allowing quotations from previously unpublished Wilde material. It didn't sound like my father's attitude to serious academic research at all, but I felt terrible about it all those years after and could only offer him a sort of family apology. Jules replied that he had never had any personal contact with Vyvyan, it was just that he had been warned by two major libraries with substantial Wilde holdings, the Clark in Los Angeles and the Harry Ransom at Austin, Texas. Vyvyan's relationship with both had been perfectly cordial until then, especially since they had co-operated over the publication of Oscar's letters. The source of the rumour can only have been someone who had frequented those libraries for research and who, for some reason, had wanted to disparage my father as a tiresome literary heir. Everything pointed to the vindictive behaviour of 'Judas' Hyde.[670]

Richard went down from Oxford in 1967 and I, as a language student, having spent time abroad as part of my degree course, stayed on for a second and final year in our scruffy 'digs' in the Cowley Road. The Lodging Houses Delegacy, long since gone, whose job it was to approve all out-of-college accommodation, had passed it but with some reluctance almost certainly on account of the sanitary arrangements. There was one bathroom, which also served as our kitchen sink, shared between four undergraduates and a family with two children. That bathroom was partly the reason I took up boxing again in my last year. So disgusting was it that I had to find another way to keep clean. The new university sports hall with wonderful hot showers had just opened on the Iffley Road close by and since I had learned the rudiments of boxing at school, I joined the university boxing club. We trained three times a week in the evenings so it was the perfect solution both to keeping fit and to keeping clean. The slightly surprising outcome of the need for regular showers was regular attendance at training sessions, being fitter than at any other time in my life, and a place on the team for the annual intervarsity match against Cambridge. I won my welter-weight bout despite 'taking more punishment than he needed' according to the *Oxford Mail* and nowhere, thank God, was there any jocular reference to Oscar and the Queensberry Rules.

In that last year at Oxford it became worryingly obvious that I needed to have some sort of gainful employment lined up immediately I came down. Having a vague idea that I might try for the very competitive diplomatic service, or failing that a job in museum work of some sort, I sat the first round of the Civil Service exam the January before my finals. I failed dismally and I realised that my future lay elsewhere. The idea of publishing attracted me, but in those days it was not really an option as salaries started at about £600 a year and even a single room in London was £10 a week. Henry Andrews, Rebecca West's husband who had become something of a mentor to me since my father's death, suggested I apply for a job in industry as the starting salaries for graduates were decent and, so long as I proved myself in the six-month probationary period, my long-term employment would be more or less secure. His advice was persuasive, particularly as my parents had done everything to discourage any form of unconventional behaviour in me during my teenage years. It felt as if everyone was terrified I would go off the rails, repeat in some lesser way the mistakes that two previous generations had made and, as far as they could, were trying to steer me into getting 'a proper job rather than messing about in the Arts.' It must have been a combination of the worry that I wouldn't earn a living, and that I would lead a sort of dissipated life, somehow finishing up in debt and bankrupt like Vyvyan, and that such waywardness, if these things ran in the family, might even manifest itself in—well, God forbid!—in homosexuality. Nor is that something which I have imagined years afterwards. In the summer of 1962, I hitchhiked my way around Ireland with another close friend from school. On the day before I left my father recorded in his diary: 'Thelma had a row with Merlin about going to Ireland with Michael Whittingham. She thinks there is rumple-frumpus going on there. I shouldn't be at all surprised, but what I say is let it run its course. More harm than good can be done by nipping it in the bud.'[671]

So, I talked my way into a sales job with Wiggins Teape who had been making paper for two hundred years which I imagined would be slightly less dispiriting than selling pharmaceuticals or fertiliser. After six months of basic training around the country, working shifts at paper mills, writing simple technical reports which stretched my 'O' level Physics and Chemistry to their limits and learning all about my new trade, I finished up in London wondering why I had spent four years studying French and German literature at Oxford. It was the start of a strange double life. I rented a furnished room in the one ugly house in Thurloe Square which overlooked the South Kensington underground station. The carpet, of a nondescript colour due to decades of ingrained filth, did not lend itself to walking around in bare feet. Alongside these squalid surroundings, there were episodes in my life that summer of 1969 which were memorable for being almost unimaginably far removed from my bedsit existence.

Henry Andrews had died the autumn before and Rebecca had moved to a mansion flat in London. Very conscious of all that the two of them had done for me over the years and what a support she had been to Vyvyan over the publishing of Oscar's letters, I would willingly accept the odd invitation to Sunday lunch knowing that if she had a fraction of the pleasure from my company as I did from hers, it went a small way to repaying a huge debt of gratitude. Shortly before my finals, she and Henry had invited me to spend a 'non-revising' weekend with them at Ibstone House. I got to know Rebecca then far better than I had ever done previously and just before leaving to go back to Oxford I remember saying to her what a treat it had been and how much she made me feel at ease with her and no longer slightly intimidated. 'Oh, I'm so glad,' she replied., 'It's been wonderful for me too as I haven't had to be on my best behaviour.'

Apart from the Sunday lunches with Rebecca I also accompanied her on a couple of occasions to the theatre or a concert, the most memorable of which was in July to hear Gina Bachauer play Beethoven at the Festival Hall. The invitation had come from Fleur Cowles, the expatriate American writer, artist and society hostess who asked us to share her box. I sat next to a man whose face seemed familiar, but I couldn't think who it was until he said 'You must be Vyvyan's son. I'm Beverley Nichols. He and I used to lunch together at a very seedy pub in Chancery Lane and eat summer oysters.' During the interval, a tall, strikingly attractive blonde woman came up and shook hands with me. We talked for a while, about what I don't recall, but I do remember asking her what she did and she replied that she was training to be a concert pianist. Later I learned that she was Princess Irene of Greece, that Gina Bachauer was her teacher and that she had made her London début three weeks earlier. Fleur, who lived in A5 Albany, which couldn't possibly have been further removed from my single room in 52 Thurloe Square, had arranged for about twenty of the concert-goers to join her there afterwards for a late supper. Apart from the Princess I must have been the only one there under thirty but Beverley, sensing my possible discomfort came to my rescue. He said that he knew I might feel 'a bit of a twerp,' as he put it, amongst the great élite of London and that I just had to go and tug his sleeve and he would introduce me to someone. He was as good as his word and mercifully didn't do it as 'the grandson of.' The names were endless: John Gielgud, Yehudi Menhuin, Lionel Bart, Michael Denison being but a few, and if one or two of them knew me as Vyvyan's son, that was fine.[672] More disturbing to me was that I now found myself trying to conceal from those who might know that Oscar was my grandfather, the fact that I was just a paper salesman living in a bedsit, and I imagined that anyone who became aware of my secret would think that I was somehow letting the family down.

Later, having delivered Rebecca back home, I returned to the dull reality of No. 52 and the 'musical' finale of the evening: the crescendo rumble of the last District Line train approaching, the grinding of the brakes, the hiss of the closing doors, the ting of the guard's bell to the driver, then off, diminuendo into the tunnel. It was a hot night so I opened the French windows onto the tiny balcony and in walked a cat asking for food and a bed for the night. I told Beverley, cat-mad that he was, when I wrote to thank him for his kindness and said that it felt like a debt I was paying back. It was a pity I didn't know then that Gina Bachauer was famous for feeding the stray cats which came regularly to her house in Athens.

Three days later I was summoned by the Wiggins Teape overseas sales director and told that I was being posted to Beirut at the end of the year. I heard the news with an odd mixture of relief, excitement, and apprehension. There was relief that I would finally stop being a trainee and start a productive job with more money, far from England where nobody would know or care about my relationship to Oscar Wilde. Then there was the excitement of rising to a challenge—that of opening up new markets in North Africa, Turkey, and Iran, but with it the knowledge I wouldn't see England again for three years. Those precious years consolidating university friendships would disappear. Looking back on it now, although I wasn't conscious of it at the time, I think there must have been a small element of wanting to escape. Leaving England, to start afresh was something the family had a habit of doing, though in my case I like to think that the reasons were far less dramatic and certainly less negative than in the past. My motives were largely materialistic. I had seen what my parents' precarious financial existence had done to their lives and I was determined not to repeat it. Even if that meant a few years of self-imposed exile while saving enough money to give me a little capital, at least I knew I would be in exotic surroundings.

From the moment I arrived in Lebanon, apart from the two other Wiggins Teape employees in the office, I went out of my way to avoid English expatriates as far as possible. My boss, Ronnie Whitfield, a remarkable man born in Cairo before the War, who spoke fluent Arabic and four other languages, was totally sympathetic over my decision since he felt much the same about close-knit groups of our countrymen abroad. He was less happy that I chose to live in a French colonial-style apartment in down-town Beirut. If I was going to give up a few years of my life to do a job merely for the financial security which had been markedly absent from my youth, I felt that at least I could do it as an immersive experience.

I lived in a mixed residential-commercial quarter in the rue Jbeil at the junction of two quiet streets. The ground floor was occupied by an Armenian shopkeeper whose only trade was in beer, kept in two enormous fridges, and cigarettes. He also acted as the bar and telephone service for the taxi rank outside and, once my patronage had been established, as a sort of unofficial concierge for me when I was away. On one corner opposite was a large ochre coloured villa with elegant architectural features and a frangipani tree in the front garden which flowered profusely all summer and whose heavy scent contrasted with the more brutal urban smells. The villa was said to be haunted and remained un-occupied the whole time I was there. On the other corner was the Hôtel La Résidence which could scarcely have been more differ-ent. Its clientele seemed to consist almost exclusively of foreign girls employed by the Casino du Liban for their floor shows or as hostesses. Each room had a balcony and from about midday these nocturnal creatures would start to open their shutters and come out to sun themselves. Unlike the offensive bling of the Casino, where we were occasionally obliged to entertain favoured custom-ers from the Gulf States, I regarded this privileged spectacle as much more honest and down to earth than having to watch horses and elephants parade across the Casino stage at Jounieh. There was nothing voyeuristic about it at all since I was on waving terms with some of the longer-staying residents.

Looking back on that period fifty years later and going through letters from friends there was a constantly recurring question in all of them: 'Are you lonely?' Yes, I was, and I obviously gave that impression in the letters I wrote to them. It was a loneliness which came from suddenly finding myself in an environment in which there was no one with whom I could discuss those mostly unspoken thoughts and minor prejudices which some of us nur-ture in secret embarrassment yet long to share. My new friends in Beirut were Greek, Egyptian, Syrian, Iraqi, and even Lebanese, but not British with whom I might have shared a common cultural bond. It was the price I paid for wanting, temporarily, to reject my background.

I would never claim that the four years which I spent in Lebanon were wasted. They taught me much about commerce and business practices in general, as well as giving me a knowledge of paper and printing which I have used off and on ever since. I talked up the job to anyone who asked. I wasn't a travelling rep for a paper manufacturer, I was an assistant manager for a British company in the Middle East providing highly specialised papers for stamps, banknotes, cheques, and lottery tickets, all of which was true but only about ten percent of the business. Most people would have been grateful for the 'good job' which I had. I wasn't, and I simply put my ingratitude and boredom down to 'bad blood' of some sort and felt guilty.

There were times in my life when I was travelling, which seemed more or less incessantly, that I felt my personal life was running away from me. I was the product of an era which taught the values of a strong work ethic and, barring accidents, one was generally expected to keep one's job until retirement which I had no intention of doing. There was a permanent conflict between what my instincts seemed to be dictating and what an older generation, whose guidance I had sought, had encouraged me to do. In those four years, I learned that if I was to preserve a degree of personal integrity, no salary could buy my commitment and loyalty to a job which I despised myself for doing.

Even two thousand miles away from London, I still couldn't avoid the fall-out from the occasional Wilde-related controversy. In the summer of 1969 before I left England, an old friend of Vyvyan's, Alec Waugh, had been in touch about a book he had written and was wanting to dedicate to my father. Alec had been very kind to me after Vyvyan's death, inviting me to dine with him on a couple of occasions and showing genuine interest in how the son of his very old friend was going to make his life. My father had had his fatal accident after lunching with Alec who may have felt vaguely responsible and his concern showed itself as a form of transferred affection. Whichever way, I appreciated it as an opportunity to speak about my father to a man who had known him since twenty years before I was born. The book, Alec told me, was *A Spy in the Family: an Erotic Comedy,* and the dedication he wanted to include was to read: 'To the memory of my deeply missed friend, Vyvyan Holland, the younger son of Oscar Wilde and very much a person in his own right as a man of letters and a *bon viveur,* I dedicate, not inappropriately, this indelicate story which contains no indelicate words.' I knew that Alec and my father had had a sort of grown-up-schoolboys-saucy-seaside-postcard correspondence for years, hence 'not inappropriately,' and I could see no real harm in it, but I knew equally what Thelma's reaction would be. I consulted Rebecca West for a balanced opinion and she expressed misgivings, but we both assumed that from Alec's past work, it would be 'an elegantly risqué book.' I steeled myself to talk to Thelma about it and we agreed that 'not inappropriately' should be replaced by 'with great affection,' the reference to Oscar Wilde should be dropped, and the dedication could then stand for the USA, but for the British edition it should simply read 'To the memory of V. H.' Alec agreed to the compromise and I told him to confirm it with Thelma for safety's sake and thought the matter was then settled.[673] Alec, after all, had been the one who had come to Vyvyan's rescue financially over the whole sordid business of Montgomery Hyde trying to steal his copyrights, and to refuse this further gesture of friendship, however eccentric, would have seemed churlish.

When a pre-publication British copy was sent to Thelma in June the following year, the full dedication had been left in and she was incensed. She wrote to me at once saying that Alec must have taken leave of his senses: 'It can undo all the good I have done the family that you and I belong to, smear your father's reputation and ruin me socially and from a business point of view . . . I hope to God you didn't give permission . . . anything to do with the family must be discussed with me as I am the executrix of his estate.'[674] I replied reminding her that we *had* discussed it but clearly Alec had not kept his word or, it would seem, written to Thelma which was unfortunate. She wrote him a pained letter and should then have let the matter drop but she didn't. She contacted the publishers through a solicitor trying to get the book withdrawn before publication and the whole affair started to escalate into another full-scale battle in her crusade to keep the family spotlessly 'clean.' The story with the full wording of the dedication was leaked to William Hickey's gossip column on the *Daily Express* (probably by the publisher sensing extra publicity for the book) and reached an even greater audience than the mere dedication in the book would have done. It also brought in Thelma's connection to the Palace and the Queen's cosmetics for added flavour, which was only to be expected.

Rebecca sent me a long letter about the whole affair saying the book was 'quite without literary merit' and that it was generally felt that Alec had gone too far, but that 'people will forget it soon.' She also reassured me that there was 'not a word against your mother for her conduct of the whole business.'[675] But thinking about it, there wouldn't have been; no one was going to take Alec's side against her in the circumstances. They probably saw it as a great deal of fuss over an unfortunate misunderstanding. The solicitor extracted an undertaking from W. H. Allen, the publishers, that the dedication would not appear in any future edition, and told Thelma there was nothing further they could do especially about the piece in the gossip column. 'I earnestly advise you to forget all about it as soon as possible. There is no really effective action you can take and you will only upset yourself if you enter into a correspondence about it.' Thelma's letters to me were still full of it: I mustn't contact Alec under any circumstances; she was going to lobby the Home Secretary to have a law passed to prevent libelling the dead (though the relevance of that in this case escaped me); this was Alec's revenge for Vyvyan stealing some of his girlfriends in the 1930s. Re-reading the correspondence made me realise what a monstrous waste of time it all was.[676] Now that Vyvyan was dead, Thelma was settling into her caricature role as a tiresome literary widow. It also put paid to any hope I may have had about becoming more friendly with Alec and learning something about my father's past life. My mother had never really approved of Alec and here was a perfect example of why she felt he needed to be brushed out of our lives. Given his generosity to Vyvyan over the bankruptcy and their long-standing friendship, I wish I could have mended the fences and still feel bad when I think about it.

Unfortunately, it wasn't the last time during my years abroad that Thelma decided her father-in-law needed defending from the wicked assaults on his reputation by the press and others. On

AFTER OSCAR · 449

31 May 1971 a cartoon by Michael Cummings appeared in the *Daily Express* prompted by Mary Whitehouse's criticism of some films put out by the BBC on sex education. It showed a queue of historical personalities waiting to be interviewed as specialist teachers in the subject, among them Casanova, the Marquis de Sade, and Oscar, whose qualification was a 'Professorship in Homosexuality.' She immediately wrote a protesting letter to the editor but, understandably, never received a reply.

In February the following year Sadler's Wells put on a ballet entitled 'O.W.' about the relationship between Oscar and Bosie Douglas. Thelma heard about it and managed to get herself invited to the opening night, writing to me 'if it is obnoxious I am going to act.'[677] Including a high camp caricature of Oscar in his heyday chasing Bosie with a butterfly net, but partly salvaged by veteran dancer Michael Somes in a masterly performance as the later disgraced Oscar, the critics largely gave it the thumbs-down. Thelma wrote that she found it 'insufferable' but after her bruising experience over Alec's dedication, this time she wisely kept her mouth shut in public.

I used to write to Rebecca while I was in Lebanon to tell her how I was getting on. I was devoted to her for all she had done for me and she seemed to enjoy getting my news. At some point I had discovered that Lady Hester Stanhope, intrepid traveller, antiquarian, and eccentric in the early years of the nineteenth century, had spent the last twenty years of her life at Joun in southern Lebanon where she was buried. I went to find her grave and must have written to Rebecca about it thinking that since there were obvious parallels between these two feisty women's lives, Rebecca would be interested. She, of course, knew of Hester Stanhope but seemed not to have made the connection with me and Lebanon. The Middle East was one region she had always wanted to visit, so Lady Hester became the inspiration for her two week visit to Lebanon and Syria in April 1971 and she very generously paid for Thelma to come with her to visit me after eighteen months of being away. It was an extremely selfless gesture since one can hardly imagine two more diverse intellects, but from the diary which she kept at the time and her later correspondence with me, Thelma at times made an exasperating travelling companion.[678] They were due to go on to Cyprus and Jerusalem but in the end Rebecca had to resort, as she told me, to the subterfuge of having a cable sent from London summoning her back on the pretext of some crisis, leaving Thelma to complete the last leg of the journey on her own. Our expedition to pay our respects to Lady Hester at her grave, picnicking among the wild cyclamen on Dahr-el-Sitt (The Hill of the Lady), was memorable. I remember, too, one particular evening spent at a Lebanese friend's house where Rebecca, on entering the sitting room and seeing the bad reproduction eighteenth century furniture, remarked to me in a whisper, 'Oh, wonderful! Louis Soixante-Quatorze!'

The final straw was when I managed, after two years of trying, to sell twenty tons of tracing paper to the State Monopoly in Algeria, and the Head Office in London sent it in all the wrong weights and sizes. Making cellulose tracing paper then was a hugely specialised operation; only about four paper companies in the world could produce it properly and we were one of them. Since its independence from France, Algeria was using its oil revenues to create a solid infrastructure and construction was taking place at an enormous rate; hence architects' need for tracing paper. Until then it had been supplied by a French company, but the Algerians were anxious to divest themselves of all French influence wherever possible, which is where I saw our chance and persuaded them to transfer their business to us. It turned into an embarrassing commercial disaster. I probably shouldn't have taken it personally, but I took a certain pride in what I had achieved and my credibility with the State Monopoly was wiped out at a stroke. I had a potential job lined up with a Swiss-American publishing company, checked that they still wanted me, gave in my notice and said goodbye to Beirut in January 1974.

CHAPTER TWO
THE ELLMANN SAGA

When I returned from Beirut in 1974, it was to find my mother in a constant state of worry; if it wasn't about money it was about 'those university professors' as she would refer to them, picking over Oscar's life. She had increasingly mixed feelings about whether publishing his correspondence had been such a good thing, as Oscar, 'warts and all,' was not really encompassed by her Holland family scheme. I think she regretted slightly that she had been persuaded by Rebecca West and others to allow the letters to appear unexpurgated, since she saw it as a definite backwards step in the clean-up of the Wilde/Holland line. It was a strange and rather contradictory attitude: she wanted the attention of being Oscar Wilde's daughter-in-law but only on her terms, so with as little scandal as possible. Only twenty years later, after her death, did I learn from my cousin Dinah that Thelma had revelled in the association all the time I had been abroad and continued to do so, unknown to me, until long after my return, bringing it up with strangers at the slightest opportunity. When invited to dinner in a restaurant and offered a liqueur to finish off the meal, she would invariably order what she referred to as 'an Oscar Wilde special.' It consisted of a potent blend of one third green and two thirds yellow Chartreuse and had been gleaned from Vyvyan's *Drink and Be Merry,* in which he recounted how Oscar had visited the Grande Chartreuse monastery and asked the Almoner the secret of the monks' apparent happiness. 'It is simple, Monsieur,' came the reply. 'One third green and two thirds yellow.' It was hard to believe that this was the woman who had been telling me since I was fifteen to keep my head below the parapet, avoid journalists, and get on with my life, having as little to do with my grandfather as possible. It would also have been hard to persuade others to believe it had not the Australian comedian Barry Humphries recalled lunching with Thelma not long after she had introduced herself to him (born and bred Melburnians that they both were) as Oscar Wilde's daughter-in-law in 1981:

> Towards the end of our lunch, she held my hand across the table.
>
> 'I can tell you're like me, Barry,' she confided with a rush of frankness, no doubt inspired by the O.W. specials. 'You don't believe all those horrible stories about O.W. either!'
>
> I wasn't sure what Thelma meant. 'What stories?' I asked.
>
> 'Oh, you know, those foul stories Montgomery Hyde put about saying that O.W. was *one of them*.' Thelma made an eloquent limp-wristed gesture.
>
> 'You mean,' I said, 'that you don't think that Oscar was homosexual? What about the trials? What about all the other . . . well . . . evidence?'
>
> 'All hearsay, Barry, as you well know. All slanders spread by that ghastly Monty Hyde. Let's have another special, shall we?'[679]

This denial of Oscar's sexuality had become absurd. The liberated 1960s, the repeal of Section 11 of the 1885 Act which had sent Oscar to prison had come and gone, Carnaby Street was flourishing and the Gay Pride rally in London was in its tenth year at the time of that lunch. Thelma, with her crusade to protect 'the family,' seemed pathetically stuck in a pre-Wolfenden era. It was all the more surprising given that she had shared my father's life for twenty-four years and they had moved in artistic, literary and theatrical circles in which they counted the likes of Norman Hartnell, Cecil Beaton, John Gielgud, Binkie Beaumont, Beverley Nichols, Nancy Spain, Dickie Buckle, and Robin Maugham as good acquaintances if not friends. She knew that she could no longer keep up this pretence with me, but it didn't stop her from attempting it with strangers or from trying to prevent me writing anything on the subject of the trials and imprisonment right up to the time of her death.[680] I began to realise that I was dealing with a hangover from her Australian youth, with what her Sunday School teachers in the Melbourne Methodist Church would have regarded as sexual deviance and therefore deeply sinful. I appealed to the exhibitionist and the bohemian in her, but to no avail. I reasoned with her saying that Wilde's private life was no longer the scandal that it had been for the first half of the twentieth century; she stood firm. I said that Oscar Wilde's 'family' no longer needed the protection which she had fought to give it (and rightly so) in the '50s and '60s and she replied that my own young son would need it now. The past—the referred pain of her husband's unhappy childhood combined with her own experience of a sensation-seeking press—made her suspicious of everyone with an interest in Oscar Wilde. There was also, undeniably, a sense of profound but quite misplaced injustice that everyone except Wilde's own family seemed to be making money out of him.

My mother's continuing preoccupation with keeping the family squeaky-clean at a time of sexual liberation and when homosexuality had become, as Oscar might have said, a perfectly normal aberration, had some other unfortunate consequences besides threatening to give what was left of his estate a caricature reputation for obstructiveness. For many years my father had collected Bamforth & Co.'s Saucy Seaside Postcards which were single scene and very much *double entendre*; for example, a bus driver looking into the engine of a broken-down bus and a voluptuous conductress behind him asking 'Would you like a screwdriver?' to which he replies 'Not now love, we're ten minutes late already.' It was a light-hearted extension of his passion for collecting stamps or fashion plates or paperweights, all of which had gone the way of the auction rooms at the time of his bankruptcy. The postcards cost next to nothing, each one in the series was numbered, and Vyvyan was trying to collect them all. He even carried a list of the missing numbers in his wallet to prevent buying duplicates, but duplicates there were because friends like Alec Waugh and James

Laver would send them to him with messages on the back which might simply be 'Have you got this one?' or something to match the sauciness of the front. I can even remember sending him a few myself. A few years after Vyvyan's death when I asked where they were, Thelma told me she had burned all those addressed to him personally, put on a scarf and dark glasses, and went incognito to sell the unused ones somewhere off the Charing Cross Road. Nobody should ever know that the son of Oscar Wilde collected saucy postcards.

Then there was the 'editing' of Vyvyan's diaries. He had kept a diary spasmodically from his schooldays, but in December 1940 he started one which he kept up almost daily until his death in 1967. In his essay on 'Keeping a Diary' he wrote that the most important rule is that it must be truthful, and truthful it certainly was—too much so for Thelma who by the mid-1970s had started removing and burning whole pages.[681] She justified it by saying that she was Vyvyan's executrix and that it is what he would have wanted her to do. I was horrified by this mutilation of what I knew he regarded as his *magnum opus*, and I felt myself being drawn into an ugly situation of entrenchment on both sides, a family civil war, with me fighting to save what remained of my 'real' father, and Thelma fighting to save her late husband's reputation. In the end she resorted to 'whiting out' various entries which, thanks to my training in the paper industry, I knew I could reverse, time consuming though it would be. I did finally take possession of the diaries in 1995 and one day, as I was laboriously restoring some the censored parts, my son, then sixteen, came into the room. Seeing the slight bloom left after removal of the correction fluid, he said philosophically, 'It may be a pain, but now we can read it again and we can also see what granny was trying to hide.' It was while I was trying to find a workable compromise between my mother's insistence on sanitising a hundred years of family history and my own view that it was a ludicrous waste of time, that Richard Ellmann came into my life.

Dick had invited my father to lunch in May 1964 and Vyvyan's only comment in his diary at the time was 'I think that everything has been said about him [Oscar Wilde] that could be said, on both sides. Why can't they let the poor fellow rest in peace?'[682] I am sure that Vyvyan would have told him little more than he had already written in his autobiography; besides, he was never too happy to talk about his own father with strangers, for it still gave him pain, and apart from the dim recollections of his childhood, most of what he knew was from third parties. Also, in a way quite unhelpful to serious researchers, he would occasionally retreat into flippancy about the whole business, which was a sort of refuge from having to think seriously about it. My father's various financial crises over the years had ensured that there were no Wilde manuscripts and not a single first edition of any of his works left in the family and precious little secondary material which anyone considered of importance, so the meeting was probably more to ascertain how cooperative Wilde's estate was likely to be.

Since the enormous critical acclaim which greeted his biography of James Joyce in 1959, Ellmann had been under gentle pressure from Oxford University Press to undertake another biography. Proposals and counterproposals were made—Henry James, W. H. Auden, Hemmingway, and then, with Rupert's edition of the letters about to appear in 1962, Dick began to think seriously about taking on Oscar. He had misgivings that my father 'would continue to withhold certain papers,' but thought that the letters might provide enough new material to make a biography possible.[683] They obviously did and by October that year he had reached an agreement with OUP for a 100,000 word biography of Oscar Wilde. It is the standard biographer's nightmare to take on a controversial life and to find that one is also taking on all the prejudices and insecurities of the left-over family who control much of the material one needs, and Ellmann was taking no chances. He wrote a courteous letter of condolence to my mother on Vyvyan's death in 1967 keeping, one cannot help feeling, the door ajar for the future and for the next eight years we heard no more from him.

Then in September 1975 he wrote to my mother requesting a 'blanket' permission to have Wilde manuscript materials copied from various archives in Europe and America. After my father's death and in the years I was abroad, whenever requests were addressed to Thelma, as they were with increasing regularity, to use extracts from letters or the odd fragments of Oscar's writing which were still protected by copyright, she would sit on them for several weeks, if not months, before passing them on to a local solicitor for reply. The solicitor would charge her ten pounds for the work and sometimes when the occasion warranted it, collect about the same as a permission fee. As I was now working in publishing and it seemed pointless paying a solicitor whose main work was conveyancing to deal with these few Wilde copyrights, I managed to persuade my mother after several months of dithering to let me take over and deal with all the negotiations and correspondence. The only condition was that she be kept informed and have the ultimate right of veto. I had no option but to accept, and in February 1976 I went to Oxford to meet Richard Ellmann.

We lunched in hall at New College and I cannot have told him anything that he did not know already. He had seen the archives and done the research; I had not. I suspect that he must have invited me to lunch largely out of curiosity as I am sure I should have done in his place. Perhaps, too, there was the thought in the back of his mind that, given my father's reluctance to talk and my mother's suspicions about all researchers into Oscar Wilde, if there was anything hidden away in a family cupboard, he would be far more likely to find it through me. We got on very well. I had not returned to Oxford since I was an undergraduate in 1968 and the last time I had sat in college rooms with an academic was probably to justify some sweeping generalisation on French Literature to my poor, patient tutor who had heard it all twice a week for as long as he could remember. This was different. I was no longer on trial. I felt immediately at ease with him, finding none of the arrogance which I often encountered with the self-appointed 'experts' on Wilde, who were so busy around that time with their 'scissors-and-paste' popularisations of his life. We talked at great length about his views on my grandfather and it was clear that his biography, when it eventually appeared, would be far better researched than anything which had yet appeared. It would be a definitive work for many years. A few days after, I was able to help him in a very small way by looking up the original of one of Constance's letters which we still had and which had been quoted rather loosely elsewhere. He needed the exact quotation. It was another ten years before we met again, but in the meantime this meeting was a catalyst which would change my whole outlook on my grandfather and the place I allowed him to occupy in my life.

I had been increasingly aware since the publication of Oscar's letters that the academic world had finally begun to take him seriously as a writer and a thinker, and an altogether different picture was taking the place of the first-rate funny man struggling to rise above the third division in literature. Dick Ellmann himself had contributed to this by publishing *The Artist as Critic* in 1970, one of the only editions of Wilde's critical writings to appear since before the First World War and in striking contrast to the regularly reprinted 'Selected Works' which simply rolled out the usual suspects: the four society plays, the fairy stories, *Dorian Gray* and *The Ballad of Reading Gaol*. There now appeared to be a depth of learning in Wilde which defied the frivolous, lightweight reputation ascribed to him for decades after his death, and those who had started to study him and write about him from this angle invariably knew far more about my grandfather's life and works than I did. It was all the more uncomfortable since I was somehow expected to be a sort of walking Oscar Wilde encyclopaedia. 'Did your grandfather read Nietzsche?' 'How on earth do you expect me to know?'[684] I later discovered that Dick Ellmann was corresponding with Rupert Hart-Davis at almost exactly this time about sources for research on his book and to one of his letters Rupert had replied, ' . . . nor is Mrs. Holland a good prospect. She has now asked her son Merlin to deal with me in her place and he is coming here shortly. But he knows nothing, and Vyvyan must have sold every scrap he ever had.'[685] Right on every count I'm afraid, and, conscious of my ignorance, I set myself to remedy it. Oscar became my Saturday job: answering the correspondence, reading around the 1890s, rereading the letters and the works and I embarked on a sort of private Odyssey to find this grandfather, from whom I had been kept at arm's length ostensibly for my own good, which was to last for the next fifty years.

In the summer of 1986 I was sorting through papers in my mother's flat and came across a bundle of Constance Wilde's letters to her brother covering the period of her engagement to Oscar as well as her exile in Italy. They were the type of letters which would have been passed over as unimportant by previous biographers, looking as they were for dramatic detail, but I knew they were exactly the sort of material which would help Dick and, on the pretext of putting them in order, I took them home and called him one morning shortly after. I was taken rather aback by his voice which was slurred as though he had been drinking, but he seemed pleased to hear from me again and I invited him to see the letters at the end of August in London. Shortly before he came, I learned that motor neurone disease had been diagnosed, and I was both ashamed and angry with myself that I could have put his impaired speech down to alcohol.

We spent a whole Saturday together and only covered about a fifth of them. Dick seemed to think that it would be worth continuing as he wrote to me: 'How very kind of you to go to so much trouble on my behalf. There's no doubt that the information in the letters is valuable and exciting . . . My thanks to Sarah [*my wife who had provided home-made hamburgers for lunch*] for her hospitality and to Lucian [*aged 7*] for his forbearance in sacrificing a playmate,' and a few weeks later: 'Is there any chance of seeing some more material? I hope so. It would make a great difference.' The problem was that I had not reckoned with Thelma's continuing worries and suspicions. Ultimately as my father's heir she could exercise her veto,[686] although I was doing all the day-to-day work and was much more likely to be able to make balanced decisions about whether 'researchers' were sensationalist muck-rakers or not. There was nothing in Constance's letters which could be interpreted sensationally. They were simply extra pieces for the jigsaw which could be used to flesh out the characters.

For two months I tried to convince her that we should let Dick use whatever parts of these letters he could. I explained that his biography would be the last word on Wilde for years to come and that we should be helpful rather than obstructive. Emotions ran high between us. Then, without telling me, at the beginning of November, Thelma invited herself to meet the Ellmanns in Oxford. I could only guess at her motives which were almost certainly fuelled by the suspicion that Dick and I were collaborating in a way which would undermine some of her reinterpreted family history. Her letter of thanks to him afterwards emphasised her role as Vyvyan's executrix and said that if she came across any papers which might be of use to him, she would tell him, all the while knowing full well that she had Constance's letters to her brother recently sorted by me. Her letter to me a few days later told a very different story: 'I then gave them a dissertation, which I am sure is true, that OW was basically heterosexual. That shook them.' I have no doubt that it did and I imagine Dick Ellmann's heart must have sunk at the thought that his book was nearing completion and that the nightmare executrix was beginning to stir. She went on to say to me that more than enough had been written about Constance and about the tragedy of Oscar Wilde and that we should encourage people just to look at the positive side of his legacy: 'The most constructive thing we as a family can do, is to forget the dead . . . we must see that his work is presented for future generations and get rid of this so-called Victorian disgrace.'[687] Thelma had already talked of burning the letters as a last resort if she felt they were ever going to be used in any sort of context of which she did not approve. 'I shall have to tread very carefully in the next few months if I am to win her over,' I had written to Dick in September, 'and I cannot let you acknowledge the source of the material until I have her permission or it will simply confirm her opinion that I am not to be trusted and I hate to think of the historical bonfire which might ensue.'[688] I saw Constance's letters as the kindling for a much greater family conflagration.

By now Dick was running out of time and his manuscript was due at the publishers early in the New Year. I cannot remember how I managed to win Thelma over; I think it was partly because by then Dick was too ill to travel and I offered to transcribe everything that was relevant and send it to him. In that way Thelma could vet the material and feel nominally in control, so with reluctance she agreed and I sent him the transcripts after Christmas.

Unfortunately, towards the end of 1986 there had appeared a slim volume of Richard Ellmann's lectures to the Library of Congress between 1982 and 1985 entitled *Four Dubliners*, one of which was on Oscar Wilde. In it he conjectures that Wilde probably caught syphilis while he was a student in Oxford and that it was later to be the cause of his death. One of my mother's busybody friends, of whom there were a number misguidedly encouraging her sanitising crusade, called the book to her attention and off we were once again. Dick had given me a copy of the book in October, but I paid little attention to the syphilis theory as it had been propounded in one form or another by several biographers since Arthur Ransome had first mentioned it in print in 1912 and a major new biography could not but discuss the question rather than ignore it. To give Thelma her due, it was one of two occasions in twenty years of quarrelling over my grandfather, that I found myself siding with her. She pointed out that what was just a paragraph or two in a lecture but described as altering Oscar's life, was likely to become a major feature of the biography.

In February 1987 Dick wrote asking for official permission to quote from Oscar's letters and certain unpublished writings. I replied that I would like to come up to Oxford and see him because I wanted to talk about the whole vexed question of syphilis and to know how he had tackled it: 'There has, as far as I know, never been any serious evidence for the allegations. It was mentioned in a couple of personal reminiscences but that appears to be all. I think it is high time that some proper evidence was produced or the matter knocked on the head once and for all . . . I should like to discuss this in some detail with you.'[689] Even face to face communication with Dick by then was almost impossible. In the hour we spent together I realised he was intending to make Wilde's syphilis one of the central themes in his book. New evidence to justify it was, as I had suspected, simply not there. On the little hand-printer which by then he was reduced to using, he printed out 'Your father was quoted by Sherard as saying Wilde had syphilis' as if this were somehow intended to be the ultimate and unquestionable proof, although my father was far less likely to have known the truth than Wilde's close friends. I still have the tape stuck in my file. Even the hoary old story about the Oxford prostitute was trotted out, the source of which I have since discovered was Francis, 11th Marquess of Queensberry and grandson of the man who triggered the whole Wilde débâcle in 1895.[690] I felt a huge sense of disappointment because I liked and trusted Dick and I had expected him to take a scholarly and informed view. Of course, the subject had to be raised but it needed objective analysis rather than just relying on dubious or questionably referenced sources and selective quotation to fit the conjecture. How could things have gone so badly off the rails? Very simply—money and commercial interests.

Back in 1964 when Richard Ellmann signed up with Oxford University Press for his Wilde biography he would probably have received a modest advance, partly because OUP has never been known for its financial generosity to authors and partly because literary biography had not yet become the fashionable genre that it was by the 1990s. As an academic, the prestige of being published by Oxford would have largely compensated for terms less lucrative than with a trade publisher, although they had agreed to an unusual 15% royalty.[691] Ellmann was, however, a very desirable 'house author' for the American branch of OUP, especially after the huge success of *James Joyce* and in recognition of this they offered him $100,000 over ten years as a retainer and in respect of four books to be delivered.[692]

Whether he accepted it or not is uncertain but, as Oxford terms went, it was an uncharacteristically generous proposal. Twenty-one years after signing the contract and with the biography still unfinished, Dick attended a Joyce conference in Monaco where he met a glamorous Brazilian artist and publisher, Rosita Fanto. Rosita and Dick were immediately attracted to each other, she to him for his intellect and he to her for her creativity and within a very short time she had persuaded him to collaborate with her in producing a pack of playing cards based on Oscar Wilde's life and works. It must have been around this time, too, that Dick became increasingly aware of the commercial potential of his Wilde biography as his letters to Rosita show. He had acquired a literary agent in New York who had succeeded in selling the rights to Knopf on the condition that he could extricate himself from the OUP contract.[693] Oxford demanded seven times their advance to release the rights, but the deal with Knopf covered that and more, and by the time Knopf had sold on rights to Hamish Hamilton and Penguin in the UK for £90,000 the advances exceeded $250,000, the highest ever paid for a biography.[694] Ostensibly the move, according to Ellmann, had been triggered by OUP's refusal to bring him from Oxford to New York in 1982 to celebrate the launch of his revised Joyce biography, but in reality you do not sue your partner of twenty-five years for divorce just because of a domestic tiff over a party.[695] In the end one cannot help but sympathise over the switch of loyalty. He had retired in 1984; his wife, Mary, was wheelchair-bound after a stroke and he had elected to remain resident in England where the costs of caring for her disability were substantially less than in the US; and he needed to squeeze every last penny out of his professional writing.

But Knopf didn't just want a reliable biography from an Emeritus Professor of English at Oxford; for their substantial advances they wanted something sensational to sell the book, something which would make headlines. By early 1986, reading between the lines of a letter to Dick from his editor at Knopf shows the direction in which matters are moving: 'I have been looking at the recent book of "new" Wilde letters and there's nothing sensational in what I've read so far. But it's fun getting ready for the main event.'[696] There was, however, the unresolved question of whether Wilde ever contracted syphilis and whether it was the cause of his death.

Since 1967 Dick had been agonising over the question of Oscar and syphilis. He wrote to the French doyen of Wilde studies, Guillot de Saix, and asked whether he had come across any evidence for it at all, saying that Edmund Wilson claimed on the scantest of evidence that it was the cause of Wilde's death.[697] De Saix did not reply as he had been dead for three years. He then corresponded with eminent medical men, among them J. B. Lyons Professor of the History of Medicine at Trinity Dublin, and Dr. Macdonald Critchley at the National Hospital for Nervous Diseases in London. Both urged caution about coming to conclusions on the very slim evidence available, views reflected in the published work of each of them.[698] Dick also wrote to Rupert Hart-Davis on the subject and Rupert recommended him to read Terence Cawthorne, an ENT surgeon and medical historian on Wilde's last illness. He, too, came down firmly on the side of cerebral meningitis.[699] From 1981 onwards Dick raised the matter on an annual basis in his correspondence with Rupert, attempting to persuade him of his theory on the 'evidence' mostly of hearsay. Rupert remained consistently sceptical 'I am still loath to accept the syphilis theory without better authority than the third-hand one—supposedly Wilde—Ross—Ransome—the World—nor is there any necessary connection between that disease and the fatal ear trouble,' and again 'There seems no doubt that Oscar died of cerebral meningitis as recorded on his death certificate. Whether this was a long-delayed after-effect of syphilis seems doubtful,' and finally in January 1987, only months before Ellmann's death:

Do you know of any concrete evidence (as opposed to vague gossip) for Oscar's syphilis and the prostitute? You mention it as though it were a proven fact. If it is not, I think you should make that clear. I am not saying there was no syphilis and no prostitute, but so much fact has now been disentangled from legend, that you should take care not to entangle them again.[700]

Clearly, though, the desire to satisfy the marketing arm of a trade publishing house was stronger than the need to establish the probable truth once and for all and giving Oscar a dose of the pox at Oxford and having it determine certain aspects of his life from then on was a neat solution.

It left me little choice but to go to the publishers and ask for sight of the typescript before I was prepared to grant permission for copyright material to be used. I made two calls to Hamish Hamilton the day after my return from Oxford asking to speak to the editor responsible for the book, but each time I met with a rebuff of such arrogance that anger replaced disappointment. I wrote to all the publishers who controlled quotation rights in Wilde's letters and asked that they temporarily withhold permissions until I could get a hearing. To Hamish Hamilton I wrote explaining that I had known Dick for a good while and that it was not my intention to obstruct publication but rather to see an end to all the speculative research of the past:

> I am not attempting to whitewash a part of Oscar's life which I find distasteful. If it is the truth and can be properly documented, then within reason, it should be said. I have not seen the typescript and should like to do so. To offer me a few words in defence is unacceptable. I am quite prepared to co-operate, but the way in which this has been handled has touched a raw nerve. We are still Wilde's family and I consider it no more than a common decency that our feelings be taken, even if minimally, into consideration.[701]

Within days I had met Christopher Sinclair-Stevenson, the Managing Director, and had been allowed sight of the typescript, but his editor clearly still regarded me as a troublemaker.[702] How dare a member of the family presume to argue with an Emeritus Professor of English? I insisted they give me a fortnight to present my case. Meanwhile Dick had turned both to Owen Dudley Edwards and to Rupert Hart-Davis to help resolve things. Rupert's reply to him came down rather firmly on my side:

> I can't help sympathising with Merlin for the following reasons. When I had read the first part of your typescript, I had complained of your putting forward the syphilis at Oxford as a simple fact without any evidence . . . You are indeed a most reputable scholar and as such you should closely respect the difference between a provable fact and some unreliable gossip.[703]

Owen Dudley Edwards, with his detailed knowledge of Wilde's letters from when he had worked on them with Rupert in the 1950s, offered to provide sources for quotations which would circumvent permissions for many of them if I proved intractable and the rest could, if necessary be paraphrased.[704] My own research was done all day and half the night for two weeks. I turned it into a closely reasoned paper.[705] I sent it to all concerned, the publishers, Dick and Rupert Hart-Davis. To Rupert I wrote:

> Between you and me I have felt very bad about taking this stand on account of Dick's health, but I feel equally upset about the idea of a major biography appearing in which Oscar is branded as a syphilitic with very little evidence at all. Family ties are strange. I have never felt this strongly about anything to do with OW before. I feel I owe it to him . . . Your letter to Dick voices my feelings exactly . . . I think he should present the facts as they are and let the reader decide for himself.[706]

Rupert's reply was that my paper 'makes excellent sense but it is more than a dying man can tackle,' and he begged me to agree to the now famous footnote in which it was said that the evidence was not decisive, but that it was Richard Ellmann's personal conviction.[707]

What could I say? I gave in to compromise for I respected Dick and was upset by his slow, wasting decline. It would always have been on my conscience if he had died not knowing whether his book's publication was safe. The finality of death is always made worse by unresolved quarrels but I like to think, as I said in one of my last letters to Dick, that we had simply agreed to disagree; his book was none the worse for stating Wilde's syphilis as a belief rather than a hard fact and I was satisfied with the compromise. In fact, he has come in for much criticism from the academic and medical worlds for his lack of proper evidence in the whole matter and toning it down slightly has done his reputation more good than harm. The whole disagreement over syphilis was blown up out of all proportion by those who came into it at the last minute, myself included, but if Dick had got in touch back in 1981, as he suggested in a letter to Rupert that he might, it would never have become a last minute issue.[708] By contrast, I discovered much later that at least Dick had had the good sense to ignore another piece of unfounded posthumous gossip: J. B. W. Polak, the Dutch scholar and bibliophile wrote to him in September 1986 maintaining that he heard that André Gide, Oscar Wilde, and Louis Couperus all met in 1890 in Tangiers at a male brothel to have sex with Arab boys. When Dick questioned the reliability of the story, Polak admitted that it might all be a fantasy as it was told to him 'by an old man whose name I am not at liberty to mention.'[709] In such arbitrary fashion these myths live or die. Then again, without the sensational 'revelation' about syphilis and the difference of opinion between the author and Wilde's heirs, about which much was made subsequently in the press, perhaps the book would have had less of an initial impact.

I was prepared more or less to close the file then. It was the period of limbo between the last flurry of refinements to the manuscript and the mass of reviews and comment which was certain to greet its publication. It wasn't my book; I had had very little to do with it. And yet because it was my own grandfather and because I had known and admired Dick, I wanted it to be a bestseller. Apart from anything else it would call a temporary halt to much of the second-rate, second-hand stuff which the Wilde industry had been churning out for fifteen years.

It was Charles Elliott, the London editor for Knopf, who told me about Dick's memorial service in New College Chapel on 22 June; I probably would not have known otherwise. It was a very personal matter for me to go, irregular Christian that I am. If there is any truth in a concept of spirit or soul or after-life it was one way in which I could say to Dick, 'See, there are no ill-feelings between us.' He had also done Oscar a great service with a hugely sympathetic biography and even if we had disagreed over a few facts, I wanted to pay my respects to him. I had never been part of the mainstream publishing or academic world and I had to steel myself into taking a cup of tea after the service was over, aware that I would know nobody. I hate such occasions. I worry about making some gauche remark and clam up completely. It becomes almost like a panic attack which feeds on its own insecurity. All I remember was shaking hands with his daughters Maud and Lucy and being made to feel very uncomfortable by his wife, Mary, and I wanted to leave as soon as I could. I heard later from Rosita Fanto, she of the Oscar Wilde pictorial playing cards, that some members of the family felt I shouldn't have come. With all the other emotions of that day I certainly hadn't reckoned with hatred as well.

There is a curious situation in which I have occasionally found myself being the unconscious object of someone else's strong emotions, whether love or hate is immaterial, while being part of a gathering. For some reason you are the only one to remain utterly unaware of it, and when you look back on the incident later, it is almost inconceivable that you could have been so blind. It happened that afternoon. I still do not understand why the Ellmann family insisted on their right to protect Dick's memory while apparently denying me the same right to protect Oscar's. Perhaps protection is only allowed for those whom you have known personally, although family to me is family of whatever generation.

Since I did not take the *Sunday Times* it was an old friend who drew my attention to Roger Lewis's article three months later in the magazine section of 13 September. Editorially, in those days, the Sunday colour supplements tended to work six to eight weeks in advance so he must have written his piece in July. Lewis, 27, Fellow of Wolfson College and ex-pupil of Dick Ellmann, was commissioned to do a 'taster' article for the supplement in advance of a two-part serialisation of *Oscar Wilde*. It was a pre-publication look at the biography and about the tragedy of Dick's death. He interviewed the family, Mary, Maud, and Lucy, about Dick in the context of the book and quoted one of them as making some disobliging remarks about Rosita such as 'She's sixty-five and has been so for quite a time,' and that she 'enjoys the accumulated wealth of a husband or so,' and about me that I had 'threatened to bring an injunction and stop everything if my father [Ellmann] said Wilde died of syphilis, which it's quite obvious he did.'[710] Rosita immediately threatened to sue and offered to join me in her writ for libel, which I could never have done on my own. I wrote and protested to the *Sunday Times* saying that I found the article offensive and misleading, and demanded an apology; there was a flurry of correspondence from both Ellmann daughters accusing Lewis of making it all up and concerned that I could somehow 'ban' their father's book as a result; and the *Sunday Times* made it obliquely clear that legal action from any side would jeopardise serialisation of the book. There was a wonderful irony in the whole affair which I appreciated: I've always fought against the artificial sensationalising of Oscar purely for commercial gain and here circumstances seemed to have intervened on my behalf. Rosita was more hurt than angry and after a couple of weeks she withdrew her action and the newspaper printed an apology to both of us. And poor Roger Lewis was left wondering into what a nest of vipers he had wandered unwittingly.

Looking back on it, I can see that the Ellmanns were deeply

distressed at Dick's death and the manner of it, and they were upset that I was disputing one of the cornerstones of his book which, understandably, had made Dick anxious about its future. What was more natural than to lash out at me and tar me with the same brush as so many other literary estates as being difficult, obstructive, and protective of Wilde's reputation? On the other hand, it would have been insane for Roger to have invented what the Ellmanns were supposed to have said to him. He would have lost any reputation he may have had both as an academic and as a journalist if it had been proved that what he reported was simply invention. It was not as if he were writing for the *Sunday Sport*. Roger Lewis was undoubtedly caught in a vicious cross-fire. There must have been a few indiscreet comments and a lot of naivety on the part of the Ellmanns to suppose that he wouldn't use them. It gave him a good angle to his story to cast Rosita as the exotic *femme fatale* and me as a tiresome, narrow-minded descendant of the lovably flamboyant Oscar, but neither characterisation could he have pulled out of thin air as Roger at that stage knew neither of us. I suppose we shall never know the truth, but it always seemed to me that Maud and Lucy Ellmann were not entirely innocent in the matter.

The best of the posthumous Oscar stories have had sequels and this one was no exception. Rosita Fanto had launched the Oscar Wilde playing cards at the Cadogan Hotel on the anniversary of Oscar's birthday the year before, an occasion which was, incidentally, my first experience of being used for publicity. My wife and I were invited to attend the reception and a dinner afterwards. Thelma was not, presumably because her reputation had preceded her, and tried to dissuade me from going. The reception part over, I realised that we were expected to pay for our dinner so, to my wife's disgust, I made some polite excuse, left and took her to a pizza restaurant around the corner. It was the first and not the last time I let my integrity get the better of me in such matters.

Rosita's loosely worded agreement with Dick entitled him to a royalty of 20% on the sales of the playing cards, but after the

article in the *Sunday Times* Rosita had wanted to disassociate herself and the project from the Ellmann estate and was prepared to
pay them off to retain all the rights and to be able to contribute the
profits to a Motor Neurone Disease charity. However, her agreement with Dick had been so vague about 'competitive ventures'
that the Ellmanns' lawyers were worried she might have a claim on
the biography royalties and approached her first with a suggestion
for a mutual renunciation of claims, they on Rosita's cards and she
on Dick's biography. She was only too happy to sign.[711]

The biography appeared at the beginning of October 1987
and was an instant success. Apart from the sensational claim that
Oscar had died of syphilis, the publishers couldn't resist another
literary scoop—Wilde as cross-dresser. Among the illustrations
was a photograph from the Roger-Viollet photo archive in Paris
captioned 'Wilde in costume as Salomé.' The rounded chin, the
heavy eyelids, the soft-looking, unmuscular flesh betraying the life
of indulgence which he was known to be leading by 1891 when
the play was written, all weighed heavily in favour of its authenticity, but to me it just didn't seem in character. The nose was too
aquiline (his mother's perhaps but not his) and the lips too thin.

In 1993 I enlisted the help of a German scholar at Braunschweig,
Horst Schroeder, in an attempt to settle the matter. He suggested
that Strauss's opera rather than Wilde's play might be the source
and within a few months we had exposed it as yet another Wildean
myth. The photograph was indisputably that of a Hungarian opera
singer, Alice Guszalewicz, playing in Strauss's *Salomé* at Cologne
in 1906, but it had become detached from its proper caption in
the photo archive under 'Wilde—General.'[712]

The first appearance of 'Wilde as Salomé,' had been in *Le
Monde* of 20 March 1987 only weeks before Ellmann's death. It
was picked up by his editor, Catherine Carver, from a review of a
new French biography on Wilde and sent to Dick Ellmann who
was said to have been delighted with the discovery, but so near to
the end of his life he was unable to verify its source personally. The
publishers, however, sensing another Wildean scandal, made sure

it was included and for several years, until Horst and I exposed the error, a whole new branch of post-Freudian Wilde research was in danger of taking root. Despite my attempts to persuade Penguin that Ellmann's biography would be much improved by correcting the considerable number of errors and omissions occasioned by his premature death, the estate was adamant that not a word should be touched.[713] As for the fall-out from the syphilis myth, it still registers occasionally on the literary Geiger-counter and contaminates the unwary. For some, no amount of referring them to the carefully reasoned medical literature on the subject will shake their conviction that Oscar's last illness was due to tertiary syphilis. In one case, an academic monograph, 'the first full-length psychoanalytic biography of Wilde' published in 1994, made it one of the premises of its main argument and as late as 2019 the author suggested that I might disinter Oscar's remains and subject a sample to genomic testing to prove the point.[714] And Roger Lewis, to his amusement, has become immortalised in Lucy Ellmann's sixth novel *Doctors and Nurses* as a psychopathic doctor of the same name. Oscar breathes new life into those endless squabbles of the 1930s—a modern dress revival and just a few changed names.

CHAPTER THREE
CLASSIFYING THE TOMB

S hortly after Robbie Ross's ashes were placed in Oscar's tomb in 1950, his heirs felt that the ownership of the tomb (until then in Ross's name) together with its key should be transferred to my father. Clearly the decision was not implemented, for John-Paul Ross, Robbie's great nephew, wrote to Vyvyan in December 1960 saying that the matter was still pending. My father's reply (he who later described the Epstein sculpture as 'a flying angel with an erection')[715] was typical of his feelings towards Oscar at the time:

> As for the key itself . . . the best thing would probably be to put it into a water-tight container and fling it into the Liffey, as near to TCD as possible. I cannot think that anyone would ever want to use it again, unless Papa were canonised at some future date and pieces of him were needed as holy relics.[716]

This flippancy in reference to his father occurs quite frequently in Vyvyan's private correspondence but, for obvious reasons, never in his published writings. He was also desperately short of money at that time and to have treated the matter more seriously would have implied that he was prepared to take his share of financial responsibility for the tomb. Writing this over sixty years later I have conflicting emotions about it. Why should he have been bothered about the upkeep of his father's tomb, the man who had destroyed his family by his reckless behaviour, who had made his wife and children's lives such a misery after 1895? The little income that Vyvyan had from writing was spent on day-to-day living and the modern rehabilitation of Oscar, especially with Parliament drag-ging its feet over the recommendations of the 1957 Wolfenden Report, was still a few years off. And yet . . . this was his father who had provided him posthumously with enough royalties from his works to live in relative comfort and earn a living as a translator in the 20s and 30s. Just another question I should have asked my father had he lived ten years longer.

It was an incident in 1961 which again raised the whole ques-tion of the tomb's future. Sometime in the late summer of that year, the genitals of 'the flying demon angel' were mutilated. The first that was known of it was a letter from the Director of Père Lachaise Cemetery to the criminal barrister C. G. L. du Cann, saying that he would be grateful if du Cann would pass on this information as he did not have Vyvyan Holland's address which, given Vyvyan's reluctance to take any responsibility for the tomb, was unsurprising.[717] Du Cann had always had an interest in Wilde, had collected a few of his letters and had attended the centenary lunch at the Savoy, so he was well-known in Wilde circles. At the same time as he forwarded the letter to my father he sent a copy to the *Evening Standard* which ran a couple of paragraphs on the subject and quoted my father as saying 'Something will have to be done about it. But unfortunately the tomb doesn't belong to me. It belongs to the Ross family.'[718] It was this shrugging off of any responsibility for his father's tomb which John-Paul Ross found intensely irritating, even if he was occasionally amused by their exchanges in correspondence:

> It seems to me as though Vyvyan Holland may well not wish to take a transfer of the ownership of this tomb, and his whole attitude towards it all along has been somewhat flippant and *sans-gêne* . . . it is a somewhat piquant situation where the Ross loyalty to Oscar Wilde appears to entail obligations continu-ing for far longer than the statutory duration of his copyright. Clearly Vyvyan Holland has as much, if not greater, obligation towards his father's burial place, but I think we shall have to wait

until the Day of Judgement before we get him to realise or act upon that fact.[719]

Several stories have grown up around the castration of the angel most of which owe more to the fertile imagination of French authors than to reality. One thing is certain: between the unveiling of the tomb in 1914 and 1961 the angel's genitals had become much smoother than the rest of the monument due to their repeated caressing by admirers.[720] Michel Dansel in his book on the stories, the secrets and the legends associated with the cemetery, maintained that it was two Englishwomen who, incensed at the sight of the polished testicles, picked up stones nearby and knocked them off. They were then retrieved by a patrolling cemetery guard and taken to the Director's office where they were used for two years a paperweight.[721] There is no source for this story, which implies that the two women were caught in the act of mutilating the sculpture, but by whom, it is not stated. Certainly not by the cemetery authorities, whose initial letter says that the culprit was unknown. If the piece or pieces had been large enough to be used as paperweights, the Director's letter would almost certainly have made mention of them with a view to restoration, French *fonctionnaires*, living by rules and regulations as they do. But as my father used to say of such anecdotes in connection with Oscar 'Why let the facts get in the way of a good story?' The French have always found what they saw as the 'persecution' of Oscar Wilde to be somewhere between hypocritical and laughable so the idea that two Englishwomen—spinsters by a further embellishment—should have been responsible for yet another outrage on the writer, must have seemed like an irresistible epilogue to the story and the added irreverence of suggesting that the balls were used as a paperweight adds a perfect touch of Gallic piquancy to the whole fabrication. An amusing sequel to the story was provided in the summer of 2000 by an American intermedia artist from Detroit, Leon Johnson, who commissioned the sculptor Rebecca Scheer to provide him with a silver prosthesis to replace the missing genitals. He then performed a forty-minute ceremony entitled 're-Membering Wilde' in which the prosthesis was temporarily installed and the whole event recorded on video.

The question of whether to repair the damage was discussed at length between my father, the Ross family, and Lady Epstein herself, and in the end all agreed that a costly restoration might well attract further vandalism, so nothing was done. My mother suggested hiding the damage with a fig-leaf, oblivious to the early history of the tomb and the fury of Jacob Epstein at having his sculpture 'sanitised' to satisfy the French authorities in a similar way in 1914, It was characteristic of Thelma to want, yet again, to cover up something even remotely sexual which could be associated with her scandalous father-in-law. John-Paul Ross gently dismissed the idea saying that the curious would no doubt want to know what lay beneath it and souvenir hunters would probably remove it entirely.[722] This discussion was still continuing when my father died six years later and led on logically to the question of whether the tomb was due for a clean, which hadn't been done since 1950, the cost of doing it, and the future of the tomb as a whole.

Already the idea was being floated that the Paris Municipality or some department of the Ministry of Culture might be persuaded to take it over. By that time I'm glad for him that my father wasn't around. He didn't have enough money to pay for his share of the cleaning, and it would have been difficult for him to brush it aside jokingly as he had done a few years before about the keys and the ownership. Handing the tomb over to the French, even if they were to accept it, would have involved even greater expense with all the complications of proof of ownership through wills, changes of name, birth, marriage and death certificates and all of it put into French by an accredited translator, not forgetting solicitors' and *notaires* fees on both sides of the Channel. Meanwhile the tomb became increasingly grubby and unkempt and since the sculpture had been deprived of what the French charmingly referred to as *les parties nobles* for visitors to caress more or less harmlessly, they started to leave messages on the stone with felt-tip pens or, worse still, scratched into it. It was around this time that public interaction with graves in Père Lachaise started to become popular. Jim Morrison of The Doors was buried in the cemetery in 1971 and his grave immediately became a place of pilgrimage for adoring fans who, even before there was a headstone, scribbled their messages on neighbouring tombs. Oscar, in death as in life, courted controversy and around this time, alongside the tributes on his tomb, I remember a smattering of political messages of the type 'Troops out of N. Ireland.' Whether it was admiration for the bad boy of the 1890s or the pop icon of the 1960s, both of whose lives fascinated by their excesses, the graffiti began to increase exponentially, and something had to be done to limit the damage.

At that time, I was living and working in Beirut and John-Paul Ross was with the UN in Jerusalem. We were a hundred and fifty miles apart only, but direct communication was out of the question. Email was a couple of decades away; telephoning between Lebanon and Israel was impossible, and letters had to be posted from a neutral country. It was only after I returned to England and John-Paul had retired and went to live in France that we could start to address the problem actively.

In 1975 John-Paul discussed the future of the tomb informally over lunch in Paris with Baron Denys Cochin, a former Paris City councillor and Philippe Jullian, a French art historian, journalist and author of a biography of Oscar Wilde which had appeared in 1967. Jullian had seemed enthusiastic at the idea of France taking an active role in the preservation and protection of Epstein's monument as a work of art and proposed writing a piece for *Le Figaro* 'to test public opinion' as he put it. When the piece appeared a few days later, despite not a word having been mentioned about the cost of its upkeep, Jullian maliciously suggested that Ross wanted to offload the tomb by gifting it to the City of Paris because he was finding the financial burden too heavy. With that, any hope of French help with the tomb had to be abandoned for more than a decade. John-Paul suspected that Jullian might have been exacting revenge for some bad reviews of his biography when it appeared in English translation, but I think that was an explanation too far. There were certainly plenty of errors, misattributed anecdotes and strange conjectures which led Rupert Hart-Davis to lament (as he would do later with Richard Ellmann) that Jullian had re-muddled up all the fact and fiction which, in seven years of working on Oscar's letters, he himself had managed to disentangle.[723] A couple of years after the appearance of the *Figaro* article, having suffered a series of personal tragedies, including the stabbing to death of his Moroccan manservant and companion, Jullian put an end to his life at the age of 58. Then we simply let the dust settle which Jullian's unsympathetic piece in *Le Figaro* had raised, wondering ineffectually what to do about the tomb's upkeep, and in the meantime its condition simply worsened. I continued together with the Ross family to explore the possibilities of getting the tomb somehow 'adopted' by the French as it was (and still is) one of the most visited tombs and main attractions of Père Lachaise Cemetery. However, the difficulty, as pointed out by the cemetery office, was that normally tombs could not be passed on to non-family members. A possible solution was to apply for its classification as a 'Monument Historique' which would afford it some legal protection against vandalism, but we had been led to believe that the Ministère de la Culture would look more favourably on the idea if the tomb was in a state of good repair.

It was during a dinner in June 1988 given at the British Embassy in Paris that I was introduced to Robert Cantoni, a director of the Conseil Franco-Britannique and, as it happened, an admirer of my grandfather. Cantoni was exceptionally well-placed in political and diplomatic circles and one of his friends, Jack Lang, had recently been appointed to the staff of the Minister of Culture. Letters were written and our dilemma finished up on the desk of the Regional Director of the Monuments Historiques where, knowing the speed at which French administrations and their endless committees work, it might have languished for months had a member of the public not written a letter to *The Times* in February

1989 horrified by the state of the tomb covered in graffiti and asked why the British and Irish governments didn't do something about it. I replied in the correspondence columns of the newspaper saying that both the Ross and Holland families were fully aware of the problem and were trying to find a solution, but that short of a twenty-four hour armed guard it was virtually impossible to prevent mindless 'fans' from scribbling or spraying their names and messages on it.[724] But it also gave John-Paul the perfect pretext to arrange a meeting with the Monuments Historiques in order to present our case for getting the tomb classified or even adopted by an official body, and one afternoon a couple of weeks later my phone rang:

'Is that Mr. Holland?'
'It is.'
'Geoffrey Keating here—Cultural Section, Department of Foreign Affairs in Dublin. We've a team of stonemasons going over to Paris to carry out repairs on the Irish College and we were thinking we might take in Oscar's grave at the same time.'

It turned out that he had read the exchange of letters in *The Times* and, as I wrote to him shortly afterwards, I was both delighted and somewhat taken aback by the friendliness of this direct approach, especially as people who had occasionally contacted the British Embassy in Paris on the subject were told rather loftily by the Cultural Attaché's office that it was the family's responsibility and nothing to do with the British Government.[725] It was an exceptionally welcome offer by Ireland to one of her more prodigal sons, especially as it involved some remedial work on the stone and not just a superficial clean. I explained that it would all have to be carefully co-ordinated with our tentative approaches to the French, and if the timing was right it could be seen as an impressive Franco-Irish collaboration with the Irish responsible for the cleaning and restoration and the French somehow taking responsibility for its future protection. As it was, that would have been far too easy. Although the Irish were supposed to be keeping me informed through their Paris Embassy, there were staff changes and a matter of such minor importance clearly slipped through the net. The team of masons from Dublin came to work on the Irish College for four months in the summer and went leaving Oscar's grave untouched. John-Paul presented a dossier to the Monuments Historiques and was told that the matter would be put before the classification committee once a study of the more noteworthy tombs in the cemetery had been completed, which it wasn't until two years later. Meanwhile, I made polite enquiries of the Ministry of Foreign Affairs in Dublin as to whether they were still interested in helping but was told that the Foreign Cultural Support Budget was tiny, and while it might have been possible, tagged onto the end of the Irish College repairs, the opportunity had gone. We had been relying on the Irish support to get the tomb cleaned and repaired so that the French would look more favourably on granting it classification and protection rather than seeing it as just a cynical move towards applying for a grant, which all classified structures are entitled to do. The unworthy motives attributed to us by Jullian for wanting to shed responsibility for the tomb had largely been forgotten, but the matter still had to be treated with extreme caution. It was a delicate balance between Irish cleaning, French classifying and everyone wanting some of the kudos.

I mentioned the whole business casually to Owen Dudley Edwards, an Irishman and Reader in History at Edinburgh who, as a young post-graduate, had done much of the research for the 1962 *Letters of Oscar Wilde*. Owen's view was that the Irish had made the gesture and should carry it through, especially as Dublin had been selected as European City of Culture for 1991 and Oscar's name, among others, had been used in the proposal documents. He wrote to his cousin, Brian Lenihan, Defence Minister in the Irish government, Tánaiste and candidate for the forthcoming presidential election, who in turn asked his colleague in Foreign Affairs if the matter could be revived. A word in the right quarters and our carefully engineered project was back on the rails. Within a few months the Irish had re-committed themselves to cleaning and repairing the tomb dependent only on its classification by the French Monuments Historiques. Further chasing of the Ministry of Culture in Paris finally extracted the news (unofficially) at the end of July 1991 that the selection committee had accepted Oscar's tomb for classification 'by a large majority' and the *arrêté préfectoral* was signed on 27 Sept 1991 almost exactly 30 years since the angel had been castrated. Although this classification only entitled it to be included (*inscrit*) on the *Liste Supplémentaire*, a sort of probationary listing, the committee, we were told, was eager to see it elevated to the full status of Monument Historique (*classé*) and if, in a year or two, we were to apply, the promotion would be a mere formality. It was, and on 10 March 1995 Oscar the writer and Jacob Epstein's sculpture together became a French historic monument.

Now that the initial classifying of Oscar's tomb was complete, at the end of November 1991 John-Paul and I made an appointment with the Architecte des Bâtiments de France in Paris to discuss urgently the approved methods and materials for cleaning it. As a listed monument the regulations were extremely strict and such crude cleaning and protection (high pressure hosing and plastification) as had been suggested a few years before and offered gratis for publicity purposes by an opportunistic Belgian firm, were out of the question. The only reason for mentioning this otherwise routine visit was that Oscar intruded, as he had a habit of doing, in the most unexpected form. I had travelled from London by car and having no small change for the parking meter in the Marais where the meeting was taking place, I went into a newsagent to buy a paper and change a note. I wouldn't normally have bought a *Paris Match* but I felt that buying a paper with a 50 franc note was a little unreasonable so I bought the magazine instead. It was only later in the day that I opened it and discovered to my astonishment that I appeared to have a distant cousin of German extraction living in Paris.[726] Claudy Wilde was a twenty-four year-old

blonde film star who claimed to be a great-great-niece of Oscar
Wilde and whose relative had emigrated from Ireland to Germany
sometime in the distant past. 'J'ai retenu les leçons d'oncle Oscar,'
(roughly 'I've followed the example of Uncle Oscar') she said in
her interview, and implied that, like him, she was a rebel who
loved travelling and breaking down barriers. Fascinated by this
very public claim, I wrote to the distributors of her latest film in
which she played a high-class call-girl, and asked (with proof of
my identity to show I wasn't some sort of groupie) if she could tell
me more as I was trying to establish a family tree. Needless to say, I
never got a reply. Wilde is not an unusual German name and even
in the 1990s people still assumed that Oscar, as a homosexual,
would have had no descendants to dispute such a claim, so someone in her family probably decided that creating this myth might
be quite beneficial. Claudy at twenty-four, making a career as a
screen actress, was happy to believe it. Since Germany in the early
years of the twentieth century did so much to re-establish Oscar's
reputation as an author and dramatist, I thought it amusing and
even strangely appropriate that one of its citizens wanted to claim
him as a relative.

Early in the next year, the Irish Government, true to its commitment, paid for the tomb to be professionally cleaned and a few
minor repairs to be carried out. I wanted to put a discreet bilingual
notice on the plinth: 'Respect the memory of Oscar Wilde and do
not deface this tomb. It is protected by law as an historic monument
and was restored in 1992 by courtesy of the Irish Government,'
but Dublin asked me to remove the last six words in case it created some sort of precedent. Reluctantly I did. The bronze plate
was made, and I sent it to the stone masons with strict instructions
to use the anti-vandal one-way screws which I provided. They
didn't and, predictably, within a year it was removed by a souvenir
hunter. More expense, more time, more hassle leaving me feeling
more ambivalent than ever about the unavoidable responsibilities
of it all. On a brighter note, once the tomb was cleaned, those who
were probably among the more articulate of the graffitists started

to leave little *billets doux* (love notes) on the step at the base of the plinth or on the shelf under the angel's wings. On my occasional visits to the tomb over the next few years I would collect whatever was there at the time and put them into an envelope. I'm not sure why. I think it was because they were a touching testimony to the affection of an anonymous public who wanted to communicate with Oscar. For them he was still alive. A number thanked him for giving them *De Profundis* which had helped them through difficult periods in their lives. These notes had no value, but they were beyond price and I felt posterity should know. The majority, judging from the signatures, were from girls or women and from the language and first names often Italian. My initial surprise rapidly gave way to seeing that it was obvious; in life his humour and his sensitivity had endeared him to many women; there was no reason for it to be any different in death. In addition, his story seemed to touch them at a deep emotional level. Once, I found a note with two cigarettes lying on it: 'Dear Oscar, One for you and one for Robbie. I hear they don't sell cigarettes in heaven. Hope you like it up there. Love, Annie xxx.' Hanging around to pick up soggy bits of paper mostly torn from diaries on the spur of the moment or more rarely written carefully and put in an envelope, meant waiting sometimes for as much as an hour until there was no one to see me and question I was doing. On one occasion I waited until a guided tour of the cemetery had moved on but couldn't resist joining the back of the group to listen to what the guide was saying. His commentary was so full of inaccurate generalisations about both Oscar and tomb that I must, involuntarily, have pulled a face, and as soon as he had finished he came straight up to me and said: 'You're not part of my group. You haven't paid, so I'll thank you not to join us.' If he'd been more a little more inquisitive and less aggressive, I might have admitted who I was and added a few colourful anecdotes for his flock to enjoy.

I can't remember exactly when the kissing started. I think it must have been about 1995 when there were various centenaries and commemorations. Exactly a hundred years since the first night of *The Importance of Being Earnest*, Oscar was admitted to Poets' Corner in Westminster Abbey and, of course, there was much in the Press remembering his trials and imprisonment. Nothing like a perceived injustice to rouse the public's sympathy, so if you're in Paris, go to the tomb and give him a lipstick kiss to make up for all that beastliness a century ago. The biopic with Stephen Fry and Jude Law in 1997 would have given it added impetus and the whole circus in 2000 surrounding the centenary of his death must have put 'kissing Oscar's tomb' firmly on the tourist circuit, like the attaching of 'love padlocks' to the Pont des Arts. For a while it was possible, though increasingly expensive, to remove the kisses as they appeared, but as their number increased exponentially, it became clear that the grease from the lipstick was sinking into the porous stone and mere surface cleaning became largely ineffective.

In April 2005, in a moment of inspiration, I wrote to L'Oréal. Given that their share of the world lipstick market was greater than that of any other cosmetics company, I suggested that until a more durable solution could be found, they might consider helping me clean and maintain the tomb. With profits in billions, a few thousand Euros a year was 'stamp-money' and we could construct an amusing 'feel-good' story for the press and link it to the publicity for the French edition of one of my books on Oscar which was being published in the autumn. After four months I received a polite reply saying that all their sponsorship money was unfortunately reserved for 'eminent women in the field of science worldwide.'[727] Reading between the lines, I felt it was like trying to find a corporate sponsor for what turned out to be the very successful centenary exhibition at the British Library in 2000: an association with Oscar Wilde was still making companies with public profiles uneasy.

I began to despair. My wife, Emma, tried to put it in context by saying that every kiss could have been a fan letter to Oscar which I, as his reluctant posthumous secretary, might have felt obliged to answer. A terrifying thought. At one moment I seriously considered concealing myself near the tomb with a camera, photographing someone in the act of planting a lipstick kiss on it, following them to the exit and having one of the Père Lachaise guards make a sort of citizen's arrest which they were entitled to do. The penalties for defacing a historic monument are severe— up to €15,000—and to make a public example of one person would certainly have discouraged others, but I abandoned the idea almost as soon as I thought of it. Although I would have been protecting what is a privately owned, listed edifice against acts of vandalism, I would have been monstered on social media and the side of me which was grateful and sympathetic to Oscar's public said firmly 'Don't.' Nevertheless, something had to be done to prevent further damage to the tomb.

Martine Lecuyer, the director of Père Lachaise, proved to be a great ally. Despite having 44 hectares of cemetery and nearly 70,000 graves under her care, she promised, unofficially, to keep an eye on Oscar and was as good as her word. Although the upkeep of graves is the responsibility of individual families, the public, all three million a year, expect to find the cemetery tidy and well-kept. The patrolling guards were instructed to pass by his tomb more often and the faded flowers and older tributes were regularly removed. It was a small personal favour by a French *fonctionnaire* which also made good PR for Père Lachaise. I was particularly touched, having told her about picking up the *billets doux* which people left, that she presented me on several occasions with an envelope full of them which she had collected personally. Martine also suggested talking to Guénola Groud, the head conservation officer and historian responsible for all the Paris cemeteries. As it turned out Guénola's contacts with the Monuments Historiques were invaluable and within a month she had organised a site visit to the tomb together with her opposite number in the Ministry of Culture, Caroline Piel. We were all agreed that urgent specialist cleaning and the application of a 'sacrificial coating' to make the removal of graffiti and kisses easier was essential and that once complete some sort of barrier should be installed, but it still didn't solve the problem of finding the money to pay for it all. Even as we were discussing it, a young woman shamelessly took out her lipstick and started to apply it to her mouth in quantity. We stopped talking and watched her pointedly. She must have realised we were not merely tourists like herself and thought better of it. I stood there and felt a mixture of frustration and anger at other people's selfishness for not realising that they were slowly destroying what they had actually come to honour. Shortly after that I met Sheila Pratschke.

Sheila had recently been appointed director of the Irish College, Ireland's cultural centre in Paris, and on our first meeting she admitted that she had never been to see Oscar's tomb. I offered to take her to Père Lachaise on my next visit but warned her that it was in a shocking state. In the event it didn't happen until another commemorative date, 20 July 2009, the centenary of moving Oscar's remains from Bagneux to their final resting place. The Irish Ambassador to France, Anne Anderson, had issued an open invitation to the Embassy before her departure for the United Nations in the summer so I suggested 20 July, explaining that Emma and I were planning to pay our respects to Oscar on the centenary of his last move. Anne, who had never seen Oscar's tomb either and whose tour of duty finished that very day, asked whether she might come too, on condition she wouldn't be intruding on a very private family affair. 'Oscar Wilde has given me such pleasure over the years and it seems so fitting for my very last function (though to call it that is too formal) in Paris.'[728] It seemed particularly appropriate to include her, since it was with Ireland's help that the tomb had been classified. Martine Lecuyer arranged for us to have access to the cemetery half an hour before public opening time and a small party of us, including Sheila and Guénola, laid flowers to mark the occasion and repaired to the Embassy for breakfast hosted by Anne. Naturally, there was much discussion about what could be done to protect Oscar from his fans and I was encouraged to apply to the Ireland Fund for France, a charitable organisation which sponsored projects of Irish interest. By this time, I had quotes for the cleaning and protection which totalled more than €50,000, a sum which the Fund certainly would not grant in its entirety, but even a small amount from them, to show that the project had some official support, would make it easier to obtain further funding. News on the Irish grapevine in Paris travels fast. By November, even before I had filled in the application form for 2010, I was told unofficially that the Ireland Fund board had been informed, that they had 'nodded agreement' and mention was being made on the Fund's website that a grant towards the tomb's restoration was going ahead. By the end of February it was official but in order to take advantage of it I had to find the rest of the money by the end of the year. At that point Sheila Pratschke took over.

Before being appointed to the Irish College, Sheila had been director of various cultural institutions in Ireland, notably the Irish Film Institute and the Tyrone Guthrie Centre and was well connected in the worlds of politics and the arts in Ireland. One of her contacts was Martin Mansergh, a Junior Finance Minister with responsibility for the Office of Public Works in Dublin. The OPW not only looked after Irish heritage sites but also properties abroad, notably the Embassies and, of course, the Irish College. It was definitely a long shot, Sheila said, but it was worth writing to ask if the OPW would consider helping, given Oscar's status as an Irish author and his PR value to Ireland. *The Picture of Dorian Gray* was, for example, the chosen work for Dublin's 'One City, One Book' festival for 2010. The reply was encouraging: a group of senior OPW officials, including John McMahon the Heritage Commissioner, would be visiting France in July and time permitting, would take a look at the grave. I'm sure that the small grant from the Ireland Fund helped matters and by September the OPW had provisionally allocated €60,000 to the project conditional on competitive quotes being received and all relevant permissions from the Monuments Historiques and the cemetery administration being in place by the end of the year.[729] Sheila's initiative couldn't have been taken at a better time as the OPW had a small surplus in its budget due to other delayed projects. I spent the next three months chasing quotations, asking favours and filling in forms; rules were bent and strings were pulled, the most remarkable of which was Guénola Groud persuading the Monuments Historiques that it was hugely in their interests to approve the project as I wouldn't be applying to them for a grant. Caroline Piel agreed and managed to pass the dossier within four days of its reception instead of the usual six months—nothing short of a miracle for anyone familiar with French bureaucracy. The last hurdle was having to convince the Architecte des Bâtiments de France that protective glass panels, only chest-high at 140cm, were worse than useless; even if Oscar's 'adoring public' could no longer kiss him, they would simply lean over and scribble messages on the stone. Practical considerations had to take precedence over aesthetics and a height of 190cm was agreed, being a little above the upwardly bent elbow of the average visitor.

For the first six months of 2011, given the Irish economic crisis and the drastic budget cuts, I was expecting the OPW's letter saying that 'Unfortunately . . . ' But I needn't have worried; Ireland's belief in the importance of fostering its culture across borders won out and Brian Hayes, the Minister who had replaced Martin Mansergh in the new government and was on a visit to Paris for rather more important affairs of state, took time out to confirm the commitment publicly at the graveside. Sheila, who was there, later recounted that three or four women 'lipstick-kissed' the tomb and then photographed the result which can only have confirmed to the Minister that the Irish decision to help was entirely the right one. On the same occasion she witnessed the following exchange between an American tourist and his teenage daughter:

Daughter: What did Oscar Wilde do Daddy?
 Father: (*after a short pause*) He was an artist.
Daughter: What did he paint?
 Father: (*after another short pause*) *A Portrait of the Artist as a Young Man.*

The Picture of Dorian Gray might have been marginally more correct.

By the autumn of 2011, after more jumping through administrative hoops and the nightmare of co-ordinating everything to be ready merely days before 30 November, the anniversary of Oscar's death, we were ready to 'unveil' the newly cleaned and protected tomb. Bertrand Delanoë, Mayor of Paris, together with Christophe Girard his deputy for cultural affairs, had been invited; I don't recall that they even bothered to reply to the invitation. Fréderic Mitterand, nephew of the former president and at the time Minister of Culture, called off at the last minute and sent a relatively junior civil servant to represent him. It was a potentially embarrassing situation since the Irish were sending over their own Minister for the Arts, Heritage, and the Gaeltacht, Dinny McGinley, to celebrate the event. My wife, in a moment of inspiration, suggested inviting Rupert Everett to speak who, although without political status, would be an excellent cultural counterpart to Minister McGinley. I didn't know him but by roundabout means finally got in touch and Rupert accepted with enthusiasm, even managing to delay a filming commitment elsewhere to take part. It turned out to be a bizarre start to our friendship. When we met in Paris the first thing he asked me was if his aunt, as it had always been said in his family, had had an affair with my father. When? What was her name? Aunt Peta. It was one of those rare moments we sometime experience when a missing piece of history drops into place; a link, previously unnoticed, brings a memory to life, gives a story a whole new dimension; the circuit suddenly seems complete . . . Peta Everett, with her blonde, bouffant hair, press officer for Lenthéric when Thelma was working for one of their cosmetic companies, who went to comfort my mother when Vyvyan was dying and paid for that taxi, so I could go and say goodbye to him in hospital. No, no affair, Rupert. Just a flashback, still astonishingly clear, to a night so long before. I'm sure I never did get to thank her personally, but to be able to thank her nephew forty-four years later was strangely emotional, and rather satisfying.

The event itself, thanks to the Embassy publicity machine (and undoubtedly to the presence of Rupert who made an elegant bilingual speech), was reported by TV, Radio, and printed media from round the world. There were at least six camera crews in evidence and a dozen journalists and press agencies. In France it figured on the national morning news programme Télématin; in the UK it made the Today Programme, the World Service, and the BBC Six O'Clock News. It was covered by all the major French, Irish, and UK newspapers, and AFP and Reuters made sure that people everywhere from Los Angeles to Sydney read about it. French politicians love publicity and contemplating Oscar's media revenge for the stand-offish behaviour of some of them was one of the more satisfying results of that day.

Naturally, the kissers were angry at what they regarded as a stuffy decision to deny them their 'right' to this exhibitionist form of self-expression and lost no time in using the internet to say so. The *New York Times* ran an article quoting an 'architectural historian' who blogged that the kisses 'enhanced the impact of Epstein's bold, modern memorial,' and continued that if it had been her ancestor's grave 'I think I'd be chuffed, actually.'[730] Not very helpful, but I suppose the *Times* was trying to be even-handed in its reporting. Overall, the 'Hands off our Oscar!' lobby was largely outnumbered by those who saw the cleaning and protection as positive.

Early next spring I went to Paris to see if the glass had been effective and I was pleasantly surprised to discover that the front panel was serving a purpose which no one had thought of. Visiting fans who now kissed the glass would see their kisses projected onto the stone as shadows by the morning sun—same effect, no damage, transitory and, in a way, rather romantic. A provincial journalist, Valérie Parlan, writing for *Ouest-France* who rang me for a quote had noticed it too. She had been to Père Lachaise and was nearly at the grave when two young women came running up and asked her where they could find 'the tomb of the artist all covered in lipstick kisses.'[731] Not Oscar Wilde's tomb, you note. When it was pointed out, they were crestfallen to find that the stone itself was now inaccessible but accepted the compromise when Valérie showed them the effect of the sunlight if they kissed the glass. Unfortunately, not all visitors have been so reasonable and simply paying one's respects to the man is not enough; exercising what they see as their 'right' to kiss the stonework, to challenge unreasonable authority, is more important. The adjacent grave provides a convenient platform from which to lean over the top of the glass and access Oscar's tomb itself and in August 2012, barely nine months after the restoration, one kisser, obviously determined to kiss higher than any before, must have tried to mount its massive granite cross and toppled it. Collateral damage from trying to protect Oscar's tomb was not something I had reckoned with. Shortly after, the cemetery office printed a bilingual 'Please desist' notice and taped it to the glass in a plastic bag. Like the bronze plate before, several replacements proved irresistible to souvenir hunters. This time I was quite relieved as part of the text read like a family whinge, but re-reading the quaint English it could only have been written by a French *fonctionnaire* with a rudimentary knowledge of the language: 'Please, respect for this memorial. Out of respect for this grave, please do not sully by any mark. The cleaning fees are exclusively paid by the family. Thanks for your visit. *La Direction du Cimetière.*' So, I had it printed in a more permanent form and attached it firmly to the inside of the glass. Even so there are traces of a visitor trying unsuccessfully to scrape it off.

Cleaning the glass panels, though easier and less damaging for the tomb, soon became an unwelcome financial burden since it had to be done monthly due to the accumulation of lipstick kisses and inscriptions. However, a solution to the problem came in a totally unexpected form. In 2009 I had been introduced to Ömer Koç a Turkish businessman, who for some time had been building up an Oscar Wilde collection. Ömer, a man of rare culture and discernment, had asked for my help in putting together an Oscar Wilde exhibition, initially in Turkey but when that had proved impracticable, we settled on Paris instead.[732] Such an exhibition involves lengthy preparations and during the course of them I discovered that Oscar was just one of his collecting passions and among the others were 20th century self-portraits, Iznik ceramics, and a remarkable library of Western European books on Constantinople dating back to 1493. My years spent in Beirut and regular visits from there to Istanbul had given me enough knowledge of Turkish culture to appreciate the importance of this library and when Ömer invited me to the launch of its catalogue in London in May 2014, of course I went. A month later, I was sorting through an old suitcase of books left in the attic by the previous owner of our house and was astonished to find a four volume set of *L'Histoire des Turcs* (1697) in its contemporary seventeenth century binding. Why they had belonged to my predecessor, a basic Burgundian *vigneron,* was difficult to imagine. I wrote and offered the four volumes to Ömer saying that I was sure he must have them, but even if he did, he might like to find a suitable home for them in Turkey. He replied that he had the first edition of 1689, but not this one and asked me how much I wanted for it. I said that I hadn't been intending to sell it, but if he wanted to give me a small contribution towards cleaning the tomb, it would be very welcome. It was then, spontaneously, that he offered me help with its maintenance for the foreseeable future: 'It is the least I can do for Oscar Wilde,' he wrote.[733] Later he told me of the little-known generosity of the Sultan Abdulmejid who sent three shiploads of grain to the Irish at the height of the Great Famine in 1847, when Anglo-Irish landlords, indifferent to the sufferings of the Irish peasantry, were shipping more corn than ever over the Irish Sea.[734] 'Clearly,' I said half-jokingly, 'the Turks have a soft spot for the Irish.' 'Yes,' replied Ömer, 'in my case sympathy with the Irish does run deep. After all, I can't forget that, as a boy, I was looked after by an Irish woman from Tipperary.'

More recently an over-simplified article about the history of repairing and protecting Oscar's tomb appeared in the *Irish Times* on 28 December 2019 as a result of Irish State Papers being released under the 30-year rule. Essentially it was based on that letter which I had written to Geoffrey Keating at the Department of Foreign Affairs in Dublin back in 1989 and from which, for some inexplicable reason, my name had been 'redacted.' It compressed thirty-odd years of nightmare dealings with the tomb into a few hundred words and as I went back to the files to remind myself of the facts, I realised that there had been moments during that time when it felt as though previous generations had drunk all the wine and I was just left with the hangover. But it would be churlish to complain. Although I must admit that being related to Oscar is occasionally a source of exasperation, even from beyond the grave he arouses feelings of affection and sympathy in his admirers of whom, inevitably I am one. Link that to a strong sense of family obligation to protect him from the misplaced but well-meaning attentions of his fans visiting Père Lachaise and duty shifts subtly into something akin to pleasure. Above all, however, this duty-pleasure has brought me into contact with people and professionals who have been hugely generous with their time and their knowledge and some of whom, thanks to Oscar, have become friends.

From the time I was old enough to take an interest in my family background, which was when I was about fifteen, until my father's death seven years later, I don't recall him ever mentioning his mother to me once. Looking back through the diary he kept almost daily for twenty-six years, he occasionally writes about his brother, remembering him on the anniversary of his death in 1915, and more frequently about Oscar, but hardly anything about Constance at all. I always found this strange given that it was his mother who provided the stability after the family débâcle of 1895 and on whose affection he was so dependent for the next three years until her death. The fact that she was torn so suddenly and so brutally out of his life after an unnecessary operation by an incompetent surgeon, that he couldn't attend her funeral and, from what one can gather, had little opportunity to grieve for her properly, may in part account for it. I can't be certain, but I don't believe Vyvyan ever visited her grave in Genoa's Staglieno Cemetery. Its location was all but unknown to people interested in Oscar back then, not least because the inscription on it was in her maiden name 'Constance Mary Lloyd.' But all that changed in 1963 when Constance's great niece, Dinah, who was married to an Italian and living in Rome, decided to have the words 'Wife of Oscar Wilde' added on the headstone. It was the most extraordinary liberty to take; I would never dream of having something done to a tomb which didn't belong to an immediate relative when the descendants were still alive, especially since she presented it to my father as a *fait accompli*, but Oscar's reputation was on the rise once more and claiming kinship with him, even by marriage, doubtless had its social advantages. Vyvyan was quite touched and even offered to pay for it, but Dinah wouldn't hear of it and I only found out about it twenty years later.

It was on a terrible February morning in 1983, the temperature a few degrees above zero and in driving sleet, that my first wife Sarah, Lucian, and I visited Constance's grave. A few weeks before I had asked the British Consul in Genoa, Michael Wicks, if he could give me directions for finding it since Staglieno is one of the largest cemeteries in Europe and I had never been to her grave before. No problem: she was buried in the Protestant section not far from the main entrance and since she now figured in the cemetery guidebook, any of the guards would know. We found it easily enough but were dismayed by the state of it. The marble cross was coated in years of accumulated city grime; one of the small conical pillars marking the perimeter had fallen over; and the grave itself was overgrown with ivy and a young rogue palm tree had implanted itself close by, threatening to lift the headstone. I managed to persuade the main cemetery office to lend me a bucket of soapy water and a sponge and we 'gave granny a scrub' as Lucian put it. It was as we were clearing away the weeds and the ivy, that we came across a tiny scent bottle with a visiting card rolled up inside on which was written: 'Whoever takes care of this tomb, please contact me. Thanks.' We finished our rudimentary maintenance and went to warm up in a restaurant where I found a public phone and called the number on the card. It had been put there by a teacher of English in Genoa called Nevia Cisotto who, it turned out, had known all about Constance's exile from England and her untimely death for years past. She used to relate the story to her students as an unexpected 'extra' when teaching them about Oscar Wilde and would encourage them to take flowers to the tomb on the anniversaries of Constance's birth and death. I still have the card, a terrestrial 'message in a bottle' which, as Nevia said, seemed to have been guided by the spirit of Constance into exactly the right hands. Unlike another visiting card left at a club eighty-eight years before and which changed the course of our family history, this one opened the door to a friendship rather than to the Old Bailey.

When I returned to London, I wrote to Michael Wicks to report on my visit and asked if he could put me in touch with someone who could do a little basic maintenance on the grave. I also floated the idea that since Constance was starting to be mentioned as one of Staglieno's notable foreign residents, maybe the Genoa municipality might like to get involved. First, however, the grave needed some basic restoration to halt any further damage and since my work occasionally took me to Italy, I planned to take a couple of days off in Genoa to meet stonemasons and make sure that the job was done properly. In the meantime, Nevia had given an interview to *Il Lavoro* to try and raise awareness among the Genovese about Constance's tragic fate and the state of the grave.[735] I felt it could do no harm, particularly if it caught the attention of an organisation or individuals who might be prepared to help whether financially or merely by keeping an eye on the grave for me. It did indeed have an outcome but not at all of the sort I had expected.

On 25 October 1985 there was a short article in the *Evening Standard* reporting that 'at a brief ceremony today . . . attended by the British Consul-General [Constance's] tomb will be re-dedicated after restoration at the expense of the Italo-Britannic Association.'[736] The fact that a local association (the Associazione Italo-Britannica) had decided to clean up the tomb, without any reference to the family and for its own glorification, was bad enough, but that the British Consul with whom I had been corresponding two years before, was clearly a party to it was intolerable. He was perfectly well aware of my existence, so I considered it outrageous behaviour on the part of an English government official to have colluded with the AIB—maybe even tipped them off that it needed doing—and not to have informed me. Apart from anything else it looked as though the family couldn't have cared less about poor Constance. I rang Nevia who had been as surprised as I was to read of it in the local press and all the more so since she had friends among the English expatriate community who knew of her interest in Constance's grave. She promised to look into it and discovered that it was a joint effort by the AIB and the local historical society A Compagna. Together they had been discussing the possibility of cleaning and repairs ever since Nevia's newspaper interview the year before and the total cost was less than £100.[737] Clearly if they had contacted me as Constance's descendant, I would have paid for it myself which, of course, would have defeated the purpose of the AIB's cheap publicity stunt. When I next visited the grave, the cosmetic nature of the repairs was obvious—a couple of buckets of cement to hold the pillars in place, a wash-down of the marble cross and headstone and some gravel on the surface of the grave to keep the weeds down. The invitation to the ceremony which Nevia later procured and sent me couldn't even get Constance's name right:

> The President of the Associazione Italo-Britannica, Mr. Astor W. Norrish, and the President of A Compagna, Dr. Enrico Carbone, in the presence of the British Consul Mr. Michael A. Wicks, together with representatives of the two Associations, will pay homage at the tomb of Oscar Wilde's wife, Elizabeth, recently restored by the combined efforts of the two Associations.

Apart from all his other sins, Oscar was now guilty of bigamy as well.

I wrote to Astor Norrish explaining that I was somewhat hurt to learn second-hand from a newspaper that my own grandmother's grave had been restored by the AIB when the British Consul, who had so obviously been party to the whole business, had been in correspondence with me about it two years before. I should have liked, at least, to have been able to send a message of thanks to be read out at the graveside However, I held out an olive branch by saying that my family joined me in expressing our gratitude for the generous gesture 'which is none the less warmly felt for coming after the event,' and hoped that I would have the opportunity to meet him on a future visit to Genoa. I copied it to the Consul but neither of them ever had the courtesy to reply and when later I saw the shoddy nature of the 'restoration,' I regretted writing such a conciliatory letter.

Twelve years later the grave was in as bad a state as ever, but in the meantime my 'eyes and ears' in Genoa, Nevia, had died or I should have enlisted her help to oversee the proper, long-term repairs which it needed in time to commemorate the centenary of Constance's death. Fortunately, an English expatriate journalist, Tracey Gambarotta, who was campaigning for the recently founded Associazione 'Per Staglieno' (the Friends of Staglieno) had been in touch just at that time and very generously gave her time to help. She arranged for a site visit with a monumental mason; I went to Genoa with a bag full of stainless steel rods to fix the pillars; a price was agreed on for restoring the grave to its original state (incidentally, six times what the AIB had spent); and it was all completed in time for the centenary of her death on 7 April 1998. It was a revelation. The marble surrounds of the plot which had sunk over the years were newly visible and made an elegant white frame for the grave. It looked, except that now his name was linked to hers, as it must have done when Oscar went to put flowers on it a year after her death and wrote to his friend Robert Ross: 'I was deeply affected with a sense of the uselessness of all regrets. Nothing could have been otherwise and Life is a very terrible thing.'[738] The commemoration ceremony was largely orchestrated by Tracey and Eugenio Bolleri from Per Staglieno whose involvement both in that and the renovation was more than just welcome, it was indispensable. It was also an opportunity to clear the air with the President of A Compagna and the British Consul, both of whom were invited to attend.

Sprucing up Constance's resting place has certainly made more people aware of her existence and the important role which Oscar acknowledged that she played in his life. I have paid my respects to her on a couple of occasions since and was surprised to see how well-tended the grave was looking. I'm sure that visitors, now knowing more about her, make sure that it remains so and people who have been to see her say there always seem to be fresh flowers—just as Nevia would have wished when she left that tiny scent bottle.

CHAPTER FIVE
POETS' CORNER

In March 1990 I received a card from Donald Sinden. He had been contacted by Commander Pat Paterson, a London Blue Badge Guide, who was frequently asked by tourists whom he took round Westminster Abbey, why Oscar Wilde had not been commemorated in Poets' Corner. Paterson had written to the Dean of Westminster, Michael Mayne, asking how best to answer such queries and received the reply that the Abbey was so full of memorials that only one or two could be considered each year, that there was already a waiting list of thirty and that, as far as he knew, only one person had ever written proposing Oscar Wilde—a widow who had been moved by hearing a play about him on Radio 4. He added that his predecessor, Edward Carpenter, 'did not believe it was right to follow up that request.' However, he also outlined what happened when someone was proposed and how letters of support from distinguished names in the relevant field were needed for the Dean and Chapter of the Abbey to consider the candidate's suitability.[739] This prompted Pat Paterson to write to Donald Sinden, who at the time was appearing in an eminently forgettable one-man show, *Diversions and Delights,* about Oscar's last days in Paris: 'If it is only a question of asking, then let's ask. But who should do the asking?' he wrote.[740]

It was around that time that I was first contacted by an art history graduate from the University of London, Joanna Crook, who as a student had been fascinated by Oscar Wilde and was involved in setting up an undergraduate society in his name. She had decided to take the Society public and was very encouraged by the response. In this first incarnation the Society's aims were to host a few jolly evenings with wine and canapés, readings from

Oscar's works and the occasional talk, as well as the odd out-
ing to a place associated with him—Oxford for example. There
was even a fancy-dress Birthday Ball planned but never held. In
short, it didn't have the established pedigree or the gravitas of the
Brontë Society, or the Dickens Fellowship. I don't know whether
Paterson contacted them or whether the Society had been talking
to Donald Sinden as a result of his show, but by the end of the
year the newly fledged Oscar Wilde Society was writing excitedly
about plans to set up an Oscar Wilde Memorial Fund Committee
and inviting me to join it.

If there is one thing I have learned about people wanting to 'do
something for Oscar,' it is that half of them wouldn't be doing it
if they had to remain anonymous about it like the admirable and
generous Helen Carew who gave the money for Jacob Epstein to
create Oscar's tomb. The Public Relations value to their organization or society is all too frequently uppermost in the mind of the
proposers. When pressed, Joanna Crook was suitably vague about
the details. No, they hadn't decided on the type of monument; it
was being done in conjunction with the London Monday Group
for Homosexual Equality; and the Oscar Wilde Society was going
to administer the project. I wrote to her in January 1991 to emphasise the difficulties (to say nothing of the cost) of putting memorials in public places and no less of maintaining them. She clearly
digested my words of caution because her next letter announced
the fact that she had already been in touch with Westminster
Abbey and the Society was forging ahead with the project, was
gathering together the necessary 'distinguished names' and would
be forwarding them to the Dean. Having Oscar in Poets' Corner
would at least overcome the problem of maintenance. This was
not at all what I had expected. Feeling that Oscar was being taken
over partly for publicity purposes, even if he had become a sort
of public property by that time, was uncomfortable, however
well-intentioned the Society's stated motives might have been.
However, unknown to me, another project had been simmering
quietly in the background.

Apart from contacting Donald Sinden, Pat Paterson had also got in touch with Ronald Mason, the former Head of BBC Radio Drama, who in turn had informed his successor, John Tydeman of the move to have Oscar 'memorialised.' A more influential team one couldn't have wanted, especially as Ronald Mason had known the Dean personally from their BBC days together when Michael Mayne was Head of Religious Programming. When I replied to Donald Sinden, I had made it clear from the start that I would give the project every possible support from behind the scenes, but I felt it might be counter-productive if a family member were seen to be lobbying openly; it would have been perfect gossip column fodder. Ronald must have taken me too literally for he now wrote to apologise for not informing me of the progress he had made.[741] In November 1990, having talked unofficially to Michael Mayne, he had written to a galaxy of names whom he knew personally in the theatrical and literary worlds and already had an impressive file of enthusiastic letters in reply to send to the Abbey. The whole affair was being coordinated at this stage from John Tydeman's office at the BBC.

I was a little surprised that the Dean hadn't mentioned this other initiative in his reply to Joanna Crook's enquiry about the procedures to be followed, though at that point discretion probably dictated in the matter. It left me with the unenviable task of going to the next Oscar Wilde Society Memorial meeting and telling them that Ronald Mason's proposal had a far better chance of success than their own. It wasn't welcome news and there was even a proposal by one member (quickly squashed by others) to fund a separate memorial since the Abbey had made it clear that there was a waiting list with several suitable candidates on it and, whatever the outcome, Oscar probably wouldn't be admitted to the Abbey for a few years anyway.

The whole affair was further complicated by the fact that Poets' Corner had been officially declared full and even if one more floor stone could be squeezed in (it was) Anthony Trollope had a prior claim to entry and was being championed by John Major, the

Prime Minister. The story was a gift for the newspapers at the start of the 'silly season' and duly appeared in *The Times* 'Diary.'[742]

Ever since the publication of Richard Ellmann's biography four years before I had made a point of not telling my mother about such things until they were more or less *faits accomplis*. The brief period of indignation about having been kept in the dark and not involved from the start was easier to handle than months of her tiresome and often uninformed interference. Unfortunately, Thelma had her 'spies' as she called them. These were meddlesome friends who were aware of the tensions which Oscar caused in the family and who took a perverse delight in stirring up trouble by sending her cuttings about him from those newspapers which she didn't read. So, I decided to pre-empt the inevitable and tell Thelma as soon as the 'Diary' piece appeared. Within two days I had a three-page letter instructing me exactly how to deal with the Dean of Westminster, to make an appointment to see him and take along a copy of *De Profundis* as a present and to give him a sort of crash course in the moral value of most of Wilde's writings. 'Please get to see him or if you don't I will,' she finished off the letter.[743] This was clearly going to become another of Thelma's crusades and I had to stop it before it started. I rang the Dean and explained as tactfully as I could that Thelma considered she had single-handedly done more to rehabilitate Oscar (for which read 'clean up') than almost anyone in the past forty years and that he might be hearing from her. Michael Mayne thanked me for the warning and reassured me that he had had to handle similar situations in the past and not to worry. I also wrote a fairly sharp letter to my mother telling her to back off:

> You will ruin everything. It is being handled by the ex-head of BBC Drama with the backing of people like Judi Dench and Alec Guinness. I have kept completely distant from it [*a small but necessary white lie*] as you should. They are perfectly capable of doing it themselves and family poking its collective nose in will seem as tiresome rather than helpful.[744]

And with that I had nearly three years' respite.

The problem of an overflowing Poets' Corner was solved in the meantime by climbing the walls—or more precisely using the windows—of the South transept. The architectural historian, Edward Hubbard, who collaborated with Nikolaus Pevsner on his monumental *The Buildings of England,* had died tragically young at 52 and his father offered a memorial window to the Abbey specifically to accommodate this overflow. It was dedicated along with its first two poets, Robert Herrick and Alexander Pope on 7 June 1994, and six weeks later the Dean announced that Oscar Wilde would be the next to be honoured.

Earlier in the year, conscious that he was a fairly long way down the list of candidates, an excellent and totally legitimate excuse occurred to me to help him jump the queue. I told Michael Mayne that 14 February 1995 would be the exact centenary of the first night of *The Importance of Being Earnest,* and it seemed a pity not to take advantage of it. A quick check on the day of the week and it was all agreed. Evensong would be celebrated at 5pm and the memorial pane dedicated immediately afterwards. I duly informed my mother and over the next six months the 'good advice' and interfering built up to a crescendo until the week before the dedication when the phone calls came almost daily. Even if my letter of three years before had temporarily discouraged Thelma from doing her seasoned-defender-of-Oscar's-reputation act with me and playing the Oscar Wilde's daughter-in-law role with others, that letter was clearly past its sell-by date and she was now determined that this public recognition of Oscar shouldn't pass without her orchestrating some of it. I started to keep a notebook with some of the more jaw-dropping exchanges I had with her as they were made:

'What day of the week is it being held on?'
'A Tuesday.'
'It's Valentine's Day. People will draw the wrong conclusions.'
'They won't; the emphasis is on the centenary of *The Importance.*'

'Was Trollope done at the same time of day?'
'Yes.'
'Why can't it be done at midday?'
'Because they want to tie it in with evensong.'

And it turned out that she thought my then wife, Sarah, and I had engineered it especially so that Lucian, aged fifteen, could be there after school which, needless to say, she disapproved of. 'I definitely think that Lucian shouldn't go to the Abbey for the unveiling. The press will start to take an interest in him.' Thinking back to my own adolescence and the family injunctions to keep my head down and feeling slightly perplexed about it all in the early 1960s, I was equally determined that he should be there. I also wondered whether Thelma somehow felt her own importance would be diluted by having not one but two direct descendants at the dedication, borne out by a letter she wrote to the Dean without telling me, suggesting that she 'say a few words' at the ceremony. He and I agreed the best solution was that she should lay a bouquet of flowers and leave the talking to the professionals: Judi Dench, Michael Denison, John Gielgud, and Seamus Heaney. The Dean's reply, emphasising the traditional format of Poets' Corner dedications and offering Thelma 'a non-speaking part, which will nevertheless be an important one,' was a model of non-negotiable diplomacy.[745]

By early December the Dean and I had decided on the 'speaking parts.' He was a good personal friend of Judi Dench and since we were hanging the ceremony on *The Importance,* it was obvious we had to have 'The Handbag Scene' with her as Lady Bracknell. I had been friendly with Michael Denison for years and his connection with the play was almost continuous since Anthony Asquith's 1952 film version. At nearly eighty, but still sprightly, I knew that he could carry off Jack Worthing. He didn't hesitate. I suggested that to counterbalance the comedy I should edit an appropriately poignant piece from *De Profundis* which pleased the Dean as he wanted to involve John Gielgud. All that was lacking was someone to give a short oration, an appreciation of Oscar the man. Ronnie Mason suggested Seamus Heaney, friend and fellow Irishman, who said he'd be delighted. Seamus generously sent me a cheque for the window fund writing apologetically that he wished it could have been more but that he was having to pay his airfare from Dublin. I was mortified to think that the Abbey had invited him without offering to pay his travel and told him I would reimburse him. He sent me a very gracious letter of thanks refusing.[746]

We couldn't have had a better cast and news of who would be participating must have spread rapidly with the Abbey fielding enquiries daily and forcing the Dean to ticket the 250 seated places in the South transept. I phoned Thelma to tell her so she could reserve some for friends which prompted the remark: 'Good. It'll keep out the riff-raff.' 'What do you mean?' I asked. 'Well, all the queers and pansies and people who want to use him for publicity.' I wish I could say I was merely quoting from memory and that I might be exaggerating, but I'm not. It's all there in my notebook, written down as soon as I hung up. And on that particular day she went on:

'Ask the Dean if we can have the full peal of bells when it's all over.'

'It's not a wedding. It's inappropriate,' I said.

'I hope you're not inviting the Douglas family. I can see the headlines "Wilde and Douglas families make up".'

'Well, Vyvyan was friendly with Francis Queensberry . . . '

'Yes, but he's dead now and the rest of them are all a bit funny.'[747]

It was around that time, too, that she told me who she did and didn't want contributing to the cost of the memorial window and the Queensberrys were definitely on her blacklist. I'm happy to say that I ignored every single one of her vetoes.

Before Michael Mayne announced his decision to include Oscar in Poets' Corner, he rang me to say that if there were descendants of the person being 'memorialised,' the Abbey needed to be sure that they would pay all the charges involved. The cost of the window itself would be about £1,500 and there would inevitably be a few extras as well. I suppose I should have anticipated it, but I was still caught unawares. Of course, I said 'Yes' at once, perfectly well aware that I didn't have the money but that I still had time to find it. A couple of months before the dedication, it occurred to me that I could write to fifty people who, as I put it: 'have long admired Oscar, written about him, played his plays, published his works or simply fought his corner against prejudice and sensationalism, to show a small token of their appreciation.' I suggested anything between £5 and £30 knowing that I could cover any shortfall. There wasn't one; I had the money within two weeks and felt quite overwhelmed by the response and the generosity. There was even a surplus, which I later proposed putting towards a memorial for Oscar's fiery Irish Nationalist mother whom he adored and who was buried in an unmarked grave in Kensal Green when her son was in prison.

Thelma's final salvo came in the middle of December advising us what clothes to wear on the day. 'If you are advising Sarah to wear bright Irish green, forget it. She would be judged for her lack of taste and elegance. Wilde and his family were Protestants as you know, and the Roman Catholics would lap it up, particularly as the ceremony is in the Anglican Church.' And definitely no green tie for me.[748] I would have loved to put my mother in her place by reminding her of Oscar's strong Nationalist sympathies, but by this time I was beyond caring so I refrained from comment. Thelma was still the custodian of family papers and Vyvyan's diaries and if she felt that my straightforward view and acceptance of Oscar's faults and all was going to undermine what she referred to in the same letter as her re-creation of the Wilde family, who knows what archival bonfire might have ensued.

Several weeks before the event, I thought we could not simply disperse after the dedication without raising a glass to the man being celebrated whose spirit would probably be feeling somewhat uneasy about being taken to the bosom of the Establishment in this way and in need of reassurance. The Dean offered space in the Jerusalem Chamber at the Abbey, but it could only accommodate sixty and I was certain we would have to cater for double that number. I approached the Café Royal, who for years had been using Oscar's frequenting of the place in the 1890s for publicity, thinking that they would be delighted to host such a reception. There would be plenty of big names as well as good press coverage the following day. Nothing doing. We could have the exclusive use of one of their bars from 6:30 until 8 but must pay for the drinks. Champagne being *de rigeur* for the newly honoured Oscar, that would have been prohibitively expensive. If I could find a champagne house to sponsor it, could the Café Royal stretch to a few canapés? Yes, the canapé menus start at £10 a head; a list is attached. Corkage charge to be discussed if you provide your own beverage. I wasn't getting very far. I was writing a regular wine column for *The Oldie* at the time and had some good contacts in the trade, so I suggested the idea to Perrier-Jouët whose champagne is mentioned by name in *The Importance*. It would only be four cases. No thanks; all our sponsorship is tied up for 1995. Already? In January? In the end I found a small champagne house, de Venoge, which was prepared to sell me the bottles at cost.

I think Michael Mayne was slightly put out that the reception couldn't take place at the Abbey and intimated that my inviting the 'performers' to the Café Royal would complicate matters as he had invited them to drinks and an early dinner at the Deanery. We compromised. I could have them for a drink and he for his dinner if I promised to get them back to the Abbey on time. It was good we had the exchange as it reminded me we'd be travelling in the middle of London's rush hour. I had to lay on two coaches from the Abbey for all the reception guests, which I would never have thought of otherwise. In death, as in life, Oscar continued to remind me that style and effect were far more important to him than vulgar considerations of cost.

The event itself drew the biggest crowd since Byron had been commemorated in 1969. Nearly 900 people attended. The 750 service sheets which I had specially printed were all given out as well as another 150 photocopies done at the last minute by the Abbey when they saw the numbers arriving for evensong. At his request I met Michael Denison before the start and we walked round the cloister together. He was slightly concerned about the exchange between Jack and Lady Bracknell when she asks him about his age and was wondering whether we shouldn't cut it:

'At my age, maintaining that I'm twenty-nine, would be carrying the suspension of disbelief beyond reasonable limits, don't you think?'

'Well, the scene is so well-known, people would probably notice the cut. Couldn't you turn it into some sort of joke?'

'What—brief look at the audience and raise my eyes with a sort of "If only!" expression?'

'Exactly!'

He warned Judi and, old pro that he was, pulled it off with perfect timing. It must have been the first time in the play's history that the line, subtly endowed with a mere look, raised a good laugh. John Gielgud's reading from *De Profundis* was particularly touching for those who remembered that he had been prosecuted in 1953 under the same law that had sent Oscar to prison. Seamus Heaney's address was prose but raised to the height of great poetry. The citation for his Nobel Prize later that year for 'works of lyrical beauty and ethical depth, which exalt everyday miracles and the living past' describes it perfectly. I am still moved every time I read his near-perfect summary of Oscar, the homage paid by one poet to another, read to a spell-bound audience of nearly a thousand people that February evening in Westminster Abbey:

His heady paradoxes, his over-the-topness at knocking the bottom out of things, the rightness of his wrong footing, all that high-wire word-play, all that freedom to affront and to exult in his own uniqueness—that was Wilde's true path to solidarity. The lighter his touch, the more devastating his effect. When he walked on air he was on solid ground. Which is why a window, 'that little patch of blue/That prisoners call the sky,' is such an appropriate memorial. A window which lets us see through, makes us look up, and lets lights in.[749]

A week after the event I received an itemised invoice from the Café Royal for 21 glasses of orange juice and 18 glasses of mineral water; they had 'most generously' waived their corkage charge on the champagne. Oscar still helps with their publicity and the legendary Grill Room has since been renamed the Oscar Wilde Bar. The Abbey sent in an unexpected bill of £863 for organist, choir, general staff, fixing of window, endowment for future upkeep and photocopies, but I managed to get the BBC to pay some of it as they were filming the event for a documentary. A little later I discovered that in December 1994, a month before I asked for their sponsorship, Perrier-Jouët had distributed 30,000 double-size post-cards round the pubs, clubs, bars and hotels of London's West End picturing a French waiter complete with moustache and bum-freezer jacket and the wording 'When Oscar Wilde called for the Champagne waiter, he was only after one thing—Perrier-Jouët Grand Brut.'[750] I've never knowingly touched a drop of it since.

The Abbey showed its generosity in an amusing and unexpected fashion. I made sure that the editor of *The Oldie*, Richard Ingrams, was included among the guests and during the course of the reception he found himself talking to Martin Neary the Abbey organist. After it was revealed that Richard played the organ in his local church, Martin Neary 'promised him a spin on the Abbey's organ in July,' a promise apparently kept as Richard told me later in the year that Oscar had indirectly helped him fulfil one of his lifetime ambitions.[751]

As for the window itself, like its recipient it generated a certain amount of controversy. The Dean mentioned to me that he had received a letter telling him that it was disgraceful to have put Wilde into Poets' Corner. He didn't send me a copy of it so I can't guarantee that my memory serves me correctly. However, he did give an interview to the correspondent of an American newspaper in London in which he said: 'I've had one letter of protest, which is astonishing. It came from an extreme conservative evangelical who said "How dare you memorialize a sodomite?"'[752] He also received a letter from someone who had obviously consulted an out-of-date edition of the *Encyclopaedia Britannica* and who wrote to say that: 'As everyone knows Oscar Wilde was born in 1856; here is a cheque for £20 to get the date on the window changed.' I reassured the Dean (with proof) that 1854 was the correct date and we composed a polite response pointing out that several reference works had the date wrong and that the one on the window was in fact correct. The reply came back: 'Well, if that's the case. Please send my cheque on to St. Paul's.' As Michael Mayne pointed out, it was an irritating conclusion due to the friendly rivalry between the two churches.[753] My own last word, given to an unknown journalist as we were leaving the Abbey was circulated far more widely than I anticipated. When asked what I thought of the window, I said that I thought it was highly appropriate as 'He is neither in nor out and looking both ways at the same time.' It finished up—doubtless my first and last time ever—in the quotations column of *Newsweek*.

Two weeks after Oscar was admitted to Poets' Corner, my mother died suddenly one morning at home from a ruptured aorta. She had been in such good health physically that her doctor ordered a post-mortem. Back in 1991 when I had first told her of the plans for Westminster and Oscar's Paris tomb had just been classified as a historic monument, she wrote to me: 'What with the Tomb and Poets' Corner, I could die happily. It would squash the Victorian hypocrisy.'[754] The fact that she died so soon after the Abbey dedication seemed to imply that she felt her 'work' was done and that it heralded a new beginning. After the reception at the Café Royal, Sarah and I had given a buffet supper at home to many of the donors for the window, where Thelma was made to feel (as indeed she was) the doyenne of the Wilde family. A few days later she wrote a charming and affectionate letter to congratulate us on the successful and stylish organization of everything, even praising Lucian for his part in fetching and handing the bouquet to her before she laid it under the window. David Queensberry, the 12th Marquess, had sat at her feet, she said, and listened to her stories about his parents Kathleen and Francis with whom Vyvyan and Thelma had been friends. I was glad that she ended her life on a high. Perhaps she finally considered me fit to look after her father-in-law's reputation without her supervision. At least she didn't have to experience the centenary of Oscar's trials and imprisonment a few weeks later and the whole media circus which it engendered.

Poor Thelma! She was, in an odd way, like Bosie Douglas tilting at windmills for the last twenty-five years of her life, and if I have been critical about her in this book, it has only been in the interests of telling the truth about our family and the lasting effect that Oscar's scandal has had on it. When she met my father during the War she always maintained that she had no idea about his connection to Oscar Wilde. No doubt that was true, but she certainly would have known by the time they were married in 1943. My father was twenty-four years older than her and could hardly have been described as a good 'catch.' Although he benefited from some royalty income from Oscar's works he was not a man of 'independent means.' Apart from the obvious emotional bond, his attraction for Thelma was the circles in which he moved— literary, artistic and, for the time, slightly Bohemian. But by the early 1950s the copyrights had expired, Montgomery Hyde's book on the trials had made a much wider public aware of the reasons for Oscar's disgrace, homophobia in Britain was sharply on the increase and there was the added stigma of Vyvyan's bankruptcy and the prurient interest of the press in it all. This was not what my mother had signed up to when she got married and however much metropolitan life had broadened her outlook, having to deal with family scandals not of her own making sat uneasily with what Vyvyan once referred to rather rudely as 'her Upper Tooting mentality.'[755] Oscar ended up bringing neither money nor prestige. He just brought trouble and, especially in the 1950s, some adverse comments in newspapers. Her solution to the problem was plenty of whitewash and a good dose of denial. For a while it was superficially effective, especially on the grounds of protecting a vulnerable husband and an impressionable teenage son, but then the Swinging Sixties arrived and with them a radical reassessment of Oscar through the publication of his letters. His homosexuality was no longer scandalous and neither he nor his family needed protecting any more. Thelma couldn't see that and after my father's death she never really moved on. So, Oscar came between us. Thelma often accused me of wanting some sort of 'reflected glory,' as she put it, by writing an article, or giving a lecture, or in some low-key way associating myself with my grandfather. We would have furious arguments about it. I had made it my job to learn about his life and his work as any researcher might have done so as not to appear ignorant of our family history.[756] I could see no harm in sharing that knowledge and sometimes even being paid to do so. For Thelma, though, it was to undermine her authority and take away her protecting role. There were even occasions when I had helped an author in a small way with some aspect of Oscar for a book and had to ask that I be left out of the acknowledgements. Thelma saw such friendly cooperation not as sharing scholarly research but more as fraternising with the enemy. Richard Ellmann's brief acknowledgement of me in his major biography of Oscar was seen almost as an act of treason and the subject of a long simmering row over family loyalty.

As I write this, I look back through the file of letters I received after her death, especially those from friends who had known her thirty or forty years before. Most seem to be commiserating with me on the death of someone I knew by reputation, who I vaguely remember meeting a long time before as a young child. One tells a little anecdote about Augustus John coming to dinner at our flat in Sloane Street and saying to Thelma: 'You cannot imagine, my dear, the effect on a man of my age of your golden hair.' Others repeat each other: 'irreverent,' 'fun-loving,' 'mischievous.' I search my memory for an image which fits the descriptions and, yes, there is one. It's a Sunday in September 1986; I know because I still have the letter she wrote afterwards. I've invited myself to cold lunch but promised to bring it. I arrive with two dozen oysters, a loaf of brown bread and two bottles of Chablis. We won't drink both, but we don't want to run out. Thelma adores oysters and we sit on the floor of the huge drawing room in her flat and eat them in the early autumn sunshine. Oysters prompt memories of her youth in Australia and I encourage her to reminisce. There is no Oscar; there are no cross words. We spend three hours together and I enjoy her company as one would that of an eccentric aunt with travellers' tales to tell. She recalls buying oysters as a girl of nineteen with friends in Melbourne for 2/6 a dozen and how on one occasion they overdid the Seppelt's 'Sparkling Burgundy' and when she arrived home her parents threatened to put her in a convent. It's the equivalent, twenty-five years on, of walking around Chelsea with my father in those summer dawns of 1961 and listening to the stories of his life in the 1930s. The image, suffused with sunlight, is still astonishingly vivid. But it's a one-off, which is probably why.

After my mother's death, apart from the usual clearing up of the 'estate' which came to the grand sum of £2,808, I had to inform the Social Security since for the last fifteen years her income had been so low that she had been claiming Supplementary Benefit from the State. The Benefits Agency then asked to see all Thelma's bank statements, including any savings accounts for the previous five years 'as a routine check' on any assets she may have had. Mindful of me having to go cap in hand to my benefactor, Henry Andrews, to get my father cremated, Thelma had been putting aside money for her funeral. These savings had taken her marginally over the limits allowed and I had no option but to refund them nearly £1,000 for the period she had been claiming. It was curiously ironic that in the space of a month, Oscar should be fêted by the establishment while the government was claiming its pound of flesh from his daughter-in-law.

For a number of years afterwards I had recurrent dreams about my parents. My father would appear seemingly from nowhere and start conversing with me as if nothing was more normal, and I would express surprise that he was still alive. I even felt, as far as one can in a dream, a sudden surge of pleasure, a wave of affection and a desire somehow to protect him. I would put him to bed and bring him something hot in a mug. That's all. And when I woke, there was no sense of disappointment. The dream sequence was oddly complete in itself and strangely calming. However, when I dreamed of my mother she would be arriving on my doorstep in full argumentative flow about something unspecified to do with Oscar Wilde. The subject would be immaterial but the effect was always the same: 'Oh God! I thought you'd finally left me in peace. Now I'll have to rethink my life all over again,' As with most bad dreams, it would be mercifully short, the momentary dread of what seemed reality quickly followed by the relief that it wasn't, but to feel like that about a parent is profoundly disturbing. I put it down to yet another aspect of the distant collateral damage from a century before, which made it easier to handle but I still wish that Oscar hadn't come between Thelma and me.

CHAPTER SIX
THE SPERANZA CENTENARY

When I wrote to sympathetic Wildeans asking for subscriptions to the Poets' Corner window, I wasn't expecting to collect more than £1,000. I'm not in the business of fund-raising, so I can't claim to know about these things, but setting parameters and limiting the donors seemed to be a sensible way of making everyone feel comfortable about whatever they wanted to give. I had suggested donations of between £5 and £30 in my letter which a few people simply ignored and—generously, touchingly—sent far more. In the end the fund came to just over £2,000 and even the Allied Irish Bank, where I had opened a special account, threw in £25 'to kick off the fund' as they said. This money had been given for a permanent memorial so it felt wrong to subsidise something as ephemeral as the post-dedication reception with the surplus, but it needed an appropriate home. The period 1895 to 1898 was filled with dramatic events in Oscar's life so there would be centenaries aplenty to commemorate, some, like his arrest and imprisonment, obviously less pleasant to remember than others. One, however, seemed the perfect choice: the death of Oscar's mother, Jane Wilde, on 3 February 1896 while he was serving his time in Reading Gaol. His layabout and alcoholic brother, Willie, who was living with her at the time, didn't even have the money to pay for her funeral, the cost of which had to be met by Oscar out of a gift of £1,000 he had been given by a friend, Adela Schuster, not long before his conviction. 'You knew, none better,' he wrote to Bosie Douglas from prison, 'how deeply I loved and honoured her. Her death was so terrible to me that I, once a lord of language, have no words in which to express my anguish and my shame.'[757] My grandmother,

Constance, had to break the news to him by travelling, ill as she was, all the way from Genoa. No headstone was ever put on Lady Wilde's burial place in Kensal Green Cemetery and no fees paid for the plot to be made permanent, though it turned out later that even a hundred years on she was still the only one buried in that grave. Now with the centenary of her death approaching it seemed more than appropriate that something should be done to commemorate her place in Irish history. She had played an active (if only literary) part in the Young Ireland movement of the 1840s and wrote inflammatory anti-British poetry in its journal, *The Nation*, under the pen-name of 'Speranza,' before settling down to produce three children and host one of Dublin's foremost nineteenth century salons.

There is a Wilde family tomb in Dublin's Mount Jerome Cemetery where Sir William Wilde, a prominent Dublin doctor and Oscar's father, is buried along with various members of his family. In fact, it is more of a vault rather than a single grave and Sir William was the last to be buried there in 1876. When I visited the cemetery office in the early 1990s, the register said rather laconically 'room for four more,' though the four who might have filled the space, Jane, Willie, Oscar, and Isola all finished up being buried elsewhere. It was surmounted by a sort of truncated obelisk, three sides of which were taken up with inscriptions on inset panels about those beneath it, but the fourth was blank and the perfect place for a memorial tribute to this remarkable woman and her children who, apart from Oscar, had nothing by which to remember them. Ever since the triumphant first night of *Lady Windermere's Fan* in 1892 when she had written to the author rather wistfully that she would henceforth have to 'pose as the Mother of Oscar,' she had remained rather overshadowed by him. The side devoted to Sir William's achievements was in marble and the others in a form of sandstone but badly weathered and with the inscriptions barely legible. The monumental masons said, rightly, that if the obelisk had to be dismantled for Speranza, it would make aesthetic sense (as well as lasting longer) to replace all the panels with marble, but that was way over my budget. Help came unexpectedly in the form of the Professor of Geriatric Medicine at Trinity College, Davis Coakley. Davis had come to the Wildes through his long-standing interest in Sir William's place in the history of Irish medicine and had recently published a groundbreaking book *Oscar Wilde: the Importance of Being Irish*. In it he had used a fair number of Oscar's letters still in copyright, but in view of our friendship I offered to waive the permission fees. When he heard about my Mount Jerome project, he insisted on making a contribution as a reciprocal gesture. It was yet another touching reminder of the affection in which Oscar seems to be held by so many who cross paths with him even posthumously.

With the restoration of the tomb assured, I felt it needed some sort of ceremony to mark the centenary of her death. The American College in Dublin, which now occupied the Wilde's former family home at No. 1 Merrion Square, said it would be happy to host an event there after the unveiling of the new memorial plaque which, it suggested, should be done by a well-known woman in the field of Irish politics or literature. Nothing like starting at the top, so we approached the president, Mary Robinson. The first time I had met her some years before, she told me that while at Trinity College she had lived at 15 Westland Row, Oscar's birthplace, known in her time there for other reasons also as 'The Wild(e) House.' A tenuous connection and not one to emphasise to the President of Ireland thirty years later, but she may have remembered it because, although she declined to perform the unveiling, she asked my family to meet her for coffee on the day at the Áras an Uachtaráin and sent a warm message of support to be read out at the event. However, the prominent Irish politician and Deputy Leader of Fianna Fáil, Mary O'Rourke, agreed enthusiastically to do it instead and commemorating 'Speranza of *The Nation*' began to take on a greater importance than we could ever have hoped for.

I left London the day before with a near life-size reproduction of Speranza's portrait accompanying me to Gatwick airport which meant taking a train from Clapham Junction. I don't remember exactly why she was visible to other passengers on the platform; I think the photographic studio must have wrapped her in a protective sheet of polythene and, while we were waiting, a man with a surreal sense of humour came up and asked to be introduced. I was happy to play along. 'This is Oscar Wilde's mother,' I said. 'She died exactly a hundred years ago tomorrow and I'm taking her back to Dublin.' As often with the general public, the idea that Oscar Wilde had had a mother and hadn't just burst into the world fully formed was odd so I gave him a sixty second résumé. A few minutes later our train drew in, but a passing traveller was at least better informed about Speranza's role in the history of Ireland and I reflected on how the wheel had come full circle at Clapham Junction in a century. In November 1895 while Oscar was being transferred from Wandsworth Prison to Reading he described how he found himself the subject of public derision in this very same station:

> From two o'clock till half-past two on that day I had to stand on the centre platform of Clapham Junction in convict dress and handcuffed, for the world to look at. I had been taken out of the Hospital Ward without a moment's notice being given to me. Of all possible objects I was the most grotesque. When people saw me they laughed. Each train as it came up swelled the audience. Nothing could exceed their amusement. That was of course before they knew who I was. As soon as they had been informed, they laughed still more. For half an hour I stood there in the grey November rain surrounded by a jeering mob.[758]

At least that was his account of the transfer. I have since discovered a Victorian engraving captioned 'Convicts leaving York Road Station for Portsmouth' which leads me to believe that this anecdote, one of the most chilling and poignant in the whole Wilde tragedy, may have owed a little more to Oscar's imagination than just to the bare facts.

The nearest railway station to Wandsworth prison was Wandsworth Station on York Road, Battersea, one stop further down the line than Clapham. It was closer to the prison and would have been far more discreet and secure a location from which to transfer convicts than Clapham Junction, which was, and still is, the busiest station in Europe. The engraving certainly shows that the York Road station was used by the prison for transfers and is much more likely to have been the one used by Oscar and his warders on their way to Reading. Although Oscar may well have been recognised while waiting for his train and laughed at by half a dozen people at Wandsworth in the way he describes, it doesn't have quite the same dramatic impact as a jeering mob on the centre platform of Clapham Junction. But my grandfather was Irish and a storyteller, and wherever it really took place, he has now earned himself a Rainbow Plaque on platform 10 at 'the Junction' to commemorate the event, hideous and traumatic occasion that it must have been.[759]

The unveiling of Speranza's 'In memoriam' panel took place at noon on 3 February 1996, the exact centenary of her death. The date happened to fall on a Saturday, which was perfect as it meant a reception could be held back at the American College in Merrion Square on the same day of the week that Jane Wilde used to hold her Dublin salons or *conversazioni* as she liked, a little pretentiously, to call them. To my astonishment there must have been about 300 people who turned up to the unveiling, but word travels fast in Dublin and it was also a weekend. Mary O'Rourke made a graceful and eloquent speech reminding those present of how Jane Elgee, as she then was, wrote those fiery Nationalist articles for Charles Gavan Duffy's paper *The Nation* in 1848 and how her writings had uplifted the Irish people for two decades afterwards. When she died the *Freeman's Journal* described her as 'a woman of the most versatile attainments, genuine intellectual power and commanding character.'[760] It was particularly pleasing to see that Duffy's 82 year-old granddaughter, Máire Gavan Duffy, had come to pay her respects among a host of eminent names in politics and the arts.[761] Ulick O'Connor recited one of Oscar's sonnets and just as he had finished a seagull flew overhead mewing loudly followed almost immediately by a swan. Ulick, never one to miss a good cue, quipped: 'It's her, with Oliver Gogarty in hot pursuit!'[762]

Before we left the cemetery, a Dubliner came up to me and said: 'You don't know me. I am nobody of any importance, but I just wanted to shake your hand and thank you for doing this for a great Irishwoman.' I told him that, on the contrary, he and about three hundred others *were* the most important people in Dublin that day for taking the time to come and be part of it. It was impossible not to be moved by such a simple, heartfelt tribute to my great-grandmother whose achievements were now properly listed for posterity on that new marble panel:

Jane Francesca, Lady Wilde
'Speranza' of The Nation
Writer Translator Poet and Nationalist
Author of Works on Irish Folklore
Early Advocate of Equality for Women
And Founder of a Leading Literary Salon

And not least 'Mother of William, Oscar and Isola.' I also added the first verse of Oscar's poem 'Requiescat' which he wrote in memory of his nine-year-old sister Isola, but was presumptuous enough to change 'daisies' to 'lilies' as this was now for his mother and sounded more exotic and in keeping with her character:

Tread lightly, she is near
Under the snow,
Speak gently, she can hear
The lilies [daisies] grow.

Needless to say a Wilde fan noticed and questioned whether this was a previously unknown manuscript variant. It was a lesson for the future in how to avoid awkward explanations.

I must have had access beforehand to the list of guests invited to the reception in the Wilde's old house after the unveiling, but I certainly hadn't examined it in detail nor had I tailored the brief speech of welcome that I was due to make to single out any of them in particular. Not very professional being so unprepared, but I wanted there to be a spontaneous feel about it, so I had a few notes and was going to quote from Speranza's proto-feminist essay 'The Bondage of Women' to illustrate just how advanced she was for her time. In it she pleads for equality of opportunity between the sexes: 'Genius in man or woman deserves national recognition, of which rank and wealth are the outward and visible signs and it is an injustice to deprive half the nation of all chance or hope of national honours,' and she goes on to say that while, admittedly, women have 'limited access to the great universities, all the profits and emoluments are still exclusively reserved for men.' Women have forced their way into literature (she was no doubt thinking of herself), but for others a life of action is more suited to their capabilities:

> Action for some, reflective work for another. Some souls speak best in deeds, in a life of rule and influence. Let such women be given stations of power and dignity—colonial government for instance . . . Any station where intellect can be evidenced by a life of energetic good might be given to women thus gifted.[763]

As things turned out, it was indeed my lack of preparation and unawareness of some of the more distinguished guests which gave my address such a genuine spontaneity that I surprised myself. Minutes beforehand I was introduced to the American ambassador Jean Kennedy Smith as well as the British ambassador Veronica Sutherland, both eminent women, occupying the highest-ranking positions in the Dublin diplomatic corps. I couldn't have asked for a more perfect and instant illustration of why we were celebrating the life of my great-grandmother and that essay of hers written over a hundred years before. Reflecting on the other parts played in the day's proceedings by Mary Robinson and Mary O'Rourke, I told the guests that day in No. 1 Merrion Square that it was something of an historic moment— just as Speranza would have wished, her century-old vision finally realised in her native city. I reminded them, too, that her name was the first on the 1892 petition of 10,000 signatures presented to Trinity College demanding the admission of women, the second being that of her daughter-in-law, Constance, probably encouraged by Oscar. And hadn't he lent his voice to the debate on women's education while he was editor of the *Woman's World*? In an editorial piece of December 1887 Oscar praised the success of a young woman who won the Literature Scholarship at the Royal University in Ireland saying that it 'shows how worthy women are of that higher culture and education which has been so tardily and, in some instances, so grudgingly granted to them.'[764]

Giving Speranza a memorial panel on the Wilde tomb in Mount Jerome and through it the place she deserves in Irish history and letters, has brought her out from the shadow of her more famous and infamous son. Recognition of her achievements has even earned her a place within the world of astronomy. Five years previously while flying across the Atlantic I read in the *International Herald Tribune* that the nomenclature committee of the Magellan Project was actively looking for eminent female names for the recently mapped topographical features on Venus. Because of its dense cloudy atmosphere, the nature of the planet had long been shrouded in mystery until the Magellan space probe successfully went into orbit around it for several years from 1990 and mapped the surface accurately by radar. I had written in November 1991 suggesting Speranza as a possible candidate and heard nothing until shortly after the Dublin event when I was asked for more details. I'm sure it was the press coverage I sent and the involvement of the distinguished names which clinched it; on 7 April 1999 I had official confirmation that the International Astronomical Union had approved her name for a *patera* on Venus.[765] It had taken a while but it was a thoroughly satisfactory outcome. I think her son, master self-publicist that he was, might have had mixed feelings of pride about the honour done to his adored mother, tempered maybe with a touch of envy that her reputation had gone interplanetary while his own was still firmly terrestrial.

Today, thanks to the generosity of a Wilde fan who at the time wished to remain anonymous, an elegant Kilkenny blue headstone carved with a Celtic motif was erected on Speranza's burial plot in Kensal Green Cemetery on 13 October 2000.[766] The occasion was marked by Vanessa Redgrave who had played Lady Wilde in the 1997 *Wilde* biopic and later in the day she also unveiled an English Heritage Blue Plaque on 146 (now 87) Oakley Street where Speranza had spent her last years in London. On 4 March 2021 the Irish postal service issued a stamp in her honour to mark the bicentenary of her birth. I was wondering why the issue date had been set more than nine months before her precise birthday on 27 December until I was told that it was chosen just in time to mark International Women's Day 2021. How utterly appropriate, I thought: exactly what she would have wanted. And good to think that a slight excess of generosity towards her son over Poets' Corner had helped Dublin to rediscover her, and others to acquaint themselves with the remarkable 'Mother of Oscar.'

S ometime around the beginning of the 1970s when he was
commissioned by George Weidenfeld to write a biography
of Oscar Wilde, Sheridan Morley asked whether it was a
good idea when so many had already appeared. 'I know,' said the
publisher, 'but the story is such a good one that it needs to be
retold every ten years or so for those who came along in the meantime.' Feature films on Oscar seem to be subject to much the same
principle except that the period is double and since two came out
simultaneously in 1960, it was reasonable not to expect another
until 1997.

It must have been a bout of centenary-itis caused by a combination of the Poets' Corner window being unveiled and the commemoration of Oscar's trials and imprisonment which prompted
the Samuelson brothers to produce a more 'honest' film than
those two bowdlerised versions of the story which had appeared in
1960. My introduction to it was an invitation to lunch at 'The Ivy,'
in June 1995 with Marc Samuelson, scriptwriter Julian Mitchell,
and director Brian Gilbert. I didn't know what to expect but I
did know that if I was to have any involvement at all in the film, I
only had a short time to establish my credentials and to reassure
them, whatever they may have heard, that Thelma was no longer
around with her whitewash bucket. I also needed to show that I
had both a reasonable grasp of the constraints of film-making and
a sensible rather than an over-protective attitude towards Oscar's
scandalous private life. The first thing they told me was that they
had bought the film rights to Richard Ellmann's biography. I think
this was said to prove how seriously they were taking the whole
project, but I expressed surprise and said that there was nothing

in it, apart from Ellmann's own words, to which his estate or his publishers could lay claim to any sort of copyright or exclusivity. All the facts had been rehearsed many times over and I could have saved them the £25,000 that it had apparently cost by pointing them in the direction of all the unprotected source material. It was a fairly standard procedure in making biopics, so they said, to buy up such rights to make sure the producers were covered against any possible claims—a sort of insurance policy. Anyway, the deal had been done so I felt I should warn them about some of the more glaring errors in Ellmann's book, in particular the whole question of Oscar dying from syphilis which had largely been discredited since its publication in 1987. I warned them that repeating that sort of sensationalist conjecture or, for example, taking as authentic the photo of Oscar in drag playing Salomé and trying to make something of it in the film could expose them to ridicule from knowledgeable critics. Julian Mitchell said he had already put the syphilis story into his first draft but would be happy to revisit it if I would send him all the detailed arguments against it. I did and he was as good as his word: 'I am convinced! Now I shall have to make a small alteration to the script. First, though, we have to find an actor worthy of the role . . . . I'm sure you will be absolutely invaluable, not just on Ellmann's errors, but on the right tone and feel.'[767] I came away from that lunch fairly confident that my 'audition' as an historical adviser had gone off reasonably well but, more importantly, that here was a team who genuinely wanted to make a no holds barred but balanced film about my grandfather. I wrote to Marc Samuelson summarising what I had said during the meeting:

> While my mother was alive, I used to have to think twice about taking on anything like this, as she imagined she had a sort of monopoly on my grandfather and would threaten the destruction of all my father's papers and diaries if she didn't like what I was doing. Families are awful when fear and ignorance rule. She meant well, God rest her, but I am now mercifully free to do as I

please . . . . whitewashing Wilde is as bad as sensationalising him. The truth needs to be told in a balanced and appealing manner; when told with warmth and sympathy, the story has a poignancy of its own.[768]

In his reply he just confirmed my impressions: 'I cannot tell you how pleased we are that you have agreed to become involved in our film. I hope it was clear that our project is a serious-minded attempt to tell the story properly, and to celebrate Oscar without trying to portray him as a saint.'[769] I felt a profound sense of relief that we (I already felt part of it) would be able to give cinema audiences a warts and all, but none the less endearing portrait of my grandfather for the first time, just as his letters had done back in 1962.

Since Samuelson Entertainment was still in the process of raising the production money, I wasn't holding my breath waiting for my involvement to be put on a formal footing. Marc wrote again in late September to say 'the project is going great guns,' and that he would be in touch in three or four weeks' time. Then, despite several calls to the production office asking to see the script, I heard nothing for nine months. Finally, on 23 July the following year Julian Mitchell wrote to me enclosing 'the script we've ended up with. It's been through many transformations . . . but the core has always been the same—the tragedy of Oscar and Bosie.' He also warned me about the way some of the secondary characters had been portrayed and about the simplifications and foreshortenings of the story and not to be surprised. I wasn't in the slightest. All of that I had taken for granted; it was an inevitable part of film-making. There were minor inaccuracies, and events taken out of their proper sequence or compressed in order to move the action along at a good pace, but so long as they weren't distorting the broad outline of the story, none of it mattered. The end of the script, though, was a distortion too far.

In reality, when Oscar was released from prison in May 1897 and went to France, he was determined never to see Alfred

Douglas again. Bosie, however, had other ideas and over the next three months in a series of letters he laid emotional siege to his former lover until Oscar finally capitulated and went to meet him in Rouen. Of course it was fatal and they then made plans to spend the autumn and winter in Naples together to the fury of Bosie's family as well as that of Robert Ross and Oscar's wife, Constance. After two and a half months in Italy they ran out of money, were forced to separate and, although they saw one another from time to time, never lived together again. The following year in April, Constance died after an operation and with that, any hope Oscar may have had of reconciliation with his family vanished. Alone, but not entirely friendless, he then slid inexorably to his death in 1900.

The last scenes in the screenplay, therefore, were a travesty of the truth. We see Oscar walking along the beach in Northern France reciting *The Ballad of Reading Gaol* to himself; next he's putting flowers on his wife's grave; then he's telling Robbie that he's decided to go back to Bosie; and finally Oscar and Bosie fall into one another's arms at Rouen railway station (doubtless with copious steam from a vintage engine), weeping and laughing.[770] The message? Well, he's sorry his wife has died but now he's free to do as he wants. I told Marc Samuelson that apart from this there were other points in the screenplay which, I felt, needed to be addressed if I were to be used as an historical adviser or there seemed little point in my taking on the role. We met for dinner to discuss it; the same crew as a year before plus Stephen Fry who by now had been offered and accepted the part of Oscar. I said in blunt terms that the ending was rubbish and proposed another. No problem with killing off Constance rather early, but the Oscar-Bosie reunion in Naples took place a good six months beforehand and it altered the whole dynamic of their relationship to have them reunited once she was in her grave. Why? To make Oscar appear more caring and sensitive? The whole point is that he wasn't. Constance was furious when Oscar went back to Bosie and temporarily stopped the small allowance she had been giving

him. But all that was, admittedly, far too complicated to depict
and would have to wait until Rupert Everett's poignant portrayal
of Oscar in exile twenty years later. As Julian Mitchell quite rightly
wrote in his afterword to the published film script: 'The true historical ending was slow, complicated, messy and lacked drama,
so we have tidied it up, and will no doubt be criticised for doing
so.'[771] The ending I suggested instead was this: Bosie is entering
a hotel, somewhere vaguely in Southern Europe, with a couple
of friends and a load of luggage. Next we see Oscar half in the
shadow of a colonnade opposite. Cut back to Bosie and friends as
Bosie notices Oscar and indicates to his friends that they should
go on into the hotel while he attends to something outside. Their
unscripted, unheard exchange seems to last a fraction too long
because when Bosie turns round all he sees is Oscar's back as he
walks into the darkness of the colonnade and disappears. Not a
word is spoken, yet everything is said. After their final break-up
in Naples, Oscar wrote to Robbie Ross: 'It is, of course, the most
bitter experience of a bitter life; . . . I know it is better that I should
never see him again. I don't want to. He fills me with horror.'[772]
My suggestion, entirely fictitious but a compact visual metaphor
for what really happened, was later adopted in part, but they still
couldn't resist having the two men fall into each other's arms instead of Oscar walking away. A nice, neat, sort-of-happy-ending,
and the epilogue text on the screen, which few will remember after leaving the cinema, tells us that they parted after three months.

Brian Gilbert spent most of that dinner making copious notes
of all that I was saying, presumably worried that this might be the
last time he would be able to pick my brains. At one moment he
asked me 'Are you really sure that Oscar loved his wife?' By then
I was already feeling that no one was likely to listen to a single
word of advice I might have to offer and until I had a signed contract I certainly wasn't going to offer any more.[773] The contract
did indeed arrive two days later, but before signing it I said that
I wanted both to clarify my own role and to discuss what I saw
as an excessive emphasis on Oscar's homosexuality in the film to

the detriment of so many other qualities which could have been shown. More than a third of the scenes in the script dealt directly or indirectly with this single aspect of his personality and one scene which I found particularly objectionable had Oscar playing voyeur to Bosie having sex with a rent-boy in some London hotel, for which there wasn't a scrap of evidence but, I was told, had been put in to show that the physical side of their relationship had been short-lived and by then was over. I couldn't see that audiences would necessarily come to the same conclusion and would be more likely to regard it as just another form of deviant sexuality on Oscar's part. It made a total nonsense of Marc's original assurance that this was a 'serious-minded attempt to tell the story properly.' I reiterated what I had said all along, namely that I had spent twenty years trying, from an objective position of knowledge rather than a subjective one of family emotions, to give balance to Oscar's life. It was only a fortnight before shooting was due to start and with hindsight it should have been perfectly clear to me that nothing was now going to be changed. Marc agreed to one more meeting to which he turned up with Julian; their alternative ending was discussed but nothing else and Marc left after twenty minutes. Julian said he felt that I wouldn't be happy with *any* script, which I told him was nonsense. He also told me that two scenes had been cut, both of which had to do with the literary side of Oscar's life: one in which he was discussing the dangers of publishing *Dorian Gray* with his old sparring partner Frank Harris and another, a little *vignette* of Oscar as editor of *The Woman's World* expressing some of his surprisingly proto-feminist views on the 'New Woman' of the late Victorian age. But these interesting and lesser known sides of Oscar's life were clearly considered a distraction from the main story which had been reduced to the tragedy of Oscar and Bosie with a bit of family life thrown in to make Oscar's fall from grace more poignant. It was a pity. Apart from the few points with which I took issue, and the over-emphasis on Oscar's sex-life, I always thought Julian's original script was rather good. After that last meeting, Julian and I shared a taxi home and before

I dropped him off I asked him what had made him depict Oscar being a voyeur. He admitted there was no source for it and it was merely conjecture, but as a gay man himself he thought it perfectly possible. However, he did say (and I wrote it down when I got home) that the Japanese who had put money into the production were very keen on 'sensuality and lots of bum-fucking' as they put it rather crudely.[774] Money, as so often, had got in the way of the truth.

At this stage I remember thinking, rather misguidedly, that I had a better chance of persuading producer and director to re-dress the balance of the film if I were working with them as a consultant than if I were not. Nevertheless, I thought I should put over one last point, something I had observed since the publica-tion of the *Letters of Oscar Wilde* thirty-five years before. I told Marc that the public was curiously protective about Oscar and far more sympathetic to his fate than it had been when the pre-vious films had come out. Of course his homosexuality was an important part of the whole story and now, in 1997, thirty years after the law had changed, it would be ridiculous to play it down. However, with too much emphasis on the sexual aspect of Oscar's life he risked alienating a general audience rather than generating its sympathy. I might as well have saved my breath; by this time I had obviously been branded as tiresome family, a sort of amalgam caricature of all descendants who don't want their ancestors por-trayed in a bad light. But the offer of a consultancy was still open with its £5,000 fee, so what did they actually want from me?

The bizarre answer from Marc Samuelson was: 'I don't know whether we "want" anything at all from you . . . . I suppose I was thinking that it might be helpful to be able to call you up and ask you the odd question . . . . but if it turns out that we don't consult you, then the fee was easily earned. Alternatively, something might come up, especially in the marketing of the film, which entailed a lot of work.' So I might be paid for doing nothing at all. It didn't sound right. I remembered Vyvyan in the 1960s doing his histori-cal advisory work on films and having to be on set at Pinewood or even on location during most of the shooting. Marketing? The contract wasn't just for the duration of the filming but continued for a year after the probable release, so it sounded ominously like being asked to smile and say what a wonderful film it was whatever I thought of it. I went through the contract again clause by clause and there it was: I had no right to speak to any third party or make any statement about the film without the prior consent of the production office. They might well not consult me, but by taking the fee I was more or less bound to keep my mouth shut—blood-money in effect, which my dictionary described as 'money paid for the murder of a relative.' I was still reluctant simply to walk away from it, feeling that Oscar deserved better than having a somewhat banal, over-simplified view of his life put before the public in this way and hiding behind the restrictions of the medium seemed like the film-maker's classic excuse for doing exactly that.

I knew that Valerie Eliot (the widow and second wife of T. S. Eliot) had not been best pleased about the depiction of her late husband in another Gilbert and Samuelson biopic, *Tom & Viv* in which he was shown as having his first wife committed to an asylum. I wrote and asked if she would speak to me about her involvement in the film which I felt she must have had. A few days later she called me to say that no one from the production company had consulted her, that she had proof the story was entirely false and that she had been deeply upset by the film. She referred me to an interview she had given when it was released in 1994 in which she described it as 'inaccurate, dishonest and malicious.'[775] They weren't words I would have used to describe the script of *Wilde* but if this was the team hoping to get me 'on board' as they described it, I was clearly better off sailing solo. At that stage in my life £5,000 would have been particularly welcome, but those who buy your silence are seldom inclined to seek your advice. My integrity got the better of me and I turned it down.

The idea of paying money 'to get people on board' now made sense of the £25,000 they had paid for the rights to Richard

Ellmann's book; it was the sprat to catch the mackerel. The application to the Arts Council for a grant to help fund the film stated that it was 'To prepare for the screen a version of Richard Ellmann's biography of Oscar Wilde' which gave it an entirely false pedigree, but what matter? The Greenlight Fund, which was administering National Lottery money for films, happily obliged and £1.5m was forthcoming. Dick's biography, which had rightly been hailed as masterly when it came out, was used in all the publicity: 'Based on the definitive biography by Richard Ellmann . . . ' it claimed, and Penguin reissued a paperback version of the book with Stephen Fry on the cover. A little maliciously I called the person responsible in the relevant department at the Arts Council querying why the grant had been made to film a largely literary biography when the script was more or less devoid of literature, even tangentially. It elicited the serious reply in part justification that 'The Selfish Giant' was voiced-over throughout. From that moment I realised it was pointless to go on fighting for anything resembling the definitive, balanced biopic which I had been hoping for and for the next twelve months, with some difficulty, I kept my opinions mostly to myself and waited.

Having detached myself from it all, admittedly with some reluctance, I enjoyed the occasional snippets of gossip fed to me by those who knew where I stood on the film. Rick Gekoski, the antiquarian book dealer, told me how the production office tried to persuade him to lend them a first edition of *The Happy Prince* from which Constance could be seen reading to her children. He refused and said that knowing how props were treated on film sets he would discourage any of his collector clients from lending one either. Such minute detail for authenticity, when more important facts were being ignored or unnecessarily twisted, made no sense. Anyway, I could have told them to use any one of the first seven editions as they were all visually identical and the later ones worth a tiny fraction of the price of a genuine first. That September, in the middle of filming, I had a call from Dalya Alberge, Arts Correspondent on *The Times*. Samuelson Entertainment were

obviously trying to drum up some advance publicity and had fed
her the story of how they were balancing Oscar's homosexuality
by bringing in scenes of his family life. When Dalya, whom I had
known for some years and who is a responsible and gifted journalist, told them she was going to talk to me as well, according to
her they weren't over-enthusiastic at the idea. They needn't have
worried. I simply told her that I was 'pleased to see that they have
brought Constance and the family in because they were an important part of his life.'[776] That was all. So, had I seen the script?
Yes. Was I happy with it? Not entirely. She pressed me for details.
I said there could have been changes and anyway it was best that
I said no more until I had seen a preview of the final version to
which I certainly wouldn't receive an invitation if I upset the producers at this stage. We agreed that I would give her an exclusive
interview shortly before the film was released.

On a sudden impulse a few days later I rang Sheila Colman,
who was Bosie Douglas's executrix. She and her husband Teddy
had looked after Bosie during his final illness and in gratitude he
had left them the few possessions he owned and the rights to his
literary works. The producers must have been in touch with her
for permission to use the extracts of Bosie's poetry which were being quoted in the film. What did she think of it? Sheila admitted
that she had given permission without seeing a script, then had
second thoughts about it and asked to see one. The producers
refused but the daughter of a friend who was working on the film
managed to 'loan' her a script for a couple of days and Sheila told
me she was horrified at the depiction of Bosie as a foul-mouthed
humper of rent-boys. She also said that she had met Jude Law who
told her that he was uncomfortable with this portrayal of Bosie,
but I only have her word for it and, to his credit, in the end his interpretation of the role was unquestionably the best Bosie ever.[777]

In November the theatre sequences were being filmed at the
Richmond Theatre and I went one afternoon to watch with Maggi
Hambling, who at that time was working on the Oscar memorial
sculpture by Charing Cross. She was a good friend of Stephen and

I suspect that my 'invitation' may have been a second-hand one through her. On that day they were filming the last scene from *The Importance of Being Earnest* and as soon as I saw the set my worst fears were realised. It was the most appalling Victorian Gothic interior with heavy dark furniture and wood panelling, everything that Oscar would have loathed. They had obviously based it on an illustration in Ellmann's book where it is wrongly captioned 'A scene from the original production, 1895,' when in fact was from George Alexander's Edwardian revival of 1909. I said so to a reporter from the BBC who was covering the filming for an arts programme and a day later she told me that the production office maintained that 'there were no photos of how it was so we had to make it up,' all clearly a lie and based on an error in Ellmann which they didn't want to admit. There is in fact a perfectly good sequence of photos of the first production in a contemporary magazine, *The Sketch,* showing the light, airy sets on which Oscar would undoubtedly have insisted to match the mood of the play.[778] Pointing such things out would seem to be what historical advisers are employed to do and it didn't bode well for the final film. After that I decided to say nothing more and waited quietly for an invitation to the press preview which took place in early May 1997.

I have to confess that I found the film quite moving, but whether that was the moody music and camerawork or a sense of family empathy with the whole tragedy, I can't say. With the exception of Bosie's mother, Sybil Queensberry, who was 48 at the time and made to look 70, the casting was excellent and Jude Law brought exactly the right spoilt, arrogant petulance to the part of Bosie which even Sheila Colman had to admit was perfect. Stephen Fry may have had all the physical and intellectual attributes to play the part of Oscar, but somehow this wasn't the remarkable wit and conversationalist who had kept dinner tables enthralled in the early 1890s and who 'altered the minds of men and the colours of things.'[779] There was a sense of foreboding in his whole performance as though prefiguring the disaster to come and I put it down to Stephen's depth of knowledge about my grandfather who wrote after his release from prison: 'I was made for destruction. My cradle was rocked by the Fates. Only in the mire can I know peace.'[780] Life, even in his days of glory, seemed to have him by the scruff of the neck instead of the reverse. There was nothing majestic—defiant even—about him in court delivering his speech from the dock about 'The love that dares not speak its name' and, incomprehensibly, they didn't include that pivotal moment in his libel action against the Marquess of Queensberry when on being cross-questioned by Edward Carson about whether he had kissed a young man he replied: 'Oh, no, never in my life, he was a peculiarly plain boy. I pitied him for it.' One smart-arse remark too many and he had virtually talked himself into prison, and it wasn't an omission which could possibly have been excused by the usual 'constraints of the cinematic art' argument either. When Oscar received Queensberry's libellous card, he sent a note to his wonderfully loyal friend Robbie Ross asking him to come the same evening to discuss what to do and saying that he had asked Bosie to come the next morning. When Robbie arrived, Bosie was already there, working his seductive magic. It is one of the great 'What if . . . ?' moments in the whole story but simply turned into a stand-off between the two young men in Oscar's life. 'I was no longer the captain of my soul and did not know it,' he would write later.[781] What happened to Oscar's feisty Irish mother whom he adored and whom we meet several times earlier on? She died while he was in prison, and one of the reasons why Constance is shown in the film returning from her exile on the Continent to visit Oscar in Reading Prison should have been to break the news to him. But she doesn't. 'My wife, at that time kind and gentle to me, rather than that I should hear the news from indifferent or alien lips, travelled, ill as she was, all the way from Genoa to England to break to me herself the tidings of so irreparable, so irredeemable a loss,' he wrote in *De Profundis*.[782] Another touching gesture by the wronged wife; another body blow to the prisoner at his lowest ebb; another thirty seconds of film for which one of the repetitious scenes of Oscar's sex-life could usefully have been sacrificed. Perhaps the most absurd error of all was to show Oscar placing flowers on his wife's grave inscribed with the words 'Wife of Oscar Wilde,' words which were only put there by my second cousin, Dinah, in 1963. How much more poignant it would have been without them and with Stephen Fry voicing over the letter he wrote to Robbie after his visit: 'It was very tragic seeing her name carved on a tomb—her surname, my name not mentioned of course—just "Constance Mary, daughter of Horace Lloyd, QC" I brought some flowers. I was deeply affected—with a sense, also, of the uselessness of all regrets.'[783] And what bemused French audiences would have made of Oscar saying: 'All my life I've fought against the English vice—hypocrisy,' I can't imagine. *Le vice anglais* in French means homosexuality.

One thing which irritated me in particular was realising that the Samuelsons had paid a hefty sum to Richard Ellmann's estate partly to cover themselves against any claim that they might have lifted original ideas from his book, but that they considered my father's description of his childhood and Oscar's playing with his sons in the nursery, which only he could have written, free to appropriate. Also, a couple of Oscar's letters, which were still in copyright, were quoted in the film and I raised the matter with Marc Samuelson after the preview. He told me that the American lawyers with whom he had dealt had assured him that everything in Ellmann's book was Ellmann's copyright, which was patently untrue as he had used several thousand words of Oscar's letters still in copyright and the fact was noted on the imprints page of his book. Anyway, there was no more money in the production budget, he said, but as a gesture he would give me £100 out of his own pocket. I was so insulted that I simply ignored the offer and legally it wasn't worth pursuing.

The charity première of the film took place on 16 October 1997—what would have been Oscar's 143rd birthday and a week before, as promised, I gave Dalya Alberge her exclusive interview and also voiced my criticisms of the silly and avoidable inaccuracies in the columns of *The Times*.[784] Marc Samuelson responded by saying, 'I don't regard Merlin Holland as a film critic of any note,' which seemed rather irrelevant since it was the sloppiness and not the cinematography which I was criticising. He also suggested that I was only going public with my comments since my pictorial *Wilde Album* was being published in the same week as their première and I was somehow riding on their publicity. Brian Gilbert came out with his well-worn statement about not being able to show literary brilliance on film: 'Had he been a composer or painter it would be easy to give evidence of his work,' which was supposed to explain the excessive emphasis on Oscar's homosexuality at the expense of other less well-known and more interesting aspects of his character. He even cited Oscar's famous self-assessment to André Gide about how he had put his genius into his life but only his talent into his works as a sort of ultimate stamp of approval from the man himself that his literary output was treated as almost incidental. It came dangerously close to an admission that the film had very little to do with Ellmann's biography. I made the point in a television discussion around the time of the film's release that with the vitriolic reception of *The Picture of Dorian Gray* and the banning of *Salomé* from the stage there would have been room to show just how subversive Oscar's works were considered at the time. It wasn't just his homosexuality which landed him in gaol; even his work represented a danger to public morals in the eyes of the Victorians. But by then, further discussion of what could and couldn't have been done in the film seemed pointless.

I refused an invitation to the screening and gala dinner at the Savoy partly on principle and partly because I couldn't face an evening of lying to anyone who asked me what I thought of the film. I'd already said all that I wanted to say in *The Times*. I also got wind of the fact that Madame Tussaud's was sending their waxwork Oscar to the Odeon West End cinema for the premiere, so to anyone who asked if I were going I was able to say quite truthfully 'No; I'm sending my grandfather in my place.' Instead, I spent the evening in Heffer's bookshop in Cambridge launching my own book and a volume of collected essays on Oscar, my own contribution to which was appropriately entitled 'Biography and the art of lying.'

Despite the requested 'plenty of bum-fucking' the film did badly in Japan. In the US it was scarcely more successful when it opened in the spring of the following year taking only $69,424 on the opening weekend and grossing $2,157,701 overall.[785] By 2005 the UK Film Council told me that it had only seen a return of £247,639 on its predecessor's investment of £1.5m.[786] The UK publicity poster showed Stephen Fry striding down a London street in his light grey suit and top-coat. By the time he had crossed the Atlantic Stephen suddenly found himself advertising the film dressed in flamingo pink. 'It absolutely does not sensationalise anything,' said Marc Samuelson of his film to *The Times*.[787] Really?

Revisiting *Wilde* twenty-five years later I have to admit that it is perhaps not as bad as I made out at the time. It's certainly more accurate and honest than either of the two-dimensional films of 1960 and my criticisms of it reflected my disappointment that it was a film of missed tricks and lost opportunities: the sort of film which, had it achieved its stated aim of being 'a serious-minded attempt to tell the story properly,' could have become a classic. Perhaps that is too much to ask of the cinema. Reducing that rich life to 118 minutes and keeping everything in balance verges on the impossible. Rupert Everett's 2018 film about Oscar's last years in exile was less ambitious in its scope and, despite a few reasonable conjectures and harmless inventions for cinematic effect, truer to the facts and far more moving as a depiction of the man. George Weidenfeld was right when he said that the story needs regular retelling, but I would qualify it by saying that each retelling needs to add to the picture. Give Oscar's 'protective public' a decent measure of what they are hoping to see and then season it with the unexpected, the surprising, the improbable, and they will thank you for giving them a few reasons more to admire him. Sadly, this film didn't fulfil what it promised and every time I watch it and the credits roll at the end, I think what a pity no one had enough humour to add in brackets after the credit for 'Best Boy' (not Bosie Douglas).

CHAPTER EIGHT
LOOKING AT THE STARS

When the multi-talented film-maker and gay rights activist Derek Jarman was dying from AIDS-related complications at the beginning of 1994, he made his friend Jeremy Isaacs promise that he would do all he could to have a London memorial set up to the memory of Oscar Wilde in the form of a statue.[788] Jeremy had been the founding chief executive of Channel Four at the beginning of the 1980s and had championed Derek's controversial work in the face of considerable resistance from others in the television company. It was this belief in the value of Jarman's creativity which led to a close personal friendship and after his death Jeremy was determined that his promise should be kept and lost no time in forming a committee to make sure that it was done. It consisted initially of some heavyweight names from the worlds of politics, theatre, and the arts, among them, at opposite ends of the political spectrum, Kenneth Baker and Michael Foot; a pair of theatre dames, Judi Dench and Maggie Smith, and a knight to balance things up a little, Ian McKellen; and Seamus Heaney and Matthew Parris made up the literary contingent. He also had the vital support of Simon Sainsbury whose involvement in the form of his Monument Trust was later to be invaluable. At that stage I don't think Jeremy even knew of my existence, but by the autumn of 1994 when the dedication of a window to Oscar in Poets' Corner had become official and my name had appeared in the press in connection with it, he got in touch and invited me to be part of his committee. Looking back over the file I kept for the next four years, if there was one lesson to be learned from it all it was this: if you're thinking of putting up a statue to the memory of a controversial figure in a public space in Central London, unless you have unlimited patience with narrow-minded bureaucracy, very deep pockets or a generous sponsor, and the skin of a rhinoceros throughout—don't.

The committee had met that summer to discuss a general plan of campaign and Jeremy and Simon then approached Westminster Council planning department informally about a statue of Oscar in theatreland. The response had been encouraging and at the first proper working meeting of the committee in November the mood was positive enough to discuss sites, likely sculptors and even possible dates for announcing the appeal for public funds. Two dates in 1995 were suggested: April 5th, the centenary of Oscar's arrest and May 25th, that of his conviction. By the time of the next meeting in January it was clear that the April date was unrealistic as we didn't even have a longlist of potential sculptors to choose from. Also, the Royal Fine Art Commission, English Heritage, and the Department of the Environment had got wind of the project and were all insisting on being consulted once site and sculptor had been chosen. Eduardo Paolozzi, a friend of one of the committee, was invited to the meeting in March, to express some views on public memorial sculpture, and further complicated matters by suggesting that we should consider a conceptual rather than a straightforward representational sculpture. 'Complicated' because from then on, the committee would be divided on the merits of each form, some insisting that its main purpose was to satisfy the public and others that its main object was to capture the spirit and wit and unconventionality of Wilde. In the end it encouraged us to commission something which successfully married the two. By the end of April we still had no site and no sculptor, so the full-blown launch of an appeal for funds as planned was out of the question. We decided to limit it to a relatively low-key announcement by a letter to *The Times* on 25 May, a sort of declaration of intent on the centenary of Oscar's conviction to unveil a memorial to him on the centenary of his release from prison in two years' time. Once sculptor and site had been settled on, an appeal for funds would be launched. Then the fun started.

I've often said that my grandfather caused more trouble after his death than he did in his lifetime and here was yet another example of it. Our letter in *The Times* elicited several positive comments as well as a totally predictable response from Peregrine Worsthorne, former editor of the right-wing *Sunday Telegraph*, saying that honouring Wilde the writer was fine but not Wilde the man whose 'addiction to the use and corruption of male prostitutes should no longer put a man in prison for two years' hard labour, neither should it necessarily justify putting him on a pedestal forever.'[789] I had always suspected Worsthorne of being a not-quite-in-the-closet homophobe, stuck in a pre-Wolfenden era, and it wasn't the first time he had expressed his distaste for Oscar's private life, though skilfully avoiding direct homophobic comments. He was at once taken to task by Christopher Hirst in *The Independent* who thanked God for Sir Peregrine, saying that without his 'sanctimonious piffle' the 'Weasel' column in the newspaper 'would have been stuck for subjects of ridicule on umpteen occasions in the past.' Jeremy, writing in the *Financial Times,* eloquently demolished Worsthorne's rather facile anti-statue arguments and put the whole affair in context emphasising that London needed more memorials to those who had achieved greatness in the arts to balance out those recognising military valour or political statesmanship. He went on to say that had it not been for Oscar's notoriety, such a statue might well have been in place already, so it should be regarded as a memorial to the man *and* his art *despite* rather than because of his homosexuality. Worsthorne had the last word for the time being, replying that Wilde was 'weak, hedonistic, deplorably and squalidly self-indulgent,' that 'the statue idea is part of a campaign to legalise and normalise homosexuality' and it was almost certain to be defaced by a member of the disapproving majority.[790] Apart from having his trademark cigarette stolen on a couple of occasions, it never has been.

For a while things calmed down, but for various reasons so too did our initial impetus to get the memorial chosen, accepted, and funded. I think it was becoming clear that both the subject and the choice of sculptor together were going to cause controversy and plenty of it. Jeremy realised that we needed expert steering through the rough waters ahead and persuaded Joanna Drew, who had served for years as a director at the Arts Council and then as director of the Hayward Gallery, to join the committee, together with Charles Saumarez-Smith, the director of the National Portrait Gallery, and by November, thanks to their professional advice, we had a long-list of twelve potential sculptors who were asked to submit one-page written proposals. From these we extracted a shortlist of seven who were asked to submit maquettes by the end of April 1996.[791] The clear front-runners were Maggi Hambling, William Pye and Michael Sandle, but the committee was still very much divided on whether to opt for the conceptual or the purely representational, with Pye's and Sandle's proposals being classical standing bronzes and Hambling's more of an avant-garde work of art and her own interpretation of the subject. Kenneth Baker, former Home Secretary and Tory Party grandee, liked both the Hambling and the Pye and suggested it might be possible to com-mission both, Hambling for the foyer of the National Theatre and Pye as a street sculpture. This brought the memorable response from the left-wing Michael Foot who shot back good-naturedly: 'That's a typical Conservative compromise solution, Kenneth, which in the end costs twice the money.'[792] Baker also felt that given the chosen site for the sculpture, the pedestrians-only Adelaide Street near Charing Cross and the Strand, Maggi's low-level, sit-upon, interactive piece would be bound to attract the drunks and the homeless from the area. I said that if that were the case then all the more reason to choose it to celebrate the man who wrote from prison: 'The only people I would care to be with now are artists and people who have suffered: those who know what Beauty is, and those who know what Sorrow is: nobody else interests me.'[793] The discussions and disagreements continued throughout the year until the middle of December when we finally chose by a clear majority Maggi Hambling's piece now entitled 'A Conversation with Oscar Wilde.' Oscar, a cigarette in his hand

and in full conversational flow, was to be depicted sitting up in his coffin of green granite on which was inscribed an appropriate quotation from *Lady Windermere's Fan*: 'We are all in the gutter, but some of us are looking at the stars.' I was pleased that together we had opted for something down-to-earth in every sense of the word, both witty in concept and mildly controversial, and thus entirely in the spirit of the man it was celebrating. The idea of Oscar on a pedestal, immortalised in the dreary accuracy and eternal silence of bronze which characterises so much of the nation's public statuary, was dreadful. He would have stood loftily over his public (although Bill Pye's version was only two feet off the ground), deaf to all but the murmured inanities of a few London pigeons, a sort of travesty of his own tale of a statue and a swallow. Instead, with his cigarette, he was at a level where visitors could sit and 'talk' to him. I can't take too much credit for the final choice, but a few days before the final meeting I made a serendipitous discovery as I was checking the text of a lecture that Oscar had given in America during his tour of 1882. On the subject of modern dress and its graceless influence on modern sculpture he said: 'looking around at the figures which adorn our parks . . . to see the statues of our departed statesmen in marble frock-coats and bronze double-breasted waistcoats adds a new horror to death,'[794] and I read it out to the committee saying, light-heartedly, that perhaps we should take his own feelings into account when deciding. It's nice to think that maybe he did have a hand, however small, in determining how he was to be remembered.

Then came the boring but necessary procedure of planning permission. Jeremy applied to Westminster Council, whom he had previously sounded out informally and who were favourably disposed to the idea, but who were nevertheless obliged to seek the advice of the Royal Fine Art Commission. This was chaired by Norman St. John-Stevas into whose presence Jeremy, Maggi, Richard Summers (the Westminster Conservation Officer) and I were summoned to present our case on 9 April 1997. Jeremy had warned me that the Right Honourable the Lord St. John of

Fawsley (as he had become after being sacked as Minister for the Arts by Margaret Thatcher and kicked upstairs to the Lords) was unlikely to find much merit in the proposed memorial since he ran the Commission very much according to his own tastes and that if questioned by him, I should be extremely careful in my replies to this former barrister. I was, but my cautious enthusiasm along with the others for what he clearly regarded as too avant-garde 'and has not been successfully realised as a work of art,' carried little weight. In his letter to Westminster's Richard Summers he strongly advised that 'The work needs to be developed fundamentally further before it should be considered for planning permission.' Undaunted, Jeremy wrote immediately to the Westminster Planning Committee to say that he didn't think much of Fawsley's letter which was totally muddle-headed and missed the whole point of this interactive memorial and ended by saying 'I hope you will be bold and grant approval.'[795] To their credit, they did. The same evening.

With that, we were almost into the home straight. All that remained was to raise the money. We had originally planned to unveil the memorial on 19 May 1997, the centenary of Oscar's release from prison but, being only five weeks away, that was out of the question. Earlier in the year, knowing that this would probably be the case, Charles Saumarez-Smith had already suggested that we should nevertheless make the most of the date and use it to launch the appeal to the public for funds. He offered the exhibition space in the National Portrait Gallery for two and a half months to show Maggi's long-term interest in Oscar and her development of the memorial concept from oils painted ten years before, up to the final maquettes and preliminary bronze casts. All the NPG asked was that we should cover their costs in building the display for the exhibits and the catering for the private view. It was a perfect means of raising public awareness for the memorial; it fitted in well with the Gallery's exhibition policy; and, most importantly, it promised to be an effective way of raising the money which by this stage was estimated at nearly £170,000. I was astonished that it could cost so much, but by the time the short-listed artists' maquettes had been paid for, consultant architects' and project managers' fees had been taken into account, the Marlborough Gallery's commission as Maggi's agents had been factored in, and Westminster Council's insistence on a lump sum endowment of £24,475 for maintenance had been added to the budget, it wasn't surprising. Without the generosity of Simon Sainsbury's own donations and the Monument Trust covering all the up-front costs before the launch and then agreeing to underwrite any shortfall at the end, we would probably never have made it to the finish. I had more luck with the champagne sponsorship for the private view than I had with the Poets' Corner post-dedication drink at the Café Royal: Joseph Perrier provided magnums at cost with two cases free and a giant Methusalem which we raffled on the evening. The mood at the launch was hugely positive. Jeremy was convinced that the donations would flow in, but they didn't. A month after the private view, and without counting Simon Sainsbury's contributions, the total was less than £9,000. It probably wasn't helped by yet another homophobic rant in the *Spectator* from Peregrine Worsthorne in which he referred to Wilde as a paedophile and to 'the plainly intolerable story of Wilde's sex life' with its 'disgusting details' and 'the ugly and immoral aspects of Wilde's homosexuality.' He went on to mount what, as I read it, I hoped was going to be a slightly tongue-in-cheek defence of those he called 'anti-homosexuals,' but which by the end was clearly serious. George Melly and I both wrote light-hearted letters pointing out that Oscar may have been a paederast but he certainly wasn't a paedophile with all the modern emotive connotations that the word evokes. They were published in the magazine the following week, effectively demolishing Sir Peregrine's specious arguments and that fortunately silenced him on the subject of Wilde's memorial for good.[796]

By the time the NPG exhibition ended on 3 August and despite the fact that donation forms were included with the catalogues and available at the reception, the memorial fund had still only reached £11,500. The nature of the memorial almost certainly had something to do with it. Any wealthy potential donor who disliked the sculpture was not going to give fifty pounds as a token gesture; rather give nothing at all on principle than be considered tight-fisted. Jeremy wrote to us all on the committee to say that an unveiling on 16 October or even 30 November, the dates of Oscar's birth and death, was now impossible and that more urgent fundraising had to be done. We were encouraged to approach possible donors individually. The list of those to whom Jeremy himself wrote and their responses makes interesting reading. One or two people who had made fortunes out of the West End theatre simply declined to contribute. By contrast Stephen Fry was immensely generous and gave a five figure sum; Nick Hytner who had directed Maggie Smith as Lady Bracknell in the acclaimed 1993 revival of *The Importance of Being Earnest* gave a very considerable amount as well. But one of the most touching contributions came from a seventeen year-old Austrian schoolgirl.

Sandra Mayer had come to London that summer to explore the city in which Oscar Wilde had written *The Picture of Dorian Gray*. She was studying English for her Matura—the school leaving certificate—and, although it was not on the curriculum, she had come across a copy of *Dorian Gray* the year before in an English bookshop at home, bought it on impulse and was utterly captivated by it from start to finish. Wanting to find an image of its author, she went to the National Portrait Gallery and was thrilled to discover Maggi's exhibition and the proposed memorial. On her return to Austria she sent me a ten-pound note which was all that was left of her holiday pocket money, saying that it wasn't much but that she'd like to know that she had contributed something to commemorate this man whose only novel had given her such pleasure. Normally I would have replied with a short, polite note of thanks, but there was something extraordinarily mature about her accompanying letter written in flowing and almost faultless English, quite apart from the generosity of her gift relative to her age, which persuaded me that she deserved something a little more personal and complimentary. Her command of English was clearly good enough to cope with Oscar Wilde's more serious critical writings and, as a result, she opted for a paper on Oscar Wilde in her final school exams. After they were over the following summer and passed with distinction, she came once more to London chaperoned by her father, telephoned, and asked if we could meet for a coffee. It wasn't the most convenient of afternoons because Maggi had invited me to the foundry to see the freshly made cast of her sculpture, but mindful of Sandra's gesture of the year before, I suggested that she and her father come along with me. Much later she admitted that being one of the first to see Oscar in his new incarnation had been a defining moment in her young life and once more she sent the remains of her pocket money for the statue fund. We have kept in touch over the intervening years, which have seen a ground-breaking doctoral thesis on the posthumous reception of Wilde's plays in Austria and Sandra as a fully-fledged Wildean scholar on the teaching staff at Vienna University and Research Fellow at the Austrian Academy of Sciences. As a story about how my grandfather positively influenced a young woman's career, I still treasure it, but especially as a lasting antidote to some of the deeply offensive articles written at the time both about Oscar and his memorial.

By the early summer of 1998 we were within sight of our target and Simon Sainsbury, as he had promised, made up the balance so that the memorial could be unveiled on 16 October. However, we hadn't reckoned with the bureaucracy of the gas, water, telephone, and electricity companies who all needed to give clearance that Oscar in his coffin in Adelaide Street would not obstruct any future maintenance to their conduits and pipes. Yet again the unveiling was postponed but finally fixed for 30 November.

It was Maggi Hambling who first proposed that my son, Lucian, should perform the ceremony and make a brief speech. It was an inspired suggestion for it meant that no one had to make the difficult decision about which celebrity to ask at the risk of upsetting half a dozen others. It also showed that the family still existed. At nineteen he was now old enough to be inducted into the 'Wilde circus' and from then on, he could decide for himself how much he wanted to be part of it or not at all.

Some years before, when Lucian was twelve and at King's College School, he came home one Friday with a class project for the weekend—preparing a short talk on a personality who had some connection, however vague, with his family. Until then Lucian had been aware that his great-grandfather was Oscar Wilde, but we had avoided putting too much emphasis on the fact simply because children of that age have a habit of boasting about such things without realising how badly it can backfire on them.

His project, however, gave me the perfect opportunity to tell him in broad detail about Oscar's life and achievements and his downfall. So, that weekend I coached him through his brief talk remembering Thelma's attempts to censor parts of the story when I had been a little older than Lucian and the trouble it had caused me. It was far better that he should have a more or less unexpurgated account from me than wonder later, when he would inevitably find out the truth, why I had been at pains to conceal some of it; equally I saw no point in going into the graphic details of the trials, the rent-boys, and the blackmailers. I explained how, after getting married and having two sons with Constance, Oscar had met and fallen in love with a beautiful young aristocrat and poet; how the young man's father violently disapproved of the relationship and left Oscar a rude card at his club; how Oscar sued the father for libel and lost and was then arrested, tried, and put in prison for two years because the Victorians thought love between two men was immoral and made it a crime. No sooner had I finished and was looking anxiously for a reaction from Lucian than he said, 'Why? It wasn't his fault. He couldn't help falling in love, could he?' and then I knew that at last, as far as our family was concerned anyway, it was all over. He was a new generation who could just take a quiet pride in his ancestor's literary gifts and perhaps shrug his shoulders and smile wryly at the injustice and hypocrisy of the Victorian age.

Seven years had passed since then and unveiling a memorial to his great-grandfather now seemed to me a good place for Lucian to acknowledge publicly and for the first time his relationship to Oscar. He wrote his own two minute speech and told me quite firmly that he wasn't going to show it to me beforehand. Far from being worried I thought it showed an admirable spirit of independence. How Thelma would have reacted had she still been alive doesn't bear thinking about. Nevertheless, by the time we arrived at Charing Cross I was beginning to feel like the skipper of the trawler throwing his son into the North Sea and saying 'Now, swim!' I hadn't realised quite how rough the sea could be. The news media had turned out in force, but I had warned Lucian what sort of questions they were likely to ask and he was largely prepared. Shortly before the speeches began I introduced him to Kenneth Baker who gave him a quick masterclass in public oratory: speak more slowly than you think necessary; look up from your text as much as possible; and, even though others may have gone before, don't assume the microphone still works. Having a former Home Secretary passing on to my son some vital tips gleaned from a lifetime of public speaking was a nice touch to start to the proceedings, considering that it was a previous Home Secretary, Herbert Asquith, who had sanctioned the arrest of Oscar in 1895. Derek Jarman would have been amused by the irony. In his 'Face to Face' interview with Jeremy back in 1993, he had said that it would be wonderful if such a memorial could be unveiled by a member of the Royal Family or even by the Prime Minister, but he got Oscar's direct descendant instead, as well as a short speech by Chris Smith, the first openly gay Member of Parliament and at that point Minister for the Arts. Lucian performed his part with poise, wit, and style which was a credit to his ancestor, an opinion borne out by several of the committee who wrote to say how splendid he had been. A few days later Matthew Parris wrote in the *Spectator*, 'Wilde did not stand for anything except, perhaps, the human spirit. That is what his great-grandson Lucian said to the crowd. It was immediately controversial, it is true, and it was the only interesting thing that was said all morning.'[797] Since the Handbag Scene from *The Importance of Being Earnest* had been done to death on public occasions and because Jeremy felt a snippet of Wildean drama would be appropriate for the occasion, I suggested that Judi Dench and Nigel Hawthorne should read an extract from *A Woman of No Importance*, the sexually charged verbal duel between Mrs. Allonby and Lord Illingworth at the end of Act One. It taxed the skill of even these most seasoned of professionals. In the open air, at midday and competing at one point with an ambulance siren and the general cacophony of Central London, Nigel was forced to deliver the line, 'One can survive everything nowadays, except death, and live down anything except a good reputation,' in a sort of theatrical bellow. Stephen Fry lent Lucian a hand with the removal of the tarpaulin, the elegant uncovering of Oscar rising from his coffin posing something of an unveiling nightmare, and then took on the press, much to Lucian's relief as well as mine. Nigel Hawthorne told the BBC that he didn't particularly like the monument and said: 'I think he should have been on a pedestal because that's really how he saw himself,' [798] which was exactly the misconception we were trying to combat with our interactive memorial. It was also the view of some of the onlookers at the ceremony: they were expecting a sort of dandified, limp-wristed Wilde with hat and cape and cane a composite of all that was sartorially striking about the Sarony photographs taken in New York in 1882. That would have been making him acceptable to the British public a hundred years on—nothing too much to remind them that he was just as much at home in the demi-monde of Soho as in the mansions of Belgravia. He needed to be humanised and that's what the memorial did for him. When I went back a week later to see how he was doing, I asked Brian, the hot chestnut seller at the junction of Adelaide Street and the Strand, how the public as a whole were reacting. 'They love it,' he said. 'He's hardly alone all day long.'

On Lord Henry Wotton's principle that the one thing in the world worse than being talked about, is not being talked about, it wouldn't have been Oscar's day without him indirectly stirring up some controversy, even a minor scandal. While Nigel Hawthorne was talking live to the BBC's News at One programme about the memorial, the presenter, Edward Stourton asked him 'Is there a wider significance to this or is it just a rather entertaining sculpture?' Nigel, himself gay, wanted to make the point that this was another step towards the acceptance of homosexuality in public life and started to bring in the name of Peter Mandelson, the Trade Secretary who had recently been 'outed' on BBC2's *Newsnight*.[799] Since then, the BBC had instituted a ban on any reference to Mandelson's private life, so Stourton cut him short and said he didn't want to discuss individuals but the general principle of tolerance. 'If you don't talk about individuals, then you miss the whole point of this,' persisted Hawthorne. 'Society picks on these individuals and turns them into martyrs very often, which is exactly what happened to Oscar Wilde.' Nigel was furious at the attempt to censor him and the story, picked up by most of the broadsheets as well as the *Daily Mail* and the *Sun*, made a juicy adjunct to the unveiling itself.[800]

On the Channel 4 News at 6 pm, the presenter, Jon Snow, interviewed Jeremy Isaacs from near his home in London's Docklands and, of all strange choices, Bruce Anderson, political editor of the *Spectator* in the studio. After some video footage of the unveiling ceremony and interviews with Chris Smith and Matthew Parris, it became clear that Anderson was there merely to stir up controversy.' The best thing that ever happened to Oscar Wilde,' he said, 'was going to gaol. He'd be forgotten if he hadn't. He was a very minor poet and playwright—much less good than Bernard Shaw.' This elicited an impassioned reply from Jeremy about Wilde's greatness as a comic playwright in which he described the memorial as 'an amusing interactive statue in the streets of London which will cheer up the Strand,' adding that it was another step in the right direction towards acknowledging rather than hiding sexual diversity. Bruce Anderson then made the outrageous remark: 'It's an awful piece of sculpture. It's worse than the Queen

Mother's Gates [at Hyde Park Corner] and they were designed by a homosexual as well,' prompting from an astonished Jon Snow the response 'That's a dreadful thing to say, not about the gates but about the designers.'[801]

The disagreements both over the aesthetic merit of the memorial as well as over the advisability of honouring Oscar at all continued in the press for the rest of the week. Brian Sewell, celebrated for his dismissal of most contemporary art, had already written that 'Even a homosexual deserves better than this tasteless insult' when the maquette was exhibited at the NPG the year before, and called it 'a gimcrack trifle, a graceless bagatelle' a remark recycled by the *Evening Standard* on the day of the unveiling.[802] Tom Lubbock, the chief art critic on the *Independent*, detested its 'whimsy and triviality . . . . It's wilful tack. The bust and hand aren't solid metal. They materialise from a sort of macaroni tangle of undulating tubey strands. The head looks silly. The technique does too . . . . It's tourist tat. Don't say it insults Wilde. It disgraces us . . . . An empty space would be better. At any event, it's got to go.'[803] Christopher Hart wrote an odious piece in the *Daily Mail* centring on Oscar's relationships with the Victorian rent-boys which could have been signed by Worsthorne himself, so full was it of half-truths, faulty reasoning and errors repeated from sensationalist biographies, and finishing up: 'Putting up a statue to him in its present location must be some kind of joke. But not a very funny one.'[804]

I don't remember the first time his cigarette was sawed off. The culprit wasn't found so we never knew whether it was gratuitous vandalism, souvenir hunting, or a protest by a fanatic member of ASH (Action on Smoking and Health). Maggi replaced it with a hardened stainless steel one only to find that it, too, disappeared as did three more. In 2005 we eventually tried to put pressure on Westminster Council to take action. Amazingly, given the endowment of £24,475 to look after the memorial in perpetuity, at first they denied all responsibility. Later they backed down but when we suggested that they cover the area with a CCTV camera they came up with a figure of £50,000 to install it and, adding in the monitoring costs, a total of £175,000 to maintain it over ten years. Westminster then asked Maggi to estimate the cost of repairing and replacing two cigarettes a year over the same period if they were manufactured as a batch so that there were always some in reserve. She and the foundry and the metal-worker came up with a figure of £500 a fag. At £10,000 for a packet of twenty Oscar would, I am sure, have been delighted to be smoking the most expensive cigarettes in the world, but there was something inherently wrong in the reasoning which just accepted vandalism as a fact rather than trying to prevent it. In between his cigarettes being stolen, the freelance copy editor whom Fourth Estate used for my previous books on Oscar provided him (and me) with some light relief. Ilsa Yardley, who said she had come to love Oscar through working on him, wrote a letter of protest to *The Times* after the disappearance of the fourth cigarette thus making the matter public.[805] At the same time she wrote to me saying that every time she was near Charing Cross she made a point (smoker that she was) of passing by him, lighting up and placing the cigarette between his fingers. Brilliant, I thought. We never considered that aspect of the monument's interactive potential.

You either love him or you hate him. He's still 'communicating' with his admirers, courting controversy, getting himself talked about, everything he wanted when he was at the height of his success, and as that Austrian schoolgirl remarked perceptively when she first saw him twenty-seven years ago freshly cast in the foundry, 'Oh, my goodness! He's alive.' In an odd way she was absolutely right.

CHAPTER NINE
MOSCOW PRIDE (& PREJUDICE)

I t was in the summer of 2000 while I was helping to prepare the Oscar Wilde centenary exhibition at the British Library that I first met Nicolay Alekseev. I'm not in the habit of being stopped by strangers in public places—I don't have that sort of media profile—so I was slightly taken aback when I was accosted at the entrance to the Reading Room by a young man with a Slavic accent who seemed to know who I was. He introduced himself as a constitutional law graduate from Moscow State University, told me he was hugely sympathetic to all that Oscar had gone through a hundred years before and asked if I'd be prepared to talk to him briefly about my grandfather. Usually my heart sinks at this point in such a meeting knowing that once again I'm the stand-in, the substitute for the real thing, but that somehow I owe it to my grandfather to be friendly and engage with admirers of his while ranging myself firmly alongside them, on their side of the fence looking in rather than the other way round and being an object of curiosity. Nicolay at once struck me as being different. Over coffee I discovered that he was gay and already making waves as a postgraduate in his department. His main interest, later published as a controversial book, was in gay marriage and the status of same-sex couples in international law. I told him of my own interest in Oscar's posthumous reputation abroad and he promised to see what he could find out when he returned to Moscow. I agreed that we should keep in touch, and I meant it.

Over the next four years we corresponded sporadically and he even ran to earth an extremely rare bibliography of writings about Oscar and translations of his works from 1892 to 2000. Only 300 copies were printed, one of which he sent me with translations of the more interesting entries. It had been published by the State Library of Foreign Literature with a subsidy from the Irish to celebrate the centenary of Oscar's death. I never knew, for example, that Leo Tolstoy attacked Oscar in a work entitled *What Is Art?* in 1898 saying that 'decadents and aesthetes like Oscar Wilde choose as themes in their work the dismissal of morality and the glorification of depravity,' nor, conversely, that others condemned his imprisonment as hypocritical and barbaric.[806]

Despite Russia having decriminalised homosexuality in 1993, I followed Nicolay's progress with increasing apprehension, but also with admiration when he took the university to court for discrimination after it refused his thesis on sexual minorities. He lost his case and consequently was forced to leave. Then in October 2005 he rang me and asked if I would be prepared to come to Moscow in May the following year and take part in the first Gay Pride March. Some groups were worried, saying that it was too early, especially as the growing neo-fascist movement in Russia had threatened violent opposition to gay people in public, but Nicolay was insistent that the timing was perfect. I was hesitant. I had never been actively involved in the gay rights movement in spite of having one of the most famously gay ancestors of all time, but I agreed to go when I heard that the first IDAHO (International Day Against Homophobia) conference was to be part of the programme. It was, after all, Victorian homophobia which brought my grandfather to prison and bankruptcy and had made such a misery of the first thirty years of my father's life. Nicolay also asked if he could publish two books on Wilde in Russian translation to coincide with the events, but without paying royalties on them—my edition of Oscar's libel trial against Lord Queensberry, *Irish Peacock and Scarlet Marquess,* and *Son of Oscar Wilde*, my father's autobiography. Publication of the two books was a perfect adjunct to the conference and the conference was the right moment for me to speak out against homophobia. Paying royalties on Russian translations can be complicated; it probably wouldn't have amounted to large sums in foreign currency anyway and it seemed better that any profits should help fund Nicolay's fledgling LGBTQ movement. He also asked if I would write an open letter to Vladimir Putin which he would arrange to publish. I did, on 7 February 2006, and said that I was shocked at the overtly homophobic attitude of the mayor of Moscow, Yuri Luzhkov, who had declared publicly that he would ban peaceful demonstrations by sexual minorities. I also reminded the President that a few of the greatest creative minds in Russia had been homosexual: 'Homosexuals are not terrorists; they are not murderers; they are not fanatics who take hostages to achieve their goals. They are simply human beings who are asking that their rights to normal lives be recognised.' Russia was due to assume the Chairmanship of the Council of Europe a week before the first IDAHO Conference and the planned Pride March, as well as hosting the G8 summit in July, and I made the point that it was the perfect time for the authorities to show respect for the human rights of sexual minorities. Knowing today how Russia treats its critics I'm not sure writing that letter was the wisest thing to do, but I was committed to attending the May events and although my influence was probably insignificant, at least it was another voice raised in support.

On 18 March Louis-Georges Tin, founder of IDAHO, wrote to me saying that it was more important than ever that I, as a non-gay participant, should come to Moscow in May since Michael Cashman, the British MEP and President of the European Parliament Intergroup for Gay and Lesbian Rights had now decided that it would be too dangerous for him to attend. Losing the support of such an influential figure was a blow. Would I co-sign a letter to him, asked Louis-Georges, to make him change his mind? I agreed but said that I understood Cashman's worry since he was under a death-threat from some lunatic homophobe in the UK. I don't think the letter was ever written and Cashman never did turn up. Nor did he attend any of the later Moscow Prides. To give him his due he attended the Warsaw one in June that year, but it was a soft option by comparison with what, by then, had happened in Moscow. By contrast, Sophie in 't Veld, MEP from the Netherlands, Clémentine Autain, Paris city councillor and now French *députée*, and Volker Beck, lawyer and member of the German Bundestag, all turned up and lent their support.

Earlier in the year leaders of the main religions in Russia had not helped matters by their homophobic declarations. The Chief Rabbi Berel Lazar said that a Gay pride march would be an attack on public morality and that it would simply be publicity for a 'form of sexual perversion which had no right to exist.' The Russian Orthodox Church expressed itself in similar terms and called it 'the propaganda of sin,' and the Grand Mufti of Russia, Talgat Tadzhuddin, declared 'Homosexuals have no rights. If they come out on the streets, they should be beaten. Any normal person would do it—Muslims and Orthodox Christians alike.'[807] Yuri Luzhkov, who was notoriously homophobic, stated in advance of any application to hold the march that he had no intention of allowing it to go ahead then or at any time in the future so long as he was mayor of the city. At the beginning of May two gay clubs were targeted by fascist thugs. One of them, the Renaissance Event Club, had announced an 'Open Party' only to find that the guests were greeted outside by an angry crowd of 150 skinheads, nationalists, and Russian Orthodox Christians who hurled bottles, bricks, eggs, and insults at the would-be partygoers for 'damaging the nation.' In the end it had to be cancelled because people couldn't get in.

On 15 May the official request for the march to take place was made with the authorities and within three days Luzhkov had announced a ban saying, 'This type of parade may be acceptable for some kinds of progressive countries in the West but it is absolutely unacceptable for Moscow.' Nicolay then lodged an appeal against this decision in the courts and applied instead to hold static demonstrations in front of the City Hall, in Lubyanka Square and in Pushkinskaya Square in protest against this suppression of human rights. This, too, had been refused but his appeal would not be heard for months. Both these decisions were in direct contravention of the Russian Constitution and of Article 11 of the European

Convention on Human Rights to which Russia was a signatory as a member of the Council of Europe, and whose presidency it assumed on the day after Luzhkov's ban.

I arrived on Wednesday 24 May, three days before the planned Saturday march. It was the first time I had been in Moscow since Christmas 1970 when I was living in Beirut and had visited my old friend Richard, then training with the Bolshoi Ballet. Memories dim in thirty-six years but even allowing for the different season and the passage of time, I might have been in a different city. Western consumerism seemed everywhere in evidence, together with the trappings of democracy and rampant capitalism—metro station walls were fly-posted with stickers advertising company registration procedures—and beside all this, the heavy hand of the state denying individuals the right to claim their sexual diversity seemed incomprehensible.

While the MEPs and other members of the various elected bodies in Europe settled comfortably into their hotel rooms on expenses, Peter Tatchell, Robert Wintemute, Professor of Human Rights Law at London University, and I were taken by the organisers to a private apartment where we were to stay. Officially we had been booked into an hotel and had month-long 'pre-paid' tourist itineraries which had been the only way to obtain our visas. It was all a pretence and a hangover from the Soviet era when tourism was rigorously controlled, but nobody checked up on us and no one seemed to care. As individual 'delegates' the Moscow Pride organisers had offered to put us up using promised sponsorship from abroad, notably from Pierre Bergé in Paris but he suddenly pulled out at the beginning of April because of the possible repercussions on the sales of Yves St. Laurent in Russia, and the whole event was having to be run on a shoestring. Naked light bulbs, dodgy wiring everywhere, self-catering, and the feeling that several people had slept in your sheets before you—that much certainly hadn't changed in thirty-six years. Peter as a hardened human rights activist had come prepared; he knew what to expect. He came with a towel and an emergency packet of biscuits. I didn't. I had been slightly wary of him since 1994 when, long before the case of Alan Turing, he petitioned the Queen to pardon my grandfather. My view then had been that a pardon, if granted, would simply make the British Establishment feel better about what it had done in 1895; it wouldn't make Oscar's or Constance's lives any longer or my father's any happier. I was content to see Oscar's fate as a permanent rebuke to Victorian morality—hypocrisy even. I also used to joke that if it happened I'd sue the Government for loss of earnings. But after three days in Peter's company I radically altered my view of the man and his courageous activism and I was glad of the chance that I could. Robert not only opened my eyes to some of the horrors to which LGBTQ communities were being subjected worldwide, but also proved to be a real brother-in-arms when all the ugliness began. We spent the first evening with several of the other delegates at a gay club called the '12 Volt.' I think I expected it to be more vibrant and loud than it was but, as Nicolay said, this wasn't London or New York, and since the recent attacks on other clubs in the city, the community was having to be extra-cautious. The mood was positive but uneasy. We talked about whether, in view of the bans, we should even be demonstrating, let alone marching. Everyone, though, was in agreement that something had to be done to show that the 2006 Moscow Pride hadn't been simply beaten into submission by the bullying tactics of Luzhkov.

On Thursday came the news that the Tverskoy District Court had convened a special sitting the following morning to consider Nicolay's appeal against the mayor's ban. Some thought that this augured well; others assumed it would merely be to uphold and even publicise the city hall's decision. Whatever the outcome, the authorities were clearly taking it very seriously. That afternoon Nicolay was summoned by the Deputy Chief of Police. He had been quoted on the news website Interfax as having said the march would go ahead regardless. He hadn't. 'If your march is legal,' said the Deputy Chief, 'I guarantee not a single hair of your head will be harmed.' The website was known for stirring up trouble and later, probably to get me into the fascist sights, it had reported me as being gay, a fact I was at pains to deny everywhere I went, not because I minded being thought gay, but to emphasise the fact that IDAHO and Moscow Pride had support from outside the LGBTQ community. Distortion, half-truths, and mischief-making were all part of the fevered climate surrounding the proposed march.

That evening, 25 May—significantly the 111th anniversary of Oscar's conviction and imprisonment—I gave a lecture at the State Library of Foreign Literature entitled 'The Wilde Family: the Aftermath' which was intended to show my audience some of the enduring consequences of Victorian anti-homosexual legislation. The Russians have long been admirers of Wilde's works from the pre-revolutionary interest in his essay *The Soul of Man under Socialism* to the playing of *An Ideal Husband* in the 1950s and 1960s as an example of the corrupt nature of Western Politics. But apart from this rather pragmatic approach, they have also enjoyed his work as an 'artist,' and I was not surprised (as was the case elsewhere in Europe until the 1980s) to discover that many people were ignorant of the cause his downfall and those who knew regarded it as of secondary importance. My elementary reasoning was that lovers of Wilde the artist would have more sympathy for Wilde the gay man if they knew the story—and that was part of the reason for associating Oscar with IDAHO. The Director of the Library, Ekaterina Genieva, had hosted controversial events before, and had indeed welcomed them in the spirit of tolerance and diversity which she said the Library represented. She seemed remarkably well-informed about Wilde's works in the conversation we had before the lecture and even went so far as to suggest that one day a bust of Oscar should be placed in the Library garden alongside those of other internationally known figures such as Abraham Lincoln and Charles Dickens. It was amusing to think that here he was still chasing Dickens's reputation from the time of his American lecture tour in 1882, through his tardy acceptance onto the Oxford English Literature curriculum, to being celebrated in a library garden in Moscow. Before we started, the

Director's secretary took me to one side and, in a somewhat conspiratorial tone, told me that the Irish cultural attaché had been invited and had agreed to attend with the Ambassador, but on learning that my lecture was being promoted by Moscow Pride, she said, 'they were shocked.' Allowing for her less than perfect English, and Ireland's interest in and generosity towards 'posthumous' Oscar, I think they were just being understandably cautious about the Ambassador's safety. Representatives of the British Council, on the other hand, were invited but didn't even respond.

Nicolay had already told me that the lecture had only been advertised discreetly and that the audience would be relatively small. There were about sixty in the auditorium as Ekaterina introduced me and another dozen or so drifted in while she was doing it. Then, just as I was about to begin, a crowd of twenty more arrived. They were young; probably students, I thought, and waited for them to settle down before starting. Ten minutes into the lecture I was interrupted by the latecomers who stood up and started chanting: 'Homosexual propaganda! Russia! Russia! Russia! This is our country!' They turned out to be a group of neo-fascists and before running out, one of them let off a canister of some sort of choking-gas. A nationalist website had got to hear of the lecture and had 'promoted' it with the sole intention of stirring up trouble. We cleared the auditorium in a hurry and for safety's sake Ekaterina suggested cancelling the event. I said I wouldn't hear of it. It would be giving in to intimidation which, the night before, we had all agreed would be wrong. The audience recovered its breath, no one left and I completed the lecture in another room. It was a mere appetiser for what was to come and the following day the fascists painted a huge bloody knife on the wall of the Library.

On Friday morning the IDAHO conference started in the Moscow Swissôtel and it was a credit to the hotel to have allowed the conference to take place on its premises given that we were a potential target for nationalist violence. By now we were all very much aware of that possibility from the moment we arrived. Security guards, insisted on by the hotel who later presented a huge bill for them to the Pride organisers, were posted outside the hotel, though none of them seemed to be actively checking delegates' credentials. Even a proper police presence at the library the night before had not prevented the infiltration by homophobic nationalists.

By late morning Nicolay had returned from the Tverskoy District Court where his appeal against Luzhkov had been heard. Nicolay argued through his lawyer that the ban was illegal, but the judge upheld the mayor's decision on the spurious grounds put forward by the mayor's office that there weren't enough police available to prevent outbreaks of violence. The afternoon conference sessions were cancelled and the time given over to discussing what course of action to adopt on Saturday, the day of the banned march and incidentally the 13th anniversary of Russia decriminalizing homosexuality. To do nothing would be to give in to neo-fascist threats and the blatantly illegal city council decisions and might be seen as a defeat. To march without proper police protection would be suicidal. Peter Tatchell was all for positive action rather than just static protests. 'The eyes of the world will be upon you,' he said, but added, 'though the world won't be able to protect you.' As an old hand in these matters he emphasised that we needed to be pragmatic along with the idealism. Could one be arrested on civil disobedience charges? If so what's the fine? How long might one spend in custody? Were there lawyers sympathetic to the cause who might be called on? Scott Long from Human Rights Watch raised the valid point that the foreign delegates to the conference, who outnumbered the Russians by about five to one, would leave after a couple more days and return to their comfortable democratic existences, leaving the Russians to cope with any consequences. Perhaps the Russian contingent should make the decision. The suggestion was welcomed by all. We left them in the conference room for an hour and they decided. There would be a demonstration but details of when and where would not be announced until shortly beforehand or we were liable to find the neo-fascist, homophobic thugs waiting for us.

That evening, I signed copies of the Russian translations of Vyvyan's and my books in a large Moscow bookstore and gave an impromptu talk about how Oscar's downfall had affected his immediate family for so long afterwards. Nicolay made a semi-simultaneous translation—never the best way to address an audience on a slightly emotive subject, but there was a strange and unexpected harmony in what we did. There were more people than had attended the lecture the night before and I was surprised by the number of children who came with their parents. One or two wanted me to sign Russian translations of *The Happy Prince*. Normally I detest having to sign Oscar's books as a sort of posthumous amanuensis, but this was different. Some people actually thanked me for coming to Moscow to lend my voice to the fight against homophobia. I remember feeling embarrassed by the compliment and saying something along the lines of how good it was that Oscar could help from beyond the grave. There could have been disruptions but there weren't. Given all that had happened so far, the manager, Katya Mosina showed admirable courage in allowing the signing to take place in her shop and the atmosphere of that evening helped to erase part of the unpleasant memories of the day before as well as strengthening our resolve for what was to come on the next.

On Saturday Nicolay organised a late-morning press conference at the hotel where the police were now very much in evidence. It meant, inevitably, that our plans for the afternoon had to be made public and would alert the neo-fascists, but that was the risk we ran if we wanted international press coverage of what was happening to the LGBTQ community in Russia. Several sources later reported that the IDAHO delegates barely outnumbered the media and that morning we numbered about eighty. There was to be no official march, but in small groups of two or three, so as not to attract more attention than necessary, we would make our separate ways to the Tomb of the Unknown Soldier in the Alexander Gardens at the Kremlin and lay flowers on it. The gesture would be significant as the tomb with its eternal flame was also a monument to the defeat of fascism in the Second World War. From there we would join up into slightly larger groups and walk up Tverskaya Street to demonstrate briefly in front of the City Hall, display rainbow flags and unfurl the Moscow Pride banner. The timing was critical as we had to finish up as a single cohesive crowd. Two-thirty at the tomb and no later than three o'clock at the City Hall.

As the conference was finishing, we rapidly put together a 'Moscow Human Rights Appeal' detailing some of the violations which had taken place in the previous months together with all that we felt had been illegally denied to the LGBTQ community in Russia. It was signed by all the major delegates with any political clout, including Edward Murzin a Liberal deputy from Bashkortostan and the only Russian politician brave enough to associate himself with the events.

Nicolay wanted me to go with him to lay the flowers. I said that as a heterosexual man it was maybe inappropriate for me to be at the forefront of what was happening and I suggested he might be better accompanied by a committed activist like Volker Beck. But Nicolay insisted. My presence was important to him. Once again it would show that the movement for LGBTQ rights in Russia not only had foreign support but also that of someone from outside the gay community who was protesting against Russian homophobia. A German television crew gave Nicolay and Peter Tatchell and me a lift to the Kremlin. We bought flowers on the way. As we passed the completely police-cordoned Lubyanka Square, circling the Kremlin for the fourth time, it started to rain heavily. 'Only Luzhkov and Putin together could have achieved this,' said Nicolay. His phone rang. 'They've shut the gates at the entrance to the Alexander Garden to prevent us getting to the tomb.' It was obviously Luzhkov's doing and he was later reported as having said: 'These gays wanted to lay flowers at the grave of the unknown warrior. This is a provocation. It is desecration of a sacred place.'

It was 2:30pm. We got out of the minibus into the rain and

started walking, flowers in hand. It couldn't have been more obvious who we were. Ed Murzin joined us. By the time we were within ten feet of the police cordon at the entrance, we were surrounded. I was suddenly aware that it was no longer just the familiar city police with their tall-crowned caps but now predominantly the OMON, the special riot militia, in their black berets and camouflage fatigues. The authorities were anticipating trouble and had ordered them in. I think it was the circle of photographers which saved us from being trampled by the fascists, chanting homophobic slogans. Ed and I tried to link arms with Nicolay, but were slowly edged apart from him by the crowd which seemed intent on crushing us. Police forced their way through from behind, relieving the pressure, but the three of us by now were totally separated. They dragged Nicolay off to a police bus, as much for his own protection as anything. He was an unmistakable figure after so much media exposure in the last days. What I didn't realise was that after the publicity posters for the lecture and the bookshop signing, and an article and photo in Moscow's highest circulation newspaper, I probably was as well.[808]

The fascists flowed away in front of the advancing riot police line and I followed, taking photographs—madness with hindsight, but acting like a tourist may have saved me from a beating. The fascists regrouped and started moving towards Tverskaya. I was recognised by a woman who had been among the disrupters at the lecture. She threw a couple of eggs and started shouting and pointing at me. This time I was saved by the fascists setting off flares and tear gas to delay the police advance. In the diversion, I found Robert Wintemute who offered me shelter under his rainbow umbrella. Strangely oblivious to the fact that this object would attract fascists like moths to a candle, we set off up Tverskaya towards the City Hall. I heard shouts from behind and the approach of running feet, followed by a tremendous kick in the back. I staggered but didn't fall. If I had, those who came behind would certainly have made their own contributions. They passed through. We felt sheepish and defeatist as we closed our rainbow brolly, but, outnumbered by about ten to one, anything else would have been foolhardy. A few supporters, principally those who hadn't tried to reach the tomb, had already grouped opposite the City Hall. Some sported rainbow flags; the banner had gone with Nicolay. Despite the riot police, there were injuries, Volker Beck among them. The job of the police was to keep the two sides apart, not to afford protection for us. In fact, they seemed more intent on corralling thugs and protesters together so as to inflict maximum damage, make plenty of arrests and subsequently lay all the blame for it on the LGBTQ community, as I discovered a few moments later when Robert and I found ourselves on the wrong side of a police line faced by a dozen thugs. The pack leader thrust his face into Robert's, held him against a car and shouted *Ubiraites iz Rossii, ebanye pidory* (Get out of Russia you fucking faggots). I had similar abuse hurled at me from further away and was hit by another egg and potatoes. The police, three feet away, just looked on. Toothless, old babushkas followed behind (someone said they were paid a few hundred roubles each to turn out) and sprayed us with 'holy water' from plastic bottles shouting *Moskva ne Sodom* (Moscow isn't Sodom). We finally retired to the safety of a café for two hours until the streets cleared. It had given me a small taste of what that afternoon 'in the grey November rain' on the station platform must have been like for Oscar as he was transferred from Wandsworth to Reading prison.

Nicolay was released at about 6:30pm in the evening, shaken but unhurt except for a cut on his hand inflicted at the moment of his arrest. It was in fact his first ever public protest and he later told me that he could not have imagined the degree of violence which erupted onto the streets of central Moscow that afternoon. Later years for him would be even worse with beatings and on one occasion a broken finger. I flew back to France as planned early the following morning and attempted to make sense of it all on the plane. One of the strangest consequences of those intense four days, when I tried to recall them a week later, was that I could not remember a single place where I had had a meal; alongside all that

I had experienced, eating was of such secondary importance that my memory seemed to have erased all recollection of doing it.

Many articles were published on the Moscow fracas in the following week. Half the world heard about it and was incensed by the Russian authorities' behaviour. The odd report that I was beaten up became exaggerated with each retelling, but obviously having 'Oscar Wilde's grandson set upon by anti-gay Russians' spiced up the news.[809] Every kick, every punch, every insult of that day was reversed, turned back on the homophobes, and did them more disservice than they could ever have imagined. Back in France I wrote to Robert to thank him for his companionship and support and added: 'One of the "scars" it left me with for twenty-four hours was constantly looking over my shoulder for denim-clad fascists. I caught myself doing it in the métro on the way home.'[810]

Was I frightened? No—but only because I was ignorant of the danger at the time. Would I do it again, knowing what I do now? I hope I could find the courage, because it would be small by comparison with the courage of those who had to stay behind and live with that hideous homophobia and the denial of their human rights. I was glad to think that Oscar may indirectly have done a little to move things on.

As it was, I didn't go back and take part in any more Moscow Prides. I nearly went in May 2009 since Nicolay and Ekaterina Genieva were indeed planning to put a bust of Oscar in the garden of the State Library of Foreign Literature around the same time as the Pride, which that year coincided again with IDAHO. It was never done because the sculptor claimed his price was for coated resin rather than solid bronze and the commission had to be cancelled. There was also some difficulty with being granted a visa, though I like to think it must have been an administrative problem. I can't believe that my 'activities' in 2006 could possibly have put me on a blacklist. Nevertheless, in the event that a bust of Oscar were ever to be unveiled in that garden and I were to be invited to take tea with the Mayor of Moscow, it might be sensible to take my own teabag.

Nicolay took his appeal against the banned marches of 2006, 2007 and 2008 all the way to the European Court of Human Rights and in October 2010 a unanimous verdict with costs was given in his favour.[811] Russia was not granted the right to appeal to the Grand Chamber of the ECHR. Moscow seems to have had the last word—for the moment at least. In what can only have been an act of revenge, in 2012 its City and District courts upheld a farcical order by the municipality to ban all gay parades for a hundred years.[812] I shall be long gone by then, but if the account of Oscar's vicarious presence at the first Moscow Pride still has an echo or two to encourage Russia's LGBTQ community to fight on in the meantime, then it will have been worthwhile taking him along.

CHAPTER TEN
CASHING IN ON OSCAR

Since the start of his 'rehabilitation' in the 1970s Oscar Wilde has become an attention-grabbing brand name in a number of fields including bars in several countries, a chain of apartment-style hotels, whiskey, gin, and Irish bottled water. A car ferry, a freight locomotive, a river cruise ship, and even an aeroplane have been named after him. He was even press-ganged into promoting a de-alcoholised sparkling wine, a form of purgatory that I always felt to be rather unfair. There seems to be no limit to the amount of products he gets called on to endorse. While all this is deeply flattering to his memory there is also a less attractive side to his popularity: no author of the last 150 years, more than Oscar Wilde, seems to have been subjected to so many attempts, both crude and sophisticated, to forge his letters, his manuscripts and the possessions that unscrupulous chancers would like to persuade us that he might once have owned.

As a family we own no manuscripts and almost none of Oscar's possessions. The few that survived were bequeathed to my father by such generous friends as Robert Ross who must have salvaged them from the Tite Street sheriff's sale in 1895 or from Oscar's hotel room at the time of his death. That some of them, like the decorated envelope he made containing a lock of his sister's hair on her death in 1867, have survived at all is almost miraculous. So when an auction house trumpets the discovery, for example, of 'Oscar Wilde's last toothbrush' (not yet happened but I feel it's only time), my first reaction is to find reasons why it shouldn't be genuine because it almost certainly isn't. This always raises the philosophical problem of 'proving the negative,' but since the overwhelming percentage of 'Oscar Wilde Owned' objects come with the flimsiest of provenance, bringing circumstantial evidence to bear on their authenticity generally tips the balance of probability quite heavily against it.

Until 1991 nothing in the way of Oscar's personal possessions, apart from books, manuscripts and the odd work of art, seems to have passed through auction salerooms but all that started to change in December of that year when Christie's offered for sale a silver visiting-card case purportedly given to him by his good friend Ada Leverson whom Oscar always referred to as 'Sphinx.'[813] The catalogue entry for the item speculated that the card case, inscribed 'For Sebastian Melmoth from Sphinx,' was given to him by Ada on his release from prison and just before his departure into European exile for the rest of his life. Melmoth was the pseudonym he decided to adopt to conceal his identity, and indeed his notoriety, from all but close friends and Ada was waiting to greet him that morning at the house of Stewart Headlam, the Anglican priest who had gone bail for him before his criminal trial. All very plausible and convincing: a parting gift for an old friend with a new name, except that Christie's cataloguing of the item was misleadingly inaccurate. I suppose it was typical of an auction house at the time to make as many positive historical links as they could with an item they were selling, especially as the provenance was fairly vague. The main problem with this neat explanation was that Oscar only told Ada about his pseudonym a day later after he had arrived in Dieppe when he wrote to thank her for coming to welcome him back to the outside world.[814] This would, of course, have been absurd if she had just given him a card case with 'Sebastian Melmoth' engraved on it. Quite apart from that, Oscar spent his first week of freedom writing to thank friends for their various kindnesses to him and their presents— and there is no mention of a card case in his letter to her. When I voiced my doubts after the sale, Christie's then changed their tune and said 'Well, she may have given it to him when she went to see him eighteen months later in Paris.' Yes, possibly, but there is still no letter of thanks for it and Ada Leverson was as meticulous a keeper of Oscar's letters to her (even down to one-line notes) as he was a thanker of people for their gifts. In 1930, she published *Letters to the Sphinx from Oscar Wilde* in which they were all included though with the exception, understandably, of a later one in which Oscar was critical of her husband Ernest's handling of his finances when he was in prison. There is no mention of the card case anywhere in those letters nor in her long introduction reminiscing about their friendship. To have given him a card-case the morning he came out of prison would have made a lot of sense and would have been a thoughtful gift, but it is clear from the circumstantial evidence that she didn't. To have given it to Oscar eighteen months later when he had largely dropped the pretence of 'Melmoth' (except when signing postcards) would have lost the charm of a spontaneous gesture.[815]

Although everything weighed against the card case ever having belonged to Oscar, I asked Christie's if they could give me more details about the provenance which might tip the balance in its favour. The vendor's father, they replied, 'obtained it in Paris after the First World War. It was this particularly that had satisfied us that it was authentic.'[816] Really? Provenance? Worse than useless by today's standards thirty years later—even suspect. All Oscar's possessions of any monetary or sentimental value were removed from his hotel room by Robert Ross after his death. So if the card case really was still around in Paris in the 1920s, and maybe purchased in an antiques shop, Oscar cannot have owned it when he died. Perhaps he pawned it when he needed money in those last years? For a piece of silver that size it would hardly have been worth it. Maybe he lost it in the street one night when he came home after too much absinthe in the Grand Café? One could go on forever trying to excuse such a hazy provenance, but I'd always come back to the improbability of Ada Leverson giving it to him for the lack of evidence which, given both her and Oscar's epistolary habits, ought to have survived.

Four years after that sale I was contacted by someone who claimed to have my grandmother's desktop blotter and wanted my opinion on it. It was made from tortoise-shell with silver corners and her monogrammed initials, also in silver, on the front. This time the provenance appeared to be more convincing. The owner explained that it had come down to his mother (recently deceased) through the Napier family and it had originally been given to my grandmother by her aunt, Mary Napier, after Constance had been forced to leave England and changed her name to Holland—hence the initials 'C.H.' On her death in 1898, her brother, Otho, had been responsible for putting her affairs in order and had given various personal items as mementos to close friends and family. He apparently returned this blotter to aunt Mary. Thus far, especially as there seemed to be a family connection, there was no reason to disbelieve it. However, there was another item which the owner had inherited which made me immediately suspicious: it was a hideous Victorian brass inkstand on which had been engraved 'Inkstand of Oscar Wilde given to Mary Napier by her beloved Constance.' In the first place this looked like provenance overkill and secondly, whoever had put the inscription there clearly had no idea of the level of disgust felt by the Napiers for Oscar after his downfall. When my father returned to England after Constance's death and stayed with the Napiers he was shocked to find a copy of *The Happy Prince* in their library with his father's name scratched off the cover and pasted over on the title page.[817] No, this was not the sort of gift that would have been welcomed in that family and Constance would have known it. It wouldn't have been hers to give before Oscar's arrest and it was hardly the sort of cumbersome object she would have packed up to take to the Continent with her after his conviction. Everything about it was wrong, but because of the 'Napier connection' my immediate and rather incautious reply to the owner was that I felt that the desk blotter might be genuine though I had doubts about the inkstand. I also asked for more details of how he was related to the Napiers which were never forthcoming. In a final brief note he said that his sister had some emerald and gold jewellery which they believed had belonged to Constance, a claim so fantastic that it made me certain I was dealing with an innocent legatee rather than a clumsy forger. The next thing I knew was that inkstand and blotter were being offered for sale by Christie's together with my letter as some sort of authentication. Also in the sale and from the same source was a silver cigarette case purporting to have belonged to my uncle Cyril and given to him by the Napiers on his 18th birthday.[818] No previous mention had been made of this, probably because I should have dismissed it immediately as false. It had three initials C. C. H. engraved on it in a monogram and Cyril was only given one first name; every official document which has survived, from birth certificate to all his Army service records, shows him merely as 'Cyril Holland.' That apart, my father inherited all Cyril's personal effects on his death at the Western Front in 1915, including the silver cups he won for athletics, and certainly wouldn't have parted with this cigarette case, let alone have sent it back to the Napiers whom he cordially disliked for their treatment of him after his parents' deaths. If anything, he might have given it to Robbie Ross as a memento, but would hardly have returned it to the family who had boycotted his wedding eighteen months before Cyril died. It was a perfect example of how British silver is a gift to anyone trying to establish a vaguely credible provenance because it is precisely hall-marked with a relevant letter of the alphabet for its year of manufacture so you can create every manner of 'gift' given to Oscar or one of his family between, say, 1884 and 1900. And if it doesn't have a suitable inscription, you can always add one. The cigarette case hall-mark was dated 1903, conveniently the year of Cyril's 18th birthday, and what matter if it had an extra initial in the monogram which was never his?

Undoubtedly encouraged by the success of this auction in which all the items reached well over their upper estimates, and with the *Wilde* film premiere already in full promotion, in September 1997 Bonhams agreed to auction a number of items which had supposedly belonged to Oscar Wilde and which 'were purchased in Paris from the family of the proprietor of the Hôtel d'Alsace sometime before 1914' by the great-grandfather of the vendor. The most 'spectacular' of them was a silver cigarette case supposedly given by Alfred 'Bosie' Douglas to Oscar sometime after its hall-mark of 1897. Nothing about it rang true. In the first place it was a personal item with a value and Robbie Ross would have removed it when Oscar died. Secondly, Bosie Douglas came to Paris for the funeral and, if Ross didn't keep it himself which was unlikely, he would have given it back to Douglas. Thirdly the inscription is on the outside of the case rather than the inside which in those days would have been considered extremely vulgar and that was not a fault which one could attribute either to Oscar or to Bosie. For example, in the first act of *The Importance of Being Earnest* before Algy returns Jack's lost cigarette case, the stage direction has him opening it to read the inscription. And lastly, instead of inscribing it with verses by John Donne, if he had done it at all, Bosie is much more likely to have used poetry of his own or something entirely simple along the lines of 'For Oscar from Bosie with love'; in fact Oscar's name appears on it nowhere. As for the claim that it was purchased by the vendor's great-grandfather directly from Jean Dupoirier, the proprietor of the Hotel d'Alsace where Oscar died, it was just a crude attempt to give a forgery authenticity by someone who wasn't familiar enough with the historical details and acquisition by a member of the vendor's family that long ago is always convenient since it is virtually unverifiable. None of that seemed to deter a wealthy collector of historical memorabilia, David Gainsborough Roberts from bidding and winning it for £14,000. In fact Dupoirier did keep a few items as mementos: there were two trunks of books and magazines, a pile of rough jottings which Dupoirier burned, a cheap China ink-bottle, an umbrella which he subsequently lost, a dress shirt, given to my mother in 1950 by his daughter and, most macabre, Oscar's set of false teeth but that was all.[819]

Even more improbable was a boxed manicure set bearing the words 'Presented to Oscar Wilde by his affectionate friends Reggie and Robbie October 16th 1900' engraved on the lid's silver label. Once again the vulgarity of two such intimate friends parading their generosity to Oscar on his forty-sixth birthday on the outside of their gift, let alone putting his surname on it, is totally out of character with what one knows of Robbie Ross and Reggie Turner. 'Presented to Oscar Wilde . . . '? For what special achievement exactly? The set was accompanied by a note to the effect that it 'was employed to help clean Wilde after death.' His fingernails, maybe? And why not 'containing the scissors which were used by Ross to cut off locks of Wilde's hair just after he died'? Since I still have one of the locks in an envelope with Robbie's handwriting on it to that effect, clearly I missed an opportunity to acquire the set and, unscrupulously, to 'authenticate' its absurd claims with a solid piece of historical evidence. Fabricating 'genuine' Wildeiana can be easy given the right accessories.

Whether all these are modern fakes or whether 'the vendor's grandfather' (the usual unverifiable provenance) was indeed duped into buying them in the 1920s isn't entirely clear. Oscar wasn't so popular just twenty years after his death that it would have been worth faking his possessions as opposed to his manuscripts which had a different appeal. The only people who would have been interested in acquiring them back then would have been those very familiar with his story and there were enough of the secondary characters still alive to verify or dispute their authenticity. Cashing in on Oscar's new popularity in the 1990s with a skilfully doctored object or two seems the more likely explanation.

Quite independently from my own views, it was probably the scepticism about these dubiously genuine objects voiced by others with in-depth knowledge of Wilde's life which stopped major auction houses dealing with them from then on and the market has moved into the hands of provincial auctioneers who seem less concerned with verifiable provenance.

Fans, admirers and even level-headed collectors of Oscar Wilde appear to abandon reason when an opportunity occurs to acquire something which he is supposed to have owned. Instead of what they should be doing, which is to look for obvious signs why the object they want cannot possibly have belonged to Oscar, they grasp at every straw to convince themselves that it did. They want the forgeries to be genuine. They want a piece of the 'True Cross,' simply ignoring any evidence which may weigh heavily against the authenticity of what is being offered.

Sometimes I ask myself why I bother to get worked up about it all. If the objects are fakes, it can't be because I feel angry about their dispersal because they never belonged to Oscar in the first place. It may be the dishonesty—even the hypocrisy of it all—that the sort of people who would probably have welcomed his downfall over a century ago are trading spurious relics for profit, fooling the gullible who don't have all the facts into acquiring them. But perhaps I should just leave both parties their pleasure: the vendor, whether conscious of the deception or not, is happy with the money and the purchaser is delighted to own the piece of Saint Oscar the Sinner, the silver cigarette case which never did contain those exotic Turkish cigarettes.

Photographs, purporting to be of 'Oscar Wilde as a young man'—always a convenient label to explain the obvious facial differences—are more easily dispatched. Most have been discovered by breathless enthusiasts in junk shops with something along the lines of '?Young Oscar Wilde' pencilled on the back and copies are sent to me or to the Oscar Wilde Society for verification. As with the crude attempts to forge his handwriting, my first instincts are invariably right, though I tend to look more carefully at those on mounts from nineteenth century Dublin photographers' studios. I hate being the bearer of disappointing news and the disappointed usually accept it with good grace, though some have tried to convince with complicated biometric analysis and in one case even threatened legal action if a negative opinion were voiced to the auction house which was considering such a photo for a sale.

In the spring of 1998 Bonham's offered for sale a group photograph purporting to be of the masters and pupils at Portora Royal School, Enniskillen, with Wilde, who attended the school between 1864 and 1871, prominently positioned amongst several hundred of his contemporaries. The catalogue entry was in no doubt: the figure was Wilde; the school was Portora; the photograph was previously unpublished. So confident were the auctioneers of its authenticity and importance that they put an estimate of £700-900 on it.[820] They were right about it being unpublished—at least in Wilde-related literature—but that was hardly surprising since the young man in question was certainly not Oscar Wilde. Admittedly the pupil said to be Oscar bore a vague resemblance to him, but everything else about the photo was wrong. When my grandfather was at Portora there were never more than eighty or a hundred pupils there: this photograph showed at least three times that number. The galleried hall in which they were standing had never been part of Portora; the coat of arms on the gallery was not that of the school; and the man in what must have been the headmaster's chair was not the headmaster of the time, the Revd William Steele. A brief call to Portora School, with a basic scan of the photo could have elicited all this information but it seems that no one thought of such a simple and definitive verification before printing the sale catalogue. The only two other institutions Oscar attended were Trinity College, Dublin and Magdalen College, Oxford. Trinity graduates assured me it was not Trinity; it appeared to be nowhere recognisable in Oxford; and anyway the boys in the background were far too young to have been undergraduates. If it was not one of the institutions Wilde attended, by deduction it could not have been Wilde. None of this sleuthing would have been necessary with a good strong provenance. Did it show the vendor's grandfather/great uncle/aunt's father-in-law? No, or we would have been told. Then why was it in the vendor's family and since when? Why were there traces of a front mount having been removed which for group photographs of this type frequently indicated the date and occasion? There were too many unanswered questions. I felt it was time for me to speak out publicly about this disturbing trend in the sale of false Wilde memorabilia at auction and contacted Will Bennett, Arts and Saleroom correspondent of the *Daily Telegraph*. We agreed that it would carry more weight coming from a respected journalist rather than looking like a whinge from Oscar's grandson, so I fed him the bones of the story. It appeared the day before the auction and Will told me that his phone from mid-morning had been red-hot with calls from old boys of Bedford School telling him that it was undoubtedly the Great Hall of the school, built in 1891 and burnt down in 1979. Later in the day the auctioneers had no choice but to announce that the lot was withdrawn. It was significant that the title of the sale was 'Printed Books . . . including Magic and Conjuring' an irony which Oscar would have been the first to appreciate.

The forging of Wilde's manuscripts and letters has always been far easier to expose, though in the 1920s even specialist dealers like Christopher Millard were fooled occasionally into thinking they were being offered the genuine article. Most of those early forgeries are now safely in institutional libraries, but some of the substantial number of them created by Brett Holland, the 'Paris Forger,' resurfaced in February 2007 in America. Bonhams in San Francisco offered for sale two letters from Oscar Wilde to the French author Pierre Louÿs which I immediately recognised as being in the same hand as the forged manuscripts of the 1920s. Having spent a good forty years familiarising myself with Oscar's handwriting, I had a definite advantage over the auction house, but in addition to the purely physical evidence, the style was too pretentious and laboured to have been Oscar's and the first of the letters was clearly dated 1886, five years before he is known to have met Louÿs who at that time was at school in Paris and only sixteen. These were all facts which the auction house could have checked with a minimum of effort. Encouraged by detailed reasoning and comparative handwriting samples from me, pressure was put on the auctioneers both by Bruce Whiteman at UCLA's Clark Library and by a Californian rare book dealer and the lot was withdrawn.[821] In fact Bruce purchased them for a fraction of the estimated sale price, partly as curiosities to add to the Library's collection of Wilde forgeries and partly as a gesture to remove them from circulation. Shortly after, in April, six 'original' Wilde manuscripts were being touted round the New York Antiquarian

Book Fair. They were in exactly the same forged hand as the Pierre Louÿs letters which Bonhams had withdrawn from sale in February and the star item was a manuscript of 'The Happy Prince.'[822] I was surprised that dealers to whom they were being offered even gave them a second glance as they, too, were clearly the work of Brett Holland. They had apparently been bought by an eminent American book collector in the 1930s and were now being sold by his descendants. I suspect that the Louÿs letters were put into the Bonhams sale in order to 'test the water'—the appearance of same source forgeries so close together had to be more than just coincidence—but due to auction houses observing strictly the confidentiality of buyers and sellers I couldn't prove it. Despite being told by the dealer with whom they had been consigned that the manuscripts were forgeries, the owners refused to accept the fact and tried to sell them through Sotheby's in New York. From East to West, America may be a large country but the Wilde world is small and eventually no one would touch them. I heard that the family was not impoverished and suggested through the dealer that they should do the decent thing and donate them to a suitable library to get them out of circulation. The suggestion was turned down so they are probably still out there somewhere. My hefty file on 'Fakes & Forgeries' continues to grow, much more slowly than before, I'm glad to say, but I like to think that after I, too, have been removed from circulation, it may be publicly accessible to ensure that there are fewer disappointed among the gullible who will always be preyed on by the unscrupulous.

More disturbing than outright forgeries are the misrepresentations by auction houses of genuine letters in order to give them a sensational slant which they never originally had. In November 1993 Christie's put out a press release about a photograph of Wilde and two of his letters, both undated, which had been consigned to them for sale.[823] They had been written to a young man in Birmingham, Philip Griffiths, who must have attended one of the lectures that Oscar is known to have given there at the end of November 1884 and who asked for a signed photograph. This,

Oscar sent on his return to London on 2 December, together with a rather effusive letter to Philip asking his young admirer for a photo in return 'which I shall keep as a memory of a charming meeting and golden hours passed together. You have a nature made to love all beautiful things and I hope we shall see each other again soon. Your friend, Oscar Wilde.' The photo which Oscar sent was clearly a pre-signed publicity one which he was accustomed to giving out and had 'To Philip Griffiths' inscribed on it in a different ink. The second, very short letter postmarked six months later was addressed to Griffiths, by then in London, arranging to meet and 'go and see pictures together'—perhaps the spring exhibition at the Grosvenor Gallery of which Oscar was an habitué—and signed 'Very sincerely yours Oscar Wilde.' Nothing particularly compromising in either of them given Oscar's occasionally florid style of letter-writing. However, the historical sequence as I have described it didn't suit Christie's Book Department and even less the PR department whose manipulation of the facts was worthy of a tabloid newspaper. They reversed the order of the letters by mis-dating one of them in order to show an increasing intimacy, though Oscar's home address on the longer one was absolute proof that it was the first to be written. 'A fascinating selection [sic] of letters written between 1884 and 1885 by the Irish poet and playwright Oscar Wilde to his lover, Philip M. Griffiths reveals the close and previously unknown relationship between the two men,' said the press release. After complaints about this totally unjustified hyping of the correspondence, Christie's toned down their publicity and corrected the miscataloguing verbally when the lots came up on the day of the sale, but the desired effect had been achieved and the letters and photo sold for over twice their high estimates. There was at least an amusing footnote to this otherwise rather tawdry business: in an ironic reversal of their historical importance the photo of Oscar adorned the front cover of the catalogue while a portrait of Queen Victoria, also included in the sale, was relegated to the back.

Far worse was the blatant attempt by the auctioneers Bamford's

of Derby in September 2010 to over-sensationalise five letters
written by Oscar Wilde to the twenty-four year-old Alsager Vian,
editor of the *Court & Society Review*.[824] There were five of them
written over a six month period from 11 April to 9 September
1887. Frustratingly for his later editors but a gift to auctioneers,
Oscar seldom dated his letters but these, all dealing with editorial matters, can be accurately dated to within a few days either
by their content or, if they survived, by the accompanying postmarked envelopes. He had already published his first short story,
'The Canterville Ghost' in the *Review* earlier in the year and had
started to write theatre reviews and feature articles for the magazine by the beginning of April. He was also, significantly, in discussions with the publishers Cassell & Co about taking up the
editorship of the *Lady's World* which he described as 'too feminine
and not sufficiently womanly' suggesting that it should 'deal not
merely with what women wear, but with what they think and what
they feel,' in other words a publication to give a voice to the so-
called 'New Woman' of that era. In the event, he did indeed take
up the editorship later in the year and had the name changed to
the *Woman's World*.

Whether Bamford's or the vendors changed the correct sequence of the letters or whether it was just bad research and
sloppy cataloguing wasn't clear, but they were presented in an order to show an increasing intimacy between the two men as well as
deliberately misquoting from one of them to make it appear that
Wilde was propositioning Vian. What he wrote was 'I think your
number is excellent, but as usual had to go to S. James's Street
to get a copy. Even Grosvenor Place does not get the *C[ourt]*.
& S[ociety]. till Thursday night! This is all wrong, isn't it?' The
exclamation mark is an expression of his astonishment that the
Review, whose publication day is stated clearly as Wednesday on
its front cover, can't be got until 36 hours later. However, the auc-
tioneer's transcription in the catalogue and statements to the press
a week before the sale, quoted the last sentences divided up so
that 'Till Thursday night! This is all wrong isn't it?' had nothing

to do with the availability of the magazine, but—and the implication was openly stated in the catalogue—with some sort of liaison between Wilde and Vian, making 'Till Thursday night!' sound like an excited 15 year-old schoolgirl on her first date. And as for interpreting his own behaviour rather than the poor availability of the magazine as 'all wrong,' he never regarded his homosexuality as 'wrong.'

In two of the letters Oscar suggests an evening meeting to discuss an article on journalism, which, given that he was also deciding whether to take on the editorship of what would become the *Woman's World* makes perfect sense. Apart from the proposed article, he would have been interested in talking to the young Vian about editing a magazine which Vian had been doing for a couple of years and Oscar never had. He was hardly likely to go to a seasoned journalist like Walter Pollock on the *Saturday Review* for advice and a few tips. Bamford's attempt when talking to the press to put a homosexual interpretation on these meetings implying that they were a prelude to seducing Vian was simply laughable.

Astonishingly the *Daily Telegraph* and *The Independent* as two respectable broadsheets swallowed this misleading rubbish without bothering to check the facts and the *Telegraph* even published an image of the misquoted letter with the critical passage carefully excised so its readers were unable to verify the accuracy of what they were being told. FOR SALE: LETTERS FROM A LOVE-SICK WILDE TO THE OBJECT OF HIS AFFECTION ran the heading in *The Independent* and in the *Daily Telegraph*: LOVELORN WILDE'S INVITATION TO DINNER: JUST OURSELVES AND A FLASK OF ITALIAN WINE.[825] Most papers tried to make out that the letters were 'being revealed/published for the first time' no doubt fed this misinformation by Bamfords. Three had already been published (including the 'revealing' one) in 1985 and again in the *Complete Letters of Oscar Wilde* in 2000.[826] Alan Judd of Bamford's was interviewed by James Naughtie on BBC4's 'Today' programme on the morning of the sale and after saying ignorantly that the letters were important because they covered a period in Wilde's life which wasn't very well-known, when he was 'writing for, I suppose, what was the equivalent of *Woman's Own*, writing quite trite articles for ladies' society magazines.' He went on to admit 'you know journalists and auctioneers are very similar, Jim. We try to take a small story and make it big, but in this case we've started with a big story and I've just tried to make it enormous.'[827] Indeed. Later in the day the five letters were knocked down for £33,900, 50% over the pre-sale high estimate, and afterwards Alan Judd told the *Yorkshire Evening Post*: 'What's interesting is that he appears to be propositioning Vian . . . There was only one intention in the letters, Wilde was hoping to meet up with him. If they could have shown anything happened, they would have made twice as much.'[828] Yes, and if they had been correctly rather than sensationally catalogued they would have been sold for half the amount which is what happened when Sotheby's put them up for sale eleven years later with accurate descriptions and a proper assessment of their literary value.[829]

Putting such a salacious interpretation on some aspect of Oscar's life entirely for crude financial gain has not been limited to irresponsible auction houses. The first that I heard of the Old Parsonage Hotel in Oxford was in *The Times* of 29 April 1991. Under the heading of 'Wilde Oats,' its 'Diary' column carried a piece about how Oscar was supposed to have spent a year there during his time at Oxford, 'entertaining ladies of dubious reputation, only to conclude that it was a losing battle against his true sexual instincts.' On its own it was a silly piece of historical gossip best ignored, but Michael Thompson, the general manager of the Hotel, which was then being renovated, had decided that the connection was an unmissable opportunity to publicise the reopening, and to give the story legs he even claimed to know in which room it all took place: 'Not to put too fine a point on it, this is the room where Wilde discovered that women were not his thing. We expect a lot of interest from his devotees.' *The Times* also printed a quote from controversial literary critic Martin Seymour-Smith who, significantly, the year before had published a biography of

Rudyard Kipling claiming that he was homosexual. Seymour-Smith, it said, had been at Oxford with Vyvyan Holland: 'Vyvyan told me his father engaged in the local Oxford practice of picking up tarts from nearby St. Ebbe's and taking them back to his hotel. Oscar Wilde first realised he preferred men when he was staying at the Old Parsonage.' This was step too far. Apart from the fact that my father had gone to Cambridge, to have been his contemporary Seymour-Smith would have had to be about a hundred and five when he talked to *The Times*, and it was utterly out of character for my father to have said such a thing anyway. It was also convenient that Vyvyan had been dead for 24 years and wasn't on hand to deny it. I wrote to *The Times* pointing out in fairly guarded terms that they had been duped by a cheap publicity gimmick, but the terms were clearly not guarded enough as they refused to print my letter. For three weeks they hid behind the 'Diary' editor being on holiday and waiting for the hotel to produce its evidence, which of course it couldn't, and by then it was stale news. In the meantime, with the help of the Magdalen College records and the University Archivist, I was able to establish that Oscar had had an unbroken sequence of college rooms for his whole time at the university and that the Old Parsonage was not a hotel then but a registered students' lodging house at 1-3 Banbury Road. Regulations at that period required colleges to make termly returns to the university authorities of all their students living outside the college and nowhere in the university archives does Oscar's name appear as lodging at 1-3 Banbury Road. Obviously. He lived in college for the four years that he was up at Oxford. Having given up on *The Times* I put this to the hotel. Ah, they said, it must have been when he was rusticated for the summer term in 1877 for coming back late from a trip to Greece. Actually, no. There's ample proof from his letters and other sources that he went straight down to London, attended the opening of the new Grosvenor Gallery, reviewed it as his first piece of journalism and went back to Dublin. Well, said the hotel, by now struggling for opportunities when Oscar might have stayed on their premises, it must have been at the end of his university career when he had to keep another term of residence and pass a divinity exam; he wasn't in college then. No, he wasn't; he was assigned rooms at 71 High Street opposite Magdalen.[830] Undeterred, the hotel announced two 'Oscar Wilde Weekends' in September and October with talks from Wilde specialists who had accepted the hotel's claims because they were said to be backed by serious historians and local researchers. In fact, the only reference anyone could produce was a brief unsourced sentence under the 'Old Parsonage Hotel' entry in Christopher Hibbert's Encyclopaedia of Oxford which had no doubt been fed to him by the previous owners. One of those due to take part was an Irishman I had met, Manus Nunan, who regularly gave a good popular lecture on Oscar. He asked me what I knew of the hotel. I told him about The Times 'Diary' piece (which he said was 'shocking') and my research, but when he rang the hotel for an explanation Michael Thompson 'absolutely denied saying these things.'[831] The Oscar Wilde Society got to hear of the claims and the weekends and protested at this shameless and unfounded use of Wilde's name for crass commercialism and warned the speakers (at least two of whom were Society members) that they might like to reconsider their involvement. This led to the hotel putting a paragraph in its December newsletter: 'Wilde Weekends: The two Wilde Weekends we had planned for September and October this year had to be postponed due to petty-minded politics and unprecedented pressure on some of our participants from the Oscar Wilde Society. I am pleased to say that we shall be resurrecting the idea in 1992 . . . '[832] As far as I know the weekends never did take place and after that I just let the matter drop as being a waste of time. I don't think that Michael Thompson, like others before and since, realised just how loyal some people are to Oscar's memory and how cross they could be to find him being used in this way without a shred of evidence to support the connection. As I write, the hotel still insists on dragging him into the promotional website though qualifying their rather nebulous claim that he stayed there that summer he was rusticated with 'traditionally said' and 'presumably sought refuge at the Old Parsonage.' As always with such stories about Oscar, there was an amusing, if slightly surreal postscript of which I should never have been aware had I not done the research on Oscar's accommodation at Oxford. When my son, Lucian, went up to Oxford in 1997, for the first year he was assigned rooms out of college—at No 71 High Street. Fortunately, no one has yet suggested that he used them for entertaining 'ladies of dubious reputation.'

I find myself in a very difficult position as Oscar's heir and for the most part I try not to become too involved in disputes of this sort, though once in a while it does no harm to be seen leading the charge. I can't help feeling a profound sense of injustice on Oscar's behalf when someone makes an unverified statement imputing some newly discovered naughtiness to him, not to increase our knowledge of him but to inflate the price of objects at auction or to increase the sales of a writer's books or the occupancy rate of a hotel. Oscar would have been the first to tell me not to destroy myths, but these are not myths; they are the gossip of the *concierges*.

Of the other hotels Oscar is known to have patronised some have been more honest and less crass about claiming their relationship to him. Top of the list must be the Hôtel d'Alsace in Paris, now known simply as 'L'Hôtel,' which sheltered him for much of the last three years of his life and whose proprietor, Jean Dupoirier, was unfailingly generous about his unpaid bills. After that, one could never begrudge the hotel for making something of the association which it does in tasteful fashion and the room in which Oscar died is always booked up months in advance.

Until its $50m makeover was complete in 2019, the Cadogan Hotel's only real claim to Oscar-fame was that he was arrested there shortly after the collapse of his libel action against Bosie Douglas's father. Actually he wasn't staying there at all; Bosie was, and the event was subsequently immortalised in John Betjeman's poem 'The arrest of Oscar Wilde at the Cadogan Hotel.' However, Oscar's fleeting acquaintance with the place hasn't prevented the new management from maintaining he was a regular overnight guest when his West End nights stretched into the next morning and charging a four-figure sum for the room in which it was all supposed to have taken place—No. 118. Pity they changed the room numbers though; it was No. 53 then.[833] And I can't recall any evidence that he stayed elsewhere than at the Savoy, the Albemarle, or the Avondale, the first of them understandably reticent about celebrating his alleged cavorting with rent-boys and the other two long since disappeared. Of all London venues the Café Royal's connection to Oscar is the strongest—apart from the Old Bailey, that is. He was a regular diner and it was there, notably, that his friend Frank Harris in the company of George Bernard Shaw tried to persuade him to abandon his disastrous libel suit against the Marquess of Queensberry. Over the years a host of other famous names bohemian, literary, artistic, and royal have passed through its doors so they have not had to push Oscar to the forefront of their publicity. Nevertheless, it was sad they had to be so parsimonious about celebrating his entry into Poets' Corner, especially as they have now renamed the long-famous Grill Room the Oscar Wilde Bar.

No hotel in Great Britain would have dreamed of using him to promote itself before the 1960s, but today he seems to be flavour of the decade and, however vague the historical association, emphasising the fact can be good for trade. The Old Monmouth B & B in Lyme Regis says he is supposed to have stayed there in 1891 and even scratched his name on a window with a diamond cuff-link. There is a notice in the hotel to that effect and his visit is commemorated by calling one of the bedrooms 'The Oscar Wilde Suite.' The Old Monmouth is pretty harmless in its claims and it can't really be proved one way or another. He did scratch a caricature of one of his Oxford friends on the window of his rooms at Magdalen in 1877 which may have influenced the story, though I still think it's rather unlikely that, aged 37 and with his ideas about aesthetics, he would have done an 'Oscar woz 'ere' on a hotel window pane, but if he brings them in a bit more business, why not?

Ironically James Whistler is definitely known to have spent time in Lyme Regis and even painted two of the locals, but the Royal Lion Hotel where he stayed makes no capital out of it at all. I suppose Whistler doesn't have quite the same appeal today as Wilde, which would be rather galling for him after their verbal duels in print in the 1880s.

Then there are the individuals who want to be 'related' to him whether by blood or just by name alone. When I hear of those claiming to be something like my third cousin I write to them (or mostly to their agents as it seems to be a peculiar quirk of the entertainment industry) expressing genuine surprise and delight that maybe I have discovered a new relation. Oscar's father is known to have fathered at least three illegitimate children, so my mind is never completely closed to the idea. The letter, carefully phrased to show my bona fide interest and to reassure them that I am not an unhinged groupie, is seldom answered. Claudine Wilde, the German actress, I felt sure must have swallowed some vague story circulating in her family when she repeated to Paris Match that Oscar was her great uncle. Amanda Burton, the Northern Irish TV actress told the Sunday Telegraph that her English mother was descended from Oscar Wilde, improbable but not utterly implausible if my uncle Cyril had had a secret liaison about which we never knew.[834] Her PA did reply to me saying that the article 'was actually slightly inaccurate—allegedly her father, not mother, was a descendant of Oscar Wilde, although she's not certain enough to state this as a fact.' Honest enough. Another hand-me-down family fable, no doubt.

Reginald Smith was discovered while singing in a London club in 1958 by the impresario Larry Parnes who signed him up and, as with all his protégés, gave him a stage name with a ring to it and turned him into the internationally famous rock star Marty Wilde. Parnes had also 'created' Tommy Steele and Billy Fury, but adopting the name Wilde at a time when Oscar was still trailing a few clouds of scandal was a calculated risk especially when starting on a career as a teenage pop idol. But it worked because the reputation of the imprisoned homosexual was giving way to the new image of a rebellious, creative individual. Forty years later an American actress of Irish descent, Olivia Jane Cockburn, changed her surname to Wilde openly saying that it was in homage to a man she admired and respected and, coming from a long line of journalists, pseudonyms were something of a family tradition.[835] More bizarre was the artist Gerald Wilde whose obituary in *The Times* of 6 October 1986 stating that he was a grandson of Oscar Wilde was sent to me by Richard Ellmann with an amusing note about the mistake. I discovered that Gerald had been a good friend of Lucian Freud to whom I wrote asking whether Gerald had ever claimed this, since *The Times* was not in the habit of getting its facts that badly wrong. His reply needs no further comment: 'Gerald Wilde never made any direct reference to his parentage while I knew him. From his conversation I formed a vague impression that he was the outcome of Oscar Wilde's relationship with Alfred Douglas.'[836]

For years I have kept a file with some of the more interesting appropriations of Oscar's name, his image and his works to promote—well—more or less anything. When I started to write about them I began to realise, just as I did twenty-five years ago in the New York Public Library checking references to him in the general catalogue, that searching for them in this digital age may be relatively easy but also leads to madness: just listing the usage of aphorisms and quotations from his works on everything from postcards to mouse-mats would fill pages. And it's not just his words; it's images of the man as well, in particular the now unmistakable series of photo-portraits taken by Napoleon Sarony at the start of Oscar's year-long lecture tour of North America in 1882. His face has become so familiar that a caption to identify it is almost superfluous; lines from his plays are even parodied without attribution in the most unlikely contexts. Several years ago I was amused to read on the sports pages of a newspaper a football report which began 'To lose one home match at the start of the season may be regarded as a misfortune; to lose two in a row seems like carelessness,' echoing Lady Bracknell's immortal comment on Jack Worthing's mysterious parentage. No need to mention the play nor the author; just the structure of the sentence, even adapted by a sports journalist, was too familiar to be mistaken.

Why is it that this man, whose name in 1900 could hardly be mentioned in polite society, is now so widely solicited to endorse and help sell such a huge variety of products and services? Consult a good dictionary of quotations and you will find that in quantity his two fellow Irishmen, Shaw and Yeats, both beat him by a short head and there's no denying that Yeats was the better poet and Shaw the more prolific playwright. His aphorisms and epigrams, both genuine and imagined, appear on greetings cards and publicity brochures the world over, combining as they do frivolity with seriousness and revealing more than a grain of truth in every paradox.[837] Although that may explain his presence in print, it doesn't answer the question of why his name and his image adorn such an enormous variety of goods and services. At the risk of employing a cliché, he does seem to be the perfect example of a man before his time—in short, a perfect lifestyle model for the twenty-first century. Add to those qualities his sheer accessibility to every age and level of society, his role as a gay icon and his endorsement of everything from racehorses to record sleeves, from beer to buildings and bookshops makes perfect sense. Perhaps, too, that by using him to promote what is positive and desirable we may even feel we are righting a wrong, correcting a century-old injustice.

EPILOGUE
(2025)

At the end of his second volume of memoirs my father wrote: 'If ever I feel depressed, I contemplate my blessings one by one and say that I am a happy man, that I have no quarrels with Fate, which has almost overwhelmed me at times, but which has in the end left me, as it were, washed up on the shores of time in the warm sunlight.'[838] Sadly, it was not something that his own father could ever have written about himself, though the two of them did share that admirable ability to shrug their shoulders and smile at misfortune. Nor could I conceivably think of applying it to my own life, as Fate has been kinder to our family down the years, but living with Oscar's legacy has had its particular problems.

Vyvyan discovered this after he married my mother during the War and she encouraged him to be more open about his heritage. He had been forced to lead a life of concealment for so long that, at the age of sixty, to become publicly 'Oscar Wilde's son' he never found easy. 'One of the most awkward things about my position in life is that a nudge in the ribs and a: "Do you see that fellow over there? That's Oscar Wilde's son!" is always good for a laugh,' he wrote in 1951.[839] I was amused to read that for the first time nearly sixty years later, and realised I felt much the same, only in the intervening years laughter had changed to curiosity, and with it had come the weight of other people's expectations. 'So, what's it like being Oscar Wilde's grandson?' is the one question that I used to dread being asked and it generally came at the end of an exchange along the lines of:

'Are you really the grandson of Oscar Wilde?'
    'Yes.'
    'A direct descendant?'

'Yes.'

'How exciting!'

'Maybe for you, but for me it's rather more of a burden.'

'But why? What's it like?'

The simple answer is 'Complicated,' and I invariably refer to him as my grandfather rather than to myself as his grandson, a subtle distinction which, I think, needs no explanation.

On one occasion this was brought home to me quite forcefully. In the autumn of 1977, I attended a party at Searcy's in London's Pavilion Road to celebrate the publication of an anthology of Rebecca West's work. Many of the good and the great from the literary and artistic world seemed to be there and I felt rather out of place as I hadn't a first novel to my name or a by-line in a magazine or newspaper. At one point the actress Margaret Rawlings came up to me, took me by the arm and said 'Come and meet Harold Pinter.' 'Harold this is Merlin Holland; he's Oscar Wilde's grandson.' 'So what?' said Pinter (although I vaguely remember that he expressed it more forcefully), turned around and continued talking to another guest. I could have killed Margaret on the spot for her well-meaning gesture, though since he and she were at opposite ends of the political spectrum, I suspect that Pinter's snub was largely directed at her. Half a dozen conflicting emotions ran through my head. I suddenly felt a little of the discomfort my father must have known from years of living in Oscar's shadow, when the scandal was still adding to the darkness. No one cared about the scandal any more but, paradoxically, the renaissance in Oscar's reputation seemed to cast a longer and darker shadow than ever. I couldn't help my lineage; playing down the relationship was liable to be misconstrued as much as playing it up. But yes, so what, I thought and decided to do something about it. I never met Harold Pinter again, but if I had, I might have thanked him.

Finding that place, that niche in which my back was protected, took a long while. At first it was easier to define where that place was not rather than where it was. It was *not* in gatherings at which

I had to wear a label which said 'Merlin Holland: Oscar Wilde's grandson' or a green carnation or even both (it has happened). The trouble was that I had my background whether I wanted it or not, so the obvious solution was to add to it something of my own. By the time of Rebecca's soirée, I had already embarked on my self-imposed course of in-depth Wildean education to be able to deal with copyright permissions from the academic world. Since the quantity of copyright material was generally minimal as were most of the fees in consequence, it became clear very quickly that I had far more to gain by co-operation than by confrontation and I absorbed, almost indiscriminately, anything Wildean which came my way. In knowledgeable academics I had some of the best tutors I could have wished for and free tuition, and after a while I realised that I was in a unique position, being in close touch with some of the latest scholarship, while at the same time having the ear of a much wider general audience if I wanted it; in due course it led me to original research of my own. I had found the key to the cage which enabled me to join the spectators rather than remaining permanently on the inside looking out. And that, I suppose, is as close as I shall come to a definition of feeling at ease with it all: if, in any gathering, it is what I can contribute which interests people, what I have done rather than merely who I happen to be, then I'm comfortable with it: the launch of a book I have written; curating an exhibition at the British Library; a conference at which I'm asked to give a paper and give it on some entirely new aspect of his life or work. That said, it would be pointless to deny that having Oscar as a grandfather has allowed me to meet many people in the theatre and the arts whom I would never have known otherwise. It's the dancing bear syndrome: people are insatiably curious to know, even at two removes from the original, what sort of grandson Oscar Wilde might have so, inevitably, their interest is not in me and what I may have done with my life, but rather in what I represent as part of the story.

One could say that I have defeated the object of the exercise by drawing even more attention to myself and my relationship to Oscar by writing about him, re-editing his letters, publishing for the first time the full libel trial transcripts, and even lecturing about him, and that is undeniably true, but it was done in the spirit of a researcher just as anyone else would have done it, and the main thing is that the door of the cage remains open. Of course, there have been exceptions to the 'contribution' rule when it would have been bad-mannered to refuse: the installation of his window in Poets' Corner or the unveiling of a monument or plaque in his honour. I could go too far in my refusal to participate and cause ill will and in such cases, even if I am there merely as a blood-relation, it is good to remind people who might have forgotten (or never even knew) that he had a family, but it still doesn't mean to say I'm always comfortable with it. That said, just as my father did before me, I feel a strange obligation towards Oscar to help make things right between him and the world, because he once suffered the prejudice of an uncomprehending and blinkered society. I have letters, for example, which fall into my letterbox out of nowhere, asking for this or that bit of information or help, or sometimes just to say how much the writer 'owes personally' (the expression recurs frequently in connection with *De Profundis*) to my grandfather. This fan-mail by proxy, these undeliverable thank-you letters seem to come with the job, and mindful of how the man himself would reply courteously to complete strangers, not to acknowledge them seems like letting the side down. Nonetheless, even if playing secretary to him is a contribution of sorts, it is a constant reminder of my inescapable position.

There have been occasions when, to my discredit, I have allowed my feelings of frustration to get the better of me, but disentangling myself from my emotions immediately afterwards, I remember that I can lay the blame at nobody's door but my own for accepting the exposure in the first place. More often than not there are valuable lessons to be learned. Once, after giving a lecture in Reading Town Hall, I was approached by a woman who wanted me to sign her ageing copy of *The Happy Prince*. It was late, I was tired, and rather snappishly I said something like 'No, I can't. It's bad enough having to live as his grandson without having to sign his books as well.' I knew it was wrong the moment I uttered it. She would have had every right to be equally rude back, but instead she just looked disappointed and said 'But Mr. Holland you should see it from our point of view.' I was mortified, apologised, and signed her book, and I have never forgotten her words. Not long after, I found myself on the other side of the fence. I had attended a lunch hosted by *The Oldie*—I was their wine correspondent at the time—at which one of the guests was Spike Milligan. Since my son was heavily into the BBC's revival recordings of the Goon Show, I went up to him and asked him for an autograph for Lucian. He obliged a little ungraciously and added after the signature 'For Lucian. Sorry about your father.' I felt as the woman in Reading must have done and it reinforced the lesson I learned in the Town Hall. The autograph, though not a pleasant reminder, was carefully preserved.

Another time, around 1980, I was invited to a production of *The Importance of Being Earnest* put on by a local repertory company in a London borough. During the interval, I remained in my seat and made polite small-talk to the mayor's wife. After a moment or two she gushed 'You must be so proud of your grandfather.' If ever a remark was guaranteed to strike conversation dead in its shoes, that was it. What could I say? I had plenty of other feelings about him. Admiration, envy even, for his remarkable facility with words; bewilderment sometimes tinged with anger at the recklessness which destroyed his family's life as well as his own; and a curious, almost possessive sense of protection about this man whom I had never known; but pride? So, I just nodded and said 'Yes' and she probably thought me rude and indifferent. Pride of that sort is a very personal emotion. It needs human warmth to grow and a sense that somehow, to whatever tiny degree, you have participated. I could feel pride for my father and how he had coped with a difficult life, and I could feel pride in his achievements, but that seemed to me only possible because I had known him and loved him. Whatever other feelings I might have had about her, I could feel pride for my mother who had gone from her modest Melbourne origins to become beauty adviser first to Princess and then to Queen Elizabeth. To be proud of Oscar Wilde meant actively laying claim to him as a grandfather and that, as had been impressed on me for so long in the past, was not sensible. My intellectual search had started to give me an understanding of him, which on occasions bordered on something deeper, but the catalyst of this simple encounter now made me want more. I carried the seed of it around for another fourteen years before it burst dramatically into life.

It was an early evening at the end of November 1994. I was in Paris advising on a BBC documentary about Oscar. That day we had covered his last, penniless years in exile. It was more disturbing than I could have imagined. I sat in the half-darkness of a side-aisle in the Église Saint-Germain-des-Prés. I could not remember how often I had come here to light a candle in the Sacré-Coeur chapel, where the very discreet funeral service for Oscar had been held in 1900. Always alone, a little mechanically, without emotion. It was not something which could be shared. I was not even certain why I did it; a sense of family duty, perhaps, like weeding a grave; or maybe out of curiosity to see if I could bring to life a small, numb feeling which I had carried around for so long, but which had always remained stubbornly unresponsive. Suddenly on that autumn evening the numbness had gone, its place taken by emotions of almost paralysing intensity. Several dozen candles were burning at the entrance to the chapel, far more than was usual and my own not yet among them. I worked out the date, expecting a popular saint's day and realised that it was the anniversary of my grandfather's death on 30 November 1900. All at once I understood the endless visitors to the newly cleaned tomb in Père Lachaise Cemetery that morning. I sat there with my unlit candle, reluctant to place it with the others, resenting what felt like a public intrusion by strangers to mark this day which I had not even remembered. I knew instinctively that I must overcome such pettiness, but for an instant I did not see how. It was then that blood and history flowed together and I found myself the unwilling conduit for a century of unwept family grief; for Oscar's two sons, Cyril and my father Vyvyan, who should have stood in this chapel ninety-four years before to pay their last respects to him, but weren't even told by their guardian; for Constance, a touchingly loyal wife, who paid first with her health and then with her life less than a year after Oscar's release; and for Oscar himself who saw neither wife nor children again after prison and who at the age of forty-six had lain here in his coffin on the way to a sixth class burial in the suburbs. For the first time I felt it was part of me, not just cold, bare facts from the past. Resentment gave way to gratitude, numbness to the realisation that I *did* have a right to claim this part of my heritage and with it a little pride and something akin to love. I lit my candle. In a few minutes it was indistinguishable from the rest, just a flickering tribute among many. I left by a side door and behind me burned some of the insecurities of twenty years.

Sadly, the one thing which has proved far more difficult to claim back has been the name. It is sad that as far as the family is concerned, it more or less died out in 1900, but life would have been intolerable for my father without his cloak of 'Holland' pseudonymity, certainly until the 1920s. His own attempt to reclaim 'Wilde' not long after he was twenty-one was short-lived and he never tried to do it again. All the same, I believe that Vyvyan suffered almost as much from having to hide behind a name which was not his own as he did from the consequences of the scandal itself. There was, for example, his cousin Dolly Wilde who was Oscar's niece and who still bore the family name and carried it around Paris between the wars as something of an asset. Vyvyan could hardly object to her use of the name, but that she could use it with impunity—indeed to advantage—in a country which cared little for a thirty year-old scandal, must have been galling. When he was asked by the MP Beverley Baxter in 1949 'Tell me Mr. Holland, if it's not too personal a question, have you ever regretted changing your name?' he replied 'No, not for a minute,' though the jocular fashion in which the incident was recorded probably hid a deeper truth.[840] Similar to Vyvyan's feelings about Dolly are my own about people in the entertainment world changing their names to Wilde 'to honour the great Irish writer' as most of them put it: for example the pop singers Marty Wilde and his daughter Kim, and the American actress Olivia Jane Cockburn who took the stage name Olivia Wilde after a stint in Dublin at the Gaiety Acting School. Touching though these tributes to Oscar are, I cannot help feeling a certain sadness that the name is mine by right, but paradoxically far more difficult for me to claim back than for them to adopt.

Around the time of my own twenty-first birthday, I remember Vyvyan telling me one day that, if I wanted to, my coming of age would be the time to change my name.[841] It was as if he were encouraging me to do what had been denied to him so long before, obliquely asking me to shoulder a responsibility and somehow to make things right again. He had just turned eighty and I am sure that he was still struggling with all the conflicting emotions about his parents which he had felt for years. Time had rubbed off the sharp edges, but love, pain, and perhaps a little resentment remained unresolved. It didn't take me long to decide: I was my father's son much more than I was my grandfather's grandson, so I said no. Other, deeper feelings told me as well that it would be a terrible slap in the face to my father to do so. Looking back on it, I have no doubt it was the right decision. Changing it back wasn't going to make my father's childhood any happier. I don't think that my mother knew anything about it and she would probably have vetoed the idea if she had. Much later, around the time that the centenary of Oscar's death was commemorated, and my own son had just turned twenty-one, I toyed briefly with the idea again. The timing would have been perfect, and I had grown bored with having to trot out the same old story whenever I was asked why my name wasn't Wilde. My answer to anyone small-minded enough to accuse me of cashing in on Wilde's ever-increasing popularity would have been to quote the passage from *De Profundis* in which Oscar talks about his parents: 'She and my father had bequeathed me a name they had made noble and honoured not merely in Literature, Art, Archaeology and Science, but in the public history of my own country in its evolution as a nation. I had disgraced that name eternally. I had made it a low byword among low people. I had dragged it through the very mire,'[842] and to say that this was being done not just for him but also for an earlier generation, still revered in Dublin to this day. A hundred years on, far from being a disgrace, the name of Oscar Wilde had become a positive asset, a useful hook on which to hang happenings of all sorts and a boon to the world of advertising. I could have taken back the name and doubtless traded on the relationship, but in the end and mindful of Robbie Ross's remark at the Ritz dinner in 1908 about living 'on ruins of another's fame,' I couldn't face having to justify myself and chose to do neither. Whether in disgrace or in fame, living with him as part of the family is far from easy. When I was in my thirties, I remember how an old friend and one of my contemporaries told me he wished he had had my family background as he would have been able to make so much more of it. Perhaps; but with that family background comes a great deal of clutter and cumbersome baggage which means that 'making the most of it' is far less simple than it might appear.

Listening to 'Desert Island Discs' one Sunday morning years ago, I heard some entirely admirable public servant or scientist describing their upbringing and the professions of their ancestors. 'On my father's side they were all doctors and nurses and on my mother's they were mostly teachers and in quite a few cases campaigners for social justice of one sort or another.' And mine, I can still remember thinking, were criminals and bankrupts. At that age, I longed to have come from a good solid middle-class family with no skeletons in the cupboard and a sort of genetic justification (and no doubt the odd leg-up) to move smoothly into an occupation similar to that which my father would have had.

In 1999 I went to America to give a couple of lectures and do some final research for my revised edition of Oscar's letters. To be paid for lectures required a particular visa which inevitably led to some precise questioning by the young immigration official about the nature of my work. Since I was last in the queue and I suspect she was bored, the questions were more detailed than usual. What was the subject of the lecture? Oscar Wilde. Was I a university professor? No. Then why was I lecturing at a university? And so on, until I had to come clean about my relationship. Wasn't he the one who said at American immigration that he had nothing to declare but his genius? Yes, that's supposed to be the story. And if I asked you . . . ? I thought for a second: 'Nothing but my albatross,' I replied. Whether she had read *The Ancient Mariner* or not I'll never know, but she smiled, stamped my passport and waved me through.

A short while afterwards, I was in the New York Public Library checking the catalogue for any Wilde letters which might have been donated or even discovered in the library's holdings since Rupert's *Letters* of 1962. Thinking that there might be other items of interest as well, I requested a print-out of everything with key-word 'Oscar Wilde' in all categories. Paper began to cascade out of the printer, and I wondered if I had entered the wrong search criteria. I hadn't; it was just that the amount of Wildeiana in the library was enormous, especially under Performing Arts and Ephemera and much of it post-1962. It was a Damascene moment: panic that half of it was unknown to me was followed by an over-whelming sense of relief. In that instant I no longer felt the need to know, as I realised he had become public property. Not that I ever really laid claim to him, but the twenty-five year Odyssey to find him was almost over. I had come as close as I would ever get and it was time to move on. But this in turn has led to another burden from which it seems equally difficult to escape.

There was a time back in the 1980s around the time that Richard Ellmann's biography came out when I felt obliged to take an interest in everything Wildean of a public nature: new productions of his plays, books both about his life and critical appreciations of his work and events, ever more frequent, involving him however peripherally. Now, in 2025, I feel I have had enough. So much is done involving Oscar Wilde that it would be impossible to keep up with it all, so I don't really care whether I have missed a totally off-the-wall production of *The Importance of Being Earnest* in a Clydesdale warehouse. But when I'm asked for my opinion about that off-the-wall *Earnest* and have to admit that I don't have one because I didn't see it and, what's worse, that I don't really care that I didn't . . . 'But you're his grandson; doesn't it mean anything to you that . . . ?' In the end I can't win.

The family heritage that I have to deal with is a true Siren, both treacherous and seductive. Despite strapping myself to the mast of the present she tries to lure me back to the past with her songs about the excitement of research and discovery, and although I respect its power and even, to an extent, my debt to that past, backwards can lead to festering and forwards is more creative. At times I long to tell her to leave me alone. It's like the worst sort of cousins and aunts; you're tied by blood but most of the time you'd much rather you weren't. But I also recognise that, more than most of us want to admit, our ancestors provide us with bits of genetic hard-wiring and to deny it is to fight a pointless battle. I grew up at a time when the British public still had a very ambivalent attitude towards Oscar. They would read 'The Happy Prince' to their children at bedtime but hope they didn't find out that he went to prison and ask why, and my parents were no exception. All that changed in the 1960s, but life took my father from me when I was twenty-one and Thelma rather discouraged me from taking much of an interest in my grandfather until I was in my early thirties, so it was little wonder that the family past started to exercise a certain fascination.

Anyone who claims not to have any regrets in the course of their life is either supremely arrogant or a liar. Among others I have two which make me particularly sad. The first is not to have been able to ask my father more about the family and his life before I came on the scene, by which time he was nearly sixty. Many of his inter-war friends survived him and from them I could have learned much but I was unaware of their existence. Almost as sad was the fate of the silver wine jugs.

In 1977 when Thelma was particularly hard up, she summoned me to her flat and told me that she was having to sell two items of family silver—a pair of Victorian wine jugs. To give her credit she asked if I wanted them and said that if I could give her the reserve auction price, she'd be happy with that. I thought practically: wine and silver don't make good bedfellows, so I told her to sell them. I wasn't particularly interested in the fact that they'd belonged to Oscar's father and goodness know how they had survived 120 years with all the family's ups and downs. Had I known their significance then, I would have done anything to raise the money. They were presented to William Wilde in 1857 by members of the British Association for the Advancement of Science whom he had taken on an expedition to the Arran Islands after their annual meeting in Dublin. One was inscribed in English and the other in Irish. It was in recognition of his work as an antiquary and Irish folklorist, interests cultivated alongside a pioneering career in medicine. They were a tribute to the man whose name Oscar said he had 'dragged through the very mire' and we had sold them off as impractical wine jugs. The Christie's catalogue entry didn't even mention Sir William's name nor the inscriptions. When I realised later what an extraordinary polymath he had been in his time and his importance in the history of Irish medicine, I tried to trace them, but the search proved fruitless.

The rise and fall of the Wilde family is an extraordinary story, even if it's a tragic one, and I'm happy to have been a small footnote in the epilogue, though occasionally I would much rather not to have been a footnote at all. My father was really the last chapter and, as he said, it nearly overwhelmed him at times. My son, fortunately for him, is lost somewhere in the index. Oscar, unsurprisingly, remains the main focus of the story even so long after his death. In his 1916 biography of Oscar, Frank Harris recalled a conversation he had with him during his last years in which Oscar, despite his still recent disgrace, predicted that in a hundred years' time 'my comedies and my stories and *The Ballad of Reading Gaol* will be known and read by millions, and even my unhappy fate will call forth world-wide sympathy.'[843] Even allowing for Harris's well-known exaggerations and inventions, there is a ring of truth to what Harris wrote and a remarkably prescient assessment by Oscar about his future popularity. More than a hundred years have gone by and I often wonder how long it can be before the Wilde bandwagon runs out of steam, but I'm beginning to realise that he has become such a fixture in British cultural life that it's unlikely to happen for a long time and his survival has partly to do with his ever-fluctuating reputation. Reputations need to be on the move constantly if they are not to grow stale and die and, as I have tried to show in this book, Oscar's has fluctuated wildly for more than a century after his death. The arguments about his life and works continue with one part of the literary world—increasingly small it must be said— insisting that he was simply a passing sociocultural phenomenon and the author of lightweight popular works, while another view has it that he was a modern thinker, bridging two centuries, an astute critic and commentator, a writer at odds with the stuffi- ness of his age, whose 'over-the-topness in knocking the bottom out of things' in Seamus Heaney's words, amused but finally en- raged his tight-laced Victorian contemporaries.

For two generations after his death, it was convenient to forget his essays and his criticism, which amount to more than a third of his published works, but which did not fit into the mould which had been made for him. It reinforced the public image which he was so fond of projecting of himself, but it concealed the fact that he was a man deeply interested in the issues of his day, carrying in his intellectual baggage a quite extraordinary classical and philo- sophical education. As this other dimension to Oscar Wilde has developed, despite his intellect—or perhaps even because of it— he has remained supremely accessible, a quality which has always been anathema to the literary critic. He has become that phenomenon of a popular author, who has somehow been able to generate and sustain scholarly interest in his work. His appeal is to a universality of human experience, which transcends social as well as intellectual status and evokes in most of us powerful feelings of personal empathy.

For the very reasons that the Victorians wanted to be rid of him, Oscar Wilde's popularity in twenty-first century continues unabated. The very sentiments and philosophy of life which are so attractive to the youth of today are precisely those which he was preaching so subversively in 1895: rebelliousness, integrity to one's principles, individualism, and sensuality. What young adult today would not like to claim that they subscribe to any or all of them?

In his 1946 review of Hesketh Pearson's *Life of Oscar Wilde*, Charles Morgan, now a largely forgotten English novelist, was perhaps one of the first to sense the role which each new generation would play in keeping him 'alive':

What gives me reasonable assurance that his work will live is the fact, of which I have had repeated evidence, that young men and women, who are themselves interested in writing, find, in decade after decade, extraordinary stimulus in the work of Wilde. Again and again they 'discover' him. What is it that they discover? His good humour, his gaiety, his wit, his challenge to encrusted opinion—all these; but above all they discover that there is such a thing as the art of writing, that it largely consists in a lucidity, a grace and an enchantment which, in supreme instances, become poetry, and that it depends, not upon self-righteousness or opinion, but upon the choice and placing of words. If Wilde can teach this to successive generations of youth and take their breath away by his lessons, it does not matter into what school of economics they go down in their middle age, *Intentions* and *De Profundis* and *The Importance* will survive them all.[844]

And it will be successive generations of young people, precisely those visitors who always seem to be in the majority whenever I go to visit his tomb in Père Lachaise, who will make sure that this 'posthumous Oscar' survives and flourishes.

Titles of books are quoted in full on first appearance and thereafter with author's surname only but with date of publication if the author appears with multiple works in the bibliography.

CL	*Complete Letters of Oscar Wilde* (2000)
AD	Lord Alfred Douglas (1870–1945)
AS	A. J. A. Symons (1900–1941)
CB	Carlos Blacker (1859–1928)
CH	Cyril Holland (Wilde) (1885–1915)
CM	Christopher Millard (1872–1927)
CW	Constance Wilde (1858–1898)
FH	Frank Harris (1856–1931)
HMH	Harford Montgomery Hyde (1907–1989)
MH	Merlin Holland (1945–)
MM	Max Meyerfeld (1875–1940)
OL	Otho Lloyd (1856–1943)
OW	Oscar Wilde (1854–1900)
RE	Richard Ellmann (1918–1987)
RH-D	Rupert Hart-Davis (1907–1999)
RR	Robert Ross (1869 - 1918)
RS	Robert Sherard (1861 - 1943
RT	Reginald Turner (1869–1938)
TH	Thelma Holland (1910–1995)
VH	Vyvyan Holland (Wilde) (1886–1967)
WL	Walter Ledger (1862–1931)

The exact call numbers are only given if it would be difficult to find the documents without them. I have made no distinction between original documents and direct copies (as distinct from transcripts), treating both as 'Manuscript' (MS) material for simplicity.

Asquith	Asquith Papers, Bodleian Library, Oxford
BL	British Library
BL Eccles	Eccles Collection, British Library
Cambridge	Cambridge University Library
Clark	William Andrews Clark Library, University of California, Los Angeles
Harvard	Houghton Library, Harvard University
Holland	Merlin Holland Papers
Holland, J.	John Holland Papers
Illinois	University of Illinois
Kew	British National Archives, Kew
Leeds	Brotherton Library, University of Leeds
Paris	Archives de la Ville de Paris
Reading	Reading University Library
Southampton	Broadlands Archive, University of Southampton
Stewart	Margaret Stewart (for Cyril Holland's letters)
Texas	Harry Ransom Humanities Research Centre, University of Texas, Austin
Tulsa	McFarlin Library, University of Tulsa
Univ. Oxon.	Robert Ross Memorial Collection, University College, Oxford
Yale	Beinecke Library, Yale University

NOTES

PART ONE (1897-1900)

Introduction

[1] For example: Derek Hudson, 'The Tragedy of Oscar Wilde,' *Daily Telegraph,* 10 Sep 1954; Lord Birkenhead 'Oscar Wilde's Son,' *Time and Tide*, 11 Sep 1954; John Connell, 'Good Reading,' *Evening News*, 11 Sep 1954; Hesketh Pearson, 'Father and Son,' *Sunday Times*, 12 Sep 1954.

[2] Merlin Holland, 'Biography and the Art of Lying,' in *The Cambridge Companion to Oscar Wilde*, ed. Peter Raby; *Private Eye*, 9 Oct–1 Nov 2018.

Chapter One: Oscar's Release

[3] OW to Robert Ross, 13 May 1897, *Complete Letters,* p. 823.

[4] F. G. Bettany, *Stewart Headlam: a Biography*, p.132.

[5] For reasons explained on pp. 517-18 this was almost certainly not Clapham Junction as Oscar recounted to Alfred Douglas in his long prison letter *De Profundis*.

[6] Correspondence from Margaret Gray, Elizabeth Norris's great niece Dec 1997–Feb 1998 to MH in which the story is related in detail (MSS Holland).

[7] The full details can be found in Ernest Leverson's letter to OW, 17 May 1897, *CL*, p. 828.

[8] Ada Leverson, *Letters to the Sphinx from Oscar Wilde*, pp. 45-46.

[9] Back in 1930 when her book was published, my father already suspected Leverson of 'improving' OW's letters to her: Vyvyan Holland to Tom Balston, 17 Jan 1930 (C. J. Sawyer catalogue No. 277, 1968 Item 551). As it turned out, when *The Letters of Oscar Wilde* was published in 1962 and the originals were consulted, he was right; she left out all Oscar's references to her husband in order to make the letters appear more intimately addressed to her alone. She probably let her imagination run away with her in this case

too. See also Raymond and Ricketts, *Oscar Wilde: Recollections*, pp. 47-49 for Oscar's state of mind at the end of his prison sentence as well as my notes of a conversation with the Farm Street archivist Fr Geoffrey Holt in 1999.

[10] Although he himself was reported to have said to a French journalist (*Echo de Paris*, 6 Dec 1891) 'Legends should never be destroyed. It is they which help us to catch a glimpse of the genuine face of a man,' I would add 'unless they are manifestly absurd or their purpose was merely to reflect advantageously on their inventor.'

[11] OW to Reggie Turner, 17 May 1897, *CL*, p. 832.

[12] Not West Croydon as most biographers state. The error was started by Montgomery Hyde in *Oscar Wilde: the Aftermath*. A quick check of Bradshaw's Railway Guide for 1897 reveals that West Croydon was not on the Victoria—Newhaven line. A trivial point but illustrative, yet again, of unquestioning follow-my-leader biography.

[13] Joseph Donohue (ed.) *The Complete Works of Oscar Wilde* Vol. X, pp. 862-63.

[14] Sebastian Melmoth was the main character in his great uncle Charles Maturin's gothic novel *Melmoth the Wanderer*.

[15] Much of the detailed description of Oscar's first day of freedom in France that follows was provided by Robert Ross in an unpublished memoir which would have served as an introduction to a projected edition of Oscar's letters to him (MS Clark).

[16] OW to RR, 28 May 1897, *CL*, p. 860. The sums amounted to £22.10s or the equivalent of £3,000 in today's money (2025).

[17] *CL*, p. 777.

[18] *CL*, p. 733.

[19] Robert Sherard, *Oscar Wilde: The Story of an Unhappy Friendship*, p. 248.

[20] OW to Henrietta Stannard, 28 May 1897, *CL*, p. 857.

[21] OW to RR, 1 Apr 1897, *CL*, p. 780.

[22] RR to Alfred Douglas, 23 Jun 1897 (MS BL Eccles).

Chapter Two: After The Fall

[23] As a result, the Liberal MP Richard Haldane visited Wilde and had extra books sent into Pentonville Prison for him. See Moyle, p. 277 and Sturgis, pp. 590-92 for full details.

[24] Constance Wilde to Emily Thursfield, 25 Jun 1895 (MS Clark).

[25] Hyde, *Aftermath*, p. 24; Sherard 1902, pp. 204-12.

[26] Otho Holland to OW, 27 Nov 1883, *CL*, p. 222.

[27] Merlin Holland, 'Le neveu d'Oscar Wilde,' in *La Règle du jeu* No. 53 (2013) p. 155.

[28] OH to Mary Holland, 9 Sep 1895 (MS Holland).

[29] CW to Mary Holland, 15 Sep 1895 (MS Holland, J.).

[30] My father gave an account of these early months of the family's exile in his 1954 autobiography including the dramatic story of how they were ejected from a hotel on account of who they were and were forced to change their name. In fact, the family stayed in the same hotel until they left in September. For a correct version of this incident see my comments on Vyvyan's book on pp. 334-35.

[31] CW to Robert Sherard, 21 Sep 1895 (MS BL Eccles).

[32] *CL*, p. 665, n. 2.

[33] CW to Emily Thursfield, 12 Oct 1895 (MS Clark).

[34] Vincent O'Sullivan, *Aspects of Wilde* (1936), p. 63.

[35] OW to RR, 13 May 1897, *CL*, p. 818.

[36] OW to RR, 10 Mar 1896, *CL*, p. 652.

[37] OW to RR, 13 May 1897, *CL*, pp. 816-17. The clearest and most detailed account of this episode can be found in J. Robert Maguire's *Ceremonies of Bravery* (2013), pp. 64-84.

[38] The Deed of Separation is now in the Eccles Collection at the British Library Add MSS 81754 B.

[39] CW to OH, 24 May 1897 (MS Holland); OH to Carlos Blacker 13 Jan 1901 (MS Maguire). She kept all Oscar's letters to her in a small blue leather case which disappeared after her death.

[40] OH to Mary Holland, 18 Apr 1898 (MS Holland).

[41] OW to RR, 29 May 1897, *CL*, p. 865.

[42] CW to OH, 20 Mar 1897 (MS Holland).

[43] AD to Muriel Sherard, 1 Apr 1940 (MS Reading).

[44] Sherard 1902, pp. 246-47; OW to More Adey, 27 Nov 1897, *CL* p. 995.

[45] Henrietta Stannard to Louise Jopling, 23 Feb 1898 (MS Private).

[46] *CL*, pp. 733-34.

[47] OW to Frank Harris, 13 Jun 1897, *CL*, p. 896.

[48] OW to RR, 1 Apr 1897, *CL*, p. 785.

[49] OW to RR, 28 May 1897, *CL*, p. 858.

[50] See page 383-84 (Part 4 Chap. 6 'Publishing Oscar's Letters') for a summary of the story.

[51] Maguire, *passim* and specifically pp. 87-91.

[52] OW to CB, 4 Aug 1897, *CL,* p. 921.

[53] OW's written answers in an American 'Confession Album' reproduced in Merlin Holland, *The Wilde Album*, p. 45.

[54] Maguire, p. 93.

[55] VH diary 17 May 1960 (MS Holland).

[56] OW to RR, 2 Mar 1898, *CL,* p. 1029.

[57] CW to OH 19 Feb 1898, *CL,* p. 1022.

[58] CW to Arthur Humphreys, 18 Feb 1898 (MS Holland).

[59] OW to CB, 28 Mar 1898, *CL,* p. 1051.

Chapter Three: Constance's & Oscar's Deaths

[60] OH draft letter to OW 24 Jul 1897 (MS Holland).

[61] Vyvyan Holland, *Son of Oscar Wilde* (1954), p. 73.

[62] Melissa Knox, *Oscar Wilde: a Long and Lovely Suicide* (1994), pp. 42-43. For the origins and refutal of the Wilde 'syphilis myth' see pp. 463-66.

[63] Ashley Robins & Merlin Holland, 'The Enigmatic Illness and Death of Constance, Wife of Oscar Wilde,' *Lancet*, vol. 385, pp. 21-22. https://www.thelancet.com/journals/lancet/article/PIIS0140-6736(14)62468-5/fulltext.

[64] CW to VH, 4 Feb 1898 (MS BL Eccles).

[65] This wealth of detail is taken from the almost daily letters which Otho wrote to his wife, Mary, during his stay in Genoa (MSS Holland).

[66] Holland 1954, p. 131.

[67] CW to VH, 24 Mar 1898 (MS BL Eccles). In his autobiography *Son of Oscar Wilde* p. 130, my father refers to another 'last letter' from his mother which in all probability didn't exist. See pp. 333-34).

[68] CH to VH, 13 Jun 1898 (MS Holland).

[69] Holland 1954, p. 165.

[70] Mary Holland to OH, 9 Apr 1898 (MS Holland).

[71] CW to Lady Mount-Temple, 18 Aug 1892 (MS Southampton BR 57/15/13).

[72] 'Il prof. Luigi Maria Bossi sospeso dall'ufficio per due anni per atti immorali e scorrettezze amministrative,' *Avanti!* (Milan), 29 Jul 1918.

[73] 'Una oscura tragedia in via Boccaccio: il prof. L.M. Bossi ucciso in suo ambulatorio,' *Corriere della Sera*, 2, 3, 4 Feb 1919; 'Wife's Mania: Light on Consulting Room Tragedy,' *Daily Mail*, 4 Feb 1919.

[74] RR to Leonard Smithers, 17 Apr 1898, *CL*, p. 1054.

[75] Alfred Douglas, *Oscar Wilde: a Summing Up*, pp. 102-3.

[76] OW to CB, 12/13 Apr 1898, *CL*, p. 1055.

[77] OW to RR, 1 Mar 1899, *CL*, p. 1128.

[78] VH to FH, 9 May 1926 (MS Texas).

[79] A fact confirmed by his close friend Alec Waugh in *My Brother Evelyn and Other Profiles*, pp. 253-54.

[80] Maguire, pp. 13-21, 127-29. The falling out between the two of them still reverberated sixty years later when Oscar's correspondence was being prepared for publication. See pp. 383-84.

[81] VH to CB, 13 Apr 1898 (MS Holland).

[82] CB diary entry 9 May 1898, Maguire, p. 128.

[83] Fr Romualdo Fumagalli to CB, 10 Apr 1898 (MS Holland).

[84] Holland 1954, p. 200; Lucien Wormser to VH pp. 340-42.

[85] Holland 1954, pp. 149 & 200.

[86] Holland 1954, p. 203.

[87] Since this is not a book about Oscar Wilde but largely about the extraordinary and lasting effect he has had on posterity, his family, his friends and even his enemies, there seemed little point in covering this period in detail. It has been done admirably enough by some of his biographers: Matthew Sturgis, Robert Maguire and Nicholas Frankel (see bibliography). Wilde's many letters from those last years also constitute a poignant record of how he spent the end of his life.

[88] OW to FH, end Feb 1898, *CL*, p. 1025.

[89] OW to RR, 25 Nov 1898, *CL*, p. 1102.

[90] The play, *Mr. and Mrs. Daventry,* was finally written by Frank Harris and performed in London in October 1900. For a list of those known to have an interest in the scenario, see *CL*, p. 1189 n. 3.

[91] OW to Leonard Smithers, 9 Jan 1898, *CL*, p. 1011.

[92] OW to Frances Forbes-Robertson, mid-May 1899, *CL*, pp. 1144-45.

[93] OW to RR, May/Jun 1900, *CL*, p. 1188.

[94] For a discussion of the causes of his death see pp. 463-66.

[95] For father Dunne's account see *CL*, pp. 1223-24.

PART TWO (1900-1918)

Chapter One: The Orphaned Wildes

[96] Laura Hope Diary for 1895, 5 Apr 1895 (MS Clark, More House Archive Box 37).

[97] VH 1954, p. 77. Although my father refers to this change of name early in the family's European 'exile,' the Royal Warrant issued by the College of Arms is dated 31 October 1903, meaning that it could only have been undertaken by Hope as the children's guardian after the death of their mother.

[98] OW to OH, [c. 15 Mar 1898] CL, p. 1036.

[99] VH 1954, p. 138.

[100] OH to Mary Holland, 26 Jun 1898 (MS Holland).

[101] MS Kew WO 339/6404.

[102] VH 1954, p. 136.

[103] VH 1954, p. 137.

[104] CH to VH, 3 Jun 1914 (MS Holland). The full text of the letter, written in reply to one which Vyvyan had written to Cyril earlier in the year, can be found on pp. 157-62.

[105] VH 1954, p. 139.

[106] CH to VH, 3 Jun 1914 (MS Holland).

[107] VH to CH, 23 Feb 1914 (Draft MS Holland).

[108] Exchange of letters between Adrian & Laura Hope 13-19 Sep 1899 (MS More House Archives, Clark Library).

[109] CH to VH, Jun 1898 (MS Holland); VH to Adrian Hope, 21 May 1898 (MS More House Archives, Clark Library); Holland 1954, p. 149.

[110] OW to More Adey, 25 Sept 1896, CL, p. 665; OW to AD, Jan–Mar 1895, CL, p. 766.

[111] A. K. Boyd, The History of Radley College 1847-1947, p. 258.

[112] Louis Wilkinson told the story of how he invented the Ipswich Dramatic Society in order to correspond with OW in Louis Marlow [pseud.], Seven Friends.

[113] Holland 1954, p. 152.

[114] CH to CB, [Dec 1900] (MS copy in the hand of RR, Clark Library). Quoted with omissions in Holland 1954, p. 153.

[115] RR to Adela Schuster, 23 Dec 1900, CL, p. 1228.

[116] These letters can be found in *CL,* pp. 1211-30 and more specifically the letter from RR to More Adey pp. 1221-22.

[117] Maguire, pp. 158-59.

[118] Maguire, pp. 161, 165.

[119] *Dundee Evening Telegraph,* 3 Dec 1900.

[120] Father Browne's and Vyvyan's letters to Father Dunne of respectively 5, 12 and 14 Dec 1900 are in the Clark Library, together with Father Dunne's narrative which was subsequently published in *CL,* pp. 1223-24.

[121] Holland 1954, pp. 154-56.

[122] CH to VH, 23 January 1904 (MS Holland).

Chapter Two: Ross Manages The Estate

[123] Holland 1954, p. 164 and a fact confirmed by Ross's first letter to VH of 1 Aug 1907 (MS BL Eccles).

[124] Oscar was adjudged bankrupt on 31 August 1895 on the petition of the Marquess of Queensberry for his costs in the failed libel action which Oscar brought against him. The complete bankruptcy files are in the British National Archives ref. B9/428 & 429, from which much of the following information about Wilde's literary estate before 1906 has been gleaned.

[125] OW to AD, [Jan–Mar 1897], *CL,* p. 734.

[126] OW to Reginald Turner, 10 Aug 1897, *CL,* p. 924.

[127] Society of Authors Archives (BL Add. MSS 86845-49).

[128] Michael Seeney in *From Bow Street to the Ritz: Oscar Wilde's Theatrical Career from 1895 to 1908* lists no less than 282 venues at which the four major plays were produced during this period.

[129] *The Candid Friend,* 14 Dec 1901, edited, incidentally, by Oscar's old sparring partner, Frank Harris.

[130] RR to FH, 1 Feb 1917 (MS Texas); RR to Adela Schuster, 3 Jan 1902, Margery Ross, *Robert Ross: Friend of Friends,* p. 75.

[131] *Salome,* (London, 1907), p. xiii.

[132] *New York Times,* 21 Dec 1924.

[133] 'A prefatory dedication,' *De Profundis* (London, 1908), pp ix-x.

[134] E. V. Lucas to RR [Nov 1904], Ross, *Friends,* p. 88.

[135] Ross, *Friends,* pp. 93-100.

[136] OW to AD [Jan–Mar 1897], *CL,* pp 729 & 758.

[137] 'A few maxims for the instruction of the over-educated,' *CW,* p. 1242.

[138] An article commissioned by the *Mercure de France* in July 1895 and which would have included three of Wilde's intimate letters to him was 'spiked' at Wilde's insistence through his friend Robert Sherard. The text was published in 2002 as *Oscar Wilde: A Plea and a Reminiscence*, ed. Caspar Wintermans; Douglas did, however, publish an article 'L'Affaire Wilde' in the *Revue Blanche* on 1 June 1896; OW to RR, 30 May 1896, *CL,* p. 654.

[139] AD to RR, 21 Jun 1897 (MS BL Eccles).

[140] Douglas 1929, p. 181.

[141] RR to FH, 1 Feb 1917 (MS Clark). See also RR to VH, 9 Jun 1918 (MS BL Eccles). In the 1950s when my father sold the letters Ross had written to him, he made and kept typescripts. Ross stated in this letter that in 1900 Douglas refused his 'sporting offer' and that it was a cause of animosity between them ever after. Vyvyan annotated it with the following explanation: 'Ross offered Douglas a half share in all future Wilde Royalties if he would pay off the bankruptcy—£800.' Even if the basic fact is correct, the details cannot be. The remaining debt was far larger. Wilde was made bankrupt in 1895 for £3,591 and between then and his death only two small dividends were paid to creditors. Secondly, Ross would never have parted permanently with half the royalties, given Oscar's instructions that they should mainly benefit his children.

[142] *The Motorist and Traveller,* 1 Mar 1905; *St. James's Gazette,* 2, 3 & 9 Mar 1905.

[143] Bernard Shaw to RR, 13 March 1905, Ross, *Friends,* p. 111.

[144] Compton Mackenzie, *My Life and Times: Octave Three,* p. 225.

[145] *The Times,* 3 Apr 1905.

[146] Hyde, *Aftermath,* p. 192. Hyde references the original correspondence in the archives of Methuen & Co which due to multiple takeovers has since disappeared.

[147] *Daily Chronicle,* 30 Aug 1905.

Chapter Three: No Longer Schoolboys

[148] CW to OH, 22 Jan 1895 (MS Holland).

[149] Holland 1954, p. 171.

[150] Adrian Hope, the boys' original guardian, had died on 10 May 1904 and his place had been taken by barrister, businessman and local politician Ernest Louis Meinertzhagen (1854-1933) until Vyvyan came of age.

[151] Holland 1954, p. 183.

[152] Holland 1954, p. 185.

[153] Helen Carew's estate was worth £232,759.

[154] The volume, the 1892 'Author's Edition' of the *Poems* is now in the British Library with the inscription duly (and improbably) attributed to 'Mrs. Carew' (MS BL Eccles 253).

[155] Sir George Kennard, *Loopy*, p. 5.

[156] 'Banquet to Mr. Parnell,' *The Times*, 9 May 1888; OW to Oscar Browning, *CL*, p. 348.

[157] Holland 1954, p. 187.

[158] A few months later one of Robbie's close friends, Christopher Millard wrote to the American publisher, Thomas Mosher: 'He [Vyvyan] is interested in his father's career and books, but says that his elder brother is "very anti the gov'nor" and always refers to him as the man "that wrote the plays".' 29 May 1908 (MS Houghton). This is confirmed in Robbie's first letter to Vyvyan, after their meeting: 'What you told me about Cyril caused me no surprise, although I was deeply pained,' 1 Aug 1907 (MS BL Eccles).

[159] CH to RR [Oct 1913] (MS Holland).

[160] Roy Kennard to VH, 30 Jul 1907 (MS Holland).

[161] VH diary 1907-1911, p. 24; Roy Kennard to VH, 28 Oct 1911 (MS Holland).

[162] RR to VH, 1 Aug 1907 (MS BL Eccles).

[163] VH diary, 1907-1911, pp. 2-8.

Chapter Four: Return From Purgatory

[164] RR to CM, 26 Sep 1906 (MS Clark).

[165] RR to WL, 1 Apr 1908 (MS Univ. Coll. Oxon.) and Mason p. 424.

[166] AD to WL, 3 Jun 1902 (MS Univ. Coll. Oxon.).

[167] *Reynolds' Newspaper*, 31 May 1895.

[168] Millard's letters to Ledger have been preserved in the Robert Ross Memorial Collection, MS Ross 13 now housed in the library of University College, Oxford. See also pp. 298-99.

[169] The sorry details of the incident can be found in Maria Roberts, *Yours Loyally: A Life of Christopher Sclater Millard*.

[170] RR to WL, 6 May 1906 (MS Univ. Coll. Ox.).

[171] RR Statement, p. 53 [Oct 1913 relating to his persecution by Alfred Douglas] (MS Clark).

[172] James Nelson in his *Leonard Smithers; Publisher to the Decadents*, p. 265 lists seventeen piracies between 1903 and Smithers' death in 1907.

[173] It was in fact written by J. F. Bloxam, an Oxford undergraduate for whose magazine, *The Chameleon,* Oscar wrote his 'Phrases and Philosophies for the Use of the Young.' See *Irish Peacock and Scarlet Marquess*, p. 306.

[174] The exchange between Ross and Le Gallienne took place in the columns of the *TLS* on 28 Jun, 3 Oct and 10 Oct 1907.

[175] Holland 1954, p. 191.

[176] Holland 1954, p. 191.

[177] *CL*, pp. 264-65.

[178] CH to VH, 1 Aug 1913 (MS Holland); CH to Laura Hope, 1 Aug 1913 (MS Clark); CH to Robert Ross, 1 Jul 1913 (MS Holland) are all an unfortunate cross between an attempt at his father's slightly 'purple prose' style and a Baedeker travel guide.

[179] *Akademos: mode d'emploi*, p. 446 n. 1 (reprint ed. N. Albert et P. Cardon, 2022).

[180] *Akademos*, vol. 1 p. 65.

[181] *La Gazzetta di Venezia*, 25 Sep 1908.

[182] See Francis Steegmuller, *Cocteau: A Biography*, p. 34. Cocteau later inscribed a copy of *Thomas l'imposteur* to my father when they met again in Paris in 1923.

[183] Cocteau's *Le Portrait surnaturel de Dorian Gray* was published posthumously in 1978; Laurent's essay was also published posthumously in his Études anglaises in 1910.

[184] *Das literarische Echo*, 1 & 15 Mar 1909. The whole detailed story of Laurent's death and my father's stay in Venice has been admirably told by Horst Schroeder in 'Suicide of Vivian Wilde,' *The Wildean* No. 30 (2007).

[185] *Die Zeit* (Vienna), 17 Oct 1903; the piece was later published as *C.3.3 und anderes* (1904).

[186] Stuart-Young's colourful life has been recorded in detail by Stephanie Newell in *The Forger's Tale*; Hesketh Pearson, *The Life of Oscar Wilde,* p. 265.

[187] *The Critic and Literary World*, Jul 1905, pp. 86-88.

[188] *New York Times Review of Books*, 1 Jul 1905.

[189] *Los Angeles Examiner*, 22 Nov 1908.

[190] *The Times,* 2 Dec 1908.

[191] John Gay, *Fables,* Fable XLV. Like Robbie, from the moment I read those lines, I have never forgotten them and they have conditioned, a century later, almost all my dealings with what is left of my grandfather's legacy.

[192] The full text of Ross's speech is reproduced in Margery Ross, *Robert Ross: Friend of Friends,* pp. 153-57. The best account of the dinner was written by Mrs. Desda Cornish, an American journalist, for the *Boston Evening Transcript,* 16 Dec 1908.

Chapter Five: Robbie & Bosie Declare War

[193] The article on *The Grey Stocking* appeared in *The Academy* on 6 Jun 1908.

[194] Ross, 'Deposition,' pp. 45-46; Ross, 'Statement,' pp. 10-11. Ross's account of these quarrels is in two documents he later prepared for use in court cases involving Douglas. The first was his 'Deposition' regarding the history of *De Profundis* when Douglas sued Arthur Ransome; the second was Ross's 'Statement' prepared for his solicitor detailing Douglas's persecution of him between 1908 and 1913 (MSS Clark).

[195] *The Academy,* 11 & 18 Jul 1908.

[196] Ross, 'Deposition,' pp. 47-48.

[197] Ross, 'Deposition,' pp. 49-49.

[198] *The Academy,* 29 Jan 1909.

[199] RR to Olive Douglas, 28 Feb 1909 & AD to RR, 1 Mar 1909 both in Ross, 'Statement,' pp. 14-17.

[200] *De Profundis,* ed. M. Meyerfeld (1909) pp. xvii & 14.

[201] Frank Harris, *Oscar Wilde: His Life and Confessions,* p. 540. The story about Ross moving Oscar's body himself continued to appear in all subsequent editions of the book until its first appearance in England in 1938 when it was dropped. Reggie Turner also told Harris that it was nonsense in February 1925: Frank Harris & Alfred Douglas, *New Preface to "The Life and Confessions of Oscar Wilde."*

[202] A letter from RR to VH, 19 Sep 1911 confirms this fear on Cyril's part (MS Holland) as does my father himself in his second volume of memoirs *Time Remembered,* p. 44. Brigadier Malden Studd, who had been a subaltern with Cyril at Woolwich, wrote to Rupert Hart-Davis in November 1962 to say that he was sure that no one was aware of Cyril's parentage at the time (MS Holland).

[203] Bernard Shaw to RR, 13 Mar 1905, Ross, *Friends*, p. 111.

[204] *Collected Works*, p. 930.

[205] The whole controversy surrounding the BMA statues is recounted in Jacob Epstein's *Let There Be Sculpture*, pp. 33-55, and an excellent summary of the affair is in Simon Wilson's *Jacob Epstein's Studies for the Tomb of Oscar Wilde*.

[206] OW to AD 23 Jun 1897, *CL*, p. 907.

[207] Ross's correspondence with Kenyon and internal memos on the subject are now preserved in the British Library Add. MS 50141. See also *Daily Telegraph*, 21 Nov 1914.

[208] The case was fully reported in *The Times* on 11, 12 & 15 Feb 1910.

[209] AD to More Adey, 23 May 1910 (MS Illinois).

[210] André Gide, *Si le grain ne meurt*, Deuxième Partie, Chapitre 2.

Chapter Six: Vyvyan Tries To Find A Purpose In Life

[211] Holland 1954, p. 195.

[212] Vyvyan's ambivalence to his father's memory was evident when he passed on to Walter Ledger the engraved plate from Oscar's first coffin given to him as a memento by Robbie when Oscar was reburied in 1909. VH's letter to Ledger accompanying the plate is dated 10 Apr 1910 (MS Univ. Oxon.).

[213] RR to VH, 1 Aug 1907. All RR's surviving letters to VH are in the Eccles Collection at the British Library (BL Add. MS 81719). Vyvyan sold them to the bookseller George Sims in 1959.

[214] These are still in my possession.

[215] Holland 1966, pp. 16, 58 & 62.

[216] Holland 1966, pp. 21-34.

[217] RR to WL, 11 Oct 1911 (MS Univ. Oxon.). According to the report with prices realised in *The Times*, 28 Jul 1911, the manuscripts included three chapters of *The Picture of Dorian Gray* and Oscar's complete essay 'The Soul of Man under Socialism.'

[218] RR to VH, 19 Sep 1911. The text of this letter exists only as a part typescript made by my father before destroying the original when he sold Ross's other letters.

[219] CH to VH, 20 Mar 1912 (MS Holland).

[220] VH Spanish Diary, 25 Jan 1912; OW to AD, *CL*, p, 730; Holland 1966, p. 57.

[221] 'How the Hudsons came together,' *Morning Post*, 8 Apr 1913; CH to VH, 1 Aug 1913 (MS Holland).

[222] Holland 1966, p. 59.

[223] Holland 1966, pp. 59-66.

[224] RR to VH, 26 Oct 1913 (MS BL Eccles).

[225] CH to RR, Sep 1913 (MS Holland).

Chapter Seven: The Brothers Exchange Letters

[226] RR to VH, 13 Jul 1914 (MS BL Eccles).

Chapter Eight: A Tale Of Two Testicles

[227] Ross 'Statement,' p. 23 and 'Deposition,' pp. 52-55; Arthur Ransome, *Autobiography*, pp. 143 & 146.

[228] Ross, 'Statement,' pp. 24-28.

[229] Ross, 'Statement,' p. 23.

[230] My father, incidentally, very much disliked the sculpture which he irreverently described as 'a flying angel with an erection,' VH to John-Paul Ross, 25 Oct 1961 (MS Holland).

[231] E. J. Shaw. 'Mr. Jacob Epstein's monument for the tomb of Oscar Wilde,' *Walsall Observer and South Staffordshire Chronicle*, 15 Jun 1912. Edward Shaw was a respected local businessman, art-lover and generous donor to the Walsall Art Gallery which now, coincidentally, houses many works by the sculptor donated by his widow Kathleen in 1973.

[232] Stephen Gardiner, *Epstein: artist against the establishment*, p. 106.

[233] 'Wilde at Père Lachaise,' *Pall Mall Gazette*, 23 Sep 1912.

[234] Wilson, *Epstein*, p. 49.

[235] *Le Temps*, 29 Sep 1912.

[236] 'Oscar Wilde: prisonnier de la Préfecture de la Seine,' *Comœdia*, 9 Oct 1912. Translation from Epstein, *Sculpture*, pp. 278-80.

[237] Jacob Epstein, *Let There Be Sculpture* (London, 1940). pp. 67-68; *Cambridge Daily News*, 23 Sep 1912.

[238] Procès-Verbal de la Réunion du 25 Oct 1912 (MS Archives du Cimetière du Père-Lachaise); Procès Verbal de la Réunion du 13 Décembre 1912 (MS Paris PER 196 1).

[239] *Chelsea News*, 28 Feb 1913.

[240] *L'Action de l'art,* Mar 1913.

[241] Aleister Crowley, *The Confessions of Aleister Crowley,* pp. 644-48; *The Times,* 6 & 8 Nov 1913.

[242] *The Times,* 3 Jan 1914.

[243] For the ultimate fate of the testicles see pp. 473-75.

Chapter Nine: The Ransome Libel Trial

[244] Sherard 1902, pp. 257-58; Leonard Cresswell Ingleby, *Oscar Wilde,* p. 85.

[245] AD to John Lane, 18 Aug 1912 (MS Clark).

[246] AD to RR, 1, 2, & 5 Nov 1912 in RR 'Statement,' pp. 30-35.

[247] The incident is described in detail in Marie Belloc Lowndes's memoir *A Passing World,* pp. 177-79 and in RR 'Statement,' pp. 36-37.

[248] Preface to T. W. H. Crosland, *The First Stone,* p. 6.

[249] W. Sorley Brown, *The Life and Genius of T.W.H. Crosland,* pp. 282-83.

[250] Sorley Brown, *op. cit.* p. 299.

[251] Ransome, *Autobiography,* p. 154.

[252] Douglas 1929, p. 249.

[253] Douglas mentions this on several occasions in books he later wrote: *Autobiography,* pp. 114, 128-29; *Without Apology,* p. 77, keeping only 25 which he described as 'comparatively colourless' and which he later sold to the London dealer Bernard Quaritch. They were purchased by William Andrews Clark of Los Angeles who made a facsimile volume of them: *Some Letters from Oscar Wilde to Alfred Douglas 1892-1897* in 1925.

[254] *The Academy,* 16 Oct 1909, p. 627. I am grateful to Caspar Wintermans for drawing my attention to this.

[255] The account of the trial, with varying degrees of accuracy, is given in the law reports of *The Times* and the *Daily Telegraph* 18, 19, 22 & 23 Apr 1913. The best summaries are given in the biographies of Alfred Douglas by Caspar Wintermans and Douglas Murray. Douglas's very one-sided account of the libel action can be found in his *Autobiography,* pp. 33-36.

[256] Ransome, *Autobiography,* Chapter 16. It would not be the last time that an innocent party was suddenly implicated in a quarrel about Oscar Wilde. See later chapters in which Bernard Shaw found himself between Frank Harris and Alfred Douglas, Rupert Hart-Davis between my father and Montgomery Hyde, and Roger Lewis between Rosita Fanto and the Ellmanns.

[257] RR to Arthur Ransome, 22 Mar 1912 (MS Brotherton, Leeds).

[258] RR to Ada Leverson, 18 November 1912 (MS Clark).

[259] *The Times*, Law Report, 13 June 1913.

[260] RR to VH, 16 Mar 1912 (MS BL Eccles).

[261] Holland 1966, p. 65.

[262] Douglas 1929, p. 250.

Chapter Ten: Kicking Oscar's Corpse

[263] RR to Ada Leverson, 18 Nov 1912 (MS Clark).

[264] RR to Edmund Gosse, 21 Oct 1913 in Gosse's copy of *The Suppressed Portion of De Profundis* (MS Univ. Oxon.); Vyvyan Holland, *De Profundis*, p. 10.

[265] Christopher Millard recorded all the recipients of the copies (MS Holland).

[266] The convoluted and disgraceful story of how Crosland and Douglas attempted to suborn witnesses is admirably told in detail by Maureen Borland in *Wilde's Devoted Friend*, pp. 189-228 and in even more detail by Edra Bogle in her unpublished PhD thesis 'The Life and Literary and Artistic Activities of Robert Baldwin Ross 1869-1918,' pp. 301-51.

[267] RR 'Statement,' pp. 53-59.

[268] RR to John Lane, 23 Dec 1913 (MS Texas).

[269] RR to Edmund Gosse, 2 & 6 Jan 1914 (MS Leeds); RR to Ada Leverson, 15 Jan 1914 (MS Clark).

[270] Sorley Brown, *Crosland*, p. 309.

[271] The basic premise behind the writing of this book was to show the extent to which the echoes of my grandfather's tragedy—self-inflicted though it may have been—have impinged upon the lives of dozens of people, even those who never knew him, for more than a century after his death. However, there are times when the details, such as those reported in these court cases, fascinating and directly related to Oscar as they are, threaten to overwhelm and I have had to resist the temptation to include them or the book would have become unmanageably long. Since the Ross/Douglas/Crosland feuding has been admirably dealt with in biographies by Edra Bogle, Maureen Borland, Douglas Murray, and W. Sorley Brown, I have had to limit myself to a few of the more dramatic highlights.

[272] Exchange of letters between Ross and Nathan (MS BL Eccles).

[273] Herbert Asquith to RR, 23 Jul 1914 (MS BL Eccles) along with many other sympathetic letters in the same collection.

[274] RR to VH and Violet Holland, 13 Jul 1914 (MS BL Eccles). RR's letters to Frank Harris around that time in Vyvyan's handwriting and signed by Ross are evidence of my father's secretarial activities (MS Texas).

[275] RR copied Cyril's letter to Frank Harris with his of 1 Feb 1917 (MS Texas).

[276] *West London Press,* 1 May 1914.

[277] Geoffrey Matthews has written up an account of the whole affair in *The Wildean* No. 60 (2022) and further details can be found in the Chelsea Borough Council Minutes for the period as well as in the *West London Press.*

[278] In 1938 in his penultimate book *Without Apology,* p. 58.

[279] Douglas 1914, pp. 62-64.

[280] *Daily Telegraph,* 25 Nov 1914.

[281] Douglas 1929, p. 44; Ralph Straus to RR, 7 Apr 1915 (MS BL Eccles).

[282] *Daily Telegraph* and *The Times,* 28 Nov 1914.

[283] Sorley Brown, *Crosland,* pp. 336-37.

[284] *The Globe,* 7 Apr 1915.

[285] AD to Andrew Bonar Law, 15 Apr 1915 (MS Parliamentary Archives BL/37/1/32).

[286] AD to Herbert Asquith, 22 Jan 1915 and to Winston Churchill, 21 May 1915 (MS Asquith).

[287] The page-proofs of 'The Wilde Myth' are now in the Harry Ransom Centre at the University of Texas.

[288] CH to VH, 22 Jan 1915 (MS Holland).

Chapter Eleven: Vyvyan & The War

[289] Lieut. H. T. Harrison note on CH's death (MS Holland).

[290] Holland 1966, p. 84.

[291] Holland 1954, p. 142; Malden Studd to RH-D, Nov 1962 (MS Holland).

[292] CH to VH, 6 Nov 1906 (MS Holland).

[293] CH to Margaret Maitland, 4 Aug 1907, 26 Oct 1909 & 1 Jul 1913 (MS Stewart).

[294] VH to T. Werner Laurie, 18 Jul & 25 Aug 1915 (MS Yale).

[295] VH to RR, 10 May 1915 & 4 Aug 1916 (MS Holland).

[296] RR to VH, 11 Feb 1918 (MS BL Eccles).

[297] RR to Charles Ricketts, 13 Jun 1918 (MS BL Eccles).

[298] *The Verbatim Report of the Trial of Noel Pemberton Billing*, p. 472.

[299] Billing, *Verbatim Report*, p. 476.

[300] Billing himself published the most complete record of the trial under the imprint of the Vigilante Office in 1918, but more concise accounts with the relevant background to the affair can be found in Philip Hoare, *Wilde's Last Stand*, and Michael Kettle, *Salome's Last Veil*.

[301] RR to VH, 3 & 9 June 1918 (MS BL Eccles). Ross gives even more detail about the massive cancellation of these contracts in his letter to Charles Ricketts of 13 Jun 1918 (MS BL Eccles).

[302] RR to Charles Ricketts, 13 Jun 1918, Ross, *Friends*, p. 333.

[303] RR to Sir Charles Mathews, 6 Jun 1918 (MS BL Eccles); RR to VH, 9 June 1918 (MS BL Eccles).

[304] Siegfried Sassoon to Edra Bogle, 6 Nov 1960, Bogle, Thesis, p. 419.

[305] Holland 1966, pp. 102-3.

[306] RR to VH, 13 Jul 1914 & 20 Jan 1915.

PART THREE (1918-1945)

Chapter One: Vyvyan Takes Control

[307] Holland 1966, p. 108.

[308] In fact he managed to get two short stories published in the *Morning Post*, 'How the Hudsons came together' (8 Apr 1913) and 'The Rajah's polo team' (13 Jul 1917).

[309] Holland 1966, p. 112. Temple died in 1958 having had a very successful career as a public relations consultant to several major British companies and London hotels. Vyvyan wrote his carefully worded obituary for *The Times*, 14 Mar 1958.

[310] The handling of the estate's copyrights and the convoluted negotiations for dramatic performances as well as publications at that time are beyond the scope of this book but can be found in the Society of Authors' archives preserved in the British Library, Add. MSS 56845-56849 & 56861.

[311] Fewer than half of the letters were published in two volumes *After Reading* (1921) and *After Berneval* (1922). An American edition of each,

with extra letters and less edited, was published in 23 copies by Paul Reynolds in the USA to secure the American copyright.

[312] The Law Reports of the *Daily Telegraph* for 25, 26, & 29 Nov 1921 give the fullest account of the trial.

[313] OW to RR, 30 May 1897, *CL,* p. 865.

[314] VH to Edward Heron-Allen, 23 Feb 1924 (MS Holland); VH to William Andrews Clark, 18 Aug 1923 (MS Clark).

[315] MM to CM, 20 Oct 1921 (MS Yale); VH to CM, 30 Oct 1921 (MS Clark).

[316] Meyerfeld published an account of his visit to London and his meeting with Vyvyan in 'Oscar Wildes Sohn' *Die neue Rundschau,* Nov 1924, pp. 1151-79 & 1200.

[317] *CL,* p. 782; Meyerfeld, 'De Profundis appears in full,' *New York Times,* 21 Dec 1924.

[318] See *CL,* p. 683 for the details.

[319] VH to his solicitor Norman Croom-Johnson, 12 Jun 1925 (MS BL Add. MS 56847).

[320] *Oscar Wilde: Letzte Briefe,* ed. Max Meyerfeld (Berlin, 1925) p. 5 (my translation).

[321] See note 315 above.

[322] VH to Norman Croom-Johnson, 9 May 1926 (MS BL Add. MS 56847).

[323] *Mercure de France,* 16 May 1913, p. 241; *CL,* p. 1029.

[324] Quoted from the July 2013 books and manuscripts catalogue of the French bookseller William Théry, 28800 Alluyes (my translation).

[325] VH to Norman Croom-Johnson, 22 Dec 1926 (MS BL Add. MS 56847).

[326] Davray published his translation in both a popular edition (Mercure de France) and a limited one (Simon Kra) in 1926. It was in the long preface to the latter that he reproduced the passages critical of Douglas. Vyvyan's correspondence on the legal aspects is in the Society of Authors' archives at the BL Add. MSS 56847 & 56848.

[327] FH to VH, 10 Dec 1927 (MS Clark).

[328] Martin Holman to Society of Authors 5 & 13 Feb 1925 (MS BL Add. MS 56847).

[329] Yoko Hirata, 'Oscar Wilde and Honma Hisao, the first translator of *De Profundis* into Japanese,' *Japan Review,* vol. 21 (2009), pp. 241-66.

[330] Honma Hisao, *Taiō Inshōki* [Impressions of Europe] is only available in the original Japanese. I am indebted to his granddaughter, Yoko Hirata, for providing me with translations of the relevant chapters on Vyvyan, Arthur Symons, and Max Beerbohm.

[331] *Eikoku Kinsei Yuibishugi no Kenkyū* [A study of Aestheticism in Modern England]. Between 1926 & 1927, in *Waseda bungaku* vols 242, 245 & 254 under Honma's editorship, Tadashi Miki published the first third of *De Profundis* in Japanese taken from Max Meyerfeld's 1925 German edition. It was probably not continued, being too far removed linguistically from the original. The first 'complete' translation, based on my father's 1949 version, didn't appear until 1952, and the first fully accurate one based on the *Letters of Oscar Wilde* (1962) was only published in 1976.

Chapter Two: Understanding Vyvyan In The 1920s

[332] VH to CM, 3 Mar 1921 (MS Clark).

[333] VH to Frank Harris, 15 Nov 1926 (MS Texas). Vyvyan's only acknowledgement of his work as a translator at the time was to sign himself somewhere discretely as H. B. V. his initials back to front.

[334] Information from O'Flaherty's estate in 2009; Charles Scott Moncrieff to VH, 3 Jun 1927 (MS Texas).

[335] Liam O'Flaherty's letters I still have and the hundred or so letters from Charles Scott Moncrieff were sold by Vyvyan in 1961 and are safely preserved in the Humanities Research Centre at the University of Texas.

[336] VH diary 29, 30 Apr & 1 May 1943.

[337] This is no mere conjecture. Both sides of his correspondence with Alec Waugh, author and brother of Evelyn, have survived and prove the point. VH's cautious description of Heron-Allen's 'double life' is in his 1966 memoir, pp. 129-30.

[338] I have their letters still. See also *The Oldie*, Spring 2024 for an account of his relationship with Kathleen Hale.

[339] Julien Green, *Journal intégral 1919-1940*, p. 1044 (my translation).

[340] The income from the Wilde estate at that time was about £1,400 a year and £100 would equate to about £5,500 in 2025.

[341] *In Memory of Dorothy Ierne Wilde*, ed. Natalie Barney, p. 135; VH to RH-D, 15 Jul 1961 (MS Holland).

[342] VH diary, 10, 11 & 17 Apr 1941.

[343] VH to WL 10 Apr 1910 (MS Univ. Oxon.) The plate is preserved in the Ross Memorial Collection at the College.

[344] See pp. 424-25.

Chapter Three: The 1920s Forgeries

[345] These details and many which follow, were recorded by one of Wilde's first French translators, Henry-D. Davray, in several articles he wrote for the *Mercure de France*: 15 Jun 1923; 1 Oct 1925; 1 Feb 1926; 1 Mar 1926; and 1 Jan 1927. He corresponded extensively on the subject with Christopher Millard but the original letters appear not to have survived. Millard's file on the subject is now in the Clark Library.

[346] *The Times*, Law Report, 11 Nov 1926.

[347] VH to William Andrews Clark, 26 Nov 1923 (MS Clark).

[348] Two years later he did exactly that, after being convinced that it was a forgery. If Methuen & Co were using Wilde's name to publish a spurious work by him, then they should pay royalties to his literary estate. CM to WL, 17 May 1926 (MS Univ. Oxon.).

[349] Millard described in detail Cosgrove's visit to him in a letter to Walter Ledger 1 Jul 1925 (MS Univ. Oxon.).

[350] CM to VH, 14 Aug 1925 (MS Clark). Both editions of the circular are preserved in the Clark Library.

[351] CM to WL, 15 Nov 1926 & 4 Apr 1927 (MS Univ. Oxon.). For a full account of the Shaw scam see Gregory Mackie, *Beautiful Untrue Things*, pp. 190-97.

[352] 'Methuen & Co. Ltd. *v.* Millard' circular dated 19 Dec 1926 (Holland).

[353] Tribunal de Première Instance, refs D1U6 5684 & 1698 (MS Paris). His personal details were taken from his hotel registration.

[354] William Figgis's account of being duped into purchasing the 'Gide' Oscar Wilde manuscripts (MS Clark).

[355] CM to William Figgis, 25 Jul 1922 (MS Clark).

[356] Several attempts have been made to tell the Fabian Lloyd/Arthur Cravan story, generally with more conjecture and hearsay than accuracy. The more reliable are to be found in *Cravan: une stratégie du scandale* by Maria Lluïsa Borràs and *'Arthur Cravan est vivant!' La Règle du jeu*. No. 53 (Paris, 2013).

[357] *New York Times Book Review*, 27 Mar 1921; *The Sun*, 6 Apr 1921.

[358] This last literary scam has been documented in an unpublished essay communicated to me by its author, Bastiaan D. van der Velden

[359] *Gastonia Daily Gazette*, 24 Apr 1934.

[360] *Sunday Times,* 8 Jul 2007.

[361] The early career of Brett Holland/Dorian Hope is covered in exhaustive detail in Mackie.

Chapter Four: Frank Harris's Life Of Wilde

[362] Frank Harris to RR, 23 Dec 1900 (MS Clark).

[363] David Holmes Autographs, Catalogue 77, Item 148; Augustus John, *Chiaroscuro,* p. 130.

[364] RR to FH, 30 Jul 1911 (MS Texas).

[365] RR to FH, 6 Sep 1913 (MS Texas).

[366] RR to FH, 19 Dec 1913 (MS Texas).

[367] Philippa Pullar, *Frank Harris,* p. 319.

[368] FH to RR, 24 Oct 1916 (MS Clark).

[369] RR to FH, 1 Feb 1917 (MS Texas).

[370] AD to Robert Green-Armytage, 20 Jan 1917 & 26 Jan 1918 (MS Columbia); AD to Charles Norton Outcault 14 Feb 1921 (MS Private).

[371] Gladys Brooke was the daughter of Walter Palmer, owner of Huntley & Palmers biscuit factory in Reading. Walter and his wife Jean has been good friends of the Wildes in the 1890s and as children Gladys and my father were playmates.

[372] Frank Harris & Lord Alfred Douglas, New Preface to *The Life and Confessions of Oscar Wilde,* pp 11-17; FH to Henry Davray, 1 Mar 1926 (MS Holland).

[373] FH to AD, 21 Mar 1925 (MS Texas).

[374] AD to Basil Willett, 6 Mar 1930 (MS Texas). The story of how the meeting was arranged was due to be told by Gladys Palmer in her memoir *Relations & Complications* but the publisher, John Lane, refused to include it on the grounds that it included libellous material. A copy of the suppressed part was given to me in 1996 by Rhoda da Pinto, who had been Gladys Palmer's secretary.

[375] AD to FH, 20 Mar 1925 (MS Texas).

[376] AD to FH, 28 Mar 1925 (MS Texas).

[377] Harris 1925, p. 53.

[378] Reginald Turner to FH, 16 May 1925 (MS Texas).

[379] The original TS of the *New Preface* with the libellous remarks about Sir Edward Clarke is in the Clark Library. They were removed by Douglas before it was printed later in the year.

[380] Douglas's letters to Harris are at the Harry Ransom Centre at the University of Texas; Harris's letters to Douglas are preserved in the Eccles Collection at the British Library.

[381] FH to George Viereck, 1 Dec 1925 (MS Clark).

[382] AD to FH, 29 Dec 1925 (MS Texas).

[383] FH to VH, 1 Mar 1926 (MS Holland). The remaining letters from Harris to Vyvyan are in the Clark library and all Vyvyan's to Harris are at the Harry Ransom Centre at the University of Texas.

[384] VH to FH, 19 Mar 1926 (MS Texas).

[385] Holland 1954, pp. 33 & 193.

[386] AD to Lucie Delarue-Mardrus 18 Feb 1930 (MS Texas).

[387] *The Times,* 17 October 1928; MS Kew, TS 27/544.

[388] FH to McHugh, 1 Dec 1927 (MS Private).

[389] Harris 1916, pp. 438-44; the illustration was almost certainly that printed in the *Illustrated London News*, 28 Jan 1899, p. 5.

Chapter Five: Inventions & False Memoirs

[390] Holland 1954, pp. 39-40; Holland, *Album*, pp. 130-31.

[391] Gladys Palmer, *Relations and Complications*, pp. 1-4.

[392] Peter Chalmers Mitchell, *My Fill of Days*, pp. 183-84; Alec Waugh, *My Brother Evelyn and Other Profiles*, pp. 7-8.

[393] 'Ein Gespräch mit dem Dichterfürsten Paul Fort, dem letzten Freund Oscar Wildes,' *Die literarische Welt*, 27 Nov 1925.

[394] 'Oscar Wilde mourait dans mes bras,' *L'Intransigeant*, 30 Nov 1930.

[395] Ross's account of Oscar's last days, his death and his funeral can be found in *CL,* pp. 1211-30.

[396] Their relationship is admirably analysed in Laura Beatty's *Lillie Langtry*, pp. 134-43.

[397] Ernest Dudley, *The Gilded Lily*, pp. 190-91.

[398] Coulson Kernahan, *In Good Company*, pp. 189-96; *CL,* p. 474.

[399] Natalie Barney, *Aventures de l'esprit,* pp. 19-20.

[400] Laurence Housman's *Echo de Paris* published in 1923 is also a reconstruction of an hour-long conversation between himself, Oscar, and three of Oscar's friends outside a Paris café. He admits that most of it is invention but that 'it has a solid basis in fact.' Although the two men were not close friends, surviving letters from Wilde to Housman in the *Complete Letters of OW* would seem to support the latter's claim.

[401] Hester Travers Smith, *Psychic Messages from Oscar Wilde,* pp. 5-71; Herbert Thurston, *Modern Spiritualism,* Chapter 3.

[402] Arthur Conan Doyle, 'The Alleged Posthumous Writings of Great Authors' in *The Bookman*, Dec 1927, p. 345.

[403] *Daily Express*, 2 Oct 1923.

[404] Martin Holman to Society of Authors, 6 Dec 1923, (MS BL Add MS 56846).

[405] 'The Ghost of Oscar Wilde,' *News Chronicle,* 3 Feb 1934.

Chapter Six: Oscar In The 1930s

[406] Douglas 1929, p. 319.

[407] *The Times*, 13 Jun 1913; British Museum Standing Committee Minutes, 12 Jul 1913.

[408] RR to Ada Leverson, 18 Nov 1912 (MS Clark); RR to British Museum, 26 Jun 1913 (MS Kew TS27/330).

[409] *Daily Express* 28 Jan 1929; Frederic Kenyon to Treasury Solicitor, 27 Nov 1929 (MS Kew TS 27/330).

[410] AD to A.J.A. Symons, 29 Apr 1930 (MS Clark).

[411] AD to AS, 21 Dec 1931 (MS Clark).

[412] AD to AS, 7 May 1938; 2 Aug 1939 (MS Clark).

[413] AD to RS, 1 Mar 1935 (MS BL Eccles); AD to Maurice Rostand, 7 Jun 1935 (MS Reading).

[414] AD to AS, 9 Oct 1939 (MS Clark).

[415] Harris 1930, pp. xliv-xlv.

[416] Sherard 1902, pp. 212-14.

[417] AD to RS, 10 Oct 1929 (MS Reading).

[418] RS to VH, 28 Mar 1928 (MS Clark); VH to RS, 31 Mar 1928 (MS Reading).

[419] Harris 1916, pp. 456-68.

[420] Sherard, *Oscar Wilde, Drunkard and Swindler*, pp. 13-14.

[421] RS to George Hill, 1 Jul 133 (MS Reading.); George Hill to RS, 6 Jul 1933 (MS Reading).

[422] RS to Reginald Turner, 3 Apr 1933 (MS BL Eccles).

[423] RS to W. H. Wagstaff, 15 Jul 1933 (MS Cambridge RSL E2) where the subsequent exchange of correspondence can also be found.

[424] Alan Sheridan, *André Gide*, p. 461-62.

[425] RS to Eamon de Valera, 6 Sep 1933; RS to Franklin Roosevelt, 17 Jan 1934 (MSS Reading Univ.).

[426] RS, 'Ultima Verba,' p. 74 (Unpublished MS BL Eccles).

[427] AD to RS, 9 Jul 1935 (MS Reading).

[428] AD to AS, 27 Jan 1937 (MS Clark).

[429] Rather than overload the text with footnotes for this correspondence, the reader is referred to the Shaw/Douglas letters which were first edited and published by Mary Hyde in 1982 (see bibliography).

[430] Shaw's preface to Frank Harris's book published by Constable & Co in 1938 simply as *Oscar Wilde*, p. x.

[431] Sherard 1937, pp. 124-25; Duke of Newcastle to RS, 2 May 1928 (MS Reading).

[432] The full story is given in Douglas 1938, pp. 258-62.

[433] David Hunter-Blair to AS, 10 Jun [1935] (MS BL Eccles); he did eventually publish his paper as 'Oscar Wilde as I knew him' in the *Dublin Review,* vol. CCIII (July 1938), pp. 90-105.

[434] Donald Cree to Michael Sadler, 13 Jan 1932. This and subsequent letters are in the University College, Oxford archives ref: UC/MA44/7/ C1/1. A fuller account was published by Robin Darwall-Smith in *The Wildean* vol. 15 (1999).

[435] Internal File Douglas and the Trustees of the British Museum 29 June–28 July 1943 (MS Kew TS 27/544).

[436] OW to AD, 20 Apr 1894 *CL,* p. 590; AD to AS, 3 Sept 1931 (MS Clark); AD to GC Williamson, 22 Feb 1940 (MS Texas); AD to Muriel Sherard, 15 Feb 1943 (MS Reading).

PART FOUR (1945-1967)

Chapter One: Australia

[437] MS Kew, B9/1507.

[438] Thelma Holland unpublished memoir (MS Holland).

[439] *Sydney Sunday Telegraph*, 19 Oct 1947.

[440] TH Press-cutting book, 19 Nov 1947.

[441] VH diary, 17 Nov 1947.

[442] 'Oscar Wilde's Son Here,' *Melbourne Herald*, 18 Sep 1947; *Sydney Bulletin*, 24 Sep 1947.

[443] *Hobart Mercury*, 20 Sep 1947.

[444] VH diary, 18 Sep 1947. In complete ignorance of what Vyvyan had written I would express myself in almost identical terms fifty years later, though I became specifically a monkey and the bun became a handful of peanuts.

[445] VH diary, 2 Jun 1948.

[446] Holland 1966, p. 182.

[447] RR to Charles Ricketts, 13 Jun 1918, Ross, *Friends*, p. 333.

[448] Christopher Millard ed, *Oscar Wilde Three Times Tried*, p. vii.

[449] For three months the book, described as 'indecent or obscene' was temporarily banned in Ireland by the Eire Censorship Board who then lifted the ban on appeal of *Northern Whig*, 29 Sep 1948 and *Belfast Telegraph,* 22 Dec 1948.

[450] *Evening Despatch* (Edinburgh), 13 Jul 1948.

[451] TH to 'Boodle' Hyde, 4 Mar 1956, written by my mother when Hyde's next book on Wilde, *Oscar Wilde in Prison* (later retitled *Oscar Wilde: the Aftermath*) was due to appear. She was even more concerned about the effect of this on me as an impressionable 11 year-old, then at boarding school (MS Holland).

[452] VH diary, 15 & 18 Aug 1948.

[453] VH diary, 7 Sep 1948.

[454] Later, in 1953, when *A Woman of No Importance* ran for five months in the West End, Binkie generously paid my father a small ex gratia royalty to help him out of his ever-worsening financial predicament.

[455] *CL*, p. 780.

[456] VH diary, 25 Jan 1949.

[457] *The Listener*, 8 Dec 1949 & 5 Jan 1950.

[458] John Gielgud to VH 25 Dec 1949 (MS Holland).

[459] VH diary, 10 July 1949.

Chapter Two: *Writing* Son Of Oscar Wilde

[460] VH diary, 28 May 1949.

[461] *Spectator*, 28 Oct 1949.

[462] *Sunday Times*, 30 Oct 1949.

[463] *Manchester Guardian*, 1 Nov 1949.

[464] *Glasgow Herald*, 3 Nov 1949.

[465] VH diary, 15-29 Nov 1950.

[466] VH diary, 5 Feb 1951.

[467] St. John Ervine, *Oscar Wilde: A Present Time Appraisal*, pp. 47, 125, 126, 175, & 336.

[468] *Spectator,* 21 Dec 1951.

[469] *Observer*, 9 Dec 1951.

[470] VH diary, 26 Feb 1952.

[471] See page p. 160.

[472] VH diary, 29 Aug 1952.

[473] VH diary, 4 Jan 1953.

[474] VH diary, 21 Jan 1953.

[475] VH diary, 9 Mar 1953.

[476] VH diary, 8 Aug 1953.

[477] Douglas Graham to VH, 24 Sep & 14 Nov 1953 (MSS Holland).

[478] Some time in the early 1930s the then headmaster the Rev. E. G. Seale had Wilde's name replaced on the board. The gold lettering, marginally larger and brighter than that of those around him, for years made Wilde's name stand out among his contemporaries.

[479] I took notes of this telephone conversation with Father Geoffrey Holt on 26 August 1999 and preserved them as part of my *Son of Oscar Wilde* research file.

[480] VH diary, 9 Nov 1953.

[481] VH diary, 3 Jan 1954.

[482] VH diary, 21 Jan & 15 Feb 1954.

[483] VH diary, 24 May 1954.

[484] For 1954, it was clearly the right decision, though when it was re-printed thirty-three years later and had become an integral and much quoted sequel to the Wilde tragedy, I felt it was only courteous to provide one for his modern readers.

[485] VH diary, 25 Jun 1954.

[486] VH to Lewis Broad, 7 Jul 1954 (MS Holland).

[487] VH to Lewis Broad, 28 Jul 1954 (MS Holland).

Chapter Three: Unpicking Son Of Oscar Wilde

[488] Vyvyan Holland, *An Evergreen Garland*, p. 150.

[489] I was subsequently able to remove the Tippex without destroying the writing beneath. See p. 454.

[490] They are now in the Eccles Collection at the BL Add. MS 81727.

[491] VH diary, 17 Jun 1951.

[492] VH diary, 19 Jan 1965, and a predictable target for my mother's Tippex brush.

[493] CH to CB, [early Dec 1900] copy in Ross's hand (MS Clark). For the unravelled history of this letter see pp. 83-84.

[494] Palmer, *Relations*, pp. 1-3.

[495] See OW to AD 23 Jun 1897, *CL*, p. 906.

[496] Holland 1968, p. 146.

[497] Lucien Wormser to VH, Oct 1955 (MS Holland).

Chapter Four: The Tite Street Unveiling

[498] *The Times*, 28 May 1948.

[499] The correspondence is in the Clark Library at UCLA.

[500] Eric Barton to VH, early Aug 1953 (MS Holland).

[501] Max Beerbohm to VH, 16 Aug 1953 (MS Texas).

[502] Max Beerbohm to Eric Barton, 14 Sep 1953 (MS Clark).

[503] VH diary, 15 Oct 1953.

[504] VH diary, 21 Oct 1953.

[505] Max Beerbohm to VH, 28 Oct 1953 (MS Texas).

[506] John Gielgud to Eric Barton, 30 Oct 1953 (MS Clark).

[507] Richard Huggett, *Binkie Beaumont*, p. 431.

[508] Pearson & Walsh Agency, Telex, 27 Oct 1953 (MS Holland).

[509] *Sunday Express,* 25 Oct 1953; *Daily Sketch,* 27 Oct 1953.

[510] VH diary, 27 & 28 Oct 1953.

[511] VH diary, 22 Oct 1953.

[512] Edith Evans to Eric Barton, 5 Nov 1953 (MS Clark).

[513] Louis Wilkinson to Eric Barton, 11 Nov 1953 (MS Clark).

[514] VH diary, 9 Nov 1953.

[515] VH diary, 16 Dec 1953.

[516] T. S. Eliot to Bartons, 19 Mar 1954 (MS Clark).

[517] Ross, *Friends*, p. 100.

[518] E. M. Forster to the Bartons, 14 Jul 1954 (MS Clark).

[519] VH diary, 23 Jul 1954.

[520] VH to Irene Barton, 23 Jul 1954 (MS Clark).

[521] Max Beerbohm to VH, 12 Sep 1954 (MS Texas).

[522] House of Lords Debate, 19 May 1954, vol. 187 cols 737-67.

[523] VH diary, 21 Aug 1954.

[524] Cecil Day-Lewis to the Bartons, 19 Aug 1954 (MS Clark).

[525] *Adam*, Nos 241-43, p.vi.

[526] 'Oscar Wilde paid dearly for being Oscar Wilde, but being Oscar Wilde was the height of luxury. It was naturally going to be expensive. We can never pay sufficient tribute to the author of *The Ballad of Reading Gaol*.'

[527] 'We should be proud that Oscar Wilde chose France as his refuge.'

[528] Lennox Robinson sent the full text of his address to Vyvyan the day after (MS Holland).

[529] VH to RH-D, 3 Oct 1954 (MS Holland).

[530] Claud Cockburn, 'Belated Oscar Award,' *Punch*, 27 Oct 1954.

[531] VH diary, 16 Oct 1954.

[532] VH diary, 27 Jul 1954.

[533] Contemporary transcript of the speeches (MS Clark).

[534] 'London Letter,' *Irish Times*, 18 Oct 1954.

[535] *West London Press,* 22 Oct 1954.

[536] 'Civic recognition. The latest tribute to Wilde,' *Manchester Guardian*, 18 Oct 1954.

[537] The text was given to Vyvyan after the lunch by Cecil Douglas (MS Holland).

[538] Their letters are preserved in the Clark Library at UCLA.

[539] Actually not so. Journalists from the *Manchester Guardian*, *The Times* and the *Irish Times* all attended the lunch as well as columnists for *Punch* and the *Spectator*.

[540] VH diary, 16 Oct 1954.

[541] Harford Montgomery Hyde, *Oscar Wilde*, p. 385.

[542] *Birmingham Daily Post*, 28 Oct 1954.

[543] Rebecca's letters to my father 1925-1928 would lead one to believe they had an affair at that time (MS Holland). His letters to her were apparently destroyed.

[544] VH diary, 16-24 Oct 1954; Rebecca West to John Van Druten, 31 Dec 1954 (MS New York Public Library, Performing Arts).

[545] MH diary, 29 Dec 1961.

Chapter Five: The Duplicitous Mr. Hyde

[546] RH-D to VH, 30 Nov 1950 (MS Holland).

[547] Julian Symons, *A.J.A. Symons: His Life and Speculations*, pp. 244-49; Methuen & Co Ltd, Contract with Symons and Holland, 11 Nov 1935 (MS Holland).

[548] Hyde admitted this later in his essay 'Oscar Wilde' in *Four Oaks Library*, ed. Gabriel Austin, p. 86.

[549] The copy correspondence is preserved in the Beinecke Library, Yale University, GEN MSS 872.

[550] *Hansard* 5th Series, vol. 529, cols 586-88.

[551] Home Office to VH, 31 Jul 1956 (MS Holland).

[552] Home Secretary to HMH, 24 Nov 1954; VH to HMH, 30 Nov 1954 (MSS Yale).

[553] VH diary, 10 Dec 1954.

[554] Vyvyan was later told this by a Home Office official when the whole dispute over Hyde's new book blew up in December the following year. Hyde's hastily made transcripts of the petitions used later in his *Oscar Wilde: the Aftermath*, are littered with errors, even missing a complete line precisely as it stands in the MS, which merely corroborates the story. In the event both Hyde and Vyvyan received transcribed copies from the Home

Office which makes Hyde's use of his own transcripts in his book the more mystifying as well as providing damning proof of his duplicity.

555 Alan White to VH, 20 Dec 1954; VH to Alan White, 22 Dec 1954 (MSS Holland).

556 VH to RH-D, 10 Mar 1956 & 25 Apr 1956 (MS Holland).

557 VH diary, 26 Jan 1955.

558 VH diary, 22/23 Mar 1955.

559 On various occasions over the next twenty years Hyde would hint darkly at this piece of dishonesty on the part of my father in correspondence, even to third parties. HMH to VH, 6 Mar 1956: 'As you know, I have always been ready to help you in any way, either connected with your father or on any other matter on which you have sought my assistance. No doubt several instances will come to your mind.' (MS Holland); HMH to Alan White, 3 Sep 1962 [In response to accusations that he had tried to buy up Vyvyan's copyrights]: 'On the contrary, I would have treated them in exactly the same way as I treated his family silver which I was glad to take care of for him while the bankruptcy business was going on.' (MS Holland); HMH to John Cullen of Methuen, 12 Jul 1976 [In response to my accusations that Hyde had 'lifted' photos from one of my father's books]: 'At the time of his father's bankruptcy I was able to render Vyvyan Holland considerable service, the precise nature of which it is unnecessary for me to specify here.' (MS Holland).

560 VH diary, 2 May 1955.

561 VH diary, 21 May 1955.

562 *The Times,* 31 May 1956.

563 VH letters to HMH, 19 Apr 1955 & 28 Jan 1956 (MS Holland).

564 VH to HMH, 4 Apr 1955 (MS Yale).

565 HMH to Home Secretary, 30 Dec 1954; Home Secretary to HMH, 19 Jan 1955; Home Office to HMH, 16 Jul 1955 (MS Yale).

566 HMH to Home Secretary, 20 Sep 1955 (MS Yale). 'Mug shots' of prisoners were definitely taken on their admission to Reading Gaol at the time. In 2003, while preparing *Irish Peacock and Scarlet Marquess* for publication, I made a thorough search of the surviving prison archives in the Berkshire County Record Office, but the relevant pages in the album at the time of Oscar's admission had disappeared.

567 VH to HMH, 28 Jan 1956 (MS Holland). Significantly, Hyde cut this last sentence out of Vyvyan's original letter at some stage before his archived correspondence was sold, presumably to avoid appearing

insensitive to my father's discomfort. The redacted original is in the Beinecke Library at Yale.

[568] VH to RH-D, 10 Mar 1956 (MS Holland).

[569] RH-D to HMH, 1 May 1956 (MS Holland).

[570] Exchange of letters between VH and Alec Waugh, 25/26 Apr 1956 (MS Holland).

[571] HMH to T.J.M. Macleod, 4 May 1956. This letter in carbon copy and the subsequent correspondence between Hyde and Macleod, 10 May to 21 Jun is preserved at the University of Texas, Austin (Harry Ransom Centre, MSS Wilde, O. Misc. Corresp. with Elles, Reeve, & Co.).

[572] HMH to Alan White, 6 May 1956 (MS Yale). Hyde's correspondence with Methuen and Macleod is divided between the Beinecke Library at Yale and the Harry Ransom Centre at Austin, Texas.

[573] Home Office to Charles Russell & Co, 17 May 1956 (MS Holland).

[574] Richard Butler to VH, 4 Sept 1956 (MS Holland).

[575] VH diary, 17 Mar 1957 and 23 Aug 1962.

[576] VH diary, 22 Jun 1956.

Chapter Six: Publishing Oscar's Letters

[577] VH to HMH, 5 Jul 1953 (MS BL Eccles Add. MS 81847).

[578] Allan Wade to VH, 22 Oct 1954.

[579] VH to HMH, 4 & 12 Mar 1956 (MS Yale).

[580] It is preserved in the Rauner Special Collections at Dartmouth College, New Hampshire.

[581] *The Lyttelton Hart-Davis Letters*, 30 Oct 1955.

[582] In fact, Symons had already sold certain legal documents from the collection to Montgomery Hyde by 4 March 1949, when Hyde and my father first met. To Hyde's credit he offered to return them to my father and reclaim his money from Symons, but for some reason this was never done. HMH to VH, 6 Mar 1949 (MS Holland).

[583] Bonhams, San Francisco offered a 'genuine' letter from Wilde to Pierre Louÿs lot 253 in its sale of 18 Feb 2007. I pointed out that both from the handwriting and the content it was an obvious Brett Holland forgery. Bonhams very correctly withdrew it.

[584] VH to Rupert Hart-Davis, 7 Apr 1960. If at all, Oscar would have written in French as Bernhardt spoke not a word of English.

[585] The whole sorry story of Oscar's friendship with Carlos Blacker is admirably and impartially told in J. Robert Maguire, *Ceremonies of Bravery*.

[586] Mark Hichens, *Oscar Wilde's Last Chance: the Dreyfus Connection*. Although not as laughably biased as St. John Ervine's hatchet job of 1951, this settling of old scores a century after the events seemed a rather pointless exercise by the family to brand Oscar as an unattractive anti-Semite.

[587] RH-D exchange with VH 5, 7 & 20 Nov 1956 (MSS Holland).

[588] VH diary, 26 Apr 1960.

[589] RH-D to VH, 26 Apr 1960 (MS Holland).

[590] VH to RH-D, 9 Jun 1960 (MS Holland).

[591] VH to Rebecca West, 23 Jun 1960 (MS Holland).

[592] Rebecca West to VH, 25 Jun 1960 (MS Holland).

[593] Rebecca West to VH, 30 Jun 1960 (MS Holland).

[594] RH-D to VH, 19 Nov 1956 (MS Holland).

[595] *Hansard*, Commons Debates, 28 Jul 1964, col. 1209.

[596] VH to RH-D, 16 May 1962 (MS Holland).

[597] RH-D to VH, 17 May 1962 (MS Holland).

[598] Rebecca West to VH, 5 Jun 1962 (MS Holland).

[599] *Western Mail*, 30 Jun 1962.

[600] *Sunday Times*, 24 Jun 1962.

Chapter Seven: Eton

[601] VH diary, 25 Nov 1956.

[602] Somtow's World, 'Things of Darkness', 20 Sep 2011. https://www.somtow.org/2011/09/?m=0. Retrieved 09/05/2025.

[603] David Simpson to VH, Dec 1960.

[604] David Simpson to VH, 15 Oct 1959.

[605] David Simpson to VH, Apr 1963.

[606] VH diary, 24 Oct 1954.

[607] *Hansard,* Commons Debates, 26 Nov 1958, cols 438-39.

[608] *Hansard*, Commons Debates, 29 Jun 1960, cols 1472-75.

[609] VH diary, 17 & 20 Nov 1959.

[610] VH diary, 22 Nov 1959.

[611] VH diary, 22 Nov 1959.

[612] David Simpson to VH, Dec 1959.

[613] I wondered for many years whether I had misremembered this or even made it up until Barry Humphries recounted in his autobiography *My Life as Me* how Thelma had also tried to convince him of Oscar's innocence in similar terms. See p. 452.

[614] VH diary, 18 Jun 1955.

[615] Alastair Graham memorably used to start off his German classes for those new to the subject, 'Fahrt means a journey, Tat [*pronounced 'tart'*] means a deed and Kant [*pronounced c***t*] was a philosopher. Laugh now; don't laugh again.' He was an inspiration to all whom he taught.

[616] Holland 1954, p. 174.

[617] VH diary, 30 Nov 1963.

[618] David Hunter-Blair, 'Oscar Wilde as I Knew Him,' *Dublin Review,* CCIII (Jul 1938), p. 93.

[619] VH diary, 19 June 1961.

Chapter Eight: The Two Oscar Wilde Films

[620] James Hodge memorandum to his solicitors, 3 Dec 1962 (MS Holland).

[621] VH diary, 18 Nov 1959.

[622] VH diary, 20 Nov 1959.

[623] VH diary, 9 & 11 Feb 1960.

[624] *Evening Standard,* 18 Mar 1960.

[625] James Hodge memorandum to his solicitors, 3 Dec 1962 (MS Holland).

[626] VH diary, 22, 23 & 31 May 1960.

[627] VH diary, 6 Apr 1960.

[628] The very first edition of *Oscar Wilde: Three Times Tried* was published in January 1912 by the non-existent 'Ferrestone Press' from the same address as Frank & Cecil Palmer's publishing house. A second edition was issued two years later over the Palmers' imprint, but given the sensitive nature of the material they probably considered it advisable to distance themselves artificially from the initial publication.

[629] *Daily Mail,* 19 Mar 1960.

[630] *Sunday Pictorial,* 24 Apr 1960.

[631] *Daily Telegraph,* 14 May 1960; *Evening Standard,* 16 May 1960; *The Times,* 17 May 1960.

[632] *Daily Express,* 20 May 1960.

[633] Earl of Birkenhead to HMH, 30 Jun 1950 (MS Public Record Office of Northern Ireland Ref. D3084/H/2/18).

[634] VH diary, 31 May 1960.

[635] *The Wildean,* No. 8, p. 3.

[636] *Sunday Express,* 29 May 1960.

[637] VH diary, 21 Aug 1960.

[638] VH diary, 11 Jul 1961.

Chapter Nine: Vyvyan's Last Years

[639] VH diary, 22 Feb 1960.

[640] Vyvyan Holland, *Oscar Wilde: A Pictorial Biography* (1960), p. 92.

[641] 'Tragedy Obscured,' *Birmingham Daily Post,* 13 Dec 1960.

[642] *The Lyttleton Hart-Davis Letters,* 26 Dec 1961.

[643] VH to RH-D, 29 Dec 1961 (MS Holland).

[644] VH diary, 29 Dec 1961.

[645] VH diary, 6 Jan 1962.

[646] VH diary, 12 Jan 1962.

[647] VH diary, 15 Jan & 2 Feb 1962.

[648] VH diary, 25 Apr 1963.

[649] My own copy he inscribed with the words 'For Merlin: this monumental translation which nearly shattered the translator, his father Vyvyan Holland, with love.'

[650] VH diary, 31 May 1965.

[651] Holland 1968, p. 146.

[652] VH diary, 6 Sep 1965.

[653] TH/VH exchange of correspondence, 23 Oct, 28 Oct, 7 Nov and 10 Nov 1965 (MSS Holland).

[654] *Marylebone Mercury,* 13 Jan 1906; *Roscommon Messenger,* 20 Jan 1906.

[655] C. B. Cochran to VH, 19 Apr 1944 (MS Holland).

[656] VH/MH correspondence, Aug–Sep 1966 (MSS Holland).

[657] VH diary, 6 Aug 1966.

[658] Even by the standards of the time it was relatively harmless 'There was

a young lawyer named Rex/With very small organs of sex/When charged with exposure/He replied with composure/'*De minimis non curat lex.*' Vyvyan's tame *An Explosion of Limericks* sold poorly having to compete with William Baring-Gould's classic and more explicit *The Lure of the Limerick* published at exactly the same time and which remained in print for over 20 years.

659 CBS Arts Programme, Camera Three: 'Aubrey Beardsley and His World,' recorded on 16 February and transmitted 12 March 1967. https://www.bridgemanimages.com/fr/noartistknown/aubrey-beardsley-discussion/footage/asset/620164?offline=1.

660 VH diary, 16 Feb 1967.

661 'Fond Memories by Wilde's Son,' *Kansas City Star*, 21 Feb 1967.

662 Boris Brasol, *Oscar Wilde: the Man, the Artist, the Martyr*, pp. xvii-xviii.

663 VH diary, 24 Jan 1967. He noted that Alec had been put on the list of 'undesirable friends' by Thelma.

664 See p. 488.

665 MH to Henry Andrews, 17 Nov 1967 (MS Tulsa).

666 TH to RH-D, 13 Jan 1968 (MS Holland).

667 A. W. J. Houghton to VH, 6 Jun 1967 (MS Holland).

PART FIVE (1968-2024)

Chapter One: (After) Oxford

668 Diana Scott-Kilvert email to MH, 8 Jan 2011 (MS Holland).

669 TH & VH to MH, 18 May 1967 (MS Holland).

670 MH email correspondence with Jules Ryckebusch, 30 March to 30 June 2011 (MSS Holland).

671 VH diary, 24 Aug 1962.

672 I kept a occasional diary at the time and found that I wrote about the evening in detail the next day. False memory is not at work in this case.

673 Alec Waugh to MH, 2 Sep 1969 (MS Holland).

674 TH to MH, 15 Jun 1970 (MS Holland).

675 Rebecca West to MH, 17 Jul 1970 (MS Holland).

676 TH & MH correspondence between 15 Jun & 12 Aug 1970 (MSS Holland).

[677] TH to MH, 22 Feb 1972 (MS Holland).

[678] Rebecca West's Notes on Lebanon (MS Tulsa) and letters to MH, mid-Apr, 5 May 1971 (MS Holland).

Chapter Two: The Ellmann Saga

[679] Barry Humphries, *My Life As Me*, pp. 339-41.

[680] TH to MH, 19 Mar 1993 (MS Holland).

[681] Holland 1968, p. 145.

[682] VH diary, 15 May 1964.

[683] Richard Ellmann to Derek Hudson, OUP, 29 Jan 1962 (MS Tulsa).

[684] Wilde 'trainspotting' in the extreme and a genuine enquiry. Unlikely before he went to prison because his German wouldn't have been up to it in the original and there were no English translations until 1899, but he might have got hold of a French translation of *Also sprach Zarathustra* when he was in Paris, where it came out in 1898.

[685] RH-D to RE, 21 Nov 1975 (MS Tulsa).

[686] TH to MH, 22 Sep 1986 (MS Holland); MH to RE, 2 Dec 1986 (MS Tulsa).

[687] TH to MH, 10 Nov 1986 (MS Holland).

[688] MH to RE, 18 Sep 1986 (MS Tulsa).

[689] MH to RE, 16 Mar 1986 (MS Tulsa).

[690] See *A Portrait of Oscar Wilde,* Chapter 2. Queensberry owned a bound volume of miscellaneous Wilde MSS which he had had transcribed and annotated on blank pages facing the tipped-in MSS; the annotations (of which the Oxford prostitute is one) are mostly as unreliable as the transcriptions are inaccurate. The original is now in the J. Pierpont Morgan Library, New York. Ellmann, without seeing the MSS, used a Maggs Bros catalogue description of the volume as evidence of his theory.

[691] RE to Rosita Fanto, 26 Aug 1985 (MS Tulsa).

[692] Whitney Blake, OUP, NY to RE, 22 Mar 1967 (MS Tulsa).

[693] RE to Rosita Fanto, Jun–Sep 1985 (MS Tulsa).

[694] *Sunday Times,* 20 Sep 1987.

[695] *Sewanee Review*, vol. 117, no. 2, p. 288.

[696] Alfred Knopf to RE, 11 Feb 1986 (MS Tulsa) in reference to *More Letters of Oscar Wilde* (1985).

[697] RE to Guillot de Saix, 18 Jan 1967 (MS Tulsa).

[698] Author's personal conversations and correspondence with both; see also J. B. Lyons *What Did I Die Of?*, pp. 123-38; Macdonald Critchley, 'Medical Reflections on Oscar Wilde' in *Medico-Legal Journal*, vol. 30 (1962), pp. 73-84, and 'Oscar Wilde's Fatal Illness: the Mystery Unshrouded' in *Encyclopaedia Britannica, Medical & Health Annual* 1990, pp. 190-207.

[699] Terence Cawthorne, 'The Last Illness of Oscar Wilde,' *Proceedings of the Royal Society of Medicine*, vol. 52, no. 2, Feb 1959, pp. 123-27.

[700] RH-D to RE, 18 May 1984; 5 Mar 1985; 12 Jan 1987 (MS Tulsa).

[701] MH to Christopher Sinclair-Stevenson, 27 Mar 1987 (MS Holland).

[702] James Woodall wrote up his side of the story in an article in *Daily Telegraph* ten years later on 11 Oct 1997. In it he maintained that I might have been motivated by the fear of hereditary syphilis, an astonishing suggestion since denying Ellmann the right to use copyright material would hardly have cured me had I inherited the disease and anyway its transmission is known to pass only through the female line.

[703] RH-D to RE, 4 Apr 1987 (MS Holland).

[704] Owen Dudley Edwards to RE, 13 Apr 1987 (MS Tulsa). Edwards has since retracted his view and declared Ellmann to be wrong, based on evidence which he later uncovered. I later came to see his support for Dick at the time as an expression of his emotion rather than a declaration of war on the Hollands.

[705] It was later published as: 'What killed Oscar Wilde?' *Spectator*, 24 Dec 1988. See also Ashley Robins & Sean Sellars, 'Oscar Wilde's terminal illness,' *Lancet*, 25 Nov 2000, for more detailed medical views on the subject.

[706] MH to RH-D, 6 Apr 1987 (MS Holland).

[707] Rupert also wrote even more forcefully on the subject to the German scholar, Horst Schroeder, author of *Additions and Corrections to Richard Ellmann's Oscar Wilde* on 1 Jul 1989. Many years later Schroeder most generously passed on the letter to me for safe-keeping. (MS Holland).

[708] RE to RH-D, 4 Feb 1981 (MS Tulsa).

[709] J.B.W. Polak to RE, Sept 1986 and 19 Sept 1986 (MS Tulsa Ellmann Box 195). He or his informant may well have been confusing this with the story related by Gide in *Si le grain ne meurt*. See p. 292.

[710] Roger Lewis, 'Declaring His Genius,' *Sunday Times*, 13 Sep 1987.

[711] Correspondence regarding Oscar Wilde Playing Cards (MS Tulsa); Rosita Fanto, *Lady of the Cards*, Chapter 26.

[712] Merlin Holland, 'Wilde as Salomé?,' *Times Literary Supplement,* 22 Jul 1994; Horst Schroeder, *Alice in Wildeland.*

[713] See bibliography for the indispensable 311 pages of addenda and corrigenda by Horst Schroeder; also email Alexis Kirschbaum to MH, 18 May 2010 (MS Holland).

[714] Knox, *Wilde* and correspondence 16 Aug and 27 Oct 2019 (MS Holland).

Chapter Three: Classifying The Tomb

[715] VH to John-Paul Ross, 25 Oct 1961 (MS Holland).

[716] VH to John-Paul Ross, 26 Dec 1960 (MS Holland).

[717] Conservateur du Cimetière de l'Est to Mr C. G. L. du Cann, 14 Sep 1961. 'J'ai le regret de vous faire savoir que la sculpture reposant sur la sépulture de feu O. Wilde a subi des détériorations (mutilation des testicules) et ce par un inconnu' (MS Holland).

[718] *Evening Standard,* 19 Sep 1961.

[719] John-Paul Ross to Giles Robertson, 7 Oct 1961 (MS Holland).

[720] According to Prof. Giles Robertson, great-nephew of Robert Ross in conversation with Michael Pennington, author of *An Angel for a Martyr,* p. 61.

[721] Michel Dansel, *Au Père-Lachaise,* p. 65.

[722] TH & John-Paul Ross correspondence, 1 Dec & 16 Dec 1966 (MS Holland).

[723] John-Paul Ross to TH, 10 Dec 1975 (MS Holland).

[724] *The Times,* 1 & 8 Feb 1989.

[725] Unpublished article by Suzanne Lowry, Paris correspondent of the *Daily Telegraph,* c. 12 Feb 1989 (MS Holland).

[726] *Paris-Match,* No. 2218, 28 Nov–4 Dec 1991.

[727] Jennifer Campbell (L'Oréal) to MH, 7 Oct 2005 (MS Holland).

[728] Anne Anderson email to MH, 15 Jun 2009 (MS Holland).

[729] Sheila Pratschke email to MH, 13 Sep 2010 (MS Holland).

[730] 'Walling Off Oscar Wilde's Tomb From Admirer's Kisses,' *New York Times,* 15 Dec 2011.

[731] Valérie Parlan, 'Au Père-Lachaise, on embrasse encore Oscar Wilde,' *Ouest-France,* 17 Mar 2012.

[732] Thanks to Ömer Koç's sponsorship it was eventually put on at the

Petit Palais in Paris between 27 September 2016 and 15 January 2017 where it attracted over 95,000 visitors.

733 Ömer Koç email to MH, 2 Jul 2014 (MS Holland).

734 https://mikedashhistory.com/2014/12/29/QUEEN-VICTORIAS-5-THE-STRANGE-TALE-OF-TURKISH-AID-TO-IRELAND-DURING-THE-GREAT-FAMINE/ (Retrieved 17 Mar 2020).

Chapter Four: Constance's Tomb

735 'A Genova la tomba di Lady Wilde,' *Il Lavoro*, 5 Nov 1984.

736 'Sad Lady's Last Home,' *Evening Standard*, 25 Oct 1985.

737 Nevia Cisotto to MH, 16 Nov 1985 (MS Holland).

738 OW to RR, 1 Mar 1899, *CL*, p. 1128.

Chapter Five: Poets' Corner

739 Michael Mayne to Pat Paterson, 24 Jul 1989 (MS Holland).

740 Pat Paterson to Donald Sinden, 7 Mar 1990 (MS Holland).

741 Ronald Mason to MH, 19 Feb 1991 (MS Holland).

742 *The Times* 'Diary,' 8 Aug 1991.

743 TH to MH, 10 Aug 1991.

744 MH to TH, 12 Aug 1991.

745 Michael Mayne to TH, 30 Jan 1995 (MS Holland). His letter to me after her death said very astutely: 'She was obviously a remarkable character and I am glad to have known her. I can guess that she must sometimes have proved a demanding presence, but I guess, too, that she will be greatly missed and grieved.'

746 Seamus Heaney to MH, 31 Jan 1995.

747 Entry for 3 Dec 1994 in my notebook kept at the time.

748 TH to MH, 15 Dec 1994.

749 Seamus Heaney, 'Oscar Wilde Dedication: Westminster Abbey, 14 Feb 1995,' in *Wilde the Irishman*, ed J. McCormack, p. 176.

750 *Daily Telegraph*, 16 Feb 1995.

751 *Independent*, 'Diary,' 21 Feb 1995.

752 'Scandal No More: Wilde Gets Honor,' *Baltimore Sun*, 14 Feb 1995.

753 Personal conversation with the Dean.

[754] TH to MH, 10 Aug 1991 (MS Holland).

[755] VH diary, 24 Jun 1962 on Thelma's reaction to some explicit reviews of *The Letters of Oscar Wilde*.

[756] A letter which my first wife, Sarah, wrote to Thelma on 9 April 1988 (MS Holland) is a perfect summary of the tense situation at the time and corroborates what may otherwise seem to the reader like exaggeration on my part.

Chapter Six: The Speranza Centenary

[757] *CL*, p. 721.

[758] *CL*, pp. 756-57.

[759] This is borne out by Oscar's friend and biographer Robert Sherard in his *Oscar Wilde: the Story of an Unhappy Friendship*, pp. 219-20, who visited Oscar several times in prison and states clearly that the station was Wandsworth and not Clapham Junction.

[760] *Freeman's Journal*, 6 Feb 1896.

[761] 'Outspoken patriot's centenary marked by unveiling of memorial,' *Irish Times*, 5 Feb 1996.

[762] For the story of Oliver St. John Gogarty's present of swans to the Goddess of the River Liffey which he claimed had saved him from assassination in 1923, see Ulick O'Connor, *Oliver St. John Gogarty*.

[763] Lady Wilde, 'The Bondage of Women' in *Social Studies* (1893), pp. 20-22.

[764] 'Literary and Other Notes,' *Woman's World*, Dec 1887.

[765] For those with a thirst for detail: 'A *patera* is an irregular or complex crater with scalloped edges-usually a volcanic feature.' Jane's is 75 kms in diameter and located at 21.3S, 266.3E and she shares the honour with the likes of Queen Boadicea, Sappho, Colette, Marlene Dietrich, George Eliot, Katherine Mansfield, and Judy Garland. https://planetarynames.wr.usgs.gov/

[766] I later learned that it was Bindon Russell, one of the founder members of the Oscar Wilde Society, who died not long after.

Chapter Seven: Wilde, The Film

[767] Julian Mitchell to MH, 30 Jun 1995 (MS Holland).

[768] MH to Marc Samuelson, 25 Jun 1995 (MS Holland).

[769] Marc Samuelson to MH, 4 Jul 1995 (MS Holland).

[770] Original filmscript 5th draft pp. 114-16.

771 Julian Mitchell, *Wilde: the Screenplay* (1997), pp. 225-26.

772 OW to RR, [2 Mar 1898], *CL*, p. 1029.

773 MH to Annie Paul, 8 Aug 1996 (MS Holland).

774 In fact it now appears that the origin of this story, according to Stephen Fry, was a lunch he had with Mishiyo Yoshizaki the CEO of the Japanese backers, NDF International. She was concerned that Stephen, better known for his comedy acting, might not be dignified enough for the part. At the end of the lunch, having convinced her to the contrary, he was most taken aback when she asked him if the film had 'plenty of bum-fucking.'

775 MH diary, 29 Aug 1996; 'What Val has to say about Tom and Viv,' *The Independent*, 23 Apr 1994.

776 'Secret Life of Wilde as an Ideal Husband,' *The Times*, 16 Sep 1996.

777 My diary entries and recollections of conversations with Sheila Colman are corroborated by notes taken at the time by John Stratford, later to become the co-executor of Sheila's and Bosie's estates.

778 *Sketch*, 20 Mar 1895. There is also a set of original photographs preserved in an album from the Eccles bequest at the British Library (Add. MS 81626).

779 *CL*, p. 729.

780 OW to CB, 4 Aug 1897, *CL*, p. 921.

781 *CL*, p. 730.

782 *CL*, p. 721.

783 OW to RR, [1 Mar 1899], *CL*, p. 1128.

784 'Wilde grandson condemns film as "gay obsessed,"' and 'Not the genuine Oscar,' *The Times*, 10 Oct 1997.

785 International Movie Database www.imdb.com (retrieved 12 Mar 2011).

786 Alan Bushell to MH, 14 Apr 2005. The UK Film Council was replaced by the British Film Institute in 2010 and the file on *Wilde* has since 'disappeared.'

787 *The Times*, 10 Oct 1997.

Chapter Eight: Looking At The Stars

788 It was first mentioned at the end of the BBC 'Face to Face' interview which they did together on 15 Mar 1993. Jeremy later gave his own account in Maggi Hambling, *A Statue for Oscar Wilde*, a catalogue for the fund-raising exhibition at the National Portrait Gallery.

[789] *The Times*, 29 May 1995.

[790] 'The Weasel,' *Independent Magazine*, 3 Jun 1995; 'For the glory of Oscar,' *Financial Times*, 5 Jun 1995; *Independent,* 10 Jun 1995.

[791] For the record they were: Frank Forster, Maggi Hambling, Andrew Logan, Eduardo Paolozzi, William Pye, Michael Sandle, and Glynn Williams.

[792] It was after that meeting that Michael invited me to have a coffee with him and asked what was new in the world of 'posthumous Oscar.' I told him that someone had tracked down the grave of Oscar's niece and my first cousin once removed, Dolly Wilde, in Kensal Green, but far from being excited my reaction was 'Oh, God! Not another family grave!' 'What a great title for a chapter!' he exclaimed, and I wish it could have been but the structure of this book didn't allow it.

[793] *CL*, p. 734.

[794] 'The Decorative Arts,' *Complete Works*, p. 930.

[795] Lord St. John of Fawsley to Richard Summers, 9 Apr 1997; Jeremy Isaacs to Alan Bradle, 10 Apr 1997 (MS Holland).

[796] 'If Mr. Isaacs were really brave, he'd want a statue to a homophobe not to Wilde,' *Spectator,* 24 May 1997 & 31 May 1997.

[797] 'How Oscar's selfishness would have coloured a London winter,' *Spectator,* 5 Dec 1998.

[798] BBC News On-Line, 30 Nov 1998 http://news.bbc.co.uk/2/hi/entertainment/224541.stm

[799] Supposedly by *The Times* columnist Matthew Parris who disputed it on Channel 4 Six O'Clock News, 30 Nov 1998 and said that Mandelson's sexuality had already been referred to publicly in the *News of the World,* the *Evening Standard* and a leading article in the *Independent*.

[800] 'Wilde has last laugh on BBC and Mandelson,' *Daily Telegraph,* 1 Dec 1998. Nigel Hawthorne published his own account 'The dangerous bigotry of the BBC,' *Independent,* 2 Dec 1998.

[801] Getty Images, ITN News at 6pm, Clip No. 721886957, 30 Nov 1998.

[802] *Evening Standard*, 12 Jun 1997 & 30 Nov 1998.

[803] *Independent,* 30 Nov 1998.

[804] 'If he lived today he would be on a paedophile register. So why are we honouring Oscar Wilde?,' *Daily Mail,* 1 Dec 1998.

[805] *The Times*, 24 Nov 2007.

Chapter Nine: Moscow Pride (& Prejudice)

806 From Y. A. Rosnatovskaya's introduction to *Oscar Wilde in Russia: A Bibliography 1892-2000.*

807 'La Sainte alliance,' *Préférences Magazine,* Mar/Apr, 2006; *The Independent,* 17 Feb 2006.

808 *Moskovskij Komsomolets,* 26 May 2006.

809 *Daily Telegraph,* 29 May 2006; *Le Figaro,* 29 May 2006.

810 MH email to Robert Wintemute, 30 May 2006.

811 https://hudoc.echr.coe.int/eng-press?i=003-3311485-3700129 (retrieved 4 Jan 2022).

812 https://www.bbc.com/news/world-europe-19293465 (retrieved 11 June 2025).

Chapter Ten: Cashing In On Oscar

813 Christie's Sale Catalogue, 'Continental and English Literature,' 16 Dec 1991, lot 329.

814 OW to Ada Leverson, 20 May 1897, *CL,* p. 845.

815 OW to Ernest Dowson 26 Oct 1897, *CL,* p. 971: 'I have retaken my own name, as my incognito was absurd.'

816 Christie's Manuscript Dept to MH, 15 Jan 1991.

817 Holland 1954, p. 136.

818 Christie's Sale Catalogue 'Autograph Letters and Modern First Editions,' 17 Nov 1995, lots 175 & 176.

819 Robert Sherard, 'At Oscar Wilde's Grave,' *Reynolds's Newspaper,* 21 Jun 1903; 'Oscar Wilde mourait dans mes bras,' *L'Intransigeant,* 30 Nov 1930; 'Par un soir d'automne, en 1900 le grand poète Oscar Wilde quitta le peitit Hôtel d'Alsace pour le cimetière de Bagneux,' *Le Journal,* 1 Nov. 1937.

820 Bonhams Sale Catalogue (London), 24 Feb 1998, lot 357.

821 Bonhams Sale Catalogue (San Francisco), 18 Feb 2007, lot 253.

822 'The Oscar Sinners,' *Sunday Times Magazine,* 8 Jul 2007.

823 Christie's Manuscripts and Printed Books Sale, 19 Nov 1993, lots 312 & 313.

824 Bamford's Sale Catalogue, 'Oscar Wilde and Terra Nova Sale,' 24 Sep 2010, lots 67-71.

825 *Independent,* 16 Sep 2010; *Daily Telegraph,* 16 Sep 2010

826 *CL*, pp. 295-96, 318. In fact all three had been transcribed with their correct postmark dates by my father and A. J. A. Symons when they were planning an edition of Oscar's letters in the 1930s.

827 BBC 'Today Programme,' 24 Sep 2010 (my transcript).

828 'Revealing Oscar Wilde Letters Sold For £30,000,' *Yorkshire Evening Post*, 24 Sep 2010.

829 Sotheby's Sale Catalogue, 27 Apr 2021, 'Collection of a Connoisseur: History in Manuscript. Part 2,' lot 126 which made £15,000 hammer price.

830 Oxford University Archives to MH, 10 May 1991; MH correspondence with Old Parsonage Hotel, 19-21 Aug 1991 (MS Holland).

831 Manus Nunan correspondence with MH, 12-26 Sep 1991 (MSS Holland).

832 Old Parsonage Newsletter, Dec 1991.

833 'Oscar Wilde's Arrest,' *Illustrated Police Budget*, 13 Apr 1895.

834 *Sunday Telegraph Magazine*, 5 May 2002.

835 'Wilde at Heart,' *New York Observer*, 15 Apr 2007.

836 Lucian Freud to MH, 24 Mar 1993 (MS Holland).

837 Misquotations and even inventions are legion. Dorothy Parker, the American humourist summed it up in her lines: If, with the literate, I am / Impelled to try an epigram, / I never seek to take the credit; / We all assume that Oscar said it.

Epilogue

838 Holland 1966, pp. 191-92.

839 VH diary, 21 Nov 1951.

840 VH diary, 2 Mar 1949.

841 I was concerned that I might have misremembered this until I came across a reference to it in a letter from Robert Ross's great-nephew, John-Paul Ross, to my parents dated 26 Sep 1966. 'The more I think about the suggestion of Merlin re-adopting his grandfather's name, the more I like it.' (MS Holland).

842 *CL*, p. 721.

843 Frank Harris, *Contemporary Portraits*, pp. 121-22.

844 *Sunday Times*, 23 Jun 1946.

Austin, Gabriel ed., *Four Oaks Library* (1967)

Barney, Natalie, *Aventures de l'esprit* (1929)

Barney, Natalie ed., *In Memory of Dorothy Ierne Wilde* (1951)

Beatty, Laura, *Lillie Langtry: Manners, Masks and Morals* (1999)

Bettany, F.G., *Stewart Headlam: A Biography* (1926)

Billing, Noel Pemberton, *Verbatim Report of the Trial of Noel Pemberton Billing* (1918)

Bogle, Edra, 'The Life and Literary and Artistic Activities of Robert Baldwin Ross 1869–1918' (Unpublished Thesis, Univ. of Southern California, 1969)

Borràs, Maria Lluïsa, *Cravan: une stratégie du scandale* (1996)

Borland, Maureen, *Wilde's Devoted Friend* (1987)

Boyd, A.K., *The History of Radley College 1847-1947* (1948)

Brasol, Boris, *Oscar Wilde: the Man, the Artist, the Martyr* (1938)

Cooper-Prichard, A.H., *Conversations with Oscar Wilde* (1931)

Croft Cooke, Rupert, *Bosie; The Story of Lord Alfred Douglas, His Friends and Enemies* (1963)

Crowley, Aleister, *The Confessions of Aleister Crowley: An Autohagiography,* John Symonds & Kenneth Grant eds, (1989)

Dansel, Michel, *Au Père-Lachaise* (1973)

Delarue-Mardrus, Lucie, *Les Amours d'Oscar Wilde* (1929)

Douglas, Lord Alfred, *Oscar Wilde and Myself* (1914)

Douglas, Lord Alfred with Harris, *New Preface* (see below)

Douglas, Lord Alfred, *The Autobiography of Lord Alfred Douglas* (1929)

Douglas, Lord Alfred, *Without Apology* (1938)

Douglas, Lord Alfred, *Oscar Wilde: A Summing Up* (1940)

Dudley, Ernest, *The Gilded Lily: The Life and Loves of the Fabulous Lillie Langtry* (1958)

Dulau & Company Limited, *A Collection of Original Manuscripts, Letters & Books of Oscar Wilde* (1928)

Epstein, Jacob, *Let There Be Sculpture* (1940)

Ervine, St. John, *Oscar Wilde: A Present Time Appraisal* (1951)

Fanto, Rosita, *Lady of the Cards* (2010)

Findlay, Jean, *Chasing Lost Time: The Life of C.K. Scott Moncrieff* (2014)

Frankel, Nicholas, *Oscar Wilde: The Unrepentant* Years (2017)

Gardiner, Stephen, *Epstein: Artist Against the Establishment* (1992)

Gide, André, *Oscar Wilde: In memoriam (souvenirs) & le 'De Profundis'* (1910)

Gide, André, *Si le grain ne meurt* (1924)

Hoare, Philip, *Wilde's Last Stand,* (1997)

Huggett, Richard, *Binkie Beaumont* (1989)

Green, Julian, *Journal intégral 1919-1940* (1919 - 1940)

Harris, Frank, *Oscar Wilde: His Life and Confessions* (1916)

Harris, Frank, *Contemporary Portraits* (1915)

Harris, Frank, *Oscar Wilde: His Life and Confessions. With 'Memories of Oscar Wilde' by Bernard Shaw* (1918)

Harris, Frank & Lord Alfred Douglas, *New Preface to the 'Life and Confessions of Oscar Wilde'* (1925)

Harris, Frank, *De Profundis* (1929)

Harris, Frank, *Oscar Wilde: His Life and Confessions. With the Full and Final Confession of Lord Alfred Douglas* (1930)

Harris, Frank, *Oscar Wilde* [Doctored by Bernard Shaw at Douglas's request] (1938)

Hart-Davis, Rupert ed., *The Lyttelton Hart-Davis Letters, 1955 - 1962* (1978 - 1984)

Hichens, Mark, *Oscar Wilde's Last Chance: The Dreyfus Connection* (1999)

Holland, Vyvyan, *De Profundis* (1949)

Holland, Vyvyan, *Son of Oscar Wilde* (1954)

Holland, Vyvyan *Oscar Wilde: A Pictorial Biography* (1960)

Holland, Vyvyan, *Time Remembered* (1966)

Holland, Vyvyan, *An Evergreen Garland* (1968),

Holland, Merlin, *Irish Peacock and Scarlet Marquess* (2003)

Holland, Merlin, *The Wilde Album* (1997)

Holland, Merlin, *A Portrait of Oscar Wilde* (2008)

Honma, Hisao, *Taiō Inshōki* [Impressions of Europe] (1929)

Honma, Hisao, *Eikoku Kinsei Yuibishugi no Kenkyū* [A study of Aestheticism in Modern England] (1934)

Housman, Laurence, *Echo de Paris* (1923)

Humphries, Barry, *My Life As Me* (2002)

Hyde, Mary ed., *Bernard Shaw & Alfred Douglas: A Correspondence* (1982)

Hyde, Harford Montgomery, *Oscar Wilde: the Aftermath* (1963)

Hyde, Harford Montgomery, *Oscar Wilde* (1976)

Hyde, Harford Montgomery, *Lord Alfred Douglas* (1984)

Ingleby, Leonard Cresswell, *Oscar Wilde* (1907)

Kennard, George, *Loopy: An Autobiography* (1990)

Kernahan, Coulson, *In Good Company* (1917)

Kettle, Michael, *Salome's Last Veil* (1977)

Knox, Melissa, *Oscar Wilde: A Long and Lovely Suicide* (1994)

Leverson, Ada, *Letters to the Sphinx* (1930)

Lowndes, Marie Belloc, *A Passing World* (1948)

Lyons, J. B., *What did I die of?* (1991)

Mackenzie, Compton, *My life and times. Octave 3, 1900-1907* (1964)

Mackie, Gregory, *Beautiful Untrue Things* (2019)

Maguire, J. Robert, *Ceremonies of Bravery: Oscar Wilde, Carlos Blacker and the Dreyfus Affair* (2013)

Mason, Stuart [Christopher Millard] *Oscar Wilde: Three Times Tried* (1912)

McCormack, Jerusha, *Wilde the Irishman* (1998)

Mitchell, Julian, *Wilde: The Screenplay* (1997)

Mitchell, Peter Chalmers, *My Fill of Days* (1937)

Moyle, Franny, *Constance: The Tragic and Scandalous Life of Mrs Oscar Wilde* (2011)

Murray, Douglas, *Bosie: A Biography of Lord Alfred Douglas* (2000)

Nelson, James, *Leonard Smithers: Publisher to the Decadents* (2000)

Newell, Stephanie, *The Forger's Tale* (2006)

O'Sullivan, Vincent, *Aspects of Wilde* (1936)

Palmer, Gladys, *Relations and Complications* (1929)

Pennington, Michael, *An Angel for a Martyr: Jacob Epstein's Tomb for Oscar Wilde* (1987)

Privaz, Étienne, *Un Malfaiteur: André Gide* (1931)

Pullar, Philippa, *Frank Harris* (1975)

Raby, Peter, ed., *The Cambridge Companion to Oscar Wilde* (2010)

Ransome, Arthur, *Oscar Wilde: A Critical Study* (1912)

Ransome, *The Autobiography of Arthur Ransome*, ed. Rupert Hart-Davis (1976)

Raymond, Jean Paul & Charles Ricketts, *Recollections* (1932)

Roberts, Maria, *Yours Loyally: A Life of Christopher Sclater Millard* (2014)

Rodriguez, Suzanne, *Wild Heart, A Life: Natalie Clifford Barney's Journey from Victorian America to the Literary Salons of Paris* (2002)

Ross, Margery, *Robert Ross Friend of Friends* (1952)

Rosnatovskaya, Y.A. & Y.G.Freedshmen, *Oscar Wilde in Russia: A Bibliography 1892-2000* (2000)

Rostand, Maurice, *Le Procès d'Oscar Wilde* [Play] (1934)

Schroeder, Horst, *Alice in Wildeland* (1994)

Seeney, Michael, *From Bow Street to the Ritz: Oscar Wilde's Theatrical Career from 1895 to 1908* (2015)

Sherard, Robert Harborough, *The Story of an Unhappy Friendship* (1902)

Sherard, Robert Harborough, *The Life of Oscar Wilde* (1906)

Sherard, Robert Harborough, *The Real Oscar Wilde* (1917)

Sherard, Robert Harborough, *André Gide's Wicked Lies about the Late Mr Oscar Wilde in Algiers in 1895* (1933)

Sherard, Robert Harborough, *Oscar Wilde 'Drunkard & Swindler': A Reply to George Bernard Shaw, Dr G.J. Renier, Frank Harris etc* (1933)

Sherard, Robert Harborough, *Oscar Wilde Twice Defended from André Gide's Wicked Lies and Frank Harris's Cruel Libels* (1934)

Sherard, Robert Harborough, *Bernard Shaw, Frank Harris and Oscar Wilde* (1937)

Sheridan, Alan, *André Gide* (1998)

Smith, Hester Travers, *Psychic Messages from Oscar Wilde* (1924)

Sorley Brown, *The Life and Genius of T.W.H. Crosland* (1928)

Steegmuller, Francis, *Cocteau: A Biography* (1970)

Stokes, Leslie & Sewell, *Oscar Wilde* [Play] (1937)

Stuart-Young, J.M., *Osrac, the Self-Sufficient* (1905)

Symons, Julian, *A.J.A. Symons: His Life and Speculations* (1950)

Thurston, Herbert, *Modern Spiritualism* (1928)

Tobin, A.I. & Elmer Gertz, *Frank Harris: A Study in Black and White* (1931)

Waugh, Alec, *My Brother Evelyn and Other Profiles* (1967)

Wilson, Simon, *From Greek Youth to Flying Demon Angel: Jacob Epstein's Studies for the Tomb of Oscar Wilde* (2020)

Wintermans, Caspar, *Alfred Douglas: A Poet's Life and His Finest Work* (2007)

Wintermans, Caspar ed., *Lord Alfred Douglas. Oscar Wilde: A Plea and a Reminiscence* (2002)

The following is an annotated but necessarily brief list of works whose battered state on my shelves is testimony to their value for any study of Oscar Wilde and his life:

Beckson, Karl, *The OW Encyclopaedia* (1998). The definitive reference work on Wilde's works and his circle.

Conrad, Tweed, *Oscar Wilde in Quotation* (2006). 3,100 thematically ordered quotations with attributions and reliably sourced.

Ellmann, Richard, *Oscar Wilde* (1987). Needs to be read with Schroeder (below).

Mason, Stuart [Christopher Millard], *Bibliography of Oscar Wilde*

(1914). Still the finest and most accurate bibliography of all Wilde's written work.

Mikhail, E.H., *Oscar Wilde: An Annotated Bibliography of Criticism* (1978). A now slightly dated but useful listing of books and articles about Wilde to 1978.

Mikhail, E.H. ed, *Oscar Wilde: Interviews and Recollections,* 2 vols (1979). First-hand recollections of Wilde from printed sources both English and foreign.

Page, Norman, *An Oscar Wilde Chronology* (1991). An invaluable and very detailed chronology of Wilde's life in 100 pages.

Pearson, Hesketh, *The Life of Oscar* Wilde (1946). Still one of the best pre-Ellmann biographies containing much original material, but infuriatingly devoid of references.

Schroeder, Horst, *Additions and Corrections to Richard Ellmann's Oscar Wilde* (2002). Essential reading to accompany Ellmann's biography.

Sturgis, Matthew, *Oscar: A Life* (2018). Now regarded as the definitive biography.

Wilde, Oscar, *The Complete Works of Oscar Wilde,* vols I – XI (in progress) in Oxford English Texts Series (Oxford, 2000 – 2021). The ultimate, scholarly, variorum edition for in-depth study of everything published by Wilde including his journalism.

Wilde, Oscar, *The Collins Complete Works of Oscar Wilde,* fifth corrected edition (2003). Also contains selected journalism and lectures. More accessible for the general reader than the OUP edition.

Wilde, Oscar, *The Complete Letters of Oscar Wilde,* Rupert Hart-Davis & Merlin Holland eds (2000).

Wilde, Oscar, *Oscar Wilde: A Life in Letters,* Merlin Holland ed. (2003). A selection of Wilde's best letters with running commentary to be read as an autobiography.

INDEX

IMAGE CREDITS

ACKNOWLEDGEMENTS

Almost everyone with whom I have dealt in writing this account of my grandfather's 'posthumous life' seems to have become imbued with the same generosity of spirit that they have found in Oscar himself. To them all I should like to express my heartfelt gratitude, especially for their patience in waiting to see if their support for my project would ever bear fruit.

First of all, I must thank the following for allowing me to use quotations from the copyright material which they control:

The late Barry Humphries for permission to reproduce from his autobiography the conversation which he had with my mother in 1981;

Catherine Heaney for permission to quote from her father's moving oration delivered at the time of Oscar's admission to Poets' Corner in 1995;

John Holland for permission to quote from his grandfather Otho Holland's correspondence with his wife Mary;

John Stratford, as Lord Alfred Douglas's literary executor, for allowing me to use extensive quotes from Douglas's unpublished correspondence;

Peters Fraser & Dunlop for permission to quote from Rebecca West's letters to my father;

Duff Hart-Davis for permitting the use of his father's correspondence with Vyvyan over the publication of Oscar's letters;

And lastly, Caroline Gould for allowing extensive quotations from the correspondence of her great-great uncle Robbie Ross.

Every attempt has been made to trace the copyright holders of quoted material especially through the WATCH (Writers, Artists, And Their Copyright Holders) database run jointly by the Universities of Texas and Reading, even in cases where the concept of 'Fair Dealing' would apply. However, if any have been overlooked, I will be pleased to make the necessary arrangements.

My greatest debt is to the staff of the various libraries and archives with extensive holdings of what must be described as 'secondary' Wilde documents, but none the less important for that description. Rebecca Fenning Marschall and Scott Jacobs from the William Andrews Clark Library at the University of California, Los Angeles, were unfailingly helpful both on my visits to the library and later over the ether. Marc Carlson and Kirsten Marangoni in the McFarlin Library at the University of Tulsa guided me skilfully through the papers of Rebecca West, Richard Ellmann, Rupert Hart-Davis, and Rosita Fanto. In the Harry Ransom Humanities Research Centre at the University of Texas, Austin, John Thomas and Eric Colleary were especially helpful with the papers of Frank Harris, Max Beerbohm, and Montgomery Hyde. At the British Library, Laura Walker, Lead Curator of Modern Archives and Manuscripts, helped me to find my way around the Eccles Collection once it had been safely transferred to the library, and Zoe Stansell, Manuscript Reference Specialist, pointed me in the direction of the Society of Authors archives, an important resource for the study of Wilde's literary legacy in the 1920s and 1930s. Elizabeth Adams, dynamic librarian of University College Oxford, reclaimed the Robert Ross Memorial Bequest for the College from the Bodleian where it had languished, largely unused, for nearly seventy years. It has since been fully catalogued and digitised, and has proved an invaluable resource for my work. Robin Darwall-Smith, archivist at Magdalen and University College, talked me through its fascinating history for this book. Vincent Giroud of the Beinecke Library, Yale University, drew my attention to some vital correspondence which Montgomery Hyde had with Alan White at Methuen & Co, throwing a whole new light onto the story of my father's bankruptcy. To Isobel Quigley, Maggie Fergusson, and John Wells at the Cambridge University Library I am indebted for helping me discover why André Gide's honorary fellowship of the Royal Society of Literature was rescinded in 1933. I am particularly grateful to Evelyne Lüthi-Graf and Elénore Rinaldi Lecciso at the Archives of the Swiss Commune of Montreux for helping to establish what really happened to the Wilde family in the summer of 1895 when Oscar went to prison, and for giving me a guided tour of the area to put it all into perspective. Steve Tabor, formerly of the Clark Library and now Curator of Rare Books at the Huntington Library, California, graciously accepted my apology for answering a letter of his ten years late which then led to my discovering an important and revealing cache of Vyvyan's letters to his close friend Alec Waugh at the Albuquerque Museum Foundation, New Mexico. There, the librarian Elaine Richardson kindly made them all available to me. Alexandra Browne, archivist at Trinity Hall, Cambridge, and Celia Pilkington, archivist of the Inner Temple, provided much useful information about Vyvyan's legal studies and his brief time at the Bar. Marcel Fleiss of the Galerie 1900-2000 in Paris allowed me access to his papers on Vyvyan's cousin, Fabian Lloyd, providing essential background to the strange history of that proto-Dadaist. Jean Fessey, House of Commons Library helped me with the Commons debates on the Wolfenden Report which led eventually to the decriminalising of homosexuality in 1967. Debra Majer, Archivist for Roman Catholic Diocese of London, Ontario, provided much useful information adding to my research on Brett Holland, the 'Paris Forger'. Michael Bott of Reading University Library was generous with his time helping me to sort through the papers of Robert Sherard.

My gratitude to various individuals is no less profound, more so even, for giving me what cannot be valued—their time:

The late Mary Eccles gave me unlimited access to her exceptional Wilde collection (since bequeathed to the British Library) in the early years of my research.

Edra Bogle gave me access to her unpublished doctoral thesis on the life of Robbie Ross and shared her extensive research on the subject.

Patricia de Montfort in her research on the artist Louise Joplin unearthed some correspondence with Henrietta Stannard, throwing new light on the relationship between Constance and Oscar after his release.

Lucia Mataro helped, through Italian newspapers, to flesh out the story of my father's visit to Venice in 1908 as 'Vyvyan Wilde' and its strange consequences.

Bob Forrest lifted the veil on Arthur Cooper-Prichard's background and activities, though as in most matters Wildean, some of the mystery remains.

Ed Maggs allowed me access to what he terms the slightly embarrassing file of forged Wilde manuscripts which his family firm of booksellers purchased from Brett Holland in the 1920s.

Marilyn Bisch and Joan Navarre, as always, gave unstintingly of their time to answer queries concerning matters Wildean in America.

The late Horst Schroeder, comrade-in-arms in my fight against Wildean myths (especially 'Wilde dressed as Salomé') generously shared his extensive knowledge of the German literary scholar, Max Meyerfeld.

Caspar Wintermans gave me unrestricted access to his files of Alfred Douglas's correspondence which was invaluable in understanding Bosie's quarrels with the rest of the World.

Noreen Doody helped with stories of Portora School in post-Wildean times.

Joe Bristow at UCLA generously shared his discovery of previously unknown correspondence between my father and Father Cuthbert Dunne who received Oscar into the Catholic Church on his deathbed.

Ashley Robins who was largely instrumental in solving the mystery of my grandmother's final illness and death.

The late Macdonald Critchley who finally nailed the myth about Oscar dying from syphilis.

Simon Wilson whose knowledge of Jacob Epstein's work and Oscar's tomb in Père Lachaise Cemetery provided invaluable background to the story of its creation.

Yoko Hirata, granddaughter of Honma Hisao, who made available in English the story of her grandfather's 'pilgrimage' to London in 1928 to find some of the survivors of the 1890s.

Jim Beach at the University of Northampton for much advice on Cyril's and Vyvyan's army careers in WW1.

Tom Wright for sharing his research on Oscar Wilde and the 'Eighty Club' and James Carew, allowing me to speculate more realistically on the reasons for Helen Carew funding the Epstein sculpture on Oscar's tomb in Paris.

Rupert Everett for helping me find a literary agent when I most needed one, and when that agent, Clare Conville, did agree to take me on, she picked me up, dusted me down, and restored my confidence.

Christopher Potter commissioned this book at Fourth Estate nearly thirty years ago and still believed in it when I was forced to change publishers and found him again at Europa Editions. This book owes its existence to him.

Millie 'the Guillotine' Guille, my editor at Europa, has been fierce in her polishing but, I have to admit, almost always right. It was a pleasure to work with her, one of an increasingly rare breed, a true publisher's editor.

Most of all, my thanks to my wife Emma and her unflagging support, since she had to live with what she has affectionately referred to over twenty years (and she was right) as 'that bloody book', correcting, suggesting, reassuring to the end.

It has, indeed, been a very long time in the making, so long in fact that rumours began to circulate querying its very existence. It used to be a painful reminder of the joke about the two Irishmen who meet for a drink in a Dublin pub and one asks the other: 'What are you up to these days?' 'Writing a book,' comes the reply. 'Neither am I,' says his friend. But now I can finally stand back from the story as I tell it, no longer in an awkward, self-deprecating way, thanks in large part to the help and kindness of all those listed here. As Rupert Hart-Davis wrote in his introduction to *More Letters of Oscar Wilde* in 1985 (and I plagiarise unashamedly) 'There must be others who have helped me along the way, but old men forget, and I can only gratefully beg the forgiveness of any such neglected benefactors.'

Thank you all.

About the Author

Merlin Holland, the only grandson of Oscar Wilde, is an author living in France. For the last forty years he has been researching his grandfather's life and works, and writes, lectures, and broadcasts regularly on the subject. During that time he has been in the unique position, through having to administer the few remaining copyrights in Wilde's writings (mostly letters and unpublished fragmentary manuscripts) of being in close touch with the latest academic research, but at the same time presenting a lively and very personal view of his grandfather to a wider, more general audience.

His publications include *Irish Peacock and Scarlet Marquess*, the first complete, verbatim record of the libel trial which ultimately brought Oscar Wilde to ruin and social disgrace, and *The Wilde Album*, a pictorial biography of Oscar Wilde which has been translated into seven languages. He is also the co-editor of *The Complete Letters of Oscar Wilde* as well as the editor of an abridged and commentated version of Oscar's letters, *Oscar Wilde: a Life in Letters,* and the author of *Conversations with Oscar Wilde.*

After Oscar's conviction in 1895, his wife, Constance, and their two sons were forced to move abroad and change their name to Holland. The family has never reverted to the name Wilde.

the Gods.

...his genius, a disting...

...illiancy, intellectual da...

...ilosophy, and philosop...

...e minds of men and

...as nothing I said or

...wonder: I took the ...

...own ~~art~~, and made it a

...pression as the Epic

...see that I widened its

...characterisation: drama,

...fantastic dialogue, w

...eautiful in a new mode

...gave what is false n

...its rightful province

...the true are merely

~~rented art as the supreme reality,~~
~~existence.~~ awoke the

...it it created myth a...

...f all systems in a ...

...in epigram.